Software Engineering

Second Edition

David C. Kung

Mc
Graw
Hill

SOFTWARE ENGINEERING

Published by McGraw Hill LLC, 1325 Avenue of the Americas, New York, NY 10019.

This book is printed on acid-free paper.

1 2 3 4 5 6 7 8 9 LCR 28 27 26 25 24 23

ISBN 978-1-265-24243-5
MHID 1-265-24243-7

Cover Image: *Shutterstock Images, LLC*

mheducation.com/highered

Dedication

To My Father

Brief Contents

Part VII

Part VIII

Appendices

Contents

Chapter 14

Activity Modeling for Transformational Systems 314

Chapter 15

Modeling and Design of Rule-Based Systems 330

Part V

Applying Situation-Specific Patterns 351

Chapter 16

Applying Patterns to Design a State Diagram Editor 352

Chapter 22

Software Configuration Management 541

Part VIII

Project Management and Software Security 553

Chapter 23

Software Project Management 554

Chapter 24

Software Security 584

Preface

BACKGROUND

Computers are widely used in all sectors of our society, performing a variety of functions with the application software running on them. As a result, the market for software engineers is booming. There is a significant gap between the demand and supply, especially for graduates with software engineering education.

Many people do not know the scope and usefulness of software engineering, and the discipline is often misunderstood. Many media outlets deem software engineering as writing Java programs. Some students think that software engineering includes everything related to software. Others think that software engineering is drawing UML diagrams, as the following story illustrates. Years ago, after the first class of a software engineering course, a student told me, "professor, you know that this will be an easy course for me because we've drawn lots of UML diagrams before." At the end of the semester, the student came to me again and said, "professor, I want to tell you that we worked very hard, but we learned a lot about OO design. It is not just drawing UML diagrams." So what is software engineering? As a discipline, it encompasses research, education, and application of engineering processes, methodologies, quality assurance, and project management to significantly increase software productivity and software quality while reducing software cost and time to market. A software process describes the phases and *what* should be done in each phase. It does not specify (in detail) *how* to perform the activities in each phase. A modeling language, such as UML, defines the notations, syntax, and semantics for communicating and documenting analysis and design ideas. UML and the Unified Process (UP) are good and necessary but not sufficient. This is because *how* to produce the analysis and design ideas required to draw meaningful UML diagrams is missing.

MOTIVATION

To fill the gap mentioned above, we need a methodology or a "cook-book." Unlike a process, a methodology is a detailed description of the steps and procedures or *how* to carry out the activities to the extent that *a beginner can follow* to produce and deploy the desired software system. Without a methodology, a beginning software engineer would have to spend years of on-the-job training to learn design, implementation, and testing skills.

This book is also motivated by emerging interests in *agile processes, design patterns,* and *test-driven development* (TDD). Agile processes emphasize teamwork, design for change, rapid deployment of small increments of the software system, and joint development with the customer and users. Design patterns are effective design solutions to common design problems. They promote software reuse and improve team communication. Patterns also empower less-experienced software engineers to produce high-quality software because patterns encode software design principles. TDD advocates testable software, and requires test scripts to be produced before the implementation so that the latter can be tested immediately and frequently.

As an analogy, consider the development of an amusement park. The overall process includes the following phases: planning, public approval, analysis and design, financing, construction drawings, construction, procurement of equipment, installation of equipment, preopening, and grand opening. However, knowing the overall process is not enough. The development team must know how to perform the activities of the phases. For example, the planning activities include development of initial concept, feasibility study, and master plan generation. The theme park team must know how to perform these activities. The analysis and design activities include "requirements acquisition" from stakeholders, site investigation, design of park layout, design of theming for different areas of the park, creating models to study the layout design and theming, and producing the master design. Again, the theme park team must know how to perform these activities to produce the master design. Unlike a process that describes the phases of activities, a methodology details the steps and procedures or how to perform the activities.

The development of an amusement park is a multiyear project and costs billions of dollars. The investor wants the park to generate revenue as early as possible, but with the above process, the investor has to wait until the entire park is completed. Once the master design is finalized, it cannot be modified easily due to the restrictions imposed by the conventional process. If the park does not meet the expectations of the stakeholders, then changes are costly once the park is completed.

Agile processes are aimed to solve these problems. With an agile process, a list of preliminary theme park requirements is acquired quickly and allowed to evolve during the development process. The amusement and entertainment facilities are then derived from the requirements and carefully grouped into clusters of facilities. A plan to develop and deploy the clusters in relatively short periods of time is produced, that is, rapid deployment of small increments. Thus, instead of a finalized master design, the development process designs and deploys one cluster at a time. As the clusters of facilities are deployed and operational, feedback is sought and changes to the requirements, the development plan, budget, and schedule are worked out with the stakeholders–that is, joint development. In addition, the application of architectural design patterns improves quality and ability of the park to adapt to changing needs– that is, design for change. Teamwork is emphasized because effective collaboration and coordination between the teams and team members ensure that the facilities will be developed and deployed timely and seamlessly. The agile process has a number of merits. The investor can reap the benefits much earlier because the facilities are operational as early as desired and feasible. Since a small number of the facilities are developed and deployed at a time, errors can be corrected and changes can be made more easily.

In summary, this text is centered around an agile unified methodology that integrates UML, design patterns, and TDD, among others. The methodology presented in this book is called a "unified methodology" because it uses UML as the modeling language and it follows an agile unified process. It does not mean to unify any other methods or to be used as a "unified" methodology for all projects.

AUDIENCES

This book is for students majoring in computer science, software engineering or information systems, as well as software development professionals. In particular, it is intended to be used as the primary material for upper-division undergraduate and introductory graduate courses and professional training courses in the software industry. This book's material evolved over the last two decades from courses taught at universities and companies domestically and internationally, as well as from applications of the material to industry-sponsored projects and projects conducted by software engineers in various companies. These allowed the author to observe how students and software engineers applied UP, UML, design patterns, and TDD, and the difficulties they faced. Their feedback led to the development of the Agile Unified Methodology (AUM) presented in this book and the continual improvement of the material.

The book describes AUM in detail to facilitate students to learn and develop analysis and design abilities. In particular, each analysis or design activity is decomposed into a number of steps, and how to perform each step is described in detail. This treatment is intended to facilitate students learning how to perform analysis and design. Once acquired the abilities, one may skip some or most of the steps.

ORGANIZATION

The book has 24 chapters, divided into eight parts:

Part I. Introduction and System Engineering. This part consists of the first three chapters. It provides an overview of the software life-cycle activities. In particular, it covers software process models, the notion of a methodology, the difference between a process and a methodology, and system engineering.

Part II. Analysis and Architectural Design. This part presents the planning phase activities. It includes requirements elicitation, domain modeling, and architectural design.

Part III. Modeling and Design of Interactive Systems. This part deals with the modeling and design of interactive systems. It consists of six chapters. These chapters present how to identify use cases from the requirements, how to model and design actor–system interaction and object interaction behavior, how to apply responsibility assignment patterns, how to derive a design class diagram to serve as the design blueprint, and how to design the user interface.

Part IV. Modeling and Design of Other Types of Systems. This part consists of three chapters; each presents the modeling and design of one type of system. In particular, Chapter 13 presents the modeling and design of event-driven systems. Chapter 14 presents the modeling and design of transformational systems. Chapter 15 presents the modeling and design of business rule-based systems.

Part V. Applying Situation-Specific Patterns. This part consists of two chapters and presents how to apply situation-specific patterns. A case study, that is, the design of a state diagram editor, is used to help understand the process.

Part VI. Implementation and Quality Assurance. This part consists of three chapters. They present implementation considerations, software quality assurance concepts and activities, and software testing.

Part VII. Maintenance and Configuration Management. This part includes two chapters and covers software maintenance and software configuration management.

Part VIII. Project Management and Software Security. The last part of the book consists of the last two chapters. One of the chapters presents software project management. The other chapter covers software security, that is, life-cycle activities concerning the modeling and design of secure software systems.

The material can satisfy the needs of several software engineering courses. For example,

1. Part I through Part III and selected topics from Part VI to Part VIII are a good combination for an Object-Oriented Software Engineering (OOSE) course or an Introduction to Software Engineering course. This could be a junior- or senior-level undergraduate course as well as an introductory graduate-level course.
2. Part II, Part V, and selected sections from the other chapters could form a Software Design Patterns course. It is recommended that the OOSE course described above be a prerequisite for this course. However, many international students may not have taken the OOSE course. In this case, a review of the methodology presented in Part II and Part III is recommended. The review of the methodology provides the framework for applying patterns. The review may take two to four weeks.
3. Part VI and Part VII could be taught in various ways. They could form one course–Quality Assurance, Testing, and Maintenance. They could be taught as two courses–Software Quality Assurance, and Software Testing and Maintenance.
4. Chapters 13–15, 19, and 20 plus selected patterns from the other chapters may form a course on modeling, design, verification, and validation of complex systems.
5. Part I, Parts VI–VIII, and selected chapters from the other parts may form a Software Project Management course.

Various teaching supplements can be found at http://www.mhhe.com/kung. These include PowerPoint teaching slides, pop quiz and test generation software, databases of test questions, sample course descriptions, syllabi, and a solution manual. Instructors who have not taught the courses may find these helpful in reducing preparation time and effort.

ACKNOWLEDGMENTS

I would like to thank my numerous students who constantly stimulate me with their questions, feedback, enthusiasm, and effort to apply AUM to real-world projects. They provided valuable improvement suggestions. Many continue to practice AUM in industry after graduation and share with me their valuable experiences. I also want to thank the reviewers and numerous instructors for their comments and suggestions. These have significantly improved the organization, presentation, and many other aspects of the book. I am thankful for the opportunities to teach on-site training courses and for-credit courses for various companies. These allow me to interact with many software developers and learn from them. Some companies let the developers apply AUM and patterns to in-house or product-development projects. All of these projects generated very positive feedback including high-quality design documentation and drastic reduction in defect rates. I want to thank the managements of various companies for their constant support to industry-university collaboration and the opportunity for me to learn from practice.

part I

Introduction and System Engineering

1

Chapter

Introduction

Key Takeaway Points

- Software engineering aims to significantly improve software productivity and software quality while reducing software costs and time to market.
- Software engineering consists of three tracks of interweaving life-cycle activities: software development, software quality assurance, and software project management activities.

Computers are used everywhere in our society. It is difficult to find a hospital, school, retail shop, bank, factory, or any other organization that does not rely on computers. Our cell phones, cars, and televisions are also based on computer-powered platforms. The driving force behind the expanding use of computers is the market economy. However, it is the software that makes the computers work in the ways we want. Software or computer programs consist of thousands or millions of instructions that direct the computer to perform complex calculations and control the operations of hardware devices. The demand for computer software has been rapidly increasing during the last several decades. This trend is expected to continue for the foreseeable future.

The proliferation of computer applications creates a huge demand for application software developers. According to the Bureau of Labor Statistics (BLS), application software developer was one of the 30 fastest-growing occupations in America (bls.gov/emp/tables/fastest-growing-occupations.htm). The number of positions was projected to grow from 1,469,200 in 2019 to 1,789,200 in 2029, an increase of 316,000, or 21.50%. The median annual wage for an application software developer in May 2019 was $110,140, much higher than the median annual wage for all occupations ($41,950). Among the 10 computer and IT occupations surveyed by the BLS, only application software developer and information security analyst enter into the 30 fastest-growing list. Its median pay was also much higher than the median pay of $91,250 for the 10 computer and IT occupations surveyed by the BLS.

There are two popular misconceptions. One equates application software development with computer programming. The other equates an application software developer with a computer programmer. However, according to the BLS, software developers create the applications or systems that run on a computer or another device.

Computer programmers write and test code that allows computer applications and software programs to function properly. The BLS survey also showed that the median pay for a computer programmer in May 2019 was $89,190, which was lower than the median pay for computer and IT occupations and much lower than the median pay for an application software developer.

Unlike a computer programmer, an application software developer is required to identify and formulate feasible and cost-effective solutions to solve large, complex real-world problems and design software to implement such solutions. The solutions and the software must take into account potential impact to public health, safety, security, and welfare as well as cultural, social, and environmental aspects (abet.org). To be able to perform the work required of an application software developer, an education in software engineering is highly desired.

1.1 WHAT IS SOFTWARE ENGINEERING?

Software systems are complex intellectual products. Software development must ensure that the software system meets the needs of the intended application, the budget is not overrun, and the system is delivered on time. To accomplish these goals, the term "software engineering" was proposed at a NATO conference in 1968 to advocate the need for an engineering approach to software production. Since then, software engineering has become a discipline and made remarkable progress. The efforts that take place in the field lead to the following:

Definition 1.1 *Software engineering* as a discipline is focused on the research, education, and practice of engineering processes, methods, and techniques to significantly increase software productivity and software quality while reducing software costs and time to market.

This definition includes several important points. First, the overall objective of software engineering is significantly increasing software productivity (P) and quality (Q) while reducing software production and operating costs (C) as well as time to market (T). These are abbreviated as PQCT in this book. In other words, significantly improving PQCT means producing higher-quality software more quickly, efficiently, and cost-effectively. These will eventually contribute to the improvement of our lives. Second, research, education, and practice of software engineering processes, methods, and techniques are the means to significantly improve PQCT.

Software development involves three tracks of interweaving activities, as Figure 1.1 exhibits. These activities take place simultaneously throughout the software life cycle:

1. Software development activities.
2. Software quality assurance activities.
3. Software project management activities.

Software development activities are a set of activities performed to transform an initial system concept into a software system running in the target environment. Like many engineering projects, software development activities include software

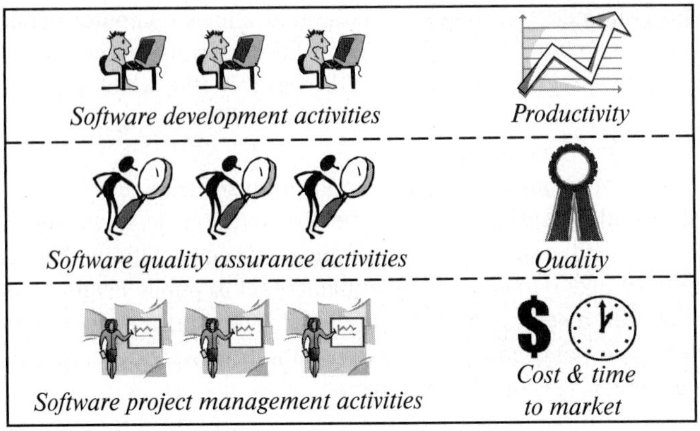

FIGURE 1.1 Three tracks of life-cycle activities

specification, software design, implementation, testing, deployment, and maintenance. Software specification determines what the customer and users want. These are specified as requirements or capabilities that the software system must deliver. Software design produces a software solution to realize the software requirements. In particular, it determines the overall software structure, called the software architecture, of the software system. The architecture depicts the major system components and how they relate, interface, and interact with each other. Software design also defines the user interfaces as well as high-level algorithms for the system components. During implementation and testing, the design is converted into computer programs, which are tested to ensure that they work as the customer and users expect. The software system is then installed in the target environment, tested and modified to ensure that it works properly. During the maintenance phase, the software system is continually modified to correct errors and enhance functionality until it is abandoned or replaced.

Software quality assurance (QA) activities are carried out alongside the development activities. QA activities ensure that the development activities are carried out correctly; the required artifacts, such as software requirements document (SRD) and software design document (SDD), are produced and conform to quality standards; and the software system will fulfill the requirements. These are accomplished through requirements review, design review, code review and inspection, as well as testing.

Software project management activities ensure that the software system under development will be delivered on time and within budget constraint. One important activity of project management is project planning. It takes place at the beginning of a project, immediately after the requirements for the software system are determined. In particular, effort and time required to perform the three tracks of activities for the project are estimated. A schedule of activities is produced to guide the project. During the development and deployment process, project management is responsible for continuous monitoring of project progress and costs, and executing necessary actions to adapt the project to emerging situations.

1.2 WHY SOFTWARE ENGINEERING?

First, software is used in all sectors of our society. Companies rely on software to run and expand their businesses. Airplanes, vehicles, medical equipment, and numerous other machines and devices rely on software to operate. Internet of Things (IoT), cloud computing, and AI applications also heavily rely on software. Software systems are getting much larger, extremely complex, and highly distributed. Today, it is common to develop systems that contain millions of lines of code. For example, the F35 fighter runs on 8 million lines of code, Microsoft's Windows operating system has about 50 million lines of code, and Google Search plus Gmail plus Google Maps consist of 2 billion lines of code. For many embedded systems, which consist of hardware and software, the software cost has increased to 90%–95% of the total system cost from 5%–10% three decades ago. Some embedded systems use application-specific integrated circuits (ASIC), system on chip (SoC), and/or firmware. These are integrated circuits with the software burned into the hardware. They are costly to replace; hence, the quality of the software is critical. These call for a software engineering approach to system development.

Second, software engineering supports teamwork, which is needed for large system development. Large software systems require considerable effort to design, implement, test, and maintain. A typical software engineer can produce on an average 50–100 lines of source code per day. This includes the time required to perform analysis, design, implementation, integration, and testing. Thus, a small system of 10,000 lines of code would require one software engineer to work between 100 and 200 days or 5–10 months. A medium-sized system of 500,000 lines of source code would require a software engineer to work 5,000–10,000 days, or 20–40 years. It is not acceptable for any business to wait this long. Therefore, real-world software systems must be designed and implemented by a team or teams of software engineers. For example, a medium-sized software system requires 20–40 software engineers to work for one year. When two or more software engineers work together to develop a software system, they face serious conceptualization, communication, and coordination challenges.

Conceptualization is the process of observing and classifying real-world phenomena to form a mental model to help understand the application for which the system is built. Conceptualization is a challenge for teamwork because the software engineers may perceive the world differently due to differences in their education, cultural backgrounds, career experiences, assumptions, and other factors. The parable of the blind men and an elephant explains this. We as software developers are like the four blind men trying to perceive or understand an application. If the team members perceive the application incorrectly, then how can they produce software that will correctly automate the application? If the team members have different perceptions, then how can they design and implement software components that will work with each other? Software engineering provides modeling languages such as the Unified Modeling Language (UML), methods and techniques to help developers establish a common understanding about an application for which the software is built.

When a team of software engineers works together, they need to communicate their analysis and design ideas. However, the natural language is too informal and sometimes ambiguous. Again, UML improves the communication among the developers. Finally, when teams of software engineers work together, how can they collaborate and coordinate their efforts? For example, how do they divide the work and assign the pieces to the teams and team members? How do they integrate the components designed and implemented by different teams and team members? Software engineering provides a solution. That is, software development processes and methodologies, software project management, and QA solve these problems.

1.3 SOFTWARE ENGINEERING ETHICS

Software is present everywhere in our society, and controls and affects every aspect of our lives. Software can do good or cause harm to our society or others. Therefore, software engineers must consider social and ethical responsibilities when designing, implementing, and testing software. In this regard, the ACM/IEEE-CS Joint Task Force on Software Engineering Ethics and Professional Practices recommended the "Software Engineering Code of Ethics and Professional Practice" (Figure 1.2) as the standards for teaching and practicing software engineering.

Software engineers should adhere to these ethical standards in their professional practice as well as daily lives. For example, a software engineer must respect the confidentiality of the client or employer. A software engineer must also respect and protect the intellectual property of the client or employer. Sometimes, a software engineer must choose one act or another. For example, a software engineer happens

Software Engineering Code of Ethics and Professional Practice (Short Version)

PREAMBLE

The short version of the code summarizes aspirations at a high level of the abstraction; the clauses that are included in the full version give examples and details of how these aspirations change the way we act as software engineering professionals. Without the aspirations, the details can become legalistic and tedious; without the details, the aspirations can become high sounding but empty; together, the aspirations and the details form a cohesive code.

Software engineers shall commit themselves to making the analysis, specification, design, development, testing and maintenance of software a beneficial and respected profession. In accordance with their commitment to the health, safety and welfare of the public, software engineers shall adhere to the following Eight Principles:

1. PUBLIC–Software engineers shall act consistently with the public interest.
2. CLIENT AND EMPLOYER–Software engineers shall act in a manner that is in the best interests of their client and employer consistent with the public interest.
3. PRODUCT–Software engineers shall ensure that their products and related modifications meet the highest professional standards possible.
4. JUDGMENT–Software engineers shall maintain integrity and independence in their professional judgment.
5. MANAGEMENT–Software engineering managers and leaders shall subscribe to and promote an ethical approach to the management of software development and maintenance.
6. PROFESSION–Software engineers shall advance the integrity and reputation of the profession consistent with the public interest.
7. COLLEAGUES–Software engineers shall be fair to and supportive of their colleagues.
8. SELF–Software engineers shall participate in lifelong learning regarding the practice of their profession and shall promote an ethical approach to the practice of the profession.

Source: https://ethics.acm.org/code-of-ethics/software-engineering-code/

FIGURE 1.2 The ACM/IEEE code of ethics

to know that a component may behave abruptly in rare circumstances, which might cause property damage or loss of lives. He also knows that his company wants to release the product quickly to gain back market share. If he reports the problem, then the release has to push back considerably, and he would become the "trouble maker." If he does not report, then devastating tragedy might happen. Such a hypothetic scenario has actually occurred again and again in our industry. Management persons also have to choose between right and wrong. If the software engineer reports the problem, would the management take it seriously? As a matter of fact, wrong doings pay big prices–companies were ordered to pay hefty fines, and individuals were jailed for their wrong acts.

Ethical dilemmas can occur in our daily lives. A college student had a job interview soon, but unfortunately his laptop broke. He wanted to borrow his girlfriend's laptop for the weekend to prepare for the interview, but the laptop belonged to her company. In this case, should she lend the laptop to her boyfriend, or not help when he needs the help? What would you think his girlfriend should do?

1.4 SOFTWARE ENGINEERING AND COMPUTER SCIENCE

What is the difference between software engineering and computer science? This question is often asked by students and working professionals. First of all, computer science emphasizes computational efficiency, resource sharing, accuracy, optimization, and performance. These can be measured accurately and relatively quickly. In the last several decades (i.e., from 1950 to the present), all efforts and resources spent in computer science research are aimed to improve these aspects. Most chapters of a computer science textbook are written about methods, algorithms, and techniques to improve or optimize these aspects.

Unlike computer science, software engineering emphasizes software PQCT. For example, obtaining an optimal solution is often the goal of computer science. Software engineering would use a good-enough solution to reduce development or maintenance time and costs. Efforts and resources spent in software engineering R&D are aimed at significantly improving software PQCT. Most chapters of a software engineering textbook are written about methods and techniques to improve these four aspects. Unfortunately, the impact of a software engineering process or methodology cannot be measured easily and immediately. To be meaningful, the impact must be assessed during a long period of time and consume tremendous resources. For example, researchers took more than one decade to realize that the uncontrolled goto statement is harmful. That is, the uncontrolled use of the goto statement results in poorly structured programs, which are difficult to understand, test, and maintain.

Computer science focuses only on technical aspects. Software engineering has to deal with nontechnical issues. For example, the early stages of the development process focus on identifying business needs and formulating requirements and constraints. These activities require domain knowledge, analysis and design experience, communication skill, and customer relations. Software engineering also requires knowledge and experience in project management. User interface design has to consider human factors such as user preference and how users would use the system.

In addition, software development must consider political issues because the system may affect many people in one way or another.

Recognizing the differences between software engineering and computer science could help in understanding and appreciating software engineering processes, methodologies, and principles. Consider, for example, the design of a software system that needs to access a database. Computer science might emphasize efficient data storage and retrieval, and favor a design in which the program accesses the database directly. Such a design would make the program sensitive to changes to the database design and database management system (DBMS). If the database schema or the DBMS is changed or replaced, then considerable changes have to be made to the program. This could be difficult and costly. Therefore, software engineering would not consider this a good design decision unless efficient database access is highly desired. Instead, software engineering would prefer a design that will minimize the impact of database change to reduce maintenance effort, costs, and time.

Despite the differences, software engineering and computer science are closely related. Computer science to software engineering is like physics to electrical and electronics engineering, or chemistry to chemical engineering. That is, computer science is a theoretical and technological foundation for software engineering. Software engineering is application of computer science. However, software engineering has its own research topics. These include research in software processes and methodologies, software verification, validation and testing techniques, among others.

Software engineering is a broad area. A software engineer should know areas of computer science including programming languages, algorithms and data structures, operating systems, database systems, artificial intelligence, and computer networks, to mention a few. Embedded systems development requires the software engineer to have a basic understanding of electronic circuits and how to interface with hardware devices. Finally, it takes time for a software engineer to gain domain knowledge and design experience to become a good software architect. These challenges and the ability to design and implement large complex systems to meet practical needs make software engineering an exciting area. The ever-expanding computer application creates great opportunities for the software engineer and software engineering researcher.

1.5 SUMMARY

Software engineering is defined as a discipline that investigates and applies engineering processes and methodologies to improve software PQCT. The need for software engineering is discussed, and software life-cycle activities are described. The chapter ends with a discussion of software engineering ethics and relationship between computer science and software engineering. That is, computer science is a foundation for software engineering. While computer science is mainly concerned with optimization and efficiency, software engineering is concerned with software PQCT. Knowing these should help understand software engineering and the rationale behind the processes, methodologies, modeling languages, design patterns, and many others. All these are designed to improve software PQCT.

1.6 CHAPTER REVIEW QUESTIONS

1. What is software engineering? Why is it needed?
2. What is a software development process?
3. What is software quality assurance?
4. What is software project management?
5. What are the differences and relationship between software engineering and computer science? Can we have one without the other?

1.7 EXERCISES

1.1 Search the literature and find four other definitions of software engineering in addition to the one given in this chapter. Discuss the pros and cons of these definitions.

1.2 A number of methods have been proposed for measuring software productivity. These include counting the lines of source code, number of classes, and number of methods delivered. Each of these has drawbacks. For example, each line of a program could be split into two to "double" the productivity although the functionality of the program has not changed. Discuss the pros and cons of each of these methods.

1.3 Describe in a brief article the functions of the three tracks of life-cycle activities. Discuss how the three tracks of activities work together during the software development life cycle. Discuss how they improve software PQCT.

1.4 Should optimization be a focus of software engineering? Briefly explain, and justify your answer with a practical example.

1.5 Identify three computer science courses of your choice. Show the usefulness of these courses in the software life-cycle activities.

1.6 There are interdependencies between software productivity, quality, cost, and time to market. For example, more time and effort spent in coding could increase productivity. This may result in less time and effort in quality assurance because the total time and effort of a project are fixed. Poor quality could reduce productivity due to rework. Identify three pairs of such interdependencies of your choice. Discuss their short-term and long-term impacts on the software development organization. How should software engineering solve this "dilemma" induced by these interdependencies?

1.7 What would you do if you were the software engineer described in Section 1.4?

1.8 What would you do if your boy/girlfriend desperately needs to use your laptop, but it belongs to your company?

2 Chapter

Software Process and Methodology

Key Takeaway Points

- A software process defines the activities and how the activities fit together over time, often with pre- and postconditions for the activities.
- A software methodology details the steps or how to perform the activities of a software process. A methodology is an implementation of a process.
- Software development needs a process and a methodology.

Writing programs that consist of a few thousand lines of code might be an unprecedented experience and a challenge for many undergraduate and graduate students. However, in the software industry, software development for systems that consist of millions of lines of code is a common practice. The difference between academic programming projects and real-world software development projects is not limited to the number of lines of code. Systems development in the real world has to overcome many other challenges. A disciplined approach for systems development is required. This is similar to all engineering disciplines. One important element of a disciplined approach is a process that defines the activities as well as when to perform each activity. For example, a process for building a custom home may involve the following activities: specification, design, build, inspection, testing, and delivery. A software process also involves similar activities. During the history of software engineering, many software process models have been proposed. Software development requires not only a process but also a methodology. While a process specifies the activities and when to perform each activity, a methodology details the steps, or how to perform the activities, of a process. In other words, a methodology is an implementation of a process.

In summary, this chapter presents the following topics:

- Challenges of system development in the real world.
- Software development as a wicked problem.
- Software process and process models.

- Software methodology and how it differs from a process.
- Agile processes and agile methods.
- An overview of the methodology presented in this book.

2.1 CHALLENGES OF SYSTEM DEVELOPMENT

Developing software systems in the lab is quite different from developing them in the real world. Real-world projects are much larger and much more complex. Besides these obvious challenges, there are others. An understanding of some of the challenges is useful for the study of software engineering. That is, it helps to understand why computer science alone is not enough, and why we need software processes and methodologies. Furthermore, it helps us to know how software processes and methodologies help overcome the challenges. First, there are project challenges. The following are just some of them:

Project Reality 1. Many system development projects have long development durations, which typically range from one year to several years. Real-world projects must meet schedule and budget constraints.

Project Challenge 1. How do we plan, schedule, and manage the project work without a complete knowledge of what the customer wants, and what will happen in the next several years?

Project Reality 2. Many system development projects require collaboration of multiple departments or development teams. For example, many large embedded systems involve both hardware and software components and require the software engineering department to cooperate with hardware departments.

Project Challenge 2. How do we divide the work and assign the interdependent pieces to the departments and teams, and how are we able to smoothly integrate the components produced by the different departments and teams?

Project Reality 3. Different departments or teams may use different development processes, methods, and tools. The departments or teams may be located at different places.

Project Challenge 3. How do we ensure proper communication and coordination among the departments and teams?

Besides project challenges, there are product challenges. Some of them follow:

System Reality 1. Many real-world systems have to satisfy a large number of requirements and constraints including stringent real-time constraints. For example, a mail-handling system has hundreds of requirements and constraints. It is required to scan and process more than 40,000 mail-pieces per hour or 12 mail-pieces per second.

System Challenge 1. How do we develop systems that will fulfill the requirements and constraints?

System Reality 2. Requirements and constraints may change from time to time. Take, for example, a small project that the author had contracted to do.

The requirements changed every week during the first three months due to change requests from the customer.

System Challenge 2. How do we cope with changes that are often inevitable and the exact changes are impossible to predict?

System Reality 3. The system under development is expected to evolve for many, many years, during which numerous changes will be made. Changes made to one component may impact other components, which must be changed as well. This creates the so-called ripple effect of change impact. Moreover, changes to the system may introduce bugs as well as deteriorate the structure of the system. All these make the system more and more difficult to understand, test, and maintain.

System Challenge 3. How do we design systems that are easy to understand, change, and test?

System Reality 4. The system may consist of hardware and software components, use third-party components and multiple implementation languages, and run on multiple platforms and machines located at different places.

System Challenge 4. How do we design systems to hide the hardware, platform, and implementation peculiarities so that changes to these will not affect the rest of the system?

The list is not complete. There are many more challenges in the real world that are not included. However, the list is enough to show that a scientific approach is not adequate to tackle the challenges. We need an engineering approach. Two important components of an engineering approach are software process and software methodology.

2.2 SOFTWARE PROCESS

Advances in computer science, especially non-numerical computation and relational database systems in the 1960s, led to a rapid expansion of computer applications in the business sector. The ad hoc development approaches that existed then could not satisfy the needs of business organizations. The notion of a software development process or software process was introduced. It is defined as follows:

Definition 2.1 A *software process* is a series of phases of activities performed to construct a software system. Each phase produces some artifacts that are the input to other phases. Each phase has a set of entrance criteria and a set of exit criteria.

For example, the waterfall process exhibits a straight sequence of development activities that begin with requirements analysis, followed by software design, implementation, testing, deployment, and maintenance. It is called a waterfall process because its straight sequence of activities resembles a waterfall when the activities are shown vertically one after another. The requirements phase produces the requirements specification, the design phase produces the design, and so on. Frequently, the entrance criteria specify the software artifacts that must be available. For example, the entrance criteria for the software design phase are that the requirements specification must have been produced and reviewed. The exit criteria specify the software artifacts that must be produced. For example, the exit criteria for software design are that the architectural design and high-level design must have been produced and reviewed.

The waterfall process has been used since the 1970s, and some organizations still use it. The straight sequence of phases of the waterfall process simplifies project planning, project scheduling, and project status reporting. Because of these, it is deemed a predictable process. Moreover, the straight sequence of functional activities allows function-oriented project organization. In such an organization, the functional teams are specialized in different functional areas such as requirements analysis, design, implementation, and testing. Projects are carried out by the functional teams in a pipeline manner. Finally, the waterfall process is appropriate for developing large, complex, long-lasting, embedded systems. Examples include mail-sorting and routing systems, process control systems, and many other types of computerized equipment. Such systems need to respond to numerous hardware-generated events, process huge amounts of incoming data, and control the behaviors of hardware devices. Usually, the capabilities or requirements of such systems are jointly defined by the equipment manufacturer and the customer. In many cases, the system to be developed is merely a major enhancement of the functionality, performance, and security of an existing system. The vendor has experience and good knowledge of the application and what the customer wants; hence, major changes to the requirements are rare. Once the purchase order is issued, the customer does not have access to the equipment until the acceptance testing stage, although the customer participates in reviews and prototype demonstrations. The phased approach allows each phase to be performed rigorously to ensure that the system runs reliably and satisfies performance and timing constraints.

The waterfall process has a number of drawbacks. First, the strict sequence of phases and related milestones makes it difficult to respond to requirements change. This is because requirements change requires considerable rework. Unfortunately, requirements change is the way of life, due to business competition, new regulations or standards, or advances in technology. For many applications, the long development duration is unacceptable because the requirements were identified long ago and business needs have changed dramatically. In addition, the users cannot experiment with the system to provide feedback until it is released. Experiences show that early user feedback helps in detecting misconception of business needs and problems in user interface design. Finally, the customer cannot reap the benefits of the new system during the long development period.

2.3 THEORY OF WICKED PROBLEMS

The problems of the waterfall process are closely related to the theory of wicked problems. The theory was first studied by Horst Rittel, a late professor at the University of California, Berkeley. Wicked problems exhibit a number of properties, making them difficult to solve. In contrast, tame problems exhibit nice properties and can be solved by using a process like the waterfall. Examples of wicked problems include urban planning and many real-world software development projects. Tame-problem examples are solving of mathematical equation systems, development of chess-playing programs, compiler construction, and operations research. Figure 2.1 compares the properties of these two types of problem.

For a tame problem such as solving an equation system, the problem has a definite formulation. Moreover, the specification and the solution can be separated. The equation system is the specification; an assignment of values to the variables is a solution. This is not true for many application software development projects. For example, the requirements specification may not specify the real requirements. This is why many projects fail because the delivered system does not meet users' expectation. Prototypes are often constructed to help identify real requirements. In this case, the prototype is both the specification and the solution because it not only specifies the features but also how to implement the features.

The number of steps to solving a tame problem such as an equation system is finite. Moreover, each step has only a finite number of possible moves. This is not the case for software design. The number of possible design alternatives is limited only by the ability of the designer. The process to solving an equation system stops when a solution is found. But software projects terminate because the developer has run out of time, budget, or patience. A solution to an equation system can be evaluated immediately and objectively as correct or wrong. But a software system can only be evaluated in terms of good or bad, and the judgment often depends on the knowledge, experience, and personal preference of the evaluator. Moreover, many software systems are subject to lifelong testing. For example, a computerized sell-off on May 6, 2010, sent the Dow Jones Industrials to a loss of nearly 1,000 points, or 10% of its value, at one time. Procter & Gamble, a stable blue-chip stock, dropped almost 37% to a seven-year low. These were caused by a simple typographical error that should have

Properties of a Tame Problem	Properties of a Wicked Problem
1) A tame problem can be completely specified.	1) A wicked problem does not have a definite formulation.
2) For a tame problem, the specification and the solution can be separated.	2) For a wicked problem, the specification is the solution, and vice versa.
3) For tame problems, there are stopping rules.	3) There is no stopping rule for a wicked problem–you can always do it better.
4) A solution to a tame problem can be evaluated in terms of correct or wrong.	4) Solutions to wicked problems can only be evaluated in terms of good or bad, and the judgment is subjective.
5) Each step of the problem-solving process has a finite number of possible moves.	5) Each step of the problem-solving process has an infinite number of choices–everything goes as a matter of principle.
6) These is a definite chain of cause-effect reasoning.	6) Cause-effect reasoning is premise-based, leading to varying actions, but it is hard to tell which one is the best.
7) The solution can be tested immediately; once tested, it remains correct forever.	7) The solution cannot be tested immediately and is subject to life-long testing.
8) The solution can be adapted for solving similar problems.	8) Every wicked problem is unique.
9) The solution process is a scientific process.	9) The solution process is a political process.
10) If the problem is not solved, simply try again.	10) The problem solver has no right to be wrong because the consequence is disastrous.

FIGURE 2.1 Properties of tame and wicked problems

been prevented. The trading system had been used for many years, but this incident was another lifelong test. While the solution to a tame problem could be adapted to solve a similar problem, every application software development project is unique. This is why application software is developed or custom made, not manufactured.

Software development is not a scientific process. In other words, many decisions are not made scientifically. For example, a good-enough algorithm is chosen instead of an optimal algorithm because it is more economical to implement and use. Sometimes, the decision to use, or not to use, a specific programming language or a third-party product is a political decision. In one project that the author was contracted to develop, the client requested not to use any product from a particular vendor because the client had had a bad experience. Finally and importantly, software failures could result in millions of dollars of property damage and loss of human lives. Therefore, software developers have no right to be wrong. Tame problems do not share this property–if the result is incorrect, the problem solver can try again.

2.4 SOFTWARE PROCESS MODELS

During the history of software engineering, many software process models have been proposed. All of them aimed to rectify the problems associated with the waterfall process. Most models adopt an iterative, rather than a strictly sequential, process of activities. This section presents some of these process models.

2.4.1 Prototyping Process

The prototyping process model recognizes the mismatch between the software and users' expectation. As a solution, a prototype of the system is constructed and used to acquire and validate requirements. Prototypes are also used in feasibility studies as well as design validation. A simple prototype shows only the look and feel and a series of screen shots to illustrate how the system would interact with a user. A sophisticated prototype may implement many of the system functions.

Prototypes are generally classified into throwaway prototypes and evolutionary prototypes. A throwaway prototype is constructed quickly and economically–just enough to serve its purpose. A throwaway prototype could be used as a reference implementation to check whether the implementation produces the correct result. Furthermore, it could be used to train users before the system is released.

2.4.2 Evolutionary Process

Throwaway prototypes imply that much effort is wasted. This is true when sophisticated prototypes are needed for feasibility study and design validation of large, real-time embedded systems. The evolutionary process model is aimed at saving the effort by letting the prototype evolve. It lets the users experiment with an initial prototype, constructed according to a set of preliminary requirements. Feedback from the users is used to evolve the prototype. This is repeated until no more extensions are required. This process is called the evolutionary process. Because the prototype is not a throwaway prototype, it is constructed with operational functionality and needed robustness.

The evolutionary process is most suitable for exploratory types of projects, where the exact requirements and algorithms are to be discovered from working with the system. Many real-world projects belong to this category, including intelligent systems and research software as well as distributed real-time embedded systems. Intelligent systems and research software are aimed to explore unknown worlds and discover unknown things such as gene sequencing. Distributed real-time embedded systems such as Internet of Things (IoT) actively interact with its complex environment. The behavior of such a system is difficult to predict. The evolutionary process allows the requirements, design, and algorithms to evolve while the system is being developed.

2.4.3 Spiral Process

The spiral process, proposed by Barry Boehm, is known for its unique feature for risk management. As its name implies, the development process looks like a spiral, as shown in Figure 2.2. Each cycle of the spiral is aimed at enhancing a certain aspect

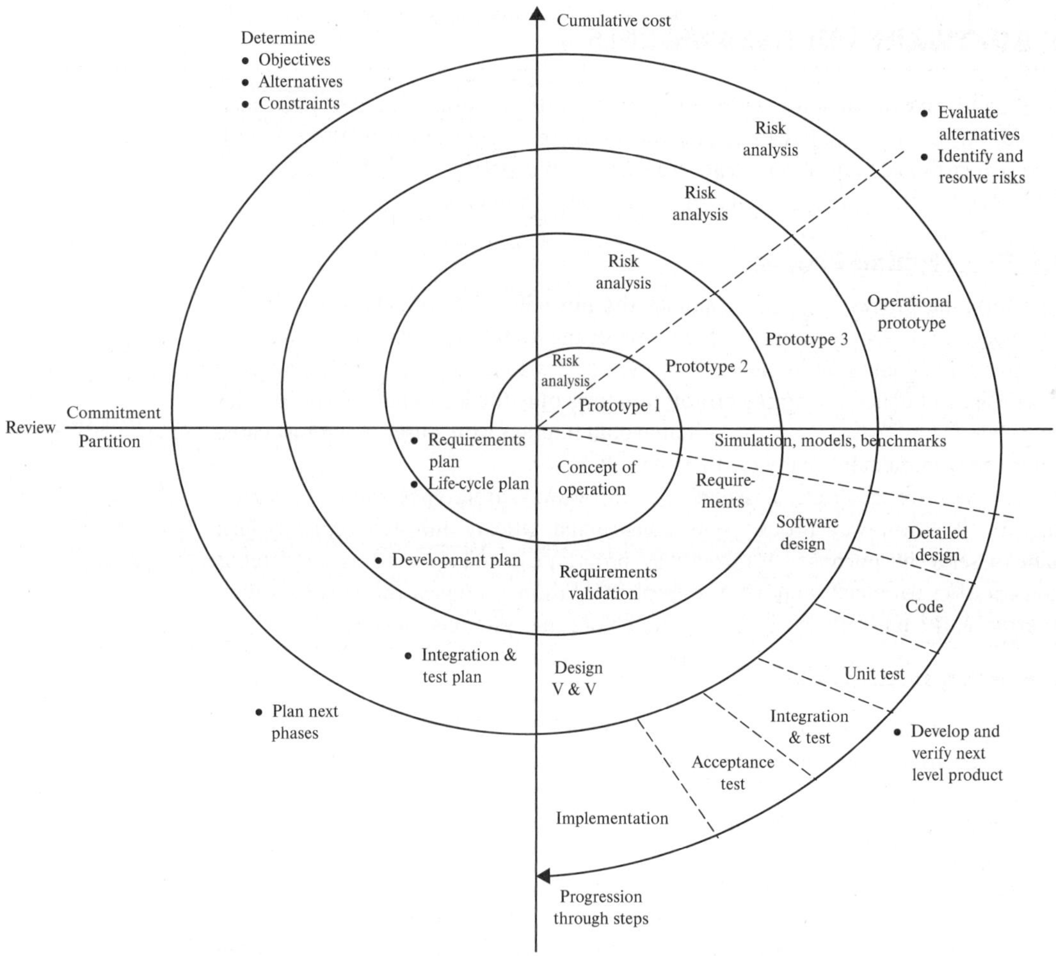

FIGURE 2.2 The spiral process

of the system under development, for example, functionality, performance, or quality. In this sense, the system evolves incrementally as the model iterates the spiral cycles. Each cycle of the spiral selectively executes some of the following steps:

1. *Determine the objectives, alternatives, and constraints for the current cycle* (the northwest corner of the spiral). The objectives, the alternative approaches to accomplish the objectives, and the constraints that must be satisfied are identified in this step. Project risk items are identified and prioritized.
2. *Evaluate alternatives; identify and resolve risks* (the northeast corner of the spiral). The alternatives to accomplish the objectives within the constraints are evaluated. Risks of not achieving the objectives are identified and ways to resolve the risks are developed. Prototyping, simulation, modeling, and benchmarking are some of the techniques for risk resolution. Depending on the outcome of risk analysis and resolution, the next step may be one of the following:
    - If there are remaining risks, then the subsequent steps would be the southwest corner, that is, planning for the next level of prototyping, followed by a new prototyping cycle.
    - If the previous cycles have resolved the major known risks, then the subsequent steps could proceed like the waterfall, as shown in the southeast corner of the model.
    - If the prototype produced during the previous rounds are operational and robust enough to evolve into a final system, then the subsequent steps would extend and use the prototype as in the evolutionary prototyping model (Section 2.4.1). That is, they would proceed toward the right in the northeast corner.
3. *Develop and verify next level system* (the southeast corner). This step proceeds like the waterfall model, as shown in Figure 2.2.
4. *Plan next phases* (the southwest corner). For either a new initiative or a continuing project, this step defines the requirements, the life-cycle activities, and the integration and test plan for the next phase.

2.4.4 The Unified Process

The Rational Unified Process (RUP) or Unified Process (UP), as shown in Figure 2.3, consists of a series of cycles. Each cycle concludes with a release of the system. Each cycle has several iterations. The iterations are grouped into four phases: inception, elaboration, construction, and transition. Each phase ends with a major milestone, at which the manager makes an important project decision as to continue or terminate the project. Each iteration goes through a series of workflow activities, including requirements analysis, design, implementation, and testing. The gray areas in Figure 2.3 are rough indications of the extent of the workflow activities that are carried out during the phases. The focuses of the four phases are described below.

- *Inception*. The first one or two iterations constitute the inception phase. This phase produces a simplified use case model, a tentative software architecture, and a project plan. In simple terms, a use case models a business process of the application for which the system is being developed. Verb-noun phrases are commonly used to describe use cases. For example, *Deposit Money*, *Withdraw Money*,

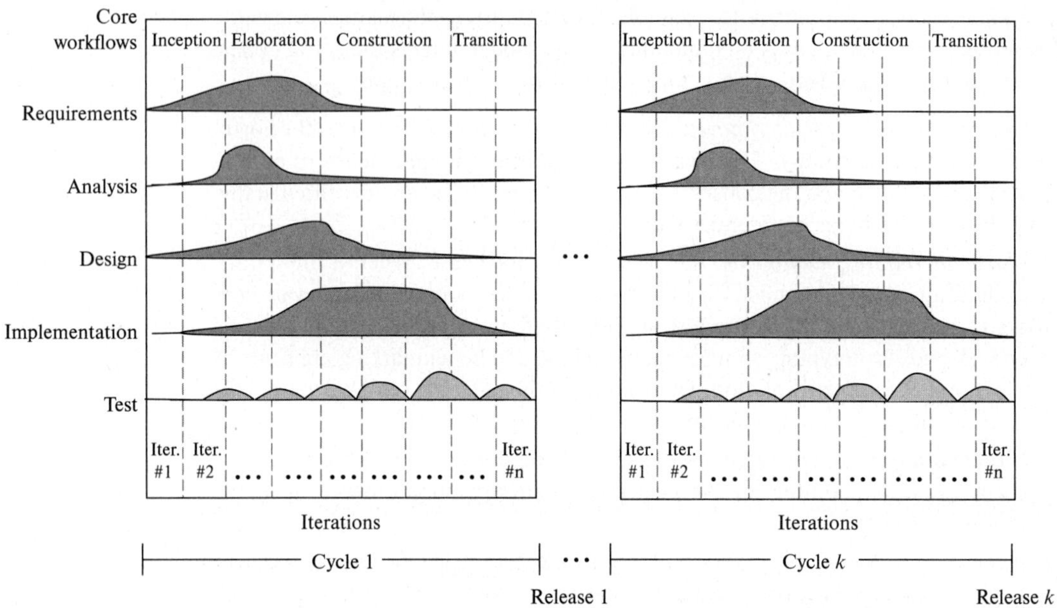

FIGURE 2.3 Illustration of the Unified Process

and *Check Balance* are use cases for an automatic teller machine (ATM). The use case model contains the most critical use cases of the software system.

- *Elaboration*. The elaboration phase consists of the next several iterations. During this phase, most use cases are specified, and an architectural design of the software system is produced. The most critical use cases of the software system are designed and implemented.
- *Construction*. During the construction phase, the remaining use cases are iteratively developed and integrated into the system. The system can be incrementally installed in the target environment.
- *Transition*. During the transition phase, activities are performed to deploy the software system. These include user training, beta testing, defect correction, and functional enhancement.

The UP focuses on identifying use cases and uses them to plan the iterations to develop and deploy the system. In this sense, the UP is characterized as *use case driven*. The UP determines the architecture or the overall structure of the system early in the life cycle and uses it to guide the development of the software system. For this reason, the UP is said to be *architecture-centric*. The other two features of the UP are that it is *iterative* and *incremental* because the system is developed and deployed iteratively and incrementally.

2.4.5 Personal Software Process

The personal software process (PSP), proposed by Watts Humphrey, is a comprehensive framework that is designed to train individual software engineers to improve their personal software processes. PSP consists of a series of scripts, forms, standards, and guidelines that the software engineer can apply to carry out a number of predefined programming exercises. Rather than enforcing a specific development method, the PSP allows the software engineer to choose the development methods. Throughout the training, the PSP helps the software engineer identify areas for improvement. It also helps the software engineer develop abilities that are useful in a teamwork environment, such as developing the ability to estimate more accurately and the ability to meet commitments. As stated above, the PSP is meant to improve the personal software process of a software engineer; it is not meant to be a software development process. That is, after the training, the software engineer is expected to develop and use his own software processes to produce high-quality software. It is believed that quality increase leads to productivity increase because the effort and time spent in testing and debugging are reduced.

2.4.5.1 The PSP Process Evolution

To facilitate learning, the PSP uses an evolutionary approach. That is, the framework is presented in a series of predefined processes, named PSP0, PSP0.1, PSP1, PSP1.1, PSP2, PSP2.1, and PSP3.0. Each of these processes introduces a couple of good software engineering techniques or practices.

The PSP0 and PSP0.1 introduce process discipline and measurement. In particular, PSP0 introduces the baseline process, time recording, defect recording, and defect type standard. PSP0.1 introduces coding standard, size measurement, and process improvement proposal. The PSP1 and PSP1.1 introduce estimation and planning. In particular, PSP1 introduces size estimation and test reporting while PSP1.1 covers planning and scheduling. The PSP2 and PSP2.1 introduce quality management and design. In particular, PSP2 presents code review and design review, and PSP2.1 introduces a design template. Finally, the PSP3.0 is designed to guide the development of component-level programs.

2.4.5.2 PSP Script

In PSP, all processes are described using *process scripts*. Each script specifies the purpose, the entry criteria, the steps or activities of the process, and the exit criteria. For example, the baseline process PSP0 consists of six phases: *planning, design, code, compile, test,* and *postmortem*. This process can be described by the script shown in Figure 2.4. It consists of three steps: (1) planning; (2) development, which encompasses design, code, compile, and test; and (3) postmortem. The entry criteria of a script specify the software artifacts that must be available before the process can begin. The steps list the activities and descriptions of the activities. The exit criteria specify the software artifacts that must be produced when the process is completed.

The postmortem step in Figure 2.4 is a unique feature of the PSP. It requires the software engineer to complete a Project Plan Summary form with the actual time, defect, and size data. This form is described in PSP Forms below. The software engineer completes the form at the end of each programming exercise. The form allows the software engineer to observe his personal software practices, identify areas to improve, and acquire data to use in estimation.

Purpose		To guide module-level program development
Entry Criteria		• Problem description • PSP0 Project Plan Summary form • Time and Defect Recording logs • Defect Type standard • Stopwatch (optional)
Step	Activities	Description
1	Planning	• Produce or obtain a requirements statement • Estimate development time • Fill the Project Plan Summary form • Complete the Time Recording log
2	Development	• Design the program • Implement the design • Compile the program; fix and log all defects found • Test the program; fix and log all defects found • Complete the Time Recording log
3	Postmortem	Complete the Project Plan Summary form with actual time, defect, and size data
Exit Criteria		• A thoroughly tested program • Completed Project Plan Summary form with estimated and actual data • Completed Time and Defect Recording logs

FIGURE 2.4 PSP activities are described by scripts

The PSP adopts a recursive view of the development process. That is, a process consists of a series of activities, and an activity can be described by a lower-level process. For example, the planning step in Figure 2.4 is a process, which can be described by another script. The script may consist of a requirements step, a resource estimation step, and a scheduling step. Similarly, the development step in Figure 2.4 can be described by a script consisting of design, code, compile, and test steps.

2.4.5.3 PSP Forms

PSP uses forms to facilitate documentation. Each form specifies the ordinary information such as student name, date, program name, program number, instructor, and the programming language. To be consistent with the forms, the following presentation will use the terms *student* and *software engineer* interchangeably. Some of the forms are described below.

The Time Recording Log. This form has seven columns, as shown in Figure 2.5. The Delta Time is the Stop Date and Time minus Start Date and Time minus Interrupt Time. Each student fills in the entries for each step/phase of the process on one line of the form. For example, after completing the baseline process PSP0, the student fills in one line of the form for each of the planning, design, code, compile, test, and postmortem steps.

The Defect Recording Log. Figure 2.6 shows the Defect Recording Log form. At the top are the 10 defect types, which are explained in Figure 2.7. Each student is required to specify the defects detected and removed during the course of a

PSP Time Recording Log

Student		Date	
Program		Program#	
Instructor		Language	

Project	Phase	Start Date and Time	Interrupt Time	Stop Date and Time	Delta Time	Comments

FIGURE 2.5 PSP time recording log

PSP Defect Recording Log

Defect Types	
10 Documentation	**60 Checking**
20 Syntax	**70 Data**
30 Build, Package	**80 Function**
40 Assignment	**90 System**
50 Interface	**100 Environment**

Student	Student 3	Date	1/19
Program	Standard Deviation	Program#	1
Instructor	Brown	Language	C++

Project	Date	Number	Type	Inject	Remove	Fix Time	Fix Ref.
1	1/19	1	20	Code	Comp.	1	

Description Missing semicolon.

Project	Date	Number	Type	Inject	Remove	Fix Time	Fix Ref.
		2	20	Code	Comp.	1	

Description Missing semicolon.

FIGURE 2.6 PSP defect recording log

Summary of PSP Defect Types

ID	Defect Type	Description
10	Document	Comments, messages, and manuals
20	Syntax	Spelling, punctuation, typos, and instruction formats
30	Build, Package	Change management, library, version control
40	Assignment	Declaration, duplicate names, scope, limits
50	Interface	Procedure calls and references, I/O, user formats
60	Checking	Error messages, inadequate checks
70	Data	Structure, content
80	Function	Logic, pointers, loops, recursion, computation, function defects
90	System	Configuration, timing, memory
100	Environment	Design, compile, test, or other support system problems

FIGURE 2.7 Summary of PSP defect types

process. For each defect, the student enters the program number, the date on which the defect was found, the defect identification number, the type of the defect, the phase in which the defect was introduced and removed respectively, the time spent to find and fix the defect, the defect number that during its fix introduces the current defect, and a brief description of the defect including the error and why it was introduced.

The Project Plan Summary Form. The Project Plan Summary form mentioned in the last section is shown in Figure 2.8. It consists of four sections. At the top of the form is the descriptive information, which specifies the student name, date, program name, program number, instructor, and the programming language used. The Time in Phase (in minutes) section specifies the planned time for the process, and the actual time, the to-date time, and the to-date % time for each of the phases. For example, if a student spent 30 minutes in the design phase for the first program and 25 minutes in the design phase for the second program, then the actual and to-date times for the first program are 30 minutes. The actual and to-date times for the second program are 25 minutes and 55 minutes, respectively. If the total to-date time for the first program is 117 minutes, then the to-date % time for the first program is 25.6% (i.e., 30 divided by 117).

PSP0 Project Plan Summary Form

Student	Student 3	Date	1/19
Program	Standard Deviation	Program #	1
Instructor	Brown	Language	C++

Time in Phase (min.)	**Plan**	**Actual**	**To Date**	**To Date %**
Planning		5	5	4.3
Design		30	30	25.6
Code		32	32	27.4
Compile		15	15	12.8
Test		5	5	4.3
Postmortem		30	30	25.9
Total	180	117	117	100.0

Defects Injected	**Actual**	**To Date**	**To Date %**
Planning	0	0	0.0
Design	2	2	28.6
Code	5	5	71.4
Compile	0	0	0.0
Test	0	0	0.0
Total Development	7	7	100.0

Defects Removed	**Actual**	**To Date**	**To Date %**
Planning	0	0	0.0
Design	0	0	0.0
Code	0	0	0.0
Compile	6	6	85.7
Test	1	1	14.3
Total Development	7	7	100.0
After Development	0	0	

FIGURE 2.8 PSP0 project plan summary form

The defects-injected section has the same columns and rows as the time-in-phase section and records the number of defects by phase. The defects-removed section is similar to the defects-injected section and records the number of defects removed by phase.

The PSP also includes methods to help the software engineer in estimation and planning. In addition, PSP presents quality assurance procedures to help the software engineer improve software quality. These are presented in Appendix A.

2.4.6 Team Software Process

The *team software process* (TSP) was developed by the Software Engineering Institute (SEI) to enable team members who are trained in PSP to work together to carry out a team project. As shown in Figure 2.9, the TSP consists of a series of cycles. Each cycle performs a series of activities. A TSP project begins with a TSP launch process to build the team and produce a project plan. The launch process is guided by a trained and qualified TSP coach. The process identifies the customer's and users' needs and assigns roles to team members. It produces an initial system concept, a development strategy, and a plan to develop the system. The TSP team also produces a quality plan and a risk management plan. The plans are presented to the management, which may approve or request changes. The last step of each cycle is the postmortem. At the postmortem meeting, the team reviews the launch process, identifies and records improvement suggestions, and assigns follow-up items to team members.

The TSP activities of each cycle are specified in a script. Figure 2.10 illustrates a script that is tailored to use the methodology presented in this textbook. That is, the methodology implements the TSP process. The script shown in Figure 2.10 is designed to fit one semester of teamwork, including learning. It can be modified or tuned to fit different situations. For example, it could run in a shorter period. In this case, there will be only one or two cycles. It could drop some topics; for example, applying

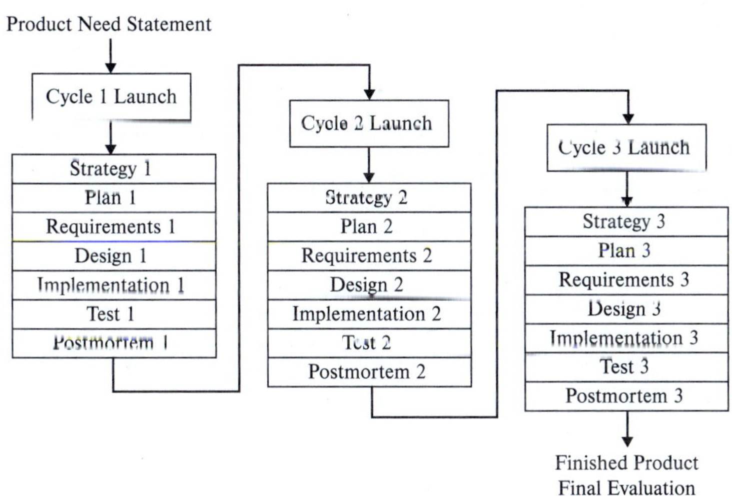

FIGURE 2.9 Team software process

A Team Software Process Script

Purpose		To guide a team through developing a software product
Entry Criteria		• An instructor guides and supports one or more five-student teams. • The students are all PSP trained. • The instructor has the needed materials, facilities, and resources to support the teams. • The instructor has described the overall product objectives.
General		The PSP process is designed to support three team modes. Follow the scripts that apply: 1. Develop a small- to medium-sized software product in two or three development cycles. 2. Develop a smaller product in a single cycle. 3. Produce a product element, such as a requirements, design, or a test plan, in part of one cycle.
Week	**Step**	**Activities**
1	Review	• Course introduction and PSP review • Read preface, introduction, and this chapter; focus on the PSP section
2	LAU1	• Review course objectives and assign student teams and roles • Read TSP and overview of the agile unified methodology in this chapter
	STRAT1	• Produce the conceptual design, establish the development strategy, make size estimates, and assess risk • Apply a software architectural design style (in most cases the N-tier architecture) • Read architectural design and project management chapters; focus on estimation and risk management sections
3	PLAN1, REQ1	• Define and inspect requirements, focus on high-priority requirements • Derive use cases from the requirements, produce use case diagrams and traceability matrix, specify high-level use cases • Allocate the use cases to the cycles, produce allocation matrix • Review the use cases, use diagrams, high-level use case specifications, and matrices • Read system engineering, software requirements elicitation, and quality assurance chapters; focus on requirements-related sections; read deriving use cases chapter
4	REQ1, DES1	• Perform cycle 1 domain modeling (brainstorming, domain concept classification, and domain model visualization) • Specify cycle 1 expanded use cases, produce use case based test cases • Review domain model expanded use cases, and use case-based test cases • Read domain modeling, actor-system interaction modeling, and software testing chapters (use case-based testing)
5	DES1	• Produce and review cycle 1 scenarios, scenario tables, and sequence diagrams • Derive and inspect cycle 1 design class diagram (DCD) and user interface design • Read object interaction modeling, deriving design class diagram, and user interface design chapters
6	IMP1	• Conduct cycle 1 test-driven development (maybe combined with pair-programming) to fulfill 100% branch coverage • Review unit test cases and code • Read implementation, quality assurance, and software testing chapters
7	TEST1	• Build and integrate cycle 1, run use case-based test cases • Demonstrate cycle 1 software to the customer and users, solicit and record feedback • Produce user documentation for cycle 1
8	PM1	• Conduct a postmortem and write the cycle 1 final report • Produce role and team evaluations for cycle 1
	LAU2	• Re-form teams and roles for cycle 2
	STRAT2, PLAN2, REQ2	• Produce the strategy and plan for cycle 2, assess risks • Update and review requirements, domain model, use cases, traceability matrix, and allocation matrix
9	DES2	• Apply GRASP patterns, and update and review cycle 1 sequence diagrams • Produce and inspect cycle 2 expanded use cases and use case-based test cases • Apply GRASP, and produce and review cycle 2 scenarios, scenario tables, and sequence diagrams • Read applying responsibility assignment patterns chapter
10	IMP2	• Conduct test-driven development and inspection of cycle 2, accomplish 100% branch coverage • Review unit test cases and code
	TEST2	• Build, integrate, and test cycle 2; demonstrate cycle 2 software to the customer and users; solicit and record feedback • Produce user documentation for cycle 2

FIGURE 2.10 TSP development script

11	PM2	• Conduct a postmortem and write the cycle 2 final report • Produce role and team evaluations for cycle 2
	LAU3	• Re-form teams and roles for cycle 3
	STRAT3, PLAN3, REQ3	• Produce the strategy and plan for cycle 3, assess risks • Update and review requirements, domain model, use cases, traceability matrix, and allocation matrix
12	DES3	• Apply situation-specific or Gang of Four patterns, update cycle 1 and cycle 2 design diagrams • Produce and inspect cycle 3 expanded use cases and use case-based test cases • Produce and review cycle 3 sequence diagrams (situation-specific patterns are applied) • Read applying situation specific patterns chapter
13	IMP3	• Conduct test-driven development and inspection of cycle 3, accomplish 100% branch coverage • Review unit test cases and code
	TEST3	• Build, integrate, and test cycle 3; demonstrate finished product to the customer and users; solicit and record feedback • Produce and review user's manual for the finished product
14	PM3	• Conduct a postmortem and write the cycle 3 final report • Produce role and team evaluations for cycle 3 • Review the product produced and the processes used, identify lessons learned, and propose process improvements
Exit Criteria		• Completed product or product element and user documentation • Completed and updated project notebook • Documented team evaluations and cycle reports

FIGURE 2.10 *(Continued)*

situation-specific patterns could be moved to another course. Another alternative is running the script to produce only the design but not the implementation.

2.4.7 Agile Processes

The waterfall process works well for tame problems because such problems possess a number of nice properties. Application software development is a wicked problem. It needs a process that is designed to solve wicked problems. Agile processes are such processes. Agile processes emphasize teamwork, joint application development with the users, design for change, and rapid development and frequent delivery of small increments in short iterations. Agile development is guided by agile values, principles, and best practices. All these take into account wicked-problem properties.

2.4.7.1 Agile Manifesto

According to the Agile Manifesto (www.agilemanifesto.org), agile development values four aspects of software development practices, which are different from their conventional, plan-driven counterparts such as a waterfall process. These are listed and explained below.

- *Agile development values individuals and interactions over processes and tools.*
- *Agile development values working software over comprehensive documentation.*
- *Agile development values customer collaboration over contract negotiation.*
- *Agile development values responding to change over following a plan.*

Agility Values Individuals and Interactions over Processes and Tools Conventional, plan-driven practices believe that a good software process is essential for the success of a software project. One conventional wisdom is that "the software quality is as good as the software process." Although the conventional wisdom still has its merits, experiences indicate that the abilities of the team members as well as teamwork are more important. After all, it is the team members who carry out the software process. If the team members do not know how to design, or they do not communicate with each other effectively, then the result won't be good. Conventional practices place significant weight on the use of tools. For this reason, many companies invest heavily in development tools and environments. Some tools are good and solve the intended problems. But these can only be accomplished by the right people, who know how. A UML diagram editor won't help if the software engineer does not know how to design. Although the editor produces nice-looking UML diagrams, these are not necessarily good designs.

Unlike conventional practices, agile methods value individuals and teamwork. This is because software is a conceptual product and the development activities are highly intellectual. If the team members have to work together to jointly build the software product, then the abilities of the team members to interact and contribute to the joint effort is essential to the success of the project. Software processes and tools certainly matter, but individuals and interactions are essential.

Agility Values Working Software over Comprehensive Documentation Before agile development, companies spend tremendous efforts in preparing analysis and design documents. This is partly due to standards audits and partly due to the beliefs that "good software comes from good design documentation, and good design documentation comes from good analysis models." These beliefs are true, but only partly. Many software engineers have experienced that in some cases it is impossible to determine the real requirements, or whether the design works, until the code is written and tested. In these cases, comprehensive documentation won't help and might be harmful because it gives the illusion that a working solution has been found. Comprehensive documentation also means less time is available to coding and testing, which are the only means in these cases to identify the real requirements and the needed design.

Consider, for example, a software to optimize the inventory for a large corporation. The inventory consists of textual descriptions of millions of items written by various employees during the last several decades. Numerous acquisition and merger activities significantly increase the number of items, categories of items, and description formats and styles. The software is required to process the inventory descriptions. The objective is to simplify the inventory and reduce inventory costs. Clearly, the requirements for the software are what the software can do to accomplish this objective. However, without implementing the software, nobody knows exactly what the software can accomplish. This is an example of a wicked problem, that is, the specification and the solution cannot be separated. Suppose that the requirements were somehow identified without needing to implement the software. Then, the design of data structures and algorithms is a grand challenge because it is extremely difficult to know what data structures to use and whether the algorithms work and to what extent. This is due to the diversity of the inventory descriptions, inconsistencies, incomplete entries, typos, and abbreviation variations. A trial-and-error approach is more appropriate.

Agile methods value working software because working software is the bottom line. After all, the development team has to deliver the working software to the customer. Only the working software can be tested to ensure that the software system delivers the required capabilities. In this sense, the working software is the requirements and vice versa. The inventory description classification project discussed above illustrates this. However, this discussion must not lead to the conclusion that agile methods do not want analysis and design. On the contrary, agile methods construct analysis and design models. Nevertheless, agile principles advocate just barely enough modeling to help understand the problem and communicate the design idea but no more.

Agility Values Customer Collaboration over Contract Negotiation Conventional processes involve a contract negotiation phase to identify what the customer wants. A requirements specification is then produced and becomes a part of the contract. During the development process, the customer only participates in a couple of design reviews and acceptance testing. Many important design decisions that should be made with the customer are made by the development team. Although the development team is good in making technical decisions, it may not possess the knowledge and background to make business decisions for the customer. For example, a requirement to support more than one DBMS may not specify which DBMSs are to be supported. Technically, the team may know which DBMSs are the best and should be supported, but the customer may consider other factors to be more important. These include the ability of its information technology (IT) staff to maintain the types of DBMSs, costs to introduce such systems, and compatibility with existing systems. If the development team makes such decisions for the customer, then the resulting system may not meet the customer's business needs.

Customer collaboration is essential for the success of a project. It improves communication and mutual understanding between the team and the customer. Improvement in communication helps in identifying real requirements and reducing the likelihood of requirements misconception. Mutual understanding implies risk sharing; hence, it reduces the probability of project failure. For many projects, the exact outcome of the system, a design decision, or an algorithm is difficult or impossible to predict. In these cases, customer collaboration is extremely important. Mutual understanding means that the development team has a good understanding of the customer's business domain, operations, challenges, and priorities. This enables the team to design and implement the system to meet the customer's business needs.

Mutual understanding also means that the customer understands the limitation of technology, that is, technology alone will not solve all business problems. The customer needs to understand the limitation of the development team, as the following experience of the author illustrates. A customer had insisted that a medium-sized software product be produced in one month, regardless that the author had indicated that this was not possible. In addition to the lack of time, the lack of qualified developers was another challenge. After six months, the team still could not deliver; the project failed. In this story, the customer wanted the system in one month, but no team could meet this demand because the system had to implement a completely new set of innovative business ideas. Customer collaboration might save the project. For example, the two parties could try to understand each other's priorities and limitations and develop a realistic agile development plan to incrementally roll out the innovative features.

Agility Values Responding to Change over Following a Plan Conventional practices emphasize "change control" because change is costly. Once an artifact, such as a requirements specification, is finalized, then subsequent changes must go through a rigorous change control process. The process hinders the team in responding to change requests. Agile methods value responding to change over following a plan because change is the way of life. In today's rapidly changing world, every business has to respond quickly to change in business conditions in order to survive or grow. Thus, change to software is inevitable. Advances in Internet technologies enable as well as require businesses to update their web applications quickly and frequently. The inflexibility of the conventional, plan-driven practice cannot satisfy the needs of such applications. Agile methods thus emerge.

2.4.7.2 Agile Principles

The agile values express the emphases of agile processes. To guide agile development, the agile community also develops a set of guiding principles called agile principles:

1. Active user involvement is imperative.

Active user involvement is required by many agile methods. This is because identifying the real requirements is the hardest part for many software development projects. Conventional approaches spend 15%–25% of the total development effort in requirements analysis. They implement rigid change control to freeze the requirements. These do not seem to solve the problem. It is not the lack of time or effort. It is the inability of human beings to know the real requirements in the early stages of the life cycle. Moreover, the world is changing, so the requirements ought to change.

Active user involvement means that representatives from the user community interact with the development team closely and as frequently as needed. For example, a couple of knowledgeable user representatives are assigned to the project. They stay and work with the team or visit the team regularly several times a week. These arrangements greatly improve the communication and understanding between the team and the users. These, in turn, ensure that requirement misconceptions are corrected early, users' feedback is addressed properly and timely, and decisions about the system are made with the users. All these imply that real requirements are identified and prioritized, and the system is built to meet users' expectations.

2. The team must be empowered to make decisions.

Agile development values individuals and interactions over processes and tools. This principle realizes this. That is, team members are required and encouraged to make technical decisions and take responsibility and ownership. To be able to do this, the team members are required to work as a team and interact with each other and the users throughout the project. Nevertheless, this principle does not mean that the team should make business decisions for the customer and users. For example, whether a nurse should be allowed, or not allowed, to update a patient's medical record is a business decision. The team must not make such a decision for the customer, even if the team had developed a similar system for another client. In this case, the "active user involvement" principle tells us that the team should discuss with the customer and users, and implement the outcome of the discussion.

3. Requirements evolve, but the timescale is fixed.

Unlike conventional approaches that freeze the requirements, agile processes are designed to welcome change. This principle means that the scope of work is allowed to evolve to cope with requirements change, but the agreed time frame and budget are fixed. This means that new or modified requirements are accommodated at the expense of low-priority requirements. That is, the extra effort is compensated by giving up other requirements that are not mission critical or have lower priorities. Of course, which requirements to be replaced should be agreed with the client.

4. Capture requirements at a high level; lightweight and visual.

Agile development values working software over comprehensive documentation. After all, the bottom line is to deliver the working system, not just the analysis and design documentation. To accomplish this, agile methods capture barely enough of the requirements at a high level, omitting details, and often come with user stories, features, or use cases written on small-size story cards. These are visualized using storyboards or sequences of screen shots, sketches, or other visual means to show how the user would interact with the system. These techniques avoid heavy documentation and make it easy to change and trade off requirements because story cards and storyboards are easy to share and manipulate.

5. Develop small, incremental releases and iterate.

Agile projects develop and deploy the system in bite-sized increments to deliver the use cases, user stories, or features iteratively. This arrangement has several advantages: Project progress is visible, the users only need to learn a few new features at a time, it is easier for the users to provide feedback, and small increments reduce risks of project failure.

6. Focus on frequent delivery of software products.

Before agile development, there are iterative approaches such as the spiral process and the Unified Process. Agile processes differ from their predecessors in frequent delivery of the software system in small, bite-sized increments. Different agile methods suggest different iteration lengths. For example, Dynamic Systems Development Method (DSDM) suggests two to six weeks while Extreme Programming (XP) uses one to four weeks. An iteration in Scrum is called a sprint and is usually set to 30 days. In the software industry, many software development teams use two week iteration intervals because developers know what can be accomplished in two weeks. The iteration duration of the methodology presented in this book is two to four weeks.

7. Complete each feature before moving on to the next.

This principle means that each feature must be 100% implemented and thoroughly tested before moving onto the next. The challenge here is how do we know that the feature is thoroughly tested? Test-driven development (TDD) and test coverage criteria provide a solution. TDD requires that tests for each feature must be written before implementation. To write the test, the programmer has to understand the features. Another benefit is that the code can be tested immediately and frequently. Test coverage criteria defines the coverage requirements that the tests must satisfy. For example, the 100% branch coverage criterion is used by many companies. It requires that each branch of each conditional statement of the source code must be tested at least once.

8. Apply the 80-20 rule.

This is also referred to as the good enough is enough rule. The rule is based on the belief that 80% of the work or result is produced by 20% of the system functionality. Therefore, priority should be given to the 20% of the requirements that will produce the 80% of work or result. This principle advises the development team to direct the customer and users to identify and prioritize such requirements. The rule also reminds team members of the diminishing return associated with the final extra miles. This applies to features that are nice to have, performance optimization that is not really needed, and so forth. For example, an optimal algorithm may not be worth the extra implementation effort if a simpler algorithm is fast enough for the data to be processed.

9. Testing is integrated throughout the project life cycle; test early and often.

This principle and principles 5–7 complement each other. That is, testing is an integral part of frequent delivery of completely implemented small increments of the system. This principle is supported by test tools such as JUnit, a Java class unit testing and regression testing tool. Using such a tool, a programmer needs to specify how to invoke the feature to be tested and how to evaluate the test result. The tool will generate the tests, run the tests, and check the test result, all automatically. The tests can be run as often as desired.

10. A collaborative and cooperative approach between all stakeholders is essential.

Conventional approaches rely on comprehensive documentation to communicate the requirements to the development team. Agile projects capture requirements at a high level and are lightweight. Therefore, collaboration and cooperation between the development team and the customer representatives and users are essential. The parties must understand each other and work together throughout the life cycle to identify and evolve the requirements. Because the new system may significantly change or affect the work habit and performance of the users, collaboration and cooperation between the team and users are essential to the success of the project.

2.5 SOFTWARE METHODOLOGY

Software development requires not only a process but also a methodology. Unfortunately, the term methodology is often left undefined. As a consequence, methodology is often confused with process. Methodology and process are two important concepts of software engineering. They are related but not the same. It is important to distinguish a process from a methodology because the distinction lets a process to use different methodologies, and vice versa. According to Cockburn, a process describes how activities fit together over time, often with pre- and post conditions for the activities ([Cockburn 2006], page 151). He uses the word methodology as found in the Merriam-Webster dictionaries: a series of related methods or techniques ([Cockburn 2006], page 149).

Definition 2.2 A *software methodology* defines the steps or how to carry out the activities of a software process.

A process in general specifies only the activities and how they relate to each other. It does not specify how to carry out the activities. It leaves the freedom to the software development organization to choose a methodology, or develop one that is suitable for the organization. The definition means that a methodology is an implementation of a process. Software development needs a process and a methodology.

2.5.1 Difference between Process and Methodology

Figure 2.11 shows the differences between a process and a methodology. While a process defines the phases of activities or *when to do what,* a methodology details the steps or *how to perform the activities.* Processes are paradigm independent, but

Process	Methodology
• Define phases of activities, or WHEN to do WHAT. • Define entrance and exit criteria for each of the phases. • Do not dictate representations of artifacts. • It is paradigm independent. • Useful for project planning and project management.	• Prescribe detailed steps, or HOW to perform the activities. • Describe procedures, techniques, and guidelines for each of the steps. • Define representations of artifacts. • It is paradigm dependent. • Useful for communication and collaboration between teams and team members.
Examples • Waterfall process • Spiral process • Prototyping process • Unified Process • Agile process	**Examples** • Structured analysis/structured design (SA/SD) • Object Modeling Technique (OMT) • Some agile methods such as Feature-Driven Development (FDD) • Agile unified methodology (AUM), the methodology presented in this book

FIGURE 2.11 Software process and methodology contrasted

methodologies are not. According to the *Online American Heritage Dictionary*, a paradigm is a style, or how people view the world.[1] For example, the structured paradigm views the world and systems as consisting of functions invoking each other. This resembles a C program or a Fortran program. The OO paradigm views the world and systems as consisting of interacting objects. As a consequence, methodologies must define representations of artifacts such as analysis models and design diagrams, but processes are not required to do this. A process may use one of several different methodologies because it is paradigm independent and does not dictate the presentation of artifacts. For example, a waterfall process may use an OO methodology or a structured methodology. A process is useful for project planning and management because they let the project manager know when to do what. On the other hand, a methodology is useful for communication and collaboration between teams and team members because everyone knows the steps and uses the same representations of artifacts. It is very useful for global software development, where the designer, programmer, and tester are geographically separated.

2.5.2 Benefits of a Methodology

The use of a good software development methodology is associated with a number of benefits, including

1. A good methodology helps the development team focus on the important tasks, and guides the team to correctly perform the tasks to produce the desired software.
2. A good methodology improves communication and collaboration between teams and team members because everyone follows the same steps and uses the same modeling and design language.
3. A good methodology improves software productivity and quality due to the guidance provided by the methodology and improved communication and collaboration between teams and team members.
4. A good methodology forms the basis for process improvement because measurements of software quality, productivity, cost, and time to market can be defined and applied to identify areas for improvement.
5. A good methodology forms the basis for process automation because large portions of the methodological steps can be mechanically carried out, making software automation much easier.
6. A good methodology facilitates training of newcomers and enables less-experienced developers to produce quality software because the methodology teaches them how to produce quality software.

2.5.3 Status of Software Development Methodologies

Methodologies fall into four categories [Maier 2021]:

1. *Normative methodologies* are based on solutions or sequences of steps known to work for the discipline.

[1] *The American Heritage Dictionary*, ahdictionary.com/word/search.html?q=paradigm.

2. *Rational methodologies* (no connection with the Rational Software company acquired by IBM in 2003) are based on methods and techniques.
3. *Participative methodologies* are stakeholder-based and capture aspects of customer involvement. Most agile methods, see next section, fall into this category.
4. *Heuristic methodologies* are based on lessons learned.

Unfortunately, "most of software development is still in the stage where heuristic methodologies are appropriate." [Cockburn 2006] Although 15 years have passed, the situation remains the same.

2.6 AGILE METHODS

All agile methods adopt an iterative, incremental development process. Agile methods emphasize short iterations and frequent delivery of small increments. Moreover, all agile methods more or less cover requirements, design, implementation, integration, testing, and deployment activities during each iteration. Nevertheless, the emphases are different from conventional approaches. For example, agile methods value working software over comprehensive documentation. This means barely enough modeling in the requirements and design phases. This section describes several of the most widely used agile methods. Figure 2.12 provides a summary of these methods, which are described in more detail in the next several sections. Each of these methods has a long list of principles, features, values, and best practices. Figure 2.12 lists only three of the most unique features.

2.6.1 Dynamic Systems Development Method

The DSDM emerged in the early 1990s in the United Kingdom as an alternative to rapid application development (RAD). It is a framework that different projects can adapt to perform rapid application development. It has been deemed by some authors to be most suited to financial services applications. DSDM is guided by a set of DSDM principles, which are similar to the 10 agile principles presented in Section 2.4.7. As shown in Figure 2.13, DSDM consists of five phases. The first two phases are performed only once, while the other three phases are iterative:

1. *Feasibility study*. During this phase, the applicability of DSDM and the technical feasibility of the project are determined. The end products include a feasibility report, an outline project plan, and optionally a prototype that is built to assess the feasibility of the project. The prototype may evolve into the final system.
2. *Business study*. During this phase, the requirements are identified and prioritized, a preliminary system architecture is sketched. The end products include a business area definition, a system architecture definition, and a prototyping plan.
3. *Functional model iteration*. During this phase, a functional prototype is iteratively and incrementally constructed. The end products include a functional model containing the prototyping code and the analysis models, a list of prioritized functions, functional prototype review documents, a list of nonfunctional requirements,

AUM*	DSDM	FDD	Scrum	XP
Key Features				
• A cookbook for teamwork using UML. • For beginners and seasoned developers. • Suitable for agile or plan-driven, large and small projects.	• A framework that works with Rational Unified Process and XP. • Base on 80-20 principle. • Suitable for agile or plan-driven projects.	• Feature driven and model driven. • Configuration management, review, inspection, and regular builds. • Suitable for agile or plan-driven projects.	• Scrum master, product owner, and team roles are clearly defined. • 15-minute daily status meeting to improve communication. • Team retrospect to improve process.	• Anyone can change any code anywhere at any time. • Integration and build many times a day whenever a task is completed. • Work ≤ 40 hours a week.
Life Cycle Activities				
Planning Phase 1. Acquire prioritized requirements, aided by domain modeling. 2. Derive use cases from requirements. 3. Assign use cases to iterations. 4. Sketch an architectural design. **Iterative Phase** 1. Accommodate requirements change. 2. Extend domain model to include iteration use cases. 3. Perform actor-system interaction modeling for iteration use cases. 4. Perform behavioral modeling for iteration use cases. 5. Derive/extend the design class diagram to include classes and relationships introduced by iteration use cases. 6. Perform test-driven development/pair programming. 7. Perform integration testing. 8. Deploy iteration use cases.	**Feasibility Study** 1. Assess suitability of DSDM for project. 2. Identify risks. **Business Study** 1. Produce prioritized requirements. 2. Produce an architectural design. 3. Determine risk resolution. **Functional Model Iteration** 1. Identify prototype functionality. 2. Build, review, and approve prototype. **Design & Build Iteration** 1. Build system. 2. Conduct beta test. **Implementation** 1. Deploy system. 2. Assess impact to business.	**Develop Overall Model** 1. Perform system walkthrough. 2. Develop group models. 3. Derive an overall model. 4. Produce a model description. **Build Feature List** 1. Identify business activities to automate. 2. Identify features of business activities. **Plan by Feature** 1. Schedule development of business activities. 2. Assign business activities to chief programmers. 3. Assign classes to team members. **Design by Feature** 1. Produce sequence diagrams to show object interaction using features. 2. Encapsulate features to form classes to implement. **Build by Feature** 1. Implement classes. **Deploy**	**Release Planning Meeting** 1. Identify and prioritize requirements (product backlog). 2. Identify top priority requirements that can be delivered within an iteration called a sprint. 3. Identify sprint development activities. **Sprint Iteration** 1. Planning meeting to determine what to build next, and how. 2. Daily Scrum meeting for team members to exchange status. **Sprint Review Meeting** 1. Increment demo. 2. Team retrospection. **Deployment**	**Exploration** 1. Collect information about the application. 2. Conduct feasibility study. **Planning** 1. Determine stories for the next release. 2. Plan for the next release. **Iterations to First Release** 1. Define/modify architecture. 2. Select and implement stories for each iteration. 3. Perform functional tests by customers. **Productionizing** 1. Evaluate and improve system performance. 2. Certify and test system for production use. **Maintenance** 1. Improve the current release. 2. Repeat process with each new release. **Death** 1. Produce documentation if project is done, or 2. Replace the system if maintenance is too costly.

*AUM: the agile unified methodology described in this book

FIGURE 2.12 Summary of some agile methods

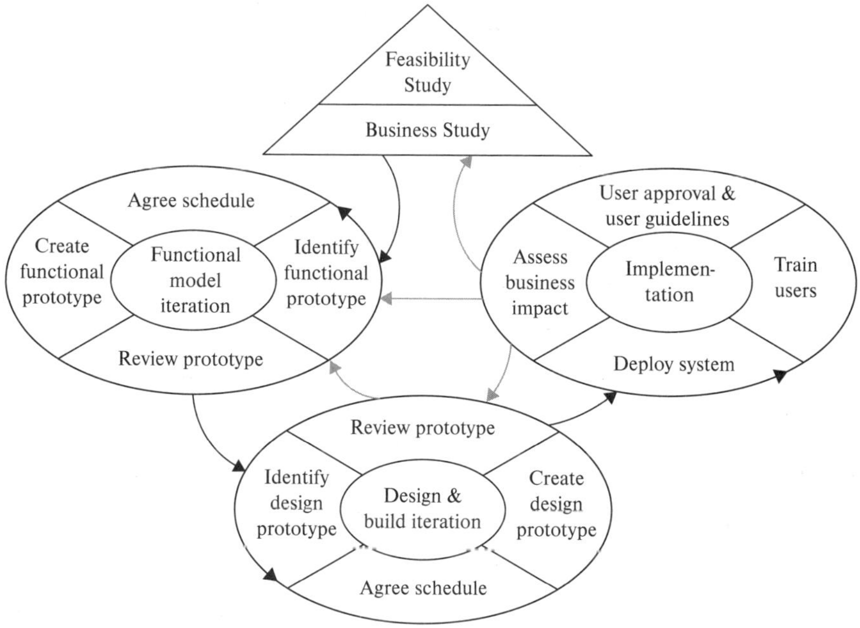

FIGURE 2.13 Process of the Dynamic Systems Development Method

and risk analysis for further development. The prototype review documents specify the user feedback to be addressed in subsequent iterations. The functional prototype will evolve into the final system.

4. *Design and build iteration*. During this phase, the system is designed and built to fulfill the functional and nonfunctional requirements, and tested by the users. Feedback from the users is documented and addressed in future development.
5. *Implementation*. During this phase, the system is installed in the target environment and user training is conducted. The end products include a user's manual and a project review report, which summarizes the outcome of the project and what to do in the future.

2.6.2 Feature-Driven Development

As shown in Figure 2.12, FDD consists of six phases. The first three are performed once and the last three are iterative. FDD is considered more suitable for developing mission-critical systems by its advocates. The six phases of FDD are briefly described as follows:

1. *Develop overall model*. During this phase, a domain expert provides a walk-through of the overall system, which may include a decomposition into subsystems and components. Additional walk through of the subsystems or components may be provided by experts in their domains. Based on the walk through, small groups of developers produce object models for the respective domains. The development teams then work together to produce an overall model for the system.

2. *Build a feature list*. During this phase, the team produces a feature list representing the business functions to be delivered by the system. The features of the list may be refined by lower-level features or functions. The list is reviewed with the users and sponsors.
3. *Plan by feature*. During this phase, the team produces an overall plan to guide the incremental development and deployment of the features, according to their priorities and dependencies. The features are assigned to the chief programmers. The chief programmer is the main decision maker of the team. This team organization is referred to as the chief-programmer team organization. The classes specified in the overall model are assigned to the developers, called class owners. A project schedule including the milestones is produced.
4. *Design by feature, build by feature, and deploy*. These three phases are iterative, during which the increments are designed, implemented, reviewed, tested, and deployed. Multiple teams may work on different sets of features simultaneously. Each iteration lasts a few days to a few weeks.

The roles and their responsibilities of an FDD project are similar to the common job titles. These include project manager, chief architect, development manager, chief programmer, class owner, domain expert, release manager, toolsmith, system administrator, tester, and technical writer.

2.6.3 Scrum

Scrum is a framework that allows organizations to employ and improve their software development practices. It consists of the Scrum teams, the roles within a team, the time boxes, the artifacts, and the Scrum rules. Scrum is an iterative, incremental approach that aims to optimize predictability and control risk. As displayed in Figure 2.14, there is a release planning meeting. It determines the product backlog and the priorities of the requirements, as well as plans for the iterations, called sprints. During the sprint iteration phase, the team performs the development activities to develop and deploy the product increments. Each sprint begins with a sprint planning meeting, at which the team and the product owner determine which items of the product backlog are to

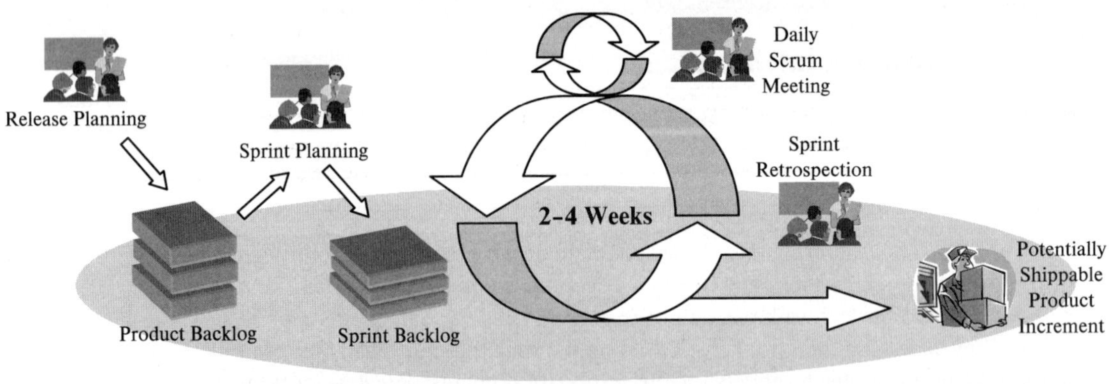

FIGURE 2.14 Scrum development activities

be delivered next, and how to develop them. Each sprint lasts 30 days, but a shorter or longer time period is allowed. One distinctive feature of the Scrum method is its 15-minute daily Scrum meeting. It lets the team members exchange progress status to improve mutual understanding. Another distinctive feature of the Scrum method is the team retrospection at the end of each sprint. This meeting allows the team to improve its practices.

2.6.4 Extreme Programming

Extreme programming (XP) is an agile method suitable for small teams facing vague and changing requirements. The driving principle of XP is taking commonsense principles and practices to extreme levels. For example, if frequent build is good, then the teams should perform many builds every day. The XP process consists of six phases:

1. *Exploration*. During this phase, the development team and the customer jointly develop the user stories for the system to the extent that the customer is convinced that there are sufficient materials to make a good release. A user story specifies a feature that a specific user wants from the system. For example, "as a patron, I want to check out documents from the library system." The development team also explores available technologies and conducts a feasibility study for the project. This phase should take no more than two weeks.
2. *Planning*. During this phase, the development team and the customer work together to identify the stories for the next release, including the smallest, most valuable set of stories for the customer. The stories should require about six months of effort to implement. A plan is produced for the next release. This phase should take no more than a couple of days.
3. *Iterations to first release*. During this phase, the overall system architecture is defined. The customer chooses the stories, the team implements them, and the customer tests the functionality. These activities are performed iteratively until the software is good for production use. Each iteration lasts from one to four weeks.
4. *Productionizing*. During this phase, issues such as performance and reliability that are not acceptable for production use are addressed and removed. The system is tested and certified for production use. The system is installed in the production environment.
5. *Maintenance*. This phase is really the normal state of an XP project. During this phase, the system undergoes continual change and enhancements, such as major refactoring, adoption of new technology, and functional enhancements with new stories from the customer. The process is repeated for each new release of the system.
6. *Death*. The system evolves during the maintenance phase until the system completely satisfies the customer's business needs and hence no more customer stories are added. When this happens, the project is done and enters the death phase, during which the team produces the system documentation for training, repair, and reference. The project also enters the death state if it cannot live to the customer's expectation.

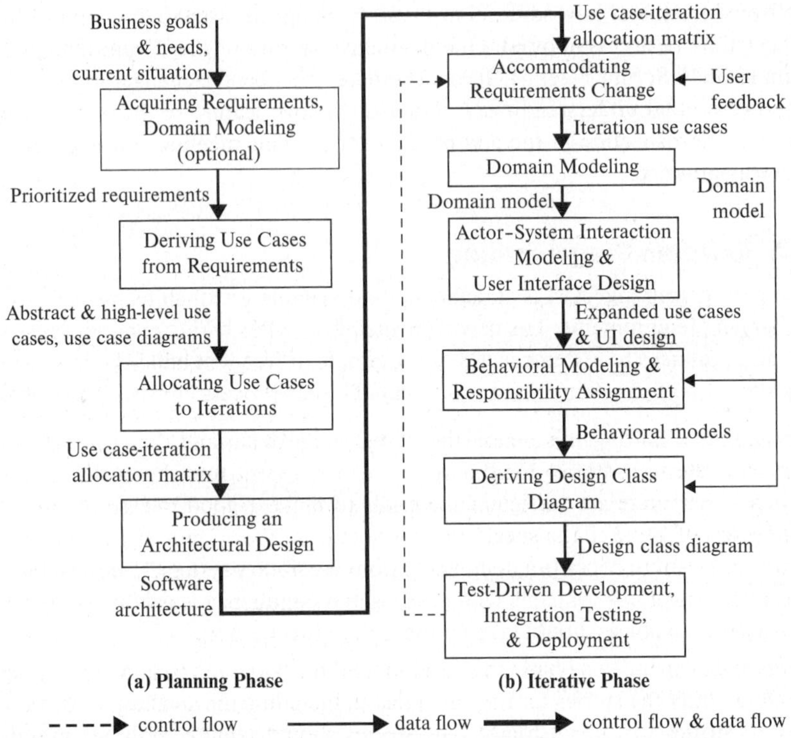

FIGURE 2.15 Overview of the agile unified methodology

2.6.5 Agile Unified Methodology

AUM is the methodology presented in Chapters 4–15 of this book. Figure 2.15 shows its phases and activities along with their input, output, and relationships. The methodology consists of two main phases: (a) the planning phase and (b) the iterative phase. During the planning phase, the development team meets with the customer representatives and users to identify requirements and derive use cases from the requirements. A traceability matrix is produced to show which use cases are derived from which requirements. Use case diagrams (Chapter 7) are produced to show the use cases and subsystems that contain the use cases. The development team also produces an architectural design and a plan to iteratively develop and deploy the use cases. During the iterative phase, the use cases allocated to each iteration are developed and deployed. Each iteration is about two to four weeks. Each iteration performs the following activities:

1. *Accommodate requirements change.* Requirements change, if any, is dealt with at the beginning of each iteration. Change to requirements may lead to change to use cases and other artifacts, as well as the plan to develop and deploy the use cases. After making these changes, the development continues with the following steps according to the changed iteration plan.
2. *Conduct domain modeling.* Domain modeling is a process to help the team understand important domain concepts. The development team acquires such domain

knowledge through communication with the customer representatives, users, and domain experts. The domain concepts are classified into classes, attributes of classes, and relationships between the classes. The result is called a domain model, visualized by using a UML class diagram (Chapter 5).

3. *Conduct actor-system interaction modeling.* Users interact with the system to obtain services provided by the system. Actor–system interaction modeling specifies how users interact with the system to carry out the use cases. The results are called expanded use cases.
4. *Perform behavioral modeling.* Behavioral modeling specifies the computation to process user requests and events that are external to the system. This step produces behavioral models, which include sequence diagrams (Chapter 9), state diagrams (Chapter 13), and activity diagrams (Chapter 14).
5. *Derive design class diagram.* Behavioral modeling and design produce sequence diagrams, state diagrams, and activity diagrams. It is difficult to see the classes, their attributes, and methods, as well as how they relate to each other. This is because a class may appear in several diagrams, which may invoke different functions of different classes in different diagrams. To obtain an integrated view, a design class diagram is produced to serve as a design blueprint to guide subsequent implementation, testing, and maintenance activities.
6. *Implement, test, and deploy the implement.* During test-driven development (TDD), the classes that implement the use cases of the current iteration are implemented and tested. The classes are integrated and tested to ensure that they work together. Finally, the iteration use cases are deployed to the target environment.

2.6.6 Kanban

Kanban is a framework for agile projects. Its centerpiece is a Kanban board, consisting of Kanban cards representing work items. Figure 2.16 shows a sample Kanban board along with other key elements of Kanban. These are explained in the following sections.

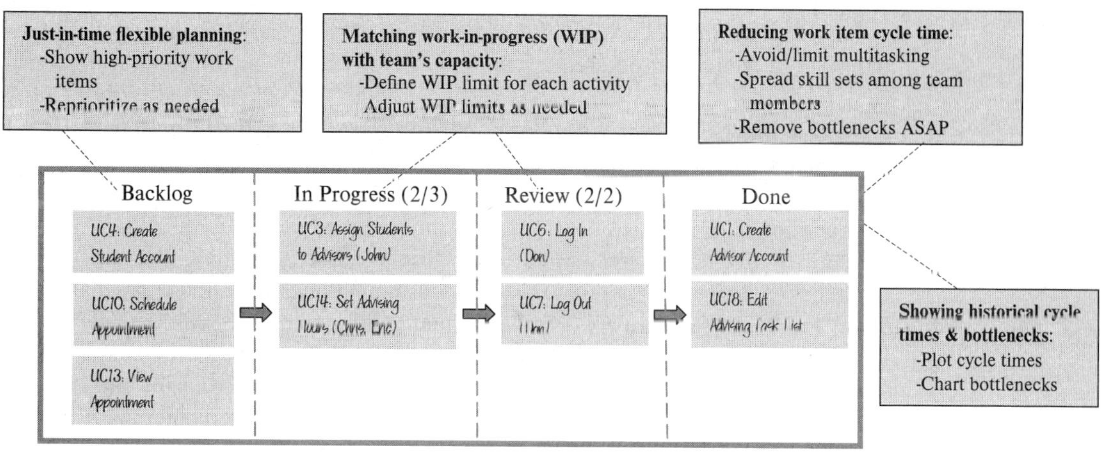

FIGURE 2.16 Key elements of the Kanban framework

2.6.6.1 Kanban Boards and Kanban Cards

Kanban boards and Kanban cards provide instant visualization and instant communication of the status of the workflow. Kanban cards can represent anything that need to be processed, such as user stories, use cases, or features. These should be bite-sized jobs that can be completed in a short time, ranging from a couple of days to a couple of weeks. Kanban boards and Kanban cards can be physical or virtual. If the team members work in the same building and see each other frequently and regularly, then physical boards and cards are convenient. On the other hand, virtual boards and cards effectively support global software development and remote work.

The board is vertically divided into columns called swim lanes. They represent the flow of activities or stages of the workflow. The work items travel from the left-most column to the right-most column. Work items in the left-most or backlog column are jobs that enter into the workflow, waiting to be processed. Work items in the right-most or done column represent jobs that are completed or delivered. Kanban does not dictate the number of columns and the workflow activities. It lets the team define them. Figure 2.16 shows the columns as backlog, in-progress, review, and done, respectively. The in-progress and review columns show the names of the team members who work on the items. When a work item is done in the current column, it is moved to the next column, to be processed by the same or different developer.

2.6.6.2 Just-in-Time Flexible Planning

Unlike the other agile methods, Kanban does not have a formal planning phase. If the project completion time is required, then the team produces an estimate, which may change as the team gains more insight about the project. Kanban planning is flexible and just-in-time. That is, the product owner places the Kanban cards in the backlog column according to their priorities. High-priority work items are placed first and on top of the backlog. When doing this, the product owner takes into account dependencies between the work items. That is, items that others depend on are placed before the other items. Team members pick work items from the backlog according to their skill sets. The product owner limits the number of cards in the backlog to ensure that they are picked and processed by team members.

2.6.6.3 Matching Amount of Work in Progress with Team's Capacity

Kanban discourages multitasking because it incurs considerable task-switching overhead and slows down the workflow. Therefore, Kanban invents the concept of limit of amount of work in progress (LWIP) to combat human temptation to start new work before existing ones are completed. In Figure 2.16, the in-progress column shows the number (2/3). This means that the maximal number of cards or LWIP for that column is 3 and currently there are 2 cards. Similarly, the number (2/2) for the code review column indicates that the limit has reached. The LWIP numbers are not set once and forever. The team may adjust the numbers whenever needed to match the team's capacity. If the number of cards in a column exceeds the limit, then other team members need to join in to clear the bottleneck.

2.6.6.4 Reducing Workflow Cycle Time

In Kanban's terminology, the cycle time is the time that work items take to go from the first column to the last column of the Kanban board. Reducing cycle time will improve workflow efficiency and team productivity. Therefore, Kanban teams should clear bottlenecks in the workflow as soon as possible. This requires that each team member possesses a wide spectrum of skills so that all team members can do all of the activities of the workflow. Some best practices can help spread the skill sets. These include peer design review and peer code review (Chapter 19), pair programming and Ping-Pong programming (Chapter 18).

In peer design/code review, one or more team members evaluate the design/code produced by others and answer a set of review questions. The results are given to the designer/programmer. Often, a review meeting is held to discuss the review results and address issues. In pair programming, the two programmers discuss how to implement the functionality. One of them writes the code and the other checks the code as it is typed and raises doubts, which are addressed right away. The two switch roles each session, which lasts one to two hours. In Ping-Pong programming, one of the two programmers writes the tests and the other implements the functionality. This effectively supports the test-early-and-often agile principle. All of these best practices require the team members to understand the functionality, design, code, and tests. Moreover, team members improve design and coding skills by sharing and learning between team members. As a consequence, knowledge and skills are widely spread among the team members.

2.6.6.5 Showing Historical Cycle Times and Bottlenecks

Kanban emphasizes continuous improvement of the workflow. To help the team identify places for improvement, Kanban uses charts to display the historical cycle times and historical bottlenecks. These help the team assess its capacity as well as identify areas to improve. For example, charting of historical cycle times helps the team understand how much time it needs to progress through the workflow. This information helps the team understand its capacity. It is useful for delivery-time estimation and improvement. Charting of historical bottlenecks helps the team understand effort and time required to perform each of the activities. It serves as the basis for defining and adjusting the LWIP values for the activities and assigning team members to the activities.

2.7 SUMMARY

Software development faces project as well as product challenges. To take on these challenges, a software process is needed. However, the conventional waterfall process is associated with a number of problems. The reason is that it is a process for solving tame problems, but application software development in general is a wicked problem. The quest for a better process leads to the creation of a number of software process models with agile processes as the latest member of the club.

While a software process specifies the phased activities, a methodology describes the steps or how to carry out each of the activities of a process. The differences between a process and a methodology are discussed in this chapter. A software methodology is influenced by the software paradigm adopted to develop the software system. This is because a paradigm determines how the development team views the real world and systems. This, in turn, determines the basic building blocks of the software system and the development methodology. For example, the OO paradigm views the world and systems as consisting of interrelated and interacting objects. This implies that the building blocks of an OO system are objects. Thus, an OO software development methodology must describe how to perform OO modeling, analysis, design, implementation, and testing activities.

The advent of agile processes and methods reflects a significant advance in recognizing the wickedness of software development. The agile manifesto, agile principles, agile processes, and agile methods are all designed to tackle software development as a wicked problem.

2.8 CHAPTER REVIEW QUESTIONS

1. What is a software process, and what are the process models presented in this chapter?
2. What is a software development methodology?
3. What are the differences between a process and a methodology?
4. What are agile processes and agile methods?
5. What are the life-cycle activities of the agile methods presented in this chapter?
6. What are the properties of tame problems and wicked problems, respectively?
7. Why is software development in general a wicked problem?
8. How do agile processes tackle software development as a wicked problem?
9. Will agile development replace the conventional approaches such as the waterfall process?

2.9 REFERENCES

[Cockburn 2006] Cockburn A. *Agile Software Development: The Cooperative Game.* Boston, MA: Addison-Wesley Professional, 2006.

[Maier 2021] Maier MW. *The Art of Systems Architecting (Systems Engineering).* 3rd ed. Boca Raton, FL: CRC Press, June 2021.

2.10 EXERCISES

2.1 What are the similarities and differences between the conventional waterfall model and the Unified Process model? Identify and explain three advantages and three disadvantages of each of these two models.

2.2 Write a brief essay on the differences between a software process and a software methodology.

2.3 Write an essay about how a good process and a good methodology would help tackling the project and product challenges. Limit the length of the essay to five pages, or according to instructions given by the instructor.

2.4 Write a short article that answers the following questions:

- **a.** What are the similarities and differences between the spiral process, the Unified Process, and an agile process of your choice.
- **b.** What are the pros and cons of each of these processes.
- **c.** Which types of projects should apply which of these processes?

2.5 Explain in an essay why the waterfall process is a process for solving tame problems.

2.6 Explain in an essay how agile development tackles application software development as a wicked problem.

Chapter 3

System Engineering

Key Takeaway Points

- System engineering is a multidisciplinary approach to develop systems that involve hardware, software, and human components.
- System engineering defines the system requirements and constraints for the system. It allocates the requirements to the hardware, software, and human subsystems, and integrates these subsystems to form the system.
- Software engineering is a part of system engineering.

Many systems are embedded systems. An embedded system consists of hardware, software, and human components. These components interact with each other to accomplish the mission of the system. An example is an airport baggage handling system (ABHS). It is responsible for moving the baggage from one place to another within an airport. Its hardware includes conveyors and destination-coded vehicles (DCV) running on high-speed tracks. Its software handles luggage check-in and controls the hardware. The human workers operate the hardware and software. Other examples of embedded systems include mail handling systems, air traffic control systems, and manufacturing process control systems. System development of such systems must consider the total system rather than the software system alone. A system engineering approach is required.

Developing a software-only system may need a system engineering approach as well. Consider, for example, an enterprise resource planning (ERP) system. An ERP system is an integrated management information system for the whole organization. It provides integrated support to all functions of the organization including marketing, sales, manufacturing, project management, supply chain management, accounting, customer support, customer relationship management, access control, and more. It automates all these business functions and the workflows among these functions. System engineering is required to develop such a system for several reasons. The system involves many business and organizational functions. The functions involve different disciplines. A multidisciplinary development team is required. The system is large and complex. It may involve legacy systems that have been developed and used for years. How to design the system and integrate with existing databases and business processes is a big challenge. A system engineering approach is needed.

System engineering is a discipline of its own. It is impossible to cover the discipline in one chapter. Therefore, this chapter only serves as an introduction. It aims to provide the software engineer a basic understanding of the processes and activities of system engineering. After reading the chapter, you will understand the following:

- System engineering process.
- System modeling and design techniques.
- Allocation of system requirements to subsystems.
- System configuration management.

3.1 WHAT IS A SYSTEM?

A system consists of components that interact with each other to accomplish a purpose. A system can be big or small, complex or simple, and can exist physically or only conceptually. For example, the universe is a very large system that has been in existence for millions of years. An ant is a very small system. These systems are natural systems. In contrast to natural systems, there are many man-made systems. Man-made systems may exist physically or only conceptually. Mathematical logic, number systems, measurement systems, and many classification systems are examples of conceptual systems. Sprinkler systems that water gardens and lawns and telephone systems that connect millions of families are examples of man-made systems that exist physically. Computer-based systems are man-made systems that include software as a subsystem or component. Examples of computer-based systems include telecommunication systems, email systems, library information systems, and process control systems. Some of these are software-only systems such as email systems. Others consist of both software, hardware, and human subsystems such as the ABHS. All systems share a set of properties or characteristics:

1. Each system consists of a set of interrelated and interacting subsystems, components, or elements. For example, the ABHS consists of several subsystems that interact with each other to accomplish the mission of the system.
2. A system may be a subsystem of a larger system, which in turn may be a subsystem of another system. For example, the conveyor system and the luggage check-in software system are subsystems of the ABHS. But the ABHS is a subsystem of the airport system. In this sense, the relationship between systems and subsystems is a recursive, whole-part relationship. This relationship forms a whole-part hierarchy. Each system or subsystem occupies a position in the hierarchy.
3. Each system exists in an environment and interacts with its environment. For example, the ABHS exists in the airport environment and interacts with the flight information system. The ABHS also works with the departing and arriving flights to load and unload luggage.
4. Systems are ever evolving due to internal or external causes. For example, if the economy is booming, then the number of business travelers as well as leisure travelers increases. The airport needs more terminals and gates. The ABHS also needs to expand. Technology advances may encourage the airport administration to replace bar code scanners with radio frequency identification (RFID)

devices. Internal causes include detected design flaws, component defect, software bugs, and the like. All these require change to the system and cause the system to evolve.

3.2 WHAT IS SYSTEM ENGINEERING?

System development for the ABHS must consider the total system rather than the software system alone. In addition, the ABHS involves multiple engineering disciplines including electrical and electronic engineering, mechanical engineering, civil engineering, and software engineering, among others. Engineers of these disciplines must work together to develop the system. In general, system development for embedded systems involves many engineering and nonengineering disciplines:

- *Electrical and electronic engineering.* Many systems use very large-scale integrated circuits (VLSIC), application-specific integrated circuits (ASIC), sensors, relays, switches, and power supply components, among many others. For example, the ABHS employs bar code printers to generate bag tags and bar code scanners at intersections of the conveyor network to read the bar codes. Electrical and electronic engineers perform analysis, design, integration, and testing of such components and subsystems.
- *Mechanical engineering.* Mechanical devices are used by many systems to perform physical work. For example, the ABHS uses conveyors to move the luggage and pushers at intersections to direct the luggage toward their destinations. The system also uses high-speed tracks to transport the luggage between the terminals. Therefore, the analysis, design, construction, testing, and installation of the ABHS require the participation of mechanical engineers and technicians.
- *Civil engineering.* Large, interconnected structures are needed by the ABHS to protect the equipment and the luggage. The conveyors and high-speed tracks must be mounted on concrete bases. The design, construction, and testing of such structures and bases, among others, are the focus of civil engineering.
- *Software engineering.* Software is responsible for performing the most critical and challenging tasks of the total system. It carries out information processing activities and controls the other equipment and devices of the total system. In the ABHS, the luggage check-in software subsystem lets an airline agent check in luggage for passengers. The luggage bar code processing software directs the mechanical pushers at intersections of the conveyor network to dispatch the luggage toward their destinations. Software engineers are responsible for the analysis, design, implementation, testing, and deployment of the software subsystems and components of the total system.
- *Computer science.* Computer and information sciences are the foundations of software engineering and provide the technologies that are used in most systems. For example, the ABHS involves at least programming languages, algorithms and data structures, database systems, analysis and design of real-time embedded systems, computer network, and computer security.

- *Business administration and economics.* Business aspects are important considerations for most system development projects. For example, system engineering for the ABHS needs to analyze the impact of local, national, and global economies on the business of the airport and the ABHS in particular. It needs to estimate the volume of luggage to be handled, future growth, revenues, costs, and return on investment. All these require knowledge in accounting, finance, management, and economics. The analysis, design, and implementation of the human resource subsystem for the ABHS require knowledge and experience in human resource management.

This is not an exhaustive list. Many systems need other engineering and nonengineering disciplines such as mathematics, natural sciences, social sciences, law, and humanities, to mention a few. In addition, system engineering must consider safety, security, reliability, and many other attributes. For example, the design of the ABHS must consider the safety of the workers working by the conveyors and high-speed tracks. The system must include equipment to check luggage for compliance of security rules. The reliability of the ABHS is critical because it affects hundreds of thousands of passengers.

In summary, system development is an interdisciplinary effort. It involves hardware, software, and human resource developments. These imply a number of challenges. For example, how do we identify and formulate system requirements for such systems? How do we design and construct such systems? How do we manage the development activities? How do we measure the performance, reliability, safety, and other factors of such systems? How do we assess the impact of the system to the society and environment? System engineering is the engineering discipline that answers these questions. System engineering addresses these challenges. In particular, system engineering emphasizes the following elements:

1. *A system engineering process that covers the entire life cycle of the system.* The system development process defines the phases and the phase activities required to develop the system. The process addresses the complete system life-cycle activities, beginning with the initial system concept to the maintenance and retirement of the system. This system-oriented approach encourages the engineering teams to focus on the customer's business needs and priorities, and develop the system to satisfy such needs and priorities.
2. *A top-down divide-and-conquer approach.* This approach decomposes the total system into a hierarchy of subsystems and components, and develops each of them separately. With this approach, the ABHS is decomposed into subsystems. Each subsystem is developed by a team of engineers. This divide-and-conquer strategy enables the engineering teams to develop very large, complex systems.
3. *An interdisciplinary approach to system development.* As discussed above, system development is an interdisciplinary effort. That is, interdisciplinary teams work with each other to carry out the system development activities.

Figure 3.1 illustrates the phases and workflows of a system engineering process. The boxes represent the phases or activities. The solid arrow lines represent work-flows between the activities. The dashed arrow lines represent interaction between the hardware, software, and human resource development activities. The type

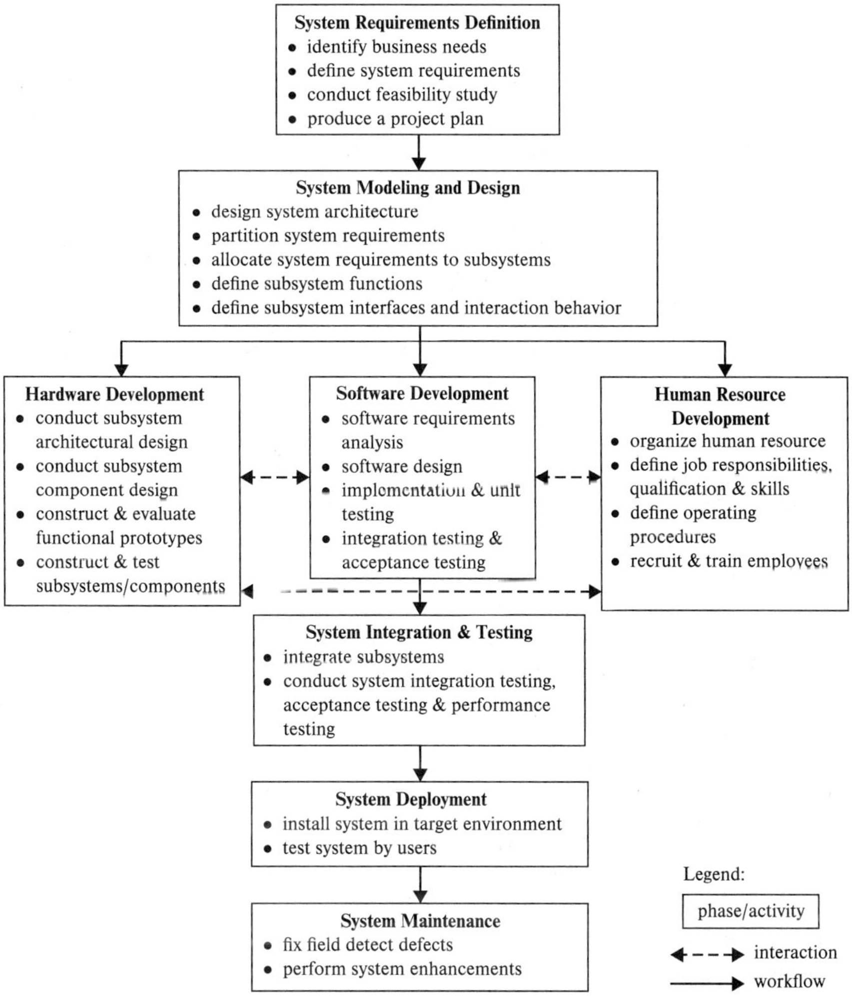

FIGURE 3.1 A system engineering process

of system influences the activities involved. For example, if the system is a software-only system, then the hardware development activities are not performed. The phases of the system engineering process are outlined below and detailed in the following sections:

1. *System requirements definition.* Systems are constructed to satisfy business needs. For example, an ABHS is developed to satisfy the needs of an airport. System requirements definition focuses on identifying business needs and specifies the capabilities of the system to meet the business needs. The result is a system requirements specification and a project plan to design, implement, test, and deploy the system.

2. *System architectural design.* The system requirements specify the capabilities of the system needed to solve business problems. They do not state how to provide the capabilities. System architectural design drafts the solution or how to provide the capabilities. In particular, this activity defines the system architecture or overall structure of the system. That is, it depicts the subsystems and the relationships between the subsystems. This activity also assigns the system requirements to the subsystems.
3. *Specify subsystem functions and interfaces.* Based on the system requirements assigned to the subsystems, the subsystems' functions and interfaces are specified. This activity also specifies how the subsystems interact with each other.
4. *Subsystems development.* After system modeling and design, the subsystems are developed by separate engineering teams simultaneously. The engineering teams refine the system requirements allocated to the separate subsystems and design and implement the subsystems to satisfy the requirements. For example, the software engineering team refines the software requirements, and designs, implements, and tests the software subsystems according to the software requirements.
5. *System integration, testing, deployment, and maintenance.* The subsystems are integrated. Integration testing is performed to ensure that the subsystems work with each other. System acceptance testing is performed to ensure that the system indeed delivers the capabilities specified in the system requirements specification. The system is then installed in the target environment and tested by users. Errors, defects, and user feedback are addressed. The system enters the maintenance phase.

3.3 SYSTEM REQUIREMENTS DEFINITION

System requirements definition identifies the business needs and specifies the system requirements. It begins with an initial system concept and expands and refines the concept. During this process, a set of capabilities that the system must deliver is identified. These capabilities are formulated as system requirements. The system requirements include functional requirements, quality requirements, performance requirements, and other system-specific requirements. This section describes the system requirements definition activity.

3.3.1 Identifying Business Needs

Identifying business needs begins with an information collection activity. That is, information about the business goals and the current business situation is collected. The team identifies the gap between the current situation and the business goals and derives the business needs. Consider, for example, a small-town airport that wants to install an ABHS. To identify the business needs, the team collects information about the current airport and business goals of the new airport. Information about the new airport may include the population and the nature of the businesses of the small town and the number of terminals, gates, and check-in areas, as well as the volume of luggage to be handled, and other factors. The information collection activity answers the following questions:

1. What is the business that the system will automate?
2. What is the system's environment or context?
3. What are the business goals or product goals?
4. What is the current business situation, and how does it operate?
5. What are the existing business processes, and how do they relate to each other?
6. What are the problems with the current system?
7. Who are the users of the current system and the future system, respectively?
8. What do the customer and users want from the future system, and what are their business priorities?
9. What are the quality, performance, and security considerations?

The information collection activity uses several information collection techniques:

1. *Customer presentation.* Customer presentation is an effective approach to gathering information. It takes place at the very beginning of the project. A management or senior personnel designated by the customer presents an overview of the current business, known problems, what the customer and users expect the system to accomplish, and what their business priorities are. The list of questions presented above may serve as the focus of the presentation. The presentation should be limited to no more than two hours including questions and answers.
2. *Study of current business operations.* The team may pay a visit to the business environment. The team may request a guided tour of the customer's business operations where they may collect paperwork forms, descriptions of operating procedures, policies, and other relevant materials. The team should study these materials carefully. These activities help the team understand the customer's business entities, business processes, and workflows. The workflows may include information flows and material flows.
3. *User survey.* User surveys are useful for acquiring users' opinions about the current system and their expectations of the new system. The survey questionnaire should be brief and focus on important issues. Use different survey questionnaires for different groups of users. Issues that require clarification are identified and addressed during user interviews.
4. *User interview.* User interviews are useful for acquiring information that is difficult to obtain through user surveys. They are also useful for clarifying issues that are not clear in the user surveys. The interviews are conducted with selected users, either jointly or individually. Each interview session should last no more than one hour. A list of items to be discussed during the interviews should be prepared beforehand. The list may be shared with the users prior to the interviews.
5. *Literature survey.* Literature survey provides additional information to help the development team understand the application domain. Literature survey should focus on similar projects, domain knowledge, business processes, government regulations, and industry standards.

3.3.2 Defining System Requirements

The next step is deriving system requirements from the business needs identified. For example, the capabilities of the ABHS are derived to satisfy the needs of the ABHS. However, not all needs are to be satisfied due to budget, delivery schedule, technology and political constraints as well as cost-effectiveness considerations. A feasibility study is sometimes performed to ensure that the team can deliver the capabilities with the budget and schedule constraints. The capabilities that the system must deliver are formulated as system requirements. In illustration, the ABHS project may identify many requirements to satisfy the needs. Some of them are stated below to serve as examples. The requirements are numbered to facilitate reference.

R1. ABHS shall check in and transport luggage to departure gates and baggage claim areas according to the destinations of the passengers.

R2. ABHS shall allow airline agents to inquire about luggage status and to locate luggage.

R3. ABHS shall check all baggage and detect items that are prohibited.

R4. ABHS shall be able to serve 20,000 passengers per day.

An end product of this phase is a system requirements specification. The specification may include constraints that restrict the solution space. For example, the ABHS may include constraints on the available space to build the conveyor and high-speed track network. It may include constraints on the types of equipment that must be used. Another product of this phase is a project plan. The project plan outlines the milestones of the project, schedules the development activities, and allocates resources to the activities. A system test plan may be produced. The test plan specifies the system test objectives, test procedures, and needed resources.

3.4 SYSTEM ARCHITECTURAL DESIGN

After the system requirements are identified, the next logical step is to design the system to satisfy the system requirements. Ideally, the system should be designed and implemented by engineers who are experts in all the engineering disciplines involved. Unfortunately, such engineers are hard to find and expensive to hire. Therefore, systems are usually decomposed into a hierarchy of subsystems, which can be developed by engineers of separate disciplines. For example, electrical subsystems are developed by electrical engineers. Mechanical subsystems are developed by mechanical engineers, and software subsystems are developed by software engineers. These subsystems are then integrated during the system integration and testing phase. This approach makes it easier to find qualified engineers. It also reduces the system development complexity and costs. System architectural design performs the following interrelated activities:

1. *Decompose the system into a hierarchy of subsystems.* This step decomposes the system into a hierarchy of relatively independent subsystems. This approach reduces the complexity and costs of system development because the subsystems are easier to design and implement.

2. *Allocate system requirements to subsystems.* This activity assigns the system requirements to the subsystems. It aims to reduce the number of requirements that are shared among the subsystems. In this way, the responsibilities of the subsystems are clearly defined. In addition, the requirements allocated to a subsystem should be functionally related. The allocation is shown in a requirement–subsystem traceability matrix.
3. *Visualize the system architecture.* This activity shows the architectural design as a diagram that consists of the subsystems and the relationships between the subsystems.

3.4.1 System Decomposition

One important task of system architectural design is identifying the subsystems of the system. A top-down, divide-and-conquer approach is often used. In particular, the approach decomposes the system into a hierarchy of subsystems. This approach reduces the complexity of system development because each subsystem is easier to design and implement. There are different ways to decompose a system. Therefore, the result is not unique. System decomposition aims at accomplishing the following goals:

1. *The result should enable separate engineering teams to develop the subsystems.* This reduces the system development costs because it reduces the number of engineers who are specialized in multiple engineering disciplines. It also simplifies the communication between the teams and reduces the communication overhead.
2. *The result should facilitate the use of commercial off-the-shelf (COTS) parts.* COTS are third-party products that can be purchased or acquired. The use of COTS increases productivity and quality while it reduces cost and time to market. For example, the design of the ABHS should consider using COTS for the conveyor systems, high-speed tracks, bar code readers, and luggage check-in software rather than developing these from scratch.
3. *The result should partition or nearly partition the system requirements.* That is, few subsystems share requirements with other subsystems. This reduces the possibility that some requirements are not fulfilled adequately due to a misunderstanding between the teams that share the requirements.
4. *Each subsystem should have a well-defined functionality.* This makes the subsystems easy to understand. For example, the luggage check-in subsystem deals with luggage check-in. The conveyor subsystem is responsible for moving the luggage within a terminal.
5. *The subsystems should be relatively independent.* That is, changing a subsystem does not affect other subsystems. Such a modular design facilitates system maintenance. For example, the luggage check-in subsystem and the conveyor subsystem are two independent subsystems. Either of them can be replaced without affecting the other.
6. *The subsystems should be easy to integrate.* That is, the subsystems should have simple interfaces and interaction behavior. This simplifies the communication between the subsystems. It facilitates subsystem integration, integration testing, and system maintenance.

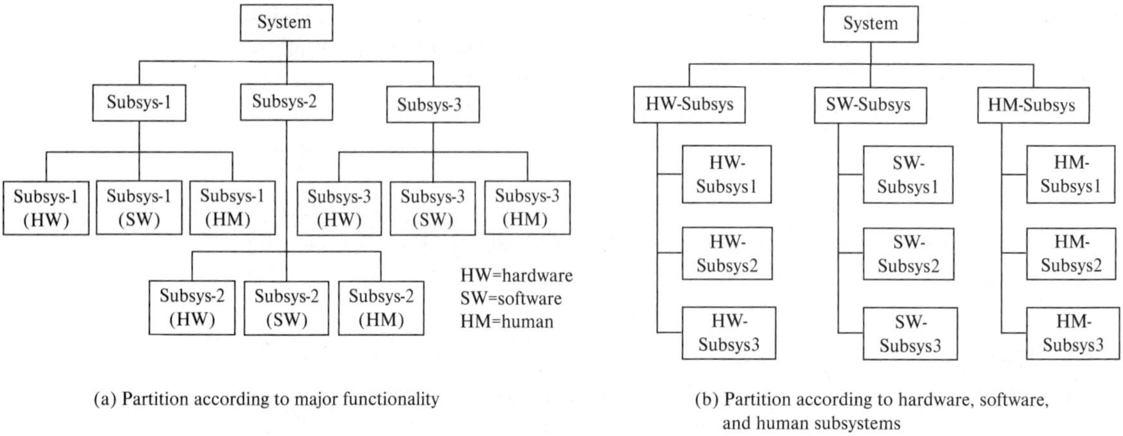

FIGURE 3.2 Partitioning a system into a hierarchy of subsystems

System decomposition applies a number of strategies, which may affect each other. Therefore, they should be applied iteratively until a satisfactory result is obtained. The strategies are to decompose the system according to

1. System functions.
2. Disciplines.
3. Existing architecture.
4. The functional units of the organization.
5. Models of the application.

Decomposing the system according to system functions is a frequently used strategy. It identifies the functions of the system from the system requirements. That is, it partitions the system requirements into nearly disjoint functional clusters. It then identifies the functional subsystems according to the functional clusters. If there are three functional clusters, then the system is decomposed into three functional subsystems. Figure 3.2(*a*) shows that the system is decomposed into Subsys-1, Subsys-2, and Subsys-3. The subsystems are then decomposed into domain-specific subsystems, that is, hardware, software, and human resource subsystems. This approach is used if there are development teams to develop the functional subsystems, or the functional subsystems can be ordered from a third party. Sometimes engineers need to decompose the system requirements into low-level requirements to make the subsystems relatively independent. To illustrate, suppose that the ABHS has the following requirement:

R1. ABHS shall check in and transport luggage to departure gates and baggage claim areas according to the destinations of the passengers.

This requirement includes several functions such as luggage check-in and luggage transportation. If the airport has more than one terminal, then the luggage transportation function involves conveyors and high-speed tracks. Therefore, the requirement should be decomposed. Requirements decomposition should ensure that the low-level requirements are equivalent to the high-level requirements. That is, the high-level requirement and the resulting low-level requirements state the same capabilities. Assume that each flight's check-in area and departure gate are located in the same terminal. So are the arrival gate and the baggage claim area. The requirement R1 can be decomposed into the following:

R1.1. ABHS shall allow airline agents to check in luggage.

R1.2. ABHS shall transport luggage to their destinations within the airport.

R1.2.1. ABHS shall transport luggage from check-in areas to departure gates.

R1.2.2. ABHS shall transport luggage from arrival gates to baggage claim areas.

R1.2.3. ABHS shall transport luggage from arrival gates to departure gates for transfer passengers.

R1.2.4. ABHS shall transport luggage within a terminal using conveyors.

R1.2.5. ABHS shall transport luggage between terminals using DCVs running on high-speed tracks.

R1.3. ABSH shall control the transportation of luggage within and between terminals.

Requirement R4 is a performance requirement and relates to several subsystems. It should be decomposed as well so that the low-level requirements can be assigned to separate subsystems. For example, the low-level requirements would specify the required speed and volume of luggage for the subsystems. This must consider the number of terminals, check-in areas, and conveyor systems per terminal, hours of operation, and the like. The decomposition must also take into account a certain percentage of redundancy to cope with extremely high demand during holiday seasons. The following are examples of the low-level performance requirements:

R4.1. Each check-in area shall handle 1,150 check-in baggages per day.

R4.2. Each check-in agent shall check in an average three passengers per minute.

R4.3. Each conveyor hardware shall scan and transport 500 check-in pieces of luggage per hour.

R4.4. ABHS control software shall process 2,300 check-in bags per day and 1,000 bar code scan requests per hour.

Next, the system requirements are partitioned into functional clusters. That is, requirements that share the same functionality are grouped together to form a functional cluster. The functional clusters are used to derive the functional subsystems. Figure 3.3 shows the functional clusters and subsystems derived from the system requirements.

Another strategy is to decompose the system according to engineering disciplines. It results in subsystems that are named after the disciplines such as electrical subsystem, electronic subsystem, mechanical subsystem, and software subsystem. In Figure 3.2(*b*), the total system is decomposed into hardware, software, and human subsystems. These are decomposed into functional subsystems. This approach is used if the hardware, software, and human subsystems are developed by hardware, software, and human engineering teams or departments.

Functional Cluster	Functional Description	System Requirements	Functional Subsystem Identified
Luggage check-in	This functional cluster processes luggage check-in.	R1.1, R4.1, R4.2	Luggage check-in subsystem
Conveyor	This functional cluster is responsible for moving luggage within a terminal.	R1.2.1, R1.2.2, R1.2.3, R1.2.4, R4.3	Conveyor subsystem
High-speed track	This functional cluster transports luggage between terminals.	R1.2.3, R1.2.5	High-speed track subsystem
Software control	This functional cluster controls the hardware to transport luggage within and between terminals.	R1.3, R4.4	Software control subsystem

FIGURE 3.3 Functional clusters and functional subsystems

Decomposing the system according to existing architecture is applied when the goal of the project is to extend or enhance an existing system. The approach could reduce the development costs and avoid potential risks due to modifying the existing system architecture. The system can also be decomposed according to the organization's functional units. For example, the manually operated baggage handling system of the small-town airport may consist of luggage check-in, transport, and baggage claim departments. These may suggest three major subsystems for the new system.

If models of the application or system are constructed to help understand the application or existing system, then these models may be used to guide the decomposition. For example, models may be constructed to understand the workflow of the existing airport luggage handling system. The models may show that baggages are manually checked in and transported to the departure gates. Moreover, bags are unloaded from arriving flights and transported to the baggage claim areas and transfer gates. From the models, subsystems may be identified and used as the initial decomposition of the system. The initial decomposition is then refined and evolved into a hierarchy of subsystems.

3.4.2 Requirements Allocation

Once the system is decomposed into a hierarchy of subsystems, the system requirements are assigned to the subsystems. The allocation considers several factors including developmental and operational costs, performance, quality of service, cost-effectiveness, and ease of change, among others. For example, some system functions may be implemented by either hardware or software. Generally speaking, application-specific integrated circuits provide better performance. If performance is not an issue, then some of the system requirements may be assigned to the software subsystems rather than the hardware subsystems. The allocation of the system requirements depends on the results of the previous steps. If the subsystems are derived from the functional clusters, then the mapping from the functional clusters to the subsystems is the allocation. This is the case for the ABHS example, as Figure 3.3 shows.

The allocation of the system requirements to the subsystems is visualized in a traceability matrix. The rows show the requirements while the columns show the subsystems. The entries indicate the allocation of the requirements to the subsystems. That is, if a requirement is assigned to a subsystem, then a cross is entered into the corresponding entry. For a real-world project, the traceability matrix is large because it involves hundreds of requirements and many subsystems. The matrix has a number of advantages:

1. *It can check that every requirement is assigned to a subsystem.* That is, each leaf-level requirement row shows at least one cross ("x"). If a leaf-level row does not contain a cross, then the system requirement is not assigned to any subsystem.
2. *It can check if the allocation is appropriate.* Assigning a system requirement to several subsystems should be avoided because it is difficult to divide the functionality among the subsystems. The traceability matrix can detect such cases by counting the number of crosses on each row. If a row contains many crosses, then the requirement is assigned to many subsystems. In this case, decomposing the requirement is desired.
3. *It shows which requirements are assigned to a subsystem.* That is, the crosses shown in each column indicate the requirements that are assigned to the subsystem represented by the column. The subsystems must satisfy the requirements, respectively.
4. *It can check if a subsystem is assigned too many responsibilities.* If a column contains many crosses, then the subsystem is assigned many responsibilities. The subsystem may be decomposed to distribute the requirements among lower-level subsystems.
5. *It can check the functional cohesion of the subsystems.* The requirements that are assigned to a subsystem should be related functionally. If the requirements indicated by the crosses on a column are not related, then the subsystem represented by the column has low functional cohesion. The requirements should be partitioned into several functional clusters. The subsystem should be decomposed into functional subsystems corresponding to the functional clusters.

3.4.3 Architectural Design Diagrams

It is a common practice to construct application models and system models during system design. These models help the team understand and analyze the application domain, business processes, and workflows to identify problems, and develop and evaluate design solutions. Various diagrams are used to depict different aspects of the application and the system. Block diagrams, UML and its extension System Modeling Language (SysML) diagrams, and data flow diagrams are widely used during system modeling and design.

Block diagrams use rectangles to represent subsystems and components, and directed edges to denote workflows between the subsystems and components. As an example, Figure 3.4 shows a high-level block diagram for the ABHS. The block diagram indicates that an ABHS consists of terminal subsystems, connected to a high-speed track subsystem. Passengers check in luggage with the terminal subsystem. The high-speed track subsystem transports luggage between the terminals. Both of these subsystems interact with the ABHS control software, which interacts with the flight

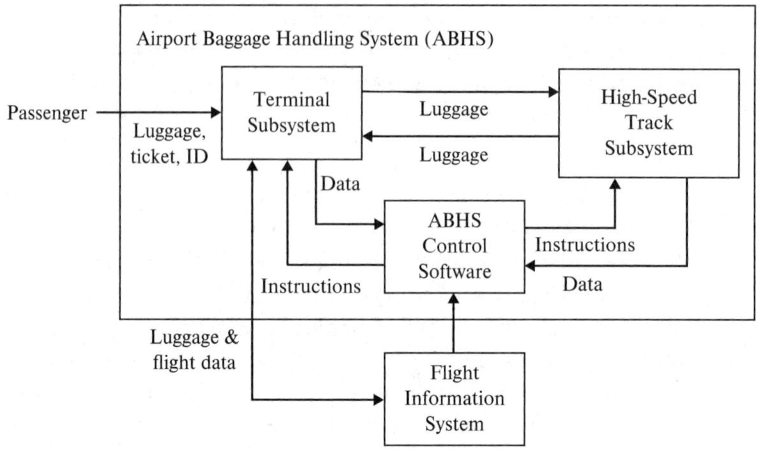

FIGURE 3.4 Block diagram for an airport baggage handling system

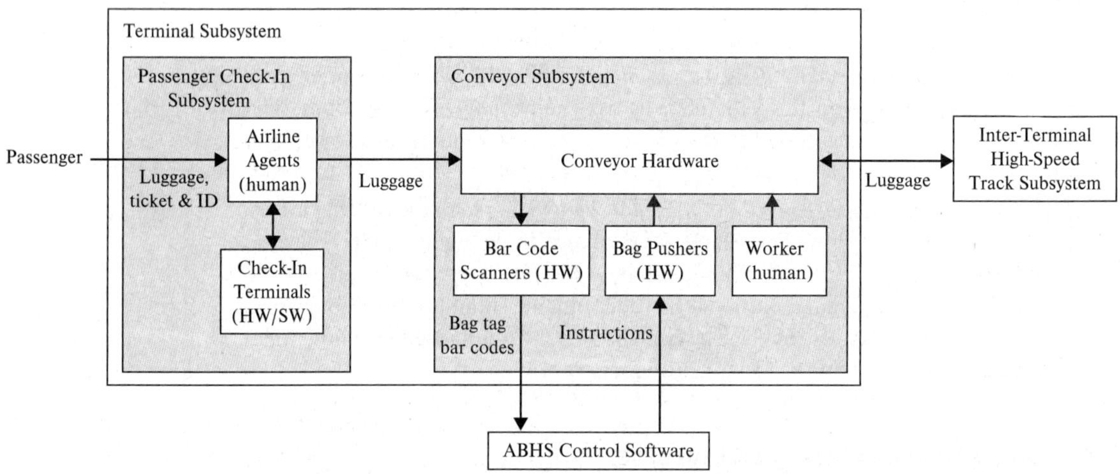

FIGURE 3.5 Block diagram showing refinement of a subsystem

information system. Figure 3.5 shows a refinement of the terminal subsystem. In the figure, hardware, software, and human subsystems are displayed.

UML was initially created for modeling software applications and systems. Its generality makes it a useful tool for system modeling as well. This is achieved by using the stereotype mechanism provided by UML. For example, Figure 3.6 shows a component diagram that models the hardware and software of a radio communication system (RCS). It uses the stereotype "<<subsystem>>" to extend the component modeling construct to model a subsystem. The diagram shows that an RCS consists of three subsystems: a base station subsystem, an account management subsystem, and a mobile units subsystem. The working of an RCS is similar to a cellular network except that it has only one base station with high-power transceivers.

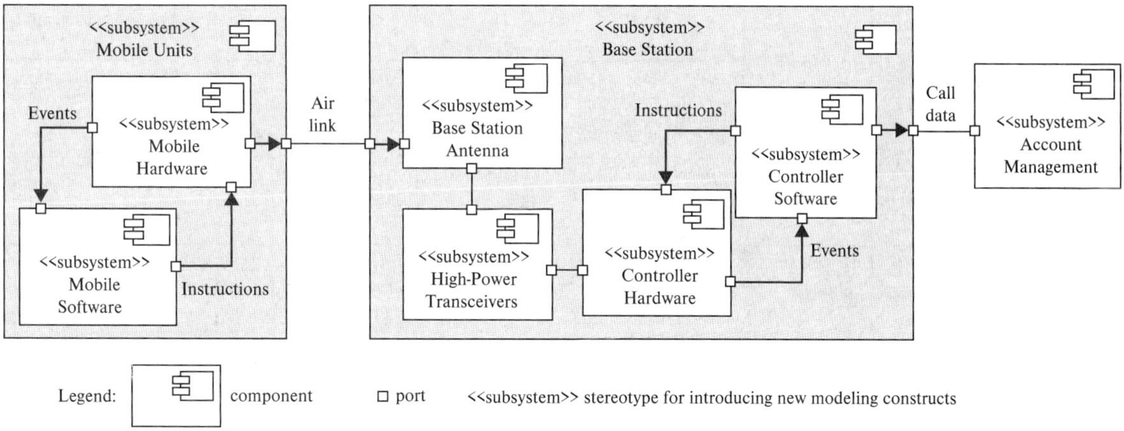

FIGURE 3.6 System modeling using a stereotyped component diagram

The high-power transceivers can service a much larger area than a single base station of a cellular network. Through the relay of the high-power transceivers, mobile units can communicate in the service area. The figure shows that each mobile unit consists of a mobile hardware subsystem and a mobile software subsystem. The hardware sends events to the software, which issues instructions to operate the hardware. For example, when the user makes a call, the event is sent to the software. The software instructs the hardware to contact the base station through a radio frequency channel, called an airlink. The high-power transceivers of the base station receive the request and forward it to controller hardware, which forwards it to the controller software. The controller software validates the call request. If the caller and callee are valid subscribers, then it instructs the hardware and the transceivers to establish a connection.

The ability of UML to support system modeling leads to an extension of UML, that is, the System Modeling Language (SysML). The nine diagrams of SysML and how they relate to UML are summarized in Figure 3.7. The last column of the table shows the chapters of this book that cover the UML diagrams. To illustrate, Figures 3.8 and 3.9 show a SysML block definition diagram (bdd) and a SysML internal block diagram (ibd) for the ABHS. These diagrams correspond to the block diagrams displayed in Figures 3.4 and 3.5, respectively.

Sometimes, it is desirable to show material flows in addition to information flows in a model. For example, the ABHS moves luggage from the check-in areas to the departure gates and the arrival gates to baggage claim areas. Such flows are called material flows. In Figures 3.4 and 3.5, material flows and information flows are represented using the same notation. The SysML diagrams shown in Figure 3.8 and 3.9 also use the same notation for information and material flows. To distinguish, material flows should be modeled differently. To illustrate, Figure 3.10 shows a data flow diagram for a library system. The block arrows represent material flows. The ovals represent tasks or processing functions. The entity or subsystem that performs that function is shown in the lower compartment of the oval. The upper compartment of the oval shows the

SysML	UML	Description	Remark	Presented in Chapter
Activity diagram	Activity diagram	Models activities that relate to each other via workflows, and exhibit sequencing, exclusion, synchronization, and concurrency relationships	SysML activity diagram extends UML activity diagram.	14
Block definition diagram	Class diagram	Models structural elements called blocks and their composition and classification	Block definition diagram extends UML class diagram.	5
Internal block diagram		Models interconnection and interfacing of internal elements of a block	Internal block diagram extends UML composite structure diagram.	
Package diagram	Package diagram	Models the logical organization of modeling artifacts and software artifacts	Same diagrams	6
Parametric diagram		Specifies constraints to support engineering analysis		
Requirement diagram		Models text-based requirements and their relationships with other requirements and artifacts such as design elements, test cases, etc.		
Sequence diagram	Sequence diagram	Models time-ordered interaction behavior between objects	Same diagrams	9
State diagram	State diagram	Models state-dependent behavior of an object	Same diagrams	13
Use case diagram	Use case diagram	Shows the functions or business processes of an application or system as well as relationships of these to external entities called actors	Same diagrams	7

FIGURE 3.7 Relating SysML and UML diagrams

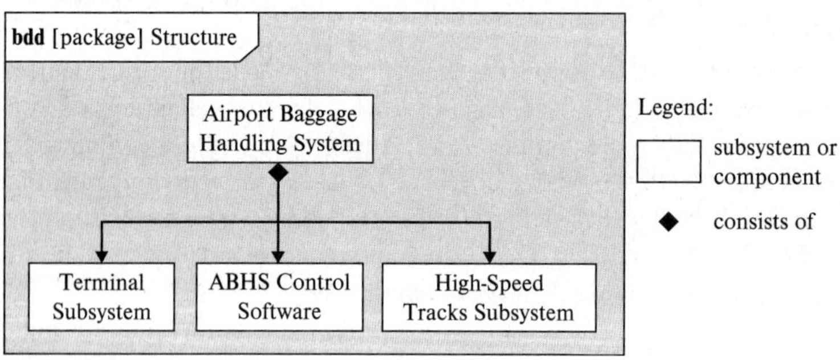

FIGURE 3.8 SysML block definition diagram for the ABHS

task ID. Material flows are useful in assigning system requirements to the hardware, software, and human subsystems. For example, the material flows in Figure 3.10 suggest that functions involving material flows such as the receiving dock, cataloging room, and book shelves should be assigned to the appropriate hardware and human subsystems.

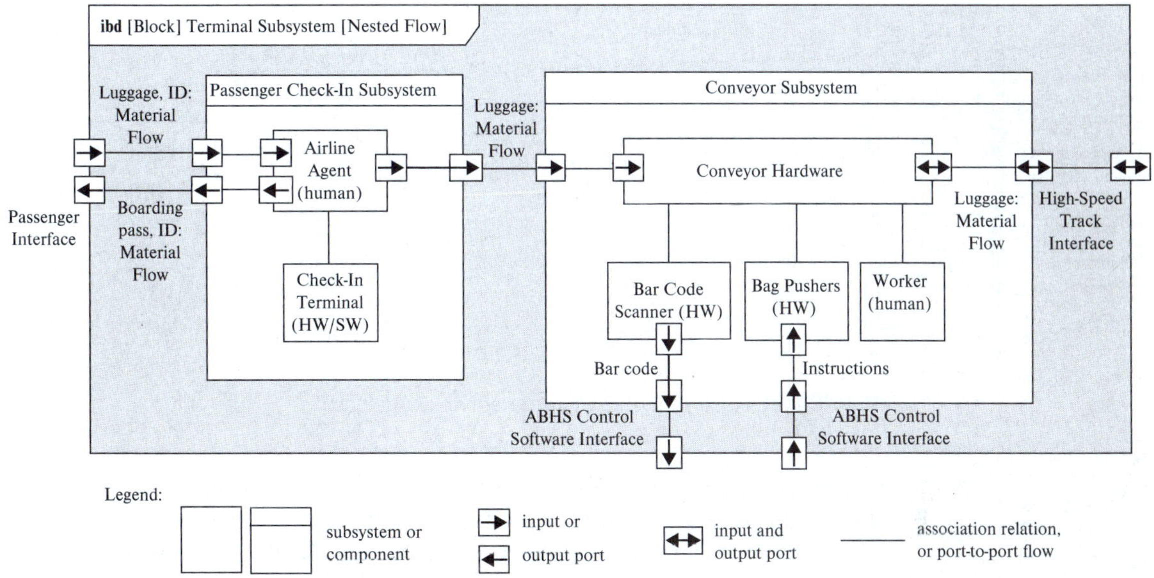

FIGURE 3.9 SysML internal block diagram for ABHS terminal subsystem

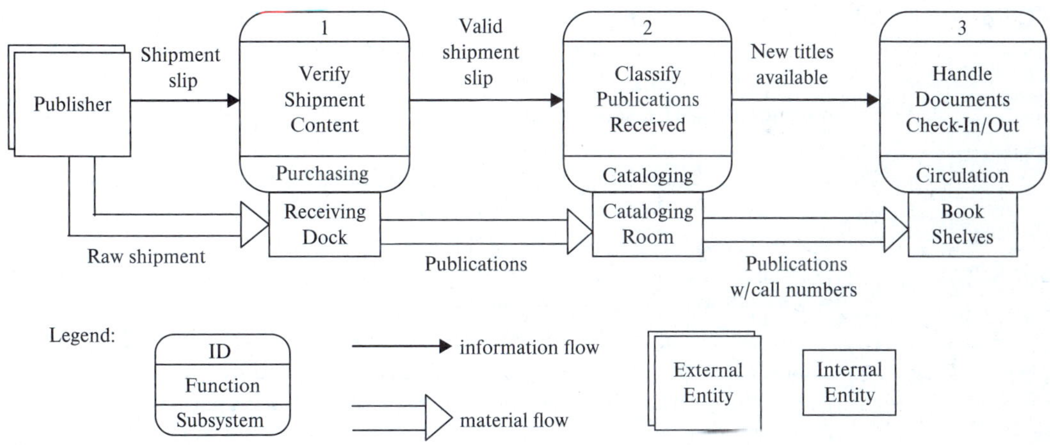

FIGURE 3.10 Data flow diagram modeling information as well as material flows

3.4.4 Specification of Subsystem Functions and Interfaces

This step specifies the functionality of each subsystem and how the subsystems interact with each other. The functionality is specified according to the system requirements allocated to the subsystem. It refines the requirements assigned to each subsystem.

The interfaces between the subsystems specify how the subsystems connect and communicate with each other. The interaction behavior specifies the sequences of messages exchanged between the subsystems. These enable the teams that

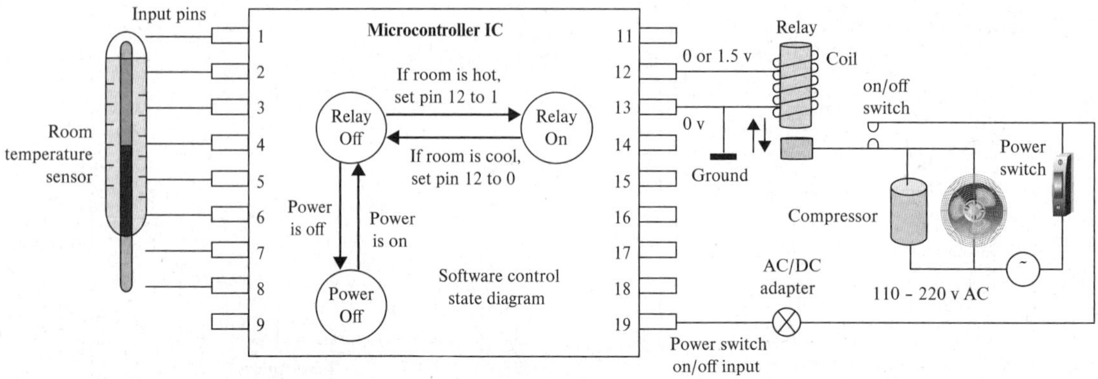

FIGURE 3.11 Illustration of software-hardware interfacing

implement the subsystems to know what interfaces and interaction behavior they can expect and need to provide. Hardware-software interfaces are the most common in embedded systems. In many cases, a microcontroller integrated circuit is used. Figure 3.11 illustrates this for an air conditioner. The figure shows only the most relevant items. For example, the unused pins should, in fact, connect to other electronic components.

The state diagram shown in Figure 3.11 represents the behavior of the software running inside the IC chip. The software enters into the Relay Off state when the power switch is turned on. The transition from the Power Off state to the Relay Off state indicates this. The software periodically reads the byte representing the eight pins that connect to the temperature sensor to obtain the room temperature. If the room is hot, the software sets pin 12 to 1. This applies a 1.5 volt direct current (DC) to the coil of the relay. The coil generates a magnetic field, which attracts the on/off switch to close the power circuit of the compressor and fan. Thus, cooling begins. When the room becomes cool, the software sets pin 12 to 0. This opens the power circuit of the compressor and fan. Thus, cooling stops.

In the case shown in Figure 3.11, the interface and interaction behavior specification defines the pins that represent the room temperature, the meaning of the byte read by the software. The specification also defines the output pins and the meaning of the output values. In this case, the output pin is pin 12. When the pin is set, the relay is engaged and the cooling begins. Besides software-hardware interface, there are human-software, software-software, human-hardware, human-human, and hardware-hardware interfaces. These interfaces and interaction behavior are specified similarly.

System design also produces a system integration test plan and an acceptance test plan. These specify test procedures to ensure that the subsystems will work with each other as expected, and the system delivers the capabilities as specified in the system requirements specification. Required resources to conduct system integration testing and acceptance testing are also specified. These test plans are used during the system integration and testing, and acceptance testing phases.

3.5 SUBSYSTEMS DEVELOPMENT

After system design and allocation, the subsystems are assigned to different engineering teams. The engineering teams construct and test the subsystems separately. In particular, the software engineering (SE) team applies software engineering processes and methodologies to develop the software subsystem. The team also performs quality assurance and management activities. The engineering teams maintain close contact, exchange progress status, and collaborate with each other to solve interdisciplinary design and implementation problems. This section presents activities that are relevant to the software engineering team.

3.5.1 Object-Oriented Context Diagram

The software development activity needs to consider the context of the software subsystem. The context consists of real-world objects and other subsystems that interact with the software subsystem. Object-oriented software engineering models the world and the software system as consisting of objects that interact with each other. For example, the context of the air-conditioning software shown in Figure 3.11 includes the room temperature sensor, the AC/DC adapter, and the relay. The context of the ABHS control software displayed in Figure 3.4 includes the terminal subsystem, the high-speed track subsystem, and the flight information subsystem. Figure 3.5 shows that the software interacts with the bar code scanners and bag pushers, which are components of the terminal subsystem. Object-oriented software development models these as objects that interact with the software under development. The result is displayed in a UML class diagram called a context domain model. It is also called a context diagram. The context domain model shows the context objects, properties of the context objects, and relationships between the context objects and the software.

To illustrate, Figure 3.12 shows a context diagram for the ABHS control software. The diagram specifies the types of objects that interact with the ABHS control software. It also specifies the interfaces and interaction protocols with these objects. The information contained in the context diagram is useful for the design of the software subsystem.

3.5.2 Usefulness of an Object-Oriented Context Diagram

The advantages of an object-oriented context diagram are as follows:

1. *It provides a unified view of the software objects and the context objects.* This helps the team understand the context objects and their relationships to the software subsystem.
2. *It highlights the interfaces and interaction with the context objects.* The context domain model treats the software as a black box, and shows only the context objects, their relationships, and attributes that are useful to the design of the software subsystem.
3. *It helps the development of the software subsystem.* For example, the attributes of the bar code scanners are useful for the design and implementation of the classes that interface with the bar code scanners. The multiplicity, such as "1..*" in

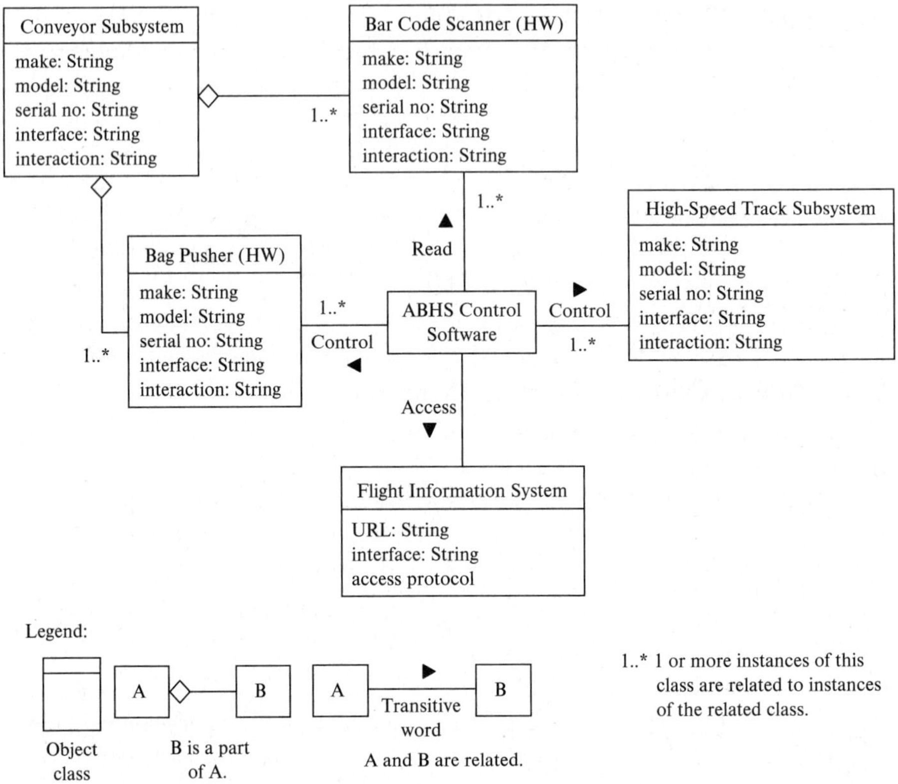

FIGURE 3.12 A context domain model for ABHS control software

Figure 3.12, specifies the number of scanners the ABHS control software must support. The information shown in the context diagram is also useful for testing and maintenance. For example, when adding a new type of bar code scanner, only the classes that interface with the new scanner need to be designed and implemented.

4. *It facilitates the communication and collaboration with other engineering teams.* The object-oriented context diagram highlights the interfaces and interaction with other engineering subsystems. This helps the software engineering team to focus on the interface and interaction issues when working with the other engineering teams.
5. *It is useful for training.* A software subsystem of a large complex system needs to interact with many other complex systems. It is not easy to understand the context. The context diagram is a useful tool for new members to learn the context of a software subsystem.

3.5.3 Collaboration of Engineering Teams

During the subsystems development process, the engineering teams maintain close contact to exchange status and solve interdisciplinary problems. Consider, for example, the design and prototyping of a radio transceiver subsystem. The electronic engineering (EE) team may discover that a certain feature should be implemented with software rather than hardware. The EE team would meet with the SE team to assess the feasibility. A change proposal is submitted if the two teams agree on the change. A change control board reviews the proposal and either approves or disapproves the change. If the proposal is approved, the change is implemented.

3.6 SYSTEM INTEGRATION, TESTING, AND DEPLOYMENT

The subsystems developed by the various engineering teams are then integrated, and integration and system testings are performed. System integration testing is conducted according to the system integration test plan produced in the system design and allocation phase. Due to changes during the subsystems development phase, modification to the test plan may be required. System integration testing refines the test procedures specified in the test plan and executes the tests to ensure that the subsystems communicate properly through the subsystem interfaces.

System testing is performed according to the acceptance test plan. It ensures that the system in fact can deliver all the capabilities stated in the system requirements. Depending on the system, integration and system testings may require special equipment. For example, test equipment for telecommunication systems can generate millions of simulated calls to test the system under development and accurately measure the throughput, performance, and response times of the system. After system testing, the system is shipped and installed in the target environment. The system is tested by the users. This is called beta testing. Defects found during beta testing are reported to the development team. The defects are removed and the system retested. After beta testing, the system enters into the maintenance phase. During maintenance, enhancements are made and more defects, if any, are removed.

3.7 SYSTEM CONFIGURATION MANAGEMENT

System engineering involves multiple engineering teams. The teams must work in a coordinated and controlled manner. Suppose that the design of a software component depends on the design of an electronic component. In this case, the design of the software component cannot be finalized until the design of the electronic component is finalized. The question is: How is the software engineering team notified when the electronic component design is finalized? Sending an email is an option, but this informal approach is problematic for a large system development project. Who should be responsible for sending the email? Who should receive the email? What if the email is not sent, or does not reach the receiver? What should be written in the email? A formal means to notify the engineering teams of such events is needed.

Change control is another issue that must be coordinated. For example, if the design of the electronic component is changed, then the design of the software component must change as well. This means that the software engineering team should be notified. A notification mechanism is needed. If the design of the electronic component could be changed frequently and arbitrarily, then the software engineering team would have difficulty coping with the changes. On the other hand, if the design cannot be changed, then how can the electronic team correct design flaws or design errors? System configuration management solves these problems.

System configuration management is based on the concept of a baseline. A baseline denotes an important stage of the project. For example, a system development project consists of system requirements baseline, system design baseline, allocation baseline, subsystem design baselines, and more. The system requirements baseline signifies that the system requirements analysis phase is successfully completed. A baseline is associated with a set of artifacts called configuration items. For example, the system requirements baseline may include the system requirements specification and the project plan. When these are produced and reviewed, and the defects found by the reviewers are removed, the system requirements baseline can be established. Before establishing the system requirements baseline, these artifacts can be modified freely. Once the baseline is established, changes to these artifacts must go through a change control procedure. That is, the proposed changes must be evaluated by a change control board representing the stakeholders. If the proposed changes are accepted, then they are implemented and the progress status is monitored. If the proposed changes are rejected, then they are archived. In summary, system configuration management consists of four main functions:

1. *Configuration item identification.* This function defines the project baselines and associated configuration items. Some examples of baselines are the system requirements baseline, system design baseline, allocation baseline, and subsystem design baselines. Example configuration items include system requirements specification, project plan, system acceptance test plan, system design specification, allocation plan, system integration test plan, and more. A configuration item can be changed freely before the baseline is established. A baseline can be established when all the associated configuration items are checked into the configuration management system. For example, if the system requirements baseline consists of the system requirements specification and the project plan, then the baseline can be established when both of these documents are checked into the configuration management system. Once the baseline is established, changes to the configuration item need to go through a change control procedure.
2. *Configuration change control.* This function defines the change control procedure and executes the procedure. Figure 3.13 illustrates the change control procedure. First, the needed change is identified and analyzed. Next, an engineering change proposal (ECP) is prepared. It specifies the change as well as its impact, duration, and cost. The ECP is evaluated by a change control board (CCB). The CCB consists of representatives of parties that may be affected by the proposed change. The evaluation either accepts or rejects the ECP. As a result, the proposed change is either implemented or archived.
3. *Configuration auditing.* This function formally establishes the project baselines. It also ensures that the proposed engineering changes are made properly. To achieve these goals, configuration item verification and validation are performed. Configuration item verification ensures that the required configuration items are produced when a baseline is established. For example, it ensures that the system requirements specification and the project plan are produced prior to establishing the system requirements baseline. Configuration item validation ensures that the configuration items are correct. For example, the system requirements specification is reviewed by the engineering teams, domain experts, customer, and users; identified defects are removed; and concerns are addressed.

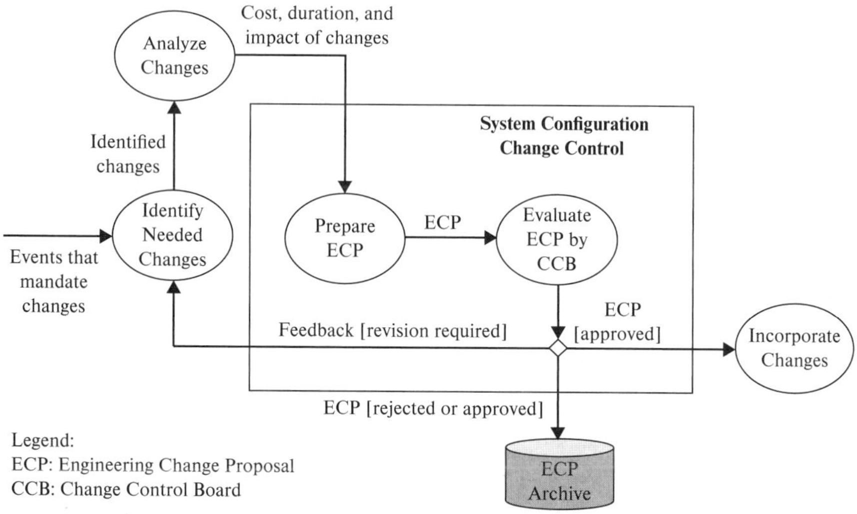

FIGURE 3.13 Configuration change control

4. *Configuration status reporting.* This function provides database support to the other three functions. The database can be queried for information about the configuration items. The function also publishes events about the system configuration. These include the establishment of a baseline and changes to the configuration items.

3.8 SUMMARY

This chapter presents system development activities that involve hardware, software, and human components. It describes the system engineering process and techniques for system modeling, design, and system requirements allocation. After allocation, the subsystems are developed by separate teams of various engineering disciplines. The subsystems are then integrated and tested to ensure that the system satisfies the system requirements and constraints. During the entire system development process, numerous analysis, design, implementation, and testing documents are produced and updated. Updating one document may affect many other documents. The updates must be coordinated, which is done by system configuration management.

3.9 CHAPTER REVIEW QUESTIONS

1. What is system engineering?
2. Why do we need system engineering?
3. Why is system engineering considered an interdisciplinary approach?
4. What are the phases and activities of the system engineering process described in this chapter?
5. What are the purposes of hardware development, software development, and human resource development, and why are they performed separately?
6. How does the system engineering process tackle the system development challenges?
7. What is the relationship between system engineering and software engineering?
8. What factors should the system engineering team consider during system design?
9. What are the applicable strategies for decomposing a system or subsystem during system design?
10. What is system modeling?
11. What is a requirement-subsystem traceability matrix?
12. What are the potential challenges of system integration and testing?

3.10 EXERCISES

3.1 Provide a brief description of the functions of a vending machine. Identify and formulate all functional and performance requirements.

3.2 Identify two embedded systems not mentioned in this chapter. For each of these systems, perform the following:

- **a.** Briefly describe the functions of the system. The description should be about a half of a page to one page including diagrams, if any.
- **b.** Identify and formulate five functional requirements and two nonfunctional requirements. One of the nonfunctional requirements must be a performance requirement.
- **c.** Decompose the system and allocate the system requirements to the subsystems.

3.3 A coin-operated car wash system is a self-service car wash system. A customer inserts the required number of quarters to buy a preset period of wash time. The customer can turn a dial to select soap, foam, rinse, and wax any time during the wash period. The system beeps when one minute is remaining. The customer can insert more quarters to prolong the wash period. Perform the following for the car wash system:

- **a.** Identify and specify the system requirements including functional and nonfunctional requirements.
- **b.** Decompose the system into functional subsystems. Decompose the system requirements if necessary.
- **c.** Allocate the system requirements to the subsystems.
- **d.** Construct a system architectural design diagram using a diagramming technique of your choice or as designated by the instructor.

3.4 A railroad crossing system employs sensors, flashing lights, sounding bells, and gates to control the traffic at a railroad intersection. When a train approaches the intersection from either direction, a sensor device senses the train and communicates with the software. The software turns on the flashing yellow warning light and the sounding bell for a given period. It then changes the light to flashing red and closes the gates. After the train has left the intersection, another sensor device detects this and communicates the event to the software. The software turns off the lights and the sounding bell and opens the gates. Perform the following for the railroad crossing system:

- **a.** Identify the hardware and software subsystems and specify the functionality of each of the subsystems.
- **b.** Describe how the subsystems relate to and interact with each other. That is, specify the subsystem interfaces and interaction behavior.
- **c.** Construct a system architectural design diagram to show the relationships between the subsystems.
- **d.** Identify and formulate safety requirements and allocate them to the subsystems. Describe how the subsystems will satisfy the safety requirements.

3.5 Managers of a department store want to expand into online retailing. This means that the company needs to develop an online system that can take orders online and ship the ordered items through a designated national shipment carrier. To reduce labor costs, the company wants a fully automated system. Perform the following for this system:

- **a.** Identify and formulate five functional requirements and two performance requirements for the system.
- **b.** Decompose the system into a hierarchy of subsystems and allocate the system requirements to the subsystems.
- **c.** Produce a system architectural design diagram.

3.6 If you have learned UML class diagramming, then produce an object-oriented context diagram for the software subsystem of the online retailing system you produced in exercise 3.5. Discuss the usefulness of the context diagram for the design, implementation, testing, and maintenance of the software subsystem.

part II

Analysis and Architectural Design

4 Chapter

Software Requirements Elicitation

Key Takeaway Points

- Requirements are capabilities that the system must deliver.
- The hardest single part of building a software system is deciding precisely what to build–i.e., the requirements. (Frederick P. Brooks Jr.)
- Software requirements elicitation is aimed to identify the real requirements for the system.

The planning phase of the agile unified methodology presented in this book accomplishes three objectives: (1) eliciting software requirements for the future system, (2) deriving use cases from the requirements, and (3) defining an iterative development and deployment plan to deliver the use cases. This chapter presents the steps to accomplish the first objective. Through the study of this chapter, you will learn the following:

- The importance and challenges of requirements elicitation.
- Types of requirement.
- Requirements elicitation activities.
- Assigning priorities to requirements.
- Requirements review techniques.
- Applying agile principles during requirements elicitation.

4.1 WHAT IS REQUIREMENTS ELICITATION?

Software systems are built for many different reasons. Most frequently, a software system is built to meet the business needs of a given customer, who pays for the development effort. For many real-world projects, there is a budget constraint. Therefore, only a subset of the business needs can be satisfied. These are formulated as software requirements, defined as follows.

Definition 4.1 *Software requirements* are capabilities that the system must deliver.

A software project is successful if the system satisfies its software requirements, the budget is not overrun, and the system is delivered as scheduled. Therefore, identifying the real requirements is necessary for the success of a software project. Identifying the real requirements, however, is not an easy task, let alone doing so within budget and development time constraints. This is because different stakeholders perceive the business priorities and needed system capabilities differently. The differences come from various factors including financial interest, educational background, experience, standpoint, and belief. For example, a stakeholder with a strong technical background may emphasize system throughput and response time while a stakeholder with a business background may give priority to costs and customer satisfaction.

Consider a health care information system that services insurance companies, health care providers such as doctors and nurses, health care facilities such as hospitals and clinics, and drug suppliers such as pharmacies and drugstores. The interests of these stakeholders are different; hence, their perception of the real requirements or their importance could be different. Insurance companies want to lower health care costs. They want the system to implement, check, and enforce rigorous claim filing rules. This creates more work to file the claims by the doctors, health care facilities, and drug suppliers. It may also incur delay in payment to them. On the other hand, doctors, health care facilities, and drug suppliers want the system to simplify the claim process as well as pay them sooner, not later. If the system involves government agencies, then it must also consider government regulations and satisfy additional requirements. Even if there are sufficient resources and time to develop the system, deciding on the real requirements to satisfy all these stakeholders is clearly not an easy exercise.

Customers or government agencies often impose restrictions on the software system. For example, the customer may require that the system be implemented in a given programming language or X% of the code must be written in that language. The customer may prohibit the use of a certain product, or any product from a given vendor. These are imposed by the customer due to political or business considerations. Restrictions as such are commonly referred to as constraints, defined as follows:

Definition 4.2 *Constraints* are restrictions on the solution space of a software system.

The main difference between requirements and constraints is that constraints reduce the number of design and implementation alternatives. Consider, for example, one extreme case, in which no constraint is imposed. In this case, the development team can choose from a broad spectrum of products, programming languages, and platforms to implement the software system. On the other hand, if the implementation language is constrained to language X, then all other programming languages are excluded. The result is that the solution space is greatly reduced.

In practice, requirements are sometimes stated as a "constraint." Consider, for example, the following statement supplied by a package shipping provider such as the U.S. Postal Service (USPS):

> Express packages are constrained to 108 inches in length or 165 inches in length plus girth (girth = 2 * (width + height)) or 150 LB in weight.

Should this be a requirement or a constraint? It contains the word "constrained." So it could be a constraint. However, a careful examination reveals that the statement actually specifies a restriction on the package to be shipped, not a restriction on the solution space. Therefore, it should be a requirement, not a constraint. In other words, the system must reject packages that exceed the dimension limit–a capability that the system must deliver.

In practice, requirements and constraints are stated in a document, called the *software requirements specification* (SRS). Also specified are the priorities of the requirements. The priorities are useful for project planning and scheduling; high-priority requirements should be developed and deployed early so that the team will have sufficient time and resources to modify the system to respond to user feedback.

For most real-world projects, the SRS is a part of the software development contract. It bears legal consequences. Therefore, software requirements analysis must ensure that the system will satisfy the requirements and constraints. Sometimes, such an assurance is difficult to assess, especially when the system uses advanced technologies, needs to meet real-time constraints, or provides innovative features. A feasibility study is often performed during the requirements analysis phase to reduce such uncertainties.

While a feasibility study ensures that the system will satisfy the requirements and constraints before the system is designed and implemented, acceptance testing ensures that this is really the case after the system is implemented. For many real-world projects, planning for acceptance testing takes place in the requirements elicitation phase. That is, an acceptance test plan is produced. It outlines test approaches and procedures, acceptance criteria, human resources and responsibilities, required equipment, test schedule, and other related elements. The test plan is a part of the overall project plan, which is produced during the planning phase to guide the subsequent software development effort.

4.2 IMPORTANCE OF REQUIREMENTS ELICITATION

Two real-world stories illustrate the importance of requirements elicitation. More than 40 years ago in the beginning of the 1970s, I had the opportunity to work on a project for the electric utility industry. We worked days and nights for two years, meeting the customer representatives, performing design, implementation, and testing. Finally, we delivered the system to the customer and celebrated the victory with a champagne party. But our joy quickly turned to grief because the customer did not pay even a dime, citing that the system did not do what they had expected. The project was a total failure. Several years later, this painful lesson motivated me to pursue software engineering as a career.

Another example took place a few years ago. It involved a state-owned health care organization as the customer and a software company as the developer. The company constructed a health care management system for the health care organization. The system was installed and operational. But the company received only a partial payment–the customer refused to pay the rest. Thus, the company sued the organization for the remaining payment. The government organization counter-sued the company, citing that the system did not satisfy the requirements. While the lawsuits were going on, new customers were scared away–who wants to be involved in such an uncertainty? In this story, both parties suffer respective losses. Therefore, identifying the real requirements are important for the developer as well as the customer.

The above two stories are not uncommon. Many projects fail because of wrongly identified or inadequately stated requirements. Speaking from his extensive software development experiences, Frederick Brooks, who received the 1999 Turing Award, tells us why: "The hardest single part of building a software system is deciding precisely what to build. No other part of the conceptual work is as difficult as establishing the detailed technical requirements, including all the interfaces to people, to machines, and to other software systems. No other part of the work so cripples the resulting system if done wrong. No other part is more difficult to rectify later."

4.3 TYPES OF REQUIREMENT

Software requirements are usually classified into functional and nonfunctional requirements. Functional requirements are statements of information processing capabilities that the software system must possess. They are formulated as declarative sentences that begin with the software system as the subject, followed by "must," "shall," or "will" and the capabilities that the system must provide. For example, a functional requirement for a car rental system (CRS) may state the following: *"CRS shall allow a potential customer to inquire about the availability of rental cars using a variety of search criteria including make, model, from date, to date, price range, and class (small size, medium size, large size, and luxury cars)."*

It is important that the statements of requirements use the terms "must," "shall," or "will" consistently throughout. In other words, if "must" has been used, then it must be used in the formulation of every requirement. The requirements specification will not look like a professionally written document if one requirement statement uses "must" and the other uses "shall." Alternatively, requirements may be formulated as abilities of users. For example, the above requirement may be reformulated as: *"Potential customers shall be able to inquire about the availability of rental cars using a variety of search criteria including make, model, from date, to date, price range, and class (small size, medium size, large size, and luxury cars)."*

Nonfunctional requirements are divided into several categories of requirements. Below are some commonly seen categories:

Performance requirements specify the effectiveness and efficiency of the system. They are statements on the system's throughput, response time, real-time processing, and resource utilization. For example, "CRS shall process 100,000 transactions per day" is a performance requirement. A road survey system "shall process 1,000,000 Kbyte of input data per second" is another example.

Quality requirements are statements of required software quality. It refers to a wide variety of desired software attributes including reliability, availability, field-detected error rate, and the like. A reliability requirement may state that "the system shall be available 99% of the time."

Safety requirements specify capabilities in preventing the system from entering an unwanted state due to unintended operations. Such an event may cause loss of lives, bodily injury, damage to properties, or other undesired consequences. For example, "the system shall save and protect transaction histories when transactions fail." Sometimes, safety requirements are derived from safety standards, defined to ensure the safety of products or services.

Security requirements specify the capabilities in protecting system resources such as data and programs from malicious attack. Such attacks can come from within or outside of the organization. An example is "the system shall encrypt all files to be transmitted over the Internet." Security requirements are described in Chapter 24.

Interface requirements specify the look and feel, interfacing, and interaction behavior that the system should provide for external entities to communicate with the system. These include user interface requirements and hardware/software interface requirements. The former concerns the layout, look and feel, user interaction behavior, and other user interface-related requirements. Hardware/software interface requirements are statements of required capabilities of the software system to operate with hardware and/or other software systems. They should specify at least what hardware and/or software systems to interface with, how to communicate with each of these systems, and when the communication will take place.

4.4 CHALLENGES OF REQUIREMENTS ELICITATION

Identifying the real requirements is the hardest single part of software development because it has to overcome significant difficulties during the requirements elicitation process. Some of these are due to the fact that *software development in general is a wicked problem,* which was discussed in Chapter 2. The difficulties include, but are not limited to, the following:

1. *The development team does not know enough about the application and application domain.* For many real-world projects, in-depth knowledge about the application and application domain is critical to the success of the project. This is because in many cases the software system either automates its manual counter-part or interacts with the application through hardware devices. This requires a good understanding of the application and application domain. However, much of the application and application domain knowledge can only be obtained by years of

working experience. This is why agile methods emphasize *customer collaboration* and *active user involvement* because these practices are effective means to acquire the needed domain knowledge.

2. *Customers and users do not know what software can do and how to express their needs.* For most users, software is both a mystery and a puzzle. They don't know what software is, how it works, what the system can do for them, how the system will work with them, and how to communicate their needs. Traditionally, software developers make such decisions for the customer and users without adequate input from them. Sometime, the developer's attitude is "you don't know, so we decide for you," or "these are nice features that you ought to like." One story shows the users' feeling toward such a software vendor. The author and his students visited a health care facility to solicit feedback on the user interface design. A senior nurse thought it was something new. She expressed her feeling about the visit, "always in the past, we were given the software to use, but this time you are listening to us." Indeed, during requirements elicitation, the development team needs to work closely with the customer and users and encourage and facilitate them to communicate what they want, what they like, and what they don't like.
3. *Lack of a common background creates a communication barrier.* The lack of an understanding of each other's field creates a communication barrier between the team and the customer and users. The same words, phrases, or expressions often have different meanings in different domains. For example, the word "security" can mean protection and safety of personnel and physical properties, or protection of information, computing resources as well as services. In the financial domain, security refers to investment products such as stocks, bonds, mutual funds, and exchange-traded funds. This is only one of the numerous examples showing that a term can mean different things in different domains, or different contexts of the same domain.
4. *Software requirements cannot be specified definitely; the specification and implementation cannot be separated.* These are properties of wicked problems. Unfortunately, software development in general is a wicked problem (see Chapter 2). Consider, for example, the requirement to provide a "user-friendly interface" for a new system. It is practically impossible to specify the requirement accurately and adequately. This is because "user-friendliness" is a qualitative attribute and there is no objective judgment. User interface prototypes are often used to help specify the requirement. But doing so is implementation, not just specification.
5. *The importance and difficulty of requirements elicitation are often underestimated by management, customers and users, as well as developers.* As a consequence, inadequate time and resources are allocated to requirements elicitation.
6. *Nonfunctional requirements are not identified or understated.* Nonfunctional requirements often refer to capabilities that concern the quality, performance, security, and reliability aspects of the system, among others. Besides these, there are nontechnical requirements that are often ignored, such as requirements to comply to regulations and industry standards. In many cases, nonfunctional requirements

are not identified or understated. The problem is usually not discovered until the later stage of the project. This could cause a significant increase in the development time and costs.

7. *Requirements change throughout the entire software life cycle, even after the software is operational in the target environment.* This challenge is a corollary of above challenges. The requirements change from day one and continue throughout the entire life cycle. Change is not limited to functional and performance requirements. User interface change is quite common and volatile, especially at the beginning of a new development project.

4.5 STEPS FOR REQUIREMENTS ELICITATION

The overall objective of software requirements elicitation is to identify capabilities for the future system. Requirements elicitation has the following steps, which may need to be repeated a couple of times.

Step 1. Collecting information about the application.
Step 2. Constructing analysis models if desired.
Step 3. Deriving requirements and constraints.
Step 4. Conducting feasibility study.
Step 5. Reviewing the requirements specification.

Requirements elicitation begins with the activity that collects information about the application and application domain. Many pieces of information are useful for understanding the application and deriving the requirements and constraints. These include business goals, current business situation, policies, regulations, and standards. The collected information is then analyzed to identify problems, from which needs are derived. Sometimes, models are constructed to help understand the application and the business processes. Due to budget and development time constraints, not all needs can be satisfied. Therefore, the team has to work with the customer and users to identify high-priority needs and derive requirements to satisfy such needs. Sometimes, feasibility study is conducted to eliminate or reduce risk items during requirements elicitation. The requirements and constraints are then reviewed by peers, domain experts, and the customer and users, respectively. The review results are used to improve the requirements specification, from which use cases are derived.

It is important to know that conventional plan-driven development and agile development perform requirements elicitation very differently. Conventional approaches spend considerable time and effort on requirements elicitation, trying to obtain 100% correct and complete requirements. This is because requirements change causes significant rework and delivery delay. Conventional approaches typically consume 15%–20% of time and effort on requirements, that is, two months or more for a one-year project. For the same project, agile development would spend only one to two weeks. It aims to gather most, such as 80% rather than 100%, of the requirements. This is guided by the good-enough-is-enough or 20/80 agile principle. That is, spend 20% effort to get 80%

of the requirements quickly. Moreover, agile projects capture requirements at a high level; leave the detail to subsequent iterations.

4.5.1 Collecting Information

Requirements elicitation is a decision-making process, deciding on the capabilities of the future system. Decision making needs to analyze information. Therefore, collecting information about the application is the first step. This section answers the following information gathering–related questions:

1. What information needs to be collected?
2. What are the available information-collection methods and techniques?
3. What are the guidelines for information collection?

Focuses of Information-Collection Activities

The information-collection activities must focus on acquiring information about the application, the business processes, and the application domain. In particular, the information-collection activities should aim to answer the following questions:

1. What is the business for which the computerized system is built?
2. What is the current business situation, and how does it operate?
3. What is the system's environment or context?
4. What are the existing business processes, their input and output, and how do they relate and interact with each other?
5. What are the problems with the current system?
6. What are the business or product goals?
7. Who are the users of the current system and the future system, respectively?
8. What do the customer and users want from the future system, and what are their business priorities?
9. What are the quality, performance, and security considerations?

Information-Collection Techniques

Information-collection methods and techniques are applied to find answers to the questions presented previously. These techniques include

1. Customer presentation
2. Literature survey
3. Study of existing business procedures and forms
4. Stakeholder survey
5. User interviewing
6. Writing user stories

Customer presentation is a good way to start. A customer presentation quickly introduces the development team to the customer's business and allows the team members to ask questions to clarify doubts immediately. The presentation may also provide the development team with an initial concept of the system under development. To be effective, a number of guidelines should be followed:

- Ensure that whoever gives the presentation knows the business and what the customer and users want, although his knowledge may not be complete or 100% correct. A manager or administrator who is responsible for the daily operation is the best choice. A new hire may not be the right one to select for this job.
- Let the customer or its representative know what should be covered. In addition, ask for pointers to gather additional information. The nine questions presented in the last section should be addressed.
- If possible, one of the team members should review the presentation slides before the presentation session to ensure that the needed information is included.
- During the presentation, only ask questions that clarify doubts; avoid implementation-related discussions. The purpose of the presentation session is to learn the business and what the customer wants the system to provide.
- Request a copy of the presentation and share it with the team members.
- Avoid long presentation sessions that run more than two hours.

Valuable insight into the customer's existing business- and system-specific information can be obtained by studying similar projects, business documents and forms, industry and company standards, relevant government policies and regulations, and other related publications. In addition, the development team can obtain information through training or attending tutorials conducted by domain experts. Information about similar projects, if available, can provide very valuable insight into the system under development. For example, the software requirements of the new system can be derived from the capabilities of similar systems. The design and implementation of the new system may also benefit from the design and implementation of similar systems.

Many business documents, procedures, operating manuals, and forms are valuable sources. By studying these, the development team can obtain a better understanding of the business processes, and the input and output of these processes. Clearly, the future system must automate some or all of these business processes. Therefore, the development team should ask the customer to provide all relevant documents and forms and study them carefully. Each industry and company has its own standards. Computerized systems must support such standards in one way or another. These standards can be used to derive requirements or constraints. Government, industry, and company-specific policies and regulations may impose restrictions on the solution space. These restrictions are often formulated as constraints in the SRS.

A survey questionnaire is a good tool to use to acquire requirements from stakeholders, which include management personnel and end users. This technique has a number of merits. First of all, wicked problem solving indicates that it is important to involve stakeholders in the decision process. An anonymous survey encourages the stakeholders to express concerns, insider information, and improvement suggestions. These might be difficult to obtain through other information-collection methods. Such information can be used to derive requirements for the future system. The following guidelines should be observed when using a survey questionnaire:

- The questionnaire should be brief and focus on important issues.
- If possible, develop different questionnaires for different groups of stakeholders to be surveyed.
- Review the questionnaire with the customer representative to ensure that the questions are appropriate and clearly stated.

Interviewing customer representatives, users, and domain experts is an effective approach to information collection. The interviews can be conducted either in person or over the phone. The interactive nature of interviews allows the two parties to engage in an in-depth discussion of issues relating to the system under development.

The following guidelines are useful when conducting interviews:

- Conduct the interview after the development team has studied the survey questionnaires submitted by the customer and users. The questionnaires may already contain the information that the development team wants to know. Therefore, conducting the interviews after the survey can save time and effort. The responses to the questionnaire can tell the development team which areas or issues should be focus during the interview.
- The interview should be prepared and focused. That is, the development team should develop a list of questions to ask during the interview. The list of questions may be derived from the survey questionnaire. The questions should focus on the critical or important issues to be solved by the computerized system.
- Each interview session should not last more than one hour.
- Respect the opinions of the customer and users; they are the experts of their business. Avoid providing advice during the interview.

Ethnography is increasing its popularity in requirements gathering. It advises the development team to observe from within, rather than outside of, the culture of the business organization for which the system is built. It is an "inside out" not "outside in" approach for requirements elicitation. To accomplish this, the team should understand the users and think like the users. Ethnography suggests that the team should observe carefully how the users work and how they solve their business problems. Agile methods advocate a similar principle. That is, active user involvement is imperative. For example, DSDM implements active user involvement with the inclusion of ambassador user and advisory user roles in the team.

User stories are widely used by agile methods as a requirements gathering method. User stories may be produced by users, or jointly with the development team. Each user story briefly describes a capability that a user role wishes to have. Each user role may have several user stories. User stories are effective because they are "inside out" rather than "outside in." The following are some of the many user stories produced in a real-world project.

1. As a medical assistant, I need to create patient records for new patients.
2. As a medical assistant, I need to search and retrieve patient records using a patient's birthday and/or the patient's last name, first name.
3. As a medical assistant, I need to keep track of a patient's medical test records.

4. As a medical doctor, I need to document all conversations with a patient.
5. As a medical doctor, I frequently need to search conversations with a patient to locate certain information.
6. As a medical doctor, I need to search a patient's medical test records.
7. As a medical doctor, I want to access the system from home or from anywhere remotely.
8. As an information security officer, I want to protect the system from unauthorized access.

This step generates a list of items that includes business goals, the current business situation, user stories or customer and users' wish lists, and government and industry, as well as company, policies, regulations, and standards. If the software system is an embedded component of a hardware-software system, then the results also include system requirements that are allocated to the software system.

As an example, consider a project initiated by the Office of International Education (OIE) of a university. Several years ago, the OIE recognized the trend of education globalization. That is, many U.S. universities observed a significant increase in the number of students enrolling in study abroad programs, which allow a student to study abroad for one or two semesters and transfer the course credits back to the United States. To meet this new demand, the OIE started a project to improve the operation of the Study Abroad Program. A summary of the result of the information collection step is as follows:

Current Business Situation

The OIE is located in a building somewhat distant from the main campus. It is difficult for students to access the OIE. The Study Abroad Program of the OIE is mainly a manual operation. It is time consuming to process student inquiries and study abroad applications.

Business Goals

1. Greatly facilitate students' access to the OIE Study Abroad Program.
2. Significantly improve the effectiveness and efficiency of the services provided by the Study Abroad Program.

Wish List

A website for the Study Abroad Program. The system is named Study Abroad Management System (SAMS). A list of similar websites was suggested by the OIE.

4.5.2 Constructing Analysis Models

Real-world applications are complex. They involve many different types of business objects, complex relationships between the business objects, and business processes. The development team needs to understand such domain knowledge to identify and formulate requirements. The domain knowledge is also useful for design, implementation, testing, and maintenance of the software system. Modeling is an effective tool to acquire domain knowledge. It is frequently used during requirements elicitation. Modeling is a conceptualization and visualization process that helps the development team understand and analyze the existing application. In particular, modeling in object-oriented software engineering views the world as consisting of objects that relate to, and interact with, each other. The result is a set of UML diagrams that visualize

UML Diagram	Description	Usefulness in Modeling an Existing System
Class diagram	A directed graph in which the vertexes represent classes and the directed edges represent different types of relationships between the classes. The vertexes also contain information that describes the properties of the classes.	Class diagrams are used to visualize domain models, which help the development team understand and communicate domain concepts and relationships between the domain concepts.
Use case diagram	A graph in which the vertexes represent abstractions of business processes and actors while the edges specify which actors interact with which business processes.	Use case diagrams are used to display an overview of the business processes of an existing application or a subsystem as well as the users that request the services of the business processes. Use case diagrams also show the boundaries of the existing application, system, or subsystems.
Sequence diagram	A directed graph in which the vertexes represent objects and the directed edges represent time-ordered messages or requests between the objects.	Sequence diagrams help the development team understand and analyze the existing business processes; that is, how the business objects process a user request in the existing business environment.
State diagram	A directed graph in which the vertexes represent system states and the directed edges represent state transitions caused by internal or external events.	State diagrams are useful for the modeling of event-driven systems or business activities.
Activity diagram	A directed graph in which the vertexes represent information-processing activities and the directed edges represent data flows and control flows among the activities. The control flows specify that the activities are performed sequentially, concurrently, and/or synchronously.	Activity diagrams are used to model information-processing activities of the existing application in which the activities relate to each other through complex data flow and control flow relationships.

FIGURE 4.1 Modeling existing applications with UML diagrams

different aspects of the existing application. Figure 4.1 shows some UML diagrams and how they model an existing application.

As another example, Figure 4.2 shows an activity diagram that describes how student applications to overseas exchange programs are manually processed. The ovals denote activities and the directed edges denote object flows and control flows among the activities. The diamond denotes a decision point and the dashed lines indicate the organizations that own the activities. As depicted in the diagram, applications for overseas exchange programs are prepared by students. The applications are reviewed by OIE advisors, who either accept or do not accept the applications. If the application is accepted, then the overseas institution is contacted, the academic department and the student are notified, and the application is archived. If the application is rejected, then the student is notified and the application is also archived.

Modeling consumes considerable time and effort. Therefore, construct models only if they greatly help understanding and analysis. Avoid constructing models just for the sake of documentation. Agile development suggests "barely enough modeling"; in other words, do minimum modeling that is just enough to serve the purpose but no more.

4.5.3 Deriving Requirements and Constraints

The main objective of this step is to derive software requirements and constraints from the information collected. To accomplish this goal, the information is analyzed

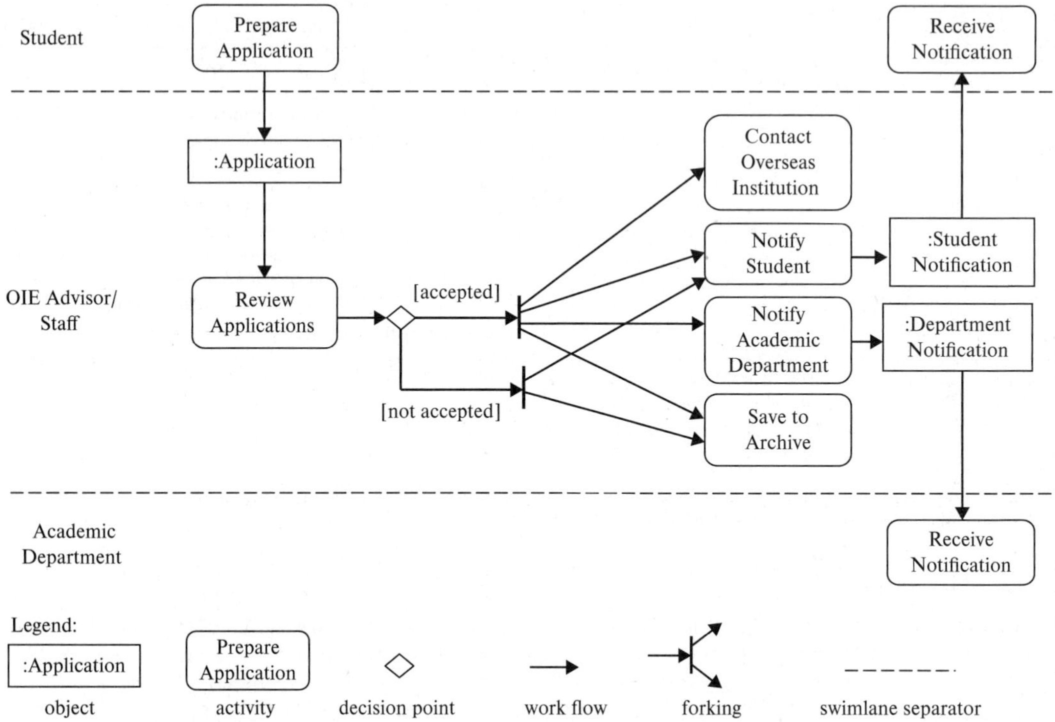

FIGURE 4.2 Activity diagram for an existing business process

to identify needs and derive system capabilities to satisfy the needs. The capabilities are then formulated as requirements. The requirements are prioritized according to business priorities. The development team works with the customer and users as well as domain experts to carry out these activities.

Identifying Needs from the Wish Lists

It is relatively straightforward to identify needs from the wish lists or user stories if they are available. Consider the OIE project discussed in Section 4.5.1. The solution is already stated in the wish list—a website for the Study Abroad Program managed by the OIE. In this case, the job of the development team is to identify what the website needs to provide to accomplish the business goals. The following are some of the needs identified:

- Students should be able to search for overseas exchange programs using a variety of search criteria.
- OIE staff members should be able to enter, edit, activate, and deactivate overseas exchange programs.
- Students should be able to create, edit, and submit applications for overseas exchange programs.
- OIE advisors should be able to process online applications.

Identifying Needs to Satisfy Business Goals

Needs are also derived from the current business situation and the business goals. First, the gap between the current situation and the business goals is assessed. This is used to identify the needs, meaning things to be done, or capabilities the business must provide to fill the gap. For example, the business goal to double sales in the next three years implies that the business has to increase its sales capability. This could be accomplished in many ways, such as by expanding its sales force, providing discounts, and/or going online, to mention a few. Often, a computerized solution is one of the possible solutions but may or may not be the most cost-effective solution for the problem. For example, going online may increase sales for some types of product, but this is not true for all types of product. The development team should work with the customer, users, and domain experts to identify the most appropriate solution for the business problem.

Deriving Requirements from Needs

From the needs, the team identifies or derives capabilities for the new system to satisfy the needs. Sometimes the needs already state the capabilities, as shown above for the OIE Study Abroad Program website. In other cases, the development team must derive the capabilities through reasoning. In either case, the capabilities identified are formulated as requirements. It should be noted that the system under development is not required to satisfy all of the needs identified. There are many possible reasons. For example, the customer and users may not want all of the needs identified by the development team. The customer may not want to pay for some of the capabilities due to budget constraints. The customer may want to have some of the features implemented in a future release due to business considerations. Each application is unique.

EXAMPLE 4.1

In illustration, after a presentation by the OIE operating director and a couple of follow-up meetings with the OIE, the SAMS project team identifies two to three dozen functional requirements for the system. The following are three of them:

R1. SAMS shall provide a search capability for overseas exchange programs using a variety of search criteria.

R2. SAMS shall provide a hierarchical display of the search results to facilitate navigation from a high-level summary to details about an overseas exchange program.

R3. SAMS shall allow students to submit online applications for overseas exchange programs.

Deriving Requirements from Analysis Models

Models are useful for understanding an existing application and its business processes, as presented in Section 4.5.2. Models are also useful for deriving requirements. The following example illustrates this.

EXAMPLE 4.2 Figure 4.2 shows an activity diagram for an existing, manual process for the Office of International Education (OIE). Identify functional requirements from the activity diagram.

Solution: The activity diagram in Figure 4.2 has the following activities:

1. *Prepare application.* This activity is performed by the student. Currently, the student fills out a form manually and submits it to the OIE.
2. *Review applications.* This activity is performed by OIE advisors. The OIE advisors review each of the applications and determine whether to accept or not accept the application.
3. *Contact overseas institution.* This activity is performed by OIE advisors, who contact the overseas institutions on behalf of the students who are accepted to exchange programs.
4. *Notify student.* This function is performed by an OIE staff, who sends letters to the students informing them of the evaluation results of their applications.
5. *Notify academic department.* This function is performed by an OIE staff, who sends a letter to each of the academic departments notifying them which students are accepted into the exchange program and which students are not.
6. *Save to archive.* This function is performed by an OIE staff, who archives the applications that are evaluated.
7. *Receive notification by student.* This function is performed by the students, who receive the notification letters sent by an OIE staff.
8. *Receive notification by academic department.* This function is performed by secretaries of the relevant academic departments, who receive and archive the notification letters sent by an OIE staff.

Although these are activities of the existing, manual system, the new system ought to provide automated means to support these activities because they are part of the business behavior of the OIE application. This suggests the following requirements for the new system.

R4. SAMS shall provide an online capability for students to prepare applications to overseas exchange programs.

R5. SAMS shall facilitate review of applications by OIE advisors.

R6. SAMS shall contact the overseas institution when an application is accepted by the OIE.

R7. SAMS shall notify relevant entities when an application is accepted or rejected.

> **R7.1.** SAMS shall notify the student when an application is accepted or rejected.
>
> **R7.2.** SAMS shall notify the academic department when an application is accepted.

R8. SAMS shall archive accepted and rejected applications.

R9. SAMS shall allow students to view and print the notification letter concerning the decisions of their applications.

R10. SAMS shall allow secretaries of the academic departments to view and print notification letters online.

Requirements are also derived from use case diagrams and class diagrams that model an existing application. The use case diagrams are useful for depicting the business processes of an existing application. That is, each use case models an existing business process. Thus, requirements to automate the business processes can be derived from the use cases. In addition, requirements are derived from what computers can do for the actor. For example, a student can only browse overseas exchange programs with the existing manual system. A computerized system can provide an online search capability using a variety of criteria. This requirement implies that information about the programs must be entered into the system. Thus, the system must provide capabilities for an OIE staff to enter, edit, activate, and deactivate overseas exchange programs. All these are functional requirements of the new system.

During the requirements elicitation phase, domain models are sometimes constructed to help the team understand the application domain. The association relationships that are labeled by a transitive verb often suggest capabilities that can be formulated as requirements. For example, a domain model for the OIE study abroad application may show an association relationship between the Faculty class and the Student class, that is, Faculty recommend Student. This relationship may suggest that the online system should allow faculty members to submit recommendation letters for students. That is, a functional requirement is derived.

In addition to requirements, some projects impose restrictions on the design and implementation. These restrictions are stated as constraints in the requirements specification. For instance, OIE may require that SAMS run on a server provided by the computing center of the university and use the database management system designated by the computing center. The OIE may choose the implementation language according to suggestions of its IT staff. These are possible constraints for the system.

Numbering Requirements and Constraints

Dotted numbers such as R1, R1.1, R1.2.1, R1.2.2, R2, R2.1, R2.2, and C1, C2, C3 are used to label the requirements and constraints. This facilitates communication, and relating the requirements and constraints to other software artifacts such as use cases and test cases. Relating the requirements to use cases helps the project manager in the scheduling of the development and deployment of the use cases. For example, it ensures that every requirement is satisfied and high-priority requirements are realized first. To facilitate identification of such relationships, a traceability matrix is widely used in the industry. The rows of the matrix represent the requirements while the columns represent the use cases. Labeling the requirements and constraints with dotted numbers makes it easy to construct and use the traceability matrix. The dotted numbers also imply a refinement or decomposition hierarchy between the requirements as well as between the constraints. In Example 4.2, requirement R6 is refined by two requirements R6.1 and R6.2. This means R6 is equivalent to R6.1 and R6.2. That is, R6 is satisfied if and only if R6.1 and R6.2 are satisfied. Such an equivalence relationship is useful because it is easier to satisfy each of the lower-level requirements.

Prioritizing Requirements

After the derivation of the requirements, an integer priority weight ranging from 1 to 5, or 1 to 10, is assigned to each requirement. Thus, use cases associated with high-priority requirements will be developed and delivered first. It is important to prioritize the requirements because time and resources are limited. The priorities help the team focus on high-priority requirements. This in turn ensures that the business priorities are met. The development team should work with the customer and users to determine the priorities of the requirements. Survey questionnaires and interviews, as described earlier, can be used.

The Delphi estimation method can be applied to determine requirement priorities. Call a meeting of customer and user representatives who are familiar with the business processes to be computerized. Explain the functionalities of the requirements one by one, and ask the participants to write down how much their company should/will pay for the requirement; a participant may choose not to deal with a requirement. Ask the highest and the lowest bids to explain why or how they come up with their dollar amounts. The participants are asked to estimate again. This process is repeated until the participants reach a consensus. The priorities of the requirements are then derived from the dollar amounts, that is, the higher the dollar amount, the higher the priority.

Requirements are used to derive use cases and use-case priorities (Chapter 7). Use-case priorities are used to plan use-case deliveries. Requirement priorities are also useful in dealing with requirements change for agile projects. For example, in the middle of an agile project, the customer wants to add two new requirements. These will not be a problem if the project budget and completion time can be extended accordingly. If budget and completion time are fixed, the team can produce estimates of costs and time to deliver the new requirements. The team also selects several lowest-priority requirements with the same/similar costs and time as the new requirements. The team then tells the customer that since budget and completion time are fixed, the solution is to trade the lowest-priority requirements for the new requirements. In most cases, the customer will agree because the new requirements are more valuable to the customer than those to be replaced.

4.5.4 Requirements Specification Standards

To avoid dispute, the requirements and constraints identified in this step must be documented. Throughout the years, the software industry has developed a number of SRS standards. Figure 4.3 exhibits and explains the IEEE Std 830-1998 SRS standard.

Section	Description
1. Introduction	Provide an overview of the software requirements specification (SRS)
1.1 Purpose	Specify the purpose of the SRS and the intended audience
1.2 Scope	a. Identify product by name b. Explain what the product will and will not do c. Describe the uses of the product including objectives, goals, and benefits
1.3 Definitions, Acronyms, and Abbreviations	Provide definitions of all items, acronyms, and abbreviations to properly interpret the SRS. It may contain references to appendixes or other documents.
1.4 References	List each document referenced in the SRS by title, report number, date, publisher, and where and how to get it
1.5 Overview	Outline the rest of the SRS and how it is organized
2. Overall Description	Provide an overview of the product
2.1 Product Perspective 2.1.1 System Interfaces 2.1.2 User Interfaces 2.1.3 Hardware Interfaces 2.1.4 Software Interfaces 2.1.5 Communications Interfaces 2.1.6 Memory 2.1.7 Operations 2.1.8 Site Adaptation Requirements	Describe the context of the product and its relations and interfaces to other components of the total system. Block diagrams may be used to show the context and relationships. Describe also the characteristics and limits on the primary and secondary memory, modes of operations, backup and recovery, and site specific requirements
2.2 Product Functions	Provide a summary of the functions of the product
2.3 User Characteristics	Describe the general characteristics of the intended users including educational level, experience, expertise, and technical skills
2.4 Constraints	Describe the restrictions on the solutions space or options of the developer
2.5 Assumptions and Dependencies	List the factors that affect the requirements
3. Specific Requirements	Describe the software requirements
3.1 External Interface Requirements	Provide a detailed description for each of the system interfaces, user interfaces, hardware interfaces, software interfaces, and communications interfaces. The description of each interface includes, for each input and output, the name, format, valid range, timing, and other relevant information.
3.2 Functional Requirements	Provide a detailed description of the functionality of each of the functional requirements beginning with "The system shall (do/perform/provide ...)." The description may include input validity checks, sequence of operations, responses to abnormal situations, and input/output relationships.
3.3 Performance Requirements	Describe all performance-related capabilities of the product
3.4 Design Constraints	Describe all restrictions on the design alternatives such as restrictions imposed by standards and hardware limitations
3.5 Software System Attributes	Describe all quality-related requirements such as reliability, security, availability, and interoperability, etc.
3.6 Other Requirements	
Appendixes	
Index	

FIGURE 4.3 IEEE Std 830-1998 SRS standard

4.5.5 Conducting Feasibility Study

The requirements specification is a part of a contract between the customer and developer and bears legal consequences. For example, two stories are presented at the beginning of this chapter. One of them results in the developer and the customer suing each other because the system does not satisfy the requirements. The system involved in the story has to provide real-time, wireless access to patient records by doctors at any time and from anywhere within the system's service area. The system has to ensure security and privacy of patient information. Even if technology can provide these capabilities, budget and schedule constraints could significantly compromise the ability of the development team to meet such requirements. Therefore, it is important that requirements elicitation evaluates the feasibility of the project taking into consideration the ability of the team, the budget and schedule constraints, the technology, and other relevant factors.

Effort estimation and scheduling methods and techniques presented in Chapter 23 are useful for assessing the feasibility relating to team ability, budget, and schedule to develop the system. Prototyping is an effective approach to evaluating technology feasibility. For example, to ensure that a timing constraint will be met, a prototype of the relevant component is constructed and used to evaluate the feasibility of meeting the constraint. Although a feasibility study reduces the likelihood of not satisfying the requirements and constraints, risks may still exist. In this case, risk management is applied to identify and analyze the risks, and risk resolution measures are developed. The risks are monitored throughout the development process. The appropriate risk resolution measures are applied if the risk conditions are detected. Risk management is presented in Chapter 23.

4.5.6 Reviewing Requirements Specification

The SRS must be reviewed by peers, domain experts, and the customer and users. These reviews are referred to as *technical reviews*, *expert reviews*, and *customer reviews*, which are briefly described in the following sections.

Technical Review

Technical review is an internal review performed by the development team. Technical review techniques include peer review, inspection, and walkthrough. Technical review is aimed to reveal a number of problems, including:

- Incompleteness such as (1) definition incompleteness (e.g., some application-specific concepts are not defined), (2) internal incompleteness (e.g., some requirement has an "if part" but no "else part"), and (3) external incompleteness (i.e., there are cases that exist in the real-world application that are not included in the requirements specification).
- Inconsistency such as (1) type inconsistency (e.g., inconsistent specification of a data type in the requirements specification) and (2) logical inconsistency (e.g., the requirements imply that two different results can be produced under the same condition).

- Ambiguity such as (1) ambiguity in the definition of application-specific concepts and (2) ambiguity in the formulation of requirements.
- Redundancy such as (1) duplicate definitions of the same concept and (2) duplicate formulations of the same requirement or constraint.
- Intractability (i.e., lower-level requirements do not correspond to the high-level requirement).
- Infeasibility (i.e., some requirements or constraints cannot be satisfied).
- Unwanted implementation details.

Expert Review

Expert review is conducted with domain experts and aims to answer the following questions:

1. Are domain-specific laws, rules, behaviors, policies, standards, and regulations correctly and accurately formulated in the SRS?
2. Is there any incorrect, inaccurate, inappropriate, or inconsistent use of jargon?
3. Is the perception of the application domain correct and accurate?
4. Are there other potential domain specific problems or concerns?

Customer Review

Customer review is performed with the customer and users and seeks answers to the following questions:

1. Does the requirements specification correctly describe the functional requirements of the application for which the system is to be built or extended?
2. Are there incorrectly stated user interface requirements?
3. Are there incorrectly stated nonfunctional requirements including performance, response time, and security requirements?
4. Are there incorrectly stated application-specific constraints relating to operating environment, government, and industry policies and regulations?

4.6 APPLYING AGILE PRINCIPLES

Conventional plan-driven development devotes considerable time and effort on requirements elicitation. For example, the requirements analysis phase of a waterfall process typically consumes 15% or more of the total development time or effort. This is because changes to requirements are difficult and costly once the requirements milestone is established.

Agile development accepts the fact that change is the way of life. It can respond to change much more quickly and responsively, thanks to short iteration intervals and small increments. Thus, requirements elicitation for agile development should consume a very small amount of time and effort, such as a couple of weeks for a small- to medium-sized project. The purpose is to produce a list of preliminary requirements, which is expected to change during subsequent iterations.

For agile projects, the following principles should be applied during requirements elicitation:

1. *Customer collaboration and active user involvement are imperative.* As discussed in the Challenges of Requirements Elicitation section, there are communication barriers between the development team and the customer and users. This is due to the lack of an adequate understanding of each others' profession. To overcome these barriers, the development team has to take initiative to involve the customer and users in the development process. This requires collaboration from the customer because it consumes considerable time and effort. Customer collaboration means that the customer understands the importance of user involvement and commits valuable employee time and effort to the project. More specifically, the customer needs to identify employees who know the application very well and assign them to work with the development team. The frequency of interacting with the development team differs from agile method to agile method, and differs from project to project. At least two to three meetings per week with the development team is desired.
2. *Capture requirements at a high level; leave the detail to subsequent iterations.* Agile methods do not specify the requirements in detail. This is because for many real-world projects, it is impossible to specify the real requirements accurately, adequately, and in detail. As the use cases are iteratively installed and operational in the target environment, the customer's business evolves, and so changes to the requirements are needed. Therefore, it is a waste of time and effort to capture and specify the details of the requirements even if it is possible to do.
3. *Good enough is enough–produce a list of software requirements quickly and move on to the next step.* You don't need to acquire every requirement up front and you don't need to have them 100% correct and accurate. The properties of wicked problems presented in Chapter 2 tell us that requirements cannot be exhaustively, accurately, and definitely identified and specified. Therefore, agile methods focus on identifying, validating, and specifying the requirements that are mission critical, with a high business priority and a high business value. This principle is often equated to the 20/80 rule, which encourages identifying the most-used functionalities of the system with a fraction of the effort. These principles are practically very useful because one cannot have everything–you give up something to get something else. This means focusing on the requirements that are the most valuable to the customer rather than spreading thin on everything.
4. *Just barely enough modeling–if models are constructed to aid requirements elicitation, then construct the minimum model quickly, just enough to serve the purpose and no more.* Agile development values working software over comprehensive documentation because the former is the bottom line. However, modeling improves understanding and communication between the team members if used properly. Just barely enough modeling means that if modeling is desired, you should then try to limit the scope to just enough to serve the purpose.

4.7 REQUIREMENTS MANAGEMENT AND TOOLS

Requirements change is common for many software projects. The changes include adding new requirements and modifying and deleting existing requirements. Changing a requirement may affect several artifacts and other requirement items. The change impact, the cost to implement the change, and the cost to address the impact need to be assessed to determine if the change is cost-effective. Requirements change is also needed during the maintenance phase to correct errors and enhance the functionality of the system. Requirements management is the mechanism to address all issues relating to requirements change. Figure 4.4 explains the major activities of requirements management.

Requirements management has to process a tremendous amount of data and complex dependencies. Many tools are available to support the requirements management activities. IBM Rational RequisitePro and IBM Rational DOORS are two such tools. RequisitePro lets the team members define the requirements and specify properties of the requirements items using a web-based interface. It supports requirements traceability including traceability between high-level and low-level requirements. It provides change impact analysis and automatic email notification whenever a requirement is changed. It checks for compliance to government and industry regulations and standards. It is integrated with other Rational tool suites.

IBM Rational DOORS is a requirements management tool. It supports requirements definition, and linking the requirements to other requirements, diagrams, tables,

Activity	Description
Definition and Prioritizing	• Identify business needs and priorities • Formulate functional requirements, nonfunctional requirements, and constraints
Quality Management	• Ensure that the requirements are clearly specified, correct, and consistent, and mission-critical requirements are included • Ensure that the requirements are linked to test cases • Collect data and compute quality metrics and trends
Risk Management	• Identify and prioritize requirements risk items • Specify risk resolution measures for high-priority risk items • Monitor risks and execute risk-resolution measurements • Update risk items and resolution measures
Traceability Management	• Track dependencies between requirements and business needs, customer documents, and all development-related artifacts such as analysis and design documents, code, and test cases
Change Management	• Identify and analyze need for requirements change • Conduct change impact and cost-benefit analysis • Ensure that approved changes are properly implemented

FIGURE 4.4 Requirements management activities

and related documents. Through its web access, stakeholders at different locations can discuss and edit the requirements and traceability information. It comes with a built-in change process that supports concurrent requirements update. It supports compliance audit in two different ways. Its traceability functions can show the auditors how the requirements, design, and tests comply with the standards and regulations. It also logs who changed what and when so there is always an audit trail of changes. The tool can integrate with other Rational and third-party tools to support enterprisewide change management, quality management, and other functions.

4.8 SUMMARY

This chapter presents the basic concepts, steps, and techniques for requirements elicitation. Also presented are the importance and challenges of requirements elicitation. The steps are (1) collecting information about the application and application domain, (2) constructing analysis models, (3) deriving requirements and constraints, (4) performing feasibility study, and (5) reviewing the requirements and constraints. Three types of requirements review are described: technical review, expert review, and customer review. Each of these reviews focuses on different aspects of the requirements specification. At the end of the chapter, agile principles for requirements elicitation are described and discussed.

4.9 CHAPTER REVIEW QUESTIONS

1. What are a requirement and a constraint? What are the differences between the two?
2. What are the objectives of requirements elicitation?
3. Why is requirements elicitation important?
4. What are the challenges of requirements elicitation?
5. What are the activities or steps of requirements elicitation?
6. What can go wrong with requirements?
7. What are the three types of requirements review? Who is involved? What is the focus of each type of review?
8. What are requirements management and requirements traceability?
9. What agile principles are applicable in requirements elicitation? What are the implications of each of these principles?

4.10 EXERCISES

4.1 Produce a software requirements specification (SRS) for a library information system that is similar to the system in use in your school. At the minimum, the system should provide functions to allow a patron to search, check out, and return documents, respectively.

4.2 Formulate functional and nonfunctional requirements for each of the following systems. For each system, limit the requirements specification to no more than three pages.

- **a.** A desktop virtual calculator that allows the user to use the mouse as well as the keyboard to enter the input
- **b.** A telephone answering machine
- **c.** A web-based email system

4.3 Identify and specify functional and nonfunctional requirements for an online course management system. The system should allow students to search, register, and drop courses, respectively. It also allows staff members of the study administration of the university to schedule classes.

4.4 Formulate functional requirements for the calendar management system described below. Limit the length of the SRS to no more than two pages.

This calendar management software allows the user to schedule personal activities such as meetings and tasks to be performed. An activity can take place on a future date during a certain period of time. An activity can take place for several consecutive days. Each activity has a brief mnemonic description. An activity can be a recursive activity, which takes place repeatedly every hour, every day, every week, or every month. A user can schedule an activity using a month-by-month calendar to select the date or dates, and then zoom in to select the begin time and end time on that the date. The calendar system shall notify the user by email, text message, or phone call the day before and on the activity day. The user can review past activities and update or delete activities.

4.5 Produce an SRS for the room reservation system described below. Limit the length to no more than two single-spaced pages.

This single-room reservation system is a resource management system that allows registered users of an organization to reserve a room for a given period of time on a given date. Moreover, the system allows the user to choose whether a reminder message will be sent automatically to a group of users and on which date(s) to send the reminder message. Because only one room is available, no search capabilities are necessary. The system allows a user to navigate to the desired day using a visual month-by-month calendar. As the monthly calendars are displayed, the time periods that are already reserved are colored red and the available time periods are colored differently, or shown with no color. The configuration of the system is used to specify a number of properties or constraints:

a. Enable or disable a display of which user has reserved which time period.

b. Enable or disable the ability for a user to reserve the room recursively for a given period of time. For example, 10:00 a.m.–12:00 p.m. every Wednesday for the whole semester.

c. Specify a constraint on the maximal period of time for recursive reservations.

d. Specify a constraint on the number of reservations that a user can make.

e. Enable or disable an automatic system reminder message.

4.6 In Appendix D.2, a National Trade Show Services (NTSS) business is described. Suppose that currently the NTSS business is conducted manually. The company wants to develop an online system to automate the business. This exercise may be an individual assignment or part of a team project. It requires the student or team to do the following:

a. From the business description, identify and list the most important business activities of the current business. These are the functionalities that the future system must provide. *Hint:* The number of such activities may differ from student to student. However, the combined functionality identified should cover at least 90% of the current business activities, which includes the most important business functions.

b. Identify other necessary functionalities for the online system so the business can run online. For example, the system needs to authenticate users.

c. Formulate the functionalities as software requirements.

4.7 Describe in concrete terms how you would conduct each of the three types of review for the NTSS SRS you produced in Exercise 4.6. Limit your answer to no more than one single-spaced page and no less than 11-point font size.

4.8 Identify and formulate requirements and constraints for the online car rental system described in Appendix D.1. Also provide priority weights for the requirements according to the nature of the car rental business.

4.9 Write an article to describe how requirements elicitation would be performed using the waterfall process and an agile process, respectively. List the differences between the two approaches, and provide a brief explanation of the differences.

4.10 What would you do if the customer wants to include two new requirements but does not want to increase budget and system completion time?

5 Chapter

Domain Modeling

Key Takeaway Points

- Domain modeling is a conceptualization process to help the development team understand the application domain and establish a common understanding among the team members.
- Five easy steps: collecting information about the application domain, brainstorming, classifying brainstorming results, visualizing the domain model using a UML class diagram, and performing inspection and review.

Mary Sanders had been working on a project for an insurance company, but she was unexpectedly reassigned to work on another project for a health care company. Her supervisor knew that she could learn this new application domain quickly, and indeed, Mary delivered the project on time and with no major issues. What is Mary's secret? How could she switch application domains so quickly?

A software engineer like Mary, who works in IT consulting, often works on projects in different application domains. Even if a software engineer is not a consultant, he or she may be required to work on new projects or novel extensions of existing systems. Software engineering is both challenging and full of excitement because engineers get to work on new applications from time to time. A good software engineer can quickly understand a new application domain. One of the tools that enables the engineer to do this is called domain modeling. Throughout this chapter, you will learn:

- Domain modeling.
- The importance of domain modeling.
- Object-oriented concepts.
- UML class diagram.
- Domain modeling steps.

5.1 WHAT IS DOMAIN MODELING?

Several years ago, I taught a class that required student teams to design and implement a cellular communication system simulator. In the class, we had learned about domain modeling, and the students were required to construct a domain model for this wireless simulator project. A hardworking student visited my office almost every week, bringing the copious notes he had taken while reading materials about wireless communication. I urged him to construct a domain model instead of taking the notes. Unfortunately, the student did not do this until the project deadline had approached. After submitting the domain model, the student came to me and said, "I regret that I did not start domain modeling earlier. It really helped me to understand wireless communication in a fast, organized way."

So, what is domain modeling?

Definition 5.1 *Domain modeling* is a conceptualization process. It aims to identify important domain concepts, their properties, and relationships between the concepts. The result is portrayed in a diagram called a domain model.

The conceptualization process involves observation, classification, abstraction, and generalization. The process is important because, in a broad sense, software is merely a conceptual product. Software development is all about *conceptualization*. Take, for instance, the construction of a banking system—the development team has to understand the banking business in the first place. This requires the development team to understand the concepts and terminologies in the banking domain, their properties, and how they relate to each other. The team has to collect application-related information, analyze the information, and construct a model to visualize the result to facilitate understanding. The process of performing these activities is called *domain modeling*. It is also called *conceptual modeling*.

5.2 WHY DOMAIN MODELING?

Software engineers are required to work on projects of different domains. Software engineers come from different backgrounds and have different working experiences, which affects their perception of an application domain. As a consequence, two software engineers may understand the same term differently. Even software engineers who have worked together in the same company and on similar projects for years may have different perceptions of their application domain. If the differences in perception are immaterial, then they will not significantly impact the design, implementation, integration, testing, and maintenance of the software product. However, if the differences are substantial, then they will surface during one of the development phases. This may result in significant rework and delay the project delivery date.

The benefits of domain modeling are the following:

- It helps the development team or the analyst understand an application and its domain because a domain model describes important domain concepts, their properties and their relationships with each other.
- It helps the team establish a common understanding about an application and its domain.
- It helps the team improve understanding of requirements because requirements specification involves domain concepts and their relationships.

- It helps the team improve communication with customer and users.
- It serves as a common basis for subsequent design, implementation, testing, and maintenance.
- It helps new members understand an application and its domain because the domain model can be used as a training tool for new comers.

5.3 OBJECT-ORIENTATION AND CLASS DIAGRAM

Domain modeling aims to identify important domain concepts, their properties, and relationships between the concepts. These are represented as classes and relationships between the classes, and can be depicted in a UML class diagram. This section reviews some of the basic concepts of the object-oriented paradigm and how these are displayed in UML class diagrams.

5.3.1 Extensional and Intentional Definitions

Domain modeling is a conceptualization process. As part of the process, the developer observes specific instances of an application and classifies, abstracts, and generalizes the observed instances to produce a conceptual model, called a domain model. One important step in this process is classification. The notion of a *class* is the end product of the classification process. To illustrate, imagine a two-year-old child out walking with his mother. The child sees a dog; his mother tells him that it is a dog, so he forms his concept of a dog. He then sees other dogs and cats of different colors. Up to this point, the child's conceptualization process is an inductive process. The approach he uses to learn new concepts is based on extensional definition, defined as follows.

Definition 5.2 An *extensional definition* defines a concept by enumerating instances of the concept.

An extensional definition of even numbers could be the set of numbers consisting of . . .,−4, −2, 0, 2, 4, . . . For the child, the extensional definition of "dog" consists of his neighbor's dog, the dog across the street, the dog that lives near the park, and so forth. As the child sees more of the world, he learns that cats and dogs are animals and they behave differently. So he knows how to abstract, classify, and generalize instances to form classes according to their characteristics. He knows how to relate classes as well.

One day the boy is excited because he is going to visit his aunt, who just moved into a garden house. He has never seen a garden house, but he is curious because the houses in his town do not have gardens. So he sketches a garden house based on his knowledge about gardens and houses. He then builds his garden house with his LEGOs. In this case, the child defines his own concept through intentional definition.

Definition 5.3 An *intentional definition* defines a concept through specification of properties and behaviors that instances of the concept possess.

Domain modeling is similar to the child's perception of the world and uses both extensional and intentional definitions. The team enters into a new application

Notion	Semantics	Notation
Class attribute operation	A class is a type; its attributes and operations characterize the objects of the class.	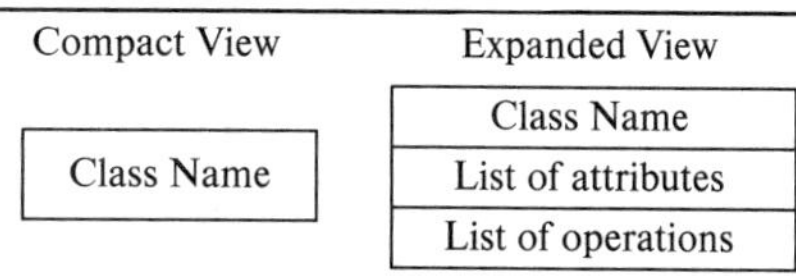
Inheritance	A generalization/specialization relationship between two classes.	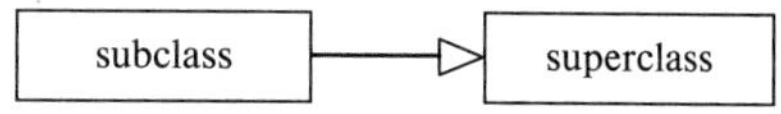
Aggregation	A part-of relation between two classes. Part-of exclusively.	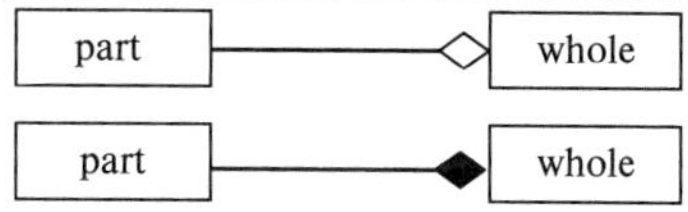
Association, direction, multiplicity, role	A binary relation between two classes.	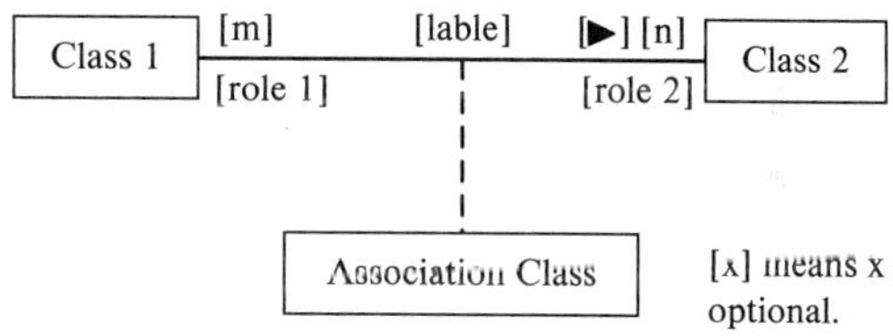
Association class	A class that describes an association.	[x] means x is optional.

FIGURE 5.1 Some commonly used class diagram notions and notations

domain. Like the child, the team enumerates things it sees and classifies them into classes, attributes, and relationships. The result is visualized using UML class diagrams, defined as follows:

Definition 5.4 A *UML class diagram* is a structural diagram that depicts the classes, their attributes and operations, and relationships between the classes.

Figure 5.1 shows some of the notions and notations of a class diagram. The next several sections explain these in detail.

5.3.2 Class and Object

Definition 5.5 A *class* is a type, an intentional definition of a concept. A class encapsulates its attributes and operations that characterize the instances of the class. An *object* is an instance of a class.

Classes can be shown using either the compact view or the expanded view, as illustrated in Figure 5.2(*a*) and (*b*). Both (*a*) and (*b*) express the same idea: an employee works on zero or one project, and a project has zero or more employees working on it. The compact view is used if there is no need to show the detail of a class. The expanded view is used to show the attributes and operations of a class. Both the compact view and the expanded view can be used in the same class diagram. That is, some classes can be shown in the compact view and others in the expanded view.

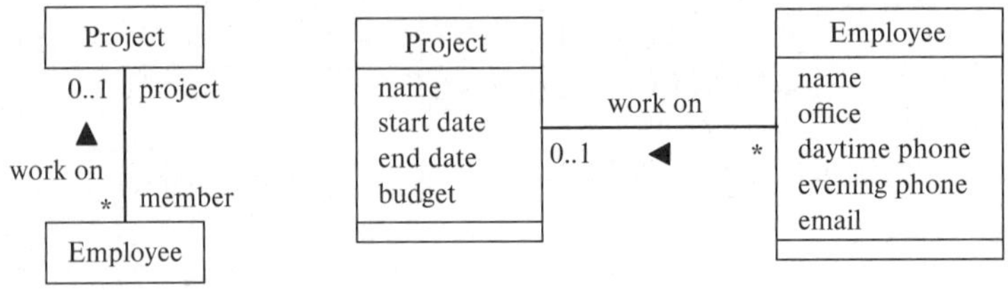

(a) Compact view (b) Expanded view

FIGURE 5.2 Representing classes in compact and expanded views

The attributes and operations of a class are also called *features of the class.* The word *feature* nicely reflects the intention to capture and highlight the most essential and necessary properties and behaviors of the class. A class is a type, be it a built-in type or a user-defined type. It is an intentional definition because a class can be defined by a predicate. For example, when the child forms his concepts of dog, cat, animal, human being, and house, he has a predicate in his mind for each of these. When he draws his garden house, he also has a predicate. In the object-oriented paradigm, the predicate that defines a class is the set of attributes and operations of the class. To facilitate discussion, the following conventions are used in this chapter:

- Class names use an initial capital and take the singular form: Customer, Bank, and Account could be used to refer to classes.
- A variable x of type X is denoted x:X. This can be applied to both scalar type and class type. For example, a variable c of the Customer class is denoted c:Customer. When no confusion can arise and the type of x is clear from the context, the colon and the type are dropped.
- An instance c of class C is denoted c:C. For example, a1:Account, a2:Account, a3:Account denote three Account objects a1, a2, and a3. When no confusion can arise and the class is clear from the context, these objects are referred to as a1, a2, and a3. It is useful to note the following: (1) :Account denotes an anonymous object of Account. It is useful in some contexts, for example, objects referenced in a loop. (2) x: denotes an orphan object, that is, an object of an unspecified class. It is useful in a polymorphic context or when the class type is not of interest.
- The set of all instances of a class C at a given point in time is denoted U(C),
  $U(C)=\{ c \mid c{:}C \}$, as a shorthand notation
  $U(C)=\{ c1, c2, \ldots, cn \}$, when the objects of C can be enumerated.
  Thus, an instance c of class C can also be denoted as $c \in U(C)$. Here, U is called the universe of discourse and U(C) the projection of U on C.
- If c is an instance of class C, then c.a and c.f(. . .) are used to refer to or access an attribute a and a function f(. . .) of c, respectively.

5.3.3 Object and Attribute

In practice, it is sometimes difficult to decide whether something should be an attribute or an object (or class). For example, color could be an attribute of car, but color can also be an object in an application that sells colors. Another example is building, which could be an object or an attribute (e.g., location of a department). The following guidelines are used to distinguish objects from attributes:

GUIDELINE 5.1 An object has an independent existence in the application or application domain; an attribute does not.

Here, *independent existence* means that the application has an interest in maintaining information or state about the object. For example, "number of seats" does not have independent existence because it could be number of seats in a car, a classroom, or an airplane, which are objects. "Independent existence" is not limited to physical existence. It includes conceptual or mental existence. For example, a book physically exists, but a discipline is a mental notion.

GUIDELINE 5.2 Attributes are scalar types (such as double, string, boolean, and char) and describe and characterize objects.

GUIDELINE 5.3 Attributes are scalar types but objects are not.

GUIDELINE 5.4 Because attributes are scalar types, they can be entered from an input device (like a keyboard), but objects cannot; objects are created by calling a constructor.

One cannot enter a student object from the keyboard. One can enter only the student name, student number, address, phone number, and other information. But these are attributes, not objects. Student objects are created by invoking a constructor of the Student class.

5.3.4 Association

Besides classes and attributes, a domain model also documents relationships between the object classes. Three relationships are commonly used in domain modeling and are defined in this and the following sections.

Definition 5.6 An *association* is a relation between one or more classes. It states that objects of one class may relate to objects of the other class.

An association defines a general relationship between the objects of one or more classes. That is, an association can be any relation that is of interest in the application. For example, in a banking system, customers own accounts. Thus, there is an association between the Customer class and the Account class. Money can be transferred between accounts. Hence, there is an association between the Account class and itself. In a university, faculty teach courses and students enroll in courses. Therefore, there are associations between Faculty and Course, and Student and Course. An

Own

Customer	Account
c1	a1
c1	a2
c2	a2
c2	a3
c3	a4

(a) Instances of a binary association

Work-Supervised-by

Student	Project	Professor
Chen	OOM	Baker
Chen	SOA	Liu
Gupta	SOA	Liu
Rosa	Security	Brown
Smith	Security	Shah

(b) Instances of a ternary association

FIGURE 5.3 Instances of an association

association between two classes is represented by a solid line connecting the two classes. In Figure 5.2, an association between Employee and Project is shown. That is, employees work on projects. The small solid triangle indicates the association direction, that is, employees work on projects but not the other way around.

A tabular representation helps understand association relationships. Consider the Customer owns Account association, denoted Own(Customer, Account). The type of Own is the pair (Customer, Account). More strictly, Own:(Customer, Account), but the colon is dropped for simplicity. Using the conventions presented at the end of Section 5.3.2, assume that U(Customer)={ c1, . . . , c4 } and U(Account)= { a1, . . . , a5 }. Assume c1 has a1 and a2, c2 has a2 and a3, c3 has a4, c4 does not have an account, and a5 is not owned by any customer. As displayed in Figure 5.3(*a*), the Own(Customer, Account) association consists of five pairs: (c1, a1), (c1, a2), (c2, a2), (c2, a3), and (c3, a4). The table together with U(Customer) and U(Account) show that a customer can own zero or more accounts and an account can be owned by zero or more customers. In fact, any subset of the set of the 20 pairs, formed by pairing each of the four customers with each of the five accounts, is allowed. That is, there are 2^{20} such subsets and each of them is a valid instance of the Own association.

The most commonly encountered associations are binary associations. Binary associations are relations between one or two classes. An association between objects of three classes, or a ternary association, can also exist. For example, a relationship among Professor, Student, and Project in which professors supervise students working on projects is a ternary association. Figure 5.3(*b*) illustrates some possible instances for this ternary association. Ternary associations are complex. They should be avoided whenever possible. From now on, we will limit our discussion to only binary association.

As illustrated in the above examples, a binary association can be denoted using the form V(X, X) or V(X, Y), where V is the name of the association and X, Y are classes. This notation will be used in this book when discussing associations. When there is no risk of confusion, the pair of parentheses and the arguments are dropped, and Own(Customer, Account) is referred to as the Own association.

5.3.5 Multiplicity and Role

The Own(Customer, Account) association states that customers can own accounts. However, it does not specify how many accounts a customer can have and how many customers can own the same account. Usually, a customer can have more than one account in a bank. Some banks allow joint account ownership, but some other banks require that each account be owned by one and only one customer. As another example, a student may work on one or more projects. But a project may have zero or more students working on it. A project may have no student because the project is either new or terminated. A student working on a project may be supervised by one or more professors. These examples demonstrate the need to identify and specify the so-called multiplicity, defined as follows.

Definition 5.7 The *multiplicity* of a class with respect to an association is an assertion on the number of instances of the class that may relate to each instance of the other class.

Consider the Own(Customer, Account) association. Suppose the bank allows joint account ownership but requires that each account be owned by at least one customer. The multiplicity of Customer with respect to the Own(Customer, Account) association is one or more because each Account object can be owned by one or more customers. In this case, Figure 5.3(*a*) is no longer valid because Account a5 does not have a customer. Adding the pair (c4, a5) to the table in Figure 5.3(*a*) will satisfy this constraint. If the bank imposes a restriction that each account can be owned by only one customer, then the Customer multiplicity is one. In this case, Figure 5.3(*a*) is no longer valid. Deleting the pair (c1, a2) from the table will satisfy this constraint.

Figure 5.4 shows the UML notations for the various multiplicity values. In a class diagram, the multiplicity is shown beside the intersection of the association and the class border. For example, Figure 5.2 shows that each employee works on zero or one project and each project has zero or more employees.

Objects play a certain role in associations. In the Own(Customer, Account) example, a customer plays the role as the account owner. Roles are displayed in a class diagram similar to multiplicity. In illustration, Figure 5.2 shows that the roles of Project and Employee in the work-on association are member and project, respectively.

5.3.6 Aggregation

An association is a general relation between one or more classes. Practical applications frequently encounter the so-called part-of relationships. For example, an engine is a part of a car; a book consists of chapters, each of which consists of sections; and so

Symbol	Meaning	Symbol	Meaning
0..1	zero or one	m..n	m to n
0..m	zero to m	m..*	m or more
,0..	zero or more	m	exactly m
1	exactly one (default)	1..*	one or more
i,j,k	explicitly enumerated		

FIGURE 5.4 Symbols for expressing various multiplicity assertions

on. The part-of relationship is a special type of association relationship and deserves a modeling concept and construct of its own. Therefore, the modeling community has long introduced the so-called aggregation relationship to accommodate this need.

Definition 5.8 An *aggregation* is a binary relation between two classes. It states that objects of one class are parts of objects of the other class.

Because aggregation is a special case of association, it is represented as Part-of(P, C) or Part-of(P1, P2, . . . , Pn, C) to denote that class C is an aggregate of classes P, P1, P2, . . . , Pn. Part-of(P1, P2, . . . , Pn, C) is in fact a shorthand for Part-of(P1, C), Part-of(P2, C), . . . , Part-of(Pn, C). Similarly, the multiplicity and role defined for association also apply to aggregation. For instance, a car has two or four doors. That is, the multiplicity of Door with respect to Part-of(Door, Car) is two or four. A line with a diamond is the UML notation for aggregation; the diamond is with the aggregate class. Figure 5.5(*a*) illustrates that a Car is an aggregate of one Engine, one Transmission, and one Brake.

5.3.7 Inheritance

Definition 5.9 *Inheritance* is a binary relation between two concepts or classes such that one concept or class is a generalization (or specialization) of the other.

Many examples of inheritance exist in various application domains. In a banking system, there are Checking Account and Savings Account, which are specializations

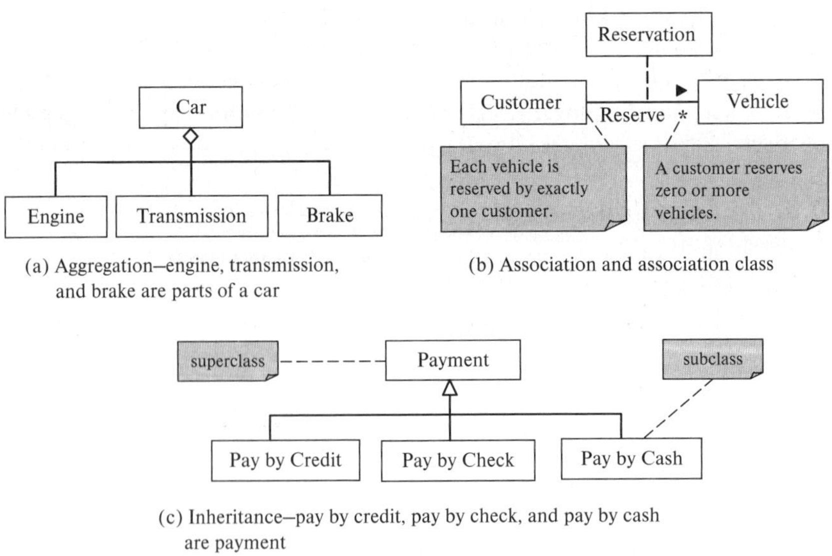

(a) Aggregation—engine, transmission, and brake are parts of a car

(b) Association and association class

(c) Inheritance—pay by credit, pay by check, and pay by cash are payment

FIGURE 5.5 Representing relationship and association class

of Account. A brokerage firm also distinguishes Margin Account and Option Account. These different types of account are similar but have different behaviors. For example, a checking account does not pay interest, but a savings account does. That is, Checking Account and Savings Account are specializations of Bank Account. Bank Account is a generalization of Checking Account and Savings Account. Similarly, Margin Account and Option Account are specializations of Brokerage Account, and Brokerage Account is a generalization of Margin Account and Option Account.

In an inheritance relationship, the class that is a generalization of the other class is called the superclass, the class that is a specialization of the other class is called the subclass, as shown in Figure 5.5(*c*). The inheritance relation is also called an IS-A relation. This is because every instance of a subclass is an instance of the superclass. For example, every checking account or savings account is a bank account. This observation implies that the properties and behaviors defined for the superclass are inherited by the subclass. This explains the use of the term "inheritance" to refer to the generalization or specialization relationships between classes.

In the above, the need to define the subclasses Checking Account and Savings Account of the superclass Bank Account is due to differences in the behaviors of objects of the subclasses. Another reason to define subclasses is due to differences in relationships. Consider, for example, Undergraduate Student and Graduate Student as subclasses of Student. An undergraduate student is required to use an undergraduate catalog to select classes, while a graduate student is required to use a graduate catalog. A full-time graduate student is required to enroll in three to five graduate courses. On the other hand, an undergraduate student may have different restrictions. Defining two subclasses will greatly facilitate the manipulation of these association relationships. Inheritance is also a special case of association. Therefore, ISA(S, C) or ISA(S1, S2, . . . , Sn, C) is used to denote that classes S, S1, S2, . . . , Sn are subclasses of class C. ISA(S1, S2, . . . , Sn, C) is in fact a shorthand for ISA(S1, C), ISA(S2, C), . . . , ISA(Sn, C).

5.3.8 Inheritance and Polymorphism

In the object-oriented paradigm, inheritance and polymorphism are like brothers or even twins. They look so alike that some authors consider them the same. But they really are not the same. To understand the difference, the following definition is introduced:

Definition 5.10 *Polymorphism* means that one thing can assume different forms.

By looking at Definitions 5.9 and 5.10, one should see the difference. Inheritance defines a relationship between two concepts or classes such that one class is more general (or more specific) than the other. Due to this generalization (or specialization) relationship, a variable of the superclass type can refer to an object of one of the subclasses. Therefore, the superclass variable can exhibit different behavior, achieving polymorphism.

Polymorphism, on the other hand, is concerned with the ability of one thing to assume different forms. Because "one thing" is unconstrained, it could be anything, not just classes and objects. The ability to assume different forms is not limited to the context of inheritance; it can be in any other contexts. For example, two or more member functions can share the same name but have different signatures. This is referred to as function polymorphism.

5.3.9 Association Class

Sometimes it is necessary to describe properties about association relationships. Consider, for example, the association that students enroll in courses. A student can enroll in one or more courses and receive a grade for each enrolled course. Clearly, the course grade is an attribute because it is a scalar type. The question is which object class should have grade as an attribute? If grade is an attribute of the Student class, then the Student class ought to have several grade attributes because a student can enroll in more than one course. If this is the case, then how do you differentiate the grades for the different courses? The following are some quick, but not necessarily good, solutions.

One possible solution is to associate each grade with a course. This can be accomplished in two different ways. The first is to use a hash table in the Student class to store the grades for the courses. This approach is undesirable because the hash table and the Enroll(Student, Course) association should have a one-to-one correspondence. However, this correspondence is implicitly assumed. The program that processes them needs to maintain this correspondence. This means that for each course grade stored in the hash table, the program must ensure that the student has in fact enrolled in the course. The program must ensure that for every course in which a student has enrolled, there is an entry in the hash table that records the grade for the course.

In addition to the above correspondence problem, it is common to record the semester in which a student received a grade for a given course. This is needed because if a student took a course many years ago, then the university usually will require the student to retake the course before the course credit can be used to satisfy the degree requirements. In this case, using a hash table to store the grade and semester for each course is not a desirable solution.

The other solution is to define a Course-Grade class to store the grade for each course and introduce a one-to-many association, say Receive(Student, Course-Grade), from the Student class to the Course-Grade class. This approach can accommodate the need to record the semester along with the grade for each course. However, it still cannot resolve the implicit assumption problem concerning the one-to-one correspondence between the instances of this Receive association and the Enroll association. That is, additional effort is required to ensure that every instance of the Receive association has a corresponding Enroll instance and every Enroll instance has a corresponding Receive instance. Similarly, if one defines grade as an attribute of Course, then one will have the same problems as discussed above. Another quick solution suggests the addition of a Grade class and two associations: One is a one-to-many association from Student to Grade, say Has(Student, Grade), and the other is a one-to-one association from Grade to Course, say Is-for(Grade, Course). But this solution still does not solve the implicit correspondence assumption problem as previously described.

A careful analysis of the problems discussed should reveal that the grade attribute is in fact a piece of information about the Enroll(Student, Course) association. Similarly, the semester in which the student had taken the course to receive the grade is also a piece of information about the Enroll(Student, Course) association. The above quick solutions attempt to store these two pieces of information not with the association itself but with other classes, creating the correspondence problem. A straightforward, and hence a better, solution would be to store the information about

Student	Course	Semester	Grade
Bachman	AI	Spr 22	A
Bachman	DB	Spr 22	A
Bachman	SE	Spr 22	A
Chang	AI	Spr 22	B
Chang	DB	Spr 22	A
Chang	SE	Spr 22	A
Chang	Compiler	Fal 23	B
Chang	Algorithms	Fal 23	A
Chang	Programming	Fal 23	B

FIGURE 5.6 Tabular representation of objects of an association class

the association with the association itself. This eliminates the correspondence problem. The question remains how to accomplish this. The following definition points toward an answer.

Definition 5.11 An *association class* is a special class that defines properties and behaviors for the instances of an association.

Consider again the Enroll(Student, Course) association. In this example, one can define an association class called Enrollment for the Enroll association between Student and Course. Enrollment will have, among others, grade and semester attributes, and setGrade(. . .), getGrade(), setSemester(. . .), and getSemester() operations. If a student takes three courses, then one needs only to create three instances of the Enrollment class, one instance for each course the student takes. Figure 5.6 shows how instances of an association class could be displayed using a tabular format, where the first two columns represent the association instances and the last two columns represent the attributes of the association instances. Association classes are indicated by a dashed line that connects the association class to the association line. In Figure 5.5(*b*), there is a reserve association between Customer and Vehicle. The Reservation class stores information about which customer reserves which vehicle. It is an association class, as indicated by the dashed line from Reservation to the reserve association line.

5.4 STEPS FOR DOMAIN MODELING

The steps for domain modeling are outlined as follows and detailed in the following sections. These steps may be iterated a couple of times to produce a good domain model.

Step 1. Collecting application domain information.

The first step to domain modeling is collecting application domain information. Techniques for collecting application domain information have been described in Chapter 4 and will be reviewed again in Section 5.4.1. The output of this step includes all relevant information/documentation about the application.

Step 2. Brainstorming.

After collecting information about the application domain, the development team members meet together to identify domain-specific or domain-relevant concepts, as described in Section 5.4.2. The output is a set of such concepts.

Step 3. Classifying brainstorming results.

The brainstorming results are then classified as classes, attributes, inheritance relationships, aggregation relationships, association relationships, and association classes. These also form the output of this step. The classification techniques are described in Section 5.4.3.

Step 4. Visualizing the domain model.

The classification result is visualized by a UML class diagram to provide an integrated view of the classes, their attributes, and the relationships between the classes. Rules for converting the classification result into a class diagram are presented in Section 5.4.4.

Step 5. Reviewing the domain model.

The domain model is reviewed to identify errors and abnormalities. Depending on the review results, some of the above steps are revisited and the domain model is revised. A domain model review checklist is presented in Section 5.4.5.

5.4.1 Collecting Application Domain Information

Information-collection is described in detail in Chapter 4 and will not be repeated here. These techniques include:

1. Customer presentation.
2. Interview with customer representatives, users, and domain experts.
3. Study of relevant literature.
4. Study of similar projects.
5. Study of business documentation and forms. (e.g., forms for various requests, invoices, purchase orders, etc.).
6. Study of government policies and regulations.
7. Study of industry standards.
8. Development and use of questionnaires.

The following documents also contain useful domain information:

- Business process descriptions.
- Operating procedures, manuals, handbooks, policies, regulations, and rules.
- Software requirements specification, which should have been produced in the acquiring requirements phase.

At the end of this step, the development team should produce a description of the application similar to the one shown in Figure 5.18. This description will greatly facilitate the subsequent steps.

5.4.2 Brainstorming

After collecting domain information, the team members get together and identify important domain concepts by highlighting, marking, or listing domain-specific/domain-relevant phrases listed below.

1. Nouns or noun phrases.
2. "X of Y," or "Y's X" expressions, where X and Y are nouns or noun phrases (e.g., make of car, engine of car).
3. Transitive verbs (e.g., "teach" in "faculty teach courses.").
4. Adjectives and enumerations.
5. Numbers and quantities (e.g., "4" and many).
6. Possession expressions (has/have, possess, etc.).
7. Constituents, part of, consist of expressions.
8. Containment or containing expressions.
9. "X is a Y" expressions, or generalized/specialized concepts.

While applying the rules, the team members should bear in mind the following guidelines:

GUIDELINE 5.5 Focus on **domain-specific** or **domain-relevant** phrases, excluding phrases that can be found in other domains.

A phrase is domain specific/relevant if it is not generic. That is, it does not belong to other applications or domains. For example, "online" and "application" are generic terms, but bank customer and bank account are application specific.

The team members should identify only *domain-specific* or *domain-relevant* phrases; otherwise, many irrelevant words and phrases will creep into the domain model, making it unnecessarily complex and less useful. This guideline in effect means that each of the rules listed above could have been preceded with "domain-specific or domain-relevant." For example, domain-specific transitive verbs and domain-specific X is a Y expressions. For simplicity, the rules are formulated without such modifiers.

GUIDELINE 5.6 Ignore design and implementation concepts.

Design and implementation concepts do not belong to any application domain; they should not appear in a domain model. Examples are graphical use interface (GUI), database-related concepts, transaction log, linked list, among others. One way to determine whether a concept is a domain concept is to ask, "if no computerized system is built for the application, will the concept exist in the application domain?" If the answer is yes, then it is a domain concept; otherwise, it is not.

To avoid only picking nouns and noun phrases, the team may divide the rules among team members and have each identify phrases using the rules assigned. If needed, shift the rules among the team members and do it again to ensure that no phrase is overlooked.

The following example uses superscript to help explain which of the above phrases is being identified. For instance, an underlined phrase with a superscript 1 means brainstorming rule 1 is applied or a noun phrase is identified. The superscripts will be used in the next section to show how the identified phrases are classified into modeling concepts. In practice, the use of the superscript is not necessary because one can easily tell the phrases from the underlined words.

EXAMPLE 5.1 Identify important application concepts from the following piece of description for a Study Abroad Management System (SAMS):

> "An undergraduate student or a graduate student can apply to no more than two exchange programs per semester. An application consists of an application form, two faculty recommendation letters, and a course equivalency form to be approved by an academic advisor.
>
> . . .
>
> An exchange program has a program name, program type, academic department, academic subject, country, region, term of study, and language."

Solution: Figure 5.7(*a*) shows the underlined phrases with superscripts to indicate which phrases are being identified. Figure 5.7(*b*) is the listing of the identified phrases, which are the input to the classification step.

An undergraduate student[1] or a graduate student[1] can apply to[3] no more than two[5] exchange programs[1] per semester[1]. An application[1] consists of[7] an application form[1], two[5] faculty[1] recommendation letters[1], and a course equivalency form[1] to be approved by[3] an academic advisor[1].

. . .

An exchange program has[6] a program name[1], program type[1], academic department[1], academic subject[1], country[1], region[1], term of study[1], and language[1].

(a) Important domain concepts underlined

undergraduate student[1]
graduate student[1]
apply to[3]
no more than two[5]
exchange programs[1]
semester[1]
application[1]
consists of[7]
application form[1]
two[5]
faculty[1]
faculty recommendation letters[1]
course equivalency form[1]
approved by[3]
academic advisor[1]
has[6]
program name[1]
program type[1]
academic department[1]
academic subject[1]
country[1]
region[1]
term of study[1]
language[1]

(b) Important domain concepts listed

FIGURE 5.7 Brainstorming result of a piece of SAMS description

5.4.3 Classifying Brainstorming Results

In the third step of domain modeling, the listed phrases are classified as classes, association classes, attributes, attribute values, and relationships. This is done by applying the classification rules shown in Figure 5.8. The second column of Figure 5.8 shows the phrases and the third column shows the corresponding object-oriented modeling concepts. When an attribute is identified, one should identify or infer the class having that attribute. Similarly, when an attribute value is identified, one should identify or infer the attribute having that attribute value. The results of this step are the classes, their attributes, and relationships.

#	Phrases Identified	Classified As
1	Noun/noun phrase, if (a) it has independent existence, or it is not a scalar type. (b) it plays a role of an object in an association. (c) it describes properties of a 1-to-m or m-to-n association. (d) it is a generalization/specialization of another concept. (e) it does not exist independently, or it is a scalar type.	 a class a role in an association an association class a superclass/subclass an attribute of a class
2	"X of Y" or "Y's X" expression (X and Y are nouns/noun phrases), if (a) X has independent existence, or X is not a scalar type. (b) X does not exist independently, or it is a scalar type. (c) X plays a role (of an object) in an association.	 Y is an aggregation of X X is an attribute of Y X is a role in an association
3	Transitive verb (must be domain-specific)	an association relationship
4	Adjective, enumeration	an attribute value
5	Number or quantity, if (a) it describes a property of an object (e.g., 4 bedrooms of a house). (b) it states the number of objects relating to another object.	 an attribute value multiplicity of a relationship
6	Possession expression (such as Y has/possesses X), if (a) X has independent existence, or X is not a scalar type. (b) X does not exist independently, or X is a scalar type.	 Y is an aggregation of X X is an attribute of Y
7	Consist of, part of, or composed of expression, if (a) part has independent existence, or it is not a scalar type. (b) part does not exist independently, or it is a scalar type.	 an aggregation relationship part is an attribute of whole
8	Containment, containing expression, if (a) contained object can be removed without changing the integrity of the containing object (e.g., removing apples from a basket). (b) otherwise (e.g., a car will not be a car without an engine).	 an association relationship an aggregation relationship
9	X is Y, or generalization/specialization expression	an inheritance relationship

FIGURE 5.8 Classification rules for classifying brainstorming results

(A):	attribute (of a class)
(AC):	association class (of an association)
(AG):	aggregation
(AS):	association
(C):	class, may be a subclass of another class
(I):	inheritance relationship
(m,n):	multiplicity of each class in a binary association
(r1,r2):	role name of each class in a binary association
(V):	attribute value (of an attribute of a class)

FIGURE 5.9 Classification codes

EXAMPLE 5.2 Classify the brainstorming result in Example 5.1.

Solution: Figure 5.10 depicts the classification result. The classification codes in Figure 5.9 are used to label the classification result. The columns of Figure 5.10 are explained as follows:

- Column 1 lists the phrases identified in the brainstorming step along with the superscripts or phrase identification numbers.

Brainstorming List	Classification Result	Rule
undergraduate student[1]	(C) Undergraduate Student	1(a)
graduate student[1]	(C) Graduate Student	1(a)
apply to[3]	(AS) apply to (Student, Exchange Program)	3
no more than two[5]	(1, 0..2)	5(b)
exchange programs[1]	(C) Exchange Program	1(a)
has[6]		6(b)
program name[1]	(A) program name	1(e)
program type[1]	(A) program type	1(e)
academic department[1]	(A) academic department	1(e)
academic subject[1]	(A) academic subject	1(e)
country[1]	(A) country	1(e)
region[1]	(A) region	1(e)
term of study[1]	(A) term of study	1(e)
language[1]	(A) language	1(e)
semester[1]	(A) Semester // same as term of study	1(e)
application[1]	(AC) Application (of apply to)	1(c)
consists of[7]	(AG) Part-of (Application Form, Application)	7(a)
	(AG) Part-of (Faculty Recommendation Letter, Application)	7(a)
two[5]	(2, 1)	5(b)
	(AG) Part-of (Course Equivalency Form, Application)	7(a)
application form[1]	(C) Application Form	1(a)
faculty[1]	(C) Faculty	1(a)
faculty recommendation letter[1]	(C) Faculty# Recommendation Letter	1(a)
course equivalency form[1]	(C) Course Equivalency Form	1(a)
approved by[3]	(AS) approved by (Course Equivalency Form, Academic Advisor)	3
academic advisor[1]	(C) Academic Advisor	1(a)
	(C) Student // added	
	(I) ISA (Undergraduate Student, Student) // added	
	(I) ISA (Graduate Student, Student) // added	

FIGURE 5.10 Classifying brainstorming result for SAMS

- Column 2 shows the corresponding classes, their attributes, and relationships between the classes. These are indicated by using the classification codes in Figure 5.9.
- Column 3 shows which classification rule is applied.
- Following industry convention, the first letter of each word of a class name is capitalized.
- The classes and their attributes are shown together. For example, the attributes of the Exchange Program class are listed under the Exchange Program class.
- In column 2, a binary relationship is displayed using the following notation

  ```
  relation-name '('class-name1, class-name2')'
  ['('[m],[n]')'] ['('[role-name1], [role-name2]')']
  ```

  where m, n are multiplicity expressions and role-name1 and role-name2 are the role names of the two participating classes. The order of the multiplicity and role specifications is immaterial. Figure 5.4 gives the various ways to express a given multiplicity.
- The multiplicity and role are listed after the relationship using the above notation. For example, the aggregation or Part-of (Faculty Recommendation Letter, Application) has a multiplicity of (2,1), which is shown on the following line. This means that an application requires two faculty recommendation letters, which is derived from the word "two" on column 1. As another example, the apply-to (Student, Exchange Program) association has a multiplicity of "(1, 0..2)" on the line following the association. This is because every student can apply to "no more than two" exchange programs per semester.
- A relationship without a multiplicity specification assumes the default value of (1, 1). For example, the multiplicity for the other two aggregation relationships is not shown. This means they both have the default value of (1, 1).
- Association classes are shown along with their association relationships, which are enclosed in a pair of parentheses. For example, Application is shown with its related association, such as apply-to, in a pair of parentheses.

One may wonder why academic department and country are attributes, not classes. This is because they are strings or scalar types that describe properties of an exchange program in the SAMS application.

Finding Missing Information

In this step, the development team examines the classification result and identifies missing information using reasoning, common sense, domain knowledge acquired elsewhere, and prior experience. The missing information includes the following:

1. Missing classes, which may be inferred from existing classes and relationships. For example, from Undergraduate Student and Graduate Student, it is useful to infer Student as a parent class of these two classes.
2. Missing attributes and types, which may be identified from a class or association class that does not have any attribute. In Example 5.2, Undergraduate Student and Graduate Student do not have attributes. The missing attributes and types can be identified from business forms, e.g., request forms, invoices, order forms, and reservation forms. For example, attributes of Undergraduate Student and Graduate Student can be obtained from student registration forms.
3. Missing relationships, which may be derived from isolated classes, i.e., classes that do not relate to any other class. In Example 5.2, Faculty is not related to any other class. The description implies that faculty provides recommendation letters; therefore, an association relationship can be identified.
4. Missing multiplicity. Some multiplicity information is important because it specifies domain laws or application-specific constraints. For example, each application must have two recommendation letters. To identify these, each of the association and aggregation relationships is examined carefully to ensure that no important multiplicity is missing.

5.4.4 Visualizing the Domain Model

In this step, the classification result is visualized by using a class diagram, called domain model class diagram (DMCD). Once the classes, attributes, and relationships are identified and documented as in Figure 5.10, it is easy to convert the classification result into a class diagram. Figure 5.11 shows the conversion rules and examples from previous sections.

EXAMPLE 5.3 Convert the classification result obtained in Example 5.2 into a class diagram.

Solution: Figure 5.12 shows the class diagram obtained.

Domain Model and Class Diagram

It is worth to understand the relationship between the classification result and the DMCD that visualizes it. First, both describe the domain model but in different forms of representation. Second, the classification result uses a textual representation, which is hard to see how the classes relate to each other. On the other hand, relationships between classes can be seen easily on a class diagram. Third, UML diagrams are widely known and used. This facilitates understanding and communication across teams, organizations, and borders. Finally, a class diagram is a directed graph, which makes it easy to apply existing algorithms to analyze a domain model. Therefore, it is advantageous to visualize the classification result in a UML class diagram.

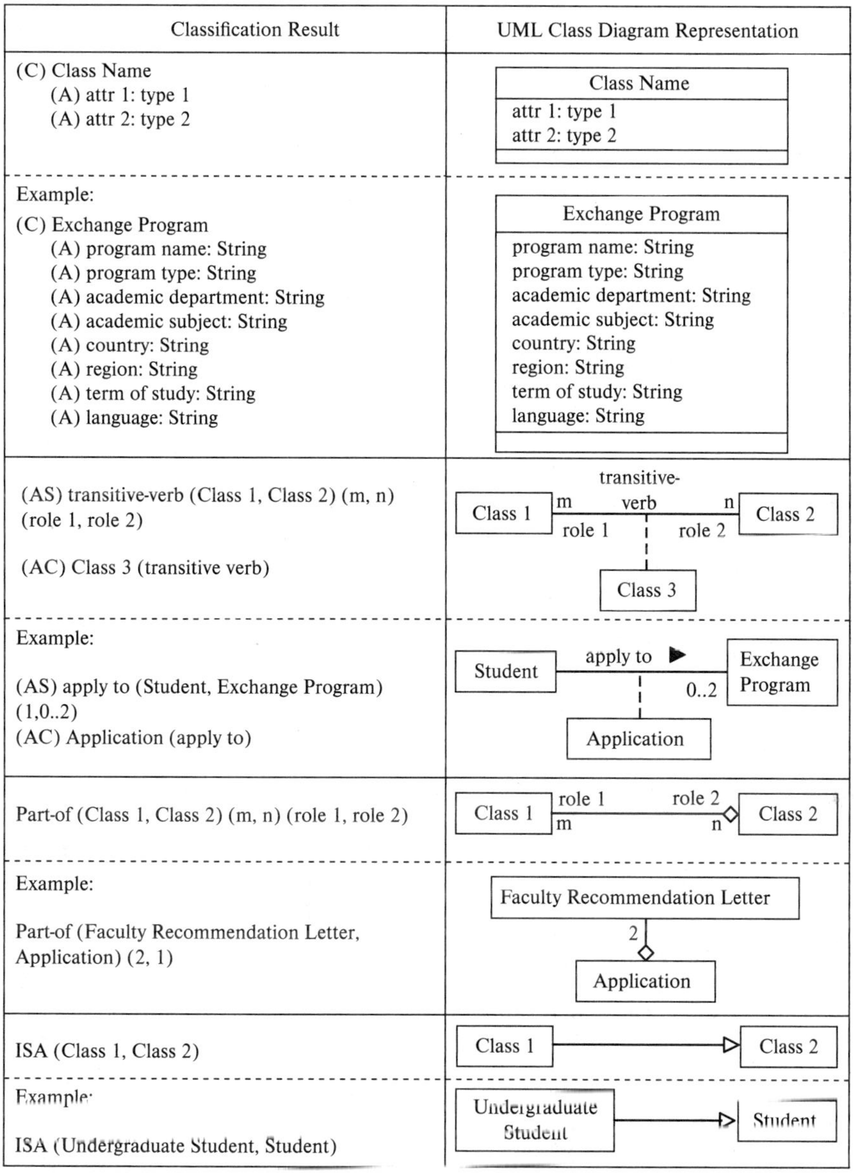

FIGURE 5.11 Conversion rules: from classified result to class diagram

A DMCD does not show any operations. Although a class diagram can show the operations of a class, a domain model should not show these. This is because assigning responsibilities or member functions to the classes is a design decision, which should be dealt with during design. Assigning operations to classes in domain modeling, without taking into consideration how the software objects should interact, is a premature decision. Therefore, it is important to refrain from assigning operations to the classes in this step.

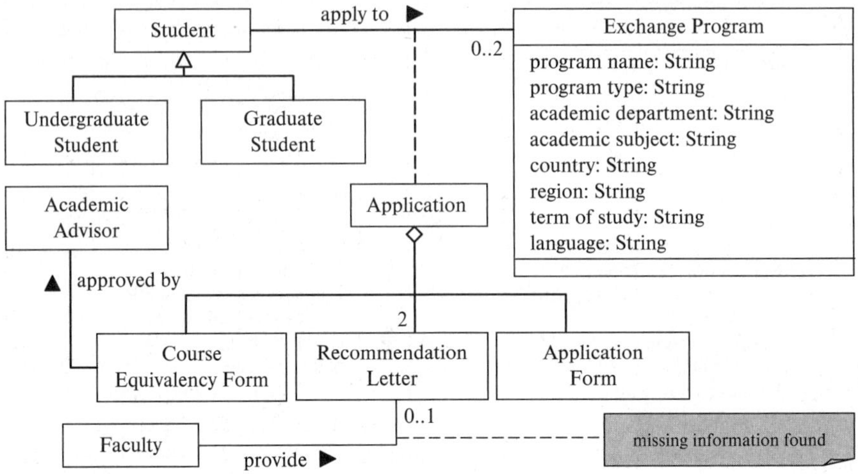

FIGURE 5.12 Converting classification result into a class diagram

Showing Aggregation Relationship

A common mistake involving aggregation is showing component classes as attribute types in a class diagram, although it is commonly seen in OO programs. For example, Engine, Transmission, and Brake are classes, but they are shown as attribute types of the Car class in Figure 5.13(*a*). As stated in Guideline 5.1, while an object has independent existence in the application or application domain, an attribute does not. Thus, treating an object as an attribute value of another object introduces a paradox. That is, something has an independent existence and at the same time it does not–and that is impossible. Therefore, it is incorrect to do so.

Figure 5.5(*a*) shows the modeling of Car as consisting of an Engine, a Transmission, and a Brake. This is correct according to common sense. In Figure 5.13(*a*), it states that an Engine object, a Transmission object, and a Brake object are attributes or properties of a Car object. This is not correct because instances of Engine, Transmission, and Brake are objects, not attributes. The attribute compartment of the class notation should show only attributes, not objects. If the business is a car rental or car dealership that is interested in maintaining information about various cars, such as the type of engine (gasoline or diesel engine), transmission (manual or automatic), and brake (disk or drum brake), then the types for these attributes should have been string, not classes. If the application is a car manufacturer or car repair shop that is interested in engine, transmission, and brake objects, then a diagram similar to Figure 5.5(*a*) should be used.

Figure 5.13(*b*) states that Engine, Transmission, and Brake are classes and attributes as well. This introduces a paradox, as pointed out earlier. Two factors may contribute to the misuses shown in Figure 5.13. First, a component of an object like an engine of a car is often implemented by a field of the Car class in object-oriented programming. Second, some IDE tools confuse or equate modeling and code generation and render aggregation relationships as in Figure 5.13(*b*). Even worse, sometimes, the incorrect way to show aggregation relationships is the only way you can do with the IDE tool.

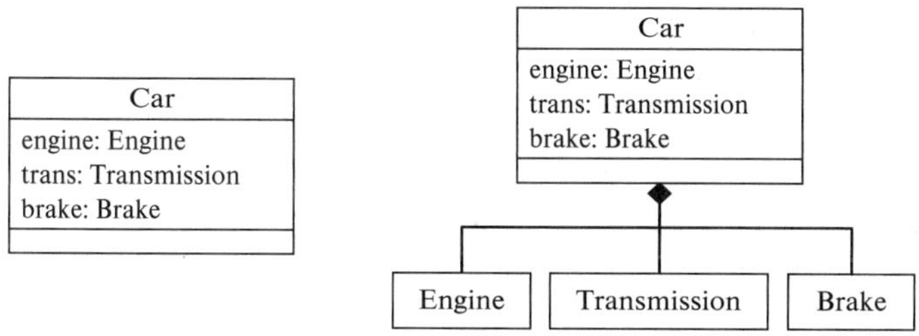

(a) Incorrect: Engine, Transmission, and Brake objects are attributes of Car.

(b) Incorrect: Engine, Transmission, and Brake are parts and properties of Car

FIGURE 5.13 Misuses of aggregation

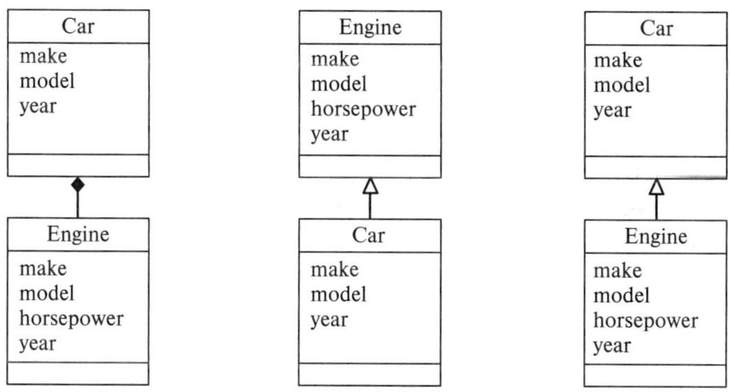

(a) Engine is an exclusive part of Car–CORRECT!

(b) Car IS-A Engine –WRONG!

(c) Engine IS-A Car –WRONG!

FIGURE 5.14 Wrongly expressed relationships

Showing Inheritance Relationship

The inheritance relationship is sometimes misused or confused with aggregation. Figure 5.14(*a*) displays a correct conceptualization. That is, a car consists of an engine exclusively. The diagram also shows that Car and Engine have similar attributes, such as make, model, and year. The fact that the horsepower of a car depends on the horsepower of its engine causes some modelers to use inheritance, as shown in Figure 5.14(*b*). This is certainly incorrect because a car is not an engine; there is no generalization or specialization relationship between the two concepts. The diagram in Figure 5.14(*c*) is also incorrect because Engine is not a Car.

The above discussion leads to the following guideline:

GUIDELINE 5.7 Use inheritance only if every instance of the subclass is also an instance of the superclass. This is called the ISA guideline.

In Figures 5.14(b) and 5.14(c), inheritance is used between Engine and Car. But instances of Engine are not instances of Car, and vice versa. Therefore, inheritance should not have been used.

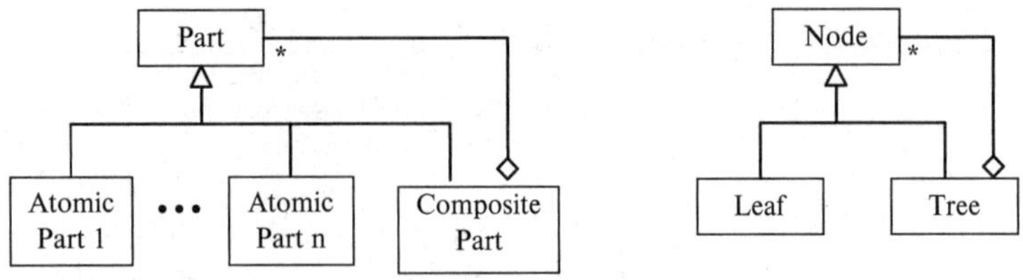

(a) A composite part is a part that consists of other parts

(b) A tree is a node that contains other nodes

FIGURE 5.15 Part and composite part

Sometimes, the ISA guideline should be understood in a generalized context. Consider, for example, a manufacturing company, where parts can be divided into atomic parts and composite parts. Atomic parts do not contain other parts, but a composite part may consist of atomic as well as other composite parts. This situation can be modeled by using the *composite pattern* as shown in Figure 5.15(a). The example in Figure 5.15(b) may be easier to understand, where a Tree is a Node and a composite of Node. Composite pattern will be discussed in detail in Chapter 16. In these generalized contexts, the ISA guideline is satisfied.

GUIDELINE 5.8 Use inheritance only if all relationships of the superclass also hold for the subclasses. This is called the conformance guideline.

Because every instance of a subclass must be an instance of the superclass, the relationships of the superclass must also be relationships of the subclass. For example, Student belongs to Department, that is, Belong-To(Student,Department). Undergraduate Student and Graduate Student are Student–that is, ISA(Undergraduate Student, Student) and ISA(Graduate Student, Student), and, therefore, Belong-To (Undergraduate Student, Department) and Belong-To(Graduate Student, Department).

Now consider Figure 5.16(a), which states that contractors are employees. According to Guideline 5.8, because employees receive benefits, so do contractors. For many companies, this is not the case; therefore, Contractor should not be a subclass of Employee. However, for many other companies, a Contractor is also an Employee. To accommodate both of these cases, Figure 5.16(b) introduces an additional subclass of Employee called Full Time to receive Benefits.

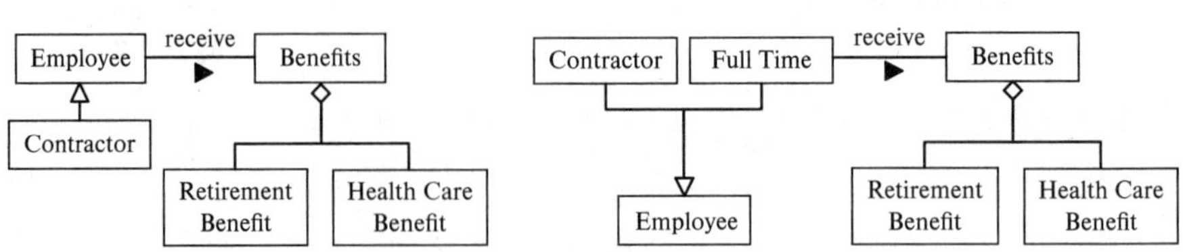

(a) Incorrect if Contractor does not receive Benefits

(b) Only Full Time receives Benefits

FIGURE 5.16 Subclass inherits relationships of superclass

5.4.5 Domain Model Review Checklist

The development team should review the domain model to detect and correct errors and abnormalities. The following is a domain model review checklist:

1. Does the domain model contain most of the important application domain concepts?
2. Does the domain model show all important application domain relationships?
3. Does each relationship in the domain model correctly represent the corresponding real-world relationship?
4. Are there any important multiplicity constraints missing or incorrectly specified?
5. Does the domain model contain any design or implementation classes?
   Remark: The purpose of constructing the domain model is to help the development team understand the application domain. The domain model is not a design or implementation document. Therefore, a domain model should contain only application domain classes, not design and implementation classes. It is incorrect to include graphical user interface classes, databases and database access classes, design patterns (except a few such as the composite), transaction logs, and the like in a domain model.
6. Does every class in the domain model show all the important attributes?
   Remark: The attributes of a class describe or characterize the objects of the class or store state information of the objects. Classes without attributes are clear indications that the attributes are missing or the classes are not needed.
7. Are classes, attributes and relationships properly named and easy to understand?
8. Are there any classes used as attribute types?
   Remark: It is incorrect to treat classes or objects as attributes in a UML class diagram.
9. Do any of the classes show operations?
   Remark: Assigning operations to classes at the domain modeling stage is premature. Responsibility assignment is a design decision and should be done during object-oriented design.

5.5 PUTTING IT TOGETHER

This section shows the domain modeling steps applied to a metropolitan car rental system (CRS) application (see Appendix D.1). The business description with the phrases underlined after brainstorming is shown in Figure 5.17. In the classification step, the phrases are classified using the classification rules in Figure 5.8. The classification result is displayed in Figure 5.18.

The figures show additional classes, attributes, and relationships added, for example, body style, number of doors, and status. These attributes were derived from the identified attribute values, such as sedan or hatchback, two or four (doors), and car status values such as "repair," and the like. The classification result is then converted into a class diagram, as shown in Figure 5.19, where missing information is added. It is quite normal for different analysts to produce different results–the classes, attributes,

Description of Car Rental Business

(1) Vehicles[1] can be taken from[3] one location[1] and returned to[3] the same
(2) location[1] or a different location with an additional charge[1]. Although
(3) the company is, at present, concerned only with passenger cars[1],
(4) it may branch out into other forms of vehicle rental[1] in the future
(5) and would like to be able to use the same reservation system.
(6) The company has several different makes of car[2] in its rental fleet,
(7) from different manufacturers[1]. Each make may have several models. For
(8) example, Toyota has Corolla, Camry, etc. The models are grouped
(9) into a small number of price classes[1]. The customer[1] must be able to
(10) select[3] the make and the model he/she wants to rent. If the selected
(11) car is not available[4], the system must display a message telling
(12) the customer that the car is rented out[4] and let the customer
(13) select another make and model or have the system suggest
(14) similar models of a different make. The company has a number
(15) of different rental plans[1] available to customers. For example,
(16) there are "daily unlimited miles plan[1]" and "weekend savings plan[1]."
(17) The company finds it important to have information available on
(18) the models of car[2], automatic[4] or manual[4] transmission[1], two[5]
(19) or four[5] doors, and sedan[1] or hatchback[1]. The rental prices[2] may be
(20) different for different options[2] and a customer[1] will want to know
(21) such information when reserving[3] a car. Currently, customers[1] make[3]
(22) reservations[1] directly with the car rental company either in person[4]
(23) or by phone[4]. The salespersons[1] process[3] the reservations[1]
(24) manually using a reservation form[1] and archive[3] them in the file
(25) cabinet. No deposit is required at the time of reservation[2]. The
(26) reservation is voided[4] if the customer[1] does not show up to sign[3] the
(27) contract[1] for more than a given period of time[2]. Such reservation is
(28) honored only if there are still cars available[4] to satisfy the request.
(29) Sometimes a customer[1] wishes to make[3] a block reservation[1] for several[5]
(30) cars and to have the invoices[1] for all rentals on the reservation
(31) handled together. As soon as a car[1] is checked out[3] to a customer[1],
(32) an invoice is opened[4]. A single invoice[1] may cover[3] one or more[5]
(33) rentals[1]. Normally a customer[1] will pay[3] the invoice[1] when the car is
(34) returned[3], but, in some cases, the invoice[1] may be sent to[3] a company[1]
(35) (such as the customer's employer). When the customer[1] pays[3] by a
(36) credit card[4], the rental charge[1] will be processed[3] through a credit
(37) card processing company[1]. A car may or may not be available[4] for
(38) rental on a given day. Rental cars need frequent preventive
(39) maintenance and, in addition, any damage to a car has to be repaired
(40) as soon as possible. The company wants to keep track of the rental car
(41) purchase[4], repair[4], maintenance[4], and disposal[4] information for
(42) business and tax purposes.

FIGURE 5.17 Partial CRS description with phrases underlined

Brainstorming List	Classification Result	Rule
vehicle[1]	(C) Vehicle	1(a)
manufacturer[1]	(A) manufacturer	1(e)
price class[1]	(A) price class	1(e)
rental price[1]	(A) price	1(e)
available[4], not available[4]	(A) available: boolean	4
rented out[4]	(A) rented out: boolean	4
	(A) status	4
purchase[4]	(V) purchase	4
repair[4]	(V) repair	4
maintenance[4]	(V) maintenance	4
disposal[4]	(V) disposed	4
car[1], passenger car[1]	(C) Passenger Car	1(a)
makes of car[2]	(A) make	2(b)
model of car[2]	(A) model	2(b)
transmission[1]	(A) transmission	1(e)
automatic[4]	(V) automatic	4
manual[4]	(V) manual	4
	(A) number of doors: integer	5(a)
two[5] or four[5] doors[1]	(V) 2, 4	5(a)
	(A) body style: String	1(e)
sedan[1]	(V) "sedan"	4
hatchback[1]	(V) "hatchback"	4
options[1]	(same as transmission, # doors, body style)	
additional charge[1]	(A) additional charge	1(e)
depreciation of the rental cars[2]	(A) depreciation	2(b)
location[1]	(C) Location	1(a)
taken from[3]	(AS) taken from (Vehicle, Location)	3
returned to[3]	AS) returned to (Vehicle, Location)	3
other forms of vehicle[1]	(TBD)	
customer[1]	(C) Customer	1(a)
select[3]	(AS) select (Customer, Vehicle)	3
rental plan[1]	(C) Rental Plan	1(d)
daily unlimited miles plan[1]	(C) Daily Unlimited Miles Plan	1(d)
weekend savings plan[1]	(C) Weekend Savings Plan	1(d)
reserving[3]	(AS) reserve (Customer, Vehicle)	3
reservation[1]	(AC) Reservation (reserve)	1(c)
time of reservation[2]	(A) time of reservation	2(b)
period of time[2]	(A) grace period	2(b)
	(A) means	4
in person[4]	(V) in person	4
by phone[4]	(V) by phone	4
voided[4]	(A) void: boolean	4
salesperson[1]	(C) Salesperson	1(a)
process[3]	(AS) process (Salesperson, Reservation)	3
archive[3]	(AS) archive (Salesperson, Reservation)	3
reservation form[1]	(same as Reservation)	
file cabinet[1] (not used)		
sign[3]	(AS) sign (Customer, Contract)	3
contract[1]	(C) Contract	1(a)
block reservation[1]	(C) Block Reservation	1(a)
make[3]	(AS) make (Customer, Block Reservation)	3
invoice[1]	(C) Invoice	1(a)
opened[4]	(A) opened: boolean	4
cover[3]	(AS) bill for (Invoice, Contract) (1, 1..*)	3
one or more[5]		5(b)
rentals[1]	(same as contract)	
checked out[3]	(AS) check out (Customer, Vehicle)	3
pay[3]	(AS) pay (Customer, Invoice)	3
sent to[3]	(AS) sent to (Invoice, Company)	3
company[1]	(C) Company	1(a)
	(AC) Payment(pay)	1(c)
rental charge[1]	(A) rental charge	1(e)
credit card[1]	(C) Pay by Credit	1(d)
processed[3]	(AS) processed by (Pay by Credit Card, Credit Card Company)	3
credit card processing company[1]	(C) Credit Card Company	1(a)
	(I) ISA (Credit Card Company, Company)	9
	(I) ISA (Pay by Credit Card, Payment)	9
	(I) ISA (Daily Unlimited Miles Plan, Rental Plan)	9
	(I) ISA (Weekend Savings Plan, Rental Plan)	9
	(I) ISA (Passenger Car, Vehicle)	9
several[5]	(AG) Part-of (Reservation, Block Reservation) (2+, 1)	7

FIGURE 5.18 Classifying CRS application concepts

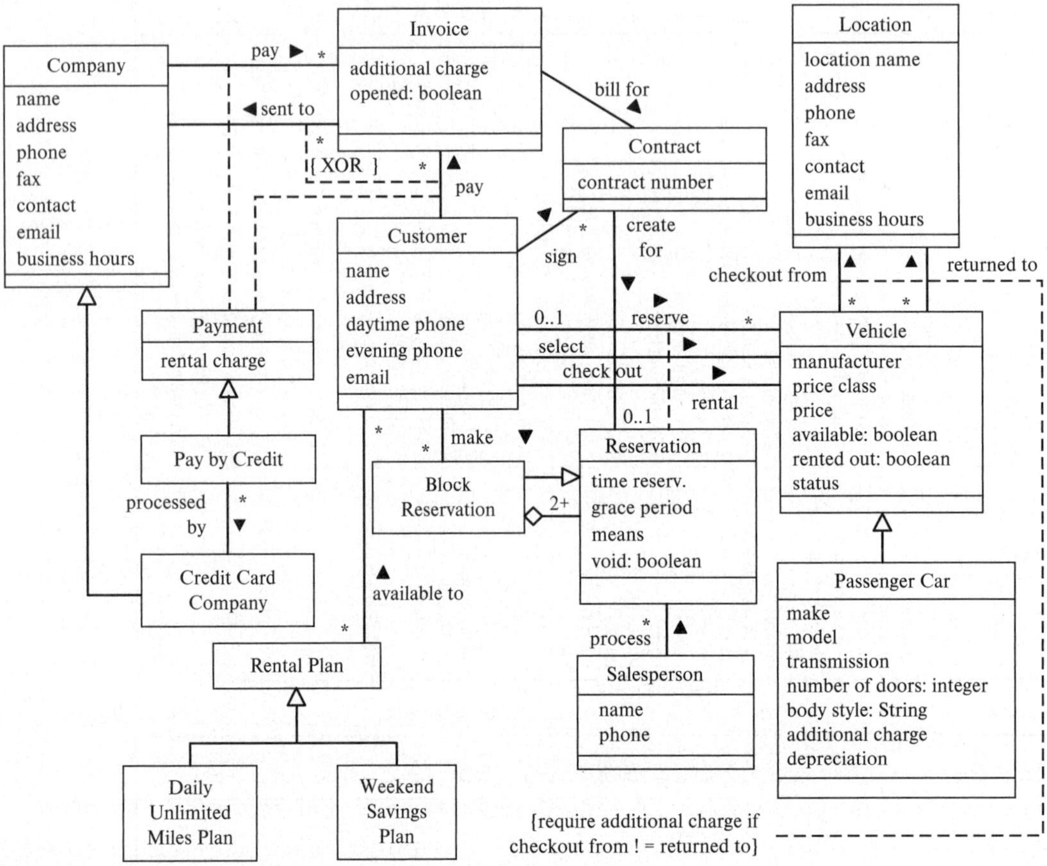

FIGURE 5.19 Visualizing car rental domain model

relationships, and association classes may differ. This reflects the differences in the perception of the application domain of the analysts; it cannot be completely avoided. It is partly due to the difference in the domain information collected by the analysts, the background and experiences of the analysts, as well as how the analysts apply the domain concept identification and classification rules.

5.6 GUIDELINES FOR DOMAIN MODELING

GUIDELINE 5.9 The team members should perform brainstorming and classification as team activities rather than individual work.

Brainstorming and classification by a group of three to five developers can help stimulate ideas and complement each other's limitations. But more significantly, the group brainstorming and classification meetings allow the team members to exchange the rationale for including/excluding a concept and how to classify it. Such meetings are critical for reaching a common understanding that forms the basis for subsequent design and implementation activities. Experiences show that teams that conduct domain modeling together produce much better design and implementation. On the other hand, teams that divide the work and assign the pieces to team members produce poor results. The lack of a common understanding of the application is the main reason.

GUIDELINE 5.10 Brainstorm first, then classify.

Do not brainstrom and classify at the same time so that the team can focus on one thing at a time. This is an application of the separation of concerns principle.

GUIDELINE 5.11 Each brainstorming and classification session should last no more than two hours.

Brainstorming needs warm-up time. It usually requires 15 to 30 minutes to ignite the brainstorming and begin productive work. The effectiveness and efficiency begin to drop after two hours for various reasons, such as participant fatigue. Before the meeting, each team member should be required to perform individually the brainstorming and classification steps and bring the results to the meeting. This improves meeting quality and efficiency. Alternatively, the team members may use the first 20 minutes of the meeting for individual work and continue with team brainstorming and classification afterwards.

At the meeting, the team members take turns recording on a whiteboard the concepts identified and classified. Draw lines to link concepts. For example, prefix "model" with "(a)" and link this to Vehicle to indicate that it is an attribute of Vehicle, and relate Weekend Savings Plan to Rental Plan with the UML inheritance link to indicate an inheritance relationship.

The whiteboard can keep the team members informed and focused on what is being discussed. At the end of the session, one team member can take a digital photo of the whiteboard and email it to the other team members. One or two members can draw the domain model and email it to the other team members to review. As an alternative to whiteboard and digital camera, the team session can also use a laptop hooked to a data projector to project the team brainstorming and classification results on a screen so that everybody can see the results. In this case, the bookkeeper can open the business description in a text editor, and use a forward slash followed by an integer to indicate which brainstorming rule is applied to identify a domain-specific phrase. If the phrase has more than one word, then highlight or underline the words.

GUIDELINE 5.12 Each brainstorming and classification session should be effectively coordinated.

One of the most time-consuming and unproductive things you can do in a meeting is to argue in circles about whether a concept should be included in the domain model or how it should be classified. Not every decision you make in software development is black and white. Many decisions are premise based and depend on the background and experiences of the decision maker. The decision about the inclusion or classification of a concept in the domain model is not always scientific. Therefore, brainstorming and classification sessions should be carefully coordinated. The session coordinator should keep the meeting focused and ensure that time is used effectively. The meeting should focus on identifying and then classifying domain-relevant concepts and relationships. Irrelevant or lengthy discussions of design and implementation issues should be discouraged and carried out after the meeting by individuals if necessary. Group time can be used more effectively by constantly monitoring the progress. If too much time has been spent on one concept or issue, then the coordinator should politely end the discussion, table that concept or issue, and suggest alternative ways to resolve the differences.

GUIDELINE 5.13 Do not draw UML class diagrams during brainstorming and classification sessions.

Drawing a UML class diagram while simultaneously trying to identify classes, attributes, and relationships is a bad idea, but many teams do this all the time. Team members should concentrate on brainstorming and classification according to the steps described in Sections 5.4.2 and 5.4.3. Once they have the needed information, drawing a UML class diagram is relatively easy. Without doing a good job in brainstorming and classification, the quality of the UML class diagram will likely be poor.

5.7 APPLYING AGILE PRINCIPLES

The following are guidelines for agile development:

GUIDELINE 5.14 Work closely with the customer and users to understand their application and application domain.

The development team needs to understand the application for which the software system is being built. This is because understanding software requirements depends on how much the team understands the application and application domain. The process to acquire domain knowledge is a communication process. Therefore, the team needs to work closely with the customer and users. The interaction with the customer and users helps the team solicit the needed domain knowledge, clarify doubts, and correct misunderstanding.

GUIDELINE 5.15 Do barely enough domain modeling and expand the domain model iteratively and incrementally.

The team must not overdo domain modeling–attempting to identify all classes, attributes, and relationships at once. Instead, the team should produce an initial domain model just enough to help understand the requirements and use cases allocated to the first iteration. The domain model is augmented during each of subsequent iterations. The attempt to capture all classes, attributes, and relationships in the domain model would result in heavy documentation, a drawback of the conventional approach that agile methods aim to avoid.

GUIDELINE 5.16 Domain modeling may be performed simultaneously with actor-system interaction modeling, object interaction modeling, object state modeling, and/or activity modeling.

It is difficult to know and understand every piece of domain knowledge at the time of domain modeling. Insisting on acquiring all of the needed domain knowledge is time-consuming and not necessary because subsequent steps may discover the missing pieces. This means that the modeling process is an iterative process that involves backtracking. It suggests that the different modeling activities may interact with each other and proceed simultaneously.

5.8 TOOL SUPPORT FOR DOMAIN MODELING

Creating and managing UML diagrams is a tedious, time-consuming job. Tool support is desirable. There are many such tools including public domain, open source, and commercial products. Some of the widely known tools are IBM Rational Modeler, Microsoft Visio, ArgoUML, and NetBeans UML Plugin. These tools provide UML diagram editors along with other features. The diagram editors let the software engineer draw, edit, and manage UML diagrams. The tools can generate code skeletons from design diagrams for different programming languages. Most tools also support reverse engineering–that is, generating UML diagrams from code. These are only a few of the features of these tools.

5.9 SUMMARY

This chapter presents the usefulness of a domain model and steps for constructing a domain model for a given application. It is important to recognize that domain modeling is not just drawing a UML class diagram. The first three and the last domain modeling steps are more significant and require educated decision making. These include collecting information about the application domain, brainstorming, classification, and finding out missing information. In this sense, drawing a domain model is the easiest step. This chapter explains intentional definition and extensional definition as two definition techniques. It reviews important object-oriented concepts including class, object, inheritance, polymorphism, aggregation, and association.

The chapter presents the UML class diagram modeling concepts and constructs, and guidelines for using some of the modeling constructs. It should be pointed out that this chapter is not meant to provide a complete coverage of UML class diagram. Rather, it is meant to present only a subset that is commonly used in domain modeling. The car rental application is used as an example to illustrate the domain modeling methodology and UML class diagram. This example is small but comprehensive enough to demonstrate the methodology and most of the UML class diagram features that are commonly used in domain modeling.

5.10 CHAPTER REVIEW QUESTIONS

1. What is the purpose of domain modeling?
2. What are the domain modeling steps?
3. What are the domain model brainstorming rules?
4. What are the domain concepts classification rules?
5. What are the modeling concepts and constructs of the UML class diagram?
6. What are the domain modeling guidelines?
7. How would you apply agile principles to domain modeling?

5.11 EXERCISES

5.1 A directed graph or digraph $G = (V, E, L)$ consists of a set of vertices $V = \{v_1, v_2, ..., v_n\}$, a set of edge labels L, and a set of directed edges $E \subseteq V \times V \times L$. Suppose you are assigned to design and implement a graph editor, that is, an editor for drawing and editing a digraph. You need to construct a domain model. This exercise requires you to perform the following:

- **a.** Produce a textual description for a graph. The description must describe the elements of a graph such as vertices and edges and relationships between the elements.
- **b.** Apply the brainstorming rules to the textual description as described in Section 5.4.2 and produce the brainstorming result.
- **c.** Classify the brainstorming result as described in Section 5.4.3 and produce the classification result.
- **d.** Convert the classification result into a UML class diagram.

5.2 Produce a one-page description of the business operation for a hotel reservation system. State practical and reasonable assumptions.

5.3 Perform the brainstorming step for the hotel reservation system using the description produced in exercise 5.2.

5.4 Perform the classification step from the brainstorming results produced in exercise 5.3 for the hotel reservation system.

5.5 Draw a UML class diagram based on the classification results produced in exercise 5.4.

5.6 Review the domain model class diagram produced in exercise 5.5 using the review checklist in Section 5.4.5. Produce a review report that answers the list of review questions.

5.7 Select another application, repeating exercises 5.2–5.6 for this application.

5.8 Suppose you are assigned to develop a graphical editor for a UML class diagram. This exercise requires you to perform the domain modeling steps and produce a domain model that describes the modeling notions depicted in Figure 5.1. *Hint:* This exercise is similar to exercise 5.1 but is a little bit more complex. The resulting domain model is a UML class diagram that describes a UML class diagram.

Chapter 6

Architectural Design

Key Takeaway Points

- The software architecture of a system refers to the style of design of the structure of the system including the interfacing and interaction among its subsystems and components.
- Different types of system require different design methods and architectural styles.

Software systems are designed and constructed to perform various functions. These functions are provided by various subsystems and components. Many software systems are meant to operate for decades. For example, many banking systems constructed in the 1960s are still in service today. Of course, these systems have experienced significant enhancements and upgrades as well as reengineering. These software maintenance experiences reveal that the structure or architecture of a software system has significant impact on a number of system properties, including performance, efficiency, security, and maintainability. It is similar to the effect of the architecture of a building to the utility, efficiency, security, safety, and maintainability of the building. According to Booch, software development should focus on the early development and baselining of a software architecture, then use the system's architecture as a primary artifact for conceptualization, constructing, managing, and evolving the system under development. In other words, the architecture of a software system plays a central role during the entire life cycle of the software system. In this chapter, you will learn:

- Software architecture and architectural design
- Importance of architectureal design
- Software design principles and how to apply them to architectural design
- Different types of system and their characteristics
- Architectural styles
- Relationships between types of system and architectural styles

6.1 WHAT IS ARCHITECTURAL DESIGN?

Architectural design for a software system is similar to the architectural design of a building. A building has rooms and subsystems such as heating and air conditioning, electric, gas and water supplies, and plumbing. Each of these serves a purpose and contributes to the overall functionality and utility of the building. The architectural design of a building highlights the major facilities and subsystems and how they relate to and work with each other. Software architectural design is similar. It is defined as follows.

Definition 6.1 The *software architecture* of a system or subsystem refers to the style of design of the structure of the system including the interfacing and interaction among its major components.

Definition 6.2 *Software architectural design*, or simply architectural design, is a decision-making process to determine the software architecture for the system under development.

A software architecture as a style of design implies that certain design decisions are already made and the architecture is the result of the design decisions. In this sense, software architecture can also be defined as a set of design decisions. There are minor differences between viewing an architecture as a style of design and a set of design decisions. The former is more tangible and facilitates understanding. It allows us to visualize a system's architecture in terms of the subsystems and their relationships. The design decisions are implied and serve as the rationale for using the architecture.

Examples of software architecture include the commonly encountered N-tier architecture, client-server architecture, and model-view-controller (MVC) architecture. The N-tier architecture structures the system as a number of layers; each uses the services of a lower level. In the client-server architecture, a server component provides services to other components referred to as *the clients*. The clients see the server, but the server does not know the clients. The MVC architecture consists of a data model, a controller, and a number of views. The controller decouples the views from the data model. It allows the data to be displayed using different views such as a table, a pie chart, or a histogram chart.

6.2 THE IMPORTANCE OF ARCHITECTURAL DESIGN

The importance of architectural design can never be overstated, as explained by the following story that took place many years ago. It was about the development of a medium to large-scale software system in C++ that accessed an Ontologies object-oriented database. Many students do not know the Ontologies DBMS, but it was red hot around 1990. Ontologies provided a C++-like query language. This means that C++ programs could directly access the database. That is, business objects and the database were "nicely integrated." However, this integration, or tight coupling, could also invite trouble if it is not dealt with properly. For example, the application code is heavily dependent on the database. If the database is replaced, then much of the application code has to be rewritten. To prevent this, a suggestion was made to develop a database wrapper to hide the database from the business objects. This provides protection to the business objects when the database is changed or replaced. If this happens, then only the wrapper, not the business objects, needs to be changed. It is much easier to change the wrapper than the business objects. The student will see in Chapter 17 that this is in fact the design of a persistence framework. Unfortunately, the development team rejected this because it was considered too complicated and inefficient and required too much work. That was at the beginning of the project.

Ten months later, after most of the system had been implemented, a rumor surfaced that the vendor of Ontologies had an internal power struggle. As a consequence, the cofounders, who were the key technical staff, threatened to leave the company and start another company. The development team that relied on Ontologies was nervous and hoped that the Ontologies personnel would stay. One month later, the rumor became a reality—the cofounders left Ontologies and formed a new company. This was disastrous to the successful completion of the project. The development team began to implement the database wrapper, but it was too late. The project was terribly behind schedule. A couple of months later, the Ontologies vendor went bankrupt. A few months later, the entire team was fired.

6.3 SOFTWARE DESIGN PRINCIPLES

During decades of software development practices, the software community learned many lessons. These led to the formulation of a set of software design principles. Architectural design can benefit from applying these principles. For example, in the 1970s, many program modules were written in such a way that each of them contained thousands of lines of code and many different functions. Such programs are difficult to understand, change, test, and reuse. Because the functions are unrelated, one does not know what a module really does—it appears to do almost everything. This type of module is said to have low functional cohesion. Similar problems occur in architectural design. For example, functionally unrelated use cases are assigned to a subsystem. In object-oriented programming, a class has low-functional cohesion if it encapsulates many unrelated functions or methods. Such classes are difficult to understand, test, and maintain. Another type of "bad program" exhibits the so-called high-coupling problem. That is, functions of the program call each other in a rather arbitrary manner, resulting in a rather complicated call graph. Clearly, such programs are difficult to understand, test, and maintain. The same problem exists in architectural design, object design and implementation: it is not uncommon to see complex dependence relationships among subsystems, components, and objects. Software design principles are proposed to solve these problems. This section presents software design principles so they can be applied during the design process.

6.3.1 What Are Software Design Principles?

Discussed above are some of the many design-related problems commonly encountered in practice. They negatively affect software productivity and quality, and significantly increase software maintenance costs. Among the remedies proposed to solve such problems are software design principles, defined as follows.

> **Definition 6.3** *Software design principles* are widely accepted guiding rules for software design—correctly applying these principles can significantly improve software quality.

Software design principles are collective wisdom acquired and validated by the software engineering community during decades of software research and development (R&D). They are valuable assets of the community. The next several sections are devoted to the study of some software design principles including *design for change, separation of concerns, information hiding, high cohesion, low coupling,* and *keep it simple and stupid* (KISS).

6.3.2 Design for Change

The *design for change* principle is rooted in the fact that change is a way of life. Numerous events could cause changes to a system. A few of these are given below to motivate:

- Changes to software requirements are needed to respond to changes in the business environment.
- Changes to the system are needed to fix problems in the system.
- Changes to the system are needed due to changes in hardware, platform, system operating environment, and the like.
- Changes to the system are needed due to changes in government and industry, as well as corporate policies, regulations, operating procedures, standards, and more.
- Changes to the system are needed to improve performance, reliability, user-friendliness, efficiency, security, and so on.
- Changes to the system are needed due to advances in technology.
- Changes to the system are needed due to changes in project schedule and budget.

A good design, if implemented accordingly, should yield a system that can adapt to change, or can be changed easily. Design for change means that the software design should come with a "built-in mechanism" to adapt to, or facilitate, anticipated change. Here, software design includes all types of design, such as architectural design, component design, module design, object design, and program design.

In Section 6.2, the Ontologies story is presented to illustrate the importance of architectural design. Viewing from a different angle, the story also shows the importance of design for change. That is, if the team had applied the design for change principle and implemented the database wrapper, the project would have been saved. Another happy-ending story is the following. More than 20 years ago, a local company awarded the author a contract to develop a web-based software, to be licensed to various organizations. At the outset, the customer representatives demanded that the product must only use an LDAP database. LDAP stands for Lightweight Directory Access Protocol–a hierarchical database management system (DBMS), which is efficient for data retrieval and widely used for web-based applications.

The design for change principle advised us that LDAP should not be the only choice. Customers of the product should be allowed to use other types of DBMS. Therefore, we applied patterns to hide the database from business objects so that the system could easily switch to other types of database without affecting business objects. However, at the design-review meeting, the customer representatives, who were seasoned developers, rejected our design. They deemed that the extra layer to hide the database was not needed and not efficient because the product would only use LDAP. At end of the four-hour meeting, we "surrendered" and told the representatives that we would drop our design. However, we did the opposite–we kept and implemented our design. We believed that this was to the best interest of the customer, who paid for the project. Several months later, we delivered the working prototype. The company's salespersons began to market the product. Despite the fact that potential customers liked the innovative features, they did not sell even one license. Why? Because customers never heard of LDAP and did not want to take the hassle, complexity and financial burden to introduce a new DBMS just for that product. Thus, the company came back to us and want the software to support all types of DBMS in the market. The company expected to pay a fortune for the change. Thanks to design for change, the company avoided a costly mistake. Many years have passed and the product is still on the market. Its architecture remains the same.

Applying the design for change principle means the design of the software architecture should consider anticipated changes and include mechanisms to accommodate such changes. In the above example, it was anticipated that the product would have to support other types of DBMS, not just LDAP. Therefore, the design of the architecture included a database manager to facilitate such a change. No rework was necessary when the product was required to support other types of DBMS.

6.3.3 Separation of Concerns

Separation of concerns was proposed by Edsger Wybe Dijkstra as a problem-solving principle, that is, focusing on one aspect of the problem in isolation rather than tackling all aspects simultaneously. UML is an excellent example of applying separation of concerns. Each of the UML diagrams focuses on the modeling of one aspect of the application or system. For example, the UML class diagram is concerned with modeling and design of the structural aspect. The sequence diagram is concerned with object interaction modelling and design. The use case diagram is concerned with use cases and their contexts.

Software design is a problem-solving activity. With respect to separation of concerns, it needs to consider the software design problem at two levels. At the higher level, the problem is concerned with how to proceed with the overall design process. At the lower level, the problem is concerned with how to design the individual components of the software system. In other words, software design is concerned with both the design process and the design product. Separation of concerns is a guiding principle for solving the design problem at both levels. With respect to the overall design process, separation of concerns tells us that the design should focus on one aspect of the overall design process in isolation and temporarily ignore the other aspects. Consider, for example, the methodology described in this book. Separation of concerns is reflected in the steps of the methodology, that is, each step focuses on one aspect of the design process. The expanded use case is concerned with the modeling and design of the actor–system interaction aspect. The high-level use case is concerned with the specification of use case scope, or when and where a use case begins and when it ends. Domain modeling is concerned with the acquisition and modeling of application domain knowledge. Object interaction modeling is concerned with how objects collaborate to carry out a business process.

With respect to the design of individual components, separation of concerns tells us that each component should focus on one aspect of the subject matter. For example, a GUI component should focus on presenting information to the end user. A database component should focus on data storage and retrieval. The business objects should focus on their respective business responsibilities. These are provided by the N-tier architectural styles. As another example, each use case should model and implement one and only one business process. Different business processes should be modeled by different use cases. The use cases of a software system should be partitioned according to their common core functionality and assigned to different subsystems. These are example applications of the principle of separation of concerns.

Applying the separation of concerns principle to architectural design means that the responsibilities of different concerns should be assigned to different subsystems. This also leads to high functional cohesion and facilitates understanding and reuse of the subsystems. At the object design level, the principle suggests that responsibilities of different concerns should be assigned to different objects. This is detailed in Chapter 10 (Applying Responsibility-Assignment Patterns).

6.3.4 Information Hiding

The *information hiding* principle was originally proposed by David Parnas as a software design principle. It shields implementation detail of a module to reduce its change impact to other parts of the software system. The design of the object-oriented programming languages like C++, Java, and C# supports this principle. In particular, information hiding is accomplished by making the data members of a class private and keeping the interface of the class stable. This effectively reduces the impact or ripple effect of changes made to the data structures and the implementation of the member functions. The introduction of the *interface* programming construct makes information hiding even more attractive. An interface can be implemented by one or more classes. A client object will not know that there is more than one implementation and which implementation is being used. Thus, the client object will not be affected if a different implementation is used. This effectively realizes the benefits of the information hiding principle.

Applying the information hiding principle to architectural design means designing the software system to shield the implementation detail of parts of the system from the rest of the system. Consider, for example, the design of a software system that uses a database. The design for change principle suggests that the design should take into consideration that the database may change. The design should hide the database from the rest of the system.

Consider, as another example, the need to apply an algorithm to elements of a data structure. The data structure could be a tree, a hash table, a linked list, or whatever. It would be nice if the algorithm could be applied to process the elements without needing to worry about the data structure that is used. The iterator pattern presented in Chapter 16 fulfills this need. That is, a common interface providing functions needed to traverse the elements of a collection is defined as follows:

- *first():* This function sets the cursor to refer to the first element of the collection.
- *next(): Object* This function returns the next available element.
- *isDone(): boolean* This function returns true if all elements of the collection are visited.

Each concrete data structure, such as tree, linked list, hash table, dictionary, and the like, implements the interface to provide concrete functions for traversing the concrete data structure. For example, a linked list would implement first() to set the cursor to the first element in the linked list, while a tree would set the cursor to the root. In this way, the concrete data structure to organize the elements and the implementation detail to traverse the data structure are hidden from whatever software client visits the elements of the collection.

6.3.5 High Cohesion

The *high cohesion* principle came from modular design in the conventional structured analysis and structured design paradigm. In structured design, the software system is decomposed into a treelike hierarchy of modules in which higher-level modules call lower-level modules and synthesize the results returned from the lower-level modules. Each module implements a component or subsystem and consists of a set of functions. Cohesion measures the degree of relevance of the functions to the module's core functionality. High cohesion facilitates understanding, software reuse, and software maintenance. The high cohesion principle suggests that the design of the modules should strive to achieve a higher degree of relevance of the functions of a module to the module's core functionality. Applying the high cohesion principle to architectural design means that the components or object classes of each subsystem should have a high degree of relevance to the core functionality of the subsystem.

Consider, for example, the design of a library information system (LIS). An LIS should let users check out documents, return documents, search documents, suggest purchase (of publications), order publications, receive order, classify publications, etc. These can be realized by use cases. A design decision is how to partition the use cases to form subsystems. The high cohesion design principle tells us that the use cases assigned to a subsystem should contribute to the core functionality of the subsystem.

This implies that checkout document, return document, and search document use cases should be assigned to a subsystem called circulation subsystem. Similarly, suggest purchase, order publication, and receive order use cases should be assigned to another subsystem called purchasing subsystem.

6.3.6 Low Coupling

The *low coupling* principle also came from the structured analysis and structured design paradigm. In structured design, coupling measures the degree of run-time effect due to dependencies and interaction between the modules. In other words, coupling measures the degree of impact of the run-time behavior of a given module on the run-time behavior of other modules. In addition to coupling through run-time behavior, the low coupling design principle also measures the change impact of one module to other modules. In other words, how many modules must be changed when a given module is changed?

High coupling increases uncertainty of run-time effect and change impact because the degree of dependency between the modules is high. It is also more difficult to test, reuse, maintain, and change the modules. It is more difficult to test because if module M1 depends on module M2 and M1 is tested before M2, then a test stub to simulate M2 needs to be constructed and used to test M1. It is time-consuming and costly to construct test stubs, especially if many test stubs are needed. Reuse is difficult because a high degree of dependency means the reuse of one module needs to include the other modules on which the reused module depends. Change and maintenance are difficult because changing one module may affect many others. Low coupling reduces the uncertainty of run-time effect and change impact and facilitates program understanding, testing, reuse, and maintenance.

One type of coupling that is commonly seen is the so-called *control coupling*. That is, modules communicate via a variable called a control variable. The value of the control variable determines which control flow will be followed at run time. For example, a parameter used as the case variable in a switch statement is a control variable. This implies that the behavior of one module is controlled by another module. Because the value is known only at run time, the behavior of the module that uses the control variable is difficult to predict, test, and debug. The following real-world story tells us how much trouble and grief a control variable could cause.

The story was about two modules developed by two programmers. The two programmers decided that the two modules would communicate via a control variable. The values and what each value was supposed to signify were agreed to at lunchtime meetings. Initially, it had three values. As time went by, the number of values increased to nine. The integration became a nightmare. It took one month to figure out that the nine values meant different things in the two modules. In the end, the programmers had to redo most of their work to fix the problem. The lesson? Use of control variables should be avoided.

Applying the low coupling principle to architectural design means reducing the run-time effect and change impact of each component to other components. In particular, the design should avoid control variables of more than two values, and use boolean variables instead of control variables. In addition, design for change and information hiding can be applied to reduce change impact.

6.3.7 Keep It Simple and Stupid

The *KISS* principle favors simple, straightforward, and easy-to-understand designs. In terms of object-oriented design, this principle may be rephrased as *designing "stupid objects."* Loosely speaking, a "stupid object" is one that is *simpleminded* and *dumb enough*, and hence, it is lovely. An object is simpleminded if it does not ask questions when it processes a request. An object is dumb enough if it knows how to do only one thing but nothing else. Consider, for example, the design of a software tool to compute various software metrics selected by the user with check boxes. One approach uses a series of conditional statements. That is, if the i-th check box is selected, then it computes the *i*-th metric. This object is not simpleminded because it asks too many questions, that is, it needs to test which of the check boxes have been selected. It is not dumb either because it knows how to compute all of the metrics.

An alternative approach that aims at *designing "stupid objects"* would define a metric interface and a number of concrete metric subclasses to compute the concrete metrics. In addition, for each check box, the design would create a concrete metric object and make it an action listener of the check box. In this way, when a check box is selected, the corresponding metric is computed; no question is asked. In this approach, each concrete metric knows only how to compute one metric but nothing else. Thus, designing "stupid objects" is accomplished. See Section 21.7.3 for a detailed description of the design and implementation.

Applying this principle to architectural design means designing the architecture to use "stupid objects." Part V (Applying Situation-Specific Patterns) provides more example applications of this principle, including the design of a persistence framework.

6.4 TYPES OF SYSTEM

As described previously, a system may consist of several subsystems, each of which may consist of lower-level subsystems or components. The architectural design for each of these is performed recursively down the hierarchy. For each of these, its system type is determined according to the characteristics of each type of system described the following sections.

The type of a system significantly influences the modeling, analysis, design, implementation, and testing of a system. Sometimes, a modeling and design methodology works well for one project but not for another project. One reason is the

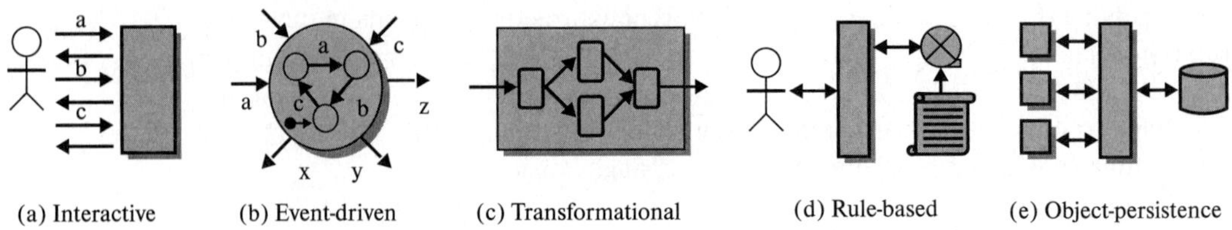

FIGURE 6.1 Types of system and behavior

mismatch between the type of system and the modeling and design methodology. Because the architecture is the result of a design methodology, this in turn causes mismatch between the type of system and the software architecture. For example, the structured analysis and structured design (SA/SD) methodology works well for traction-processing or transformational systems. Such systems are typically modeled by a network of transforms or processes connected by data flows they produce and consume. These systems are called transformational systems because they transform the original input to the final output. To be able to implement in a structured programming language like C, the model is converted into a tree or lattice during structured design. The resulting design is the so-called *main program and subroutine* architecture. The root represents the main program and the other nodes represent the subroutines. The edges represent parent subroutines calling their children. SA/SD is not suitable for real-time embedded systems, which exhibit event-driven behavior. It requires a different analysis and design methodology and leads to a different architecture, called event-driven architecture. This section describes types of commonly seen application systems and their behavior (see Figure 6.1). These are *interactive system, event-driven system, transformational system, rule-based system*, and *object-persistence subsystem*. The term "type of application system" is used to distinguish them from an infrastructure type of system like file servers and file transfer systems. For simplicity, this text uses "types of system" instead of "types of application system."

6.4.1 Interactive Systems

An interactive system typically exhibits the following properties:

1. The interaction between the system and the actor to carry out a business process consists of a relatively fixed sequence of actor requests and system responses, as illustrated in Figure 6.1(*a*).
2. The system has to process and respond to each request from the actor.
3. Often, the system interacts with only one actor during the process of a use case.
4. The actor is often a human being, although it can also be a device or another subsystem.
5. The interaction begins and ends with the actor.
6. The actor and the system exhibit a kind of "client-server" relationship in the sense that the actor requests services and the system provides the services. This relationship becomes more apparent when the actor is another system.

7. The system's state typically reflects the progress of the business process represented by the use case.

Interactive systems are the most common due to the widespread of desktop, mobile, and web-based applications. The relatively fixed sequence of interaction can be seen from a typical log-on process. To log on to a system, the user clicks the Log On link, the system shows the Log On page, the user enters the login ID and password, and the system displays the Welcome page or an error message if the login ID or the password is not valid.

To see that the system state reflects the progress of the business process, consider the process of online shopping. The customer logs on, selects the items, then checks out. If the customer has not logged on,then he or she won't be able to check out because the system maintains the state of progress. During checkout, the customer has to provide the shipping address, select the payment type, and provide payment-related information. Again, the system state reflects the state of progress of the business process. This state has been utilized by the system to prevent the customer from performing operations that do not follow the steps of the business process.

Modeling and design of interactive systems typically begin with the identification and specification of use cases representing business processes that are initiated by an actor and end with the actor. These are detailed in Chapters 7 and 8. The use cases are then refined in object interaction modeling to specify how the objects in the system will interact with each other to carry out the background processing of the business tasks. Object interaction modeling is studied in Chapter 9.

6.4.2 Event-Driven Systems

Event-driven systems typically exhibit state-dependent, reactive behavior, and the following properties:

1. Event-driven systems receive events from, and control external entities.
2. In general, event-driven systems do not have a fixed sequence of incoming events, which arrive at the system randomly.
3. Event-driven systems do not have to respond to every incoming event. Its response is state dependent–the same event may result in a different response if the system is in a different state. The system may also ignore an incoming event.
4. Event-driven systems often interact with more than one external entity at the same time.
5. The external entities are often hardware devices or other software components rather than human beings.
6. The system's state may not reflect the progress of a computation. The states may represent the recurrences of system conditions. For example, the system may be in the idle state, then enter into the "process event A" state, and return back to the idle state.
7. The system may need to meet timing constraints, temporal constraints, and timed temporal constraints such as the processing time for each digit dialed must not exceed N milliseconds (a timing constraint).

Event-driven subsystems are commonly seen in embedded systems, where the software subsystem is embedded in a total system that consists of both hardware and software. Aircraft software, vehicle self-driving software, elevator software, and telecommunication software are examples of embedded software. Hardware components of these systems capture changes in the environment and report such events to the software component, which processes the events and issues instructions to control hardware devices. Event-driven systems are modeled by state diagrams, as shown in Figure 6.1(*b*), where *a*, *b*, and *c* denote randomly arriving events and *x*, *y*, and *z*, the corresponding responses to control the devices. Modeling and design of event-driven subsystems are the topics of Chapter 13.

6.4.3 Transformational Systems

Transformational systems typically exhibit the following properties:

1. Transformational systems can be conceptually viewed as consisting of a network of information-processing activities, each of which transforms its input into its output, as Figure 6.1(*c*) illustrates.
2. The network of activities may involve control flows that exhibit sequencing, conditional branching, and parallel threads as well as synchronous and asynchronous behavior.
3. During the transformation of input to output, there is little or no interaction between the system and the actor–it is more or less a batch process.
4. Transformational systems are usually stateless.
5. Transformational systems may require number crunching or computation-intensive algorithms.
6. The actors of a transformational system can be human beings, devices, or other systems.

Transformational systems are commonly seen in scientific computation and engineering computation but can also occur in business applications like workflow management and business data mining. A familiar, simple example is a compiler, which transforms a source program into executable code in four stages: (1) lexical analysis, which transforms the source program into a stream of tokens, for example, identifiers, operators, operands, and reserved words; (2) syntax analysis, which transforms the token stream into program statements; (3) code generation, which produces executable code for each program statement; and (4) code optimization, which improves the performance and efficiency of the executable code. During this process, the actor and the compiler have little or no interaction.

A more complex example is workflow management, where requests or jobs may go through several stages of processing by different departments and may require decision making, synchronization, and concurrent processing. At each department, the staff may interact with the subsystem that automates the activities of the department. In this sense, the subsystem is an interactive subsystem of the transformational system. Modeling and design of transformational systems are the topics of Chapter 14.

6.4.4 Rule-Based Systems

A rule-based system stores knowledge and human intelligence in its rule base, and uses an inference engine to evaluate the rules. Each rule consists of a conjunction of conditions and a sequence of actions (e.g., if C1 && C2 && ... && Cm do A1, A2, ..., An). If all of the conditions are evaluated to true, the sequence of actions is executed. Rule-based systems have the following properties:

- Rule-based systems can derive new knowledge from the knowledge stored in the rule base.
- Rules can be modified and rearranged during system operation and the update can take effect immediately once the modification is committed.
- Each rule-based system intends to work for a specific area such as diagnosis of machine problems.
- As the rule base grows and improves, the system can become more powerful and more valuable.
- Some rule-based systems work with users interactively, others don't.

Rule-based systems are used by artificial intelligence applications and decision-support systems. Examples are expert systems, knowledge-based systems, and business decision-support systems. Chapter 15 presents modeling and design of rule-based systems.

6.4.5 Object-Persistence Subsystems

An object-persistence subsystem provides capabilities for storing and retrieving objects with a database or file system, while hiding the storage media. Due to its use of a database, it is also called a *database subsystem* for convenience. A database subsystem exhibits the following properties:

1. It hides the database from the rest of the system and shields the rest of the system from changes to database implementation.
2. Unlike the other types of subsystem, a database subsystem is responsible only for storing and retrieving objects with a database. It does little or no business processing except in a few cases when doing so can substantially improve performance, such as when a large number of records need to be updated.
3. A database subsystem is capable of efficient storage, retrieval, and updating of a huge amount of structured and complex data.

6.4.6 System and Subsystem

The concepts of system and subsystem are relative to each other. That is, a system is a subsystem of a larger system. A subsystem is a system of its own and may consist of other subsystems. In general, a large system may consist of several different types of subsystem. For example, an interactive system may contain an event-driven subsystem, a transformational subsystem, and a database subsystem. An event-driven subsystem may contain an interactive subsystem, a transformational subsystem, and a database subsystem. This means that one needs to apply the design method that matches the type of subsystem under development.

6.5 ARCHITECTURAL STYLES

Architectural styles are generic architectural designs that can be reused when designing the architecture of a system or subsystem. As discussed previously, different types of system influences the choice of an analysis and design methodology and the architectural design. For example, if the system is an interactive system, then the N-tier architectural style is selected. The number of tiers for the architecture can vary depending on the requirements of the application. For example, a 3-tier architecture consists of a presentation (or graphical user interface) layer, a controller layer, and a business objects layer. If a database is used to provide object persistence, then a 4-tier architecture is required. As another example, if the system is a transformational system, then the main program and subroutine architectural style is selected and the SA/SD methodology is applied. The resulting architectural design is a tree or lattice.

This section describes a number of commonly-used architectural styles and relates them to the types of system. The architectural styles covered in this section include:

1. *N-tier architecture.*This architectural style arranges the system components into a number of relatively independent, loosely coupled layers. Each layer has a well-defined functionality. It reduces change impact to other layers. It is useful for the design of interactive systems.
2. *Client-server architecture.* This architectural style consists of one server that provides services to a number of clients. The clients know the server, the server does not know the clients, and the clients do not know each other. In this sense, it reduces the coupling of the clients and the server.
3. *Main program and subroutine architecture.* This architectural style organizes the components of the system into a tree structure, in which computation begins with the root or main program and is carried out by the descendants recursively down the tree. It is useful for designing transformational or workflow-oriented systems.
4. *Event-driven system architecture.* This architectural style consists of a state-based controller that interacts with and controls a number of components. The controller knows the components and vice versa, but the components do not know each other. Interaction between the components is mediated by the controller. It is useful for designing event-driven, embedded systems.
5. *Persistence framework architecture.* This architectural style hides the databases and file systems by decoupling them from the objects that use them. That is, the objects are unaware of the existence of such storage devices; and hence, all changes to the databases and file systems have no impact to the objects. This architectural style is presented in Chapter 17.

Figure 6.2 outlines the characteristics of each type of system and how it differs from the other types. The table is useful for determining an architectural style to apply according to the type of system to be developed. In recent years, security patterns and security architectural styles are increasing their popularity due to concerns of computer security. Security patterns and architectural styles are presented in Chapter 24.

6.5.1 N-Tier Architectural Style

In the *N-tier* architecture, the system is structured into a number of layers or tiers as shown in Figure 6.3(*a*). Requests for services are sent from one layer to the next lower layer. Requests from a lower layer to a higher layer should be avoided. Figure 6.3(*b*) shows an example, where the classes and objects are grouped into five layers. The graphical user interface (GUI) layer is a group of objects that are responsible for presenting information as well as menus and buttons to the user. These objects invoke functions of a controller object in the controller layer. Each controller is responsible for handling events relating to a given use case. In most cases, there is

Type of System/ Subsystem	Highlight of System Characteristics	Architectural Style	Distinction
Interactive	Actor initiates and interacts with the system to jointly carry out a business process, using predefined interaction protocols.	N-tier	Differs from event-driven subsystems in that: 1. System interacts with only one actor during each session. 2. System events arrive in a predefined sequence. 3. System must respond to each system event.
Event-driven	System exhibits state-dependent, reactive behavior. It processes events from external entities and issues instructions to external entities.	Event-driven system architecture	Differs from heuristic problem-solving, client-server, and object persistence in that: 1. It demonstrates state-dependent, reactive behavior. 2. External entities may or may not collaborate.
Transformational	A set of interconnected information-processing activities produces an output for a given input–i.e., the input is transformed into the output.	Main program and subroutine	Differs from other subsystems in: 1. Emphasis on a series of information-processing activities. 2. Transformation of input into output.
Object-persistence	Providing object persistence and sharing between applications as well as shielding business objects from changes in database implementation.	Persistence framework	Differs from heuristic problem solving in that: 1. It provides object persistence and sharing. 2. It deals with a large number of records. 3. It hides the database from business objects.
Client-server	A dedicated, high-performance subsystem provides services that can be requested by other subsystems or components through a network.	Client-server	Differs from heuristic problem solving in that: 1. The server does the requested work. 2. The clients do not share anything 3. Clients use the services for different purposes.
Distributed, decentralized	Distributed and independent subsystems communicate over a network to use services of, and provide services to, each other.	Peer-to-peer	Differs from blackboard and client-server in that: 1. Peers are clients and servers. 2. Peers solve their own problems.
Heuristic problem solving	Intelligent, problem-solving components communicate and collaborate through a shared data repository to develop a solution to a given problem.	Blackboard	Differs from client-server in that: 1. The components carry out the work. 2. Blackboard is only a shared data repository. 3. Components solve a problem jointly.

FIGURE 6.2 Mapping system types to architectural styles

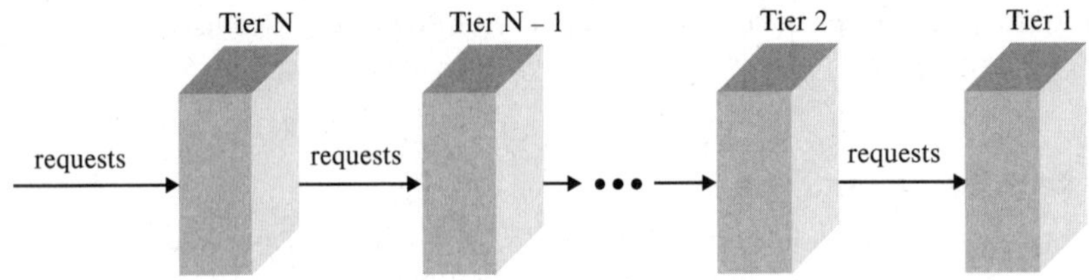

(a) N-tier architectural style

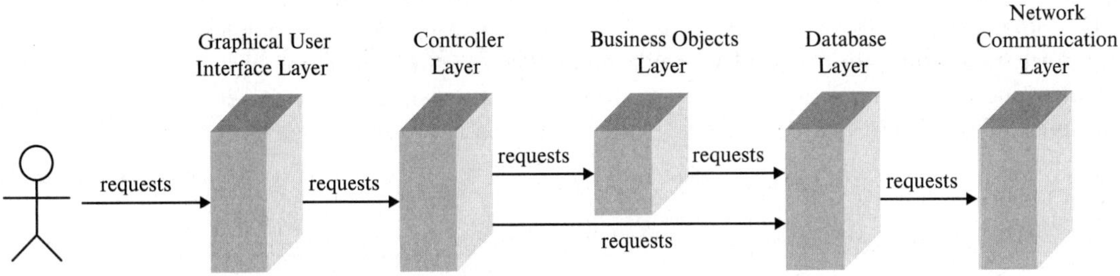

(b) An example N-tier architecture

FIGURE 6.3 N-tier architecture

a one-to-one correspondence between the use cases and the controller objects, and the controller classes are named after the use cases. For example, a library information system has a Checkout Document use case. This means there is a Checkout Document Controller class. The objects of this class are responsible for handling checkout document-related requests.

When the user clicks a button to submit a request, the GUI layer delivers the request to the appropriate use case controller. For example, if the user wants to check out a document, then the request is sent by the GUI to the Checkout Document Controller object. The latter requests the database layer to retrieve the corresponding User and Document objects from the database. The controller creates the Loan object and updates the status of the Document object to "checked out." It then saves the objects to the database through the database layer. If network communication is required, for example, the database is located at a remote site, then the network communication layer is also involved.

The N-tier architecture shown in Figure 6.3(*b*) is often used as the architectural design for interactive systems. Such systems interact with the user through use cases as illustrated by the Checkout Document use case previously described. The N-tier partitions the objects of the interactive system into layers, where each is assigned a number of related responsibilities. For instance, the GUI layer presents information and GUI widgets, the controller layer handles use case-related events, the business objects layer is a collection of business objects, the database layer stores and retrieves objects with a database, and the network communication layer is used for communicating with a remote site.

Nevertheless, the N-tier architecture is not limited to interactive systems. For example, the ISO Seven Layer Model is a seven-tier architecture used for network communication. The N-tier architecture is also used in the design of operating systems and secured systems. One approach to designing secured systems requires the layers to authenticate to the next lower layer. This creates N obstacles for an intruder and protects the valuable data and program resources. The N-tier architecture codifies several software design principles, which are presented in Section 6.3. For example, *separation of concerns* is realized by grouping objects of different concerns into different layers. As a consequence, *high cohesion* and *designing "stupid objects"* are achieved. *Information hiding* and *design for change* are supported by the fact that each layer hides the lower layer and shields the change impact of the lower layer.

6.5.2 Client-Server Architectural Style

The *client-server* architecture consists of a server and a number of clients, as shown in Figure 6.4. The diagram shows the architectural design for part of the Airport Baggage Handling System (ABHS) presented in Chapter 3. The ABHS has passenger check-in computers located at different terminals of the airport. These computers need to access the flight information system to retrieve flight information as well as update passenger check-in and flight status. In this case, the passenger check-in computers are the clients and the flight information system is the server. The clients send service requests to the server, through remote procedure calls or other network communication protocols. The server processes the requests and sends the results to the clients. The clients know the server, but the server does not know the clients. This means that clients can be added to or removed from the system freely without impacting the work of the server (except performance impact). Usually, the clients and the server reside on different machines at different locations.

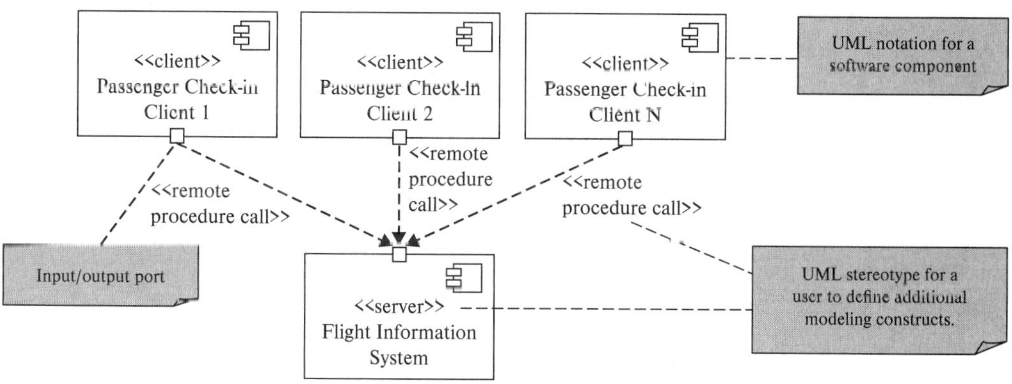

FIGURE 6.4 Applying client-server architectural style

The client-server architecture is useful for applications that require a designated subsystem to provide services to other subsystems, which may be located on other machines. The clients can be made lightweight if most of the needed services are provided by the server. For example, in the ABHS, the passenger check-in clients are lightweight clients. Besides the ABHS, many other examples of the client-server architecture are found in real-world applications. These include most web-based applications, file servers, and file transfer protocol (ftp).

6.5.3 Main Program and Subroutine Architectural Style

The *main program and subroutine* architecture has a tree or lattice shape, as shown in Figure 6.5(*a*). It consists of a main program and a number of subroutines. The main program calls its child subroutines, which, in turn, call lower-level subroutines, from left to right. The main program and subroutine architecture may have a lattice shape if two parent nodes call the same child subroutine. Students who have programmed in a procedural language such as C or Fortran should be familiar with this architecture.

The main program and subroutine architecture is often used as the architectural design for transformational systems. It is derived from a data flow diagram in SA/SD. In illustration, the following paragraphs describe how the architecture in Figure 6.5(*a*)

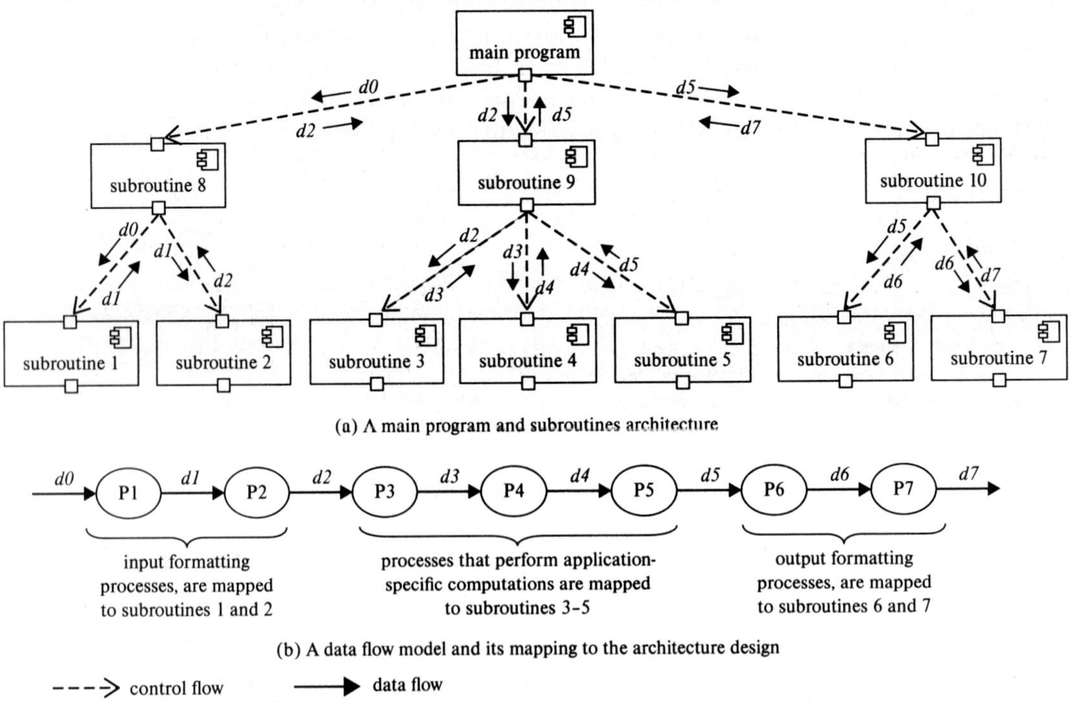

FIGURE 6.5 Main program and subroutine architecture

is derived from the data flow diagram shown in Figure 6.5(*b*). Before proceeding, it is useful to know that the processes of a data flow diagram can be classified into three broad categories:

Formatting processes. Each of these converts its input to produce an output with a different format. For example, a submitted html form is converted into a struct. Formatting processes only change the representation, not the content.

Transform processes. Each of these performs an application-specific processing, which transforms the input into an output that is semantically different. For example, the input is search criteria and the output is a list of products satisfying the search criteria.

Dispatching processes. A dispatching process analyzes its input and, according to the transaction type, redirects the input to one of the successor processes, which handle different types of transactions.

The derivation of the main program and subroutine architecture from Figure 6.5(*b*) starts from the initial input d0 and traces the processes P1, P2, ... in turn until a transform or dispatching process. For example, assume that process P3 is a transform process. The tracing continues until a formatting process is found, say P6. Thus, the tracing identified input formatting processes P1 and P2; transformational processes P3, P4, and P5; and output formatting processes P6 and P7. These are mapped to the lowest-level subroutines in Figure 6.5(*a*). Note that subroutines 8-10 are driver routines, which invoke the input formatting, transform, and output formatting subroutines. The data flow diagram in Figure 6.5(*b*) is called a transform-centered data flow diagram. On the other hand, a transaction-centered data flow diagram is one that involves a dispatching process, which has outgoing data flows to different transform processes that handle different types of transaction. The derivation of a main program and subroutine architecture from a transaction-centered data flow diagram is similar, except that the dispatching process is mapped to the main program or a subroutine that invokes one of its child subroutines according to the transaction type.

Consider, for example, the design of an integrated development environment (IDE). The functions of the IDE include, among others, compiling source programs and reverse-engineering source code to produce UML diagrams. The diagrams to be produced are selectable by the user. For simplicity, only one programming language is considered. To compile the source code to generate the executable code, a compiler performs the following tasks, implemented by four components:

1. *Lexical analysis.* This task analyzes the words of the source program and classifies them into different types of tokens. For example, "1stYear" is not valid, and "year1," "static," and "++" are recognized as identifier, reserved word, and operator. The output of this task is a stream of tokens, each of which has attributes such as type and value. The output goes to syntax analysis, which is described next.
2. *Syntax analysis.* This task analyzes the syntax of the program statements and produces a syntax tree to represent the program. The syntax tree is the input to the code generation task.

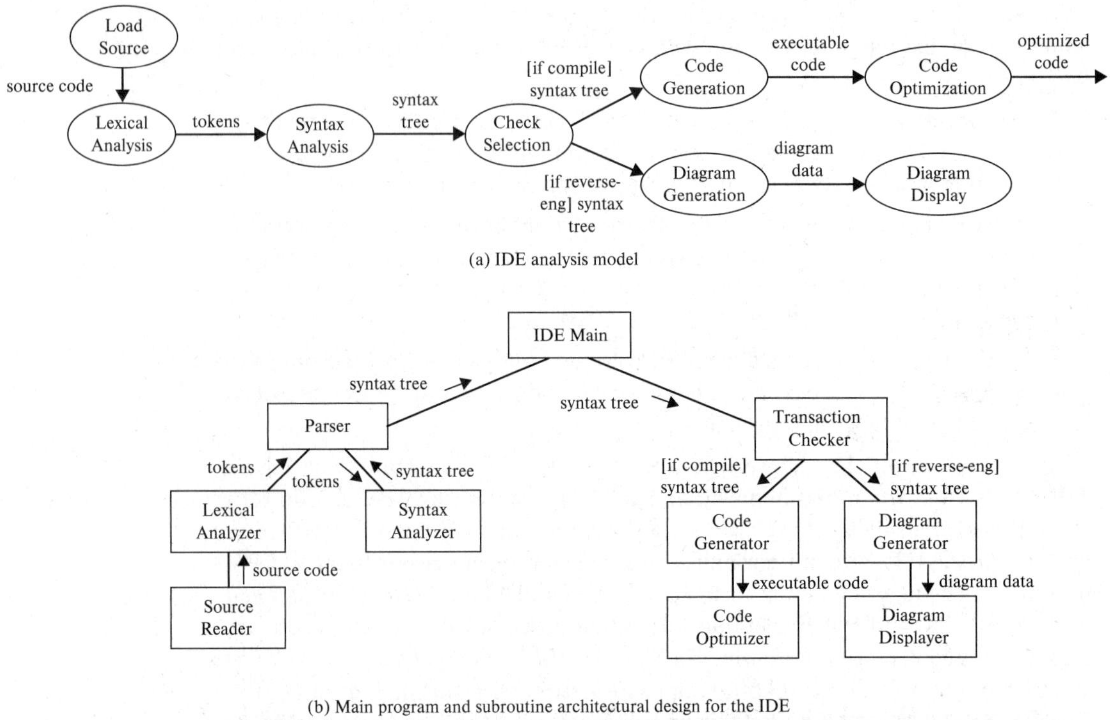

FIGURE 6.6 Applying main program and subroutine architectural style

3. *Code generation.* This task performs a post-order traversal of the syntax tree and generates the executable code when each node is visited. For instance, when nodes a and b are visited, their values are loaded in some way. When node + is visited, an addition is performed on the values of its two children and the result is stored. The output of this step goes to code optimization, as described next.
4. *Code optimization.* This task performs optimization of the generated executable code using code optimization techniques. The optimized code is the result of the compiler.

The reverse-engineering functions are similar, except that code generation and code optimization are replaced by diagram generation and diagram display, respectively. However, there is a concrete diagram generator and a concrete diagram displayer for each type of UML diagram supported. Figure 6.6(*a*) shows a data flow diagram for the IDE described above. The main program and subroutine architectural design for the IDE is shown in Figure 6.6(*b*), where only one diagram generator and diagram displayer are depicted.

6.5.4 Event-Driven System Architecture

The *event-driven system* architecture (EDSA) consists of a state-based controller and a number of components under its control. Figure 6.7 depicts such an architecture.

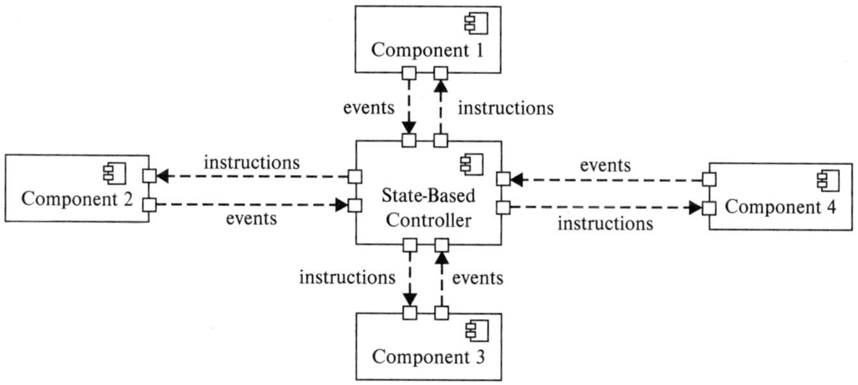

FIGURE 6.7 Event-driven system architecture

As discussed earlier, an event-driven system exhibits state-dependent behavior. This behavior is implemented by the controller. The components under control send events to the controller, which processes the events according to the state behavior and sends instructions to the components under control.

Figure 6.8 illustrates the architectural design of the software system for a basic window air conditioner. The software implements a simple state machine. It receives events from the AC unit switch and the room temperature sensor and issues instructions to control the fan and the condenser. The condenser cools the air and the fan circulates the air to cool the room. The software is stored and run on a microcontroller integrated circuit (IC) chip. The IC chip has input pins and output pins. The input pins are connected to the AC unit switch and room temperature sensor. The output pins are connected to the fan and condenser. Each pin represents one bit; its value is determined by the voltage; for example, high is 1 and low is 0. By reading and setting the pins of the IC chip, the software receives the incoming events or data and controls

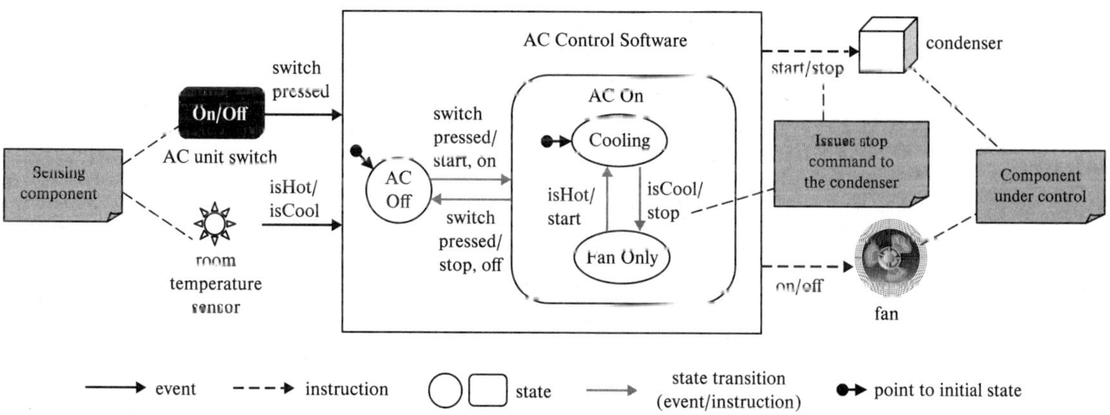

FIGURE 6.8 Illustration of an event-driven system

the fan and condenser. For example, to start the condenser, a designated pin is set to 1; to stop the condenser, the pin is set to 0.

Each time the AC unit switch is pressed, the software changes state from AC Off to AC On, and vice versa. That is, the switch toggles on and off. The software also issues the corresponding on/off and start/stop commands to control the fan and the condenser. In the AC On state, the temperature status from the room temperature sensor is used by the software to start or stop the condenser. If the software is in the Fan Only state and the room temperature is hot, the software changes to the Cooling state and at the same time starts the condenser. If it is already in the Cooling state, then the isHot event is ignored. The other transitions can be interpreted similarly.

Neither the N-tier architecture nor the client-server architecture is an appropriate architectural design solution for the control problem discussed above. The reason is that the problem and the software are event driven and state dependent. For instance, it would be difficult for the N-tier to handle the on/off events from the AC unit switch because the N-tier architectural style does not remember the previous state. It does not have the next state. One could add a state variable, but doing so changes the architecture. It is no longer an N-tier. In the client-server architecture, the clients know the server, but the server does not know the client. If it is used as the architecture for the window AC, then when the room temperature sensor triggers a state transition, it would not know to which device to send the control command. The AC control software can ignore an event if it is not in an appropriate state. However, each layer of the N-tier and the server of the client-server architecture must respond to every request they receive. They do not know which event should be processed and which one should be ignored–they must process every request.

6.5.5 Persistence Framework Architectural Style

Object-oriented systems need to save objects to a database and retrieve them afterwards. This is commonly referred to as object persistence. The *persistence framework* architecture provides such a capability that satisfies several software design principles. These include separation of concerns, information hiding, design for change, high cohesion, and keep it simple and stupid. Figure 6.9 illustrates this architectural style applied to access different types of DBMS, including relational databases, network databases, hierarchical databases, and object-oriented databases. Moreover, the databases may come from different vendors. Without using the persistence framework architectural style, each of the business objects must know how to access different types of database from different vendors. The business objects must also know how the data are organized in the databases. These increase the complexity of the business objects.

The persistence framework architectural style uses the database manager to provide an object-oriented interface to the business objects. The database manager delegates the requests from the business objects to the database access objects, which communicate with different types of database from different vendors. This

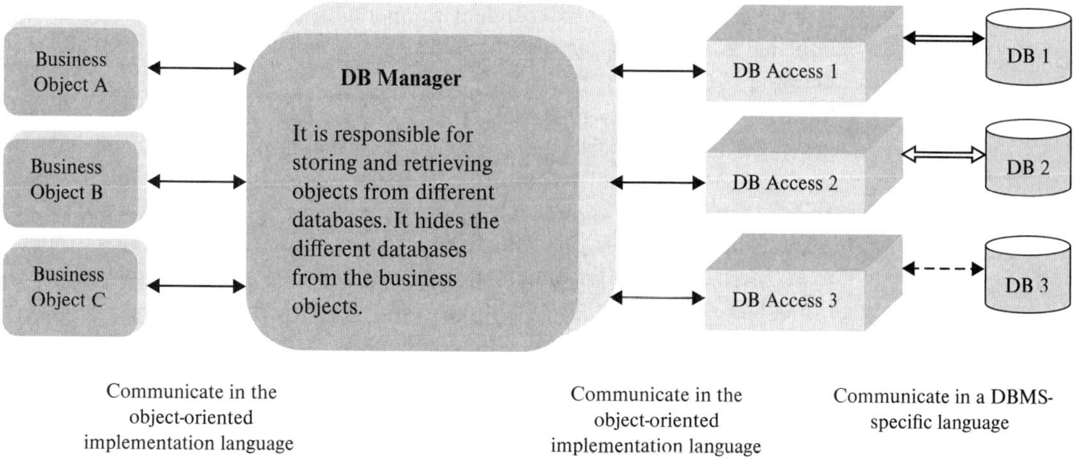

FIGURE 6.9 Persistence framework architectural style illustrated

greatly simplifies the design, implementation, testing, and maintenance of the business objects.

6.5.6 Other Architectural Styles

Besides the architectural styles presented in the previous sections, there are other architectural styles that are commonly mentioned in the literature. Below is a partial list. Others are presented in Part V (Applying Situation-Specific Patterns).

- *Peer-to-peer.* The peer-to-peer (P2P) architecture consists of independent components connected through network protocols. It is often used in decentralized or distributed computing applications. Systems built using this architecture are highly robust because the failure of one component has little impact on the operation of the system. It is also highly flexible and scalable because components can be added or removed easily.
- *Pipe-and-filter.* The pipe-and-filter architecture consists of a series of programs, called filters, interconnected by data streams, called pipes, in a pipeline fashion. Therefore, it is also referred to as the pipeline architecture. It is widely used in shell programming to do batch processing where the output of one executable program is piped to the next. The simplicity of interprocess communication facilitates novel combinations of programs to accomplish desired computation tasks.
- *Blackboard.* The blackboard architecture has a global data repository, called the blackboard, and independent components that communicate through the repository. The independent components may update the data directly or through the services provided by the blackboard. In some sense, this arrangement simplifies

interaction between the independent components. However, if not designed and implemented properly, undesirable side effects may result from concurrent updates.

- *Service-oriented architecture (SOA).* SOA is viewed as comprising the policies, practices, and frameworks that enable business functions to be provided and consumed as services. An SOA consists of the *service providers*, the *service consumers*, and the *service architecture* that manages the services between the two. A service is an abstraction and implementation of a business function in a domain, similar to an interface and an implementation. Unlike function calls, services are invoked through the use of http protocol and XML.
- *Cloud computing architecture.* Cloud computing is an extension of SOA to the entire application software as a service (SaaS) rather than a business function as a service. The service provider licenses an application software to the service consumer as a service on demand. The service consumer may be charged according to the actual use of the software. An example of SaaS is Google Apps.

6.6 ARCHITECTURAL DESIGN PROCESS

The architectural design process for a software system or subsystem is a decision-making, cognitive process. It needs to consider many factors. The type of the system to be developed is an important consideration. Experiences show that the type of system influences the selection of the architectural style. Architectural design is also a recursive process. This is because a system consists of subsystems, which in turn consist of lower-level subsystems or components, and so forth. The design process needs to be performed recursively down the hierarchy until the leaf node components are relatively easy to design and implement. Unfortunately, there is no clearly defined stopping rule–it depends on many factors, including the size and complexity of the system, the experience of the development team, and the design objectives.

Figure 6.10 shows the architectural design process, which should be performed recursively for the system as well as the subsystems identified during this design process.

1. *Determine design objectives.* In this step, the overall design objectives are identified and specified. For example, the design is aimed to provide software fault tolerance, safety, security and maximize performance. The overall design objectives may be found or derived from the requirements.
2. *Determine type of system.* In this step, the type of the system or subsystem is determined. The type of system and design objectives are used to select an architectural style from a repository.
3. *Apply an architectural style or perform custom architectural design.* If an architectural style can be applied, then this step applies the architectural style to produce a "standard" architectural design; otherwise, a custom design is produced.

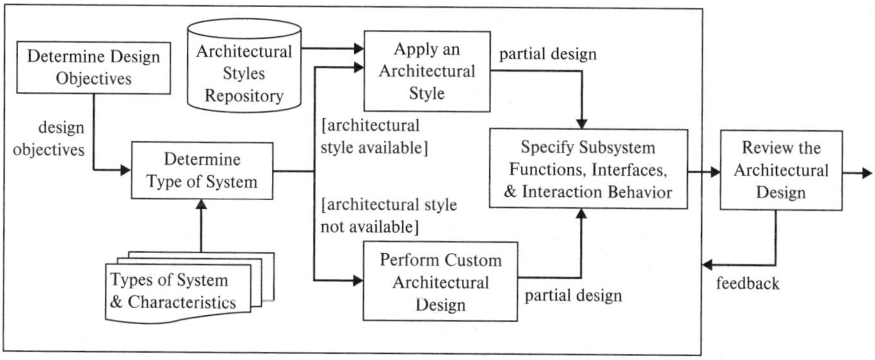

FIGURE 6.10 Architectural design process

4. *Specify subsystem functions, interfaces, and interaction behavior.* In this step, the interfaces between the subsystems are defined and the interaction behavior between the subsystems are specified.
5. *Review the architectural desgin.* In this step, the architectural design is reviewed to ensure that it satisfies the requirements, design objectives, and software design principles.

6.6.1 Determine Architectural Design Objectives

Architectural design aims to produce an overall structure for the software system. However, this objective is too abstract to be useful. A good architectural design for one system is not necessarily good for another system. Therefore, the architectural design objectives for the system to be developed should be determined and used to guide the design process. An architectural design objective specifies a system attribute or aspect that is to be accomplished by the design. Different applications have different business objectives and priorities, which influence the design decisions. Therefore, they should be taken into account when deciding on the design objectives. Sometimes the architectural design objectives can be derived from the software requirements including the quality and security requirements. A partial list of such requirements or factors that should be considered is as follows:

1. *Ease of change and maintenance.* Does the application require frequent changes to the system, such as changes to requirements?
2. *Use of commercial off-the-shelf (COTS) parts.* Does the project require or prohibit use of COTS, and what is the extent of such reuse?
3. *System performance.* Does the application require high performance, for example, to process real-time data or a huge volume of transactions?
4. *Reliability.* To what extent does the application require the system to correctly perform its intended functions under assumed conditions?
5. *Security.* What is the extent of protection to data and program resources required by the application?

6. *Software fault tolerance.* To what extent does the application require the system to continue operation when a software problem occurs?
7. *Recovery.* To what extent does the application require the system to return to a previous state after a system crash?

6.6.2 Perform Custom Architectural Design

Reusing an architectural style is always preferred because it not only saves time and effort but also brings quality to the system. The necessary condition is that the right architectural style is selected and correctly applied. However, not all application system development can reuse an existing architectural style.

Consider, for example, the design of a mission-critical subsystem. One of the design objectives requires the subsystem to continue operation when a software fault occurs. If no architectural style satisfies the design objective, then a custom design of the architecture is needed. One way to accomplish software fault tolerance is to use object diversity, that is, to design and implement very different versions of the subsystem, run one of them as the active version, and switch to one of the backup versions when a fault occurs. To accomplish this, the mission-critical component of the subsystem that requires software fault tolerance is identified. A common interface for the component is defined. Diverse teams are employed to implement the interface to produce multiple implementations of the component. The implementations are required to use different data structures and algorithms. One of the implementations is selected to run until it is replaced.

Software design patterns are useful for custom design of the architecture for a software system. For instance, an architectural design for the aforementioned mission-critical component that requires software fault tolerance can apply the *bridge* pattern presented in Chapter 17. The bridge pattern enables the system to switch to a different implementation of the mission-critical component transparently, which means the client of the mission-critical component is not aware of the switching. In this way, the replacement implementation can initialize itself to the stored state to rerun the operation.

6.6.3 Specify Subsystem Functions and Interfaces

In this step, the software requirements and design objectives are allocated to the subsystems and components of the architecture. Sometimes, it is necessary that some of the requirements are decomposed into lower-level requirements to facilitate the allocation of requirements to subsystems. The functionality of each of the subsystems and components is then specified according to their requirements and design objectives. For example, the requirement to reverse-engineer OO code to produce UML class diagram, sequence diagram, activity diagram, and state diagram is assigned to the Diagram Generator component in Figure 6.6. A performance requirement is allocated to one or more performance-related subsystems or components. A fault-tolerant design objective is allocated to a mission-critical subsystem that is required to provide such a capability.

The interfaces between the subsystems are specified in this step. The specification of the interfaces defines the input and output of each subsystem, including the number, types, and order of the input parameters, and similarly for the output. The interaction behavior between the subsystems is also specified–that is, the specification of the sequences of messages to be exchanged between subsystems.

6.6.4 Review the Architectural Design

The architectural design is reviewed to ensure that the design objectives and software requirements are satisfied. The review also verifies that the design follows the software design principles, which are described in Section 6.3.

6.7 ARCHITECTURAL STYLE AND PACKAGE DIAGRAM

The software architecture defines the structure of the software system in terms of the subsystems and their interrelationships. As pointed out at the beginning of this chapter, the software architecture is the primary artifact for conceptualizing, constructing, managing, and evolving the system under development. The implications of these are as follows:

1. *Conceptualization.* The architecture defines the overall structure of the system. Therefore, in subsequent development activities, the architecture helps the development team to think of the system in terms of its overall structure. Consider, for example, the N-tier architecture. It depicts the system as consisting of N layers of components, with each higher layer requesting services from the next lower layer. This overall picture of the system is referred to as the conceptualization of the system. The software architecture, once defined, helps the team to unify their conceptualization of the system structure.
2. *Construction.*The architecture facilitates the construction of the software system because it lets the team members know how to organize the software artifacts produced during the development process. Consider again the N-tier architecture for an interactive system. It has at least the following layers, listed from high to low:
    a. *The presentation layer.* This layer is responsible for presenting the graphical user interface and system responses to the users.
    b. *The business objects layer.* This layer is responsible for processing the business transactions represented by the use cases.
    c. *The persistence storage layer.* This layer consists of objects that provide database-related functions such as object storage and retrieval.
    d. *The network communication layer.* This layer provides network communication-related functions.

    The responsibilities of, and the dependencies between, the layers help in the construction process. For example, the task to develop a layer should be assigned to team members who possess the knowledge and skills to perform the work. The layers should be constructed according to their dependencies. That is, a lower layer should be developed before the next high layer so that the implementation and testing of the classes in the higher layer can proceed without needing to construct test stubs that simulate the unimplemented or untested lower-layer objects.

3. *Managing.* The software architecture provides an architectural view for organizing the software artifacts produced during the development process. For example, the software artifacts such as classes, web pages, and images created for an interactive system may be organized according to the layers of the N-tier architecture. Such an organization is usually referred to as the logical organization or logical architecture. It is logical, not physical, because the elements are not executables.
4. *Evolving.* The architecture provides a basis for evolving and expanding the system. For example, a library information system is an interactive system. Initially, the system is not designed to support interlibrary loan, probably due to budget limitations. Sometime later, the system is required to provide interlibrary loan capabilities. In this case, the N-tier architecture facilitates the evolution of the system by requiring the addition of a network communication layer.

To reap the benefits of the software architecture for the development activities, the team needs a way to organize the software artifacts that are produced during the development process. The UML package diagram provides a mechanism to achieve this. The notions and notations of a UML package diagram are shown in Figure 6.11(*a*).

EXAMPLE 6.1 To illustrate, suppose that a library information system is designed to use the N-tier architecture. The four layers of the architecture are as described in point 2 above: the presentation layer, the business objects layer, the database layer, and the network layer. The corresponding package diagram is displayed in Figure 6.11(*b*). The diagram shows that the library information system has four packages, each corresponding to a layer in the architecture. The GUI package owns four classes: Main, Main Frame, Checkout Dialog, and Return Dialog. Among these, the first two are public classes while the last two are private classes. The business package owns five classes: Checkout Controller, Return Controller, Loan, Document, and Patron. The first two are public and the last three are private. The GUI package imports the business package. This means the public classes of the business package–not the private classes– are imported. The database package owns only one class–Database Manager–which is imported to the business package. The classes of a package can be shown by using textual format or visual format. While the GUI, business, and database packages show the package names in the folder tabs, the network package shows its package name in the folder body. This is because the first three packages show the package contents while the network package does not show the content.

The package diagram in Figure 6.11(*b*) defines a logical organization or logical view of the classes of the library information system. During the development process, numerous classes and other software artifacts such as web pages and images are produced. Package diagrams help the team members understand which artifacts belong to which packages. Thus, the packages and the artifacts that they own can be checked into, or checked out from, a configuration management system (Chapter 22). The package hierarchy (wherein one package can own other packages) facilitates change control because the packages to be changed and the packages impacted can be identified at any

Notion	Semantics	Notation	Relationships
Package	A logical grouping of software artifacts including classes, other packages, and other software artifacts of interest.	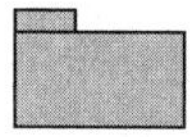	• A package may own software artifacts such as classes and other packages. • A package may import other packages.
import	A stereotyped relationship between two packages. The source package at the arrow tail imports the public elements of the destination package pointed to by the arrow head.	<<import>> - - - - - - ->	

(a) Package diagram notions and notations

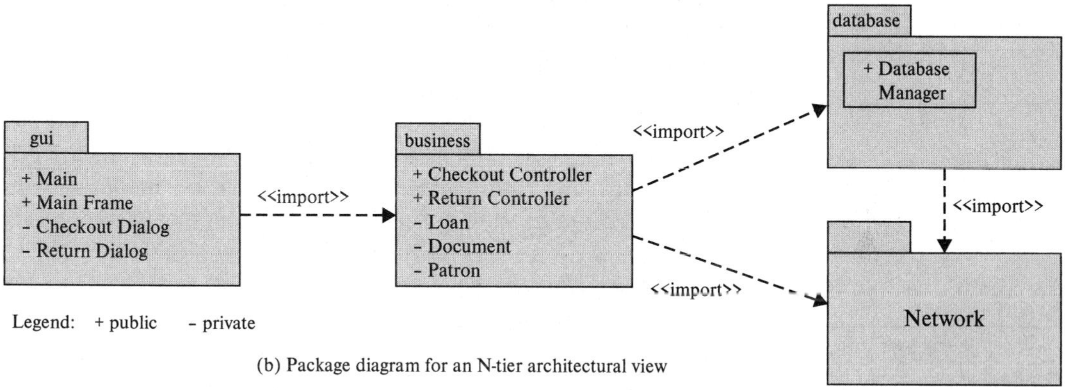

(b) Package diagram for an N-tier architectural view

FIGURE 6.11 Package diagram for a library information system

level of the hierarchy. Without such a logical organization, configuration management of the classes and other artifacts would be difficult.

6.8 GUIDELINES FOR ARCHITECTURAL DESIGN

Although they are already stated in the above steps, the following design guidelines are worth reiterating:

1. *Adapt an architectural style when possible.* Many applications can use or adapt an architectural style. This saves time and effort. Adapt an architectural style according to the type of subsystem under development.
2. *Apply software design principles.* As stated earlier, software design principles are the guiding rules for software design. They bring quality and desired features to architectural design. The design of a software architecture should strive for *design for change, separation of concerns, high cohesion, low coupling, information hiding, and keep it simple and stupid.*
3. *Apply design patterns.* Design patterns solve common design problems while codifying software design principles. Thus, applying patterns during architectural design saves time and effort as well as brings quality to the design. More importantly, patterns can be combined in innovative ways to solve challenging design problems. This is illustrated in Part V (Applying Situation-Specific Patterns).
4. *Check against design objectives and design principles.* The architectural design should be checked against design objectives such as hiding the database from

business objects, providing software fault tolerance, and maximizing performance, and the like. Similarly, the architectural design should be checked with design principles to ensure that desired design principles are followed.

5. *Iterate the steps if needed.* Architectural design has significant, long-lasting impact to software productivity and quality. The design process is a cognitive process. Therefore, it is worth the time to iterate the steps a few times to produce a good design.

6.9 ARCHITECTURAL DESIGN AND DESIGN PATTERNS

Design patterns are proven design solutions to commonly encountered design problems. As such, design patterns are widely used in architectural design and architectural styles. For example, the N-tier architecture shown in Figure 6.3(*b*) uses the *controller* pattern presented in Chapter 10 (Applying Responsibility-Assignment Patterns) to decouple presentation and business objects. The persistence framework presented in Part V applies several design patterns to accomplish a number of design objectives such as design for change, low coupling, high cohesion, separation of concerns, and designing "stupid objects."

Some design patterns are considered architectural styles. For example, the model-view-controller (MVC) pattern and the observer pattern are architectural styles. The MVC pattern consists of a data model, a controller, and a number of views. The controller decouples the views from the data model and allows the data to be displayed by using different views. The observer pattern is similar to the MVC pattern, but it does not have a controller. It consists of an observable and a number of observers. The observable is the data model in the MVC pattern. The observers are the views. The observable provides an interface for the observers to register themselves for events that are of interest to them. When such events take place, the observable notifies the observers.

Each pattern has a number of benefits and liabilities. If an architecture uses a pattern, then most of the time the benefits of the pattern are also benefits of the architecture. Patterns can be combined to mitigate the liabilities. For example, concurrent update to the observable may occur because an observer may not know the presence of other observers. This problem could be solved by combining the observer pattern with the proxy pattern, which controls the update to the observable.

Knowing the relationships between architectural design and design patterns as described above helps a developer understand the merits and liabilities of an architectural style. It also enables the developer to design architectures to serve the needs of specific applications.

6.10 APPLYING AGILE PRINCIPLES

During architectural design, the following agile values and agile principles should be applied:

GUIDELINE 6.1 *Value working software over comprehensive documentation.*

The architecture evolves during the iterations as feedback and changes are incorporated into the system. Although architectural design is important, overdocumenting the architecture must be avoided. Comprehensive documentation consumes valuable time and resources and pushes back the implementation activity. Often, the most appropriate architecture for the system is discovered during implementation. During this actual problem-solving process, the team increases its understanding of the problem and refines the solution. This in many cases changes or refines the architecture. Therefore, valuing working software over comprehensive documentation can improve the architectural design.

GUIDELINE 6.2 *Apply the 20/80 rule–that is, good enough is enough.*

There is no optimal architecture for a system because architectural design is a wicked problem–it satisfies all the properties of a wicked problem. That is, there is no stopping rule; one can always improve. However, to a certain point, the return for further improvement diminishes. Therefore, good enough is enough. For many real-world projects, a combination of several architectural styles and design patterns can be quickly selected and applied based on the types of the system and its subsystems. The architecture is then changed, refined, and improved during the iterations.

6.11 SUMMARY

This chapter presents the architectural design process and the importance of architectural design. The chapter also presents in detail five types of systems and their characteristics. These are interactive systems, event-driven systems, transformational systems, rule-based systems and persistence storage systems. A software system may include one or more of these systems as its subsystems. The design methods or techniques are different for different types of systems. In this chapter, the implication of type of system to the choice of design methods is discussed. This chapter also presents different software architectural styles and their merits and limitations. The architectural styles include the N-tier, client-server, main program and subroutine, event-driven, persistence framework, and other architectural styles. Also presented is the choice of an architectural style according to the type of system and/or subsystem under development. Software design principles are presented in this chapter. These include design for change, separation of concerns, information hiding, high cohesion, low coupling, and keep it simple and stupid. Software design principles guide the entire design process, not just architectural design.

6.12 CHAPTER REVIEW QUESTIONS

1. What is architectural design?
2. Why is architectural design important?
3. What is the architectural design process?
4. What is an architectural style?
5. What is the relationships between the types of system and the architectural styles?
6. What are software design principles?
7. How are software design principles applied to the design of the architectural styles?

6.13 EXERCISES

6.1 Construct a table with rows corresponding to the architectural styles in Figure 6.2, and columns corresponding to the design principles presented in this chapter. Fill in the entries to show which design principles are applied in which architectural styles.

6.2 For each architectural style listed in the previous exercise, briefly explain how it applies the design principles and what the benefits are.

6.3 In exercise 4.4, you produced the software requirements specification (SRS) for a calendar management system. In this exercise, do the following:

- **a.** Identify the type of system and briefly justify your answer.
- **b.** Produce an architectural design for the system.
- **c.** Specify the functionality and interface for each of the subsystems and components in the architectural design.
- **d.** Discuss which software design principles are applied, how they are applied, and the benefits of each of the principles. Also, indicate the potential problems, if any.

6.4 Do the following for the Study Abroad Management System (SAMS) presented in Chapter 4.

- **a.** Identify the type of system and briefly justify your answer.
- **b.** Identify an architectural style and produce an architectural design for the system.
- **c.** Specify the functionality and interface for each of the subsystems and components in the architectural design.
- **d.** Discuss which software design principles are applied in the design, how they are applied, and the benefits of applying each of the principles. Also point out the potential problems associated with the application of the design principles, if any.

6.5 Consider the Airport Baggage Handling System discussed in Chapter 3. The conveyor subsystem employs bar-code scanners and pushers to guide the pieces of luggage to travel toward their destinations on the conveyor belts. There is a software subsystem that works with these two types of devices. Determine the type of this subsystem. Note that the subsystem may involve more than one type of subsystem. Select the architectural style(s) to apply. Also, produce a sketch of the architectural design and specify the functionality for each of the subsystems and components.

6.6 In exercise 4.5 you produced the SRS for the web-based single-room reservation system. In this exercise, you are required to identify the type of system and sketch an architectural design for the system. Also, briefly specify the functionality for each of the subsystems and components in the architectural design.

part III

Modeling and Design of Interactive Systems

7 Chapter

Deriving Use Cases from Requirements

Key Takeaway Points

- A use case is a business process. It begins with an actor, ends with the actor, and accomplishes a business task for the actor.
- Use cases are derived from requirements and satisfy the requirements.
- Planning the development and deployment of use cases and subsystems to meet the customer's business needs and priorities.

Chapter 4 presents methods and techniques for requirements acquisition and specification. Requirements are capabilities that the system must deliver. Requirement statements are declarative sentences that state what capabilities the system must deliver, not how the system will deliver them. This gives the developer the freedom to design and implement the best software solution. However, due to the lack of business insight and domain knowledge, the best software solution from the developer's point of view may not meet the users' expectations.

Use cases offer a solution to this problem. Consider, for example, a library information system (LIS). One requirement may state that the LIS must allow a patron to check out documents. A use case derived from this requirement specifies how the system will interact with the patron to deliver the capability. In addition to this actor-system interaction part, a use case also involves a background processing part. For example, to check out a document, a Loan object must be created and saved in the database. The Document object and the Patron object must be updated and saved back to the database. Actor-system interaction modeling and design are presented in Chapter 8 and background processing or object interaction modeling is presented in Chapter 9. In this chapter, you will learn:

- How to derive use cases from requirements.
- How to specify a use case's scope, that is, when and where a use case begins and when it ends.
- How to visualize use cases and their relationships to actors and subsystems using UML use case diagrams.

7.1 WHAT IS AN ACTOR?

Software systems process information for intended applications. The system receives requests and input from users and delivers results to the users. In some cases, a software system may be embedded in a larger system, which may be a hardware-software system or consist of other subsystems. In these cases, the system under development also receives requests from and delivers results to hardware devices or other subsystems of the total system. Because the term "user" has traditionally been used to refer to human users, a neutral term with a broader scope is needed to refer to both human users and nonhuman users. This is introduced by the following definition.

Definition 7.1 An *actor* is a (business) role played by and on behalf of a set of (business) entities or stakeholders that are external to the system and interact with the system.

This definition indicates that an actor is a role played by some entities, not the entities themselves. The distinction is useful when an entity plays two or more roles at the same time. For example, a librarian checks out a book and handles the checkout transaction. Here, the person plays two roles, a librarian role as well as a patron role.

7.2 WHAT IS A USE CASE?

Users interact with the system to perform a certain business task. Often, the interaction follows a certain pattern. For example, to withdraw money from an automated teller machine (ATM), the bank customer inserts her or his ATM card, the ATM displays the login screen, the customer enters the pin number, the ATM displays the main menu, and so on. . . . Such a sequence of steps describes a business process, or how a user uses the system to carry out a business task. System development should focus on identifying such business processes, which is modeled by use cases, defined as follows:

Definition 7.2 A *use case* is a business process. It begins with an actor, ends with the actor, and accomplishes a business task for the actor.

Definition 7.2 captures four important attributes of a use case:

1. *A use case is a business process.* This is the most essential property of a use case. Consider an ATM application that allows a customer to deposit money, check balance, withdraw money, and transfer money between bank accounts. These suggest that there are four business processes: *Deposit Money, Withdraw Money, Check Balance*, and *Transfer Money*.
2. *A use case must begin with an actor or be initiated by an actor.* An ATM customer must insert an ATM card to begin the ATM business processes.

3. *A use case must end with the actor* so that the actor knows that the business process has completed successfully. For example, the *Deposit Money* business process ends with the ATM customer receiving the deposit slip. The *Check Balance* business process ends with the ATM customer pressing the OK button to confirm seeing the expected balance.
4. *A use case must accomplish a business task for the actor.* For example, *Withdraw Money* lets the ATM customer withdraw money from her or his account.

The above discussion indicates that *Deposit Money, Withdraw Money, Check Balance,* and *Transfer Money* possess the four attributes of a use case; therefore, they are use cases for the ATM application.

7.3 BUSINESS PROCESS, OPERATION, AND ACTION

A use case is a business process, not an operation or an action. Consider the ATM application again: one might think that "Get Balance from Database," "Contact Bank Server," and "Enter Password" are use cases. But a careful examination shows that they are not *business processes*; they are steps or operations of a business process. Consider, for example, "Enter Password." It is a step of the login process, which is a use case. "Get Balance from Database" is not a business process and does not begin with the actor. It is an operation of the *Check Balance* or *Withdraw Money* use case. To distinguish between business process, operation, and action, the following definitions are introduced:

Definition 7.3 A *business process* is a series of information processing steps that are necessary and sufficient for accomplishing a complete business task (with a specific business purpose).

Here, "accomplishing a *complete business task (with a specific business purpose)*" is essential because it distinguishes a business process from an operation or action.

Definition 7.4 An *operation* is a series of actions or instructions to accomplish a step of a business process.

An operation does not accomplish a business task. It only accomplishes a step of a business process. For example, "get balance from database" does not accomplish a business task, although it accomplishes part of a business task. Similarly, "enter pass-word" only accomplishes a step of the login process. Therefore, they are not use cases.

Definition 7.5 An *action* is an indivisible act, movement, or instruction that is performed during the performance of an operation.

Figure 7.1 shows examples of use case, step, operation, and action.

Application	Use Case	Steps/Operations	Actions
Text Editor	Edit Report	Open Report	Click File, select Open, navigate to directory, select file, click OK button.
		Make Changes Add texts Delete texts Modify texts	 Place curse at where to insert text, and type texts. Highlight texts to be deleted, and press Delete key. Highlight texts to be replaced, and type new texts.
		Save Report	Click File, select Save.
		Exit Editor	Click File, select Exit.
Class Diagram Editor	Edit Diagram	Open Diagram	Click File, select Open, navigate to directory, select file, click OK button.
		Make Changes Add class Delete class Modify class	 Right click in canvas, select Add Class, fill in class information, click OK. Click a class to select it, press Delete key, press OK button to confirm. Double click a class, change class information in the pop-up dialog, click OK.
		Save Diagram	Click File, select Save.
		Exit Editor	Click File, select Exit.
ATM	Deposit Money / Withdraw Money	Start	Insert card.
		Authenticate	Enter password, press Enter key.
		Do transaction	Select transaction type, enter deposit/withdraw amount, insert cash/take cash, take deposit/withdraw slip.
		Finish	Press Exit key, take ejected card

FIGURE 7.1 Example use cases, operations and actions

EXAMPLE 7.1

Consider the design and implementation of a graphical editor for drawing UML class diagrams. The editor allows the user to create new diagrams, save diagrams, delete diagrams, and edit diagrams. What are the use cases for the editor?

Solution: The application domain of the editor is *software tool/graphical editor/ UML class diagram editor*. At first glance, one may identify "create new diagram," "save diagram," "delete diagram," and "edit diagram" as use cases. Determining whether these are use cases needs careful analysis. Consider "create diagram" first. The question to ask: Is it a business process? If so, then what is its business purpose? Does the user create the diagram just for the sake of creating it? Normally, the user creates a new diagram; performs editing operations such as adding, changing, and deleting classes and relationships; and then saves the diagram. Therefore, the business process should be "edit a diagram." "Create new diagram" and "save diagram" are operations of the "edit a diagram" use case.

However, an analyst may consider that "create new diagram" and "save diagram" are business processes. There is nothing wrong with this because different analysts may perceive the world differently. The question is which one is better. To determine this, let us assume that "create new diagram," "save diagram," and "edit diagram" are use cases. Because incremental delivery allows the team to deliver some use cases before the other, let us assume that "create new diagram" is delivered first. In this case, the user won't be able to do anything that is meaningful, such as editing the diagram. This means that "create new diagram" should not be considered a use case. Similarly, "save diagram" is not a use case either.

A user can edit a new diagram or an existing diagram. These two cases may be treated as two separate use cases: (1) edit a new diagram and (2) edit an existing diagram. Alternatively, these two cases may be treated as options of the edit diagram use case. The KISS principle suggests that it is better to treat them as two use cases.

To edit a class diagram, the user may add, update, or delete classes or relationships. These must not be identified as use cases because they are not business processes; rather, they are operations of the *Edit Class Diagram* use case.

EXAMPLE 7.2 Referring to Example 7.1, what are the actions that need to be performed to add a class to a class diagram?

Solution: To add a class to a class diagram, the following actions are performed:

1. The user right-clicks in a clear area of the drawing area (called the canvas).
2. The system shows a pop-up menu that includes Add Class as one of the options.
3. The user selects the Add Class option.
4. The system shows a dialog box for the user to enter information about the class to be added.
5. The user enters the information and clicks the OK button.
6. The system verifies the information entered and draws the class (or displays an error message).

7.4 STEPS FOR DERIVING USE CASES FROM REQUIREMENTS

As discussed previously, use cases refine requirements and specify a design of system behavior. As such, use cases should be derived from requirements and satisfy the requirements. This section presents the steps for deriving use cases and subsystems from the requirements and allocating them to iterations. There are six steps:

Step 1. Deriving use cases, actors, and subsystems. In this step, verb-noun phrases representing business processes are identified from the requirements. Also derived are actors that use the use cases and subsystems that contain the use cases.

Step 2. Constructing use case diagrams. In this step, the use cases, actors, subsystems, and their relationships are visualized using UML use case diagrams.

Step 3. Specifying use case scopes. In this step, the scope of each use case is specified, producing a high-level use case, which specifies when and where the use case begins and when it ends.

Step 4. Producing a Requirement-Use Case Traceability Matrix. In this step, a Requirement-Use Case Traceablity Matrix is produced to show the correspondence/relevance between the use cases and the requirements.

Step 5. Reviewing use case specifications. In this step, the use case diagrams, use case scopes, requirement–use case traceability matrix, and use case–iteration allocation matrix are reviewed.

Step 6. Allocating use cases to iterations. In this step, the use cases are assigned to iterations according to use case priorities, their dependences and the team's capacity.

7.4.1 Deriving Use Cases, Actors, and Subsystems

To identify use cases, actors, and subsystems, the team members work together and read through the requirements one at a time. They look for or infer domain-specific verb-noun phrases that represent domain-specific business processes. Focus is on top-level requirements such as R1, R2, . . . because they tend to specify business processes to automate. Lower-level requirements tend to describe steps of business processes as refinements of top-level requirements. A verb-noun phrase so identified is a use case if the answers to all of the following questions are yes.

1. Is it a (complete) domain-specific business process? If it is only an operation or an action, then the answer is no.
2. Does it begin with an actor?
3. Does it end with the actor?
4. Does it accomplish a business task for the actor?

If the verb-noun phrase is a use case, then the team members also identify the actors and the system/subsystem that contains the use case. To identify the actors, look for or infer nouns and noun phrases that represent business roles played by external entities that initiate the use case, or for which the business task is performed. To identify the system or subsystem that contains the use cases, look for or infer nouns and noun phrases that represent a system, subsystem, or aspect of the business to which the use case belongs. Note that the requirements may not always show explicitly, exactly, or literally a verb-noun phrase. For example, "startup system" and "shutdown system" are often abbreviated to "startup" and "shutdown" in requirements specification documents. In some cases, the team may need to infer the business processes from the requirements and then derive the use cases. Fortunately, if the requirements specification is written properly, then the derivation of use cases is not difficult.

GUIDELINE 7.1 Use cases should be derived from and satisfy functional requirements.

GUIDELINE 7.2 Use cases may also be derived from nonfunctional requirements (e.g., security requirements).

GUIDELINE 7.3 Carefully select the verb-noun phrases to communicate exactly what the use cases will accomplish for the actors.

EXAMPLE 7.3 Derive use cases from the following requirements for a library information system (LIS):

R1. The LIS must allow a patron to check out documents.

R2. The LIS must allow a patron to return documents.

Solution: Figure 7.2 shows how use cases, actors, and subsystems are identified, where the dog-eared notes are UML notation for comments. The decision table illustrates how to determine whether a verb-noun phrase is a use case. For example, it indicates that "Checkout Document" and "Return Document" are use cases because the answers to the four questions are positive. The table also shows the requirements that derive the use cases. "Allow a Patron" is not a use case because all of the answers are no, and one negative answer is sufficient to conclude that it is not a use case. Because of this, the three dashes ("-") in the table mean indifference or "do not matter." Thus, the two requirements produce the following use cases, actors, and subsystems:

UC1. Checkout Document (Actor: Patron, System: LIS)

UC2. Return Document (Actor: Patron, System: LIS)

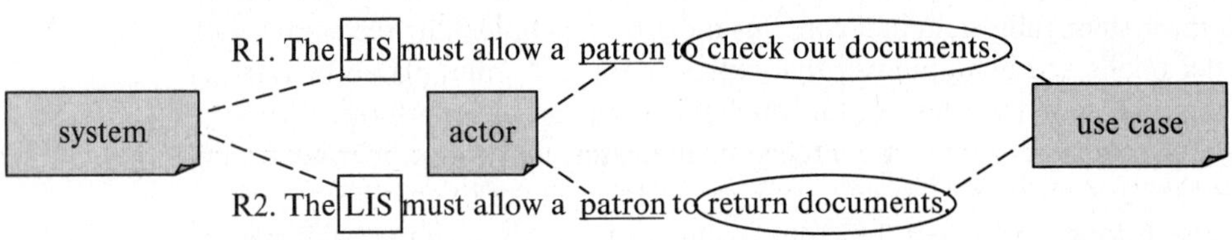

Rqmt	Verb-Noun Phrase	Is it a domain-specific business process?	Does it begin w/ an actor?	Does it end w/the actor?	Does it accomplish a business task for the actor?	Is it a use case?	Actor	Sub-system
R1	Checkout Documents	Y	Y	Y	Y	Y	Patron	LIS
R2	Return Documents	Y	Y	Y	Y	Y	Patron	LIS
R2	Allow a Patron	N	-	-	-	N	NA	NA

FIGURE 7.2 Identifying use cases for LIS

EXAMPLE 7.4

The Office of International Education (OIE) of a university wants to develop a web-based Study Abroad Management System (SAMS). The following are three of the functional requirements:

R1. SAMS must provide a search capability for overseas exchange programs using a variety of search criteria.
R2. SAMS must provide a hierarchical display of the search results to facilitate navigation from a high-level summary to details about an overseas exchange program.

R3. SAMS must allow students to submit online applications for overseas exchange programs.

Identify use cases, actors, and subsystems from these functional requirements.

Solution: Figure 7.3 shows how use cases, actors, and subsystems are identified. The verb-noun phrase representing a business process is not obvious in R1. In this case, some inference is needed. Basically, R1 states that SAMS must allow users to search for (overseas exchange) programs. Thus, the use case is "search for programs." Similarly, "display program detail" is derived from R2. One cannot literally identify the actors from R1 and R2. In this case, the requirements are examined carefully to infer the actors. It seems that every web user can use the search and view program detail functions; therefore, the actors for these two use cases are web users, which include students as well as OIE staff. From R3, one can identify Student as the actor for the *Submit Online Application* use case.

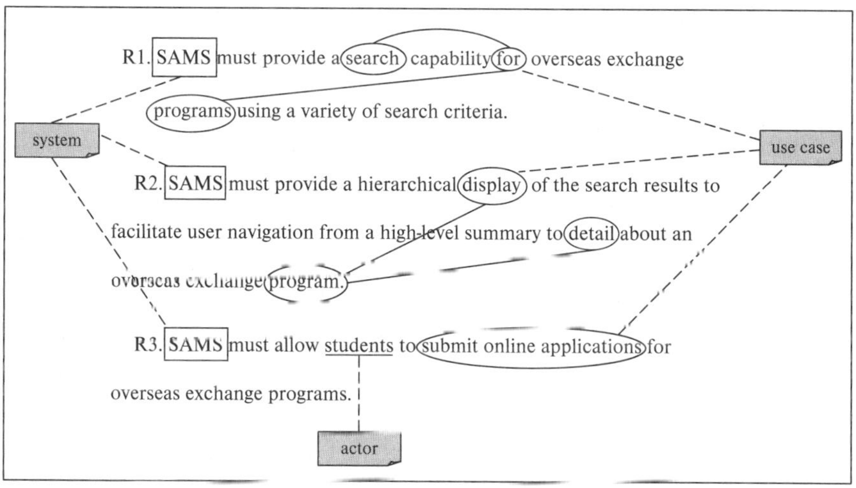

FIGURE 7.3 Identifying use cases for SAMS

In summary, the use cases derived from above requirements are:

UC1. Search for Programs (Actor: Web User, System: SAMS)
UC2. Display Program Detail (Actor: Web User, System: SAMS)
UC3. Submit Online Application (Actor: Student, System: SAMS)

This example illustrates that not every requirement clearly and literally shows the verb-noun phrase that indicates a use case, the actor, or the system; inference is required to derive them from the context. Note that "provide search capability" and "facilitate user" are not use cases because the answers to the four questions are not yes.

EXAMPLE 7.5 Which of the following are not use cases and why?

1. Press the Submit Button
2. Search a Linked List
3. Process Data
4. Query Database
5. Startup System

Solution: These phrases are analyzed as follows:

1. "Press the Submit Button" is not a use case because it is not a business process. It is an action of a use case.
2. "Search a Linked List" is not a use case. It is a process in the computer science domain.
3. "Process Data" is not a use case. It is too general, hence, it cannot be clearly associated with a business process. Who is the actor? What is the business task? These questions cannot be answered.
4. "Query Database" is not a use case. It is a database operation, not a business process.
5. "Startup System" is a use case. At first glance, one might think that it is too general, but in fact it is not. The specific system to be started is implicit. For example, it could have been *Startup LIS System, Startup SAMS*, and the like. As a general principle, every system needs a startup use case and a shutdown use case.

There is a simple test for determining whether a verb-noun phrase is domain specific. If the verb-noun phrase cannot be found or is not valid in a different domain, then it is domain specific; else, it is not. In Example 7.1, we identified the verb-noun phrase "checkout document." To determine whether it is domain specific, we see whether it can be found in a different domain, say retailing. The answer is not; therefore, it is domain specific. In Example 7.4, we identified "facilitate user." But this verb-noun phrase can be found in numerous applications in many domains; therefore, it is not domain specific.

Partitioning Use Cases to Form Subsystems

When a system is developed from scratch, the requirements often refer to the system as a whole and mention no other subsystems. In this case, all the use cases identified in the last section are assigned to the system. Therefore, we need to partition the use cases according to their functionality and form subsystems based on the partitions. The goal is to form subsystems that exhibit high functional cohesion, that is, the use cases of each subsystem should exhibit a core functionality. Moreover, no subsystem contains a large number of use cases so that each subsystem is easy to design, implement, test, and maintain. Use cases are partitioned according to the following rules:

Role-based partition. Use cases for a common actor tend to exhibit role-based functionality. This is called *role-based* partition (of use cases). Examples are *Deposit Money, Withdraw Money, Transfer Money*, and *Check Balance*–all of these have bank customer as a common actor. Use cases for a system administrator tend to perform system administration tasks such as *Startup (System), Shutdown (System), Edit Configuration*, and so on.

Note that role-based partition may produce partitions that still contain many use cases. This can happen if the actor can execute many use cases. Often, the use cases of a large partition can be further divided using the following rules or according to their functionalities.

Communicational partition. Use cases that process a common object tend to perform object-specific tasks. This is called *communicational* partition because the use cases communicate via the common object they process. Consider, for example, a graphical editor for UML diagrams. The use cases may include *New Project, Edit Project (properties), Open Project, Close Project, Delete Project, Edit New Diagram*, and *Edit Existing Diagram*. These use cases can be partitioned into two sets of use cases, one dealing with projects and the other dealing with diagrams.

Type-based partition. Sometimes, the object that modifies the noun of the use case name may be used to partition the use cases. Consider, for example, a UML diagram editor that includes use cases for editing various types of UML diagrams such as *use case* diagrams, *class* diagrams, and *sequence* diagrams. These use cases can be partitioned by the diagram type, resulting in subsystems that process use case diagrams, class diagrams, and sequence diagrams, respectively. This is called *type-based partition*.

In addition to the above, the inheritance relationship between actors can be utilized to rearrange the use cases among subsystems:

1. To reduce the number of use cases of a subsystem, use cases for an actor subclass can be separated from use cases for the actor superclass to form two subsystems. This is in fact role-based partition applied in the inheritance context.
2. Use cases for an actor subclass can be merged with use cases for an actor superclass to reduce the number of subsystems if desired.

EXAMPLE 7.6 Partition the following use cases of the Study Abroad Management System to form appropriate subsystems:

UC01. Search for Programs (Actor: Web User, System: SAMS)
UC02. Display Program Detail (Actor: Web User, System: SAMS)
UC03. Submit Online Application (Actor: Student, System: SAMS)
UC04. Login (Actor: Student, System: SAMS)
UC05. Logout (Actor: Student, System: SAMS)
UC06. Edit Online Application (Actor: Student, System: SAMS)
UC07. Check Application Status (Actor: Student, System: SAMS)
UC08. Submit Recommendation (Actor: Faculty, System: SAMS)
UC09. Approve Course Equivalency Form (Actor: Advisor, System: SAMS)
UC10. List Applications (Actor: Staff, System: SAMS)
UC11. Create User Account (Actor: Admin, System: SAMS)
UC12. Delete User Account (Actor: Admin, System: SAMS)
UC13. Update User Account (Actor: Admin, System: SAMS)
UC14. Edit System Settings (Actor: Admin, System: SAMS)
UC15. Login/Staff (Actor: Staff, System: SAMS)
UC16. Logout/Staff (Actor: Staff, System: SAMS)
UC17. Edit Personal Preferences (Actor: Account User, System: SAMS)
UC18. Add Program (Actor: Staff, System: SAMS)
UC19. Delete Program (Actor: Staff, System: SAMS)
UC20. Update Program (Actor: Staff, System: SAMS)
UC21. Upload Programs (Actor: Staff, System: SAMS)
UC22. Submit Feedback (Actor: Student, System: SAMS)
UC23. View Feedback (Actor: Web User, System: SAMS)
UC24. Startup System (Actor: Admin, System: SAMS)
UC25. Shutdown System (Actor: Admin, System: SAMS)

Solution: As listed, SAMS has 25 use cases. These use cases are not closely related. Therefore, the functional cohesion of the system is low. The use case diagram that displays all these use cases will appear very complex and difficult to comprehend. Role-based partition is applied to partition the use cases. This results in Figure 7.4.

EXAMPLE 7.7 Partition the following use cases

UC1. New Project (Actor: User, System: GED)
UC2. Edit Project (Actor: User, System: GED)
UC3. Open Project (Actor: User, System: GED)
UC4. Close Project (Actor: User, System: GED)
UC5. Delete Project (Actor: User, System: GED)
UC6. Edit New Diagram (Actor: User, System: GED)
UC7. Edit Existing Diagram (Actor: User, System: GED)

SAMS/Admin, Actor: Admin UC11. Create User Account UC12. Delete User Account UC13. Update User Account UC14. Edit System Settings UC24. Startup System UC25. Shutdown System	SAMS/Student, Actor: Student UC03. Submit Online Application UC04. Logon System UC05. Logoff System UC06. Edit Online Application UC07. Check Application Status UC22. Submit Feedback	SAMS/Staff, Actor: Staff UC10. List Applications UC15. Logon System UC16. Logoff System UC18. Add Program UC19. Delete Program UC20. Update Program UC21. Upload Programs
SAMS/Account User, Actor: Account User UC17. Edit Personal Preference	SAMS/Reference, Actor: Faculty, Advisor UC08. Submit Recommendation UC09. Approve Course Equivalency Form	SAMS/Web User, Actor: Web User UC01. Search for Programs UC02. Display Program Detail UC23. View Feedback

FIGURE 7.4 Subsystems identified by actors

GED/Project Manager	GED/Diagram Manager
UC1: New Project UC2: Edit Project UC3: Open Project UC4: Close Project UC5: Delete Project UC6: Edit Diagram	UC6: Edit New Diagram UC7: Edit Existing Diagram

FIGURE 7.5 Subsystems resulting from communicational partition

Solution: The subsystem and actor components of these use cases are the same. Applying communicational partition produces two partitions, as displayed in Figure 7.5.

7.4.2 Constructing Use Case Diagrams

Textual description of use cases, actors, and subsystems works well only for small applications that involve only a few use cases, actors, and subsystems. Many real-world applications involve many use cases, actors, and subsystems. Software development for large complex systems requires a way to organize and visualize this information. UML use case diagram fulfills this need.

UML Use Case Diagram

Definition 7.6 A *use case diagram* is a UML *behavioral diagram* that depicts the following:

- Use cases of a system or subsystem.
- Actors that use the use cases.
- The system or subsystem boundary.
- Inheritance relationships between actors.
- Relationships between use cases.

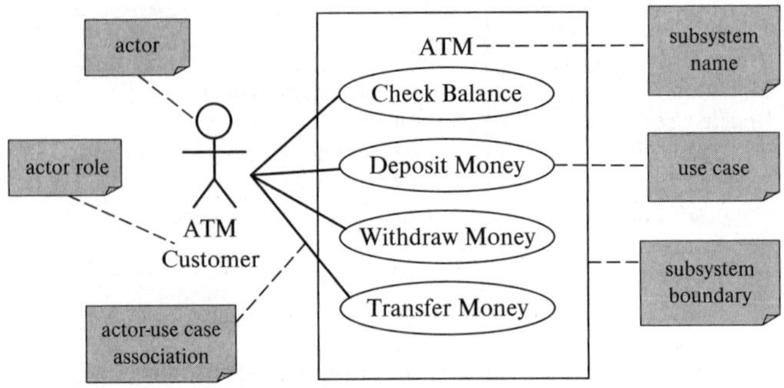

FIGURE 7.6 Use case diagram for the ATM example

Figure 7.6 shows a use case diagram for an ATM application. The use case diagram says that the ATM has four use cases. The actor of these use cases is the ATM Customer. The ATM Customer uses these use cases to accomplish four business tasks: Check Balance, Deposit Money, Withdraw Money, and Transfer Money.

Notions and Notations for Use Case Diagram

Notion and notation are closely related concepts. Notations are symbols proposed for a language to represent modeling concepts or notions. Notions are the underlying concepts or meaning of the modeling constructs or notations. Unfortunately, many UML beginners learn only the notations, not the underlying notions, resulting in beautifully drawn but meaningless diagrams. For this reason, both notions and notations for use case diagrams are shown in Figure 7.7. The student should consult the table from time to time to ensure that the notations are used with their intended meaning.

EXAMPLE 7.8 Depict use case diagrams for the use cases of the web-based SAMS in Example 7.4.

Solution: The use cases, actors, and subsystems are already identified in Example 7.4. It is relatively easy to convert these into a use case diagram, as shown in Figure 7.8.

A use case diagram should show the subsystem boundary. Doing so has a number of advantages. By examining what the use cases accomplish, the cohesion of the subsystem is assessed–that is, the use cases should exhibit a core functionality rather than unrelated functionalities. One can identify mission-critical subsystems, which should be developed and deployed as early as possible so these subsystems can be tested early and more often. One can determine whether to build the subsystem from scratch or reuse a *commercial off-the-shelf (COTS)* component.

Showing Actor Inheritance Relationships

Definition 7.7 *Inheritance* is a binary relation between two concepts such that one concept is a generalization (or specialization) of the other.

Notion	Meaning/Semantics	Notation
Use case	A use case is a named business process that begins with an actor, ends with the actor, and accomplishes a business task for the actor.	use case name
Actor	An actor is a role played by and on behalf of a set of business entities or stakeholders that are external to the system and interact with the system.	role name
System/subsystem boundary	System/subsystem boundary encloses use cases and depicts the capabilities of the system/subsystem.	system name
Association between actors and use cases	An association between an actor and a use case indicates that the actor uses the use case.	————
Inheritance	A binary relationship between two concepts such that one is a generalization (or specialization) of the other.	Pointing from specialized concept to generalized concept.
Extension relationship between use cases	A binary relationship between two use cases such that one can continue the business process of the other.	- - - - - - - - -> <<extend>> From extension use case to extended use case
Inclusion relationship between use cases	A binary relationship between two use cases such that one includes the other as a part of its business process.	- - - - - - - - -> <<include>> From including use case to included use case

FIGURE 7.7 Notions and notations for use case diagram

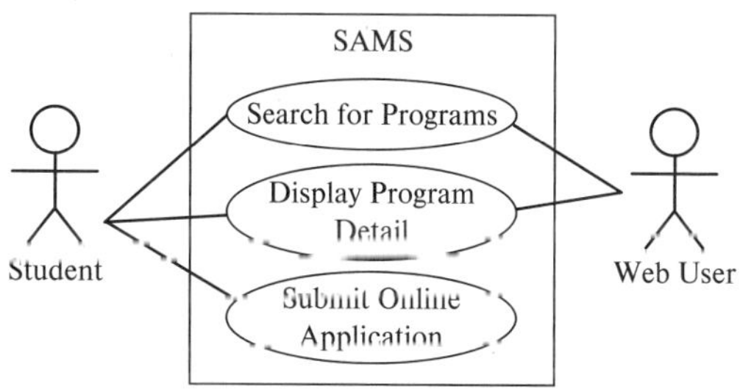

FIGURE 7.8 Use case diagram for SAMS

The inheritance relationship is also called IS-A relationship because every instance of the specialized concept is an instance of the generalized concept. Thus, the behavior and relationships of the parent class are also the behavior and relationships of the child class. Steps for identifying inheritance relationships are presented in domain modeling in Chapter 5. Exploring the inheritance relationships between actors can simplify a use case diagram. Figure 7.9(a) is a use case diagram without using

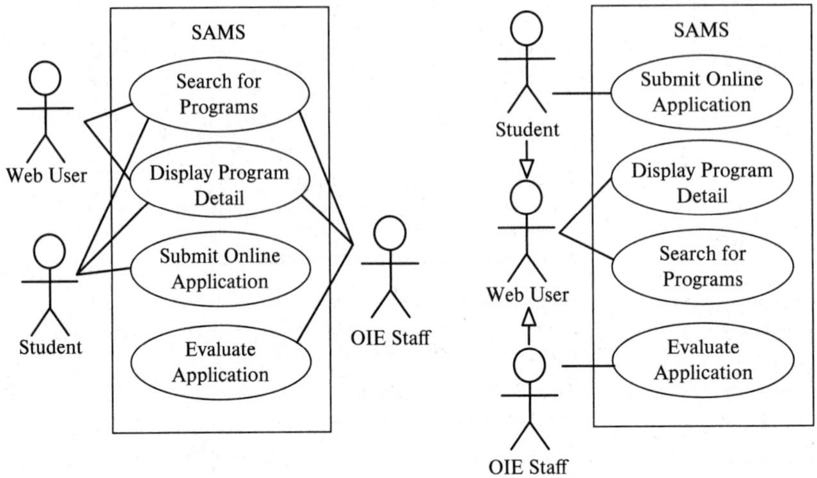

(a) Use case diagram without using actor inheritance

(b) Use case diagram using actor inheritance

FIGURE 7.9 Using actor inheritance to simplify use case diagrams

actor inheritance and Figure 7.9(*b*) uses actor inheritance. We can apply inheritance to simplify a use case diagram because the association relationships for the parent actor are also association relationships of the child actor.

Showing Relationships between Use Cases

This section presents relationships between use cases. Beginners should skip this section because showing relationships between use cases is not always required. Beginners often misunderstand the relationships and misuse them in modeling. They are presented here because they are used in some cases.

In OO programming, inheritance relationships exist between object classes. Inheritance relationships also exist between use cases. It can be used to show alternate business processes to accomplish a business task. As illustrated in Figure 7.10, the *Deposit Funds* use case for a brokerage application can be accomplished by either one

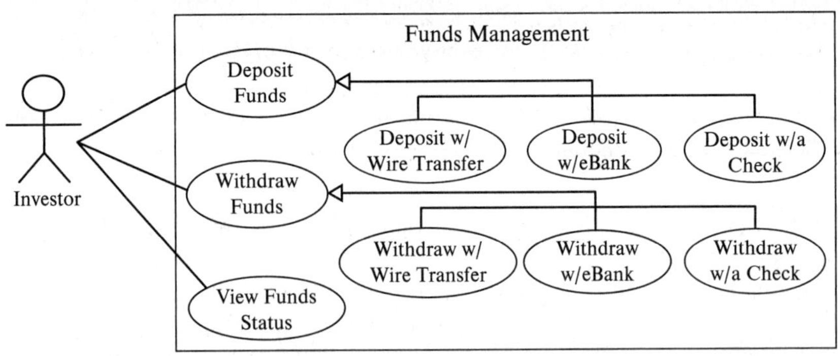

FIGURE 7.10 Showing alternative processes with use case inheritance

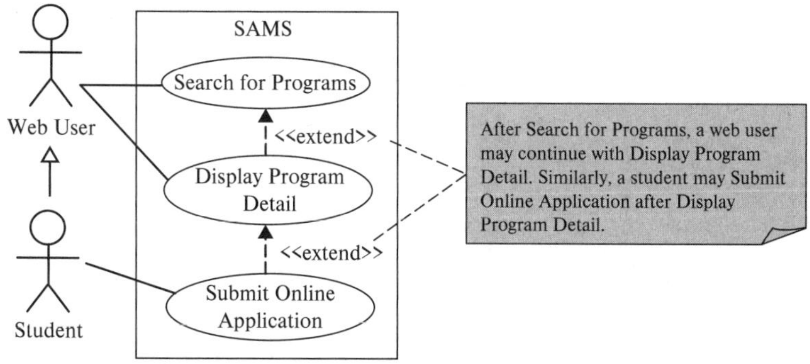

FIGURE 7.11 Extend relationship between use cases

of the following use cases: *Deposit w/Wire Transfer*, *Deposit w/a Check*, and *Deposit w/eBank*. Similarly, *Withdraw Funds* can also be accomplished by either one of three use cases.

Use cases are business processes. The execution of one business process may continue with the execution of another business process. In the web-based SAMS, a student may want to *Display Program Detail* for one of the programs listed by the *Search for Programs* use case. The student may decide to *Submit Online Application* after viewing the details of an overseas exchange program. These examples illustrate the extend relationship between use cases (see Figure 7.11). That is, the actor may optionally choose to extend the business process of a use case with the business process of another use case.

Note that in these cases, the student may continue with *Display Program Detail* after *Search for Programs*, but the student is not required to do so. Similarly, the student may choose not to continue with the *Submit Online Application* use case after viewing the program detail. That is, the extend relationship cannot be used to express that the execution of one use case requires prior execution of another use case. As one can see, showing the extend relationships is not much different from not showing them. If the relationships are not shown, then the student still can do Display Program Detail as continuation of Search for Programs. Similarly, the student still can Submit Online Application as continuation of Display Program Detail. Following the keep it simple and stupid principle, we recommend not to show the extend relationships unless it is absolutely necessary.

A business process may include another business process. So may use cases. Consider, for example, a *Reset Password* use case and a *Change Password* use case. If a user forgot his password, he uses *Reset Password*. After authentication, the user is required to change the temporary password. In this case, the *Reset Password* use case includes the *Change Password* use case, as shown in Figure 7.12.

GUIDELINE 7.4 Avoid showing the following:

- Many use cases in one diagram.
- Many use case diagrams each containing only one use case.
- Many relationships between use cases.
- Overly complex use case diagrams.

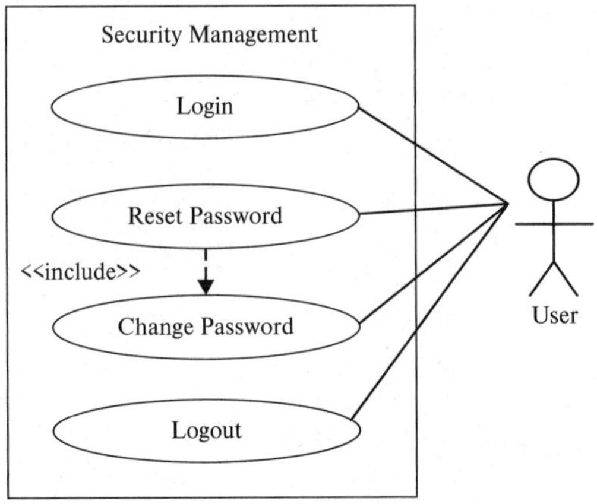

FIGURE 7.12 Showing use case include relationship

Figure 7.13 shows an overly complex use case diagram that should be avoided.

GUIDELINE 7.5 Carefully partition the use cases into groups of use cases that are closely related.

See Section 7.4.1 for some partition techniques. As an example, applying role-based partition to the diagram in Figure 7.13 produces the diagram in Figure 7.14. This significantly reduces the complexity of the use case diagrams while at the same time improving the functional cohesion of the subsystems. Note in Figure 7.14, a forward slash ("/") is used to show the subordinate relationship between subsystems. For example, "SAMS/Staff" and "SAMS/Student" denote the Staff subsystem and the Student subsystem of the SAMS system.

GUIDELINE 7.6 Show only use cases and actors that are relevant to a subsystem or aspect.

GUIDELINE 7.7 Provide a meaningful name for each subsystem based on the subsystem's functionality.

GUIDELINE 7.8 Use actor inheritance to reduce the number of actor–use case links in a use case diagram (as illustrated in Figure 7.9).

GUIDELINE 7.9 Actor–use case relationships are always association relationships.

GUIDELINE 7.10 Only use cases and their relationships can be shown within the system boundary.

Figure 7.15 shows two incorrect use case diagrams. One of the diagrams incorrectly places the actor inside the system boundary. The other diagram incorrectly includes a database inside the system boundary.

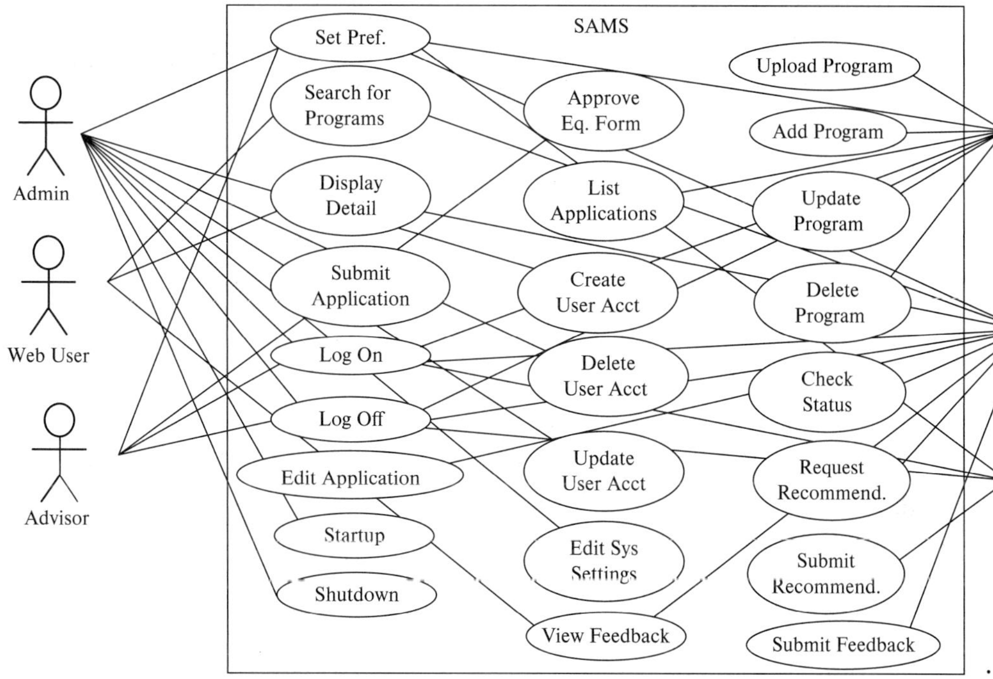

FIGURE 7.13 Overly complex diagram to avoid

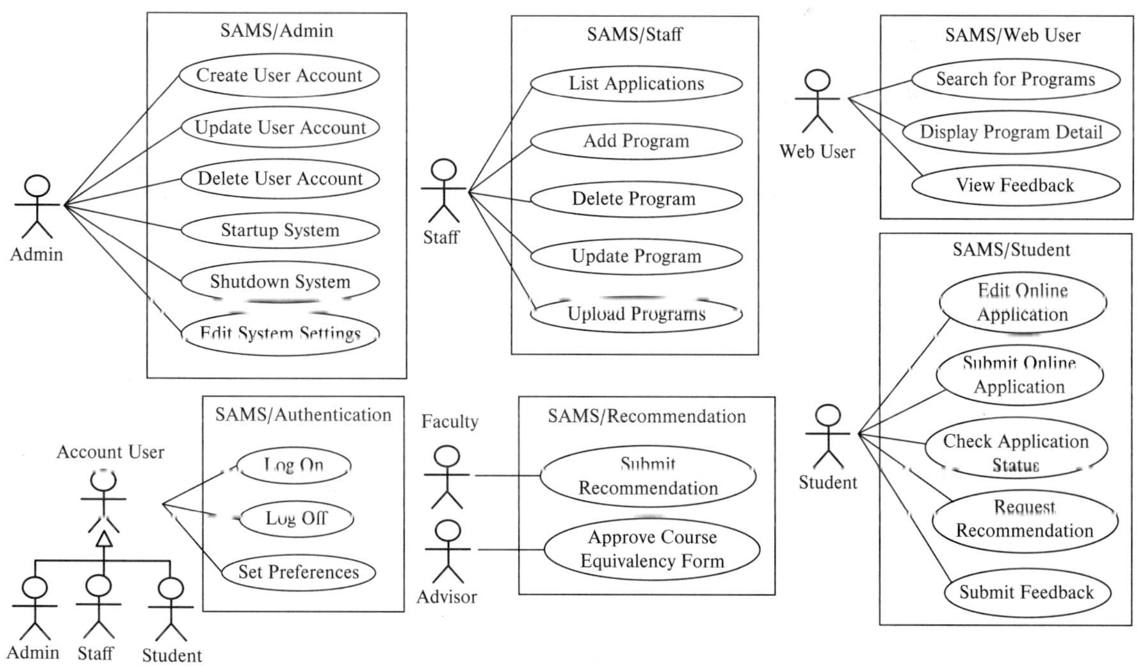

FIGURE 7.14 Role-based partition reduces complexity, improves cohesion

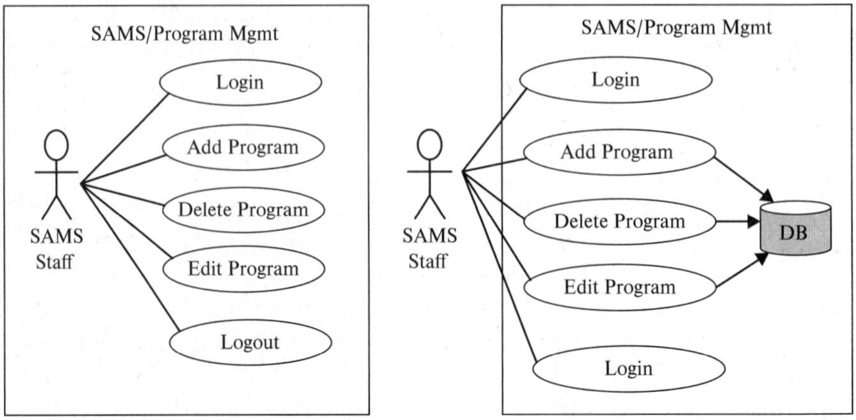

(a) Incorrect–actors must be outside of system boundary

(b) Incorrect–only use cases and use case relationships can be in system boundary

FIGURE 7.15 Incorrectly drawn use case diagrams

7.4.3 Specify Use Case Scopes

Systems development in general is a wicked problem (see Section 2.4). One property of a wicked problem is that *there is no stopping rule–you can always do it better*. Think about how many occasions you have sacrificed your holidays or sleep hours to improve on your design and implementation up until the last minute. Therefore, the team needs to know when to stop. High-level use case provides a solution. A high-level use case is a refinement, or a more detailed description, of a use case. To distinguish, the use case that is referred to by the verb-noun phrase is called an *abstract use case*. This is because the verb-noun phrase abstractly specifies the functionality, or business process, of the use case. For example, "checkout document" is an abstract specification of a business process of a library. According to Definition 7.2, a use case must begin with an actor and end with the actor. But when and where does the use case begin? And when does the use case end? A high-level use case provides the answers:

Definition 7.8 *A high-level use case* specifies when and where a use case begins and when it ends. In other words, it specifies the use case scope.

The specification of use case scopes in effect defines the stopping rule. For each use case, three decisions are made:

1. When does the use case begin? That is, what is the *actor action* that causes a stimulus or a system event to be generated and delivered to the software system being developed? For example, an ATM user *inserts an ATM card*, a SAMS user *clicks the "Search for Programs" link*, or a caller *picks up the handset*.
2. Where does the actor action take place? For example, a SAMS user clicks the "Search for Programs" link on *the SAMS home page*. If the SAMS home page is not specified, then the SAMS user would not know where to find the "Search for Programs" link. The programmer would not know where to include the search link.

3. When does the use case end? This involves the specification of explicit or implicit *actor action* to acknowledge the *completion* of the use case. For example, the caller *hears the ring tone* when the *Initiate Call* use case ends successfully. The web user *sees a listing of overseas exchange programs* when *Search for Programs* use case completes. As an example that requires an explicit actor action, consider an ATM application. The ATM customer may be required to *press the OK button* to confirm seeing a "transaction completed successfully" message.

Use case scopes are specified in two declarative sentences:

1. The first sentence is formulated as "this use case begins with (TUCBW)" followed by the actor performing the actor action and where the actor action takes place. Always use third-person, simple present tense.
2. The second sentence is formulated as "this use case ends with (TUCEW)" followed by the actor explicitly or implicitly acknowledging that the use case accomplishes the intended business task (for the actor). Again, always use third-person, simple present tense.

EXAMPLE 7.9

Specify high-level use cases for (1) *Search for Programs* and (2) *Display Program Detail* for the SAMS web-based application.

Solution: The high-level use cases are:

UC1. Search for Programs
TUCBW a web user clicking the Search for Programs link on the SAMS home page.

TUCEW the web user seeing a tabular listing of programs satisfying her or his search criteria.

UC2. Display Program Detail
TUCBW a web user clicking the View Detail link of a program in the tabular listing of programs.
TUCEW the web user seeing the program detail for the selected program.

EXAMPLE 7.10

Specify high-level use cases for (1) *Initiate Call* and (2) *Receive Call* use cases of a telephone system.

Solution: The high-level use cases are:

UC1. Initiate Call
TUCBW the caller picking up the handset from the phone base.
TUCEW the caller hearing the ring tone.

UC2. Receive Call
TUCBW the callee (hears the ring tone and) picking up the handset from the phone base.
TUCEW either the caller or the callee putting the handset on the hook.

GUIDELINE 7.11 High-level use case specifications should end with what the actor wants to accomplish.

Guideline 7.11 lets the development team focus on the design, implementation, and testing of use cases that will accomplish what the actors expect.

GUIDELINE 7.12 A use case should accomplish exactly one business task for the actor (functional cohesion).

For example, "Login and Place Trade" should be two use cases: *Login* and *Place Trade*. Similarly, "Check Balance and Inventory" should be *Check Balance* and *Check Inventory*.

GUIDELINE 7.13 High-level use cases should not specify background processing activities.

This guideline supports two software design principles–*keep it simple and stupid*, and *separation of concerns*, which were described in Chapter 6. A high-level use case is meant to specify only the use case scope or when and where it begins and when it ends.

7.4.4 Producing a Requirement–Use Case Traceability Matrix

The fact that a use case is derived from, or relevant to, a given requirement is entered into a Requirement-Use Case Traceability Matrix (RUTM). Figure 7.16 shows a dummy RUTM, where the rows represent requirements and the columns represent use cases. The second column shows the priorities of the requirements, with 1 being the highest and 5 the lowest. The priorities may have been obtained during the requirements phase. If a use case is derived from, or relevant to, a requirement, then the corresponding requirement-use case entry is checked. The UC Priority row shows the priorities of use cases. It is the highest priority of the associated requirements.

Requirement	Priority	UC1	UC2	UC3	UC4	UC5	UC6	UC7	UC8
R01	1	x							
R02	4		x			x		x	
R03	3					x			
R04	5		x				x		
R05	5			x			x		x
R06	1			x					
R07	2				x				
R08	4	x	x		x				
R09	5	x						x	
R10	3								x
UC Priority		1	4	1	2	3	5	4	3

FIGURE 7.16 Sample requirement–use case traceability matrix

The use case priorities are useful for planning the iterations. That is, use cases with the highest priority are developed and deployed first.

Note that a use case may support more than one requirement. For example, the *Search for Programs* use case of SAMS supports "R1. SAMS must provide a search capability for overseas exchange programs using a variety of search criteria." This use case must display the search result in a hierarchical manner, as stated in R2. Therefore, this use case also supports R2. Suppose that SAMS is required to support multiple database management systems (DBMS). Then the fact that *Search for Programs* must access a database is relevant to this requirement. In this case, the corresponding entry in the RUTM is checked.

The RUTM has a number of merits. It can be used to identify use cases that realize a given requirement. It can also be used to identify requirements that are realized by a given use case. This bidirectional traceability offers three advantages. First, it ensures that each requirement will be delivered by some use cases (i.e., there are no blank rows). It is easy to verify whether the use cases satisfy the requirement, that is, whether some use cases are missing. Second, it ensures that all the use cases are required (i.e., there are no blank columns). Finally, it ensures that high-priority use cases are developed and deployed as early as possible.

Often, we as developers like to implement nice features or use cases that are not required. We think that the customer would love to have them for free. Unfortunately, most customers do not think so because the extra features and use cases incur unnecessary learning curves. I have encountered cases where the customers explicitly requested that these be dropped because they do not need them and would never use them. The traceability matrix helps us identify such use cases.

7.4.5 Reviewing Use Case Specifications

In this step, the abstract use cases, high-level use cases, use case diagrams and requirement–use case traceability matrix (RUTM) are reviewed using the following checklist.

Abstract use cases

1. Does each use case name consist of a verb-noun phrase and communicate what the use case accomplishes for the actor?
2. Does each use case represent a business process?
3. Can any of the use cases be split into two or more use cases?
4. Can any of the use cases be merged?

Requirement–use case traceability matrix

1. Is there a RUTM?
2. Is every requirement listed in the RUTM?
3. Is there a blank row or blank column in the RUTM?
4. Are the use cases listed for each requirement necessary for the requirement?
5. Are the use cases listed for each requirement sufficient for the requirement?

High-level use cases

1. Is there a high-level use case specification for each use case identified?
2. Does the TUCBW clause of each high-level use case clearly specify when and where the use case begins?

3. Does the TUCEB clause of each high-level use case clearly specify when the use case ends and ends with what the actor wants to accomplish?
4. Does each high-level use case correctly specify the scope of the business process?

Use case diagram

1. Does each use case diagram show the subsystem boundary?
2. Is the subsystem name appropriate for communicating the functionality of the subsystem?
3. Is there a one-to-one correspondence between the use cases in the use case diagrams and the use cases in the RUTM?
4. Is there any use case diagram with an excessive number of use cases?
5. Is there any use case diagram containing only one use case without a good reason?
6. Is there any use case diagram containing an isolated use case or actor?
7. Is there any actor that does not have a role name?
8. Is each use case linked to the appropriate actor?
9. Is each use case assigned to the appropriate subsystem?

7.4.6 Allocating Use Cases to Iterations

Now the use cases are identified and visualized. Their priorities are derived from the priorities of the requirements. The next step is to produce an iteration plan to develop and deploy the use cases. This is called *planning the iterations with use cases*. It involves a few steps. First, the effort required to develop and deploy each use case is estimated. This is done using the estimation methods described in Chapter 23. In particular, the Poker-game estimation method is widely used by agile projects. Next, the dependencies between the use cases are identified so that they will be deployed according to their dependencies. For example, "checkout document" is deployed no later than "return document." Finally, an iteration schedule is produced using the planning and scheduling techniques presented in Chapter 23. The generation of the schedule takes into account a number of factors, in descending order of importance:

1. *The priorities of the use cases.* High-priority use cases should be developed and deployed as early as possible to satisfy the customer's business needs and priorities.
2. *The dependencies among the use cases.* If use case B depends on use case A, then B must not be deployed before A because the users won't be able to use B without A.
3. *The team's capacity to develop and deploy the use cases.* The effort required by the use cases allocated to an iteration must not exceed the capacity of the team to develop and deploy them.

Figure 7.17 shows a sample schedule, called use case to iteration allocation matrix. The rows are the use cases and the columns are the iterations. The entries show the effort distribution of the use cases to the iterations. Care should be given to ensure that the sum of the efforts of each column must not exceed the capacity of the team, which is nine person-weeks in this example. The sum of the efforts of each row must not be less than the required effort to develop and deploy the use case. The dependencies and the priorities of the use cases are satisfied.

Sometimes, a use case requires more than one iteration to develop and deploy. In such cases, each of the iterations may develop and deploy some of the features or

Use Case	Priority	Effort (person-week)	Depend On	Iteration 1 3 wks 9/15/08-10/3/08	Iteration 2 3 wks 10/6/08-10/24/08	Iteration 3 3 wks 10/27/08-11/14/08	Iteration 4 3 wks 11/17/08-12/5/08
UC1	1	5	None	5			
UC2	4	4	UC8			4	
UC3	1	2	UC1	2			
UC4	2	5	UC3	2	3		
UC5	4	3	UC4			3	
UC6	5	6	UC4				6
UC7	4	5	UC2		1	1	3
UC8	3	5	None		5		
Total Effort		35		9	9	8	9

Team size = 3 persons

FIGURE 7.17 Allocating use cases to iterations

functionality of the use case. For example, if *Edit Class Diagram* use case cannot be deployed in one iteration, then the first iteration may deploy features that allow users to add and delete classes and relationships, the second iteration will allow users to modify classes and relationships, and so on.

7.5 APPLYING AGILE PRINCIPLES

GUIDELINE 7.14 Work closely with the customer and users to understand their business processes and priorities, and help them identify their real needs.

Use cases are business processes. Only the customer and users know the business processes, how they work, and their priorities. Therefore, the development team needs to work closely with the customer and users to identify and validate the use cases.

GUIDELINE 7.15 The team members should work together to identify use cases, actors, and subsystems, and specify the use case scopes.

The process to derive and specify use cases is not just for the sake of documentation. Through the process, the team members understand and communicate their understanding about the business processes. This provides the basis for the components developed by the team members to work with each other. This is one of the reasons that agile approaches value individuals and interaction. Experience shows that dividing the tasks among team members and work separately produces poor result. This is because communication is either missing or inadequate.

GUIDELINE 7.16 Requirements evolve, but the timescale is fixed.

Agile development tends to use a fixed timescale for the iterations. This makes it easier for the team members to work with the iterations. For example, after a few iterations, the team members would know how much can be done in one iteration. Thus, the team would move forward with a constant speed. If the iteration cannot complete all the features, then take out low-priority features or move them to the next iteration after consulting with the customer and users.

GUIDELINE 7.17 Focus on frequent delivery of small increments, each of which deploys only a couple of use cases.

This increases the visibility. That is, it is easier to decide how much can be done in two weeks than how much can be done in two months. Moreover, frequent delivery of small increments reduces the risk of requirements misconception. It supports continuous testing by users and reduces users' learning curve.

GUIDELINE 7.18 Do not attempt to derive an optimal set of use cases. Good enough is enough.

First, there is no optimal set of use cases because the criteria cannot be defined. Moreover, requirements change all the time. This means the use cases ought to change. Therefore, it is sufficient to identify and specify most of the high-priority requirements and use cases. It is more important to move on to implementing the use cases and solicit users' feedback. That is, good enough is enough.

7.6 TOOL SUPPORT FOR USE CASE MODELING

Tools for drawing and managing use case diagrams include IBM Rational Modeler, Microsoft Visio, ArgoUML, NetBeans UML Plugin, and many others. These tools provide editing capabilities and other related features. Most tools also support reverse engineering and code skeleton generation from UML diagrams.

7.7 SUMMARY

This chapter presents how to identify use cases, actors, and subsystems from requirements, as well as requirement–use case traceability matrix (RUTM). The RUTM also shows the priorities of the requirements and use cases. These are used to generate an iteration plan so that high-priority use cases are developed and deployed as early as possible. The allocation of the use cases to the iterations is shown in a use case–iteration allocation matrix. High-level use cases specify use case scopes or when and where a use case begins and when it ends. The use cases, actors, and subsystems as well as the relationships between them are visualized using UML use case diagrams. This chapter signals the completion of the planning phase. In the iterative phase, the use cases are developed and deployed according to the schedule of the iterations.

7.8 CHAPTER REVIEW QUESTIONS

1. What is a use case?
2. What are the four properties of a use case?
3. Is every verb-noun phrase a use case, and why?
4. What are a business process, an operation, and an action? How are they related?
5. What is an actor? Is a person an actor?
6. From where should the use cases be derived, and why?
7. How does one derive the use cases, actors, and subsystems?
8. What is a high-level use case?
9. How does one specify a high-level use case?
10. What is a use case diagram?
11. How does one partition the use cases to improve the functional cohesion of a subsystem and reduce the number of use cases of a use case diagram?
12. What is a requirement-use case traceability matrix? What is the usefulness of such a matrix?
13. What is a use case-iteration allocation matrix? What is the usefulness of such a matrix?

7.9 EXERCISES

7.1 You produced a requirements specification for a desktop virtual calculator, a telephone answering machine, and a web-based online email system in exercise 4.2. Derive use cases, related actors, and systems for each of these applications. Also specify the high-level use cases and draw use case diagrams for the use cases.

7.2 Derive use cases from the functional requirements for the calendar management system you produced in exercise 4.4. Also specify the high-level use cases.

7.3 For the National Trade Show Services (NTSS) requirements specification you produced in exercise 4.6, do the following:

- **a.** Derive use cases from the requirements specification.
- **b.** Specify the high-level use cases.
- **c.** Draw use case diagrams.
- **d.** Apply the use case partition rules if necessary to reduce the number of use cases allocated to each subsystem.

7.4 Do the following for the Car Rental System (CRS) given in Appendix D.1:

- **a.** Derive use cases from the requirements you produced in exercise 4.8.
- **b.** Construct a requirements-use case traceability matrix.
- **c.** Specify the high-level use cases.
- **d.** Draw use case diagrams.

7.5 Formulate your functional requirements for a use case modeling tool that implements the methodology described in this chapter. Limit the specification to no more than a couple of pages. Derive use cases, specify high-level use cases, and produce use case diagrams. Review these using the review checklist presented in Section 7.4.5 and produce a review report.

8 Chapter

Actor–System Interaction Modeling

Key Takeaway Points

- Actor-system interaction modeling is modeling and design of how the system interacts with actors to carry out a use case.
- Actor-system interaction modeling and object interaction modeling (Chapter 8) deal with foreground processing and background processing (of a use case), respectively.

Chapter 7 presented how to derive use cases from the requirements and how to specify the scope of each use case. The results are referred to as abstract use cases and high-level use cases, respectively. As defined in Chapter 7, a *use case* is a business process and accomplishes a business task for the actor. To do this, the system must interact with the actor to jointly carry out the use case. This interaction is called *actor-system interaction* (ASIM). This chapter focuses on the modeling and design of such behavior. As mentioned in previous chapters, use cases are modeled with three levels of abstraction:

1. **Abstract Use Case.** An abstract use case is a verb-noun phrase that highlights what the use case will accomplish for the actor.
2. **High-Level Use Case.** A high-level use case consists of a TUCBW clause that specifies when and where a use case begins and a TUCEW clause that specifies when it ends. TUCBW and TUCEW stand for "this use case begins with" and "this use case ends with," respectively. In other words, a high-level use case specifies the scope of the use case.
3. **Expanded Use Case.** An expanded use case specifies how an actor will interact with the system. It is a continuation and refinement of a high-level use case. It specifies the interaction using a two-column table. The left column specifies the actor input and/or actor actions, and the right column specifies the system responses.

For simplicity, abstract use cases are referred to as use cases in this book. Abstract use cases and high-level use cases were described in Chapter 7 (Deriving Use Cases from Requirements). This chapter presents expanded use case specification. When you complete this chapter, you will learn:

- What is ASIM?
- The importance of ASIM.
- How to perform ASIM.

8.1 WHAT IS ACTOR–SYSTEM INTERACTION MODELING?

ASIM is the modeling and design of how the system interacts with actors to carry out use cases. As shown in Figure 8.1, the left column specifies the actor input and/or actor actions and the right column specifies the corresponding system responses. More specifically, the two-column tabular specification of an expanded use case illustrates the following:

1. **Use case ID and name.** This is shown at the top of the table in Figure 8.1.
2. **The actor role and system/subsystem name.** This is displayed in the first row of Figure 8.1.
3. **The initial state of the user interface.** Step 0 in the right column specifies the initial state of the user interface before the use case begins. It is important to specify the initial state of the user interface because (a) it tells the developer what the system should display to the actor and (b) it tells the actor what he or she will see before the use case begins.

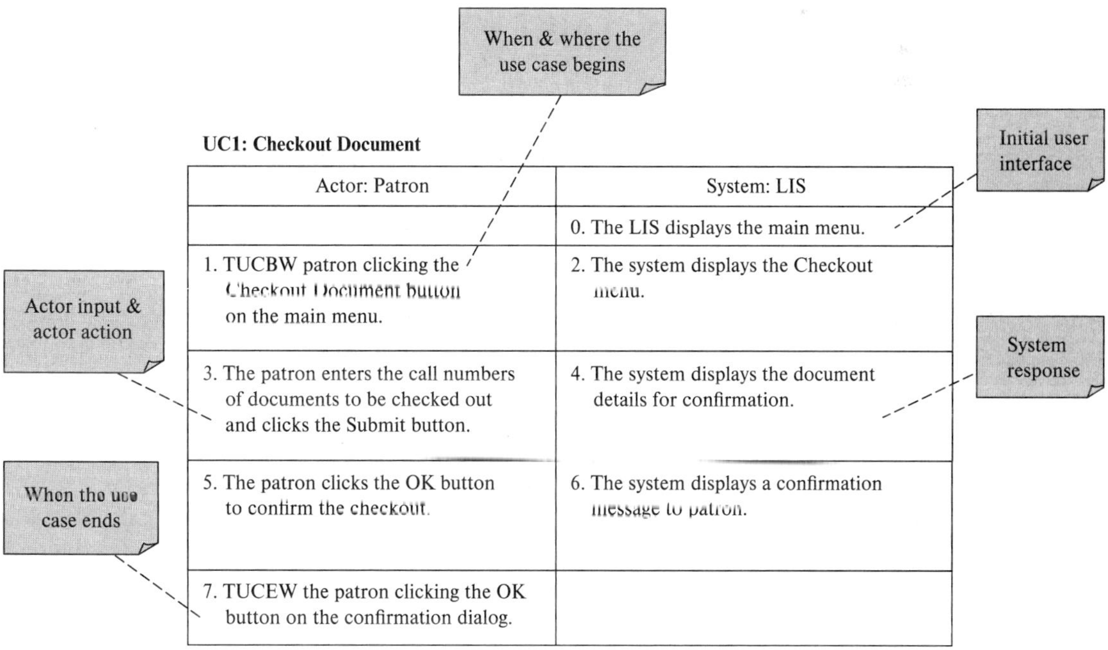

UC1: Checkout Document

Actor: Patron	System: LIS
	0. The LIS displays the main menu.
1. TUCBW patron clicking the Checkout Document button on the main menu.	2. The system displays the Checkout menu.
3. The patron enters the call numbers of documents to be checked out and clicks the Submit button.	4. The system displays the document details for confirmation.
5. The patron clicks the OK button to confirm the checkout.	6. The system displays a confirmation message to patron.
7. TUCEW the patron clicking the OK button on the confirmation dialog.	

FIGURE 8.1 Expanded use case for a library information system

4. **When and where to start the use case.** Step 1 in the left column specifies when and where the use case begins. This is the TUCBW clause of the high-level use case.
5. **The actor input and actor action at each step of the interaction.** This is specified in the left column on each row of the two-column table.
6. **The corresponding system response.** This is specified in the right column on the corresponding row of the two-column table.
7. **When the use case ends.** The last entry of the left column specifies when the use case ends. This is the TUCEW clause of the high-level use case.

8.2 IMPORTANCE OF ACTOR–SYSTEM INTERACTION MODELING

The usefulness of the expanded use case specification includes the following:

1. It specifies the actor-system interaction or system's interactive behavior that the subsequent design, implementation, and testing can follow.
2. It can be used to communicate to future users about the actor–system interaction behavior. It is useful for acquiring user feedback.
3. It can be used to generate a preliminary user's manual. This is because the expanded use case describes exactly how the user will use the system to accomplish a business task. The preliminary user's manual facilitates a potential user to experiment with a prototype of the system.
4. If updated timely according to changes in subsequent design and implementation phases, the expanded use case specification can be used to generate the as-built user's manual. This reduces the increment or system deployment effort, cost, and time.
5. It can be used to generate use case–based test cases or test scripts. This will be described in Chapter 20 (Software Testing).

8.3 STEPS FOR ACTOR–SYSTEM INTERACTION MODELING

The main activity of ASIM is constructing expanded use cases for the use cases allocated to the current iteration. It involves the following steps:

Step 1. Initialize a two-column table for the expanded use case being constructed.

Step 2. Specify each of the actor–system interaction steps until the system produces the response specified in the TUCEW clause.

Step 3. Review the expanded use cases using a review checklist.

8.3.1 Initializing a Two-Column Table

Draw a two-column table and show the use case ID and use case name at the top of the table. Name the headers of the left and right columns with the role name of the actor and the system/subsystem name, respectively. Enter the TUCBW and TUCEW clauses of the corresponding high-level use case as the second and third entries of the left column, and label them step 1 and step 3, respectively. The step number 3 will increase as more steps are inserted. Next, infer the initial system display according to the TUCBW

UC1: Checkout Document

Actor: Patron	System: LIS
	0. The LIS displays the main menu.
1. TUCBW patron clicking the Checkout Document button on the main menu.	2.
3. TUCEW patron clicking the OK button on the confirmation dialog.	

FIGURE 8.2 Initializing an expanded use case

clause of the use case and specify this in the first entry of the right column. Label this step as step 0. Figure 8.2 shows the result of this step for the Checkout Document use case of a library information system (LIS). Note that main menu is referred to in the TUCBW clause in step 1; therefore, step 0 is "0. The LIS displays the main menu."

8.3.2 Specifying Actor–System Interaction

In this step, the actor–system interaction steps are specified. It begins with the TUCBW clause in step 1. The corresponding system response is derived and entered as step 2 in the right column. The result is written as "the system displays . . . " In general, the system displays the result, or a dialog to acquire actor input. If actor input is required, then a row is inserted and the actor input and actor action are specified. This process is repeated for the remaining steps until the system produces the response specified in the TUCEW clause.

Sometimes, the system requires the actor to enter information about a domain concept. Such information is usually found in the domain model. Figure 8.3 illustrates this. In this example, program information is requested in step 4; this information is

UC7: Add Program

Actor: Staff User	System: SAMS
	0. System displays the Welcome page.
1. TUCBW staff user clicking the Program Management link on Welcome page.	2. System shows the Program Management menu.
3. Staff user clicks the Add Program link.	4. System shows the Add Program Form with name, type, department, ...
5. Staff user fills the form and clicks the Submit button.	6. System displays a message stating that the program is successfully added.
7. TUCEW staff user seeing the program is successfully added message.	

(a) Expanded use case

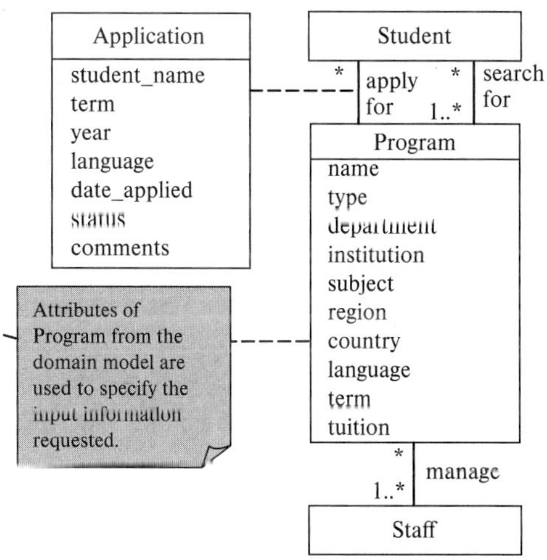

(b) Part of domain model

FIGURE 8.3 Reusing information from the domain model

usually described by the attributes of the corresponding class, i.e., the Program class in the domain model. Similarly, the attributes of the Application association class in Figure 8.3(*b*) can be used in the specification of the Apply Online expanded use case. If the domain concept is not found in the domain model, then the domain model should be updated. If the domain concept is found but the information is incomplete, then the attributes of the class should be updated.

In above, a forward reasoning approach is described. It begins with the TUCBW step and infers the next step from the current step. Sometimes, backward reasoning may be easier. It begins with the TUCEW step and infers the previous step from the current step. To do this, let n be the step number of the TUCEW step. Because the TUCEW step always shows what the system produces in step n-1, we can infer step n-1. For example, if step n is "TUCEW staff user seeing the program successfully added message," then step n-1 will be "system displays a message stating that the program is successfully added." To infer step n-2, the designer should know that for the system to produce such a message what it needs from the actor. The answer is then used to formulate step n-2, for example, "staff user fills the (add program) form and clicks the Submit button." After all of the steps are inferred, the steps are renumbered accordingly.

8.3.3 Reviewing Expanded Use Cases

The expanded use cases produced in the current iteration are reviewed using the following review checklist:

1. Are there a use case ID and a use case name for each of the expanded use cases? Do they match with the use case ID and name in the requirement–use case traceability matrix and the corresponding high-level use case?
2. Are the actors and systems correctly specified, and matching with the their counterparts in the high-level use cases and use case diagrams?
3. Does every expanded use case specify the initial system display in step 0?
4. Are the TUCBW and TUCEW clauses matched with their counterparts in the high-level use cases?
5. Does every use case begin with an actor and end with the actor in the left column?
6. Are there blank steps between the TUCBW and TUCEW steps? If so, the specification is incorrect.
7. Does every expanded use case correctly and adequately specify the actor–system interaction to carry out the business process?
8. Do the left-column steps clearly and correctly specify the actor input and actor actions?
9. Do the right-column steps clearly and correctly specify the corresponding system responses?

8.4 SPECIFYING ALTERNATIVE FLOWS

For many real-world applications, the interaction between the actor and the system involves alternative flows. That is, the system may allow the actor to choose from a number of choices in a given step of the interaction. As an example, suppose that a staff user can add a program using one of two methods: (1) filling an add-program form, and

UC7: Add Program

Actor: Staff User	System: SAMS
1. TUCBW staff user clicking the Program Management link on welcome page.	2. System shows the Program Management menu.
3. Staff user clicks the Add Program link.	4. System shows a dialog with two options: (a) fill a form (b) upload a file
5. Staff user selects (a) fill a form, or (b) upload a file	6. System displays (a) an Add Program form, or (b) a dialog for uploading a file
7. Staff user either (a) fills the Add Program form and clicks the Submit button, or (b) locates the program file and clicks the Upload button	8. System displays a message stating that the program is successfully added.
9. TUCEW staff user seeing the program successfully added message.	

FIGURE 8.4 Specifying alternative flows in expanded use cases

(2) uploading a structured file. Figure 8.4 shows the modified expanded use case, which uses "(a)" and "(b)" to distinguish the two options and the corresponding system responses.

Note in this example, the alternative flows are normal cases of the add-program business process. They are not exceptions such as the password entered is incorrect, or the user clicks the Cancel button. Expanded use cases should specify only normal cases, not exceptions.

8.5 USING USER INTERFACE PROTOTYPES

"A picture is worth a thousand words." Appropriate user interface (UI) prototypes can be used to improve the specification of expanded use cases. That is, the system responses in the right column of the expanded use case specification can be augmented by exhibits of UI prototypes, as shown in Figure 8.5. Step (2) states that "the system shows the Program Management menu." A UI prototype is used to show the appearance of the menu. Similarly, step 3 shows another UI prototype. UI prototypes can be shown by using pointers to increase readability, as illustrated in Figure 8.6 through Figure 8.8. Other presentation techniques such as URL links can also be used. Using UI prototypes in expanded use case specification has the following merits:

1. It is extremely helpful in obtaining customer and user feedback in the early stages of the development life cycle.
2. Using UI prototypes in the expanded use case specification facilitates the preparation of the user's manual.
3. Using UI prototypes helps in early preparation of use case–based test cases.

A significant challenge of software requirements analysis and software design is determining user interface requirements. It is extremely difficult to describe the layout, look and feel, color scheme, and fonts using a natural language. This problem can be easily solved by using UI prototypes in expanded use case specifications, as illustrated in Figure 8.5. As a matter of fact, the UI prototypes in Figure 8.5 were obtained after customer comments on an earlier version, which was not consistent with the customer's

Actor: Staff User	System: SAMS
	0. System displays the welcome page.
1. TUCBW staff user clicking the Program Management link on the welcome page.	2. System shows the Program Management submenu.
3. Staff user clicks the Add Program link.	4. System shows the Add Program Form.
5. Staff user fills the form and clicks the Submit button.	6. System displays a message stating that the program is added successfully.
7. TUCEW staff user seeing the "program is added successfully" message.	

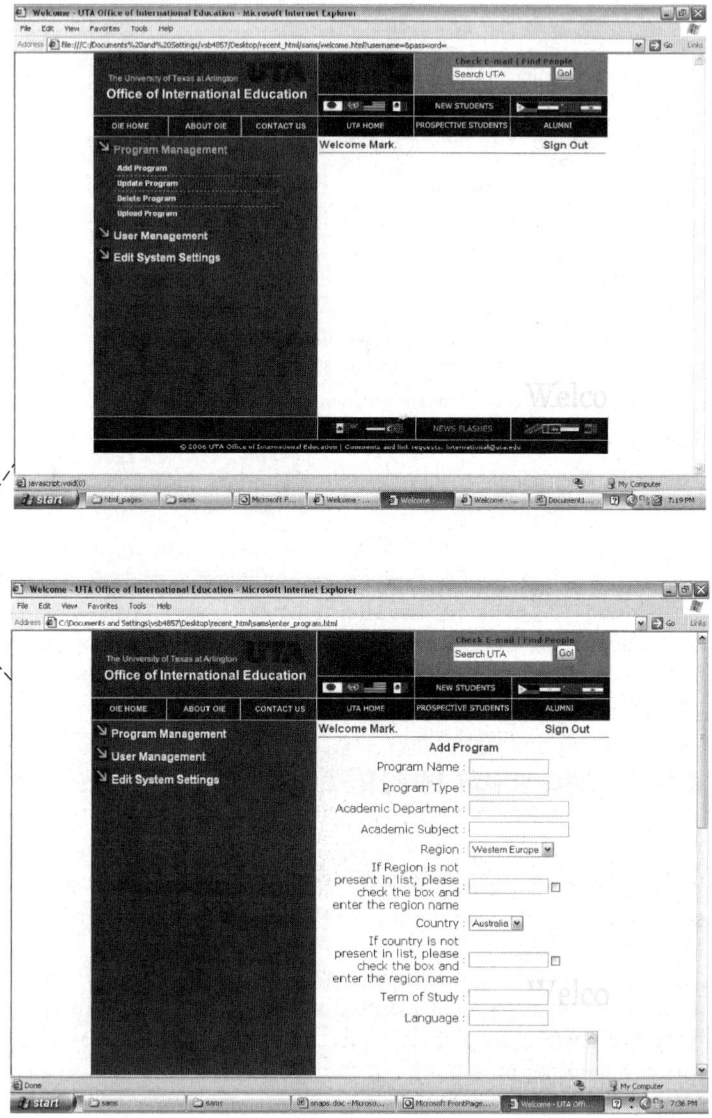

FIGURE 8.5 An expanded use case and UI prototypes

existing website in layout, look and feel, color scheme, and font. Because feedback was received early when the expanded use cases were presented to the customer, the development team avoided considerable rework. Customers and users like to see the UI prototypes because they help them understand what they will get when the system is implemented. It facilitates the customers and users to provide feedback. Customers and users hesitate to provide feedback on expanded use cases that only use textual descriptions of system responses because they are not sure if they understand the descriptions correctly.

As mentioned in an earlier section, a preliminary user's manual can be easily generated from the expanded use case descriptions. The UI prototype exhibits can be reused

Actor: Staff User	System: SAMS
	0. System displays the Welcome page.
1. TUCBW staff user clicking on Program Management link on welcome page.	2. System shows the Program Management submenu.
3. Staff user clicks on Add Program link.	4. System shows the Add Program Form.
5. Staff user fills the form and clicks on the Submit button.	6. System displays a program is successfully added message.
7. TUCEW staff user seeing the program is successfully added message.	

See Exhibit 1: Program Management Submenu

See Exhibit 2: Add Program Form

FIGURE 8.6 Expanded use case with references to UI exhibits

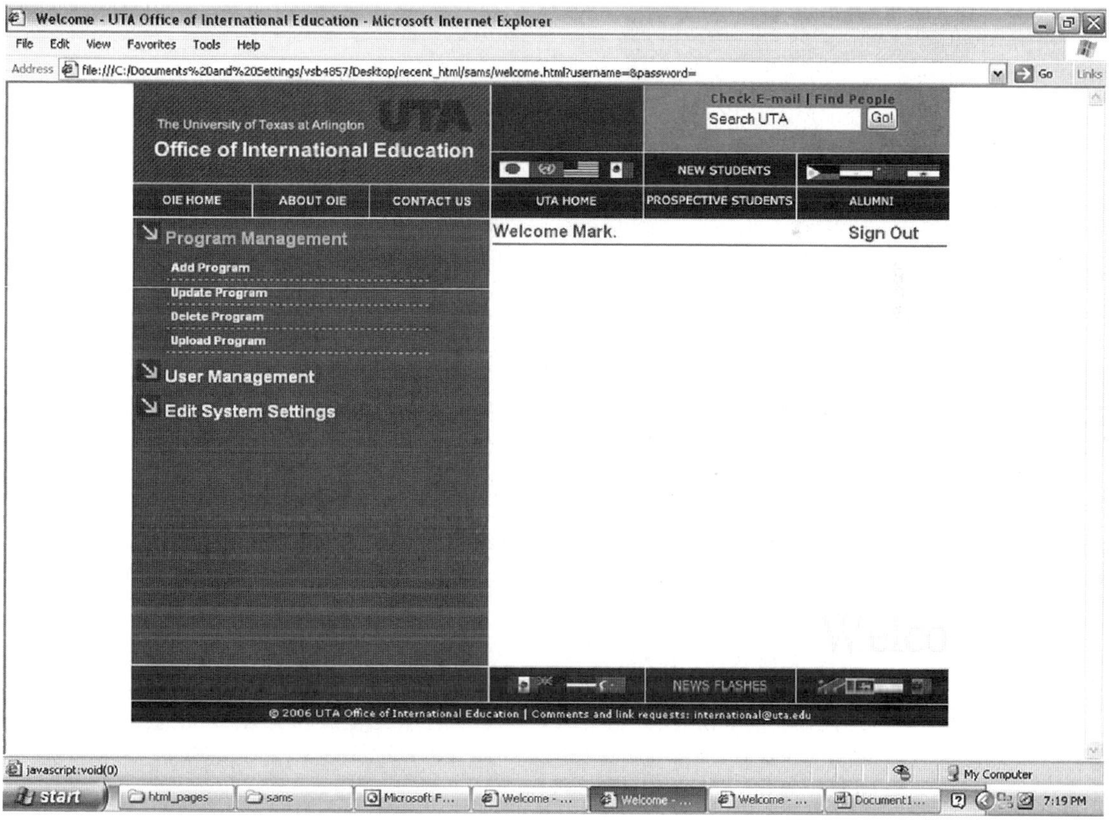

FIGURE 8.7 UI prototype exhibit 1

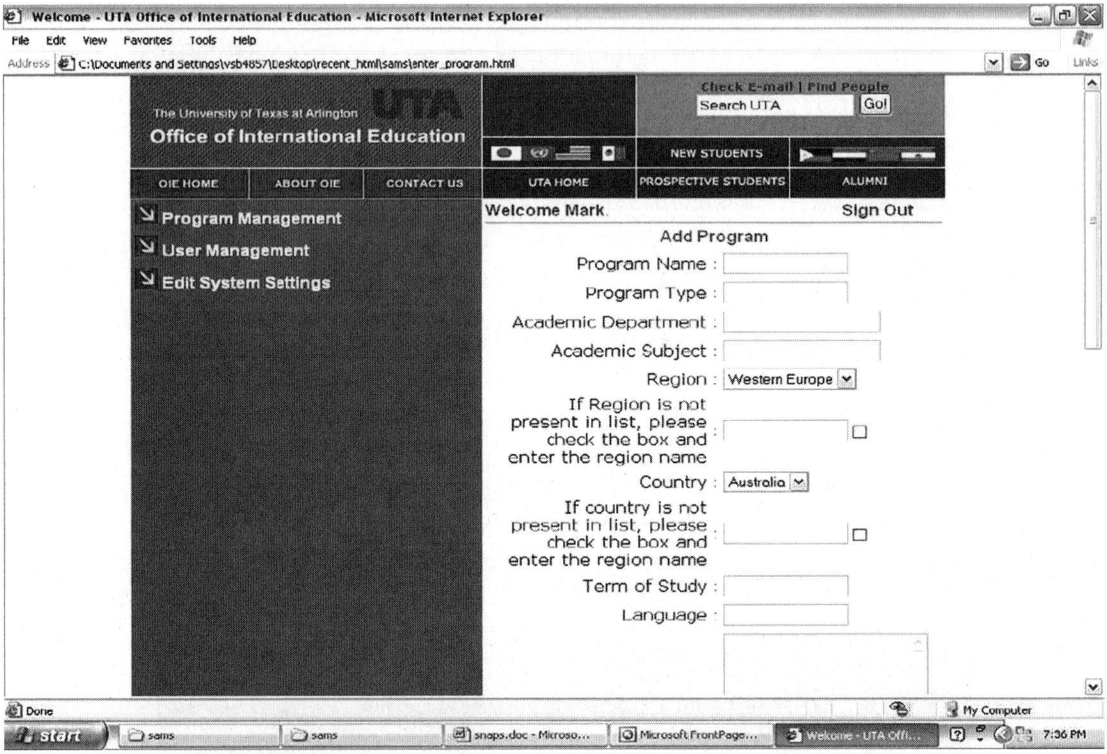

FIGURE 8.8 UI prototype exhibit 2

when generating the preliminary user's manual. Because UI exhibits are a necessary component of a user's manual, the construction of the UI prototype exhibits does not necessarily create additional effort. As a matter of fact, producing the UI prototype exhibits during ASIM could greatly save development effort because (1) early user feedback avoids rework, (2) the user's manual preparation effort is reduced, and (3) the effort to generate test cases is reduced. The expanded use case specifications that are augmented by UI prototype exhibits facilitate test case generation because they visually describe the expected graphical user interfaces. These are part of the test case descriptions. Test cases should be generated and run to ensure that the system correctly displays the windows, dialogs, and computation results. Testing is described in Chapter 20.

8.6 DO NOT SHOW EXCEPTION HANDLING

An expanded use case specifies the normal interaction between an actor and the system. Therefore, the specification should not include exceptional cases and their handling for the following considerations:

- Exceptional cases and alternative flows are different. The latter are normal business workflows, while the former are abnormal circumstances that should be dealt with at a lower level: the implementation level, not the use case specification level.

UC1: Login

Actor: User	System: WebApp
	0. WebApp displays homepage.
1. TUCBW user clicks the Login link on the homepage.	2. WebApp displays the login page.
3. User enters user name and password and clicks the Login button.	4a. If user logs in for the first time, TUCCW Reset Password; 4b. Else WebApp displays the welcome page.
5. TUCEW user sees the welcome page.	

FIGURE 8.9 Expanded use case that includes another use case

- Although exceptional cases are uncommon situations, the number of exceptional cases for a given system is numerous. For example, the network could be down, an account could have expired, the power could be off, the computer could get infected by a virus, or other problems. Specifying exceptional cases in an expanded use case is not desirable because the specification looks complex and the normal flow of interaction is more difficult to comprehend.

8.7 INCLUDING OTHER USE CASES

Use cases are business processes. It is common that one business process includes another business process as a subprocess. For example, when a new user logs on for the first time, many systems require the new user to reset the temporary password. In this case, the Login use case conditionally includes the Reset Password use case. Figure 8.9 illustrates how this expanded use case is specified, where TUCCW stands for "this use case continues with."

8.8 CONTINUING WITH OTHER USE CASES

The technique described in the last section can be used to specify alternative flows that would branch to other use cases. For example, an investor may use different ways to transfer funds. The Transfer Funds Online use case allows an investor to transfer funds from one account to another within the same brokerage firm. The Transfer Funds with a Check use case allows an investor to write a check to transfer funds from a bank account. The Transfer Funds with a Transfer Form use case allows an investor to fill in, print, sign, and mail a form to transfer funds from one brokerage firm to another. As ASIM is concerned, Transfer Funds Online, Transfer Funds with a Check, and Transfer Funds with a Transfer Form can be viewed as special cases of Transfer Funds. Thus, the Transfer Funds use case may be realized by either one of the three use cases. Figure 8.10 illustrates how this is specified.

The expanded use case specification serves as a prelude to the three different ways of fund transfer. After the investor clicks the Transfer Funds link, the system shows

UC3: Transfer Funds

Actor: Investor	System: Fund Manager
	(0) System displays Fund Management page.
(1) TUCBW investor clicking the Transfer Funds link on the Fund Management page.	(2) System displays fund transfer options: (a) Transfer Funds Online. (b) Transfer Funds with a Check. (c) Transfer Funds with Transfer Form.
(3) Investor selects one of the fund transfer options: (a) Transfer Funds Online. (b) Transfer Funds with a Check. (c) Transfer Funds with Transfer Form.	(4) TUCCW the selected fund transfer use case: (a) UC4: Transfer Funds Online. (b) UC5: Transfer Funds with a Check. (c) UC6: Transfer Funds with a Fund Transfer Form.
(5) TUCEW investor seeing: (a) Online fund transfer is completed message. (b) Fund Transfer slip. (c) Fund Transfer Form to print, fill, sign and mail.	

FIGURE 8.10 Specifying alternative flows to other use cases

the alternative ways to transfer funds. Instead of directly dealing with each of the choices that the investor may select, the expanded use case in Figure 8.10 specifies in step 4 that this use case continues with (TUCCW) one of three use cases.

8.9 COMMONLY SEEN PROBLEMS

With reference to Figure 8.11, this section presents commonly seen problems in expanded use case specifications and how to fix these problems. First, the use case ID and use case name are not shown. Second, there is no specification of the initial system display. The TUCBW clause does not specify where or which page contains the Register button, as indicated by note (a) in Figure 8.11. Without these the actor would not know where to find the button and the programmer would not know where to show the button. Therefore, explicitly specifying where a use case begins is desired. The interaction between the actor and the system should be a continuous flow of interactive actor requests and system responses, not intermittent, as pointed out by notes (b) and (e). Note (c) indicates that the actor input and actor action should be performed in one step, not two. Note (b) indicates that there is no system response to the actor input and actor action. The actor would not know whether the step is performed successfully. If the system were implemented accordingly, the actor would wait indefinitely for the system response. Steps 5 and 6 specify the background processing, which should be avoided in expanded use case specifications. Background processing should be described during object interaction modeling (Chapter 9). In addition, these steps do not specify the expected system displays. Finally, the expanded use case does not specify the TUCEW clause, as indicated by note (g). The TUCEW clause should state what the use case accomplishes for the actor. To fix these problems, step 4 should be merged into step 3, steps 5 and 6 should be deleted, step 7 should be step 4, and a TUCEW step should be added. Other commonly seen problems are the following:

- Specifying exception handling in expanded use cases.
- Missing actor input or actor action, as indicated by the blank entries in the left column in Figure 8.11.

Actor: Student	System: SAMS
1. TUCBW the student clicking the "Register Button."	2. System shows a registration screen.
3. Student fills the registration form.	
4. Student clicks the "Submit" button.	5. System retrieves student record from database, validates the information provided by the student.
	6. System sends an email to the address with a password.
	7. System displays a "Registration is successful and the password is sent via email" message.

(a) No specification of which page.

(b) Should not contain a blank entry during interaction.

(c) Steps 3 and 4 should be merged into one step.

(d) Should not specify background processing.

(e) Should not contain a blank entry during interaction.

(f) Should not specify background processing.

(g) Missing TUCEW clause here.

FIGURE 8.11 A problematic expanded use case specification

- Making the specification unnecessarily complex, as shown in Figure 8.12. It may be simplified by combining steps 2 to 15 into one step, such as "3. User enters first name, last name, email, phone number, user name, password; retypes password in the registration form; and clicks the Submit button."
- Ambiguous specification of actor input or actor action.
- Not using third-person, simple-present tense.

8.10 GUIDELINES FOR EXPANDED USE CASES

GUIDELINE 8.1 Keep it simple and stupid.

An expanded use case should contain only a few steps. Moreover, each step should be simple, clear, and straightforward. If an expanded use case has more than half a dozen steps such as in Figure 8.12, then there are two possibilities. It is likely that lower-level operations are treated as steps of the process. Another possibility is that the use case is in fact a concatenation of two use cases. In these cases, the expanded use case should be examined carefully to determine the appropriate improvement. That is, the expanded use case should hide the lower-level operations and show only the steps of the business process. For example, steps 3 to 15 in Figure 8.12 should be merged into one step. If the use case has combined two or more consecutive business processes, then the use case should be decomposed. For example, Purchase Item and Make Payment are sometimes combined into one. They should be two separate use cases.

UC1: Register a New User

Actor: User	System: NTSS
	0. NTSS displays the homepage.
1. TUCBW user clicks the Register link.	2. NTSS prompts the user to enter first name.
3. User enters first name.	4. NTSS prompts the user to enter last name.
5. User enters last name.	6. NTSS prompts the user to enter email address.
7. User enters email address.	8. NTSS prompts the user to enter phone number.
9. User enters phone number.	10. NTSS prompts the user to enter user name.
11. User enters user name.	12. NTSS prompts the user to enter a password.
13. User enters password.	14. NTSS prompts the user to reenter the password.
15. User reenters password.	16. NTSS verifies the information entered and a. displays the "Account is successfully created." message; or b. prompts the user to reenter the incorrectly entered information.
17. TUCEW user sees the "Account is successfully created." message.	

FIGURE 8.12 Unnecessarily complex actor–system interaction

GUIDELINE 8.2 Use alternative flows with care.

An expanded use case with many alternative flows increases the complexity of actor-system interaction and users' learning curve. It is more difficult to understand, implement, test, and maintain. It is likely that the use case is not one business process but several business processes combined. The alternative flows in fact reflect the selections of the business processes. To determine this, try to produce a one-sentence functional description of the use case. If the description is long, or has to list the things it does, then it is likely that the use case has been assigned too many business processes. Split the use case according to the things it does.

GUIDELINE 8.3 Do not show background processing and exception handling in expanded use cases.

Background processing and exception handling are not part of the actor-system interaction behavior. Therefore, they should not appear in an expanded use case. Leave background processing to object interaction modeling, and exception handling to implementation.

GUIDELINE 8.4 Good enough is enough. Quickly move on to software implementation.

There is no optimal design of actor-system interaction behavior. Only the customer and users have the final say, and they won't be able to decide until they have experience with the software. Therefore, it is important to quickly move on to implementation because it enables the customer and users to evaluate the design with real system. This means a good enough design is enough.

8.11 SUMMARY

This chapter presents how to use expanded use cases to model actor-system interaction and the steps for constructing expanded use cases. It also describes how to use user interface prototypes to facilitate solicitation of user feedback. The chapter presents how to specify the expanded use cases for different situations including alternative flows, inclusion of one use case in another use case, and continuation with another use case. Commonly seen problems of expanded use case specifications are discussed to help beginners avoid such problems.

The expanded use cases specify the foreground processing of use cases as they are carried out by the actors and the system. The background processing of use cases are purposely left out and assigned to Chapter 9 (Object Interaction Modeling).

8.12 CHAPTER REVIEW QUESTIONS

1. What is an expanded use case, and why it is needed?
2. What do the left column and right column of an expanded use case specify?
3. What are the three levels of use case specification, and how do they relate to each other?
4. Where does one place the TUCBW and TUCEW clauses in an expanded use case, and why?
5. Are blank entries allowed between the TUCBW step and the TUCEW step? Why?
6. Should background processing be specified in an expanded use case? Why?
7. How are alternative flows specified in an expanded use case?
8. How does one show user interface prototypes in an expanded use case? What is the usefulness of doing so?

8.13 EXERCISES

8.1 Write expanded use cases for the Deposit Money, Withdraw Money, Check Balance, and Transfer Funds use cases of an automatic teller machine (ATM) application.

8.2 Write expanded use cases for the Edit Report use case for a typical word processor.

8.3 Write expanded use cases for the Make Payment use case of a retail business. Assume that the customer can Pay with Check, Pay with Credit Card, and Pay with Cash.

8.4 Write expanded use cases for the Search Car, Reserve Car, and Cancel Reservation use cases for the online car rental application described in Appendix D.1.

8.5 In Appendix D.2, a National Trade Show Services (NTSS) business is described. In exercise 4.6 and exercise 7.3, you produced the requirements and derived use cases for this application. Now write the expanded use cases.

8.6 Formulate several requirements for a state diagram editor. Derive use cases from these requirements and produce the corresponding expanded use cases.

9

Chapter

Object Interaction Modeling

Key Takeaway Points

- Object interaction modeling (OIM) develops high-level algorithms specifying how objects interact with each other to produce system responses from actor input.
- Object interaction behaviors are specified using UML sequence diagrams.
- OIM deals with background processing of use cases while actor–system interaction modeling (Chapter 8) deals with foreground processing.

A use case is carried out jointly by the actor and the system in two parts: the foreground actor–system interaction part and the background system processing part. Chapter 8 presents actor–system interaction using expanded use cases. This chapter deals with background processing or how objects interact with each other to carry out the business processes. In this chapter, you will learn:

- Focus of OIM.
- UML sequence diagram.
- Analysis sequence diagram and design sequence diagram.
- How to perform OIM.

9.1 WHAT IS OBJECT INTERACTION MODELING?

In the object-oriented paradigm, the basic building blocks are objects. The real world as well as the system is viewed as consisting of objects relating to and interacting with each other. The objects relate to each other through inheritance, aggregation, and association relationships. They interact with each other by requesting services from, or performing actions on, other objects. Clearly, the objects must not interact with each other arbitrarily. They must interact in some way to accomplish the business processes of the use cases. As for the software development concerns, there are two issues to consider:

1. **The analysis issue.** How do the objects interact with each other to accomplish the business tasks in the existing, possibly manual, business processes?
2. **The design issue.** How should the objects interact in the proposed system to improve the business processes?

The analysis issue is important because the development team may not know the existing business processes. In this case, the development team may need to collect information and construct models to understand the existing business processes. In addition, the development team may need object interaction models to identify problems or weaknesses in the existing business processes. Therefore, it is helpful to construct object interaction models for analysis purposes.

The design issue is important because the existing business processes were designed years ago. They may be manual or outdated because the business may have expanded considerably, the business environment may have changed drastically, and technologies may have advanced significantly. The existing processes may need to be redesigned. Therefore, it is necessary to construct object interaction models for the design purpose. This brings us to the following definition.

Definition 9.1 Object interaction modeling (OIM) is a process to

1. Help understand how objects interact in the existing system or existing business processes.
2. Help identify problems and limitations of the existing system or existing business processes.
3. Design and specify high-level algorithms that describe how objects interact in the proposed software system to process the use cases.

In this definition, the first two objectives address the analysis issue while the last objective addresses the design issue. More specifically, OIM addresses the following analysis and design problems:

1. **Modeling and analysis.** This addresses the first two objectives stated above.
2. **Object interaction design.** This addresses the last objective, that is, designing object interact behaviors to solve these design problems:
   a. **Design of object interaction behavior.** This concerns the design of sequences of messages between the objects or how objects collaborate to improve the existing business processes.
   b. **Object interfacing.** This concerns the design of the signatures and return types of the functions of the objects.
   c. **Design for better.** This concerns the application of design patterns to produce a design that meets specific needs and exhibits desired properties, including low coupling, high cohesion, proper assignment of responsibilities to objects, and easy adaptation to changes in requirements and operating environment.

According to the principle of separation of concerns, this chapter is purposely limited to modeling, analysis, and design of object interaction behavior. Applying patterns to produce better designs are covered in sebsequent chapters.

9.2 UML SEQUENCE DIAGRAM

UML sequence diagrams are widely used to model object interaction. Another UML diagram for OIM is called *communication diagram.* Because these diagrams are intended for OIM, sequence diagram and communication diagram are called *interaction diagrams.* This section introduces the sequence diagram, which will be used when the OIM steps are presented. A sequence diagram depicts object interaction as a sequence of ordered messages that are sent and received between objects. Unlike sequence diagrams, communication diagrams are useful for showing what messages are sent from one object to another. Sequence diagrams and communication diagrams are semantically equivalent. This book only uses sequence diagrams.

9.2.1 Notions and Notations

Figure 9.1 shows the commonly used modeling notions, notations, and their meaning for sequence diagrams. The valid connections between the symbols, or the syntax, are described in the last column of the figure.

9.2.2 Representing Instances of a Class

OIM needs to refer to objects and process them. For example, it needs to create an object, change the object, and save the object to a database. Therefore, a named object instance is needed so the object can be accessed by using the name. As another example, a class diagram editor needs to insert diagram elements into a collection of diagram elements. Therefore, a notation for representing a collection of objects is needed. Figure 9.2 shows how various instances of an object class are represented in UML.

The first case shows an unnamed instance of a class. This representation is used when there is no need to refer to that instance elsewhere in the same sequence diagram. For example, if the instance is not passed as a parameter of a function call or as a return value, then there is no need to refer to that instance in the sequence diagram. The second case is a named instance of an unnamed class. This representation is used when the class name has not been decided during the design process, or the exact class can only be determined at runtime. In these cases, the instance must be named; otherwise, it is not possible to access it. The third case is a named instance of a named class. The fact that the instance is named does not mean that the instance must be referenced elsewhere. However, if the instance is referenced elsewhere in the sequence diagram, then the instance must be named; otherwise, how could one refer to that instance? The fourth case shows a collection of instances of a class, such as an array of book objects. The representation does not say anything about the type of the collection, that is, whether it is an array, a linked list, or a hash table. If it needs to indicate the collection type, then a stereotype or a UML note can be used. The last case is a stereotyped instance. A UML stereotype allows users to define their own classifiers

Notion	Notation	Semantics	Connectivity
Actor		A role played by a set of entities or stakeholders that are outside of the system and interact with the system.	
Stereotyped message	<<data/info>>	A stereotype, enclosed in a pair of double-angle brackets, "⟨⟨" and"⟩⟩," lets the modeler introduce a modeling concept not in UML, such as a design pattern or a database. A stereotyped message is a message between an actor and an object that has an application-specific interpretation.	object:Class ⟨⟨input⟩⟩ ⟨⟨output⟩⟩
Object Collection	(a) objcct:Class (b) :Class	(a) An object of a class. (b) A collection of objects of a class. These are placed on top of the lifeline. The colon indicates an object, or a collection of objects. The object name is placed before the colon and the class name after the colon.	object:Class :Class
Lifeline		Indicating that the object exists in the system but it is not executing a method.	object:Class
Method execution		Indicating, by the rectangular shape, that the object is executing one of its methods.	
Message passing	m	A message m is sent from one object to another object, i.e., one object calls a function m of another object.	obj1: obj2: m
Object destruction		The cross at the tip of the lifeline indicates that the object is destroyed or ceases to exist.	object:Class
Combined fragment	operator	A combined fragment expresses repetition or conditional execution of a portion of a sequence diagram, where operator can be **loop, opt** or **alt;** opt mean if-then and alt means alternate such as if-then-else.	

FIGURE 9.1 Sequence diagram notions and notations

:Car	An unnamed instance of the Car class.
car:	A named instance of an unnamed class.
car:Car	A named instance of the Car class.
:Car	A collection of instances of the Car class.
<<JSP>> LoginPage:	A stereotyped object.

FIGURE 9.2 Various instances of an object class

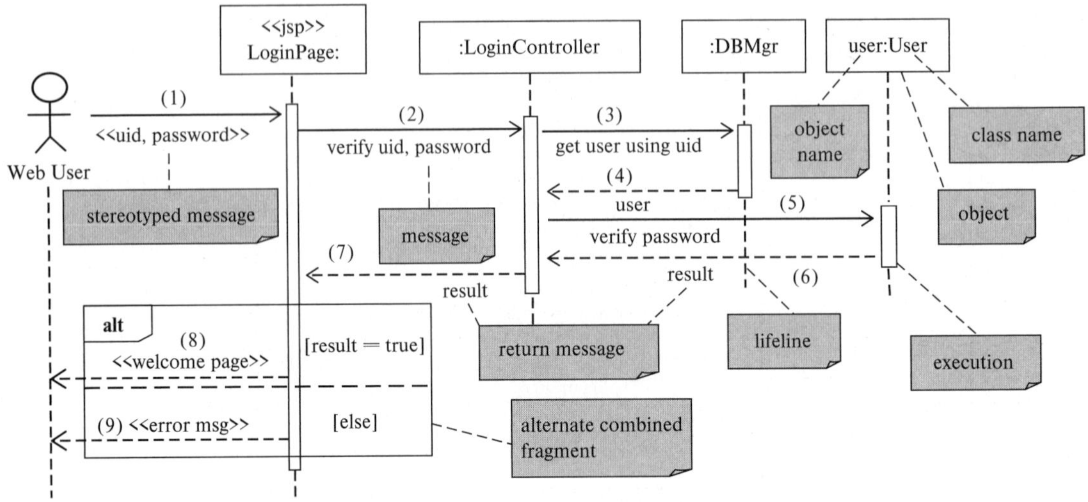

FIGURE 9.3 Sequence diagram for a Login scenario

that extend the standard UML modeling concepts and constructs. For instance, in the last row of Figure 9.2, a stereotyped object such as a LoginPage Java server page (JSP) is illustrated. The string <<JSP>> indicates that the LoginPage is not an ordinary object, it is a JSP page.

9.2.3 Sequence Diagrams Illustrated

Figure 9.3 shows a sequence diagram for a part of simplified Login use case. The diagram is a visual representation of the following scenario. Note numbers are used to indicate the correspondence between the scenario and the sequence diagram.

1. Web user submits uid and password to LoginPage.
2. LoginPage verifies uid and password with LoginController.
3. LoginController gets user (object) from the database manager (DBMgr) using uid.
4. DBMgr returns user (object) to LoginController.
5. LoginController verifies password with user (object).
6. User (object) returns result to LoginController.
7. LoginController returns result to LoginPage.
8. If result is true, LoginPage shows the WelcomePage.
9. Else, LoginPage shows an error message.

This example illustrates that from a (carefully constructed) sequence diagram one can reproduce the scenario. Similarly, from a carefully written scenario one can produce the sequence diagram.

9.2.4 Sequence Diagram for Analysis and Design

In Figure 9.3, the messages that are passed between the objects are informally specified using English texts. This style may be used in the initial stage of OIM or in the modeling of an existing application. During the analysis phase or the initial stage of object interaction design, the development team is trying to understand the existing business processes or proposing improvements to existing business processes. During this stage of OIM, it is impossible to formally specify the interfacing or the signatures of the functions for several reasons. First, the object interaction model being constructed represents an existing manual system. In this case, it is meaningless to formally specify the messages because there are no software objects. Even if the existing system is not a manual system, it is often adequate to specify the messages informally to save effort and time. Another reason to specify the messages informally at this stage is when the design idea is still vague, and hence, it is difficult to formally specify the messages. In all these cases, the development team wants to focus on learning and exploring ideas, not to be bothered by the specification of the exact interfaces between the interacting objects. As such, the sequence diagram in Figure 9.3 is referred to as an analysis or informal sequence diagram.

To facilitate subsequence design and implementation, informal sequence diagrams should be converted into formal sequence diagrams, also called design sequence diagrams, in which all messages between objects are converted into function calls. For example, Figure 9.3 can be converted into the design sequence diagram in Figure 9.4, where the integer numbers enclosed in a pair of parentheses are the corresponding scenario step numbers. Note that the dashed arrow lines representing return values disappear in the design sequence diagram. They are replaced by the return values of function calls. In such cases, the arrow line has two integer numbers enclosed in parentheses, for example, (2)(7), (3)(4), and (5)(6).

The difference between analysis and design are contrasted in Figure 9.5. First, analysis is application problem-oriented while design is software solution-oriented. This means that during the analysis phase, the development team focuses more on understanding the application domain, identifying problems in the existing application, and proposing possibly innovative solutions. During the design phase the development

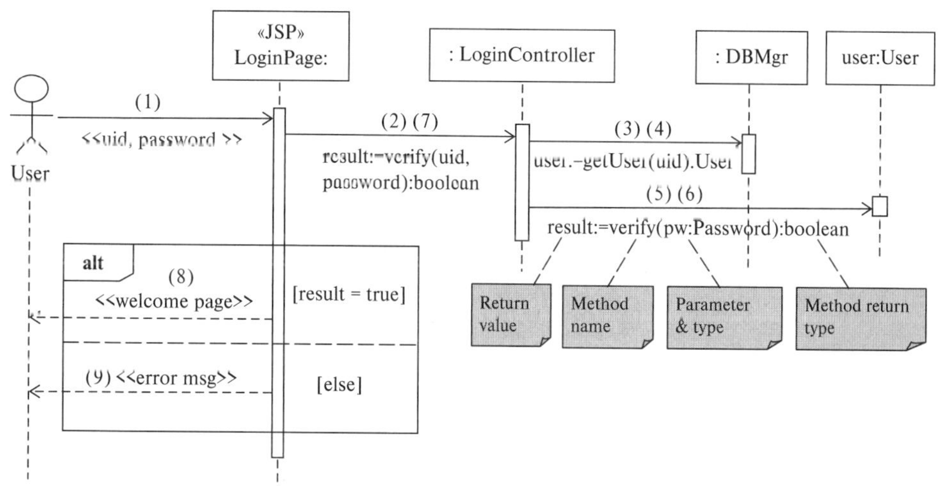

FIGURE 9.4 A design sequence diagram for a login scenario

Analysis	Design
• Application problem-oriented • Models an application domain • Classes and objects are domain concepts and instances • Describes what the world is • Allows multiple design alternatives	• Software solution-oriented • Models the software system • Classes and objects are software classes and software objects • Prescribes a software solution, or what the world should be • May reduce implementation choices

FIGURE 9.5 Difference between analysis and design

team focuses more on developing and specifying an appropriate software architecture and its elements to realize the proposed solution. The software solution should take into consideration software design principles, such as high cohesion, low-coupling, separation of concerns, and design for change.

The second difference between analysis and design is what is being modeled. During the analysis phase, the development team constructs models about the application domain to help understand the application. During the design phase, models of the software system are constructed. For example, during the analysis phase a domain model and possibly sequence diagrams for existing business processes are constructed to help the developers understand the existing application. During the design phase, sequence diagrams are constructed to specify how objects interact to carry out a use case.

The third distinction between analysis and design is the difference between perception and computerized representation of the perception. The classes and objects in the analysis model are perceptions of domain concepts and their instances. In the design model, the classes and objects are software classes and software objects. They are computer or digital representations of the perceived domain concepts and instances.

Another distinction is that analysis models describe the world as it is while design models prescribe a software solution. This is because analysis models describe the application domain and help the development team understand the application. Therefore, they are descriptive. On the other hand, the design models prescribe a software solution because the design has taken into consideration proposals to improve the existing system.

Since analysis models describe "what the world is," they should not impose any restrictions on the design space. Therefore, an ideal analysis model should allow all possible design alternatives. On the other hand, design models are the result of design decisions; therefore, they may reduce the implementation space. Consider, for example, a design decision to allow business objects to access a relational database directly. This decision may be made because of its simplicity and efficiency. But it also makes it difficult for the software product to access a different database because the business objects and the database are tightly coupled.

9.2.5 Using the Notations Correctly

UML is a language. It has its vocabulary, syntax, and semantics. A sequence diagram is a UML diagram. Its vocabulary, syntax, and semantics are subsets of their

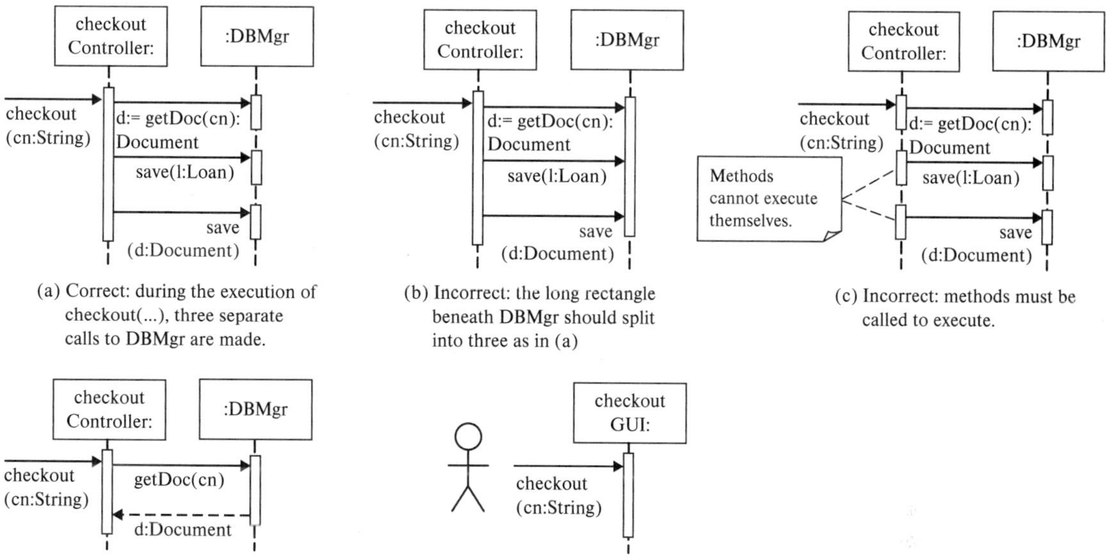

(a) Correct: during the execution of checkout(...), three separate calls to DBMgr are made.

(b) Incorrect: the long rectangle beneath DBMgr should split into three as in (a)

(c) Incorrect: methods must be called to execute.

(d) Not preferred: the back dashed arrow line can be interpreted differently. (a) is preferred.

(e) Incorrect: an actor cannot call a function of an object; should use a dashed line and stereotype message.

FIGURE 9.6 Correct and incorrect uses of notations

UML counterparts. It is important that these are used correctly when constructing sequence diagrams; otherwise, the resulting sequence diagram could be ambiguous, incorrect, or difficult to understand. It is possible to make numerous mistakes in sequence diagram drawing because there is no limit on the number of ways to abuse the diagramming technique. Figure 9.6 shows one correct use and several incorrect uses of sequence diagram modeling notations.

Figure 9.6(*a*) shows a correct sequence diagram. That is, during the execution of the checkout function of the checkout controller, three separate calls to functions of the DBMgr object are made. The sequence diagram in Figure 9.6(*b*) is incorrect because three calls to methods of the DBMgr object are represented by only one method execution. Figure 9.6(*c*) is incorrect, or difficult to understand, because the second and the third calls from the controller to the DBMgr object do not have incoming calls, which are required to trigger the execution of these two "anonymous" methods. In Figure 9.6(*d*), the dashed arrow line from the DBMgr object back to the controller should only be used in an analysis sequence diagram. Figure 9.6(*d*) is a design sequence diagram; therefore, the dashed arrow line and the "d:Document" label should be removed, and the call from the controller to the DBMgr object should be labeled by "d:=getDoc(cn:String):Document." In Figure 9.6(*e*), the solid arrow line should not be used because it represents a function call, which cannot come from an actor. It should be replaced by a dashed arrow line. The dashed arrow line should be labeled by a stereotyped message such as "<<check out cn>>."

9.3 STEPS FOR OBJECT INTERACTION MODELING

The steps for OIM are the following. They are performed for the use cases that are allocated to the current iteration.

Step 1. Collect information about existing business processes.

Step 2. Identify nontrivial steps from the expanded use cases assigned to the current iteration.

Step 3. Write object-interaction scenarios for the nontrivial steps.

Step 4. Convert the scenarios into scenario tables. This step is optional.

Step 5. Convert scenarios or scenario tables into sequence diagrams.

Step 6. Review the object interaction models.

The following sections describe each of the steps in detail.

9.3.1 Collecting Information About Business Processes

OIM requires the development team to possess sufficient knowledge about existing business processes of the use cases. To acquire such knowledge, the development team works with the customer and users to collect information about the business processes. The information gathered during the requirements analysis phase may be reused, and additional information is gathered in this step. The following is a partial list of items to focus on:

1. What is the current business situation and how does it operate?
2. What is the business for which the computerized system is built?
3. What are the business goals, or product goals?
4. What existing business processes are used to accomplish the goals? What is the functionality of each of these processes?
5. What are the input and output of each of the existing business processes?
6. How do existing processes work?
7. How do existing processes relate and interact with each other?
8. What are the improvements or enhancements expected by the customer and users?

9.3.2 Identifying Nontrivial Steps

An expanded use case (Chapter 8) is a two-column table that describes how an actor interacts with the system to carry out a business process. More specifically, the left column of an expanded use case specifies the actor input and actor actions while the right column specifies the system responses. Some of the system responses require background processing. That is, they require software objects to interact and collaborate with each other to produce the system responses. The right-column step that specifies such a system response is a nontrivial step. For example, step 4 in Figure 9.7 is nontrivial because it requires the system to retrieve the documents

UC1: Checkout Documents

Actor: Patron	System: LIS
	0) System displays the main GUI.
1) TUCBW patron clicking the Checkout Document button on the main GUI.	2) The system displays the Checkout GUI.
3) The patron enters the call numbers of documents to be checked out and clicks the Submit button.	4) The Checkout GUI displays a checkout message showing the details.
5) TUCEW the patron seeing the checkout message.	

FIGURE 9.7 Checkout Document expanded use case

from the database, create Loan objects, update the documents, and save all these to the database.

Nontrivial steps are identified as follows:

1. If the system response requires background processing, then the step is nontrivial.
2. If the system response simply displays a menu or input dialog, then the step is trivial. For example, step 2 in Figure 9.7 displays the checkout GUI, therefore, it is trivial.
3. If the system response is different for different actor of the use case, then the step is nontrivial; else, it is trivial. For example, step 4 in Figure 9.7 is nontrivial because the documents checked out by different patrons are different. On the other hand, step 2 in Figure 9.7 displays the same checkout GUI to different patrons, therefore, it is trival.

Note: Every expanded use case must have at least one nontrivial step. This is because every use case requires background processing. A use case may have more than one nontrivial step. For example, two-factor login needs to verify the password and then the passcode.

9.3.3 Writing Scenarios for Nontrivial Steps

Scenarios are widely used to describe how objects interact with each other to accomplish a task. The scenarios are then converted into UML sequence diagrams. In this book, scenarios are produced only for nontrivial steps. This simplifies the construction of the sequence diagrams and make them easy to understand and implement.

What Is a Scenario?

Object interaction is similar to the interaction between actors and actresses in a play. The actors and actresses interact according to the script of the play to act out the scenario. The software engineering community borrowed the word *scenario* to describe how objects interact with each other to carry out background processing. Object interaction scenarios are restricted to a small subset of the natural language. The sentences of the language are defined as follows.

Definition 9.2 An atomic *object interaction statement* is a declarative sentence in third-person, simple-present tense. It consists of a subject, an action of the subject, an object that is acted upon, and optionally, data or objects that are required by the subject action.

EXAMPLE 9.1 The following are examples of object interaction statements:

- The user enters user ID and password on the Login graphical user interface (GUI).

  In this case, "the user" is the subject, "enters" the action of the subject, and "user ID" and "password" are data required by the subject action. The object acted upon is the Login GUI.
- The checkout controller gets the document from the database manager using the document call number.

  In this case, the subject is the "checkout controller," the subject action is "get document," the object that is acted upon is the "database manager," the data or object required by the subject action is the "document call number."

Note in these examples, the sentences are in third-person, simple-present tense.

Compound object interaction statements can be composed from atomic object interaction statements with commonly used if-then-else, repetition, and other meaningful composition operators.

Definition 9.3 A compound object interaction statement is recursively defined as follows.

- An atomic object interaction statement is a compound object interaction statement.
- If S1, S2, . . . , Sn are compound object interaction statements and OP an n-nary composition operator, then the statement resulting from applying OP to S1, S2, . . . , Sn is a compound object interaction statement.

In this book, unless otherwise specified, statement, object interaction statement, atomic object interaction statement, and compound object interaction statement are used interchangeably.

Definition 9.4 A *scenario* for a nontrivial step is a sequence of object interaction statements. It begins with the statement in the step that precedes the nontrivial step in the expanded use case. It ends with the statement in the nontrivial step in the expanded use case.

EXAMPLE 9.2

Produce a scenario for the expanded use case in Figure 9.7.

Solution: According to the criteria presented in Section 9.3.2, step 4 is nontrivial. A scenario for the step is shown in Figure 9.8.

3) The patron submits the call numbers of documents to be checked out to the Checkout GUI.
4.1) Checkout GUI checks out documents with checkout controller using the call numbers.
4.2) For each document call number:
  4.2.1) Checkout controller gets the document from database manager (DBMgr) using the call number.
  4.2.2) DBMgr returns the document to checkout controller.
  4.2.3) Checkout controller creates a Loan object using patron and document.
  4.2.4) Checkout controller saves loan with DBMgr.
  4.2.5) Checkout controller sets document to not available.
  4.2.6) Checkout controller saves document with DBMgr.
4.3) Checkout controller returns a confirmation message to Checkout GUI.
4.4) Checkout GUI displays the confirmation message to patron.

FIGURE 9.8 Scenario for step 4 of Figure 9.7

9.3.4 Constructing Scenario Tables

Deriving sequence diagrams from scenarios is not an easy task for beginners because the relationship between the two is not obvious. A solution to this problem uses an intermediate representation called a scenario table. It can be easily derived from a scenario and easily converted into a sequence diagram. A scenario table has five columns. The first column denotes the object interaction statement number. The other columns correspond to the subject, subject action, data or objects required by the subject action, and the object acted upon, respectively. In other words, a scenario table is a tabular representation of a scenario. It separates the components of the scenario sentences into the columns of the scenario table. This tabular representation facilitates the conversion of the scenario into a sequence diagram. Another reason to construct the scenario table is that it facilitates automatic generation of sequence diagrams because the mapping from the table to a sequence diagram can be carried out mechanically.

Converting a scenario into a scenario table involves identifying the subject, subject action, data or objects required by the subject action, and the object acted upon. These are then entered into the scenario table row by row and column by column. The following example illustrates this.

EXAMPLE 9.3

Convert the scenario in Figure 9.8 into a scenario table.

Solution: Figure 9.9 shows the scenario table for the scenario in Figure 9.8.

#	Subject	Subject Action	Object or Data Required by Subject Action	Object Acted Upon
3	The patron	submits	call numbers	Checkout GUI
4.1	Checkout GUI	checks out documents	call numbers	Checkout Controller
4.2	For each document call number			
4.2.1	Checkout Controller	gets document	call number	DBMgr
4.2.2	DBMgr	returns	document	Checkout Controller
4.2.3	Checkout Controller	creates	patron and document	Loan object
4.2.4	Checkout Controller	saves	Loan object	DBMgr
4.2.5	Checkout Controller	sets available	false	document
4.2.6	Checkout Controller	saves	document	DBMgr
4.3	Checkout Controller	returns	confirmation message	Checkout GUI
4.4	Checkout GUI	displays	confirmation message	patron.

FIGURE 9.9 Scenario table for Figure 9.8

The conversion result shows that textual scenario descriptions and scenario tables are equivalent representations. Therefore, the team may choose to construct both, or only one of the two.

All scenario descriptions and scenario tables must satisfy the following:

Verification rule. *Except the first row, the subject of every row must be the object acted upon on the previous row or the subject of one of previous rows.*

As an exercise, the reader should check whether Figures 9.8 and 9.9 satisfy this verification rule. It is important to apply this rule to verify all scenarios or scenario tables you produce in the future. The rule is called a verification rule because it ensures that a scenario or scenario table is written correctly, meaning that others can understand the sequence diagram derived from the scenario or scenario table. Nevertheless, it does not ensure the correctness of the scenario or scenario table. The correctness is checked by design/code review and/or software testing.

9.3.5 Scenarios: How to Write Them

Writing a scenario is writing a high-level algorithm. It needs to make following decisions:

1. What are the tasks that need to be performed to produce the system response from the actor input? The result is a list of tasks such as get document and set document availability to false.
2. What is the desired order to carry out the tasks? The result is an ordered list of tasks.
3. For each of the tasks, determine the object to carry out the task, that is, the object that is acted upon.
4. For each of the tasks, determine the object that issues the request to perform the task. That is, the subject of the scenario sentence.

5. What are the data or objects, if any, required to perform the task?
6. How to obtain the data or objects required to perform the task if the subject does not have them?

Once these decisions are made, the logic for the high-level algorithm or scenario is developed. The remaining job is writing the scenario sentences using the results of these decisions.

EXAMPLE 9.4

What are the tasks required to produce the system response in the nontrivial step in Figure 9.7?

Solution: The only nontrivial step in Figure 9.7 is step 4. The task to begin with is "check out documents," which is the name of the use case. This task is broken into a number of subtasks, which are derived from the business process of the library application. For example, the checkout documents task needs to retrieve documents from the database, create the Loan objects, update the documents, and save the documents and Loan objects to the database. The task also returns a checkout message, as hinted by the description of step 4. These subtasks are ordered and listed as follows:

```
Checkout documents
   Get documents from database
   Create Loan objects
   Set documents to unavailable
   Save Loan objects to database
   Save documents to database
   Return a checkout message
```

To identify object to perform each of the tasks the worksheet in Figure 9.10 is used. The task and its subtasks are displayed in the third column. The nontrivial step is displayed in the last row. Examine each of the tasks and determine which object

#	Subject	Subject Action	Other Data/Objects	Object Acted Upon
		checkout documents		
		get documents (from database)		
		create Loan objects		
		set documents to unavailable		
		save Loan objects (to database)		
		save documents (to database)		
		return a checkout message		
		display checkout message		

FIGURE 9.10 Worksheet for scenario development

should perform the task. Enter the result in the last, or Object Acted Upon, column. Also specify the required input. To determine which object performs the task, look it up in the following places:

1. *First, look up the object in the second and the last columns of the current worksheet.* These are the objects that already participate in the current scenario. If the desired object is found, then there is no need to introduce a new object into the current scenario. This simplifies the design and implementation.
2. *Second, look up the object in the design class diagram.* The design class diagram, to be presented in Chapter 11, shows the classes that are designed and implemented in previous iterations. Therefore, they should be considered next. If the desired object is found, then there is no need to introduce another object into the design class diagram. This reduces the number of classes to implement.
3. *Third, look up the object in the domain model.* The domain model specifies the domain classes, their properties and relationships. It is a valuable source to identify the object to perform the task.
4. *Finally, look up the object elsewhere.* If the object is not found in above places, then look up the object in other places such as code and related business documents.

EXAMPLE 9.5 Determine the objects to perform the tasks in Figure 9.10 and the data or objects, if any, required by the tasks.

Solution: The first task in Figure 9.10 is to checkout documents. Which object should perform this task? One possible candidate is the checkout GUI because it knows when the patron clicks the Submit button. However, letting the checkout GUI perform this task may overload the checkout GUI object with responsibilities that are not relevant to a GUI object. A better design assigns the task to a checkout controller. This design lets the checkout GUI focus on its responsibility–that is, presenting information to users. This in effect applies the high-cohesion software design principle. Moreover, because the GUI object does not interact directly with the business objects. The design also supports low-coupling and design for change software design principles. To check out the documents, the controller needs to know the document call numbers. Therefore, the required input is document call numbers.

The second task in Figure 9.10 is to get documents from the database. This requires connecting to the database, querying the database, and processing the query result. If the task is assigned to the checkout controller, then the controller could become overloaded with database-related operations. Therefore, the decision is to assign the task to a database manager (DBMgr). This design supports high cohesion because the controller is only responsible for checking out documents, not other responsibilities. The required input is the document call numbers. For the same reason, the other two database-related tasks, save Loan objects and save documents, are also assigned to the database manager. The required inputs of these two tasks are the Loan objects and documents, respectively. Loan objects are created by calling the constructor of the Loan class. The input parameters are the patron and the documents to be checked out. Following object-oriented programming practice, the set documents to unavailable task should be carried out by the documents themselves. The results of all of these design decisions are displayed in Figure 9.11.

#	Subject	Subject Action	Other Data/Objects	Object Acted Upon
		checkout documents	call numbers	Checkout Controller
		get documents (from database)	call numbers	DBMgr
		create Loan objects	patron, documents	Loan
		set available	false	documents
		save	Loan objects	DBMgr
		save	documents	DBMgr
		return	checkout message	Checkout GUI
		display	checkout message	

FIGURE 9.11 Assigning tasks to objects

Now determine which object should issue the request to perform each of the tasks. As a rule of thumb, the object to issue the request is either the subject on one of the previous rows or the object acted upon on the previous row (the verification rule presented on page 208). This is detailed as follows:

1. If the task on the current row is a subtask of the task on the previous row, then the requesting object is the object acted upon on the previous row.
2. If the task on the current row is not a subtask of the task on the previous row, then the requesting object is the subject on one of the previous rows. Often, the requesting object is the subject of the previous row.
3. For the first task, the requesting object is the GUI object that receives the actor request. This GUI object is usually named after the name of the use case. Examples are login JSP for the Login use case and checkout GUI for the Checkout Document use case.

EXAMPLE 9.6

Determine the objects that issue the requests to perform the tasks in Figure 9.11.

Solution: The first task in Figure 9.11 is to check out documents. Which object should issue the request to perform this task? The answer is the checkout GUI because it receives the actor request to check out documents, as shown in step 3 of Figure 9.7. Next, which object should issue the request to get documents? Since get documents is a subtask of checkout documents, checkout controller should issue the request because it is the object acted upon on the previous row. The controller also issues the requests for the next five tasks because none of these is

#	Subject	Subject Action	Other Data/Objects	Object Acted Upon
	Checkout GUI	checkout documents	call numbers	Checkout Controller
	Checkout Controller	get documents	call numbers	DBMgr
	Checkout Controller	create Loan objects	patron, documents	Loan
	Checkout Controller	set available	false	documents
	Checkout Controller	save	Loan objects	DBMgr
	Checkout Controller	save	documents	DBMgr
	Checkout Controller	return	checkout message	Checkout GUI
	Checkout GUI	display	checkout message	

FIGURE 9.12 Specify the subjects that issue the requests

a subtask of the previous task. Finally, which object should display the checkout message? Since the task is not a subtask of the task on the previous row, it should be the subject of one of the previous rows. In this case, it is the checkout GUI on the first row. It is not checkout controller because the controller just returns the checkout message to the GUI. The results of these design decisions are displayed in Figure 9.12.

Two other tasks are needed to complete the scenario. First, for each task that returns a result, insert a row to return the result from the object acted upon to the requesting object. There are two such tasks in Figure 9.12–checkout documents and get documents. The get documents task should return the documents that are requested, as the name of the task suggests. Thus, a row indicating that the DBMgr returns the documents to the checkout controller is added after the get documents row. The checkout documents task should return a checkout message because the checkout GUI displays the message to the patron. Thus, a row indicating that the checkout controller returns a checkout message to the checkout GUI is inserted. This row is already there. Therefore, no row is added. In addition, one inserts conditional and loop statements at appropriate places if necessary. Finally, statement numbers are entered in the first column. The result is similar to the scenario table shown in Figure 9.9.

9.3.6 Converting Scenario Tables into Sequence Diagrams

Textual descriptions have a number of limitations. First, it is not easy to see which object sends which messages to which other objects and what is returned from the receiver objects. Second, it is not easy to see what actions the receiver object would perform when it receives a message. It is not easy to produce a software design from the textual, informal descriptions of scenarios. Finally, the informal style of scenario specification is not suitable for design verification and code skeleton generation. Since the scenario table is merely a tabular representation of a scenario, it also suffers the same set of problems. To overcome these problems, it is beneficial for the developer to visualize the scenarios of object interaction with UML sequence diagrams. This involves the following steps:

Step 4.1. Converting scenario tables into sequence diagrams. In this step, an informal sequence diagram is derived from each scenario table using the conversion rules in Figure 9.16.

Step 4.2. Deciding on instance names and types. In this step, the names and types of the object instances that send and receive messages are defined.

Step 4.3. Deciding on object interfacing. In this step, the function names, parameters, and return types are determined.

Converting Scenario Tables into Sequence Diagrams

Converting the scenario tables into sequence diagrams is guided by the conversion rules shown in Figure 9.13. In particular, each row of the scenario table is converted into a message between two objects, or between an actor and an object. There are four cases, which are processed differently as shown in Figure 9.13.

Case 1. The subject is an actor. In this case, the object acted upon can only be an object. This case represents an actor issuing a request to the software system. The request is entered in some way through the keyboard, mouse, touchscreen, or other hardware input devices. This converts into a stereotyped message from the actor to the object. The stereotyped message is a dashed arrow line with its label enclosed in a pair of double-angle brackets, as shown by the first case in Figure 9.13.

Case 2. The subject is an object and the object acted upon is an actor. This case represents the system delivering the system response to the actor. Most of the time this is accomplished through displaying a menu, a dialog, or information on the screen. This converts into a stereotyped message from the user interface (UI) object to the actor, as illustrated by the second case in Figure 9.13.

Case 3. The subject is an object and the object acted upon is another object. This case represents a function call from one object to another object. It is widely referred to as message passing. The call may involve a returned result from the object being called to the object that issues the call. This case converts into a solid arrow line, labeled by indicative texts, from the caller to the callee. The returned result, if any, is modeled by a dashed arrow line, labeled by the returned result, from the callee back to the caller. The third case in Figure 9.13 illustrates how to convert this. The dashed arrow line is used to distinguish the returned result from a function call, which is modeled by a solid arrow line. Note that the use of the dashed arrow line in this case and in Cases 1 and 2 causes no confusion because in this case two software objects are involved while in Cases 1 and 2 there is an object and an actor.

Case 4. The subject and the object acted upon are the same object. This case represents a call from a function of an object to another function of the same object. It is modeled by a solid arrow line from the object back to itself, as shown in the last case of Figure 9.13.

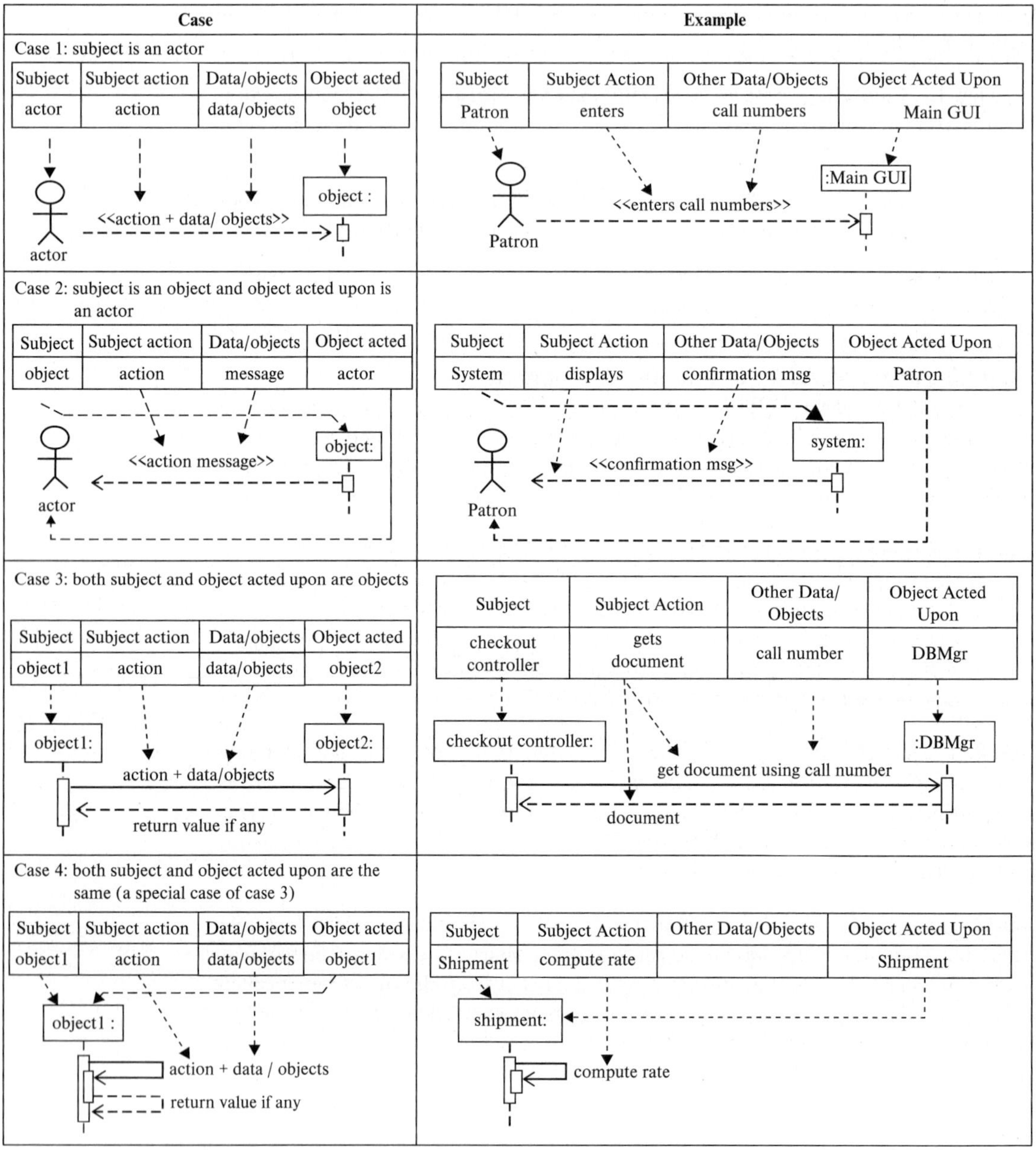

FIGURE 9.13 From scenario table to sequence diagram

EXAMPLE 9.7

Construct a sequence diagram from the scenario table shown in Figure 9.14.

Solution: The scenario table converts into the sequence diagram shown in Figure 9.3.

#	Subject	Action	Required Data/Objects	Object Acted Upon
(1)	Web user	submits	uid, password	LoginPage
(2)	LoginPage	verifies	uid, password	LoginController
(3)	LoginController	gets user	uid	DBMgr
(4)	DBMgr	returns	user	LoginController
(5)	LoginController	verifies	password	user
(6)	User	returns	result	LoginController
(7)	LoginController	returns	result	LoginPage
(8)	If result is true, LoginPage	displays	WelcomePage	Web user
(9)	If result is false, LoginPage	shows	Error message	Web user

FIGURE 9.14 Login scenario table with row numbers

EXAMPLE 9.8

Construct a sequence diagram from the scenario table in Figure 9.9.

Solution: Figure 9.15 depicts the informal sequence diagram obtained from the Checkout Document scenario table in Figure 9.9.

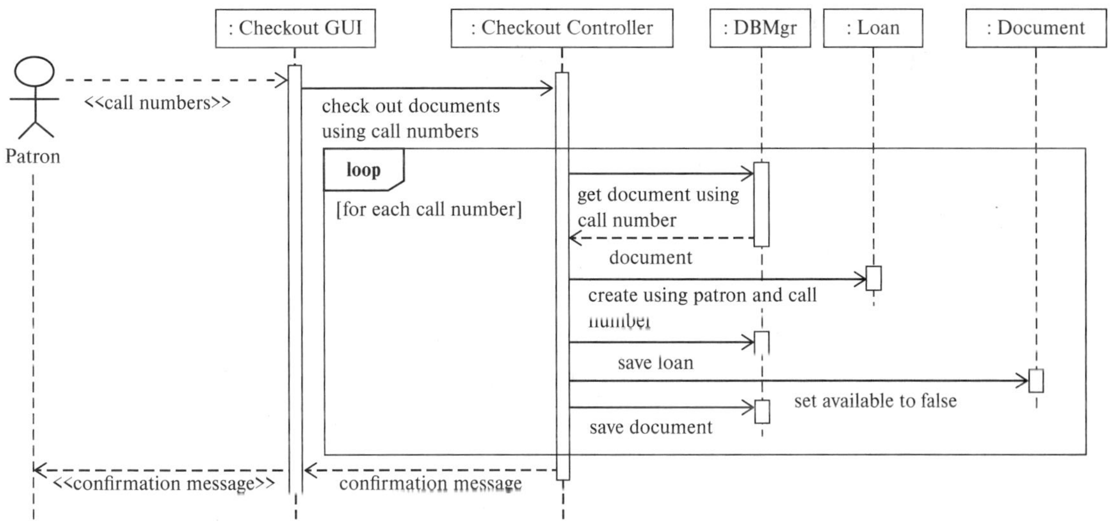

FIGURE 9.15 An informal sequence diagram with a loop

Deciding on Instance Names and Instance Types

Recall that when a scenario table is converted into a sequence diagram, the instance names and instance types are not specified. This step specifies the instance names and types by applying the following rules:

1. If an instance is used as a parameter or return value in the sequence diagram, then give the instance an instance name so that the instance name can be used to refer to that instance.
2. If an instance is not an instance of a class–if it is a JSP page–then give the instance an instance name and make the instance a stereotyped instance. Do not give the instance a class name because this could cause confusion.

The following rules are applied to determine the instance types:

1. When deciding on the class for an instance, look it up first in the current sequence diagram, then in the design class diagram, and finally in the domain model. If the needed class is not found in all of these diagrams, then introduce a new class and give it a meaningful class name.
2. When deciding on the class for the elements of a collection, two cases are considered:
   a. If the elements of the collection are instances of only one class, then that class is the class for the elements of the collection.
   b. If the elements of the collection are instances of subclasses of a superclass, then the superclass is used as the class for the elements of the collection.

Deciding on Object Interfacing

This section describes how to convert informally specified messages into formally specified messages. This converts informal or analysis sequence diagrams into design sequence diagrams, also called formal sequence diagrams. It is useful to note that one needs only to consider messages that are passed between two software objects. One does not need to consider messages that are passed between an object and an actor. The exception to this is that the actor is a software subsystem/component that requires a formally defined interface. There are two cases to consider. The first case is that the software actor already exists. In this case, the external interface must have been defined. The development team is obligated to use that interface. The other case is that the software system under construction can define its actor interface such as an application programming interface (API) to the potential clients. In this case, the development team will have the freedom to define the actor interface.

An informally specified message is translated to a formally specified message as follows. The subject action is converted into a function call, and the data or objects required by the subject action are converted into parameters. If the function returns a result, then the result is saved in a variable, which is introduced for this purpose. If more than one piece of information is returned, then additional calls to appropriate get functions are introduced to retrieve the results. In most cases, the conversions are straightforward. Figure 9.16(*a*) shows the general rule and Figure 9.16(*b*) an example.

Deciding on parameter types and return types is an application-dependent issue as well as a software design decision. This means domain knowledge is required and may be found in the domain model. It is a design decision because there are different

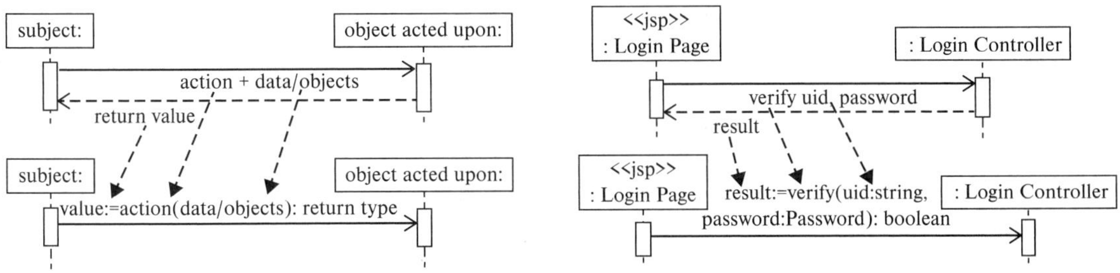

(a) General conversion rule (b) Example

FIGURE 9.16 Deciding on function names, parameters, and return variables

ways to pass data between two objects. In this regard, it is desirable to accomplish low coupling as described by the following guidelines:

GUIDELINE 9.1 Use data coupling whenever possible and appropriate.

Data coupling means that a single data value is passed as a parameter or return value from one function to another. The data value is only used in a computation to produce some result, not in selecting a path or control flow in a program.

GUIDELINE 9.2 Prefer object coupling over stamp coupling. Make sure that the update functions implement the necessary integrity checks.

Stamp coupling means that a data structure is passed as a parameter or return value from one function to another. Similarly, object coupling means that an object is passed as a parameter or return value. Often,the data structure has semantics and assumptions. These may not be obvious. Therefore, the data structure could be used incorrectly. Object coupling is preferred because functions of an object could implement integrity checks to ensure that its data structure is used correctly.

GUIDELINE 9.3 If several attributes of an object are passed as parameters to a function call, then use object coupling instead.

GUIDELINE 9.4 Avoid control coupling, common coupling, and never use external coupling.

Control coupling means that two functions are coupled with a control variable, which determines the program path or control flow at runtime. For example, a parameter used as the case variable in a switch statement is a control variable. Its value determines which case to be executed. Control coupling means that the behavior of one object is controlled by another object. The runtime behavior is very difficult to predict, test, and debug. Therefore, control coupling should be avoided.

Common coupling means that functions communicate through a global data area or a global variable. Concurrent updates to such variables may produce unpredicable behavior. In object-oriented programming, the use of a public static data member constitutes a common coupling because that data member can be accessed and updated by all objects. External coupling means that functions communicate via the memory space of an external device. This type of coupling should be avoided because the external memory space could be modified by external programs, resulting in unpredictable behavior.

EXAMPLE 9.9 Discuss the design in Figure 9.17 and make necessary improvements.

Solution: The design in Figure 9.17 exhibits control coupling due to the use of the control variable r. The value of r is computed by the User object and influences the runtime behavior of the JSP page. Figure 9.18 shows the improved sequence diagram in which the three-value control variable r is replaced with two boolean variables. The semantics of the boolean variables and the sequence diagram is clearer.

Suppose that the verify function of the User class is changed to return four values instead of three values, with the additional value to indicate that the user's account has been revoked. Suppose for some reason, that the meaning of the return values is reassigned, for example, 0 means valid login, 1 means need to change password, 2 means invalid login, and 3 means account revoked. In this case, the system implemented according to the design in Figure 9.17 will no longer work. However, the system implemented according to the design in Figure 9.18 will still work except that the newly added case will not be in effect until the design and the JSP page are changed accordingly.

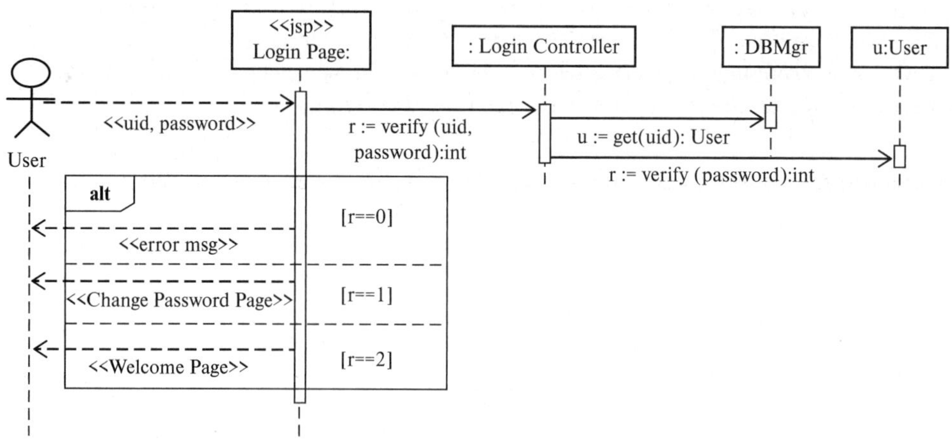

FIGURE 9.17 Object interfacing via a control variable (not a good design)

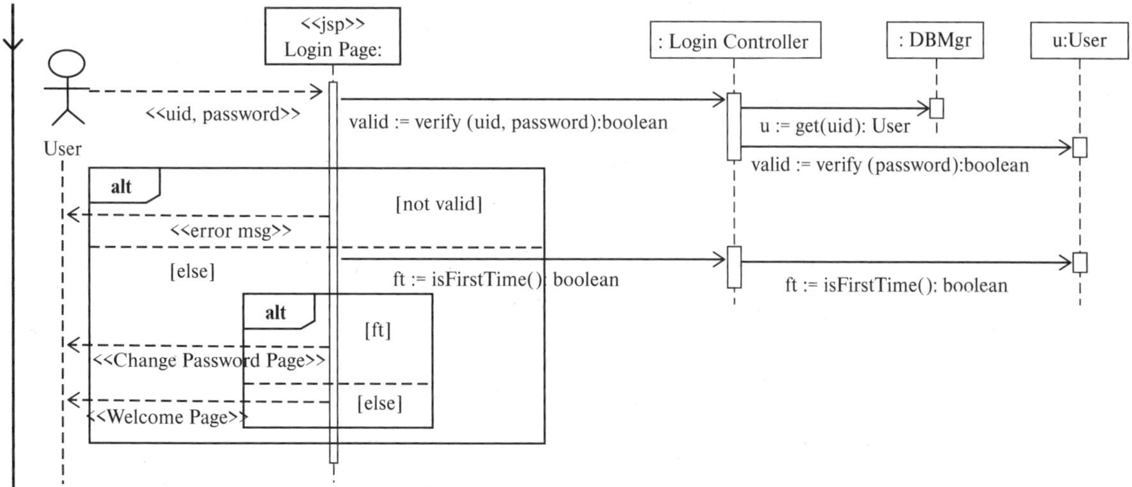

FIGURE 9.18 Improved: using boolean variables instead of control variables

EXAMPLE 9.10

Convert the informal sequence diagram in Figure 9.15 into a design sequence diagram.

Solution: Figure 9.19 shows the resulting design sequence diagram.

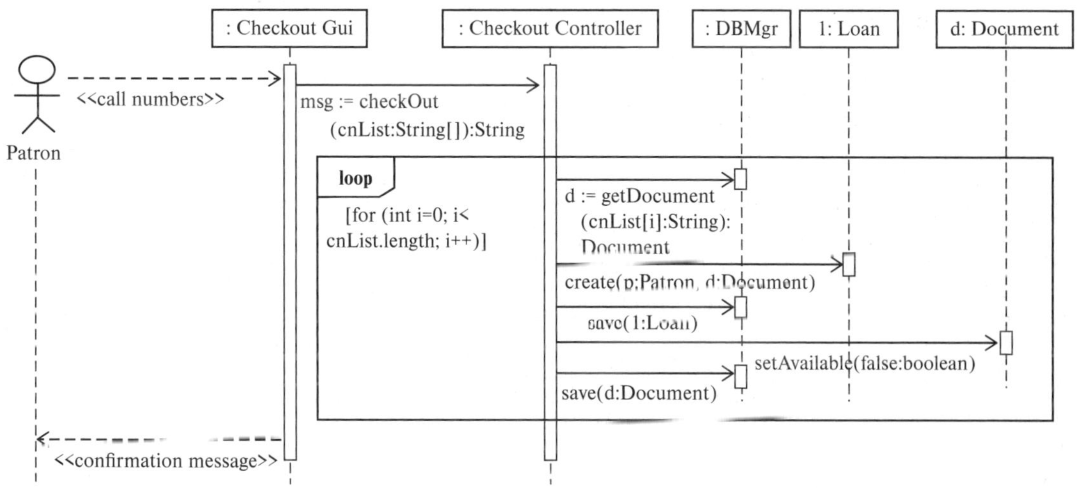

FIGURE 9.19 Checkout Document design sequence diagram

9.3.7 Object Interaction Modeling Review Checklist

1. Ensure that the scenarios satisfy the verification rule presented at the end of Section 9.3.4 as well as the sequence diagrams correctly and adequately describe the high-level algorithm to process the actor requests.
2. Ensure that all messages of a design sequence diagram are formally specified and there is no use of dashed arrow lines to return a result to an object.
3. Ensure that all required parameters and return values are present and the parameters are defined before being used in a function call.
4. Ensure that all objects retrieved from a database and updated are saved back to the database.
5. Ensure that all function names properly communicate their intended functionalities.
6. Ensure that each sequence diagram satisfies all of the following conditions:
   a. *The sequence diagram speaks*—that is, the sequence diagram is syntactically correct.
   b. *The sequence diagram speaks the right ideas*—meaning that the sequence diagram correctly describes the algorithm or scenario that you intend to express.

9.4 APPLYING AGILE PRINCIPLES

Modeling is a useful tool to improve understanding and communication between team members. The models produced are an important part of system documentation, which are a valuable aid for system maintenance. However, extensive modeling could do more harm than good. Modeling should serve its purpose; it is wasting time and effort to produce the diagrams just for certification audits. This section presents guidelines for OIM, taking into consideration agile modeling principles.

GUIDELINE 9.5 Work closely with the customer and users to understand their business processes, especially how the business processes the transactions.

Agile development emphasizes active user involvement during the entire development process. In particular, with active user involvement, information about the existing business processes could be obtained more easily and more accurately. This information is useful for constructing object interaction models to help the development team understand the current processes. Users can help the development team analyze the current business processes to identify problems and develop viable solutions. Another benefit of active user involvement is validating that the proposed computerized solutions would solve their business problems. It should be noted that although UML sequence diagrams are relatively easy for the development team to understand, they are not easy for most users. Therefore, scenarios rather than sequence diagrams should be used to communicate with users.

GUIDELINE 9.6 The team members should write the scenarios and construct the scenario tables together. Do not do these individually and separately.

A common understanding of the business processes among the team members is crucial to the success of the software project. Working together to develop the scenarios is an effective means to establish such an understanding. During this process, the team members exchange views and design ideas, and debate issues. The end results are scenarios or scenario tables. An important distinction is that the process leads to the result, but the result is not equivalent to the process. The process establishes the common understanding, which is the most crucial part of modeling. An alternative to developing the scenarios together is letting the team members write the scenarios separately. This approach produces the scenarios, but the process to exchange views and ideas is missing. It often happens with student team projects, where the team members do not want to spend time working together, so they divide the task among themselves. Numerous such projects fail because the scenarios produced by different members are not consistent with each other. It requires tremendous time and effort to correct such problems. The team encounters tremendous difficulties in subsequent design, implementation, integration, and testing phases due to the lack of a common understanding.

GUIDELINE 9.7 No need to construct the scenario, scenario table, or sequence diagram if the team members understand the business process very well.

The "barely enough modeling" principle tells us that modeling is performed only when it is needed. Therefore, if the team has a good understanding of the business process, then OIM can be skipped unless that documentation is compulsory. This is because modeling is aimed to help understanding and communication. If the team already understands the business process, then models are redundant. Modeling could be skipped if the business process is simple enough or the team has prior experience.

GUIDELINE 9.8 Converting the scenario table or scenario into a sequence diagram should be done off-line and be a one-person job.

Once the scenario or the scenario table is produced, drawing the sequence diagram is the easiest thing of all. In fact, the sequence diagram can be produced by a computer program. Therefore, drawing the diagrams should be performed by a team member off-line.

GUIDELINE 9.9 Keep it simple and stupid. Leave detail and exception handling to coding. If needed, outline these in a UML note.

GUIDELINE 9.10 Remove doubt by prototyping.

OIM is behavioral modeling. Writing a scenario is similar to writing a high-level algorithm. One challenge of algorithm design is that sometimes one does not know whether the algorithm would solve the intended problem and the performance is good enough. In cases like these, an executable prototype can be constructed to ensure that the algorithm satisfies its design objectives.

9.5 TOOL SUPPORT FOR OBJECT INTERACTION MODELING

Tools for drawing and managing sequence diagrams include IBM Rational Modeler, Microsoft Visio, ArgoUML, NetBeans UML Plugin, and others. These tools provide editing capabilities and other related features. The tools also support reverse engineering and code generation.

9.6 SUMMARY

This chapter presents the OIM methodology and UML sequence diagram. *Scenario* and *scenario table* are used to facilitate sequence diagram construction. A scenario is produced for each nontrivial step of an expanded use case. The scenario is then converted into a scenario table, which is converted into an informal sequence diagram. The informally specified messages of an informal sequence diagram are translated into formally specified messages, resulting in a design sequence diagram.

OIM is an important step of object-oriented analysis and design. It concerns the analysis and design of one of the three behavioral aspects of an object-oriented system—that is, object interaction modeling, state modeling (Chapter 13), and activity modeling (Chapter 14). This chapter does not present application of design patterns. This is done on purpose to let the student focus on one aspect at a time. The next chapter will present how to apply responsibility assignment design patterns during OIM. Design patterns codify object-oriented design principles. Therefore, when design patterns are applied correctly the design principles are applied as well.

9.7 CHAPTER REVIEW QUESTIONS

1. What is OIM?
2. What is the usefulness of OIM?
3. What is a sequence diagram?
4. What is the relationship between OIM and sequence diagrams?
5. What are analysis, and design sequence diagrams, respectively? What are the uses of these diagrams?
6. What is the relationship between an expanded use case and a design sequence diagram with respect to a given use case?
7. What are a scenario and a scenario table, respectively?
8. What are the relationships between scenario, scenario table, analysis sequence diagram, and design sequence diagram?
9. What are the steps of OIM?
10. How are agile principles applied during OIM?

9.8 EXERCISES

9.1 Write a scenario for the Order a Dish use case of a manually operated restaurant. For simplicity, assume that only one dish is ordered.

9.2 Highlight the subjects, subject actions, the objects acted upon, and data and objects required by the subject actions in the Order a Dish scenario.

9.3 Represent the Order a Dish scenario using a scenario table.

9.4 Construct an informal sequence diagram for the Order a Dish scenario.

9.5 Produce scenarios, scenario tables, informal sequence diagram and design sequence diagrams for the Deposit Money, Withdraw Money, Check Balance, and Transfer Money expanded use cases you produced for the ATM application in exercise 8.1.

9.6 For the online car rental application described in Appendix D.1, produce scenarios, scenario tables, informal sequence diagrams and design sequence diagrams for the nontrivial steps of the Search Car, Reserve Car, and Cancel Reservation expanded use cases you produced in exercise 8.4.

9.7 Produce scenarios, scenario tables, informal sequence diagrams and design sequence diagrams for the nontrivial steps of the expanded use cases you produced for the state diagram editor problem in exercise 8.6.

9.8 Suppose that you are to design and implement a software tool for OIM using the methodology presented in this chapter. The tool should support the methodology steps and automatically generate the design artifacts whenever possible. This includes automatic generation of sequence diagrams from the scenario tables–that is, there is no need for the user to draw the sequence diagrams manually although the user may need to edit the generated diagrams. The following are some of the analysis and design tasks:

a. Produce a list of requirements for this software tool.

b. Derive use cases from the requirements.

c. Construct a requirements-use case traceability matrix.

d. Construct a domain model for this application.

e. Specify the high-level and expanded use cases.

f. Perform OIM for some of the nontrivial use cases.

Which of the OIM steps can be fully or highly automated and how?

9.9 Verify the scenario table in Figure 9.14 using the verification rule presented at the end of Section 9.3.4.

9.10 Explain why the verification rule presented in Section 9.3.4 can ensure that the sequence diagram derived from a verified scenario or scenario table can be understood by others.

9.11 Apply the verification rule in Section 9.3.4 to check the scenarios and scenario tables you produce in previous exercises.

10 Chapter

Applying Responsibility-Assignment Patterns

Key Takeaway Points

- Design patterns are abstractions of proven design solutions to commonly encountered design problems.
- The controller, expert, and creator patterns are applicable to almost all object-oriented systems.

Chapter 9 presented the basic methodology for object interaction modeling (OIM). It is a basic methodology because it does not take into account the various software design principles. This is done on purpose to make the steps easy to understand and easy to follow. This chapter presents how to apply certain software design patterns during OIM. It will discuss relevant software design principles to help understand what is considered a good design. In particular, it will discuss problems associated with some of the commonly seen design sequence diagrams. The problems will be explained in terms of violation of software design principles. To solve these problems, several design patterns are introduced and how to apply these patterns to improve the design is illustrated. Throughout this chapter, you will find answers to the following questions:

- What are design patterns?
- What are situation-specific patterns?
- What are general responsibility-assignment software patterns (GRASP)?
- What is the singleton pattern?
- What are the benefits of applying patterns?
- How does one apply three of the GRASP patterns to improve a design, and how does one evaluate the resulting design?

10.1 WHAT ARE DESIGN PATTERNS?

Human beings have used patterns for a long time. For example, farmers have used cloud patterns to predict weather, and stock market investors use chart patterns to predict price movements of stocks and mutual funds. The architectural design patterns were first studied by Christopher Alexandra, who discovered that buildings that can withstand severe natural disasters have something in common. They all exhibit a set of design ideas, which he formulated as design patterns.

Definition 10.1 *Design patterns* are abstractions of proven design solutions to commonly encountered design problems.

First, a pattern is a *design abstraction*, as opposed to a concrete design. This enables a pattern to solve many similar design problems. Each pattern is also a *design solution*; it solves a design problem or a class of similar design problems. The design problem is unique to the pattern. A pattern is a *proven* design solution—that is, its effectiveness is established by practical applications, not claimed. Finally, a pattern solves a *commonly encountered* design problem; hence, it can be applied again and again to solve many similar design problems in a wide variety of applications.

The software engineering community recognized the idea and began the R&D in software design patterns in the 1980s. To date, the most well-known and influential collection of software design patterns remains the 23 so-called Gang of Four (GoF) patterns [Gamma 1995]. These patterns are called Gang of Four patterns because the book collecting them has four authors. Each pattern has a name, comprised of an abstraction of the design problem and the design solution. For example, the *singleton* pattern solves the following design problem: "How does one design *a class that has at most one globally accessible instance*?"[1]

This design problem is common in many practical applications. For example, a system needs only one system configuration object and many components need configuration information. Therefore, it is desirable to make it globally accessible. A system log file and the catalog of a library are other applications of singleton. Figure 10.1(*a*) displays a UML class diagram that describes the pattern. The Subject class is the application class that should have at most one globally accessible instance, for example, the System Configuration, the System Log, or the Library Catalog class. It has a private static instance of its own type. This instance is initially null. The Subject class has a private constructor. This ensures that no other object can create an instance of the Subject class. The static getInstance() function ensures that at most one instance is created. It allows other objects to access the instance globally through static calls. Figures 10.1 (b) and (c) show two different implementations in Java. Patterns are often described using class diagrams and also sequence diagrams. The class diagram specifies the participants, their roles and responsibilities, and how they relate to each other. The sequence diagram describes how the participants interact with each other to solve the design problem. UML notes are commonly used to provide additional information, as illustrated in Figure 10.1(*a*).

[1]Strictly speaking, a singleton can have a limited number of globally accessible instances.

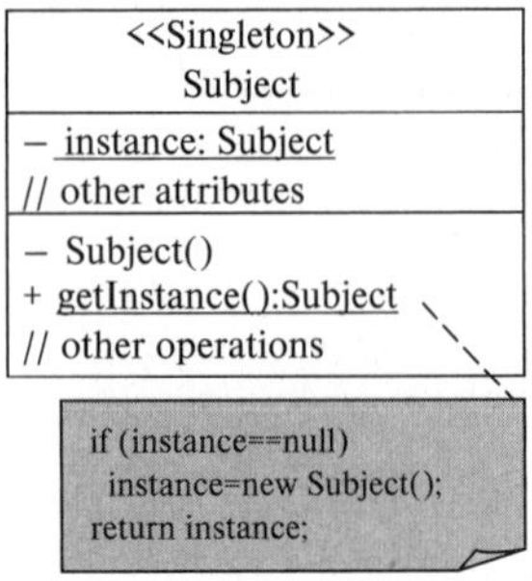


```
public class Subject {
  private static Subject instance;
  // other attributes
  private Subject() { ... }
  public static Subject getInstance()
  {
    if (instance==null)
      instance=new Subject();
    return instance;
  }
  // other operations
}
```

```
public class Subject {
  private static Subject
    instance=new Subject();
  // other attributes
  private Subject() { ... }
  public static Subject getInstance()
  {
      return instance;
  }
  // other operations
}
```

(a) UML specification (b) Java implementation (c) Another Java implementation

UML legend: –: private +: public underlined: static

FIGURE 10.1 The singleton pattern

10.2 WHY DESIGN PATTERNS?

Patterns are proven design solutions to commonly encountered design problems. Patterns can be combined to solve large complex design problems. In addition, patterns offer a number of benefits. First, patterns improve communication because the pattern names effectively convey the design problems and solutions. For example, without using patterns, one has to explain the design problem, the design idea, and how to realize it. By mentioning the pattern(s) applied, one can communicate all of these effectively. Improved communication leads to improvement in teamwork and elevates team moral. Patterns improve face-to-face communication, communication between teams or team members at different locations, and communication across time. Second, many patterns implement software design principles. Therefore, patterns improve the quality of software systems. Components designed and implemented with patterns are easy to understand, test, and maintain. Third, patterns are reusable designs. Successful reuse of well-designed and well-tested software components improve software productivity and software quality. Many experiences indicate that the use of design patterns significantly enhances the development team's ability to tackle complex design problems. Patterns empower less-experienced developers because patterns enable them to produce high-quality software. Finally, patterns effectively support agile development because patterns reduce design, implementation, testing and change efforts.

10.3 CATEGORIES OF PATTERNS

The GoF patterns are situation-specific patterns, meaning that each pattern solves a specific class of design problems. For example, there are many applications of the singleton pattern. In addition, two or more patterns can be combined in an infinite number of ways to solve countless design problems. The GoF patterns are classified into three categories–that is, creational patterns, structural patterns, and behavioral patterns. Creational patterns are useful for creating objects to solve different design problems. The singleton pattern is one such pattern. Structural patterns are useful for solving design problems concerning class structures. An example is how to represent a complex class structure such as a block diagram. Behavioral patterns are used to solve behavioral or algorithmic design problems. Examples are how to schedule the execution of operations, how to process events, and how to perform analysis algorithms on elements of a complex class structure.

Another set of well-known software design patterns is the General Responsibility-Assignment Software Patterns (GRASP), published by Craig Larman [Larman 2004]. Unlike GoF patterns, GRASP patterns are general responsibility-assignment patterns. General, because they can be applied to design almost every software system. Responsibility-assignment, because they address an important object-oriented design problem. That is, which object should be assigned a given responsibility or function so that the resulting design will satisfy software design principles. This chapter presents singleton and three GRASP patterns: controller, expert, and creator. Chapters 13, 15–17 and 21 present the remaining 22 GoF patterns.

10.4 PATTERN SPECIFICATION

A pattern specification includes structural and behavioral descriptions of a pattern to facilitate understanding and application of the pattern. For example, Figure 10.2 shows the specification of the singleton pattern discussed earlier. A pattern specification describes the important, or useful aspects of a pattern:

1. *Name and type.* These specify the name and the type of the pattern. The pattern type indicates the family of the pattern. For example, GoF, GRASP, or other type of patterns. Following [Gamma 1995], GoF patterns are further divided into creational, structural, and behavioral patterns.
2. *Specification.* This section specifies the design problem and design solution of the pattern.
3. *Design.* This section describes the structural design and the behavioral design of the pattern. A UML class diagram is used to describe the structural design. The behavioral design is described by a sequence diagram. In addition, the classes are described in terms of their roles and their responsibilities in solving the design problem.
4. *Benefits and liabilities.* These describe the advantages of applying the pattern, and any potential problems or price to pay.
5. *Guidelines.* Sometimes useful information for applying the pattern is provided.
6. *Related patterns.* Patterns that are related in various ways are described here.
7. *Uses.* General or specific applications of the pattern may be described.

10.5 THE CONTROLLER PATTERN

The *controller* pattern is used with every use case. It addresses the problem of how to design software systems that allow their user interfaces and business objects to change independently without affecting one another. Another design problem addressed by

<table>
<tr><td>Name</td><td>Singleton</td></tr>
<tr><td>Type</td><td>GoF/Creational</td></tr>
<tr><td>Specification</td><td></td></tr>
<tr><td>Problem</td><td>How to design a class that has only a limited number of globally accessible instances?</td></tr>
<tr><td>Solution</td><td>Make the constructor of the class private and define a public static method to control the creation of the instances.</td></tr>
<tr><td>Design</td><td></td></tr>
<tr><td>Structural</td><td>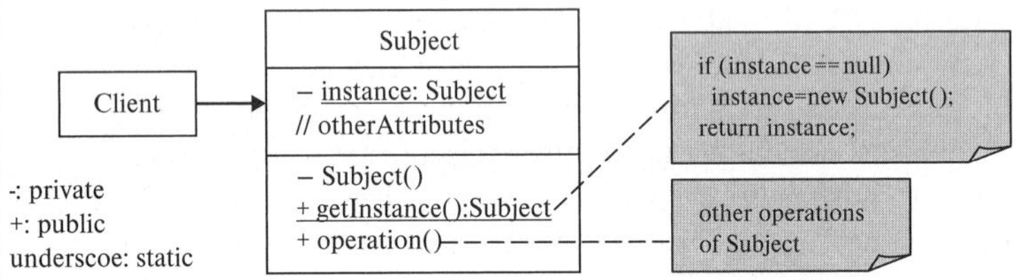
</td></tr>
<tr><td>Behavioral</td><td>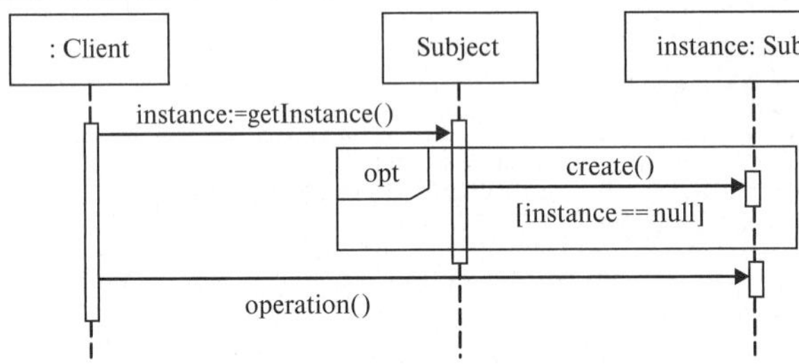
</td></tr>
<tr><td>Roles and Responsibilities</td><td>• Subject: It provides a public static getInstance() method for the client to retrieve its instance.
• Client: It calls the getInstance() method of Subject to retrieve the instance and calls its operation().</td></tr>
<tr><td>Benefits</td><td>• It limits the number of instances of the singleton class.
• It supports global access to the instance(s).</td></tr>
<tr><td>Liabilities</td><td>• Concurrent update to the shared instance may cause unwanted effect.</td></tr>
<tr><td>Guidelines</td><td>• Singleton must not be used when multiple threads or objects can update the single instance(s).</td></tr>
<tr><td>Related Patterns</td><td>• Singleton limits the number of instances of a class. Flyweight supports numerous occurrences of an object. Prototype reduces the number of classes.
• Concrete visitors and concrete factories can be singletons.</td></tr>
<tr><td>Uses</td><td>Singleton is used in many applications, e.g., system configuration, system log and the Java Calendar API.</td></tr>
</table>

FIGURE 10.2 Specification of the singleton pattern

the pattern is how to support multiple user interface technologies such as desktop user interfaces, web-based interfaces, or others. The controller pattern is a special case of the well-known model-view-controller (MVC) pattern. That is, it is an application of the MVC to handling of actor requests of a use case.

10.5.1 A Motivating Example

To motivate, Figure 10.3 shows a commonly seen design sequence diagram for the Checkout Document use case, which checks out a document with a given call number. The design in Figure 10.3 has the following problems:

1. **Tight coupling between the presentation and the business objects.** In Figure 10.3, the Checkout GUI object is commonly referred to as the presentation because it

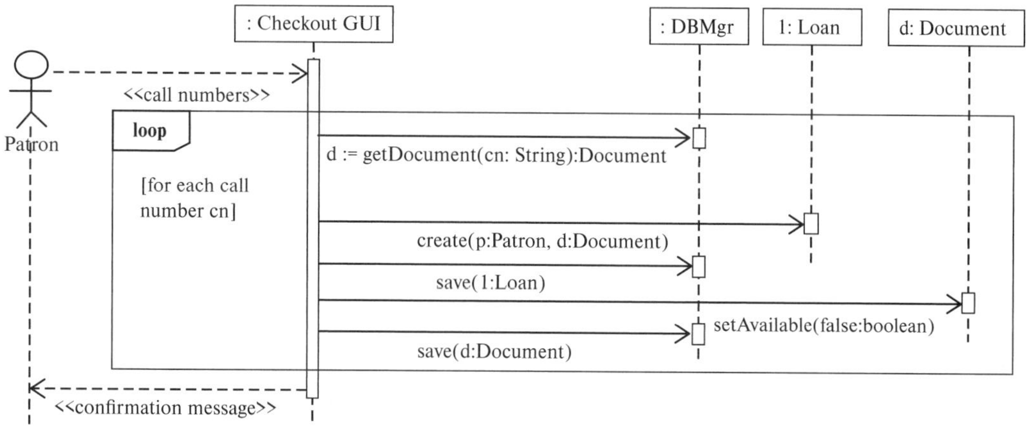

FIGURE 10.3 A commonly seen Checkout Document sequence diagram

is responsible for presenting information to the actor. The Document and Loan objects are called business objects or domain objects because they are objects of the application domain, which in this case is the library domain. The figure shows that the presentation directly accesses the business objects. For example, the Checkout GUI creates the Loan object and calls the isAvailable() and set-Available(false) functions of the Document object. These function calls create tight couplings between the presentation and the business objects. These tight couplings are not desirable, for the following reasons.

Tight coupling means that changes to the business objects may require changes to the presentation and vice versa. It is obvious that changes to the interfaces of the business objects will require changes to the presentation. However, changes to the functionality may also require changes to the presentation. Consider, for example, a function of a business object that originally returns an integer of two values is changed to return more than two values. If this integer is used as a control variable by the presentation to determine which path to follow or what to display to the user, then the presentation has to be changed to take into account the additional values. Another case is that the number of returned values is not changed, but the implications of the returned values are changed. Such changes happen all the time in practice. For example, someone thinks that it makes more sense to rearrange the values. In this case, changes to the presentation are also required.

The tight coupling between the presentation and business objects makes it difficult and costly to support multiple presentations. These include desktop user interface, web-based user interface, and smartphone user interface, to mention a few. This is because the business logic must be duplicated in each of the presentations. That is, every message or function call in Figure 10.3 has to be duplicated for each of the presentations. As a consequence, changes to the business logic are difficult because every presentation has to change. If the multiple presentations are not changed consistently, then the software system will behave inconsistently or produce inconsistent results.

For the simple example shown in Figure 10.3, these do not seem to be a problem. But the scale of the problem should be understood by multiplying the effort to make the changes and the difficulty to maintain the consistency with the number of use cases that a real-world application could have. This number easily adds up to more than 20 use cases for a very small application and hundreds of use cases for a large system.

The tight coupling creates problems for software evolution or maintenance. One type of evolution is enhancement. For example, consider a system that was originally designed as a desktop application. Later on the business wants to make it an online application. In this case, a web-based interface is added. The tight coupling between the presentation and business objects makes it difficult and costly to add a web-based interface because everything must be duplicated in the implementation of the new interface. This is one of the reasons that companies finally decide to reengineer their software systems to make them easier to enhance in the future.

2. **The presentation has to handle actor requests.** The design in Figure 10.3 indicates that the presentation has to handle actor requests that require background processing. For example, the presentation in Figure 10.3 processes the document checkout request from the patron. It should not be the responsibility of the presentation to handle such actor requests because the functionality of the presentation is to display the user interface and system responses.

   In Section 6.3.3 of Chapter 6, the principle of *separation of concerns* was discussed. The principle was originally proposed by Dijkstra as a problem-solving principle, that is, focusing on one aspect of the problem rather than tackling all aspects at the same time. With regard to software design, this principle suggests that each component should focus on one aspect of the subject matter. According to this, the responsibility to handle actor requests that require background processing should be assigned to a business object rather than the presentation.

3. **The presentation is assigned too many responsibilities.** As a consequence, the presentation is assigned too many responsibilities. That is, it is assigned the responsibility to present system responses as well as the responsibility to process business logic. It is not a "stupid object" because it knows how to do both. It also violates the principle of high cohesion because the two sets of responsibilities are not related and should not be assigned to one object.

10.5.2 What Is a Controller?

As discussed above, the design sequence diagram in Figure 10.3 has three problems: (1) the presentation is tightly coupled with business objects, (2) the presentation has to handle actor requests that require background processing, and (3) the presentation is assigned too many responsibilities.

A solution to these problems should (1) decouple the presentation and the business objects, (2) remove the responsibility to handle an actor request from the presentation and assign it to another object. The question is which object should be assigned the responsibility to handle actor requests? The answer is the *controller*, as displayed

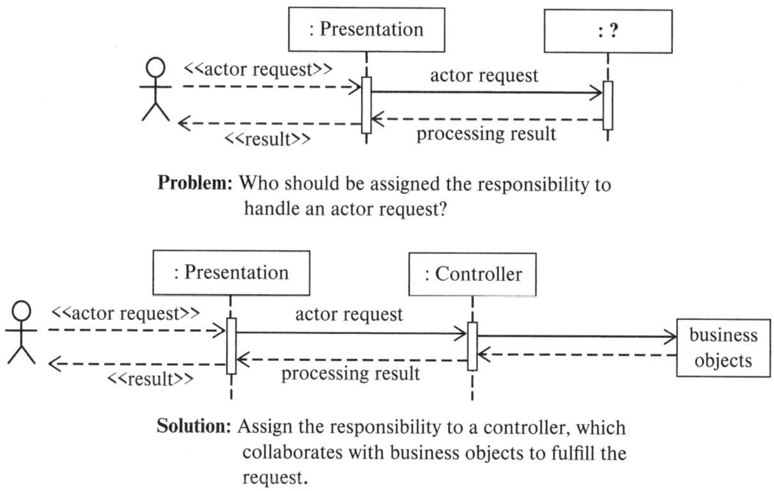

FIGURE 10.4 The controller pattern illustrated

in Figure 10.4. The figure shows that a controller is introduced and placed between the presentation and business objects. The presentation captures the actor request and delivers it to the controller. The controller collaborates with business objects to handle the actor request. The controller delivers the result to the presentation, which displays the result to the actor. Figure 10.5 provides more detail about the controller pattern.

The controller pattern nicely solves the problems discussed in Section 10.5.1. The presentation and business objects are now decoupled. The responsibility to handle an actor request is removed from the presentation and assigned to the controller. As a consequence, changes to one will not affect the other. Supporting multiple types of presentation technologies is easy. To add a new type of presentation, one needs only to design and implement the new presentation and have it deliver the actor request to the controller. This greatly facilitates software evolution or enhancement maintenance.

10.5.3 Applying the Controller Pattern

To apply the controller pattern to the design in Figure 10.3, one simply introduces a controller in between the presentation and the business objects. In addition, the business logic is removed from the presentation and assigned to the controller. Figure 10.6 shows the result. Notice that the Checkout GUI object now is only responsible for presenting information to the patron. The responsibility to process the checkout request is assigned to the Checkout Controller object, which interacts with the DBMgr and business objects to fulfill the responsibility.

10.5.4 Controller and Software Design Principles

It is instructional to briefly discuss the design in Figure 10.6 with respect to the software design principles presented in Section 6.3 of Chapter 6. The discussion is aimed to illustrate how to evaluate a design using software design principles. In addition, the discussion helps the student understand the design principles.

Name	Controller
Type	GRASP
Specification	
Problem	Who should be responsible for handling an actor request?
Solution	Assign the responsibility to handle the request to a dedicated class called controller.
Design	
Structural	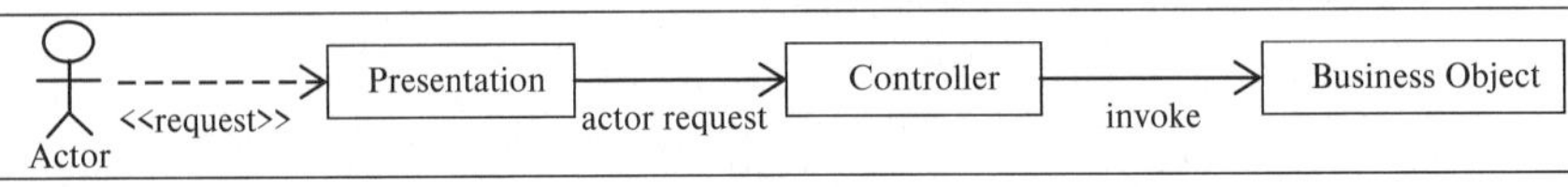
Behavioral	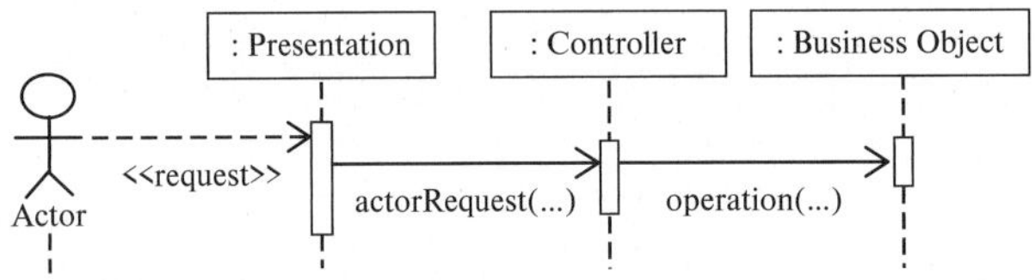
Roles and Responsibilities	• Business objects: Domain objects of the application. • Controller: A class dedicated to handling actor requests or background processing of a use case. It takes requests from the presentation and works with business objects to fulfill the request. A use case controller is dedicated to handling all actor requests of a given use case. • Presentation: An actor interface responsible for interacting with an actor. It delegates the actor requests to the controller and displays system responses from the controller to the actor.
Benefits	• It decouples the presentation and business objects. • It reduces change impact of business objects to presentation and vice versa. • It supports multiple presentation technologies such as desktop, web-based and smartphone user interface technologies. • It keeps track of the state of a use case and detects out-of-sequence actor requests.
Liabilities	A controller may be assigned too many responsibilities, resulting in a bloated controller. A bloated controller is complex, difficult to understand, implement, test and maintain.
Guidelines	• Apply use case controllers whenever possible. • Avoid using one controller for more than one use case. • Do not implement a controller class as a singleton in multithreading or multiuser applications such as web applications.
Related Patterns	• It is a special case of the model-view-controller or MVC pattern. • It is also a special case of the façade pattern (not to confuse with the façade controller). The facade pattern simplifies the client interface and decouples the client and the components accessed. The controller pattern simplifies the interface for the GUI and decouples the GUI and business objects. • The state behavior of a use case is maintained by a use case controller. The state pattern should be used to design and implement such behavior.
Uses	In the design of all interactive systems to decouple the presentation from business objects.

FIGURE 10.5 Specification of the controller pattern

1. **Design for Change.** Changes to the business logic or business objects will have little impact to the presentation, provided that the interface and interaction behavior of the Checkout Controller are not changed.

   Changes to requirements can be dealt with easily. Suppose that the library information system is extended with additional requirements to support multiple user interface technologies like web interface, smartphone interface, and voice interface. With the design in Figure 10.3, one has to design and implement the new user interfaces as well as the business logic in each of these presentations. Changes to the business logic or business objects will require changes all of the presentations. With a sizable number of use cases, the effort to making the changes and maintaining the consistency is enormous.

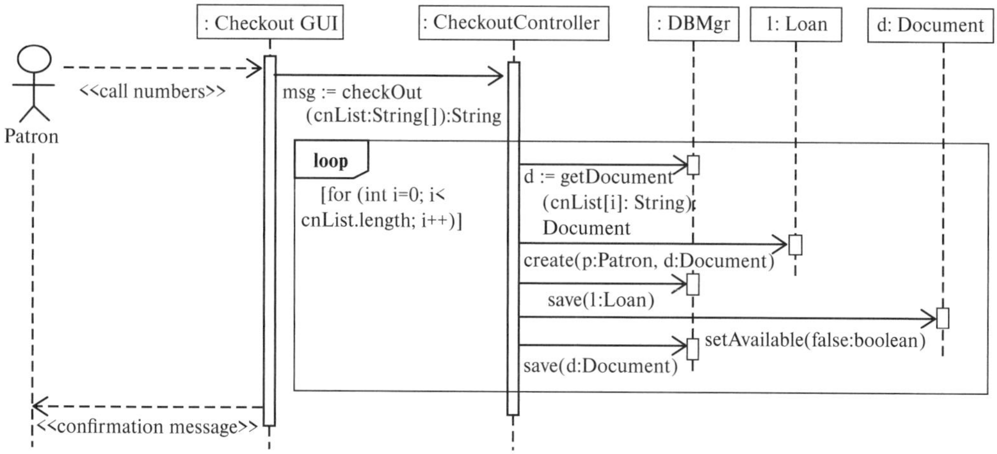

FIGURE 10.6 Applying the controller pattern

The design in Figure 10.6 only needs to add the new user interfaces and have each of them invoke the checkOut function of the Checkout Controller. Changes to the business logic or business objects would have little impact to the user interfaces. This is attractive when the number of use cases is large.

2. **Separation of Concerns.** Separation of concerns is well supported by the design. The Checkout GUI object now deals with only the presentation aspect while the Checkout Controller is responsible for processing the Checkout Document use case. In the previous design, both concerns are assigned to the Checkout GUI.
3. **High Cohesion.** Previously the responsibilities of presenting information to the patron and processing the Checkout Document use case are assigned to the Checkout GUI. But these two sets of functionality do not belong to a single core function. Therefore, the previous design exhibits low functional cohesion. In the new design, both the Checkout GUI and the Checkout Controller exhibit high functional cohesion for obvious reasons.
4. **Designing "Stupid Objects."** Previously, the Checkout GUI knew how to present information to the patron as well as how to process the business logic. In the improved design, each of the Checkout GUI and the Checkout Controller knows only one thing, presenting information and processing the Checkout Document use case, respectively.

10.5.5 Types of Controller

There are two types of controllers. (1) use Case Controller and (2) Facade Controller. A *use case controller* is responsible for handling all actor requests that are associated with a use case. The controller in Figure 10.6 was intended to be a use case controller for the Checkout use case. This is indicated by the name of the controller—that is, "Checkout Controller," which implies that the controller is for the Checkout use case.

Use case controllers are the most frequently used and preferred because they exhibit high cohesion, separation of concerns, design for change, and information hiding. This is because there is a one-to-one correspondence between the use cases and the use case controllers. That is, a use case controller is designed and implemented for each use case of the system. Therefore, each use case controller tends to exhibit functional cohesion, separation of concerns, and design for change. If new requirements are added and new use cases are introduced, it only needs to add the corresponding use case controllers. Changes to existing requirements are limited to changing the relevant use case controllers and business objects. Information hiding is supported because changes to the business objects are shielded from the presentation, provided that the interfaces of the controllers are kept stable. Thus, systems that are designed and implemented by using use case controllers tend to be easier to comprehend, implement, test, and maintain. As a naming convention, use case controllers are named after the use cases, for example, Login Controller for the Login use case, Checkout Controller for the Checkout use case, and Make Payment Controller for the Make Payment use case.

A facade controller (not to confuse with the GoF facade pattern) represents a system or organization. It is responsible for handling all requests (submitted to a system). It is used when there is only a few actor requests, or the user interface cannot redirect the actor requests to different use case controllers. An example application of a facade controller is interlibrary loan, where library A wants to checkout a document from library B on behalf of a patron. In this case, the library A information system may use a facade controller to interact with the library B information system.

10.5.6 Keeping Track of Use Case State

By definition, use cases are business processes. Some business processes exhibit state-dependent behavior. It is important for the system to keep track of use case state so that the system knows the state of the use case and the expected actor requests. The system can detect actor requests that are out of sequence. The use case controller is the best place to implement such state-dependent behavior of a use case.

Consider the Reserve Flight use case of a web-based flight reservation system. The use case begins when the customer clicks the Flight Reservation link. The system displays the Flight Reservation page. The customer selects Round Trip or One Way and enters the departure airport, destination airport, and dates of travel. The system displays the available flights. The customer selects the desired flight and clicks the Continue button. The system asks the customer to enter the passenger information. The customer enters the passenger information and clicks Continue. The system asks the customer to select Purchase or Hold. If the customer selects Hold, then the system will display a reservation success message and hold the reservation for the customer for 24 hours. If the customer selects Purchase, then the system will ask the customer to select payment options. The customer selects the payment option. The system asks the customer to enter payment option-related information. The customer enters the requested information. The system asks the customer to select ticketing option. The customer selects ticketing option. The system displays a flight reservation success message. The use case ends when the customer sees the flight reservation success message.

The use case controller will be responsible for handling all actor requests for this use case. This means each of these actor requests will be delivered to the same use case controller to process. The processing of all these requests comprises the business process of purchasing a flight ticket. In the above scenario, there are seven use case-related actor requests: (1) the customer selects Round Trip or One Way and enters the departure city, destination, and travel dates, (2) the customer selects the flight and clicks the Continue button, (3) the customer enters the passenger information and clicks the Continue button, (4) the customer selects Purchase or Hold, (5) the customer selects the payment option, (6) the customer enters the payment information, and (7) the customer selects the ticketing option.

As each of the actor requests is successfully processed, the state of the use case changes. Figure 10.7 illustrates the state transition diagram for the Reserve Flight use case. With this state model, the system can be made more user friendly and robust because the system knows what the user can do next and what will be the resulting state. Thus, the system can show only the links or buttons that the user can click at each step. This effectively eliminates the out-of-sequence requests and makes the system more robust.

10.5.7 Bloated Controller

The merits of a controller, especially a use case controller, are high cohesion, separation of concerns, design for change, and information hiding. However, if not used properly, a controller may be overloaded with excessive responsibilities and defeat the purpose. Figure 10.8 shows a controller that does everything itself rather than working with business objects and a database manager. The controller creates a loan record in the database, updates the document record by setting its availability to false. The controller is assigned too many responsibilities, as discussed previously. It violates several software design principles including design for change, separation of concerns, high cohesion, low coupling, information hiding, and keeping it simple and stupid.

Design for change The tight coupling between the controller and the database makes it difficult to work with a different database. The design in Figure 10.6 solves this problem. Since the database is hidden behind the DBMgr, changes to the database will have little impact to the controller and business objects.

Separation of concerns The controller in Figure 10.8 has all the responsibilities to process the Checkout use case. On the other hand, the controller in Figure 10.6 is

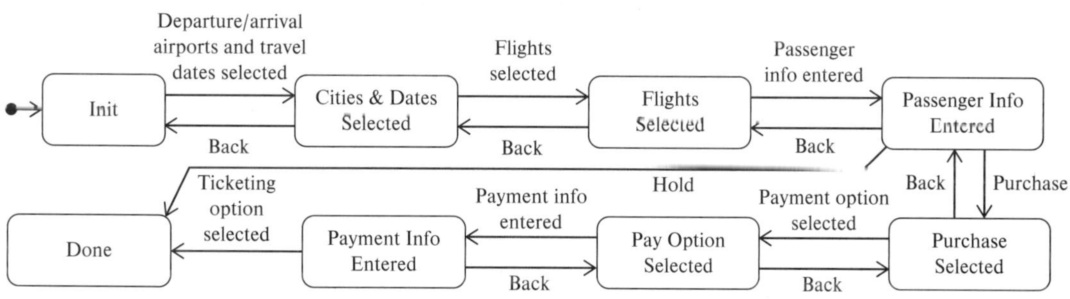

FIGURE 10.7 State transition diagram for the Reserve Flight use case

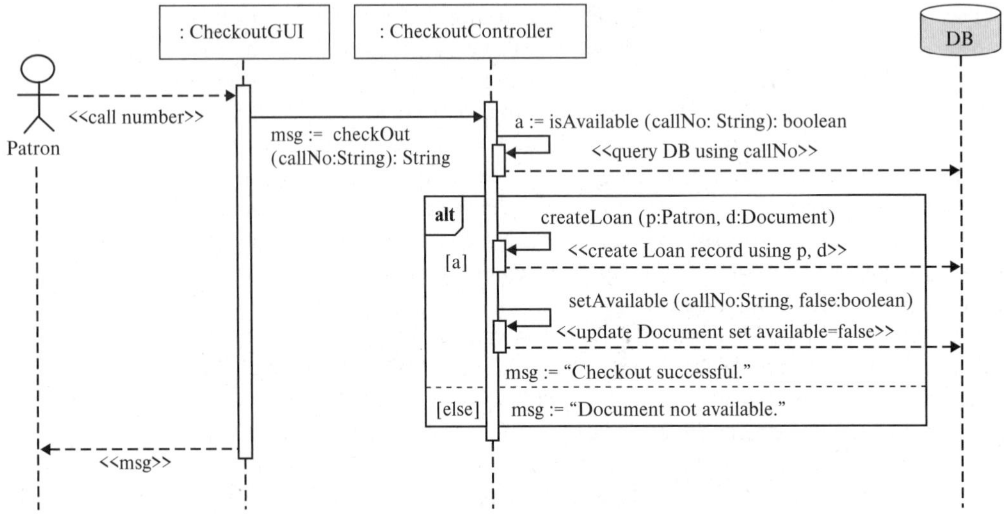

FIGURE 10.8 A bloated controller that does everything itself

assigned the responsibility to carry out the check-out procedure only. The database-access responsibilities are assigned to the DBMgr and the business objects are responsible for maintaining the states of the business objects. Therefore, separation of concerns is well-supported by the design in Figure 10.6 but not the design in Figure 10.8.

High cohesion In Figure 10.8, various responsibilities are assigned to the controller. These responsibilities are functionally divided and distributed to various objects in Figure 10.6. Therefore, the design in Figure 10.6 exhibits high cohesion.

Low coupling The tight coupling between the controller and the database in Figure 10.8 means significant change impact if the database is replaced or the database schemes are changed. Low coupling is not accomplished. On the other hand, the DBMgr in Figure 10.6 decouples the controller from the database. Therefore, change impact is low.

Information hiding The DBMgr in Figure 10.6 hides the database from the controller. The database implementation details are not shielded from the controller in Figure 10.8, which violates the information hiding principle.

Keep it simple and stupid The controller in Figure 10.8 knows the steps of the business process of the Checkout use case. But it also knows the database organization and how to update a database. It also knows the states and behaviors of the business objects (so that it can update the business objects appropriately). The controller is not "stupid" and not simple because it has to implement all these responsibilities. On the other hand, the design in Figure 10.6 yields "stupid objects," each of which has only one cohesive set of functionality.

10.5.8 When to Apply the Controller Pattern?

The controller pattern can be applied during object interaction modeling in the given order as follows:

1. *Apply when writing use case scenarios or scenario tables.* The best time to apply the controller pattern is when the use case scenario is being written. The designer bears in mind that a use case controller is needed to decouple the presentation and business objects. Therefore, the designer applies the controller pattern when writing scenarios. The advantage is that no rework is needed.
2. *Apply by modifying an existing scenario.* Often, an appropriate use case scenario is written previously, for example, during the analysis phase to describe the business process of the use case. In this case, the scenario can be modified to include a use case controller. In addition to the aforementioned merits, this approach also allows reuse of existing scenarios.
3. *Apply when constructing sequence diagrams.* Another choice is to apply the controller pattern when sequence diagrams are constructed. This option is usually used by experienced designers who can produce sequence diagrams without having to describe the use case scenarios.
4. *Apply by modifying a sequence diagram.* Sometimes, a sequence diagram may have been constructed, but it does not use a controller. In this case, the sequence diagram can be modified to include a controller to decouple the presentation from the business objects.

10.5.9 Guidelines for Applying Controller

GUIDELINE 10.1 Apply use case controller unless there are only a few actor requests and the system will not expand in the future.

GUIDELINE 10.2 Avoid overloading a controller.

GUIDELINE 10.3 Properly assign the responsibilities to process a use case to the controller, the business objects, and other resource management objects.

By definition, a use case is a business process, which consists of a series of steps. Some of these steps execute business algorithms or procedures and interact with database and/or network access objects and business objects. Thus, the responsibilities to process a use case should be properly assigned. In general, the responsibilities to carry out the business algorithms or procedures should be assigned to the controller, which may delegate some of these responsibilities to other objects. The responsibilities to retrieve objects from, and save objects to, a database should be assigned to a database access object like a database manager. Similarly, the responsibilities to access the network should be assigned to network access objects or a network manager. The responsibilities to retrieve and update the states of business objects should be assigned to the objects themselves. In particular, the expert pattern to be presented next provides an effective solution to assigning responsibilities to the business objects.

10.6 THE EXPERT PATTERN

Section 10.5.9 presents guidelines for applying the controller pattern. If the guidelines are not followed then a controller may be assigned irrelevant responsibilities. This results in a bloated controller as discussed in Section 10.5.7. The solution is removing the excess responsibilities from the controller and assigning them to other objects. That is, the controller would call these other objects rather than doing everything itself. The question is, which object should be assigned the responsibility to handle a request (from an object)? The answer is the expert pattern, shown in Figure 10.9. Clearly, the object that is responsible for handling the request should have the information to fulfill the request. As illustrated in Figure 10.10, the request to

Name	Expert
Type	GRASP
Specification	
Problem	Who should be responsible for handling a request from an object?
Solution	Assign the request to the "information expert" objects that have the information to fulfill the request.
Design	
Structural	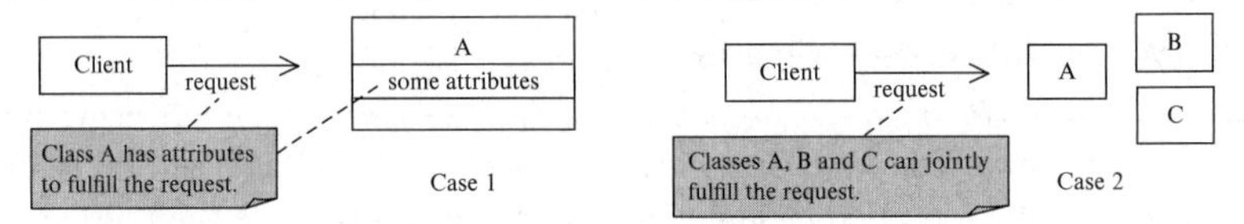 Classes in the domain model or design class diagram
Behavioral	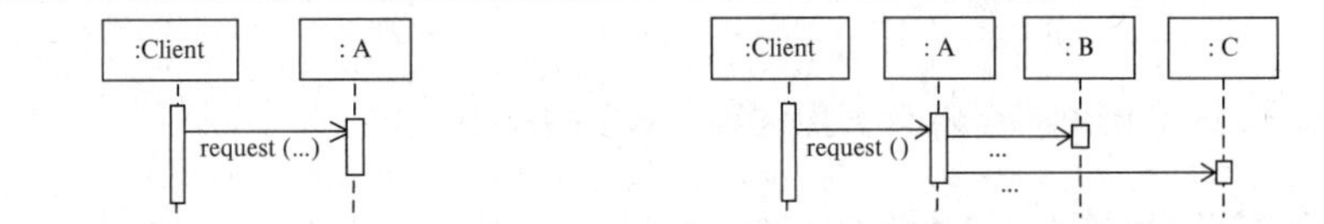 (a) Assign the request to class A in case 1. (b) Assign the request to class A, B or C, and let it collaborate with the other two classes to fulfill the request.
Roles and Responsibilities	• Classes A, B and C: The domain classes or design classes that have the information to fulfill a given request. • Client: Any class that issues the given request.
Benefits	• Low coupling because the given request is handled directly by the object that has the information to fulfill the request. • High cohesion because responsibilities are assigned to objects that can fulfill the responsibilities. • Easy to understand and change due to high cohesion and low coupling. • Designing "stupid object."
Liabilities	
Guidelines	• Most responsibility assignment decisions should apply the expert pattern. • Look for information experts in the following order: (1) sequence diagrams produced in current iteration, (2) design class diagram, and (3) domain model. • The expert pattern may involve more than one object/class.
Related Patterns	
Uses	• During behavioral modeling (object interaction modeling, state modeling, and activity modeling).

FIGURE 10.9 Specification of the expert pattern

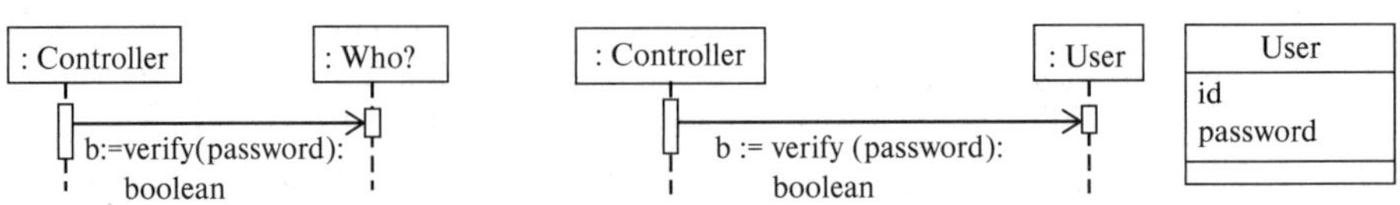

(a) The design problem: which object should be assigned the responsibility to handle a request from another object?

(b) The design solution: assign the responsibility to the object that has the information to fulfill the request.

FIGURE 10.10 The expert pattern illustrated

verify whether a password is valid should be assigned to a User object. This is because the User object has password as one of its attributes; hence, it can use that attribute to check the validity. If the responsibility were assigned to another object, not the User object, then that object would have to query the User object to obtain the password and use it to check the validity, or that object would have to ask the User object to check the validity. In either case, unnecessary coupling is created and the security of the application may be compromised.

10.6.1 Expert and Antiexpert

Consider the Login sequence diagram in Figure 10.11. Unlike Figure 10.8, the controller in Figure 10.11 does not do everything itself. It asks the DBMgr to retrieve the User object and gets the password from the User object. It then verifies whether the submitted password matches the stored password. The design is not uncommon. However, it exhibits some problems. First, the responsibility to verify whether the submitted password matches with the stored password should be the responsibility of the User object, not the Login Controller. The design violates the expert pattern; this is also called antiexpert. The reader might wonder why it is the case. Shouldn't the Login Controller be responsible for processing the Login use case and hence verify the password? This is because only the User object has the password information to verify the submitted password. The controller does not have this information. If this responsibility is assigned to the controller, then the controller has to ask the User object to give it the password so that it can verify the validity of the submitted password. However, this violates the principle of make it simple and stupid because letting the User object verify the password is a simpler solution.

Second, security requires that the passwords should be encrypted. In this case, the Login Controller in Figure 10.11 has to know password encryption and password decryption. Another security problem is that the getPassword():Password function of User allows an object to retrieve the password of a user. If the password is not encrypted, then a security vulnerability is present. Applying the expert pattern solves these problems. The result is shown in Figure 10.12, in which only one call to the verify (password):boolean function of a User object is enough.

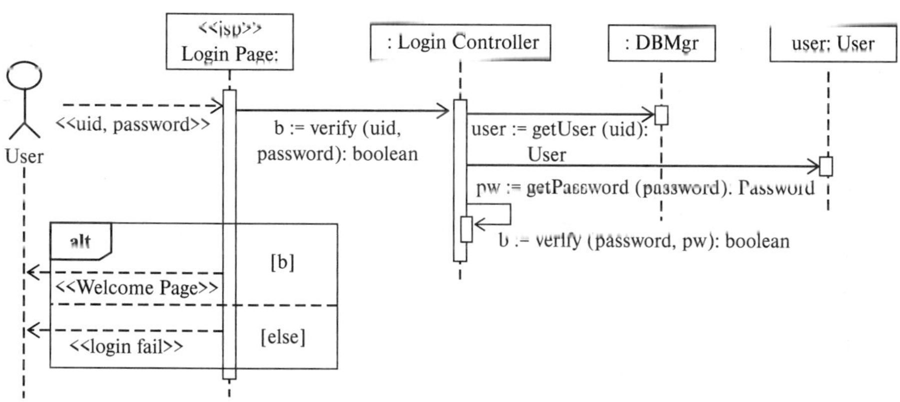

FIGURE 10.11 A Login sequence diagram that is anti-expert

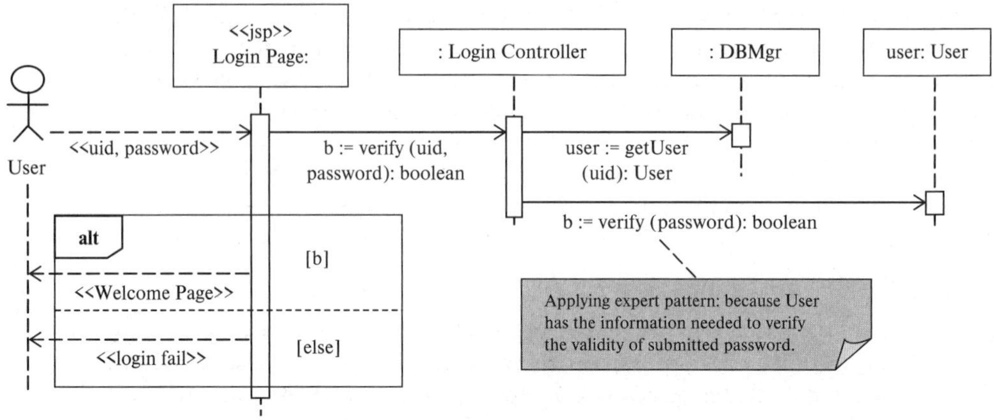

FIGURE 10.12 Applying the expert pattern

10.6.2 Expert Pattern Involving More Than One Object

Often, more than one object needs to collaborate to fulfill a request. Consider, for example, the Checkout sequence diagram in Figure 10.6. It is well known that when checking out a document from the library, the system computes the due date for the loan. In the sequence diagram, this is accomplished within the constructor of the Loan class, that is, create (p: Patron, d: Document), where "create" is a UML reserved word to refer to the constructor of a class. However, the due date depends on the patron because faculty, staff, and student have different checkout durations. The due date also depends on the type of document; for example, a student can check out a book for one month and a journal for two weeks. A reserved book can only be checked out for a given period of time specified by the instructor who reserved the book for a given course.

The above discussion indicates that the request to compute the due date has to involve at least three objects: the patron, the document, and the calendar. Since the Loan object has access to all these objects that have the needed information, it is appropriate to assign this responsibility to the Loan object.

10.6.3 When to Apply the Expert Pattern?

There are several stages in which the expert pattern can be applied. These stages are the same as applying the controller pattern described in Section 10.5.8. However, instead of introducing a use case controller, the designer identifies the information expert and assigns the request to the information expert.

10.6.4 Guidelines for Applying Expert

GUIDELINE 10.4 Look for the information expert in the current sequence diagram, then in the design class diagram, and finally in the domain model.

GUIDELINE 10.5 The information needed to fulfill a request may be distributed among two or more objects. In this case, the responsibility should be assigned to the object that has access to these objects.

Consider the example discussed in Section 10.6.2. The information to fulfill the compute due date request is distributed among several objects. The Checkout Controller and the Loan objects have access to relevant objects. If the responsibility is assigned to the Checkout Controller, then the controller has to interact with the Patron object, the Document object, the Calendar object, and the Loan object (to set the due date). That is, four function calls or four dependencies are needed. If the responsibility is assigned to the Loan object, then only three function calls or three dependencies are needed. Therefore, the responsibility should be assigned to the Loan object.

10.7 THE CREATOR PATTERN

In the example discussed in Section 10.6.2, the Checkout Controller object creates the Loan object. The reader might wonder why letting the Checkout Controller create the Loan object. And who should create the Checkout Controller, the DB manager, and so on. The creator pattern answers these questions. The specification of the creator pattern is given in Figure 10.13.

Name	Creator
Type	GRASP
Specification	
Problem	Who should be responsible for creating objects of a class (i.e., calling the constructor of the class)?
Solution	Assign the responsibility to the class that (1) consists of, (2) contains, (3) updates, (4) uses, or (5) has the information to create, objects of the class.
Design	
Structural	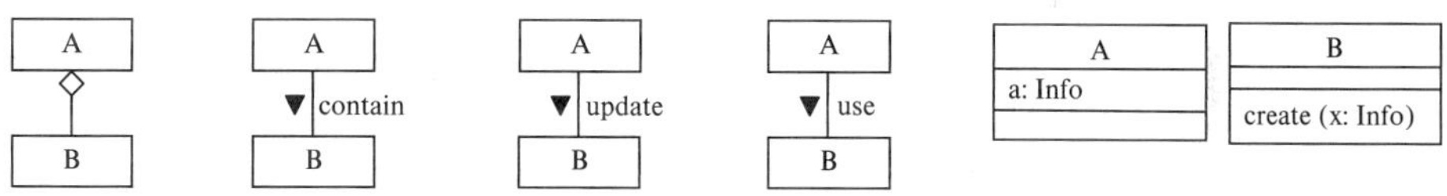 Cases in domain model or design class diagram that class A should create objects of class B
Behavioral	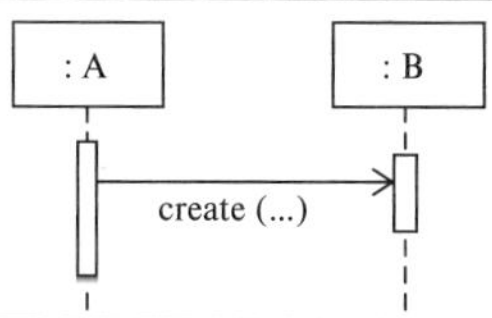
Roles and Responsibilities	• A, B: Classes that exhibit any of the relationships shown in the structural design. • A: The class that should be assigned the responsibility to create objects of class B. • B: Class of objects to be created.
Benefits	• Low coupling because the coupling already exists. • It is easier to reuse classes A and B compared to letting another class to create objects of B (in that case, one must also reuse that class).
Liabilities	
Guidelines	• Apply the creator pattern whenever the constructor of a class is invoked.
Related Patterns	
Uses	• During behavioral modeling (object interaction modeling, state modeling, and activity modeling). • It is widely applied in OO design and programming.

FIGURE 10.13 Specification of the creator pattern

10.7.1 What Is a Creator?

Object creation is a common activity of an object-oriented system. It is accomplished by calling the constructor of a class to create an object of that class. The design question is: which object should be assigned the responsibility to create an object of a class? The creator pattern addresses this problem as illustrated in Figure 10.14. The creator pattern suggests that the responsibility to create an object of Class B should be assigned to an object of Class A if one of the following holds in the given order:

1. *Class A is an aggregation of Class B.* Because objects of Class A consist of objects of Class B, it is simple and straightforward to assign the creation responsibility to Class A. The dependency of Class A on Class B already exists, the call to the constructor of Class B does not introduce additional dependencies. Reuse of Class A is easier than letting another class to create objects of Class B because the latter requires that the class be reused as well. For example, Book class should create Chapter objects because a book consists of chapters.
2. *An object of Class A contains objects of Class B.* The fact that objects of Class A contain objects of Class B implies that the former may need to use or update the latter frequently. If this is the case, then letting objects of Class A create objects of Class B may result in a simple and easy-to-understand design. For example, one should let Dispenser class of a vending machine to create vending items because the former contains the latter.
3. *An object of Class A records objects of Class B.* There are many cases where an object of Class A updates objects of Class B. For example, a patient's medical folder records the lab tests for the patient, a file check-in/check-out log records the check-in and checkout activities, and a purchase history records the details of each purchase item. In these cases, it is simpler and more convenient to pass the required parameters to the medical file, the log, and the purchase history, respectively, and let them create the objects.
4. *An object of Class A closely uses objects of Class B.* There are many cases where an object of Class A closely uses objects of Class B. Examples are a controller uses a database manager to store and retrieve objects, GUI objects use controllers to handle actor requests. Letting a controller create a database manager and a GUI object create a controller is a straightforward solution. These are illustrated in Figure 10.15.

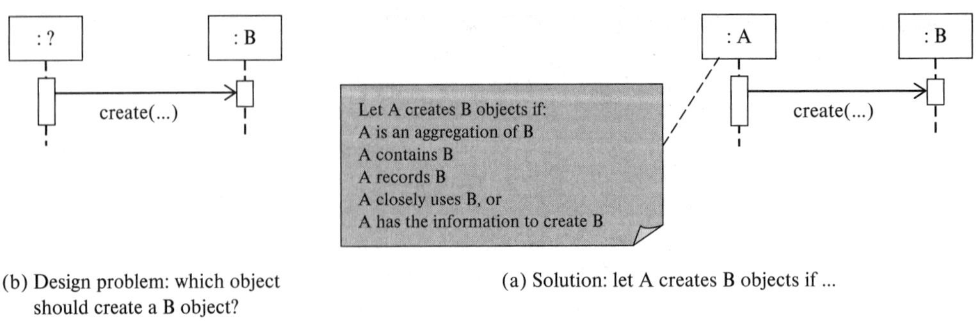

FIGURE 10.14 The creator pattern illustrated

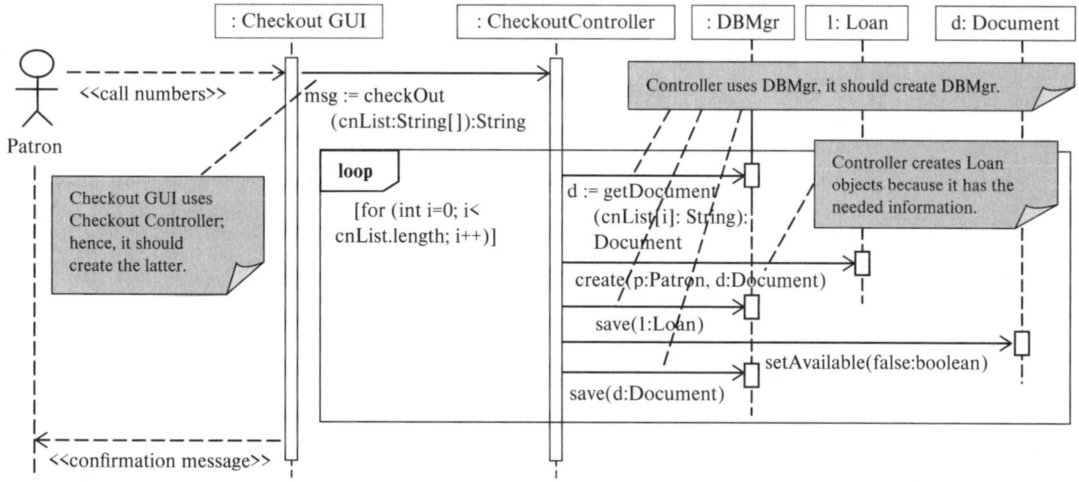

FIGURE 10.15 Who should create Controller, DBMgr and Loan objects, respectively?

5. *An object of Class A has the information to create objects of Class B.* In many cases, parameters must be passed to the constructor of a class. In such cases, it may be more convenient to let the object that has the parameters to call the constructor. In Figure 10.15, the constructor of the Loan class requires a patron object and a document object. The checkout controller has these. Therefore, the creator should be the checkout controller.

10.7.2 Benefits of the Creator Pattern

The creator pattern results in low coupling and better software reusability. The dependency of the creator on the object it creates already exists. The creator does not introduce additional dependency. Therefore, it results in low coupling. It facilitates the reuse of the creator because the creator creates its dependent objects–in other words, there is no need to reuse anything else to create the dependent objects.

10.7.3 When to Apply the Creator Pattern?

The stages to apply the creator pattern is similar to the expert pattern. That is, depending on the development context, the pattern can be applied when the designer writes or modifies scenarios, or during the construction of sequence diagrams.

10.8 SUMMARY

This chapter presents the controller, expert, and creator patterns. These patterns address a common design problem–how does one assign responsibilities to objects? In particular, these patterns answer the following questions:

1. *Who should be assigned the responsibility to handle an actor request?* The answer is the controller.
2. *Who should be assigned the responsibility to handle a request from another object in the business object layer?* The answer is the expert.
3. *Who should be assigned the responsibility to create a given object?* The answer is the creator.

The controller pattern decouples the presentation from the business logic by assigning the responsibility

Name	Problem	Solution
High Cohesion	How to keep objects focused, easy to understand and manage?	Apply the cohesion software design principle described in the architectural design chapter.
Indirection	How to assign responsibilities to avoid direct coupling?	Assign the responsibility to an intermediate object to mediate between the objects to be decoupled.
Low Coupling	How to support low dependency, low change impact, and high reusability?	Apply the low coupling software design principle described in the architectural design chapter.
Polymorphism	How to handle behavior variations without conditional statements?	Define in a parent class an interface for the behaviors that vary, and let the subclasses implement the behavior variations.
Protected Variations	How to design objects to avoid undesirable impact to other objects?	Design a stable interface to wrap the internal variation or instability so that other objects are not affected by the variation or instability.
Pure fabrication	Who should handle responsibilities that cannot be assigned to objects that represent domain concepts because doing so would violate high-cohesion or low-coupling?	Partition such responsibilities into cohesive subsets of responsibilities and assign each of the subset to an artificial class called pure fabrication.

FIGURE 10.16 Summary of other six GRASP patterns

to process an actor request to a controller rather than the presentation. The expert pattern suggests that the responsibility to handle a request from another object should be assigned to the information expert, which has the information to fulfill the request. The creator pattern suggests that the responsibility to create a given object should be assigned to the object that is an aggregate of, depends on, or has the information to create the given object.

This chapter discusses problems associated with commonly seen designs that do not apply the controller, expert, or creator patterns. It then shows how these patterns are applied to improve the design. These discussions should help the student understand not only *what* the controller, expert, and creator patterns are and *how* to apply them, but more importantly, *when* to apply these patterns and *why*. Knowing these enables the student to properly apply these patterns in the practical field of software development.

This chapter presents only three of the nine GRASP patterns. Figure 10.16 summarizes the other six GRASP patterns. They are not presented for the following reasons. High cohesion and low coupling are widely regarded as software design principles, which have been presented in Chapter 6. Polymorphism is an object-oriented feature, which has been discussed in Chapter 5. The remaining three GRASP patterns can be substituted by Gang of Four (GoF) patterns, e.g., indirection by proxy or mediator, protected variation by proxy, facade, bridge, and pure fabrication by visitor, strategy, decorator, etc.

10.9 CHAPTER REVIEW QUESTIONS

1. What are software design patterns?
2. What is a controller, a use case controller, an expert, and a creator, respectively?
3. When and how does one apply the controller, expert, and creator patterns?
4. What are the benefits of the controller, expert, and creator patterns? What are the potential problems if these patterns should be applied but are not applied?
5. Can a sequence diagram have more than one use case controller? Explain why.
6. What is a bloated controller, and how does one cure a bloated controller?

10.10 REFERENCES

[Gamma 1995] E. Gamma, R. Helm, R. Johnson, and J. Vlissides, *Design Patterns: Elements of Reusable Object-Oriented Software.* (Boston, MA: Addison-Wesley, 1995).

[Larm 2004] C. Larman, *Applying UML and Patterns: An Introduction to Object-Oriented Analysis and Design and Iterative Development*, 3rd ed. (Hoboken, NJ: Prentice Hall, 2004).

10.11 EXERCISES

10.1 Construct a table with columns for the controller, expert, and creator patterns and rows for the design principles presented in Chapter 6. Check the entries to indicate which patterns support which design principles. Provide explanations to justify the result.

10.2 See the Online Car Rental application described in Appendix D.1. Its use cases include Search for Cars, Reserve Cars, and Cancel Reservation. Do the following and apply the controller, expert, and creator patterns whenever appropriate:

a. Specify the expanded use cases and identify the nontrivial steps.

b. Produce scenarios, scenario tables, and sequence diagrams for the nontrivial steps.

10.3 Identify and explain the improvements that the controller, expert, and creator patterns introduce to the behavioral design for the Online Car Rental system. *Hint:* Compare the design with one that does not apply the patterns to identify the improvements.

10.4 Do the same as in exercise 10.2 but for the Edit Class Diagram use case for a UML Class Diagram Editor.

10.5 Identify and explain the improvements that the controller, expert, and creator patterns introduce to the behavioral design for the UML Class Diagram Editor. *Hint:* Compare the design with one that does not apply the patterns to identify the improvements.

10.6 Which classes in the UML Class Diagram Editor design could be a singleton? Justify your answer.

10.7 Write an essay to discuss the similarities and differences of the controller, expert, and creator patterns.

10.8 Describe three realistic, not dummy or hypothetic, situations to apply the controller, expert, and creator patterns.

10.9 In exercise 8.6, you produce the expanded use cases for a state diagram editor. In this exercise, you are required to identify the nontrivial steps. For each nontrivial step, write a scenario, construct a scenario table, and convert the scenario table into an informal sequence diagram and a design sequence diagram. Apply the controller, expert, creator, and singleton pattern if appropriate during this process. Preferably, the patterns should be applied when you describe the scenarios.

11 Chapter

Deriving a Design Class Diagram

Key Takeaway Points

- A *design class diagram* (DCD) is a UML class diagram, derived from the behavioral models (design sequence diagrams, design state diagrams, and design activity diagrams) and the domain model. It serves as a design blueprint for test-driven development, integration testing, and maintenance.
- Package diagrams are useful for organizing and managing classes of a large DCD.

In previous chapters, modeling, analysis, and design activities of the methodology are presented. These activities are interrelated in terms of the order to perform them, and the dependence of one activity on the software artifacts produced by previous activities. To help motivate what is needed next, the following briefly reviews the activities presented so far:

1. *System engineering (Chapter 3).* During this activity, the system requirements specification for the total system as well as the overall system architecture are produced. The overall system architecture depicts hardware, software, and human subsystems and their interrelationships. The system requirements are allocated to the subsystems.
2. *Software requirements analysis (Chapter 4).* In this activity, the system requirements that are allocated to the software subsystem are analyzed and refined, and additional software requirements are added, if any.
3. *Domain modeling (Chapter 5).* In this activity, a domain model is constructed or extended to help the development team understand the application domain and requirements. Often, domain modeling is performed during requirements analysis and subsequent iterations. The domain model is visualized using a UML class diagram.
4. *Deriving use cases from requirements (Chapter 7).* In this activity, use cases are derived from the software requirements as well as partitioned to form subsystems.

UML use case diagrams are produced to visualize the use cases, subsystems, and actor-use case relationships. Moreover, the use cases are assigned to iterations.

5. *Architectural design (Chapter 6).* This produces the architectural design for the software system, which is used to guide the subsequent design, implementation, and testing of use cases, subsystems, and components. The artifacts produced during the subsequent activities are organized according to the architectural design. This activity concludes the planning phase.
6. *Actor-system interaction modeling (Chapter 8).* During this activity, the expanded use cases for the current iteration are produced. These specify how actors will interact with the system to carry out the use cases. The domain model provides information needed to specify the actor input and system responses.
7. *Object interaction modeling (chapters 9 and 10).* In this activity, nontrivial steps of actor-system interaction are identified and sequence diagrams are produced to specify how software objects interact to process actor requests. Controller, expert and creator patterns are applied to produce high-quality designs.

The UML diagrams produced by the above activities describe different aspects of the application as well as the system under development. However, the collection of these diagrams does not provide a class structure and a road-map to guide the subsequent test-driven development (TDD) and integration testing. For example, either conventional implementation or TDD needs to know the classes that must be implemented as well as their behavior and relationships. Such information is scattered in several diagrams. Consider, for example, a library information system project. The Loan class appears in the domain model as well as more than one sequence diagram. That is, it occurs in the checkout document sequence diagram and the return document sequence diagram. Similarly, the database manager appears in all sequence diagrams that access the database. Thus, the team members must examine all the UML diagrams to look up the classes, their functions and attributes, and relationships between the classes. This is only feasible for a very small project. The effort to look up these is tremendous for most real-world projects. If classes or operations are overlooked, then the problem will surface during integration testing. This will significantly slow down the progress of the entire project.

The discussion indicates that the team needs a diagram to serve as a design specification of the classes and the class structure. This diagram is called a *design class diagram* (DCD). The DCD is a UML class diagram that depicts the classes, their operations and attributes, as well as relationships between the classes. All these are derived from the diagrams produced in the current iteration and added to the DCD. There is only one DCD for the whole system, not a DCD for each iteration or each sequence diagram. How to derive the DCD from the collection of diagrams is the focus of this chapter. In particular, you will learn the following:

- What is a DCD, and how does it differ from a domain model?
- What is the usefulness of a DCD?
- How does one derive the DCD from the analysis and design diagrams?
- How does one manage a large DCD using UML package diagrams?

11.1 WHAT IS A DESIGN CLASS DIAGRAM?

Definition 11.1 A *design class diagram* is a UML class diagram, derived from behavioral models (design sequence diagrams, design state diagrams, and design activity diagrams) and the domain model. It is a design blueprint to facilitate subsequent implementation, testing, and integration activities.

The DCD is derived from the behavioral models and the domain model. The behavioral models include sequence diagrams (Chapter 9), state diagrams (Chapter 13), and activity diagrams (Chapter 14). They are constructed to help develop, communicate, and validate design ideas, which are otherwise distributed among the team members. The processes of design review and inspection ensure that the diagrams satisfy the requirements and constraints. If the team derives the DCD from the behavioral models, then the DCD should contain all the classes, operations, and relationships that are needed to satisfy the requirements. The team implements and deploys all and only the classes in the DCD. That is, all classes required to satisfy the requirements are implemented and no more.

Due to encapsulation and information hiding, the classes of object-oriented programs implement the ordinary get and set methods, also called getters and setters or accessors. These methods simply return or set the appropriate attribute values. Since there are many such methods, if all of them are shown in the DCD, then the DCD will be crowded with such methods and obscure the other more important behavior of the classes. Therefore, as a convention, the DCD must not show the accessors. It should be pointed out that this convention should not be applied to all classes of the DCD. For example, the database manager class is responsible for retrieving from, and storing objects to the database. If the retrieving object operations are named getX(. . .):X, getY(. . .):Y, . . . , where X and Y are class names, then these operations must not be suppressed from the interface specification of the database manager class. This is because they are not the ordinary getters and setters.

11.2 USEFULNESS OF A DESIGN CLASS DIAGRAM

The usefulness of a DCD includes the following:

1. *It brings together the most significant design artifacts in one diagram.* As discussed at the beginning of this chapter, the classes and information about the classes to be implemented are distributed in a collection of analysis and design diagrams. The DCD integrates these design artifacts into one design blueprint. This integration facilitates understanding, implementation, integration testing, and maintenance.
2. *It facilitates quality measurement and assurance.* The DCD provides a basis for the definition and calculation of design quality metrics, which are useful for assessing a design and identifying potential design problems. For example, if a class has a large number of operations, then it is likely that the class is assigned too many responsibilities. A class with many outgoing edges means that it depends on many other classes; hence, it is difficult to reuse the class.

3. *It is useful for effort estimation.* Based on the operations in each class, it is possible to derive a rough estimate of the effort required to implement and test each of the classes. These estimates are useful for assigning the classes to the team members to implement and test, as described next.
4. *It is useful for assigning classes to team members to implement and test.* A DCD shows the dependencies between the classes. Implementation and testing, especially test-driven development, should take into account such dependencies. Consider two classes A and B. If A calls functions of B, then A depends on B. This suggests that B should be implemented and tested before A to avoid the construction of a so-called test stub to emulate the called functions. Besides function call dependency, A depends on B if: (1) A extends B, (2) A is an aggregation of B, (3) A calls a function that has B as a parameter type or return type, and (4) A is an association class for an association between B and some class. The dependencies between classes can be used to compute an order to implement and test the classes so that the number of test stubs need to be constructed is minimal.

11.3 STEPS FOR DERIVING A DESIGN CLASS DIAGRAM

The steps for deriving a DCD from the design sequence diagrams and the domain model are: (1) identifying classes, (2) identifying methods, (3) identifying attributes, (4) identifying relationships, and (5) reviewing the DCD. These steps are explained in the next several sections. The sequence diagram shown in Figure 10.6 will be used as the running example. Note that there is only DCD. The first iteration creates the DCD, and subsequence iterations expand the existing DCD by adding classes, attributes and relationships.

11.3.1 Identifying Classes

Classes to be included in the DCD are identified from the design sequence diagrams produced in the current iteration. These diagrams specify how software objects interact and collaborate to carry out the background processing of the use cases assigned to the current iteration. The use cases are derived from the requirements. Therefore, the classes of the objects that participate in the design sequence diagrams must be included in the DCD so that they will be implemented and deployed to deliver the capabilities specified by the requirements. The classes of objects are identified from the following four places in a design sequence diagram:

1. **Identify classes of objects that send or receive messages.** Object interaction is modeled by a sequence diagram as message passing between the objects. The objects that send or receive messages are represented by rectangles with object names and types separated by a colon. These rectangles are placed at the top of each design sequence diagram. Figure 10.6 shows five such classes: Checkout GUI, Checkout Controller, DBMgr, Loan, and Document.
2. **Identify classes of objects that are passed as parameters.** Passing an object as a parameter to a function call is commonplace in object-oriented programming. This also holds for design sequence diagrams because design sequence diagrams

are "programs in the large." More specifically, in a design sequence diagram, messages passed between objects resemble function calls from one object to another object. Since the classes that are passed as parameters must be implemented and delivered, they must appear in the DCD. Such classes are identified from the parameters passed in messages sent or received by objects in the design sequence diagrams. In Figure 10.6, three such classes are identified, i.e., Patron, Document and Loan, although Document and Loan are identified previously.

3. **Identify classes that serve as return types.** Returning an object from a function call is a common practice in object-oriented programming. This is also true for design sequence diagrams. Classes that are return types are identified from the return types of messages between objects in the design sequence diagrams. In Figure 10.6, Document is the only class that is used as a return type.
4. **Identify classes from the domain model.** Classes in the domain model that are parent classes or aggregation classes of classes identified may be added to the DCD if doing so facilitates understanding, implementation, and testing.

Figure 11.1 shows the classes identified by applying above rules. While identifying the classes, one must bear in mind the following: (1) the above rules should be applied to all of the design sequence diagrams produced in the current iteration, not to just one of the sequence diagrams produced; (2) a class may be identified by more than one rule, therefore, once a class is identified, it will not be identified again; (3) since the DCD serves as the design blueprint for the system, one needs only one DCD for all the behavioral models such as sequence diagrams and all iterations, not one DCD for each sequence diagram, or each iteration.

11.3.2 Identifying Methods

In a design sequence diagram, a message x:=m(. . .):X that is sent from an object A to another object B indicates that A calls the m(. . .) function of B and saves the result in the variable x of type X. Therefore, the methods of a class are identified from all such messages from all of the design sequence diagrams produced (in the current iteration). More specifically, the methods for a class B are the messages that label the arrow lines going to a B object in any of the design sequence diagrams. From the labels of the arrow lines, the methods of B are identified. For example, three such arrow lines go to the DBMgr object in Figure 10.6. They are labeled by "d := getDocument (cnList[i]: String):Document," "save(l:Loan)," and "save(d:Document)," respectively. Figure 11.2 shows the DCD with methods identified.

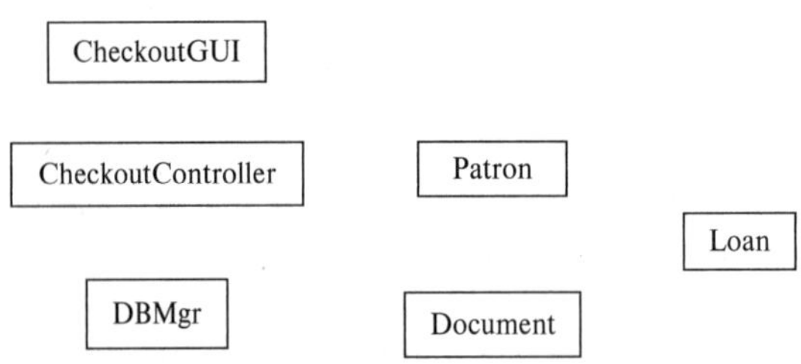

FIGURE 11.1 DCD with classes identified

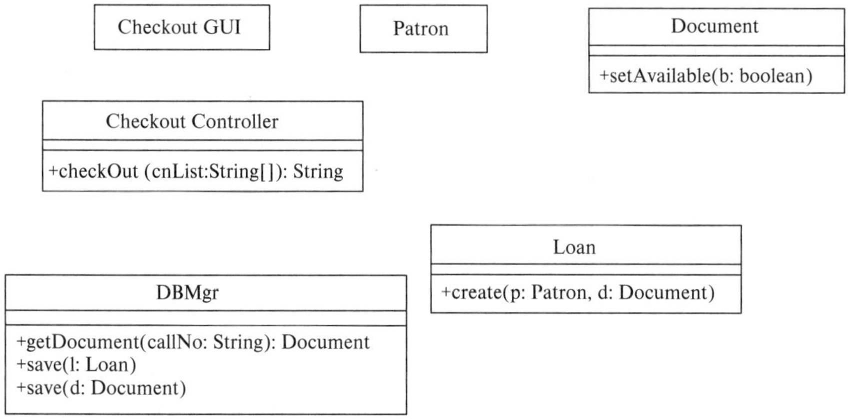

FIGURE 11.2 DCD with methods filled in

11.3.3 Identifying Attributes

It is important to bear in mind that attributes are not objects. Attributes do not have independent existence in the application or application domain. Attributes are scalar types, not object class types. Attributes are identified from messages in the design sequence diagrams and the domain model using the following rules:

1. *Identify attributes from methods that retrieve objects.* A message of the form getX-(a:T):X, where X is a class and T is a scalar type, suggests that a is an attribute of X and the type of a is T. However, whether a is an attribute of X or not should be verified using the domain model or domain knowledge. For example, in Figure 10.6, the d := getDocument (cnList[i]: String): Document message from Checkout Controller to DBMgr suggests that callNo is an attribute of Document.
2. *Identify attributes from accessor methods.* In object-oriented programming, the ordinary get and set methods are used to retrieve and update attributes of an object. This observation suggests that attributes of a class can be identified from messages such as t := getX( ):T and setX(x:T) that are sent to an object of a class, where X and x are a noun or intended to be a noun and T is a scalar type. These messages suggest that the noun X or x is an attribute of the class and the type of the attribute is T. For example, a t := getTitle():String message that is sent to a Document object suggests that title is an attribute of Document and the type of that attribute is String.
3. *Identify attributes from isX():boolean and setX(b:boolean) methods, where X is an adjective.* Recall from the domain modeling chapter, an adjective could be an attribute or attribute value. Methods that are named isX():boolean or setX(b: boolean), where X is an adjective, often suggest that isX is a boolean attribute of the object that receives the message. For example, in Figure 10.6, the setAvailable (false:boolean) message to the Document object suggest that available is a boolean attribute of Document.

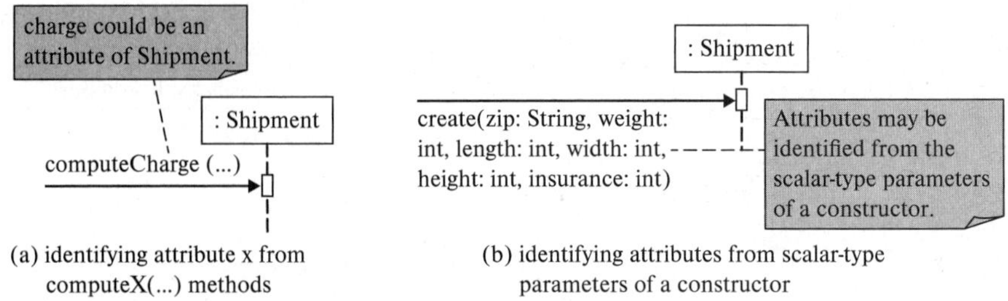

FIGURE 11.3 Identifying attributes using rules 4–5

4. *Identify attributes from methods that compute a scalar type value.* A message of the form computeX(. . .) or x := computeX(. . .):T, where T is a scalar type and computeX(. . .) is a computation that produces a scalar type value, may suggest that X is an attribute of the object that receives the message. The type of the attribute is T. In Figure 11.3(*a*), a Shipment object receives a computeCharge(. . .):double request to calculate the shipment charge. If the Shipment object stores the value of the computed charge, then charge is an attribute of Shipment and double is the type of this attribute.
5. *Identify attributes from the parameters to a constructor.* Most often, the scalar-type parameters that are passed to a constructor are used to initialize the object to be created. Consider, for example, a create(callNo: String, title: String, author: String, year: String, . . .) message that is sent to a Document object, where create is chosen by UML to mean the constructor of a class. In most cases, the parameters of this message are used by the Document class to initialize the attributes of the object that is created. Therefore, from these parameters, one can identify callNo, title, author, year and the like as attributes of Document. The type of these attributes are String. Another example for this rule is illustrated in Figure 11.3(*b*). Again the identified attributes and types should be verified with the domain model or domain knowledge.

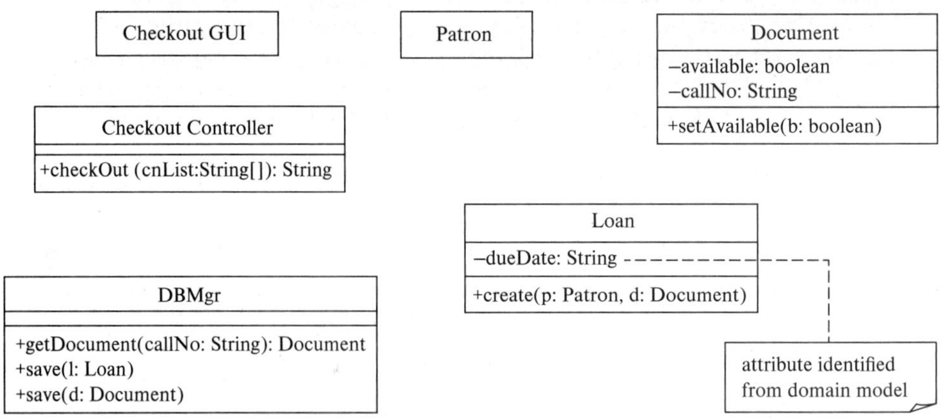

FIGURE 11.4 DCD with attributes identified

6. *Attributes are identified from the domain model.* For each class of the DCD, examine the corresponding class in the domain model and identify attributes that are needed to implement the operations of the DCD class. For example, the implementation of the constructor of the Loan class may compute the due date of a loan. The due date attribute may be found in the domain model because this is a piece of domain knowledge. A notification will be sent to the patron when the due date is approached.

The identified attributes are entered into the DCD as shown in Figure 11.4, where the minus sign ("-") is the UML notation for the private scope.

11.3.4 Identifying Relationships

Relationships between classes are identified from the design sequence diagrams produced in the current iteration and the domain model by applying the following rules:

1. *Identify create relationships.* If an object of A invokes a constructor of B or the criteria for applying the creator pattern (Chapter 10) holds, then A creates B. In Figure 11.5, one such relationship is identified: Checkout Controller creates Loan.
2. *Identify call relationships.* If an object of A calls a function of B, then A calls B. From Figure 11.5, several such relationships exist, for example, Checkout GUI calls Checkout Controller.
3. *Identify use relationships.* A uses class B if one of the following holds:
   a. *A passes an object of B as a parameter in a function call.* In Figure 11.5, the Checkout Controller calls the save(l:Loan) and save(d:Document) functions of the DBMgr. Therefore, Checkout Controller uses Loan and Document.

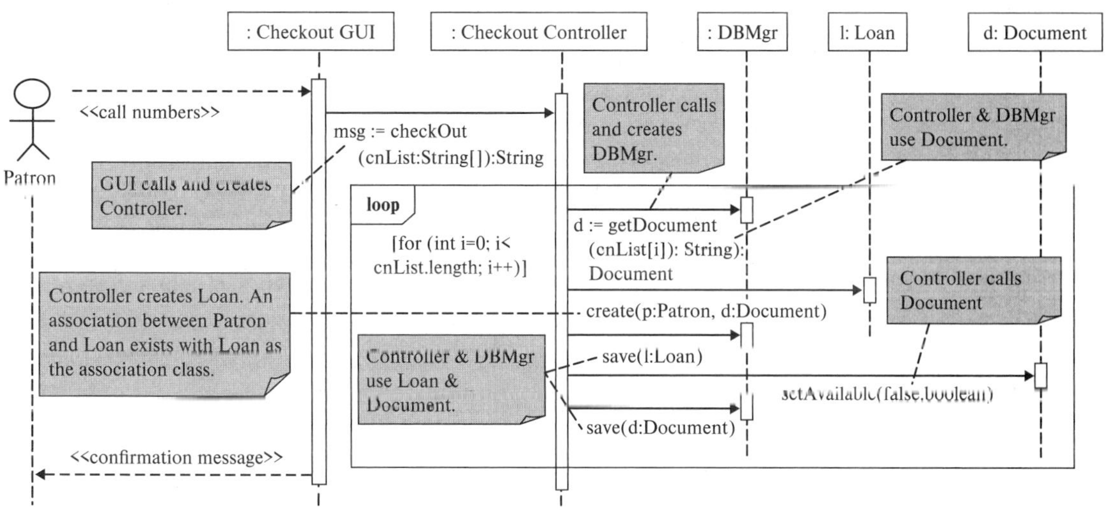

FIGURE 11.5 Identifying relationships

b. *A receives an object of B as a return value.* In Figure 11.5, there is one such relationship, that is, Checkout Controller uses Document, due to the d := getDocument(cnList[i]: String): Document call from the Checkout Controller to the DBMgr.

c. *A receives an object of B as a parameter from a call to a function of A.* In Figure 11.5, there are two such relationships: DBMgr uses Loan and Document because save(l: Loan) and save(d: Document) are functions of DBMgr.

4. *Identify association relationships and association classes.* If an object of B and an object of class C are used as parameters to invoke a constructor of A, then it is likely that an association relationship exists between B and C with A as the association class. These should be verified with the domain model or domain knowledge. In Figure 11.5, a Patron object and a Document object are used to invoke the constructor of Loan. Therefore, an association exists between Patron and Document, and Loan is the association class. The Loan object stores the checkout-related information such as which patron checks out which document and the due date. Indeed, these are true according to the library domain knowledge.

5. *Identify relationships from get object and set object messages.* If getB(. . .):B or setB(b:B) is a message to an object of A, and A and B are user-defined classes, then

   a. A is an aggregation of B if an object of B is a part of an object of A. For example, a message e := getEngine(): Engine to an object of the Car class signifies such an aggregation relationship. Such a relationship must be verified with the domain model, or domain knowledge. Sometimes, it should be verified with design decisions. For example, design patterns often use aggregation and inheritance relationships to provide behavioral variations. Such relationships usually do not exist in the application domain; hence, they cannot be verified with domain knowledge.

   b. A uses B, as explained in item 3 above.

   c. A associates with B if A and B are not aggregates of, or do not use each other. The relationship so identified should be verified with the domain model, domain knowledge, or design decisions. An example of such an association relationship is Student enrolls Course. This association relationship could be identified from the c:=getCourse():Course message that is sent to an Enrollment object.

6. *Identify containment relationships.* A containment relationship between class A and class B, such that A contains B, is identified if A receives a message of the form: add(b: B), get(. . .): B, getB(. . .): B, or remove(b: B), where A and B are user-defined classes. For example, if add(v: VendItem), get(id: String): VendItem, and remove(v: VendItem) are messages to the Dispenser class of a vending machine, then a Dispenser contains VendItem relationship is identified.

7. *Identify other relationships from the domain model.* Inheritance, aggregation, and association relationships can be identified from the domain model. For instance, one may identify User as a parent class of Patron from the domain model. This makes it easy to include other subclasses of User such as Staff and System Administrator in the future.

Figure 11.6 shows the DCD with the identified relationships.

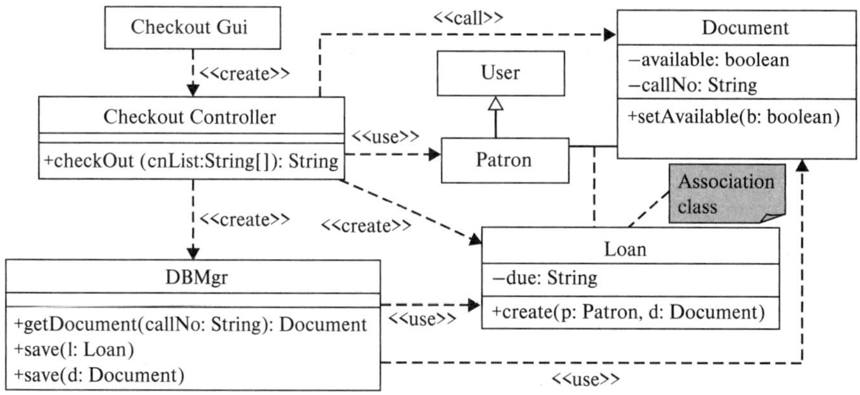

FIGURE 11.6 DCD with relationships

11.3.5 Design Class Diagram Review Checklist

To ensure quality, the DCD must be reviewed by the team members using the following review checklist:

1. Ensure that the classes, attributes, operations, parameter types, return types, and relationships in the DCD are derived correctly according to the steps and rules presented in this chapter.
2. Does the DCD contain unnecessary classes, operations, or relationships?
3. Does the naming of the classes, attributes, operations, and parameters communicate concisely the intended semantics or functionality and is it easy to understand?
4. Does the DCD clearly indicate the design patterns used? (This helps in the implementation and maintenance phases.)
5. Compute metrics such as fan-in, fan-out, class size, depth in inheritance tree, and coupling between classes and identify potential problems. See Chapter 19, Software Quality Assurance, for more detail.

11.4 ORGANIZE CLASSES WITH PACKAGE DIAGRAM

The DCD may contain numerous classes, making it difficult to understand and manage. In this case, UML package diagram, presented in Chapter 6, is useful for organizing the classes into logical partitions called *packages*. The packages may be organized in different ways. Two commonly used organizations and their combination are:

1. Functional subsystem organization.
2. Architectural style organization.
3. Hybrid organization.

The functional subsystem organization partitions the classes according to the functional subsystems of the software system. This results in packages that correspond to the functional subsystems of the software system. For example, the functional subsystems of a library information system include circulation subsystem, cataloguing subsystem, purchasing subsystem, interlibrary loan subsystem, and user support subsystem. Besides these, the system also has a persistence storage or database subsystem. Using this approach, six corresponding packages are defined. In addition to these packages, there is a package that contains classes belonging to the library information system as a whole including Main GUI, Login and Logout GUI, and Configuration. One advantage of the functional subsystem organization is that it is easy to reuse the subsystems and packages because each of these is relatively independent from the rest. A disadvantage is that various categories of classes are included in one package. For example, each package contains GUI classes, business object classes, controller classes, and the like.

The architectural style organization groups the classes according to the architectural style of the system. Consider the library information system again. It is not difficult to see that the system is an interactive system. According to the correspondence discussed in Chapter 6, the system should use an N-tier architecture. Therefore, the classes of the system are organized into packages that correspond to the layers of the N-tier architecture. One advantage of this approach is that each package encapsulates one type of classes, for example, the GUI package contains only presentation-related classes, the controller package contains only controllers, the business objects package contains only business object classes, and so on. Reusing each type of objects is easy. For example, library business classes are reused by reusing the business objects package. However, reusing a subsystem, such as a circulation subsystem, in this approach, is difficult.

The hybrid approach combines the architectural style organization and the functional subsystem organization. It can apply one of the following two approaches:

1. *Architectural style functional subsystem organization.* In this approach, the classes in each of the architectural packages are organized according to the functional subsystems of the system. For example, the classes in the GUI package are organized according to the subsystems of the library information system. This results in gui.circulation, gui.cataloguing, gui.purchasing, gui.userhelp, and gui.interlibraryloan subpackages.
2. *Functional subsystem architectural style organization.* In this approach, the classes in each functional package are organized according to the architecture of the system. For example, applying this approach to the circulation package would result in circulation.gui, circulation.controller, circulation.businessobjects, circulation.database, and circulation.network subpackages.

11.5 APPLYING AGILE PRINCIPLES

The following guidelines should be followed when deriving the DCD:

GUIDELINE 11.1 Value working software over comprehensive documentation.

The DCD is derived from the design diagrams, which are derived from the requirements and reflect the team's design ideas. For wicked problems, the implementation and the specification cannot be separated. The specification and the design ideas need testing by the working software. Therefore, the team should not spend a lot of effort to make the DCD complete for the application domain. The DCD should add only classes, attributes, methods, and relationships for the use cases allocated to the current iteration, not for future iterations.

GUIDELINE 11.2 Good enough is enough.

The DCD derived according to the steps and rules described in this chapter will include most of the classes, features, and relationships needed for the current iteration. It is good enough for test-driven development of the current iteration in many cases. Therefore, the team should not need to add many other classes and relationships.

11.6 TOOL SUPPORT FOR DESIGN CLASS DIAGRAM

Creating and managing UML diagrams is a tedious, time-consuming job. Tool support is desirable. There are many such tools including public domain, open source, and commercial products. Some of the widely known tools are IBM Rational Modeler, Microsoft Visio, ArgoUML, and NetBeans UML Plugin. These tools provide UML diagram editors along with other features. The diagram editors let the software engineer draw, edit, and manage UML diagrams. The tools can generate code skeletons from design diagrams for different programming languages. Most tools also support reverse engineering–that is, generating UML diagrams from code. These are only a few of the features of these tools.

11.7 SUMMARY

This chapter presents the steps for deriving a DCD from design sequence diagrams and domain model. The DCD serves as the design blueprint that integrates the design artifacts produced in previous activities. The chapter also presents how to use package diagrams to organize the classes in a DCD.

11.8 CHAPTER REVIEW QUESTIONS

1. What is a DCD?
2. Why do we need a DCD?
3. What are the rules for identifying classes, methods, attributes, and relationships, respectively?
4. What are the functional subsystem organization, and architectural style organization of classes? What are the hybrid organization and its merits?

11.9 EXERCISES

11.1 Derive a DCD from the design sequence diagram in Figure 9.18.

11.2 Derive a DCD from the design sequence diagram you produced for the Order a Dish use case in the exercises of Chapter 9. If you have not produced the sequence diagram, do the relevant exercises in Chapter 9 and then produce the DCD.

11.3 Derive a DCD from the design sequence diagrams you produced for the state diagram editor in exercise 9.7.

11.4 Derive a DCD from the design sequence diagrams that you produced for the ATM application in exercise 9.5.

11.5 Derive a DCD from the design sequence diagrams that you produced for the car rental application in exercise 9.6.

Chapter 12

User Interface Design

Key Takeaway Points

- User interface design is concerned with the design of the look and feel of user interfaces.
- The design for change, separation of concerns, information-hiding, high-cohesion, low-coupling, and keep-it-simple-and-stupid software design principles should be applied during user interface design.

The user interface of a software system is the means and mechanism through which a user interacts with the system to carry out business tasks. The users use the interface to request system services, provide user input, and receive system responses. Their feeling about the interface greatly influences the acceptance of the system and success of the project. If the user interface is easy to learn and use, then the users are more likely to use the system and use it correctly. This leads to an increase of productivity and acceptance of the new system. On the other hand, if the user interface is complex, confusing, or difficult to use, then the users are more likely to feel frustrated and make mistakes. Therefore, user interface design is a crucial activity in software development. Its importance can never be overestimated.

Chapter 8 presents actor–system interaction modeling, describing how users will interact with the system to perform the use cases. It is part of user interface design, that is, design of the user interface behavior. Chapter 8 did not cover the appearances of the user interface and other user interface interaction behavior that is specific to graphical user interface widgets, for example, using a text field to enter data is different from using a selection list.

This chapter presents the basic concepts and steps for user interface design. In particular, you will learn the following:

- Components of a user interface design
- Importance of user interface design
- User interface design process
- User interface design principles
- Guidelines for user interface design
- Agile principles for user interface design

12.1 WHAT IS USER INTERFACE DESIGN?

As stated previously, the user interface is the means and mechanism through which users interact with the system. As time goes by, the means and mechanism become much more sophisticated as the enabling technologies advance rapidly. Several decades ago the user interface was extremely primitive. To input a program and feed data to it, one used a special typewriter to punch holes on a black tape or punch cards. The punch tape was then mounted on an optical device, which read the tape and sent a bitstream to the computer. The output devices were the console typewriter and a line printer. Batch processing was the dominant mode of computing. In terms of today's standard, such a user interface is not user friendly at all, but at that time, it was a luxury to use a computer; therefore, nobody complained about it.

Today's software systems offer graphical user interfaces (GUI) and interactive mode of processing. Characteristics of such systems include:

- *Window-based multitasking.* Users can open multiple windows to work on and keep track of different tasks at the same time.
- *Easy to learn and use.* Proper design of the look and feel using graphical widgets makes the user interface intuitive and easy to learn and use.
- *Multimedia presentation.* The ability to use graphics, sound, animation, and movies greatly enhances information presentation and communication.

User interface design is aimed to use these features to facilitate user interaction and delivery of system capabilities. To achieve these goals, user interface design normally includes the following design activities:

1. *Layout design for windows and dialog boxes.* This is concerned with the overall partitioning of the display areas of windows and dialog boxes to facilitate user interaction, and working on different tasks. For example, most window-based applications partition the display area to include a menu bar and a toolbar on the top and a status bar at the bottom. Most integrated development environments (IDEs) partition the remaining area to include a project pane, a navigation pane, and a content pane to facilitate the user working on a project.
2. *Design of interaction behavior.* This is concerned with the design of sequences of messages exchanged between the user and the system. For example, an IDE user presses File, and then selects New Project to open a Project Specification dialog.
3. *Design of information presentation schemes.* This is concerned with the design of the presentation of information processing results. For example, using a bar chart to highlight differences in monthly sales of different products, or a pie chart to display the sales percentage of each product in the sales total.
4. *Design of online support.* This is concerned with the design of an online user guide, a user's manual, error messages, help facility, undo and redo, backup and restore, recovery, as well as many other support capabilities.

12.2 WHY IS USER INTERFACE DESIGN IMPORTANT?

Businesses and government organizations invest in computer hardware and software with the expectation to increase productivity and quality of service while lowering operating costs. The return on investment (ROI) depends on the design of the user interface because it is the sole communication channel between the user and the system. Through the user interface, users utilize the computer system to carry out business tasks. If the user interface is easy to use, then the user's productivity and work quality are increased. These in turn reduce operating costs. On the other hand, if the user interface is difficult to understand and use, then the users would avoid using the system, or their job error rates would be higher. Thus, the ROI is low. Unfortunately, the importance of user interface design is often underestimated. This results in products that offer excellent functionality and performance but do not sell because of poor user interfaces. Here are real-world stories.

The first story was a rapid application development software that allowed a software engineer to quickly compose a software system in a certain business domain using reusable components from a repository. The idea and implementation worked well on pilot studies. But the product did not sell very well despite an intensive marketing effort. One major obstacle was the graphical user interface, which was ad hoc. It displayed all kinds of icons that overwhelmed and confused the users. Another story is about a retail software that calculates shipping costs for sending mail and packages, and prints a self-adhere label for package shipping. It is used by the individually owned retail shipping stores, which are the private counterparts of the United States Postal Service (USPS). Unlike USPS and the brand name national chain stores, these retail stores allow the customer to ship with a variety of carriers including USPS as an option. Thus, the customer has the choices of carrier, air or ground shipping, overnight or express saver as well as affordable price. Another feature of such stores is speedy service to reduce customer waiting time. The retail software used by the retail stores requires a store employee to open four dialog windows to ship a package. Each window is flooded with colorful icons and buttons that confuse users and cause them to make mistakes. Correcting a mistake is a nightmare. As you might expect, the software does not sell well–it has a small customer base.

In comparison, a competing software uses only one window. It requires the store employee to enter only the package weight and destination zip code; package weight may be provided by a digital scale connected to the computer. Unlike the previous software that requires the user to select a carrier and a service of that carrier to calculate the shipping costs, this competing software displays the shipping costs for all services of all of the carriers in one screen, as shown in Figure 12.1. The store employee enters the ship-to name and address after the customer makes a selection. At that time, the corresponding button is clicked to print the shipping label. This UI design applied the keep it simple and stupid design principle. For example, instead of four windows, one window is used. Rather than requiring the user to enter all pieces of information regardless whether it is required, this app uses default values. It requires the ship-to name and address only when the customer decides to ship, in other words, lazy evaluation.

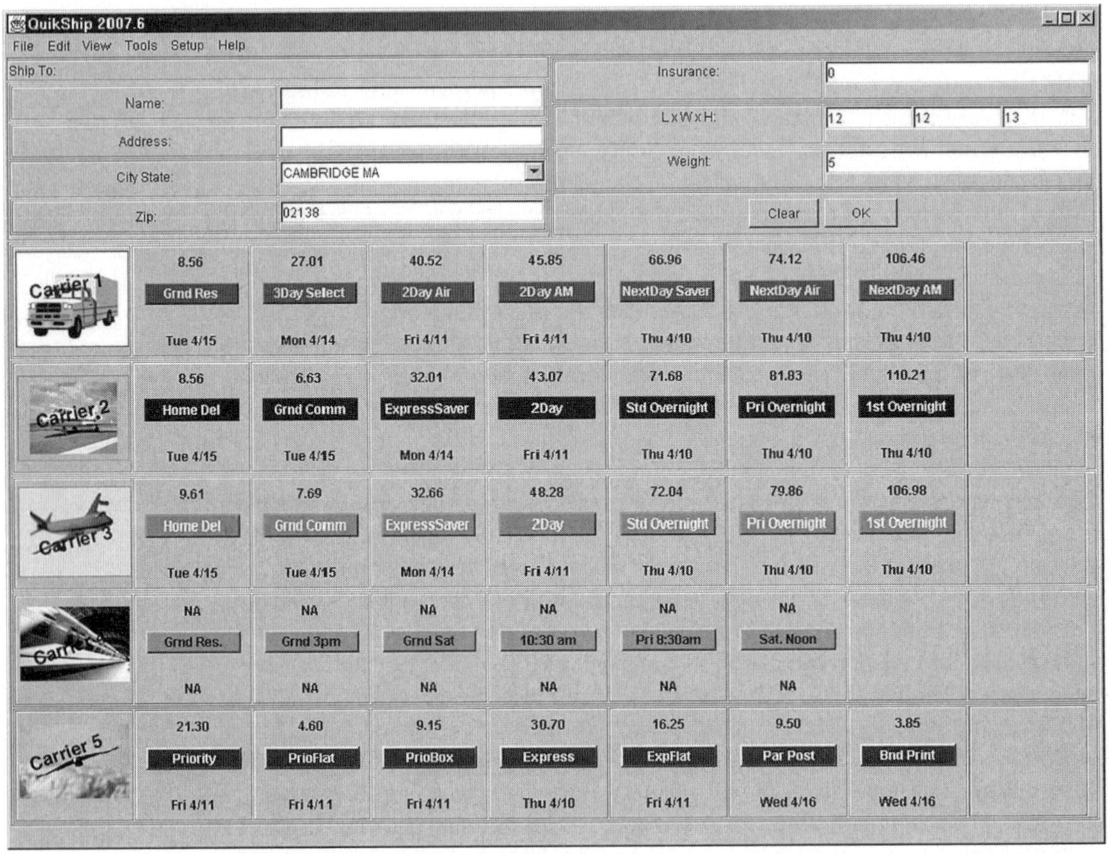

FIGURE 12.1 A shipping software that simplifies user operation

12.3 GRAPHICAL USER INTERFACE WIDGETS

Graphical user interfaces are composed of GUI widgets or widgets, such as windows, dialog boxes, menus, menu items, buttons, and many others. Different widgets serve different purposes, and proper use of the widgets is important. To save space and for simplicity, this section presents only widgets that are widely used and those used by user interfaces of stand-alone applications. In terms of design considerations, most of the widgets for web-based applications are similar to their desktop application counterparts. However, web user interface (WUI) implementation is different.

12.3.1 Container Widgets

Container widgets include window, dialog box, scroll pane, tabbed pane, and layered pane, among others. Windows are often used to present the main display or main window of a stand-alone application or its subsystems. When a software system starts, the main window is created and exists along with the application. It can be displayed anywhere in the user's desktop. Closing the window terminates the application and exiting the application closes the window. In Java, windows are decorated by frames to provide title bars, borders, and other window management buttons and menus. From a user's point of view, a window and a frame are not different; and hence, these are not distinguished in this chapter. A dialog box is a window that is launched by a window to engage the user in a dialog. Closing a dialog box does not terminate the application software.

A scroll pane provides a horizontal scroll bar and a vertical scroll bar to facilitate viewing different portions of a large object such as a long list, a big diagram or image. Tabbed panes and layered panes are useful for presenting different aspects or different instances of a subject to support the design principle of separation of concerns. For example, an IDE displays the source code of each class in a separate tabbed pane. A configuration setting dialog box may use different tabbed panes to define different aspects of the configuration of a system.

Menus and menu items, including pop-up menus, are used with windows to organize and display actions that the user can invoke. Buttons and other input/output widgets are used by windows, dialog boxes, tabbed panes, and layered panes to solicit input from, and display results to the user. Input/output widgets are described in the next two sections.

The following guideline should be observed when using container widgets:

GUIDELINE 12.1 Minimize the number of windows and dialog boxes that need to be opened to complete a business task while keeping the user interface easy to understand and use.

Reducing the number of windows improves the user experience. However, this must not lead to increased complexity of the windows and dialog boxes and make them difficult to understand and use. In this regard, creative thinking is needed. The GUI shown in Figure 12.1 illustrates how. For instance, although the software uses only one window, it does not make the user interface more difficult to understand and use. This is because it displays the choices in a well-organized, easy-to-understand manner. The display helps the customer select a shipping option, or a store employee to answer the customer's inquiries. The software uses default values for insurance and package dimension, these are the same for 90% of shipments. It does not require the user to enter the ship-to name and ship-to address until they are required.

12.3.2 Input, Output, and Information Presentation Widgets

Figure 12.2 shows some commonly used widgets for user input and information presentation. These widgets are classified into several categories:

Text-Oriented Input/Output Widgets

These are texts input/output methods. They let the user enter texts up to a predefined number of characters. They are widely used in dialog boxes or html forms to solicit text input information from the user. One advantage of these input widgets is that the input domain is extremely large. They let the programmer specify the valid length of the texts and the valid set of input characters. One disadvantage of these input

Category	Widget	Use	Type of Data	Description
Text-Oriented	• Text Field • Formatted Text Field • Password Field	Input	Single line of texts	Lets the user enter a single line of texts up to a specified number of characters. A formatted text field lets the programmer specify the valid set of characters. A password field is like a text field except that it hides the texts that are typed.
	• Text Area • Formatted Text Area	Input/ output	Multiple lines of texts	Lets the user enter, edit, or view multiple lines of text. A formatted text area allows styled texts while text area supports only plain texts. Styled texts may contain characters of different fonts, and images.
Selection-Oriented	• List • Drop-Down List • Combo Box	Input	Single or multiple items	Lets the user select from a list of choices. Multiple selections are allowed. A drop-down list displays a list of choices when it is clicked. A combo box combines the features of a list and a text field, allowing the user to select from a list or type in a value.
	• Check Box • Radio Button	Input	Boolean	Lets the user select one or more items or answer yes/no questions. Selecting one of the radio buttons of a group automatically deselects the other choices.
	• Spinner • Slider	Input	Single selection from an ordered list or a range of values	A spinner lets the user step through an ordered list of elements to make a selection, or type a valid input directly. It is sometimes preferred over combo boxes because no drop-down list is displayed that could block the view of important data. A slider is useful for selecting continuous types of input such as volume control and sensitivity.
	• File Chooser • Color Chooser • Location Chooser • Calendar	Input	File, item, or value	Lets the user select the file, color, location, or calendar date through browsing or clicking on a map or calendar.
Table-Oriented	• Table	Input/ output	Table or form	Lets the user view, edit, or enter data using a table or form.
Diagram-Oriented	• Canvas	Input/ output	Drawing	Lets the user view or edit a diagram in a drawing area.
Structure-Oriented	• Tree	Input/ output	Hierarchical	Information is organized and displayed as a tree to facilitate viewing and navigation.
Chart-Oriented	• Bar Chart • Pie Chart • Line Chart • Histogram	Input/ output		Information is displayed using appropriate charts to highlight difference, distribution, trend, and other attributes.
Image-Oriented	• Image	Input/ output	Pictorial	Information is input by click on an image, or displayed as an image.

FIGURE 12.2 Widgets for user input and result display

widgets is input error rate caused by typos, which is higher than selection-oriented input widgets. The input speed is also slower than other types of input widget. Another disadvantage is frequent switching between keyboard mode and mouse mode if the interface is not designed properly. Therefore, text-oriented input widgets should only be used for "free text" input.

Selection-Oriented Input Widgets

These input widgets let the user input information by selecting one or more of a finite number of known choices. They differ in the selection methods to satisfy the needs of various input requirements. The advantages of selection-oriented input widgets are high input accuracy and faster input because no typing is required. Switching between the keyboard and the mouse could be eliminated or substantially reduced if use of text-oriented input is restricted. A disadvantage of selection-oriented input method is that the selections may not include what the user wants. This can be resolved by adding an "Other, please specify" text field to allow the user to enter the selection. Another, potential, disadvantage is overwhelming, confusing, or difficult-to-understand choices. If used properly, selection-oriented input improves user experience. It should be a preference in user interface design.

Other Featured Widgets

The other widgets shown in Figure 12.2 provide specific features to satisfy various needs.

12.3.3 Guidelines for Using GUI Widgets

The following guidelines should be observed when using widgets:

GUIDELINE 12.2 To reduce human error, use selection input whenever possible and appropriate.

Example. People may mistype state names. Therefore, a combo box or spinner is preferred. However, a text field, possibly a formatted one, is a preferred choice for entering zip code because it is extremely difficult to locate the desired zip code from a list of thousands of zip codes.

GUIDELINE 12.3 Properly partition a long list into a hierarchy of shorter lists to facilitate navigation and selection.

Example. Partitioning all countries according to their continents facilitates the user to locate a country. Sometimes, an enormous amount of information needs to be displayed. In these cases, abstraction and classification techniques should be applied. Abstraction means suppressing unnecessary detail to focus on a high-level view of the information. It allows for navigation from a high-level view down to detail. Classification partitions the information into a number of categories and subcategories. The following guidelines should be observed when designing information displays.

GUIDELINE 12.4 Apply abstraction when the information to be displayed is of the same kind.

Example. The Search for Overseas Programs use case of the Study Abroad Management System (SAMS, presented in Chapter 4) may return many programs. In this case, the application of abstraction would display a list of high-level summaries of the programs and let the user click a program link to view the program detail.

GUIDELINE 12.5 Apply classification when the information to be displayed is of different kinds or belongs to different categories.

A well-known example of classification is the catalog of a library. The catalog classifies the documents of a library according to different subject categories and their subcategories. This classification makes sense because a library patron usually would look for documents in a specific subject category. Classification facilitates the search for needed information.

In many cases, the design of information display must take into consideration the need of the application and its users. The design of the shipping costs displayed in Figure 12.1 takes into account the needs of the retail shipping business–that is, it lets the user view the shipping cost and arrival date for each service of each carrier in one window. Abstraction and classification may not be the best approach in this case because they may require the user to open multiple windows.

12.4 USER INTERFACE DESIGN PROCESS

The user interface design process takes the expanded use cases produced in the current iteration. The output is the user interface design. The steps of the process are outlined as follows and detailed in subsequent sections

Step 1. Identify major system displays. In this step, the system displays, user input and user actions are identified from the expanded use cases produced in the current iteration. These form the basis for the design of the look and feel in the next two steps.

Step 2. Produce a draft design of windows and dialog boxes. In this step, a draft layout design of the windows and dialog boxes corresponding to the system displays is produced. This step designs the "look" of the user interface.

Step 3. Specify interaction behavior. In this step, a state diagram is produced to specify the navigation relationships between the windows and dialog boxes. This step designs the "feel" of the user interface.

Step 4. Construct a user interface prototype. This step is optional. It produces a user interface prototype to show the look and feel as designed in the last two steps.

Step 5. Evaluate the design with users. In this step, the user interface design and the prototype are presented to a group of user representatives to solicit their feedback, which is used to improve the design.

12.4.1 Case Study: User Interface Design for a Diagram Editor

The case study is to design the user interface for a state diagram editor. The state diagram editor is a stand-alone application. It allows the user to draw or edit a state diagram. For simplicity, only flat state diagrams are considered in this version of the editor. A flat state diagram is one in which all states are atomic–meaning they do not contain other states. Composite states, or states that contain other states, are considered an extension.

A part of the requirements for the state diagram editor that serves our purpose is given as follows: *"The state diagram editor shall allow a user to edit a new diagram or an existing diagram. The editor shall allow the user to add, delete, and edit states and*

Actor: User	System: State Diagram Editor
	0) System displays the editor main window.
1) TUCBW user clicking File on the menu bar and selecting • New Diagram, or • Open Diagram User locates the diagram file and clicks the OK button.	2) System accordingly displays: • a blank diagram, or • a State Diagram Selection dialog System displays the state diagram selected.
3) User repeatedly performs any of the following operations: • User clicks the State button. User clicks somewhere in the drawing area. • User clicks the Transition button. User presses the mouse in a state, drags to the destination state and releases the mouse. • User double-clicks a state or transition. User edits the state or transition and clicks the OK button. • User clicks Edit button on the menu bar then selects Undo or Redo.	4) System accordingly responds as follows: • System changes the cursor to a crosshair. System depicts a state shape with a dummy name. • System changes the cursor to a crosshair. System depicts a transition, from the source state to the destination state, with a dummy transition label. • System displays an Edit State/Edit Transition dialog. System displays the modified state diagram. • System displays the state diagram with last operation undone or redone.
5) When done, user clicks File on the menu bar then selects • Save, or • Save As User fills in the requested information and clicks the OK button.	6) System accordingly responds as follows: • System displays "Diagram Saved" in the status bar, or • System displays a Save State Diagram As dialog. System displays "Diagram Saved As ..." in the status bar.
7) TUCEW user seeing diagram saved message in the status bar.	

FIGURE 12.3 Edit State Diagram expanded use case

transitions as well as undo and redo these operations. The editor shall allow the user to perform other editing operations including saving a diagram and saving a diagram as."

As described above, the information needed by the user interface design steps is derived from the expanded use cases produced in actor-system interaction modeling. To illustrate, Figure 12.3 shows the Edit State Diagram expanded use case, where each bullet in the right column presents the system response for the corresponding bullet in the left column. For simplicity, it does not show delete operations.

12.4.2 Identify Major System Displays

In this step, the major system displays, the displayed information, as well as associated user input and user actions are identified from the expanded use cases produced in the current iteration. A major system display is one that requires user input, or displays system processing results. An error message or a confirmation dialog is not a major system display. The following rules are applied in this step. The results are shown in Figure 12.4.

1. Examine the steps in the right column of each expanded use case. A major system display is identified if
   a. the step displays system processing result, in this case, the displayed information is also identified, or
   b. the step requests the user to supply input (see Figure 12.2 for various types of input).
2. Examine the steps in the left column of each expanded use case to identify user input and user actions associated with each system display.

Above two rules imply that the quality of the expanded use cases affects the quality of the UI design. If the expanded use cases are poor, then the UI design derived from the expanded use cases could not be good.

Expanded Use Case Steps	User Input or User Action	System Display
0)		• Editor Main Window
1) & 2)	• Click File on the menu bar • Select New Diagram • Select Open Diagram • Locate diagram file and click OK button	• Dropdown menu (inferred) • Blank diagram • State Diagram Selection dialog (File chooser) • State diagram selected.
3) & 4)	• Click State button then click drawing area • Click Transition button, press mouse in drawing area, then drag and release mouse • Double-click a state or transition • Edit state/transition information then click OK button • Click Edit button on the menu bar then select Undo or Redo.	• State diagram with a new state • State diagram with a new transition • Edit State/Edit Transition dialog • Modified state diagram. • State diagram with last operation undone or redone.
5) & 6)	• Click File • Select Save • Select Save As • Enter file name and click OK button.	• Dropdown menu (inferred) • "Diagram Saved" message in the status bar • Save State Diagram As dialog • "Diagram Saved As ..." message in the status bar

FIGURE 12.4 User input and system displays for edit state diagram use case

EXAMPLE 12.1 Identify system displays, the information they display, and user input and user actions for the Edit State Diagram expanded use case shown in Figure 12.3.

Solution: Applying above rules identifies the system displays, the information displayed, and the user input and user actions as shown in Figure 12.4.

Note that in many cases, the expanded use case specifications may not be as detailed as the use case displayed in Figure 12.3. For example, the interaction steps may not show the lower-level options. However, the expanded use case still specifies the system displays although not all of the lower-level widgets are explicitly specified. In such cases, the lower-level widgets are identified from experience, similar projects, or during the draft layout design.

12.4.3 Producing a Draft Layout Design

In this step, two activities are performed: (1) deriving windows and dialog boxes for the system displays identified in the last step, and (2) producing a draft layout design for these windows and dialog boxes. That is, windows and dialog boxes are derived from the system displays identified in the previous step according to the criteria described in Section 12.3.1. Note that some windows or dialog boxes may already be implemented in previous iterations, or identified in the previous step. The widgets to be contained in the windows and dialogs can be derived from the information displayed, user input and user actions shown in the expanded use cases.

EXAMPLE 12.2

Identify windows, dialog boxes, and their widgets from Figure 12.4.

Solution: The result is shown in Figure 12.5. The windows and dialog boxes are already identified. But some of them can use a file chooser. A diagram canvas is used to display a state diagram. Two edit dialog boxes are used; one for editing a state and the other for editing a transition. These dialog boxes contain text fields and text areas to allow the user to edit state and transition attributes. The state and transition attributes are found from either the expanded use cases or the domain model. The solution shown in Figure 12.5 assumes that a state has a name and a state condition and a transition has a name and transition code. The attribute type is used to look up the widget from Figure 12.2.

Window/Dialog	Widgets or Components Contained in the Window/Dialog
Editor Main Window	Diagram Canvas (for blank diagram and selected diagram) Status bar Menu bar File (New Diagram/Open Diagram/Save/Save As) Edit (Undo/Redo) Buttons: State, Transition, Pointer (inferred)
State Diagram Selection File Chooser	File browser Buttons: OK, Cancel
Edit State Dialog	Text fields (state name and editable state attributes from domain model) Text areas (state condition, etc.)
Edit Transition Dialog	Text fields (transition name and editable transition attributes from domain model) Text areas (transition code, etc.)
Save State Diagram as File Chooser	File browser Buttons: Save, Cancel

FIGURE 12.5 Windows, dialogs, and widgets identified

The next activity is producing a draft layout design for the windows and dialog boxes. This is a creative activity, depending on the application on hand. As a rule of thumb, the layout design should follow the widely used layout design in the industry or the application domain if that standard layout exists. This reduces the user's learning curve. For example, there are consensus layout designs for the user interfaces of IDEs and document editors. For some other applications, custom look and feel is needed, taking into account the nature of the application.

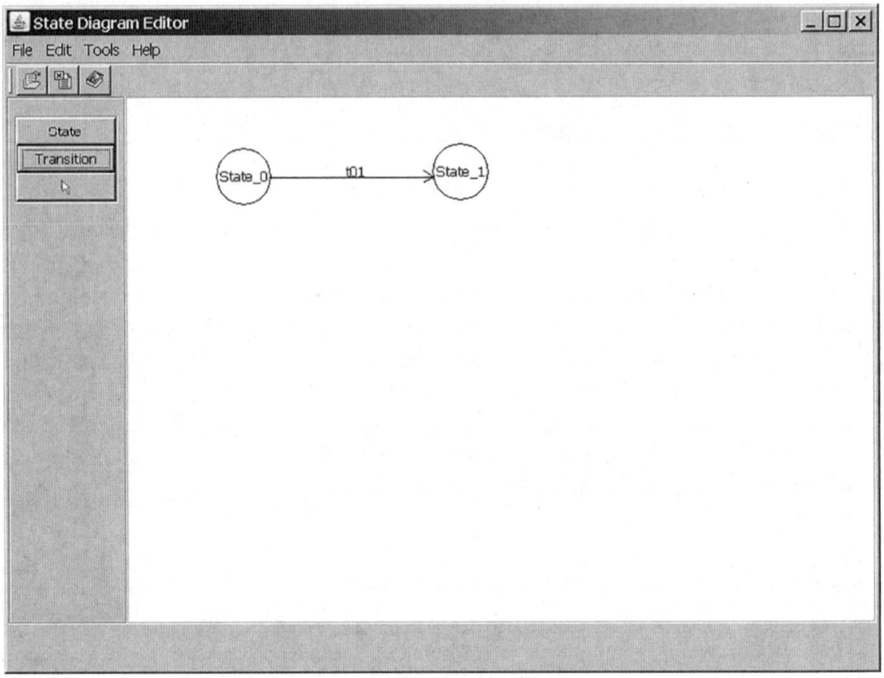

FIGURE 12.6 Design of the main window for a state diagram editor

The draft design produced in this step could be a set of drawings on a piece of paper, produced by using a slide show tool or a word processor, implemented using a prototyping tool, or implemented in the target implementation language. Figure 12.6 shows a Java implementation of a layout design for the Editor Main Window. If the user double-clicks a state or transition, a dialog appears, letting the user edit the state or transition. Figure 12.7 displays the Edit State Dialog when the user double-clicks the State_0 state.

12.4.4 Specifying Interaction Behavior

In this step, the interaction behavior of the user interface is designed and specified using a state diagram. The states of the diagram represent the windows and dialog boxes and the transitions represent the user input and user actions that cause the change from one window or dialog box to another.

In illustration, Figure 12.8 shows a partly completed state diagram for the expanded use case in Figure 12.3, where the arrow with a dotted tail points to the initial state. Additional states and transitions from other expanded use cases may be included in the state diagram. It is important to ensure that the state diagram and the expanded use case describe the same behavior.

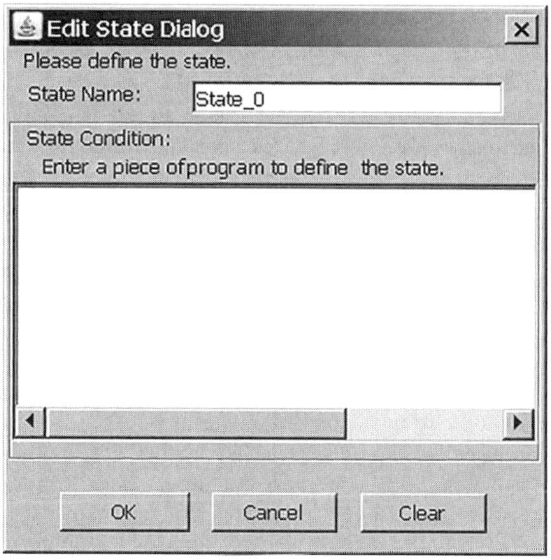

FIGURE 12.7 Design of a dialog for editing a state

The states may be annotated with the windows and dialog boxes they display, as shown in Figure 12.8 for the initial state. This technique has a number of advantages:

- It helps the developer to visualize the transition from one display to another.
- It is useful for checking the correctness of the state diagram—that is, does the state diagram correctly model the transition from one display to another as system's response to the user input and user action?

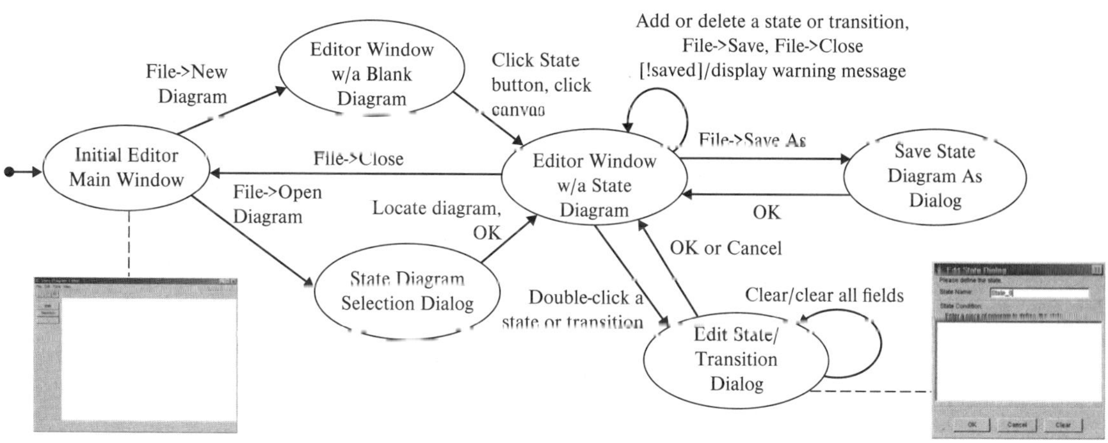

FIGURE 12.8 A partly completed user interface state diagram

- It is useful for completeness checking to ensure that there is an outgoing transition for each important user action that can be performed in the state. For example, the Edit State Dialog has three buttons, therefore, the annotated state should have three outgoing transitions. The state labeled "Edit State/Transition Dialog" in Figure 12.8 indeed has three outgoing transitions that correspond to these three user actions.
- Tools can be used or implemented to generate an animated prototype to demonstrate the behavior of the GUI.

12.4.5 Constructing a Prototype

Users may judge the user interface differently depending on factors that include personal preference, past experience, job responsibilities, and cultural background, to mention a few. Therefore, it is important to involve users in the evaluation of a user interface design. Prototyping is an effective means because it serves the purpose of "seeing is believing."

The usefulness of prototyping is similar to the use of model homes in the custom home market. Without the model homes, most home buyers would have a hard time figuring out what to expect from the floor plans. Model homes effectively communicate the look and feel to potential home buyers and facilitate them to express their change requests. Approaches to user interface prototyping can be classified as follows:

1. *Static approaches* generate nonexecutable prototypes. That is, the layout design of windows and dialog boxes are depicted on paper, using a slide show tool, or a word processor. The drawings are presented to users while the designer explains the functionality and behavior of the system. Sophisticated slide shows can animate the behavior to improve communication. Static prototypes are similar to architectural models in the construction industry. These scaled-down physical models are created to communicate the design ideas for major construction projects. Static prototypes are relatively inexpensive to construct and serve to communicate the layout design. However, they are not effective in showing the behavioral aspect of the system. Another drawback is that the prototype cannot evolve into the final system.
2. *Dynamic approaches* generate executable prototypes using a prototyping tool, implemented in a scripting language or the implementation language. Dynamic prototypes can demonstrate the interaction behavior at different levels of sophistication, ranging from simple animated behavior to fully implemented behavior. The executable feature provides more realistic interaction experience. Some approaches allow the users to experiment with the prototype. This increases the usefulness of the evaluation result. If the prototype is implemented in the target language, then it is possible to evolve the prototype into the final product. However, dynamic prototypes require more time and effort to design and implement. It is also time-consuming to incorporate major changes, which tend to occur during the initial stage of prototype development, especially for new systems.

3. *Hybrid approaches* construct static prototypes during the initial stage of prototype development and switch to dynamic prototypes after the users are more or less satisfied with the look and feel of the static prototypes.

12.4.6 Evaluating the User Interface Design with Users

In this step, the user interface design is evaluated with the users. This is, in fact, an application of agile principles–involving users in the development process. User interface design has to consider many factors, some of which can be determined only by working with the users. Factors that influence the acceptance of a user interface design include the following:

- *User interfaces of existing systems.* Users are used to the existing system because they have worked with the existing system for years. Users may not be willing to change switch to the new user interface.
- *The nature of the business.* Some applications emphasize processing speed, such as the retail shipping business discussed above. Mother's Day, Valentine's Day, and Christmas Day are the busiest shipping seasons of the year in United States. Fifty percent of the shipping volume of the year occurs during the Christmas season, and the last three days are the busiest of the year. Speed is critical to the retail shipping stores because customers may run away if it takes a long time to ship a package. Some other applications emphasize accuracy, reliability, and security. For instance, medical record management systems must ensure accuracy and security of the medical records. These systems must also ensure that alert messages are correctly scheduled and timely delivered to doctors and nurses. Some applications emphasize other aspects. Only the users can tell whether a user interface design can meet their needs.
- *User psychology.* User psychology is a combination of many factors including tradition, community culture, educational background, work experience, and gender. For example, the color red gives a striking effect and is used as a warning color in the United States. If the price of a stock, mutual fund, or exchange-traded fund is lower than yesterday, the price of the security is displayed in red. However, red is a lucky color in Asia, especially in China, Japan, Korea, and Southeast Asia. It is used to color the prices of up securities in the stock market. These are well-known cultural conventions and are easy to determine. Only the users can decide whether a user interface design violates, or is inconsistent with, organization-specific conventions. For example, hospitals and clinics use different colors to highlight items in a medical record. If a user interface design provides such a capability, then the use of color must be consistent with the existing convention. This can only be verified by users.
- *Personal preferences of the users.* Different users have different preferences, which influence the acceptance of the user interface design. Again, only the users can tell.

The above discussion indicates that it is important to evaluate the user interface design with users, solicit their feedback, analyze the feedback, and modify the design according to the feedback. The following are some of the approaches to evaluate the interface design with the users:

1. *User interface presentation.* This evaluation approach is used with static prototypes. Beginning in the initial state, a developer presents the functionality of the system by showing the windows and dialog boxes while tracing the transitions of the state diagram. The users are encouraged to ask questions, make comments, and provide change requests. These are noted and addressed later.
2. *User interface demonstration.* This approach is used with static prototypes as well as dynamic prototypes. In this approach the developer explains and demonstrates the features of the system using the prototype. User feedback is collected and used to improve the design.
3. *User interface experiment.* This approach is used to evaluate a dynamic prototype. The developer demonstrates the prototype and lets the users experiment with the prototype for a period of time. The users then provide feedback and change requests. These are addressed by the development team later. Well-written lab manuals, user training sessions, and/or user support personnel can improve the user experience and the effectiveness of this method.
4. *User interface review meeting.* This approach involves user interface design experts, domain experts, user representatives, and developers. Before the review meeting, the participants are required to attend a user interface presentation, experiment with the prototype, or review the layout and behavior design. The participants should answer a list of review questions (see Section 12.4.7). At the meeting, the participants exchange their review results and discuss possible ways to improve the design. Action items are identified and assigned to individual developers, who are required to report how the action items are resolved.
5. *User interface survey.* This approach uses a survey questionnaire to solicit feedback from the users, user interface design experts, and domain experts. The questionnaire should be brief and focus on important issues of the user interface. Review and survey questions should focus on obtaining feedback about: (1) ease of learning and using the system, (2) overall appearance of the interface, (3) effectiveness and efficiency of carrying out business tasks with the system, (4) use of language and terminology, (5) error handling and error messages (i.e., is error handling effective, are the error messages helpful to the users?), and (6) help facility and documentation (such as tutorial and user guide). The participants should be asked to choose an answer from a relative scale such as "very good," "good," "average," "below average," and "poor."

12.4.7 User Interface Design Review Checklist

1. Is the overall user interface design consistent with the standard user interface design in the industry?
2. Does each window, and dialog box have a simple appearance to allow the user to focus on the main theme of interaction?
3. Is the user interface behavior (such as the state diagram produced in step 3) consistent with the behavior specified in the expanded use case?

4. Does the user interface design make the system easy to learn and use?
5. Are the GUI widgets used correctly and consistently, and do they conform to industry standards or convention?
6. Are the labeling of the GUI widgets and descriptive texts precise and informative from a new user standpoint?
7. Are the icons used properly and informative of their functions?
8. Is the system output logically and properly structured and organized to facilitate understanding?
9. Are the messages clear and clearly displayed?
10. Are the error messages informative and helpful to users, and free of implementation detail?
11. Are color, blinking, and other user interface techniques used carefully, properly, and in a restrictive manner to avoid distraction of focus?

12.5 DESIGNING USER SUPPORT CAPABILITIES

User support capabilities include online documentation, context-dependent help, error messages, and recovery. Online documentation should include at least a user guide and a user's manual. The user guide should provide a high-level description of the system functionality and what the system can accomplish for different categories of users. A description of the functionality of each use case and how the use cases can be used together to accomplish certain business goals should be included in the user guide. A user's manual describes how to carry out each use case and how to perform certain operations. The user's manual can be produced from the expanded use case specifications relatively easily. That is, the steps of the expanded use case are converted into one-column text. Screen shots of the windows and dialogs are included to show the system responses.

A user-friendly design of online documentation should let the user find the needed information easily and quickly through browsing the table of contents and indices, navigating from one place to another, and searching for a desired topic. These features can be easily provided by the use of web pages. Context-dependent help provides help information that is relevant to the context. For example, the user may right-click in the State Condition text area in Figure 12.7 and select Help in the pop-up menu. The system should display the help information that is specific to the editing of a state condition. If the help information about the State Condition text area is not available, then the system should display help information about the Edit State Dialog, or help information about the State Diagram Editor.

The subsystem to provide context-dependent help consists of a hierarchy of help request handlers, organized as a tree or lattice. Each handler is responsible for providing help information for a given topic and knows only its parent node as its successor. The root of the tree provides information about the software system and has no successor. The leaf nodes of the tree provide information about the most specific topics such as the State Condition text area. When requested, a handler returns the help information if it has it; otherwise, it forwards the request to its successor node. In this way, the most specific help information can be provided by the chain of handlers.

The *chain of responsibility* pattern presented in Part V (Applying Situation-Specific Patterns) facilitates the implementation of this context-dependent help capability.

The design of error messages is another important task of user interface design. Many software engineers confuse an error message with a debugging message. Error messages such as "a bug has occurred in the script function foo() . . . " or " illegal operation in line 429" are useful for the developer to locate the bug but are not informative for the end user at all. Error messages should be user-oriented, not developer-oriented. They should tell the user what goes wrong and what the user can do to move on.

One important capability of a software system is its ability to recover from an undesired state. The most common and easy-to-achieve recovery capability is the ability to undo and redo certain operations. This can be accomplished by using the *command* pattern. A more sophisticated capability to recovery is the provision of automatic backup of important data sets as selected by the user. This allows the data to be restored when it is so desired. Finally, the system may be designed with software fault tolerance to provide the capability of automatic recovery from an undesired state, which is entered for various reasons, including exceptions, erroneous operations, or software fault.

12.6 GUIDELINES FOR USER INTERFACE DESIGN

Guidelines for using different kinds of widgets are described in Section 12.3. This section presents user interface design principles and guidelines. Design principles are more general and require the designer to interpret and apply them properly. Guidelines are more specific and provide more concrete advise on how to carry out a specific task. In this sense, a guideline is a lower-level principle. For example, "keep it simple and stupid" is a design principle because it provides general advice and requires the designer to properly apply it in different contexts. In comparison, "windows, dialog boxes, and web pages should have a simple and easy-to-understand look and feel" is a guideline because it provides specific advice on the design of look and feel.

The design for change, separation of concerns, information hiding, high cohesion, low coupling, and keep it simple and stupid software design principles are applicable to user interface design. These principles imply that GUI objects should be decoupled from business objects. This prevents changes to one of them from affecting the other. An example that violates these design principles is a GUI object that is responsible for presenting the widgets as well as handling action events. Such a tight coupling makes it difficult to modify the software to respond to requirement change. How to decouple the GUI from business objects was discussed in detail in Chapter 10 (Applying Responsibilities-Assignment Patterns).

As another example, the separation of concerns principle suggests that buttons and menu items of a user interface should be grouped according to different concerns. For example, it is a common practice to classify menu items into File, Edit, View, Tools, Help, and other concerns. The keep it simple and stupid principle advises us that the user interface should be easy to learn and use. In this regard, several guidelines should be followed.

GUIDELINE 12.6 User interface design should be user-centric.

This means user interfaces should be user friendly–they should provide a user-familiar look and feel, use user's language and terminology, be easy to learn, understand, and use, keep the user informed about what is going on, supporting undo and redo, and support different levels of users.

GUIDELINE 12.7 The user interface should be consistent.

This means consistency in the look and feel of windows, dialogs, and widgets, consistency in the use of terminology, consistency in information-processing activities and their results, and consistency with the overall system. For example, although there is more than one way to perform a copy-and-paste operation, the requests should be processed in the same way and produce the same result. As an example of consistency with the overall system, consider, for example, the Study Abroad Management System (SAMS). Its web pages should have the same look and feel as the web pages of the Office of International Education (OIE) because OIE operates SAMS. This provides the user a pleasant navigation experience.

GUIDELINE 12.8 Minimize switching between mouse mode and keyboard mode.

Frequent switching between mouse clicking and keyboard typing during the performance of a business task makes the user busy and less productive. Therefore, a user-friendly interface should reduce the need to switch between the two input modes.

GUIDELINE 12.9 A nice feature may not be that nice.

Software engineers have a tendency to give the users "nice features" regardless of whether the users want them or not. This happens to functionality as well as to user interfaces. For example, some software comes with an intelligent assistant wizard that automatically pops up all the time to offer help. The fact is that it really did not help much. A pop-up message that constantly reminds the user to do something such as run an update is disturbing and counterproductive. One version of UNIX for example, offers automatic command line correction. But 99% of the time, the suggested correction does not make any sense. The worst thing is, there is no way for the user to turn off this "nice" feature.

GUIDELINE 12.10 Eat your own cooking.

Many products are not user friendly because the designer never seriously uses the product. This guideline suggests that the user interface designer and programmer, or someone acting on their behalf, should seriously use the software, and have the user interface problems corrected, before releasing it to end users.

12.7 APPLYING AGILE PRINCIPLES

GUIDELINE 12.11 Active user involvement is imperative. A collaborative and cooperative approach between all stakeholders is essential.

The user interface affects all users' interaction with the system as well as the users' productivity and work quality. These, in turn, affect all stakeholders including the employer of the users. Therefore, user interface design should actively involve a variety of users. Moreover, the team should focus on users of the use cases that implement high-priority business processes. Today, all businesses are highly competitive. This means that the users may not have the time to review and experiment with the user interface and provide feedback. Therefore, collaboration of the stakeholders is essential. The project should seek support of stakeholders to allocate user representatives to actively work with the team to design the needed user interface and help the team collect users' feedback. This should significantly reduce the need to change the user interface later.

GUIDELINE 12.12 Requirements evolve but the timescale is fixed.

Change to the user interface requires considerable rework. This agile principle suggests that the iteration duration must not be extended due to rework. Instead, the team should negotiate with the customer and users to identify low-priority requirements to take out in order to make room for the rework. The 80/20 rule suggests that there are always such requirements. This also illustrates the importance to prioritize the requirements and update the priorities after each iteration.

GUIDELINE 12.13 Develop small, incremental releases and iterate. In addition, focus on frequent delivery of software products.

These principles help reduce the amount of rework because the users' needs and the real user interface requirements can be identified early and quickly. That the increment is small implies that the problem can be addressed easily.

GUIDELINE 12.14 A good enough user interface design is enough. Value the working software over the design.

Identifying the real user interface requirements is a true challenge. Although user interface sketches and prototypes are useful, they are not the actual software. The problem is not because of lack of time or effort but due to the nature of how users decide what interface they want. That is, they decide through "seeing is believing." Therefore, a good-enough design is enough. The working software is more important because it enables the users to nail down what user interface they want.

GUIDELINE 12.15 Capture requirements at a high level; lightweight and visual.

Applying this principle to a user interface means capturing the user interface requirements at a high level, making them lightweight and visual. As discussed in Guideline 12.14, the users know what they want through "seeing is believing." Therefore, capturing the requirements at a high level and making them lightweight is good enough. The nature of the user interface means that it is more effective to capture these requirements using a visual means such as sketches, user interface prototypes, and screen shots.

12.8 TOOL SUPPORT FOR USER INTERFACE DESIGN

There are many tools to support user interface design for desktop, web-based, and mobile applications. Examples are Eclipse WindowBuilder, Microsoft Visual Studio Windows Forms Designer, and NetBeans GUI Builder plug-in for desktop applications; Microsoft Visual Studio Web Designer, and NetBeans Visual Mobile Designer for designing touch-enabled user interfaces for Java ME Devices. Most tools can design the user interface by dragging and positioning the GUI widgets from a palette onto a canvas. That is, they accomplish "what you see is what you get" (WYSIWYG). The tools also allow the user to toggle between the design view and the source code view. The design view allows the user to edit the GUI visually while the source code view allows the user to edit the code directly. Finally, all the tools generate code from the design.

12.9 SUMMARY

This chapter begins with an introduction to user interface design and the importance of a user interface to the success of a software project. GUI widgets are then presented along with their usages. The chapter also presents a user interface design process and guidelines. The process is explained with a case study that produces a user interface design for a state diagram editor. GUI design is a supplement to the actor-system interaction modeling presented in Chapter 8. GUI prototypes are used along with expanded use cases to facilitate solicitation of user feedback. GUI design and actor–system interaction modeling should be performed simultaneously for them to benefit from each other.

12.10 CHAPTER REVIEW QUESTIONS

1. What are the functions of a user interface?
2. Why is user interface design important?
3. What features are offered by graphical use interfaces?
4. What are the design activities of user interface design?
5. What are the broad categories of graphical user interface widgets? What are the functions of each of these categories of widgets?
6. What are the specific categories of input, output, and information presentation widgets? What is the usefulness of each of these?
7. What are the advantages and disadvantages of text-oriented widgets?
8. What are the advantages and disadvantages of selection-oriented widgets?
9. What are the guidelines for using graphical user interface widgets?
10. What are the steps of the user interface design process presented in this chapter?
11. What is a user interface prototype? Are there different types of user interface prototype? If so, what are they?
12. What is the usefulness of a user interface prototype?
13. What is the usefulness of a state diagram in user interface prototyping?
14. What are the approaches to evaluating a user interface design with the users?
15. Why is it important to evaluate a user interface design with the users?
16. What are the user support capabilities described in this chapter?

12.11 EXERCISES

For each of the following use cases, first produce an expanded use case description if you have not done so in previous chapters. Then perform the user interface design steps to produce a user interface design for the use case.

12.1 The *Reserve a Car* use case for an online car rental application. A description of such an application is presented in Appendix D.1.

12.2 The *Login* use case. When the user logs in the first time, the system shall direct the user to a page to define authentication questions to be used when the user wants to reset password in the future. Assume that each user needs to define five questions and provide the answers to these questions.

12.3 The *Checkout Books* and *Return Books* use cases of an online library system that allows the patrons to check out and return books. The precondition for these two use cases are that the patron has logged into the system. The books that are checked out are mailed to the patron. The patron returns books by mail.

12.4 In Appendix D.4, a class diagram editor application is described. Perform a user interface design for this application.

12.5 Check the design of the above user interfaces using the user interface design review checklist presented in Section 12.4.7. Document any problems detected. Modify the design to fix the problems.

part IV

Modeling and Design of Other Types of Systems

13

Chapter

Modeling and Design of Event-Driven Systems

Key Takeaway Points

- Object state modeling (OSM) is concerned with the identification, modeling, design, and specification of state-dependent, reactive behavior of systems and objects.
- The state pattern reduces the complexity of state behavior design and implementation, and makes it easy to understand, test, and maintain.

In previous chapters, object interaction modeling (OIM) and how to apply responsibility assignment patterns were presented. OIM deals with interactive systems, in which objects interact with each other through a sequence of time-ordered messages. Since OIM is concerned with behavior between objects, it can be regarded as modeling of interobject behavior. Often, objects and systems exhibit "state-dependent behavior" or "state behavior." State behavior means that an object behaves differently in different states. For example, if the cruise control of a car is in the **Cruise Deactivated state,** then *pressing* the *ON-OFF button* of the cruise control causes it to enter into the **Cruise Activated** state. However, if the cruise control is in the **Cruise Activated** state, then *pressing the ON-OFF button* causes it to enter into the **Cruise Deactivated** state. In this discussion, bold face fonts are used to indicate states and italic font to indicate stimuli or events. This convention will be used throughout the chapter.

There are other examples of state behavior. A car can move forward, backward, or not move at all when the *gas pedal is pressed,* depending on the state of the engine and the state of the transmission. *Pushing an element onto a stack* may increase the size of the stack by one, or cause a runtime exception if the stack is full. Many event-driven systems, including embedded systems, such as the cruise control of a car and the thermostat of a house, exhibit state behavior. Modeling and analysis of state-dependent behavior and designing objects to handle such behavior are the focus of this chapter. Since OSM deals with the internal behavior of an object, it can be viewed as modeling, analysis, and design of intra object behavior.

As presented in Chapter 6, there are five types of system: interactive systems, event-driven systems, transformational systems, rule-based systems and database systems. OIM is a tool for the modeling and design of interactive systems. OSM is a tool for the modeling and design of event-driven systems. Activity modeling (Chapter 14) is a tool for modeling and design of transformational systems. While the design of interactive systems is centered around use cases, the design of event-driven systems is focused on state-dependent reactions of objects to events of interest. In this chapter, issues addressed by OSM and the need for OSM are discussed first. Steps for OSM and UML state diagram are presented next. The presentation of the state pattern for the design and implementation of state behavior concludes the chapter. After completing this chapter, you learn the following:

- What is OSM?
- The usefulness of OSM.
- How to conduct OSM.
- How to model state behavior with a state transition table.
- UML state diagram.
- How to apply the state pattern in object state design.
- How to model and design real-time embedded systems with state behavior.

13.1 WHAT IS OBJECT STATE MODELING?

OSM is concerned with the identification, modeling, analysis, design, and specification of state-dependent reactions of objects to external stimuli. OSM, like the other modeling tasks presented in this text, is not just drawing UML state diagrams. Drawing UML state diagrams is only one of the activities of OSM. The other activities have to answer a number of questions including the following:

- What are the external stimuli of interest? What are the states of an object? How does one characterize the states to determine whether an object is in a certain state?
- How does one identify and represent the states of a complex object that is an aggregate of other objects, just as a car is an aggregation of an engine and a transmission, among other components?
- How does one identify and specify the state dependent reactions of an object to external stimuli, especially when several objects are involved and their reactions affect each other?
- How does one check for desired properties of a state behavioral model including fulfillment of requirements and constraints of the application?

OSM is aimed at addressing these problems. It deals with the identification and representation of events and states of interest as well as their interdependencies. It provides analysis techniques to study the state-dependent reactive behavior of objects.

13.2 WHY OBJECT STATE MODELING?

First, OSM requires the team to collect information about object state behavior, classify the information, and construct the state diagrams. This process helps team members understand the state behavior. This common understanding is crucial to the success of a software project because a team member must know the state behavior of the objects being designed and/or implemented by other team members. Second, the state models enable the team members to communicate and collaborate more effectively because a UML state diagram is designed for modeling object state behavior. As a unified modeling language, UML state diagrams are understood by most software engineers. This means that a software engineer can implement state diagrams produced by another software engineer at another location. Without using state diagrams, the engineers have to rely on other communication and collaboration means that may not be as effective and widely used as UML.

Third, the object state models can be checked for desired properties, for example, to ensure that the event-driven subsystem processes each stimulus and sends the desired messages to the other objects or hardware devices. As another example, it is desirable to ensure that every state of a state diagram is reachable from an initial state. Application-specific properties can be checked by verification techniques. Finally, the object state models can be used to generate test cases to test an implementation as well as fault analysis to identify transitions that exhibit improper behavior. These systematic testing and fault analysis methods are more effective than casual approaches.

13.3 BASIC DEFINITIONS

Definition 13.1 An *event* is some happening of interest or a request to a subsystem, object, or component.

For example, *"ON-OFF button pressed"* and *"an element pushed"* onto a stack are events because they are happenings that are of interest to the cruise control subsystem and the stack object, respectively. The definition implicitly classifies events into two categories: (1) happenings, and (2) requests. Happenings are events that already occurred. They often come from outside and are reported to the software subsystem, expressed using past tense such as *"ON-OFF button pressed"* or *"gas pedal pressed."* Unlike happenings, requests are commands and actions to be performed, or queries. As such, they are formulated using imperative phrases such as *"turn on"* an air-conditioner. Requests often come from within the event-driven subsystem, that is, from one component or object of the subsystem to another.

Definition 13.2 A *state* is a named abstraction of a subsystem/object condition or situation that is entered or exited due to the occurrence of an event.

In the above example, **Cruise Deactivated** and **Cruise Activated** are two states of the cruise control subsystem because they are two conditions of the cruise control. They are entered or exited when the *"ON-OFF button pressed"* event occurs. As for a stack, **EMPTY, FULL**, and **IN-BETWEEN** are states because they denote three conditions of the stack and they are entered or exited when a request to the stack is executed.

13.4 STEPS FOR OBJECT STATE MODELING

OSM has five steps. They are performed for each system, subsystem, or object that exhibits state behavior. For simplicity, a system, subsystem, or object is referred to as a "subsystem" from time to time.

Step 1. Collecting and classifying state behavior information. In this step, information about state behavior of the subsystem is gathered and classified into states, events that trigger state transitions, guard conditions that govern state transitions, and response actions. This task might have been performed during the requirements analysis phase. The output of this step is the classified state behavior information.

Step 2. Constructing a domain model. In this step, a domain model showing the subsystem and its context as well as the states of the subsystem is constructed if desired. The domain model may have been constructed earlier. This step is optional but it greatly facilitates the conceptualization of the state behavior. The output of this step is the domain model.

Step 3. Constructing a state transition table. In this step, a state transition table is constructed to specify the state transitions. This step is optional. It facilitates the construction and verification of complex state diagrams. The output of this step is a state transition table.

Step 4. Visualizing the state behavior in a UML state diagram. In this step, the information shown in the domain model and the state transition table is converted into a UML state diagram. The output of this step is a design state diagram.

Step 5. Reviewing the state behavior model. In this step, the design state diagram is checked for desired properties. The output of this step is the design state diagram that possesses the desired properties.

13.4.1 Collecting and Classifying State Behavior Information

In this step, information about the events and event sources as well as states and state-dependent reactions of the subsystem is collected and classified. To facilitate this task, Figure 13.1 presents the identification and classification rules. The first column shows what to look for in the documentation. The second column shows examples. The third column shows the corresponding state modeling concepts. The last column is the rule ID, which is used in the following examples to illustrate how the rules are applied. Note: some of the rows are tautologies, which express the same thing differently. For example, S2 and S6 are similar because different modes of operation are associated with different system activities. Another example, S4 and S7 are the same because each of these identifies states with discrete state values. Figure 13.1 includes such redundancies because a modeling concept may be perceived or expressed differently in the documentation.

What to Look for	Example	Classify to	Rule ID
Something of interest happened (outside the system)	A cruise control turned on/off; user clicked a draw-shape button of a graphical editor.	Event	E1
Something of interest detected	High blood pressure detected; an obstruction detected.	Event	E2
A request to act from within the same system	A season switch object requests a compressor relay object to turn on/off the compressor; self-driving software instructs the vehicle control component to turn left/right.	Event	E3
Something that signals/informs	A timer goes off (to signal that x seconds elapsed).	Event	E4
Conditions that partitions the value space of an attribute	Stack size: size==0, size==MAX, size>0 && size<MAX	State	S1
Mode of operation	A cruise control operates in activated/deactivated modes.	State	S2
Position of a switch	The season switch of a thermostat is at off, heating or cooling position.	State	S3
Status of something	A relay is open or close.	State	S4
Period of time waiting for something to happen	System is waiting for a timer to go off, or system is waiting for an approval.	State	S5
An interval during which some activity is carrying out	A thermostat is heating; a cruise control is cruising.	State	S6
Enumeration of terms representing conditions of a system or object	A stack is EMPTY, FULL or IN-BETWEEN.	State	S7
A condition that determines whether the system will respond to an event	When the timer goes off, turn on the compressor only if room temperature is higher than the set temperature.	Guard condition	G
An action to be performed as a system/object response to an event	Call compressor relay to turn on (as a response to room temperature higher than preset temperature); start/stop timer (as a response to an on/off event).	Action	A

FIGURE 13.1 State behavior identification and classification rules

A guard condition is a conditional expression. It must be true for a state transition to take place when an event occurs. Guard conditions and state conditions are different. State conditions are conditional expressions on attributes of the object. For example, that "the size of a stack is equal to zero" is an expression on the size attribute of a stack. Guard conditions may involve variables of other objects as well as invocations of functions of an objects.

Note that it may happen that two analysts may identify a concept using two different rules because Figure 13.1 contains redundancies. For example, the states of a stack may be identified using rule S1 or S7. They may also identify different sets of concepts for the same application. This is normal because software development is a wicked problem and the solution to a wicked problem is not unique. In the following examples, the classification of a phrase is shown by a forward slash followed by a classification code. If a phrase has more than one word, the words are underlined. The classification codes are: "C" for class, "a" for attribute, "AS" for association, "AG" for aggregation, and "Ei," "Si," "G," "A" for event, state, guard condition, and response action, where i = 1, 2, . . .

EXAMPLE 13.1 Figure 13.2 shows the description of a thermostat with classes, attributes, and relationships identified using the rules presented in Chapter 5 (Domain Modeling), and events, states, guard conditions, and response actions identified using the rules presented in Figure 13.1. Figure 13.3 lists the concepts identified.

A household thermostat/C is a device that controls/AS the operations of the furnace/C and the air conditioner/C of a residential dwelling. It consists of/AG a season switch/C, a fan switch/C, two temperature up/down buttons/C, an LCD/C, and a temperature sensor/C.
The season switch can be set to Heat, Cool, or Off/E1 to control/AS the furnace, air conditioner, or not to control them.
Setting the fan switch/E1 to Auto/S3 runs the system's blower/C only during heating/S6 or cooling/S6. Setting this switch to Fan/S3 runs the blower all the time.
Press the temperature up/down buttons/E1 to set desired temperature/a,A. The LCD displays/AS the desired temperature while the buttons are pressed. The LCD displays/AS the room temperature/a when the buttons are not pressed/E1 for more than two seconds/a.
With the season switch at Heat/S3 or Cool/S3 position, the thermostat monitors/AS the room temperature by reading/AS the temperature sensor/C periodically/E4. If the season switch is at Heat position (respectively Cool position) and the room temperature is lower or higher (respectively higher or lower) than the desired temperature/G, the season switch closes/AS,E3 or opens/AS,E3 the furnace relay/C (respectively the AC relay/C).

FIGURE 13.2 Description of a thermostat with modeling concepts identified

Classes with attributes shown in parentheses:
Thermostat(desired temperature: int), AC Relay, Blower Relay, Furnace Relay, Fan Switch, LCD, Season Switch, Temperature Down Button, Temperature Up Button, Temperature Sensor(room temperature: int).

Association relationships:
control(Thermostat, Furnace Relay, AC Relay, Blower Relay), read(Thermostat, Temperature Sensor), close(Thermostat, Furnace Relay), open(Thermostat, Furnace Relay), close(Thermostat, AC Relay), open(Thermostat, AC Relay), close(Thermostat, Blower Relay), open(Thermostat, Blower Relay).

Aggregation relationships:
Part-Of(Season Switch, Fan Switch, Temperature Up Button, Temperature Down Button, LCD, Temperature Sensor, Thermostat).

Events:
set Season Switch to Heat/Cool/Off, set Fan Switch to Auto/Fan, press Temperature Up Button, press Temperature Down Button, timer off.

States, shown in parentheses:
Season Switch(Heating, Cooling, Off), Fan Switch(Fan, Auto), Furnace Relay(Close, Open), AC Relay(Close, Open), Blower Relay(Close, Open).

Guard conditions:
room temperature is lower than desired temperature, room temperature is higher than desired temperature.

Response actions:
set desired room temperature.

FIGURE 13.3 Listing of identified modeling concepts

EXAMPLE 13.2

Figure 13.4 shows the description of a cruise control with modeling concepts identified.

A cruise control/C consists of/AG a lever/C and an ON-OFF button/C at its tip. Press the ON-OFF button/E1 to activate or deactivate the cruise control. In the activated mode/S2, accelerate or decelerate to the desired speed and push the lever down/E1 to set the cruising speed/a,A. To increase or decrease the cruising speed/S6, push and hold the lever up or down/E1 until the desired speed is reached then release the lever/E1. To cancel/S6 the cruise control, pull the lever backward/E1 or apply the brake/E1. To resume cruising/S6, push the lever up/E1.

Classes: Cruise Control(cruising speed: int), Lever, ON-OFF Button, Brake.
Aggregation: Part-Of(Lever, ON-OFF Button, Cruise Control).
Events: press ON-OFF button, push lever down, push lever up, push and hold lever down, push and hold lever up, release lever, pull lever backward, apply brake.
States: cruise activated, cruise deactivated, cruising canceled, increasing speed, decreasing speed, cruising.
cruising, decreasing speed, increasing speed.
Response action: set cruising speed.

FIGURE 13.4 Description of a cruise control with concepts identified

13.4.2 Constructing a Domain Model to Show the Context

In this step, a domain model is constructed to depict the relationships between the event-driven subsystem and its context. Domain modeling is described in Chapter 5. For an event-driven subsystem, one needs to include modeling of states and the relationships between the states. For instance, the state of a car (at any given moment) is a combination of the states of its state-dependent components including the engine, the transmission, and the brake. In this case, the state of a car is an aggregation of states of its components. Besides aggregation relationships, inheritance relationships also exist between the states of an event-driven subsystem. Consider, for example, the cruise control subsystem in Figure 13.4. The cruise control may be activated or deactivated. In the **Cruise Activated** state, the cruise control is in one of four states: **Cruising, Cruising Canceled, Increasing Speed**, and **Decreasing Speed**. These states are specializations of the **Cruise Activated** state. In other words, they are subclasses of the **Cruise Activated** state class.

EXAMPLE 13.3 Figure 13.5 depicts a domain model for the thermostat subsystem shown in Figures 13.2 and 13.3. As shown in Figure 13.5, the environment or context of the Thermostat Control software receives input from, and controls hardware devices. For the software to work properly, it must keep track of the states of the hardware

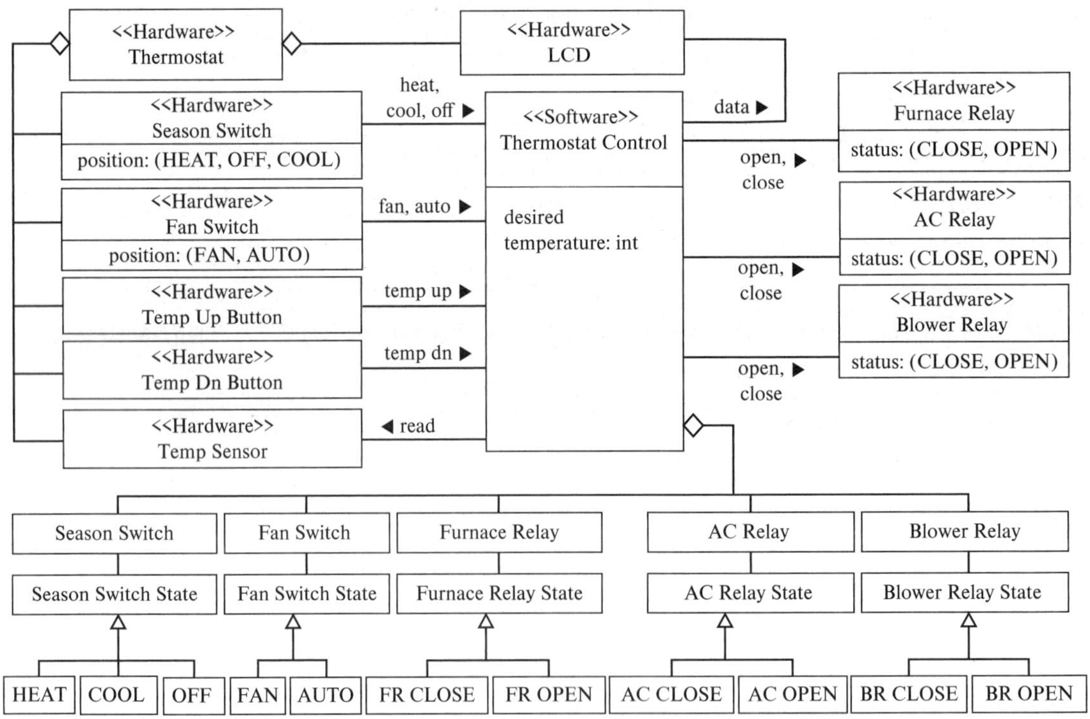

FIGURE 13.5 Thermostat domain model

devices. Therefore, the software consists of a number of classes that mirror their hardware counterparts and maintain the states of the hardware devices. Note that some of the hardware devices do not have states (e.g., Temp Up Button) or have only one state (e.g., Temperature Sensor). Therefore, the software does not need to maintain states for such devices.

The states of each of the hardware devices are identified in the last step. They can also be identified from the attribute values of classes that represent the hardware devices. For example, the position attribute of Season Switch has three values: HEAT, OFF, and COOL. This implies that the Season Switch has three states: HEAT, OFF, and COOL, as shown in Figure 13.5. The states of the other devices can be derived similarly. Figure 13.5 also depicts the events going into the software subsystem and the responses going out of the software subsystem to control the hardware devices. These are also useful for checking the consistency of the state diagrams.

EXAMPLE 13.4

Figure 13.6 shows the domain model for the cruise control system discussed in Example 13.2. It depicts the cruise control software subsystem and its relationships to the event sources and response destinations as well as the relationships between its states and substates. Note that although the Throttle Sensor class has a position attribute, it does not imply a state because the attribute type is double, a quantity value, not an indication of a state. As shown in Figure 13.4, the system can be in one of two states: **Cruise Activated** or **Cruise Deactivated**. The **Cruise Activated** state has four substates. These are displayed using inheritance relationships in Figure 13.6.

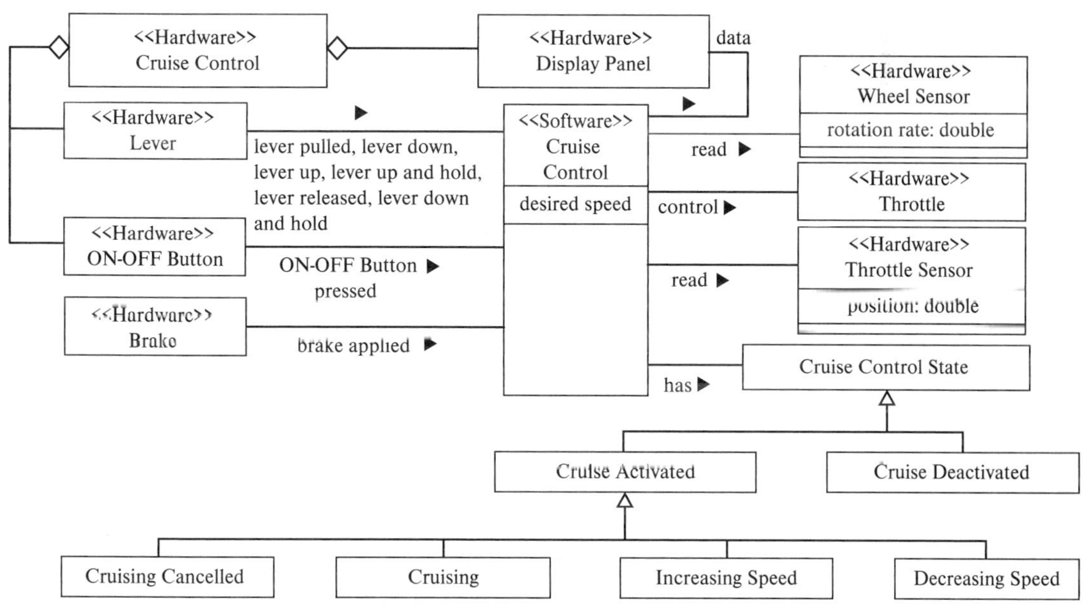

FIGURE 13.6 Cruise control domain model

The examples illustrate that there are two types of relationships between the states of an event-driven subsystem:

1. *Aggregation relationship:* A state is a *component substate* of another state because there is an aggregation relationship between the corresponding hardware/software components. For example, **Season Switch State** is a component substate of the state of Thermostat Control because Season Switch is a component of Thermostat.
2. *Inheritance relationship:* A state is a *specialization substate* of another state because the former is a subclass or a kind of the latter. For example, in Figure 13.5,**OFF, HEAT,** and **COOL** are subclasses or a kind of **Season Switch State**, therefore, they are specialization substates of **Season Switch State**.

The notions of a specialization substate and a component substate will be used in the following sections when state transition tables and UML state diagrams are presented.

13.4.3 Constructing State Transition Tables

With the information collected in step 1 and the domain model constructed in step 2, one can construct the state diagrams. However, the state behavior of some subsystems may involve many states and complex transitions between the states. How can one ensure that no state or transition is missing and that every event is processed? To accomplish these, a systematic approach to state diagram construction is needed. A state transition table offers a nice solution. Figure 13.7 shows a dummy state transition table, which is explained as follows. The columns represent events and the rows represent states and substates. Specialization substates are separated by single-lines and component substates are separated by double-lines. An initial state and a final state are indicated by "(init)" and "(final)" under the states, respectively. There are three types of table entries:

TBD entries. Initially, all of the entries of a state transition table are "TBD" (to be determined) entries.

Transition entries. These entries specify the state transitions caused by the occurrences of events. Each transition entry specifies the destination state S, an optional guard condition G, and an optional response action A, represented as S[G]/A. It means that the occurrence of an event designated by the column causes a state transition from the source state designated by the row to the destination state S only if the guard condition G is true, and if the transition takes place then the response action A is executed. A transition may execute several response actions. In this case, the actions are separated by semicolons, meaning that they are to be executed sequentially. If you want the actions to be executed in parallel, then you can use a parallel-execution symbol (such as "&"). An entry may contain more than one transition. In this case, all of these transitions must have a guard condition, and all of these guard conditions must be mutually exclusive.

NA entries. If event E does not cause a transition in state S, then the entry at row S and column E is "NA" (not applicable).

In practice, there are cases that a transition automatically takes place when the source state finishes its task, or when the state machines of a composite state reach their final states. To accommodate this, a UML state diagram allows transitions without a triggering event, which means that the destination state is entered when the source state finishes its activity. "Event-absent" transitions are treated in a state transition table by a special

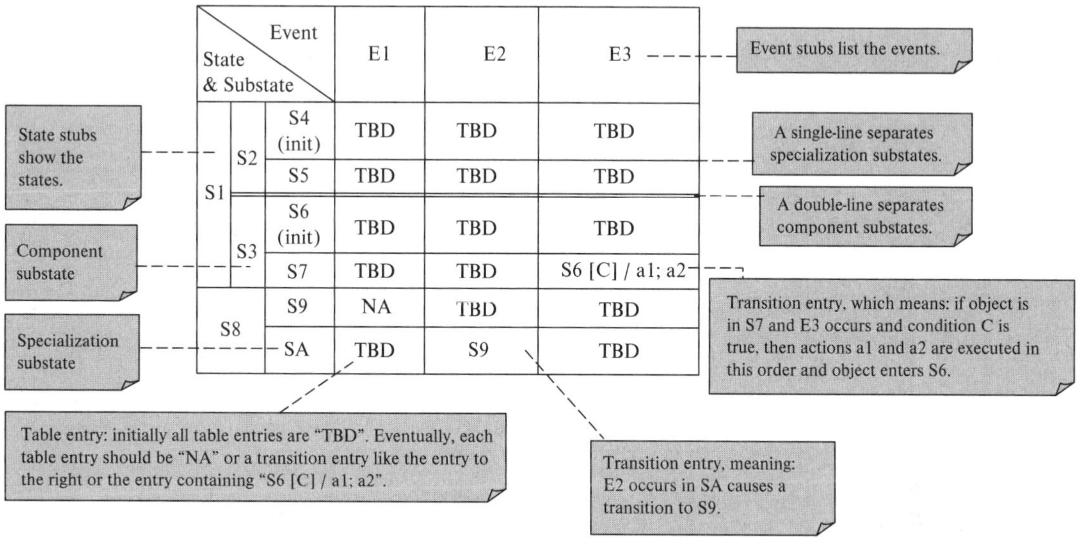

FIGURE 13.7 A dummy state transition table

column that denotes no-event. Note that a transition entry for a no-event may contain a guard condition and/or response actions. This means that the no-event transition can take place and the response actions are executed only if the guard condition is evaluated to true.

EXAMPLE 13.5

Construct a state transition table for the cruise control system discussed previously.

Solution: The state transition table is shown in Figure 13.8. In Figures 13.4 and 13.6, there are eight events coming into the cruise control software. These are shown as the column headings in Figure 13.8. There are five states, and these are used to label the rows. In the domain model,**Cruise Canceled, Cruising, Increasing Speed,** and **Decreasing Speed** are specialization subclasses of **Cruise Activated**. These are shown in the state transition table by dividing the **Cruise Activated** state into four substates and labeling them accordingly. The table also indicates the initial states with "(init)."

The first row of the table indicates that in the **Cruise Deactivated** state, the occurrence of the *ON-OFF button pressed* event will cause the cruise control to enter the **Cruise Activated** state. Since the **Cruise Canceled** substate is the initial state of the **Cruise Activated** state, the cruise control in effect enters the **Cruise Canceled** substate. In this state, if the *lever down* event occurs, then the cruise control enters the **Cruising** state and at the same time sets the desired speed (to the current speed). However, to enter into the **Cruising** state, the current speed must be greater than or equal to the minimal cruising speed. This is specified by the gard condition "[speed>=min speed]." The reader can interpret the other entries similarly. Note that the last entry of the last column is a merged entry. It indicates that the *ON-OFF button pressed* event causes a transition from the **Cruise Activated** state to the **Cruise Deactivated** state, regardless of which substate the cruise control is in. Figure 13.9 sketches an algorithm for systematically constructing a state transition table.

State & Substate \ Event		Lever down	Lever up and hold	Lever down and hold	Lever released	Lever pulled	Brake applied	Lever up	ON-OFF button pressed
Cruise deactivated (init)		NA	NA	NA	NA	NA	NA	NA	Cruise activated
Cruise Activated	Cruising canceled (init)	Cruising [speed>=min speed] / set desired speed	Increasing speed	Decreasing speed	NA	NA	NA	Cruising	Cruise deactivated
	Cruising	Cruising [speed>=min speed] / set desired speed	Increasing speed	Decreasing speed	NA	Cruising canceled	Cruising canceled	NA	
	Increasing speed	NA	NA	NA	Cruising [speed>=min speed] / set desired speed	NA	NA	NA	
	Decreasing speed	NA	NA	NA	Cruising [speed>=min speed] / set desired speed	NA	NA	NA	

FIGURE 13.8 Cruise control state transition table

13.4.4 Usefulness of the State Transition Table

There is no need to construct the state transition table if the state behavior is not complex. For complex state behavior, the state transition table exhibits a number of advantages as follows:

1. It allows systematic construction of the state model, as evidenced by the algorithm in Figure 13.9. This systematic approach ensures internal completeness, that is, it ensures that every state-event combination is analyzed.

```
State Transition Table Construction Algorithm
Input: Known states, events, responses, and state behavior
Output: A state transition table

n=number of states; k=number of events; i=0; j=0;
while (i<n) {
if (state i accepts an event e not labeling a column)
 { append a new column labeled by e; k++; }
 while (j<k) {
   if (state i accepts event j) {
     enter into table[i, j] the guard condition, the resulting state s, and the responses;
     if (the resulting state s is not labeling a row)
     { insert a new row labeled by s; n++; }
   } j++;
} i++;
}
```

FIGURE 13.9 Transition table construction algorithm

2. It allows automatic generation of state diagrams because the state transition table is an equivalent, tabular representation of a state diagram.
3. It facilitates detection of the following abnormalities:
   - **Dead state.** A dead state is a state that has no outgoing transitions. If an object enters into a dead state then it will be in that state forever. A dead state is present if there is a blank row and the state is not a final state. A dead state should be analyzed carefully to ensure that it is intended.
   - **Unreachable state.** All states that can be reached from an initial state are reachable states. A state is an unreachable state if it is not a reachable state. The transitive closure of the initial state contains the reachable states. A state that is not in the transitive closure of the initial state is an unreachable state.
   - **Neglected event.** A blank column indicates that the event is not accepted by any state. It is worthwhile reviewing each entry of that column. If the review still does not find a state that will accept that event, then it is possible that some state is missing or the event is not needed for the state transition table.
   - **Impossible transitions.** A transition is an impossible transition if its guard condition can never be true.
   - **Nondeterministic transitions.** Nondeterministic transitions exist if there is a transition entry that contains two or more transitions that satisfy the following conditions:
     a. Their destination states are different.
     b. Their guard conditions are not mutually exclusive.

     Nondeterministic transitions should be avoided.
   - **Redundant transitions.** Redundant transitions exist if a transition entry contains two or more transitions that differ only in their guard conditions. These transitions can be replaced by one transition as follows:

     Let S[C1]/A, S[C2]/A, . . . , S[Ck]/A be the transitions that differ only in their guard conditions and none of Ci is always false. If C1 OR C2 OR . . . OR Ck is always true, then replace the transitions by S/A, else replace the transitions by S[C1 OR C2 OR . . . OR Ck]/A. Moreover, a condition can be dropped if it is implied by other conditions.
   - **Inconsistent transitions.** Inconsistent transitions exist if a transition entry contains two or more transitions with equivalent guard conditions. These transitions are inconsistent because the same event, under the equivalent guard condition, can cause the object to enter into different destination states or perform different response actions.

13.4.5 Converting State Transition Table into Analysis State Diagram

Definition 13.3 A *UML state diagram* is a behavioral diagram that shows state behavior as a hierarchy of concurrent, communicating state machines, each of which depicts the states, state transitions, and response actions associated with the state transitions.

	Notion	Notation
Basic State Diagram	Simple state: A state that does not contain other states. A state is a condition or situation of a subsystem/object.	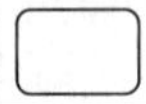
	Initial state: A pseudo state to start with.	●
	Final state: A state that indicates the completion of the state machine.	◉
	Transition: A transition from one state to another caused by an event.	⟶
	Transition label: It indicates that when event *e* occurs and the guard condition *expr* is true, then the state transition takes place and the response actions *a1; a2* are executed.	*e[expr] /a1; a2*
Advanced Features	Composite sequential state (CSS): A state that is composed of one region of states related by state transitions. At most one of the states can be active at any given point in time. Specialization substates and their parent state are visualized with CSS.	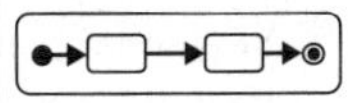
	Composite concurrent state (CCS): A state that is composed of more than one region of states related by state transitions. Two or more states, each from a different region, can be active at the same time. Component substates and their aggregate are visualized with CCS.	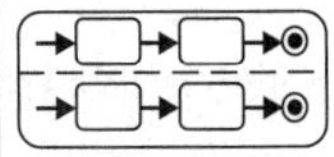
	Shallow history state: It indicates to return to the most recently active substate of its containing state but not the substates of that substate.	(H)
	Deep history state: It indicates to return to the most recent configuration of active substates of its containing state and recursively all of the substates of the containing state.	(H*)

FIGURE 13.10 Commonly used UML state diagram notions and notations

The last three steps collect and classify state behavior information, construct a domain model to show the event-driven subsystem and its context as well as relationships between the states. State transition tables to document the state behavior are also constructed. In this step, the state behavior are visualized using UML state diagrams. Figure 13.10 shows the commonly used notions and notations of a UML state diagram. Converting a state transition table into a state diagram is an easy task. First, the states and their substates are drawn. Specialization substates are placed within the boundary of their parent state. Component substates are represented by dividing their aggregate state into N regions separated by dashed lines, where N is the number of component substates. Next, for each transition S1[C1]/a1 at row S and column E, a transition from state S to state S1 is drawn and the transition is labeled with E[C1]/a1. The following examples illustrate this.

EXAMPLE 13.6 Convert the cruise control state transition table in Figure 13.8 into a state diagram.

Solution: Figure 13.11 shows the resulting state diagram. This example illustrates the representation of specialization substates.

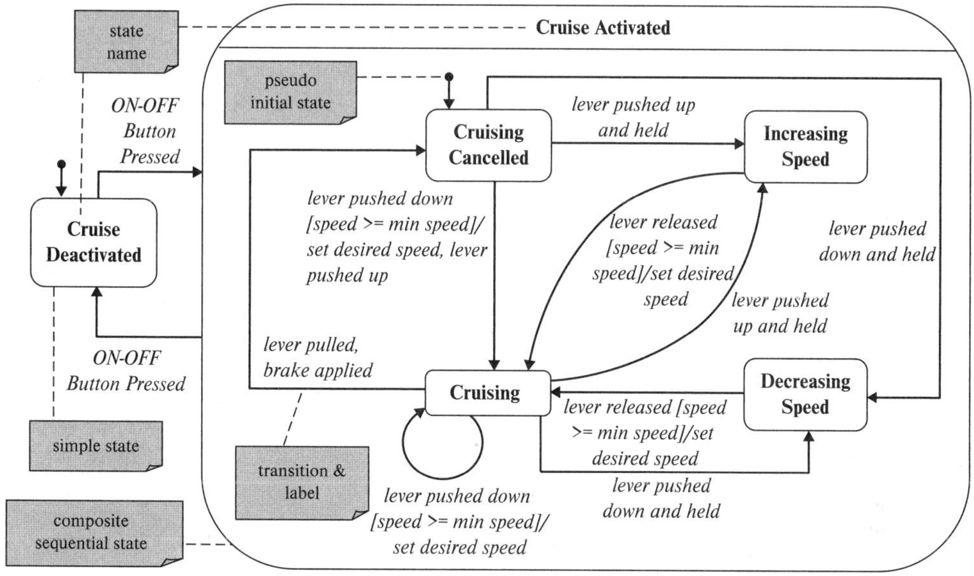

FIGURE 13.11 Cruise control state diagram

EXAMPLE 13.7

Draw a state diagram for the Thermostat Control in Figure 13.5.

Solution: Figure 13.12 shows the state diagram. The large oval represents the Thermostat Control state. The Thermostat Control has five independent components;

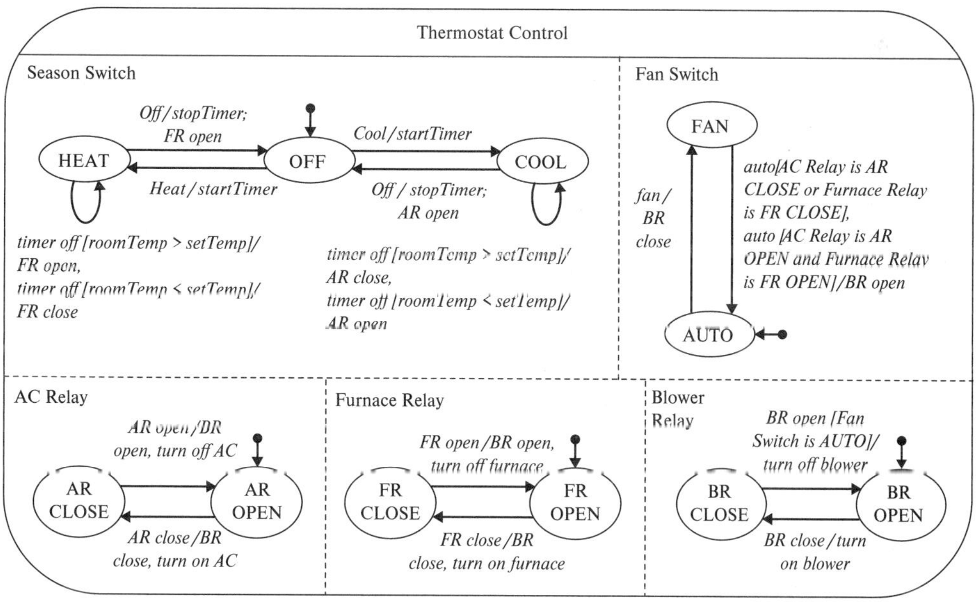

FIGURE 13.12 Thermostat Control state diagram

each has its own component state. Therefore, the oval is divided into five regions separated by dashed lines. Each region in turn shows its specialization substates and the transitions between them. Finally, the initial states are indicated.

13.4.6 Converting Analysis State Diagram into Design State Diagram

The differences between an analysis sequence diagram and a design sequence diagram are discussed in Section 9.2.4. The same distinctions are also true for analysis state diagrams and design state diagrams. In an analysis state diagram, the transitions are informally specified using English texts. This style of informal specification may be used in the initial stage of OSM, or in the modeling of an existing application. The transitions in a design state diagram are formally specified as function calls with guard conditions as conditional expressions as in a programming language. Figure 13.13 shows the design state diagram for the informal thermostat state diagram in Figure 13.12. The conversion rules are explained as follows:

- Translate each event into a function signature, that is, a function name, followed by a pair of parentheses enclosing the parameters and types, followed by a colon and the return type, where the parameters and return type are optional, for example, off(), cool(), and auto().

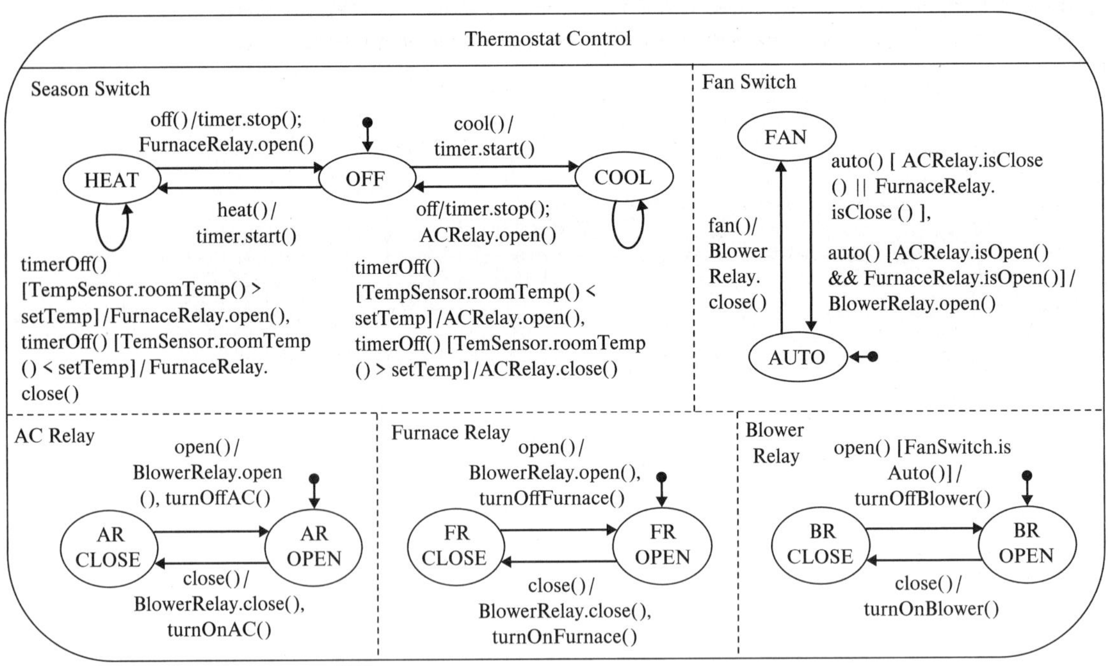

FIGURE 13.13 A design state diagram for the thermostat control

- Translate each guard condition into a conditional expression with function calls, relational operators, and logical operators. For example, "[AC Relay is AR CLOSE or Furnace Relay is FR CLOSE]" is translated into "[ACRelay.isClose () || FurnaceRelay.isClose ()]."
- Translate each response action into a function call. For example, timer.stop() and ACRelay.open().

The state diagram in Figure 13.13 is explained as follows to help the reader understand the notations. First, the Thermostat Control has five concurrent states, as shown by the five state machines separated by dashed lines. This means that all of the five state machines are active at the same time. Each of them is in an active state of its own. These state machines mirror the state behaviors of their hardware counterparts. Eventually, they are implemented by software to keep track of the state of the Thermostat.

The figure shows that initially the Season Switch is in the **OFF** state; the AC Relay, Furnace Relay, and Blower Relay are in the **OPEN** state. The fan is in the **AUTO** state. If the Season Switch is turned to the cool position, then this hardware event results in calling the cool() function of the Season Switch. Thus, the transition from the **OFF** state to the **COOL** state takes place, and at the same time, the timer is started. In other words, the Season Switch sends a message to the timer, i.e., timer.start(). When the timer goes off because the preset time has elapsed, the Season Switch reads the room temperature and compares it with the set temperature. If the room temperature is lower than the set temperature, then the Season Switch calls the open() function of the AC Relay (to stop cooling). Since the AC Relay is initially in the **AR OPEN** state, the ACRelay.open() message has no effect. However, if the room temperature is higher than the set temperature, then the Season Switch calls the ACRelay.close() function. This results in the AC Relay enters into the **AR CLOSE** state. At the same time, the BlowerRelay.close() function is called and the AC is turned on (to cool the house). The cooling will continue until the room is cool enough, then the ACRelay.open() is called to stop the AC and the Blower. Since the state machines in Figure 13.13 run simultaneously and send messages to each other, therefore, they are call concurrent and communicating state machines.

13.4.7 State Modeling Review Checklists

The state models are reviewed by using a checklist like the following:

1. Is there any event or response missing in the domain model, state transition tables, or state diagrams?
2. Are the events and responses correctly identified?
3. Do any of the abnormalities described in Section 13.4.4 exist in the state transition tables or state diagrams?
4. Are the state transitions correct? That is, are their triggering events, guard conditions, destination states, and responses correct?
5. Does every state machine have an initial state and the required final state(s)?
6. For each event going into the software subsystem in the domain model, is there a transition that accepts the event?
7. For each response going out of the software subsystem in the domain model, is there a transition that generates the response?

13.5 THE STATE PATTERN

Several conventional state machine implementation approaches exist and some of them are widely used by programmers. However, the conventional approaches are associated with a number of drawbacks. The state pattern is a better alternative to the conventional approaches. This section reviews some of the conventional approaches and points out their drawbacks. It then presents the state pattern and shows its applications to the cruise control and the thermostat examples.

13.5.1 Conventional Approaches

Conventional approaches to implementing state behavior include:

1. Using nested-switch statements.
2. Using a state transition matrix.
3. Using method implementation.

The nested-switch implementation approach is widely used by programmers. In this approach, the current state is stored in a state variable. One switch statement is used to represent the states of the state machine. Another, nested, switch statement is used to represent the events. The cases of the inner switch are responsible for implementing the state transitions, that is, evaluating the guard conditions, invoking the response actions, and setting the state variable to the destination state. At runtime, the value of the state variable and the incoming event are used to select the appropriate case of the inner switch to execute.

The transition matrix approach stores the state transitions in the entries of a two-dimensional array, which is similar to the state transition table described in Section 13.4.3. Each array entry is either null or stores the guard condition, response actions, and destination state. The current state is kept in a state variable, which together with the incoming event, determines the array entry. If the array entry is not null, then the guard condition is evaluated; if it is true, the response actions are executed and the state variable is updated.

In the method implementation approach, the state behavior of a class is implemented by member functions that denote an event in the state diagram. The current state of the object is stored in a state variable, which is an attribute of the class. A member function may evaluate the state variable and the guard condition and execute the appropriate response actions and update the state variable.

The conventional approaches are associated with a number of drawbacks. First, the nested-switch approach has high cyclomatic complexity, a measure of the number of independent control flow paths in a program. For example, if a state machine has five states and five events, then in the worst case, there are 5 by 5 or 25 independent paths. The method implementation approach has the same problem, although it is slightly better; the complexity is the number of states in the state machine. High complexity makes the code difficult to comprehend, test, and maintain. The transition matrix uses an interpretation approach rather than a compilation approach. Therefore, it is not as efficient.

Second, changes are difficult to make. For example, using the nested-switch approach, each case of the outer switch must be changed in order to add or delete an event. If the changes are not made consistently, the system will not behave properly. Third, it is not easy to implement in the conventional approaches state diagrams that contain composite states. One problem is higher cyclomatic complexity introduced by composite states. Another problem is the difficulty in implementing concurrent state machines using the conventional approaches.

13.5.2 What Is State Pattern?

The state pattern, described in Figure 13.14, overcomes the drawbacks of the conventional approaches. The sample state machine shown in the structural design section is used to help understand the design of the pattern. The mapping between the sample

Name	State
Type	GoF/Behavioral
Specification	
Problem	How to design and implement state-dependent behavior of an object.
Solution	Define a State class that implements operations to correspond to the state transitions. Each of these operations simply returns self, that is, the current state. Define a State subclass for each state in the state diagram. Each State subclass overrides the parent-class operations corresponding to the outgoing transitions to implement the state behavior associated with these transitions.
Design	
Structural	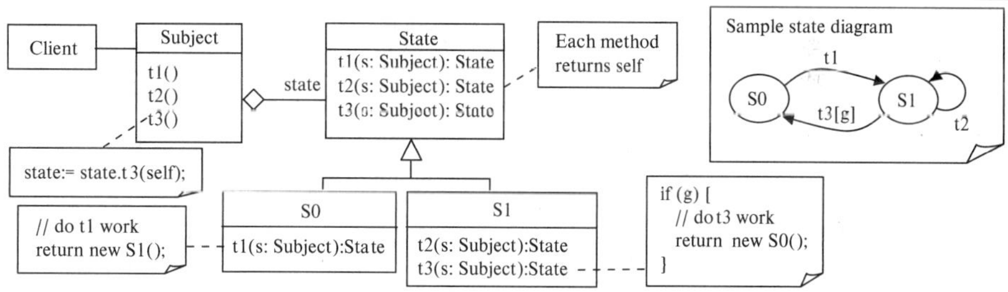
Behavioral	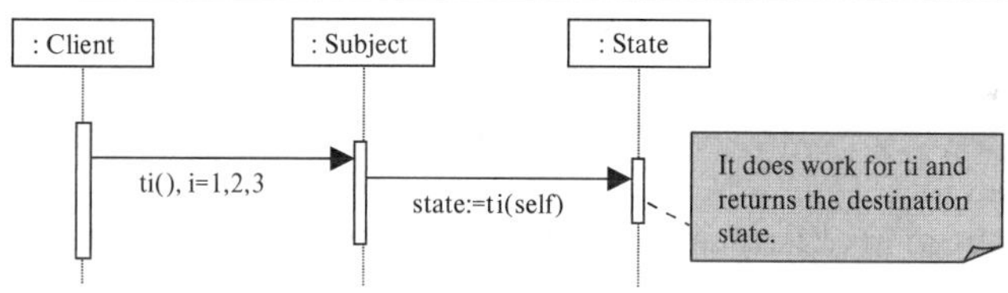
Roles and Responsibilities	• State: It defines a method for each transition in the state diagram and implements it as "return self." • S0, S1: These are the State subclasses. There is one such subclass for each state in the state diagram. Each such subclass implements the transitions that go out of the state. The implementation does the work for each transition and returns the destination state. • Subject: It represents the object that possesses the state-dependent behavior. It provides the client interface and defines an operation for each of the transitions in the state diagram. It maintains a reference to a State object, which represents the state of the Subject. It delegates the client requests to the corresponding operations of the state object. The call automatically updates the state of the Subject. • Client: It represents the event sources such as window events, sensors, etc. It calls the operations of Subject that correspond to the events.
Benefits	• It reduces the complexity of the design and implementation of the state-dependent behavior. • It is easy to add and remove states and transitions. • It makes the state behavior easy to understand, implement, test and maintain. • It facilitates test-driven development because the behavior is easier to test.
Liabilities	More classes to design and implement.
Guidelines	• Apply the state pattern to objects that have nontrivial state behavior, or the state behavior will evolve in the future. • It is not necessary to apply the state pattern to state behavior that is trivial and not expected to evolve.
Related Patterns	• A use case controller may use state pattern to maintain use case states. • State subclasses are often implemented as singletons. • State and mediator patterns are often used together; the behavior of a mediator can be modeled by a state diagram, which is designed and implemented by using the state pattern.
Uses	The pattern is useful for design and implementation of event-driven systems, especially embedded systems.

FIGURE 13.14 Specification of the state pattern

Pattern Classes and Methods	Description	Sample State Diagram States and Transitions
State	An abstract state to represent all possible states.	
t1(): State t2(): State t3(): State	Methods of abstract State to correspond to the state transitions in the state diagram. Currently, there are only three transitions in the state diagram.	t1, t2, t3
S0, S1	Concrete states; for each state in the state diagram, there is a concrete State subclass in the pattern.	S0, S1
Subject	It represents the system, subsystem, device or object (e.g., a cruise control, a thermostat) whose state-dependent behavior is being modeled by the state diagram.	(implicitly assumed)
Client	It represents the environment of the Subject. It delivers the triggering events to the Subject by calling the corresponding functions of the Subject.	(implicitly assumed)

FIGURE 13.15 Mapping between state pattern and sample state machine

state machine and the pattern classes is displayed in Figure 13.15. In practice, the concrete state objects may be created and stored in a static array in the State class. These can then be used to update the state of the subject to reduce the number of state objects created. Another approach uses the singleton pattern to implement the concrete states.

13.5.3 Applying State Pattern

As described in the previous section, the state pattern consists of two main parts: a subject with state behavior and a hierarchy of state classes that implements the state behavior for the subject. The subject defines the client interface and delegates client requests to the state object that keeps track of the state of the subject. Thus, the key to apply the state pattern is defining the hierarchy of state classes. This section illustrates the application of the state pattern to the cruise control and thermostat examples, respectively. Figure 13.16 shows the state pattern for the Cruise Control in Figure 13.11. It includes UML notes to explain the various parts. Note in Figure 13.14, the state of the subject is updated by the return values of the functions of the State class. In Figure 13.16, the same effect is achieved in the body of the functions of the State class. For example, the UML notes attached to the Cruise Deactivated and the Increasing Speed classes show that the state of the Cruise Control is updated to Cruise Activated and Cruising, respectively. This example illustrates how to map a CSS and its substates to a state class and its subclasses in the state pattern. Note that a state machine itself is a CSS. The main points of the mapping are outlined as follows:

1. Define a Subject class with client interfaces to correspond to the state machine. The interfaces are identified from the events coming into the subject or one of its components in the domain model constructed in Section 13.4.2. Each of these client interface functions delegates the request to the State object. For example, the domain model in Figure 13.6 shows eight events going into the Cruise Control software; therefore, the Cruise Control subject class in Figure 13.16 has eight functions. The functions can also be identified from the state diagram, that is, from the events that label the transitions in the state diagram.

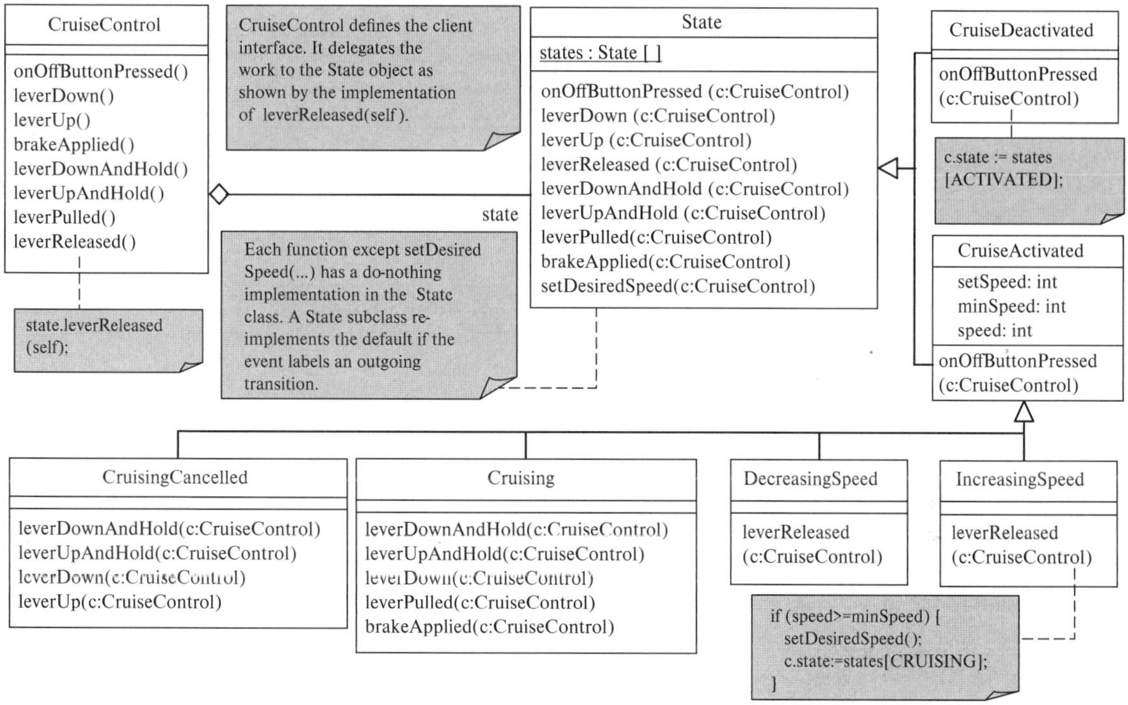

FIGURE 13.16 Cruise control state pattern

2. Create a root class for the hierarchy of state classes to represent the states of the Subject. The member functions of this root class are identified from the client interfaces of the Subject class, the domain model, or the state machine as described above. Each of these member functions has a do-nothing implementation.
3. For each CSS of the state machine, create a state class with subclasses representing its substates and name the state class and the subclasses accordingly. If the CSS is a substate of another CSS, then make this newly created state class a subclass of the state class representing the containing CSS. For example, the substates of **Cruise Activated** are mapped to subclasses of the Cruise Activated class in the state pattern. The **Cruise Activated** and **Cruise Deactivated** states are mapped to two subclasses of the State class because the state machine itself is a CSS. For each substate S and each triggering event that labels a transition going out of S, override the corresponding member function in the state class corresponding to S.

Figure 13.17 shows the state pattern for the Thermostat Control state diagram in Figure 13.13. This example shows that applying the state pattern to a state diagram containing a CCS is similar. The differences are as follows:

- The Subject class maintains N component state objects; each corresponds to a component substate of the CCS. Each client interface function delegates the request to the corresponding component state object.
- Each component has its own hierarchy of state classes as shown in Figure 13.17.

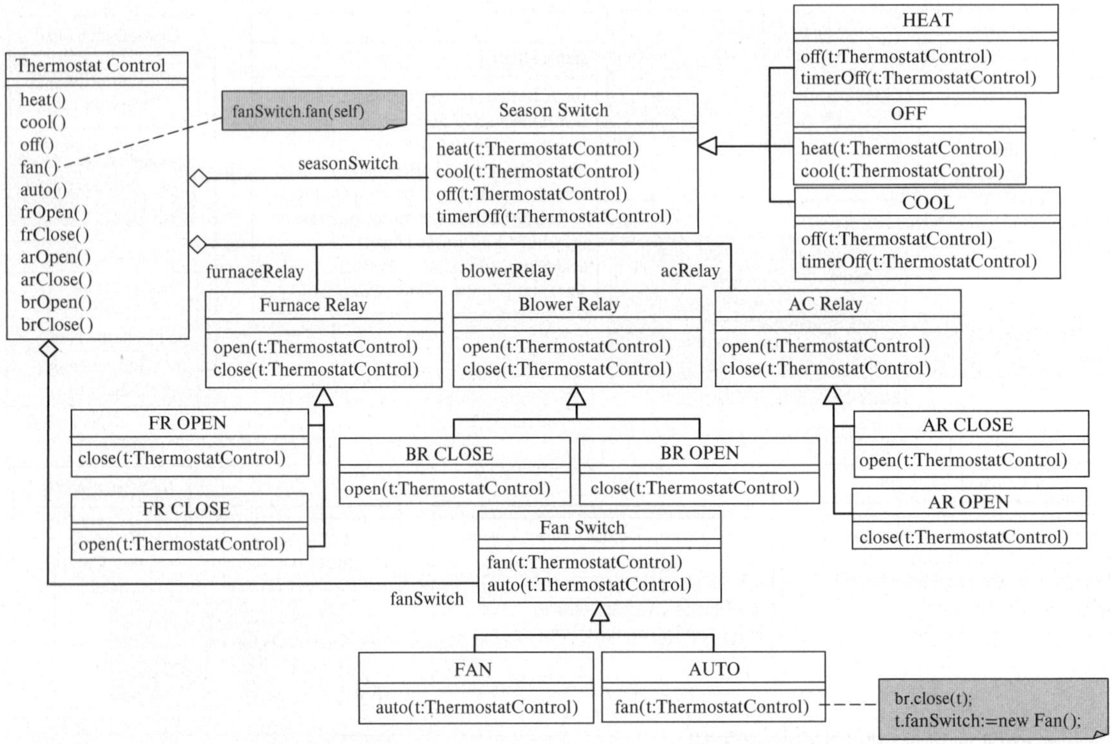

FIGURE 13.17 State pattern for the Thermostat Control

EXAMPLE 13.8 An automatic mower can mow a rectangular lawn one row after another starting from the upper-left corner. Figure 13.18 shows a state diagram describing the state behavior of the lawn mower. It uses a timer to generate a timer off event every second. When this happens, the mower checks if a border is ahead. If not, it cuts forwards, else it makes a right turn or left turn and moves down to cut the next row. Figure 13.19 shows the application of the state pattern to the state diagram in Figure 13.18 and Figure 13.20 shows the implementation of the state pattern in

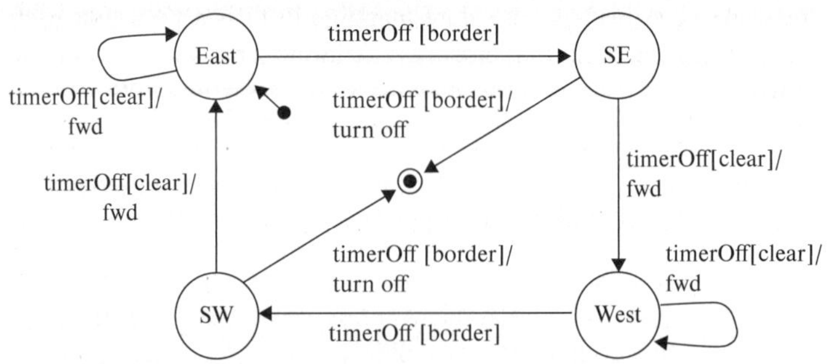

FIGURE 13.18 State behavior of the automatic mower

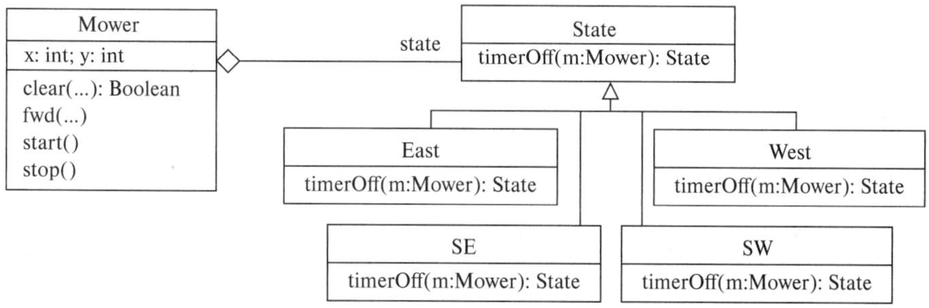

FIGURE 13.19 Applying state pattern for the automatic mower shown in Figure 13.18

Figure 13.19. The Frame1 class provides a window that contains a start and stop buttons. The Canvas class is responsible for displaying the movements of the mower and the lawn being cut. The Mower class holds its position, cuts the grass, and moves forwards, as well as checking the borders of the lawn.

13.6 REAL-TIME SYSTEMS MODELING AND DESIGN

State machines are widely used in the modeling, design, verification, validation, and testing of real-time embedded systems. This section briefly describes some of the approaches.

13.6.1 The Transformational Schema

The transformational schema was proposed by Ward and Mellor as an extension of the conventional data flow diagram to model real-time embedded systems. The transformational schema has two types of processes: control process and transform process. A transform process performs data processing tasks while a control process handles events and controls the transform processes. The behavior of a control process is modeled by a Mealy type state machine. Figure 13.21 shows the modeling concepts and constructs of the transformational schema.

A key component of the transformational schema is a control process, which is a state machine that processes the incoming events and controls the other processes. There are three types of flow between the processes:

1. *Ordinary data flow.* These are the ordinary data flows between transform processes. For example, in a cruise control system, the ordinary data flow is the driver-preset rotation rate data used to maintain the coasting speed.
2. *Control flow.* These are the flows between a transform process and a control process. A control flow represents either an event sent to a control process or a command from a control process to a transform process. An event may trigger one of the transitions of the state machine. The state transition may issue a command to control a transform process.
3. *Real-time data flow.* These are continuous data flows that must be processed in real time to prevent the data in the buffer from being overwritten by incoming data, for example, the continuous tire rotation data collected by the sensor.

```
public class Mower extends Observable
  implements ActionListener {
  public static final int WIDTH=500, HEIGHT=300;
  private Timer timer=new Timer(1000, this);
  private int x=0, y=0;
  State state=new East();
  public void actionPerformed(ActionEvent ae) {
    state=state.timerOff(this);
  }
  public int getX() { return x; }
  public int getY() { return y; }
  public boolean clear(East e) { return x<WIDTH-50; }
  public boolean clear(SE e) { return y<HEIGHT-50; }
  public boolean clear(West e) { return x>0; }
  public boolean clear(SW e) { return y<HEIGHT-50; }
  public void fwd(East e) {
    x+=50; setChanged(); notifyObservers(); }
  public void fwd(West e) {
    x-=50; setChanged(); notifyObservers(); }
  public void fwd (SE e) {
    y+=50; setChanged(); notifyObservers(); }
  public void fwd(SW e) {
    y+=50; setChanged(); notifyObservers(); }
  public void stop() { timer.stop(); }
  public void start() { x=0; y=0; timer.start(); }

class State {
  public State timerOff(Mower m) { return this; }
}

class East extends State {
   public State timerOff(Mower m) {
    if (m.clear(this)) {
      m.fwd(this); return this;
    } else { return new SE(); }
   }
}

class West extends State {
   public State timerOff(Mower m) {
    if (m.clear(this)) {
      m.fwd(this); return this;
    } else { return new SW(); }
   }
}

class SE extends State {
   public State timerOff(Mower m) {
    if (m.clear(this)) {
      m.fwd(this); return new West();
    } else { m.stop(); return this; }
   }
}

class SW extends State {
   public State timerOff(Mower m) {
    if (m.clear(this)) {
      m.fwd(this); return new East();
    } else { m.stop(); return this; }
   }
}}
```

```
public class MowerGUI extends JFrame {
  Mower am; Canvas canvas; JButton start, stop;
  public MowerGUI() {
    am=new Mower();
    start=new JButton("Start");
    start.addActionListener(new ActionListener() {
      public void actionPerformed(ActionEvent e) {
        canvas.cuts.clear(); canvas.x=0; canvas.y=0;
        am.start(); canvas.repaint(); }});
    stop=new JButton("Stop");
    stop.addActionListener(new ActionListener() {
      public void actionPerformed(ActionEvent e) {
        am.stop(); }});
    getContentPane().setLayout(new BorderLayout());
    JPanel leftPane=new JPanel(new FlowLayout());
    getContentPane().add(leftPane,
      BorderLayout.NORTH);
    leftPane.add(start); leftPane.add(stop);
    canvas= new Canvas(); am.addObserver(canvas);
    canvas.setPreferredSize(new
      Dimension(Mower.WIDTH, Mower.HEIGHT));
    getContentPane().add(canvas,
      BorderLayout.CENTER);
    canvas.setVisible(true);
  }
  protected void processWindowEvent(WindowEvent e)
  {  super.processWindowEvent(e);
     if (e.getID()==WindowEvent.
       WINDOW_CLOSING) System.exit(0); }
  public static void main(String[] args) {
    MowerGUI frame=new MowerGUI();
    frame.setSize(new Dimension(Mower.WIDTH,
      Mower.HEIGHT+100));
    frame.setLocation(200, 200);
    frame.pack(); frame.setVisible(true); }

public class Canvas extends JPanel implements
Observer {
  int x, y; ArrayList cuts=new ArrayList();
  public Canvas() {
    setBackground(new Color(0,100,0)); }
  public void paintComponent(Graphics g) {
    super.paintComponent(g);
    Cut s=new Cut(x, y); cuts.add(s);
    for(int i=0; i<cuts.size(); i++) {
      Cut x=(Cut)cuts.get(i); x.draw(g);
    }
  }
  public void update(Observable o, Object arg) {
    x=((Mower)o).getX(); y=((Mower)o).getY();
    repaint(); }
}

public class Cut {
  int x, y;
  public Cut(int x, int y) {
    this.x=x; this.y=y; }
  public void draw(Graphics g) {
    g.setColor(Color.GREEN);
    g.fill3DRect(x, y, 50, 50, false); }
}}
```

FIGURE 13.20 Implementaion of the state pattern in Figure 13.19

Notion	Notation	Semantics
Transform Process		A transformational process, representing a computation or information processing activity
Control Process		A control process, which is modeled by a Mealy type state machine and represents the state-dependent behavior of a system
State Machine		A state machine that is encapsulated in a control process and models the state dependent behavior of the system
Data Flow		An ordinary or discrete data flow
Control Flow		An event flow or control flow that triggers a transition of the state machine of a control process, or a command from a control process to a transformational process
Real-Time Data Flow		A continuous data flow, which must be processed in real time to avoid buffer data being overwritten by subsequent input data
Conjunctive Input	*a* *P* *b*	Both data flow *a* and data flow *b* are required to begin executing process *P*
Disjunctive Input	*a* + *P* *b*	Either data flow *a* or data flow *b* is required to begin executing process *P*
Split Flow	*z* *x* *y*	Two subsets of *z* are used by two different successor processes
Share Flow	*z*	All of *z* is used by two different successor processes
Conjunctive Flow	*x* *z* *y*	*z* is composed of two subsets provided by two different predecessor processes
Disjunctive Flow	*z*	All of *z* is provided by either one of two predecessor processes

FIGURE 13.21 Modeling constructs of the transformational schema

Besides these, the transformational schema also provides constructs for modeling conjunctive and disjunctive inputs as well as conjunctive and disjunctive flows (see Figure 13.21).

EXAMPLE 13.9

Figure 13.22 shows the modeling of a cruise control software and the processes that interface with the hardware components. In the figure, the control process represents the cruise control software while the transform processes represent the interfaces to the hardware components. The figure also illustrates the use of control flows and real-time data flows. The behavior of the control process in Figure 13.22 is modeled by a state machine, as shown in Figure 13.23. Note the correspondence

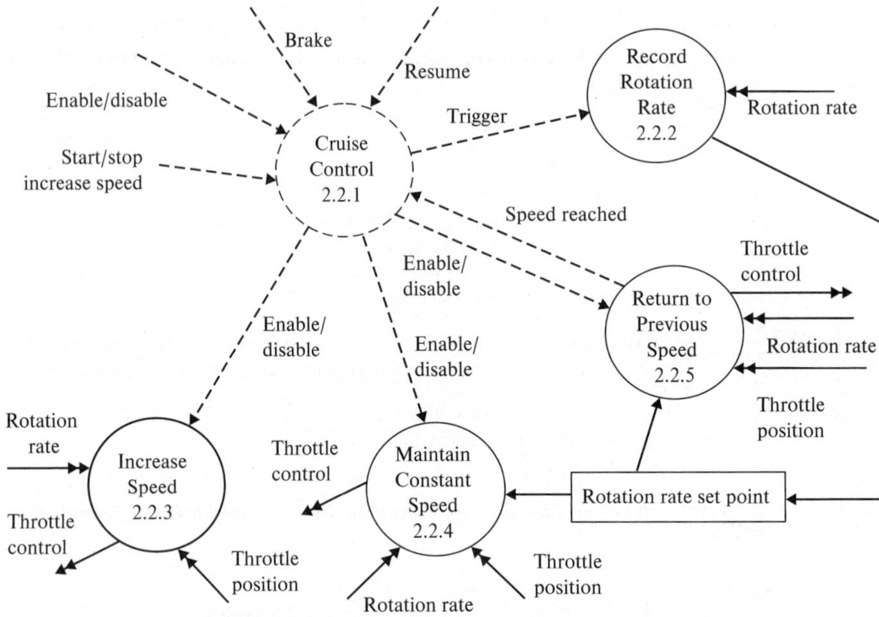

FIGURE 13.22 Modeling of a real-time embedded system

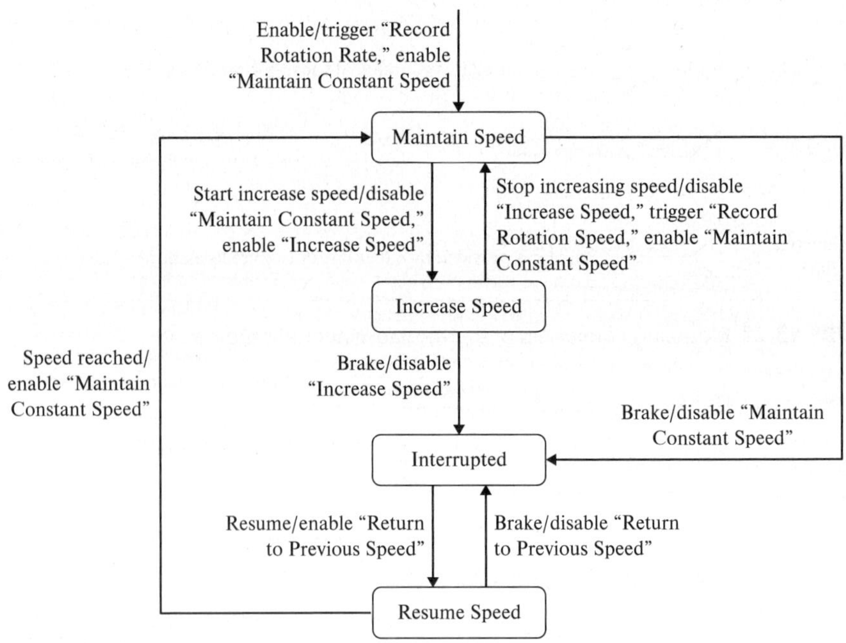

FIGURE 13.23 Modeling of real-time system state behavior

between the control flows that go into the control process and the events that trigger the state transitions of the state diagram. For example, the *resume* control flow into the control process corresponds to the state transition from the Interrupted state to the Resume Speed state. In addition, there is a correspondence between the responses or actions of the state transitions and the control flows from the control process to the transform processes. These represent the commands sent from the control process to control the hardware components.

13.6.2 Timed State Machine

The design of real-time systems sometimes requires the ability to model and analyze time and timing constraints. For example, a mobile device is required to scan a number of channels within a given period of time. It is also required to process any incoming control signal within a very brief time interval. These require the specification of processing time and timing constraints. A timed state machine (TSM) is an extension of the ordinary state machine with timed states and timed transitions. That is, a timing lower bound(lb) and a timing upper bound (ub) are specified for some of the transitions and states. For a transition, these mean that the transition must take at least lb time units and at most ub time units to process the event and execute the response actions. For a state, they specify the timing lower bound and upper bound for the state activity, or the time period to be in the state.

EXAMPLE 13.10

In illustration, Figure 13.24 shows the processing of items on a pipeline. After initialization, the system enters the Waiting state. When an item arrives, the system engages the robot to process the item. This must not take more than 5 time units. The robot then processes the item, which takes from 20 to 80 time units. When the processing is done, the system dispatches the item, which must not take more than 5 time units.

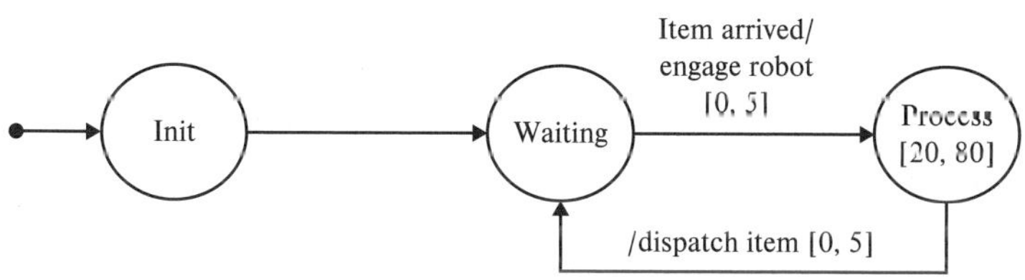

FIGURE 13.24 Modeling of time with a timed state machine

The specification of timing lower bound and upper bound allows analysis of timing constraints, which specify the required timing lower bound and upper bound between the occurrences of one event and another follow-up event. For example, some types of target tracking system need to process radar returns, update the target tracks, and display the tracks of multiple targets on the screen in real time. The constraint on the total time to complete such a sequence of operations must be specified and enforced. If the system is modeled by using a timed state machine and the transformational schema, then the total time to complete the required sequence of operations can be analyzed to ensure that the timing constraint is satisfied. The complexity of timing constraint analysis comes from the fact that many real-time systems are embedded systems, which involve hardware, software, and human subsystems. Hierarchical, concurrent, communicating state machines are used to model the state behavior of components of the system. These state machines run concurrently and communicate with each other. It is a challenge to identify and specify the sequences of transitions and the timing constraints on such sequences as well as the analysis to ensure that the timing constraints are fulfilled. Due to these, timing constraint modeling, specification, and analysis are special topics, which are beyond the scope of this book.

13.6.3 Interrupt Handling

Interrupt handling and exception handling are common in real-time embedded systems. What is needed is the ability to return to the previously active state to resuming the processing of whatever was interrupted. UML provides the history state modeling concept for this purpose. It is explained with an example as follows. Figure 13.25(*a*) shows a portion of an online test system (OTS). OTS allows students to take tests online. When a student submits the completed test, the system adds the test to a queue and returns to the **Process Tests** state. However, without using a history state, each time the system enters the **Process Tests** state, it has to start with the initial state, that is, the **Get Next Test** state. It cannot continue with the previous state when the interruption occurred.

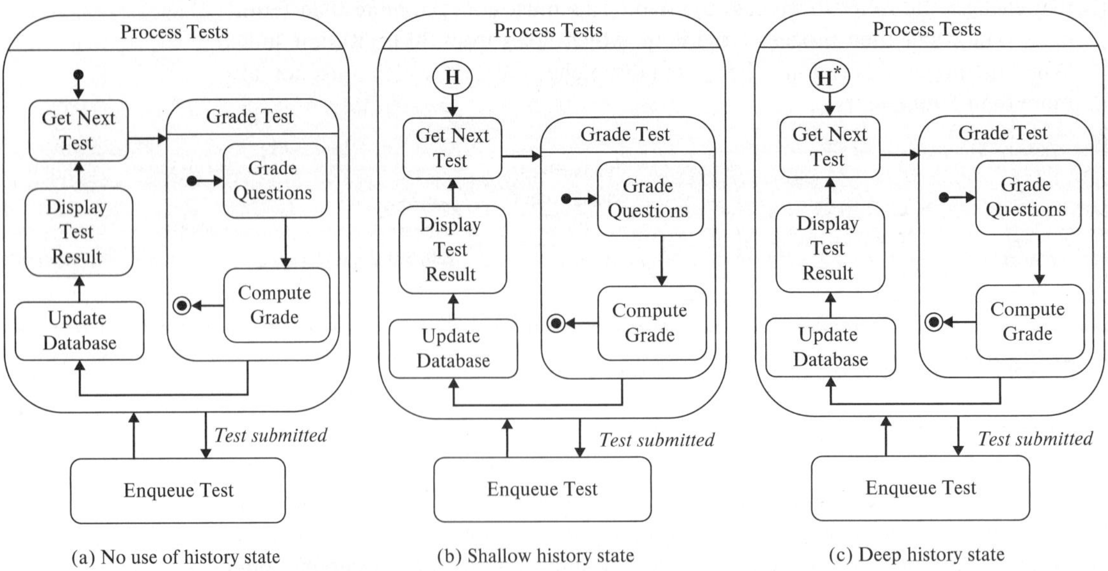

FIGURE 13.25 State diagram for a part of an online test system

Figure 13.25(*b*) uses a *shallow history state,* indicated by an H enclosed in a small circle, instead of the pseudo-initial state. This means that each time the **Process Tests** state is entered, the system resumes with the most recently active substate of the composite state. However, a shallow history state does not remember the substates of the most recently active substate. That is, if the most recently active substate is **Compute Grade**, then the system will not be able to resume with this state. Instead, the system resumes with the initial state of the composite state that contains the **Compute Grade** state, that is, the **Grade Questions** state.

A *deep history state* solves the problem. It is indicated by an H* enclosed in a small circle. It allows a composite state to return to its most recently active state configuration. In Figure 13.25(*c*), if **Compute Grade** is the most recently active substate, then when **Process Tests** is entered, it will resume with the **Compute Grade** substate rather than the initial state of **Grade Tests**.

13.7 APPLYING AGILE PRINCIPLES

GUIDELINE 13.1 Work closely with the customer and users to identify and model the state behavior.

In most cases, the state behavior of an object is application dependent. Therefore, the team needs to work closely with the customer and users in identifying and modeling the state behavior. Prototypes are useful for seeking user feedback. They should be used instead of the state diagrams, which many users do not understand.

GUIDELINE 13.2 Capture the state behavior at a high level, lightweight, and visual.

The state behavior of an object could be modeled in great detail, or at a high level and visual. This principle suggests that state modeling should avoid the details if a high-level, lightweight model is sufficient. For example, error handling and exception handling are not part of the normal state behavior. These should not be included in the state diagram–leave them to implementation.

GUIDELINE 13.3 Value working software over comprehensive documentation–do barely enough modeling.

Not all objects with state behavior need a state diagram. A state diagram is needed only if the state behavior is complex or if the team needs to gain a better understanding of the state behavior. Complex behavior is due to a large number of states, complex state transition relationships, or composite state behavior. In these cases, OSM helps the team understand, communicate, and analyze the state behavior. For many objects, the state behavior consists of only one or two states and a few simple transitions. For example, a book is checked out or not checked out. In such cases, constructing a state diagram is a waste of time. State modeling should also be guided by the "good enough is enough" principle. That is, move on to implementation when you have gained sufficient knowledge of the state behavior.

13.8 TOOL SUPPORT FOR OBJECT STATE MODELING

IBM Rational Modeler, Microsoft Visio, ArgoUML, and NetBeans UML Plugin provide state diagram editing capabilities along with other features. The diagram editors let the software engineer draw, edit, and manage state diagrams. Some tools can also generate code from the state diagrams. The IBM Rational Statemate solution is a design, simulation and prototyping tool for real-time embedded systems.

13.9 SUMMARY

OSM is concerned with the identification, modeling, analysis, design, and specification of state-dependent behavior of objects. OSM is needed because it helps the development team understand the state behavior. It facilitates team communication and collaboration, which are crucial for project success. The state models produced by OSM forms the basis for verification and test case generation. OSM is carried out in five steps. In the first step, the team collects and classifies state behavior information using a set of rules. Each rule specifies the phrases to look for in the relevant documents and the corresponding modeling concepts, that is, event, state, guard condition, and response actions. Also identified are classes, and their attributes as well as relationships between the classes, as described in Chapter 5. Both sets of information are used to construct a domain model for the event-driven subsystem. The domain model shows the event-driven software subsystem, its context or environment, and its states and the relationships between the states. These relationships determine how to structure the states in the state diagrams, that is, when to use CSS and when to use CCS.

The state transition table is presented as an aid to state diagram construction. While the domain model specifies the structural aspect and the relationships between the states, the state transition table provides a systematic approach for specifying the state transitions or state behavior. The state transition table facilitates detection of abnormalities, including dead state, unreachable state, neglected event, impossible transitions, nondeterministic transitions, redundant transitions, and inconsistent transitions.

Event-driven systems are normally associated with interrupt handling. Interrupt handling forces an object to exit a state and return to it after the interrupt is processed. A deep history state can be used to specify that recursively all active substates of a composite state must be saved so that the system can resume with this state configuration later. If there is no need to remember the chain of active substates, then a shallow history can be used. This chapter presents rules for converting an informal state diagram into one in which the state transitions are formally specified, that is, the guard conditions, the triggering events, and the response actions are specified using a programming language like syntax. The state pattern is a better design for complex state behavior, especially for state diagrams with composite states. The conventional implementation approaches and their draw-backs are discussed. The state pattern is applied to the cruise control and thermostat examples to illustrate its usefulness. Finally, the transformational schema and the timed state machine for the modeling of real-time systems are presented.

13.10 CHAPTER REVIEW QUESTIONS

1. What is OSM?
2. What are the OSM steps?
3. What are the basic and advanced features of a UML state diagram?
4. What is the state pattern, and what are the benefits of the state pattern?
5. What is the transformational schema, and how does it model a real-time embedded system?
6. What is a timed state machine, and what are the advantages of a timed state machine?

13.11 EXERCISES

13.1 Refine the cruise control state diagram in Figure 13.11 with lower-level state diagrams. Check for consistency between the external events and the triggering events of the transitions as well as the response actions and messages to the external entities.

13.2 Construct a domain model to explain a UML state diagram that includes CSS and CCS.

13.3 Apply the steps presented in this chapter to the railroad crossing system (RCS) described as the following:

An RCS includes a central control that controls the traffic light, the bell, and the gate at the crossing. When a train approaches the crossing from either direction at a certain distance, a sensor device senses the train's arrival and communicates this to the central control. The central control informs the traffic light control, bell control, and gate control.

After receiving the signal from the central control, the traffic light control turns on the flashing yellow warning light for a given amount of time, which must be long enough to allow the traffic to stop before the crossing. It then changes the light from flashing yellow to flashing red. The bell control turns on the bell. After the red light begins to flash, the gate begins to close. During this process, the train continues its course with its own speed within the specified speed limit.

After the train has completely passed the crossing, another sensor device at the other end of the railroad senses the train's departure and communicates this event to the central control. The central control instructs the gate control to lift up the gates, the traffic light control to turn off the light, and the bell control to turn off the bell.

13.4 Construct a state diagram for a typical digital watch, described as follows:

A digital watch has four modes: the display mode, the set-alarm mode, the stopwatch mode, and the set-time-and-date mode. It has three buttons: a mode button to go to different modes, a start-stop button for advancing values in different modes, and a light button for selection, lighting, and stopping the buzzer. In the display mode, press the mode button once to go to the set-alarm mode, twice to go to the stopwatch mode, three times to go to the set-time-and-date mode, and four times to go back to the display mode. In each of the above modes, use the light button to step through different values that can be set. For example, set hour, then set minute, and so on. Use the start-stop button to increment the values. Use the mode button to exit and return to the display mode.

13.5 Produce a mapping between the cruise control state diagram in Figure 13.11 and the state pattern in Figure 13.16. An example mapping is shown in Figure 13.15.

13.6 A simple lawn mower agent is capable of mowing a rectangular shape area. The lawn is conceptually viewed as consisting of 2 foot by 2 foot squares, fitting the size of the solar-powered mower. Actions of the agent include:

- Move forward: the mower moves forward one square.
- Turn left: the mower makes a left turn.
- Turn right: the mower makes a right turn.
- Cut (grass): the mower cuts the grass in the current square.
- Percept: the agent perceives the environment.
- Turn on-off: the agent turns on-off the power of the mower.

The garden landscape consists of lawns, trees, shrubs, buildings, pools, and more. The landscape be represented by an $m \times n$ array of integers:

- A[i,j] = 10 means that an obstacle is in the square.
- A[i,j] = 9 means that there is a trap, such as a pool.
- A[i,j] = 2 means that there is grass in the square that needs to be cut.
- A[i,j] = 1 means that the grass is already cut.
- A[i,j] = 0 means that the square is pavement and it is safe to cross over it.

At any given time, the agent knows its direction (N, S, E, W) and location (i, j). Initially, the agent is at A[0,0], facing east, and the mower is off. After mowing the lawn, the agent returns to the initial state that is, it is at location A[0,0], facing east, and the mower is off.

The agent maintains a set mowing schedule, for example, mowing once a week during the high-growth season, biweekly during the rest of the growing season, and not mowing during the rest of the year. The agent wakes up and mows the lawn according to the schedule.

Do the following for this exercise:

a. Construct a domain model for the mowing agent application.

b. Construct a state diagram for the mowing agent.

c. Apply the state pattern to this application.

d. Implement the mowing agent state pattern and demonstrate that the software works by printing the traversal of the agent on a 20 square by 20 square area.

13.7 A pizza vending machine is capable of producing personal-size pizza according to the choices of the customer, although the number of selections are limited. The machine consists of the following components:

a. A freezer, which is capable of dispatching frozen pizza, one at a time, into the defroster under software control.

b. A microwave defroster, which defrosts the frozen pizza and dispatches it to the oven.

c. An oven, which bakes the pizza for a given period of time under software control. It dispatches the baked pizza into the delivery window.

d. A delivery window, which allows the customer to pick up the baked pizza.

e. A bill and coin acceptor, which accepts one dollar and five dollar bills, and quarters. It returns the current dollar amount to the software upon request.

f. A keypad, which consists of five letter keys A, B, C, D, E; ten digit keys 0–9; an Enter key and other error correction keys. The customer uses the keypad to enter selections, and the operator uses it for programming the vending machine.

g. An LED for displaying instructions and system responses.

The vending machine works as follows. There are two modes of operation: the programming mode and the operating mode. The programming mode is entered by pressing a small button on the control board, which can only be reached when the door of the vending machine is open. The door is usually locked and only the operator has the key to unlock it. In the programming mode, the operator presses one letter key and one digit key to program a selection. The LED displays the blinking bake temperature. The operator enters the new temperature or leaves it unchanged, and presses the Enter key. The LED dis-plays the blinking bake time in minutes. The operator enters the new bake time or leaves it unchanged, and presses the Enter key. The LED displays the blinking price. The operator enters the new price or leaves it as it is and presses the Enter key. The operator repeats these steps to program all of the selections. The programming mode is exited when the operator presses and holds down the E key for five seconds, or when there is no keypad activity for more than ten seconds.

In the operating mode, a customer inserts the valid bills or coins into the slots of the bill and coin acceptor. Each time a bill or coin is inserted, the LED displays the total current amount received. When the required amount is inserted, the customer presses one letter key and one digit key to enter his selection. Once the selection is entered, the freezer dispatches the selected pizza into the microwave. The microwave defrosts the frozen pizza while the LED displays "Defrosting." When the pizza is defrosted, it is dispatched into the oven. The oven heats up while the LED displays "Heating." The oven begins baking and the LED displays the remaining bake time when the desired temperature is reached. The pizza is baked for the predefined period of time and dispatched into the delivery window.

Apply the steps described in this chapter to develop the pizza vending machine. Modify the description to take care of exceptions and error conditions.

13.8 Extend the pizza vending machine to allow online ordering and perform the development for the extended vending machine. The system needs a compartment to keep the baked pizza warm and moist. To use this feature, the customer must open an online account with a credit card payment or online payment service. The customer must login to place an order. The system displays an approximate pick-up time. The customer may choose if a notification message will be sent when the pizza is ready. The customer must login and use the pass code to retrieve the pizza that is ordered.

13.9 Design and implement the monkey and bananas game. Initially, a monkey and a banana are placed at different locations in a rectangular yard. When the game is started, the monkey, operated by the up, down, left, and right keys on the keyboard, goes to the banana and eats it immediately. A new banana is placed at a randomly determined position immediately. The monkey goes to consume the banana as soon as it can. This is repeated until the game is over. A game built-in timer may be used to measure the performance of the player in terms of how many bananas the monkey can consume per unit time.

14 Chapter

Activity Modeling for Transformational Systems

Key Takeaway Points

- Activity modeling deals with the modeling of the information processing activities of an application or a system that exhibits sequencing, branching, concurrency, as well as synchronous and asynchronous behavior.
- Activity modeling is useful for the modeling and design of transformational systems.

Chapters 9 and 13 presented object interaction modeling (OIM) and object state modeling (OSM). These are two of the three behavioral modeling tools of UML. OIM is concerned with the modeling and design of interactive systems while OSM addresses the modeling and design of event-driven systems. In this chapter, the other behavioral modeling tool–activity modeling–is presented. Activity modeling is concerned with the modeling and design of transformational systems that exhibit sequencing, conditional branching, concurrency, and synchronous as well as asynchronous behavior. A compiler is an example that exhibits a sequence of activities. These activities include lexical analysis, syntax analysis, code generation, and code optimization.

Another area to apply activity modeling is workflow management such as system engineering (Chapter 3). System engineering begins with system requirements analysis activity, which produces the system requirements specification, a system architectural design, and an allocation of system requirements to the hardware, software, and human subsystems. After system requirements analysis, three concurrent activities take place. These are hardware subsystem development, software subsystem development, and human subsystem development. System integration and testing take place when all these three development activities are completed, that is, a joining of three threads of activities. During system integration and testing, the team may discover major requirements or design problems. If this is the case, then the team should backtrack to a previous activity. This is called a *conditional branching.* If no problem is discovered during integration and testing, then the next activity, such as system acceptance testing, is performed–another conditional branching. After completing this chapter, you will understand the following:

- Activity modeling.
- Usefulness of activity modeling.
- The evolution of activity modeling techniques.
- UML activity diagram.
- Steps for activity modeling.

14.1 WHAT IS ACTIVITY MODELING?

Activity modeling focuses on the modeling and design of systems that perform complex information processing activities. Such systems possess characteristics of a transformational system as described in Chapter 6. These characteristics are listed here for convenience:

- A transformational system can be conceptually viewed as consisting of a network of information processing activities, each of which transforms its input into its output.
- The network of activities may involve control flows that exhibit sequencing, conditional branching, and parallel threads, as well as synchronous and asynchronous behavior.
- During the transformation of the input into the output, there is little or no interaction between the system and the actor, that is, it is more or less a batch process.
- Transformational systems are usually stateless.
- Transformational systems may require number crunching or computation-intensive algorithms.
- The external entity of a transformational system can be a human being or a device.

Workflow management systems are such systems where a request may go through several stages of processing by different departments, and may require decision making, synchronization, and concurrent processing. Consider, for example, the processing of an online application in the Study Abroad Management System (SAMS). After an online application is submitted, a number of information processing activities take place. These include obtaining faculty references and academic advisor approvals, reviewing the online-application package by an advisor of the Office of International Education (OIE), scheduling an interview with the student, contacting the overseas program, and conducting a post acceptance orientation seminar for the students who will study at an overseas institution. Each of these activities takes place at a certain point in time and requires a certain amount of time to process. Some of these activities may take place simultaneously and some of them may need to be synchronized. For example, obtaining faculty references and obtaining academic advisor approvals may take place simultaneously while the post acceptance orientation seminar needs to synchronize with the processing of all of the applications.

14.2 WHY ACTIVITY MODELING?

First, activity modeling addresses a unique problem that is not dealt with by OIM or OSM. OIM deals with the modeling and design of inter object behavior or how objects interact with each other through message passing to accomplish the business process of a use case. OSM focuses on the modeling and design of intra object behavior or how objects react to external stimuli. Activity modeling is concerned with the modeling and design of complex information processing activities, information/object flows among the activities, conditional branching, synchronization, concurrency, and workflows that move among various departments or subsystems. Second, the development team members need to construct models to help them understand and communicate analysis and design ideas about the information processing activities and the relationships between the activities. A UML activity diagram is an effective tool for the modeling and design of information processing activities of a system. Finally, activity modeling is a useful tool for the refinement of high-level requirements and the identification of use cases from the refinement. An activity model is useful in showing the workflow and control flow relationships between use cases.

Activity diagrams are useful for the modeling and design of enterprise resource planning (ERP) systems. These systems are integrated management information systems. They automate the information processing activities and workflows throughout the whole organization. The activities are carried out by a wide variety of performers including internal and external organizational units, human actors, systems, subsystems, and components. During the analysis phase, activity diagrams are used to visualize the activities and workflows as well as the activity performers of an organization. These models help the development team understand the organization's information processing activities and workflows. Requirements for the ERP system can be derived by identifying the activities and workflows that must be automated. During the design phase, activity diagrams are useful for communicating design ideas and visualizing the design of the ERP system.

14.3 ACTIVITY MODELING: TECHNICAL BACKGROUND

A UML activity diagram integrates the modeling techniques and features of three prominent modeling tools in the history of computing. These tools are flowchart, Petri net, and data flow diagrams. This section reviews these tools because a basic knowledge of these tools helps the student understand the semantics of a UML activity diagram. Moreover, it shows how modeling tools evolve and nicely integrate into a UML activity diagram.

14.3.1 Flowchart

Flowcharts are used to model information processing activities for a long time. A flowchart is a graph consisting of processing nodes, decision nodes, and directed edges between these two types of node. A processing node represents a computation or information processing activity. A decision node evaluates a condition and branches to a particular node according to the outcome of the evaluation. A directed edge

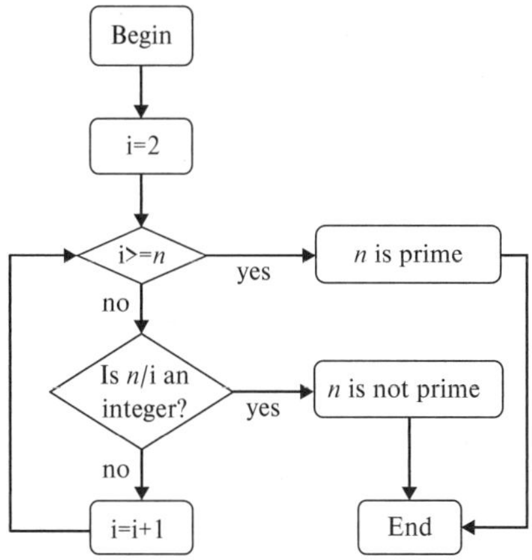

FIGURE 14.1 A sample flowchart for determining a prime

represents a control flow from one node to another. Figure 14.1 shows a flowchart for determining if an integer *n* is prime, where a processing node is represented by a round-corner rectangle, and a decision node by a diamond. The flowchart has two special nodes to indicate the begin and end of the procedure.

14.3.2 Petri Net

Petri net was proposed by C. A. Petri for modeling complex systems. A Petri net has two types of node, called places and transitions. A node can be connected to another node by a directed edge if the two nodes are of different types. Figure 14.2(*a*) shows a Petri net, where places are represented by circles and transitions by bars. Figure 14.2(*b*) assigns meaning to the places and transitions. In particular, the places represent conditions while the transitions represent events. Tokens can be assigned to

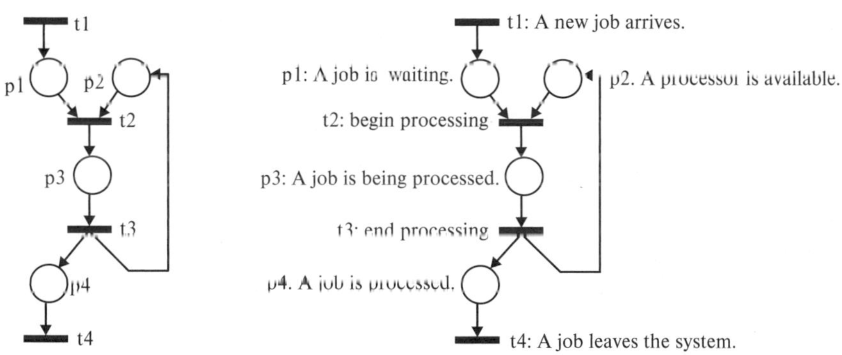

(a) A Petri net (b) The Petri net with annotations

FIGURE 14.2 A Petri net for processing jobs

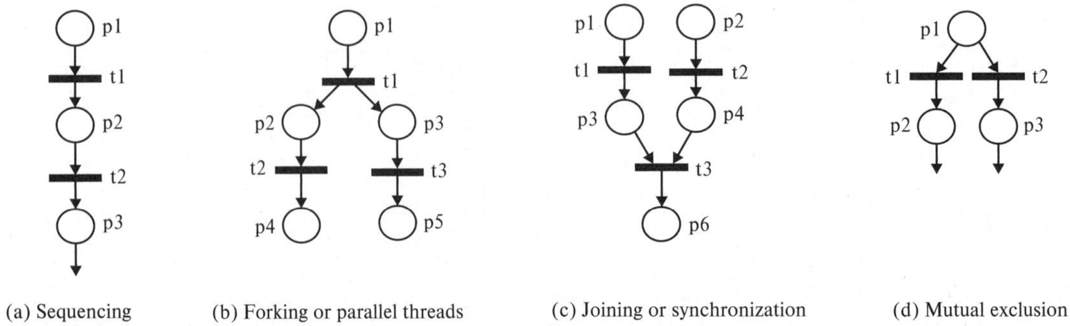

FIGURE 14.3 Modeling different situations in Petri net

places. If a place contains a token, then it is active and the condition is true; otherwise it is inactive and the condition is false. A transition can fire if each of its input places contains a token. A transition fires by removing one token from each of its input places and places a token into each of its output places.

Petri net can model different system behavior including sequencing, parallel processing, synchronization, and mutual exclusion, as shown in Figure 14.3. In particular, Figure 14.3(*a*) means that the two transitions must fire in sequence. That is, the events must occur in sequence. Figure 14.3(*b*) indicates that after t1 fires, p2 and p3 become active; and hence, t2 and t3 can fire. That is, the two events can occur in parallel. This is also called *forking*. Figure 14.3(*c*) means that t3 cannot fire until t1 and t2 have fired. It merges the two concurrent threads; hence, it is called *joining*. Figure 14.3(*d*) represents mutual exclusion because only one of t1 and t2 can fire if p1 contains only one token.

14.3.3 Data Flow Diagram

Data flow diagrams are widely used to model information processing systems in the last several decades. A data flow diagram is a directed graph consisting of three types of node: process, data store, and external entity. A process represents an information processing activity, a data store represents a data repository, and an external entity represents an entity that is outside of the system and interacts with the system.

Unlike either the flowchart or Petri net, where the directed edges represent control flows, the directed edges of a data flow diagram represent data flows. They connect the nodes and represent the input/output of the processes. This implies that a directed edge can only connect two processes, a process and a data store, or a process and an external entity.

Figure 14.4(*a*) shows a data flow diagram in which processes are presented by round-corner rectangles, external entities by squares, and data stores by wide rectangles with the right sides open. The diagram indicates that a student will provide application information for the Fill Application Form process. A partially completed application is sent, through the *partial application* data flow, to the Obtain Support Materials process. That process obtains the support materials and stores

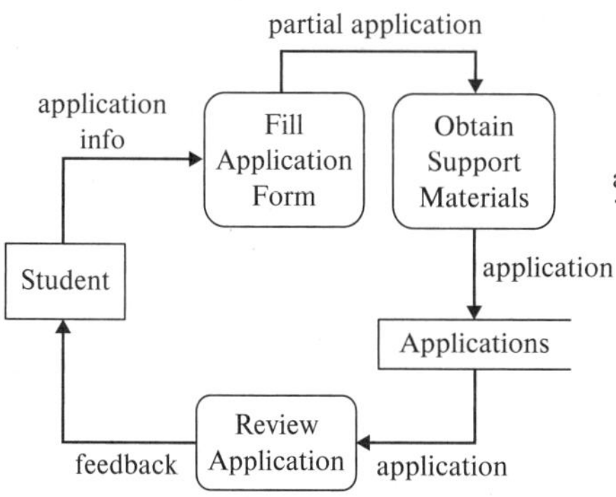

(a) A data flow diagram

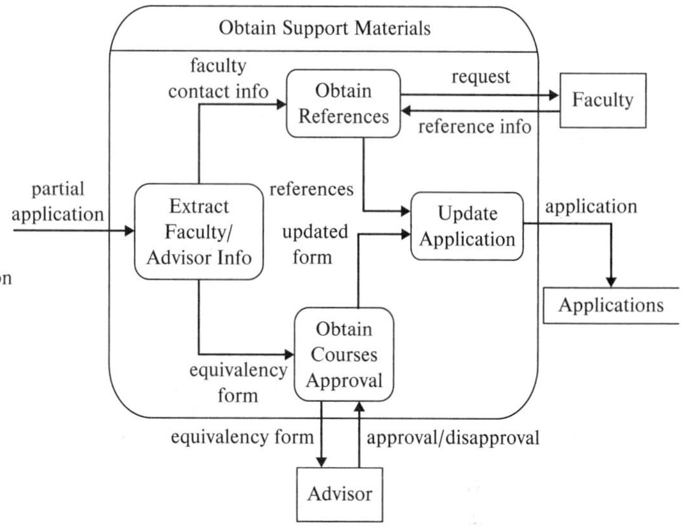

(b) A decomposition of Obtain Support Materials

FIGURE 14.4 A data flow diagram and a decomposition of a process

the (completed) application in the Applications data store. The Review Application process retrieves and reviews the applications and provides feedback to the Student, an external entity.

The data flow diagram modeling tool supports the divide-and-conquer software engineering principle. That is, a process can be decomposed into or refined by a network of lower-level processes. In illustration, Figure 14.4(*b*) shows a decomposition of the Obtain Support Materials process. The diagram shows that the high-level process is refined by four lower-level processes, each of which performs a specific task. The decomposition of a process must obey consistency rules:

1. For each data flow going into the higher-level process, there must be a corresponding data flow going into the lower-level data flow diagram resulting from decomposition.
2. For each data flow going out from the higher-level process, there must be a corresponding data flow going out from the lower-level data flow diagram resulting from decomposition.

Consider, for example, the decomposition in Figure 14.4(*b*). The higher-level process in Figure 14.4(a) has one input flow and one output flow. These two flows are present in Figure 14.4(*b*); therefore, the decomposition is consistent with the higher-level process. Note that the lower-level diagram introduces two new flows: "request" to Faculty and "reference info" from Faculty. This does not violate the consistency rules because a lower-level diagram is a refinement of a higher-level process. Refinement often reveals more detail including introduction of new flows.

14.4 UML ACTIVITY DIAGRAM

Figure 14.5 shows the commonly used activity diagram notions and notations. As an illustration, Figure 14.6 shows an activity diagram for a portion of a project management workflow. The activity diagram involves four organizational units: Project Team, Management, Accounting, and Human Resource. Project Team prepares a project proposal and submits it to Management. Management evaluates the project proposal. If the proposal is rejected, it is archived and the workflow ends. If the proposal is approved, the Management establishes the project. These two possible outcomes of the Management decision are modeled by using a conditional branching, which is represented by a diamond shape symbol. Notice that the two outgoing arrows of the diamond are labeled by "[approved]" and "[else]," respectively. The pair of brackets are used by UML to enclose a condition. That is, the branch that is labeled by "[approved]" indicates that if the project is approved, the Establish Project activity is performed. Similarly, the branch that is labeled by "[else]" indicates that if the project is rejected, the Archive Proposal activity is performed. The Archive Proposal activity has

Notion	Semantics	Notation	Connectivity
Activity or action	A computation or information processing activity	Activity name	Connects to any other nodes except an initial node or a flow final node
Conditional branching	Evaluating a condition to select one of a number of alternative threads	[C1] [C2]	Connect to/from an activity, object, forking, and joining; from an initial node, or to a flow final node
Merging alternative threads	Defining a single exit point for alternate threads created by a conditional branching.		
Control flow	Defining a precedence relation between two activities	→	Connect two activities
Object flow	Denoting objects that travel from one activity to another	object : Class	Connect to/from an activity, diamond, forking, and joining
Forking	Creating concurrent threads		Connect to/from an activity, object, or diamond; from an initial node, or to a final node
Joining	Synchronizing concurrent threads		
Initial node	A psuedo-activity to begin with	●	No incoming edge
Final node	A special node to denote the end of a network of activities	◉	No outgoing edge
Flow final node	Defining an end point for a control flow or object flow	⊗	No outgoing edge; an incoming edge only from a diamond node
Swim lanes	A mechanism for grouping or arranging activities according to organizations or subsystems		

FIGURE 14.5 UML activity diagram notions and notations

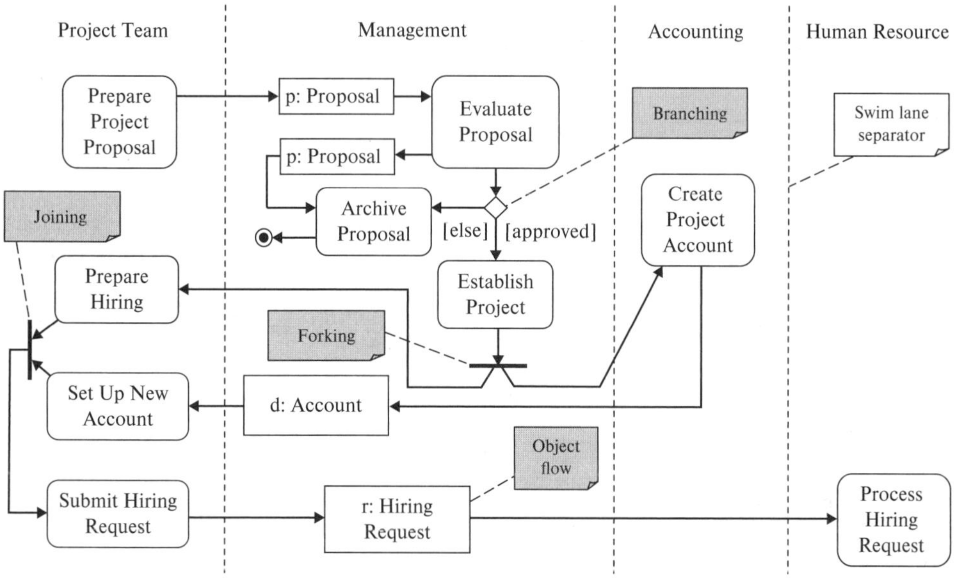

FIGURE 14.6 Activity diagram showing portions of project management activities

an outgoing arrow to a final node. This means that the workflow is terminated when the Archive Proposal activity is completed.

Now turn to the Establish Project activity. It has an outgoing edge to a forking node. This means that after the Establish Project activity is completed, the control flow splits into two concurrent threads. One of the threads is executing the Prepare Hiring activity by the project team. The other thread is performing the Create Project Account activity by the accounting department. Since these two activities are performed by two different organizational units, they tend to finish at different times. However, the joining node in the leftmost swim lane indicates that the project team must wait until both of the Prepare Hiring and Create Project Account activities are completed to perform the Submit Hiring Request activity. This is because the human resource department requires that the hiring request to contain both a job description and an account number to process the Hiring Request.

14.5 STEPS FOR ACTIVITY MODELING

For each business process that exhibits transformational characteristics, the development team performs the following steps. These are described in more detail in the following sections.

Step 1. Identify information processing activities as well as their input and output. The output of this step is the activities identified along with their input and output, and the organizations that perform the activities.

Step 2. Sketch a preliminary activity diagram. The output of this step is an activity diagram showing the activities and the control flows and object flows.

Step 3. Introduce conditional branching, forking, and joining. In this step, the preliminary activity diagram is augmented with conditional branching, forking, and joining to express alternative flows, concurrent processing, and synchronization. The output of this step is an activity diagram that adequately describes the business process.

Step 4. Refine complex activities, if desired. In this step, activities that are too complex to understand, design, or implement are refined by additional activity diagrams. The output of this step is a hierarchy of activity diagrams.

Step 5. Review the activity diagrams. In this step, the activity diagrams are reviewed to ensure correctness and consistency.

14.5.1 Identifying Activities and Workflows

Activity modeling requires that the development team possesses sufficient knowledge about the current activities. Therefore, collecting information about the activities and workflow of the business task being modeled is performed first, using the techniques described in Chapter 4. The information gathered during the requirements analysis phase may be reused. Additional information is gathered in this step if needed. First of all, the development team works with the customer and users to acquire information about the business activities. In particular, the information collection process focuses on answers to the following questions:

1. What is the business for which the computerized system is built?
2. What are the business goals and challenges to reach the goals?
3. What are the current business activities, their functions, known problems, and possible solutions?
4. What are the relationships between the business activities? How do they interact with each other?
5. What are the input and output of the business activities? Where does the input come from, and the output go to? What are the representations of the input and output?
6. When and how are the business activities performed? Who is responsible for the business activities?
7. What business activities exhibit any of the following characteristics? These are the candidates for activity modeling.
   a. The activities require considerable time and/or effort to perform. For example, it takes time to prepare a proposal, review an application, or hold meetings to reach a decision. It is not like a function call that can produce a result quickly.
   b. The activities are related by information, data, or workflows.
   c. The activities are performed by two or more organizational units.
   d. The activities are performed conditionally, sequentially, concurrently, and synchronization is sometimes required.
8. What are the improvement or enhancement expectations of the customer and users?

1. Talk to your academic advisor to **discuss internship options** in your specific *degree program.*
2. **Interview** and **get an** ***offer letter*** for an INTERNSHIP position.
3. **Submit Prospective Employer's Information** to the company and **get a** ***letter*** **from the company**.
4. **Enroll in the corresponding internship course**. Your department can provide details.
5. Have your academic advisor **fill out the** ***CPT Academic Advisor Recommendation form***.
6. **Fill out the** ***CPT Student Form***.
7. **Submit completed forms to OIE** with your *current I-20.*
8. Within 7-10 business days, OIE will **determine eligibility** and **issue a** ***new I-20*** authorizing the employment for the specified dates.
9. Once you receive your *new I-20,* you may **begin working** on the start date listed on page 3.

Legend: Activity=boldface Performer=underlined Input/output=italic Timing=double underlined

FIGURE 14.7 CPT description with activities, performers, and input/output highlighted

To identify activities and workflow between the activities, the development team looks for verb-noun phrases that indicate that something must be done to accomplish a business-specific task. The team also looks for the performer of the activity and/or the organization in which the activity is performed. Moreover, the information or data required and produced by the activity are identified. To illustrate, Figure 14.7 shows a description of the workflow for obtaining Curricular Practical Training (CPT), where activities are in bold, performers underlined, timing double-underlined, and activity input and output are in italic.

An activity table, shown in Figure 14.8, is useful for organizing the information identified. The table has the following columns, which are filled while reading the workflow description such as in Figure 14.7:

1. The number (#) column specifies the activity ID number.
2. The Activity column specifies the activity name.
3. The Performed By column specifies who or which organizational unit performs the activity.
4. The Input (from) column specifies the activity input and optionally its source activity ID number, that is, the activity that produces the input.
5. The Output (to) column specifies the activity output and optionally the destination activity ID number.
6. The Next Activity column specifies the successor activity ID number. If the completion of the current activity forks into two concurrent threads of activities, such as activity 5 Get Internship Letter, then the concurrent successor activities are separated by the "&&" signs. For example, the last entry of activity 5 is "6 && 7." This means that the completion of activity 5 forks into two threads, one goes to activity 6 and the other goes to activity 7.

#	Activity	Performed By	Input (from)	Output (to)	Next Activity
1	Discuss Internship Options	Student Academic Advisor	Degree Program		2
2	Interview	Student			3
3	Get an Offer Letter	Student		Offer Letter	4
4	Submit Prospective Employer's Information	Student			5
5	Get an Internship Letter	Student		Internship Letter (7)	6 && 7
6	Enroll in Internship Course	Student			8
7	Fill Out CPT Academic Advisor Recommendation Form	Academic Advisor		CPT Academic Advisor Recommendation Form (9)	9
8	Fill Out CPT Student Form	Student		CPT Student Form (9)	
9	Submit Completed Forms	Student	• CPT Academic Advisor Recommendation Form (7) • CPT Student Form (8)	• Current I-20 (10) • CPT Academic Advisor Recommendation Form (10) • CPT Student Form (10)	10
10	Determine Eligibility {within 7–10 business days}	OIE	• Current I-20 (9) • CPT Academic Advisor Recommendation Form (9) • CPT Student Form (9)	[eligible]/[else]	11/ Final Node
11	Issue New I-20	OIE	[eligible]	New I-20 (12)	Begin CPT
12	Begin Working	Student	New I-20 (11)		Final Node

FIGURE 14.8 A tabular summary of activity information

14.5.2 Producing a Preliminary Activity Diagram

In this step, the information obtained in the last step is used to produce a preliminary activity diagram. The table shown in Figure 14.8 is useful for this task. Using the table, the activity diagram is produced by using the following steps, which are explained using Figure 14.9:

1. Draw a swim lane for each of the unique activity performers listed in the Performed By column. The table lists three performers; therefore, three swim lanes are drawn and labeled accordingly. The swim lanes are drawn either horizontally as in Figure 14.9 or vertically. The development team makes the decision to better fit the diagram into the drawing media. In case there is only one performer, then drawing the swim lane is not necessary.
2. Draw the activities for the performers. If the activity table is filled while reading a workflow description, then the activities tend to appear chronologically in the table. In this case, draw the activities according to the order listed but place each of them in the swim lane that the activity belongs to. Figure 14.9 is produced this way. Number the activities if desired using the activity ID listed in the first column. The activity ID number is useful for tracking and checking the decomposition of complex activities.
3. Draw the control flows and object flows using the information listed in the Input, Output, and Next Activity columns. In most cases, the Next Activity column

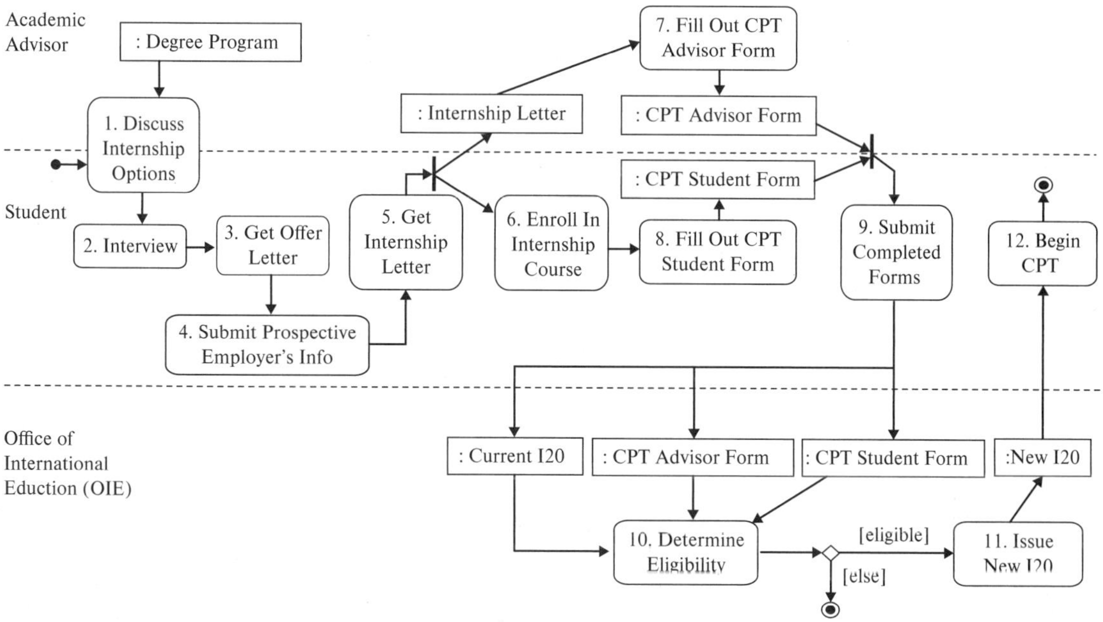

FIGURE 14.9 Curricular Practical Training activity diagram

contains only one activity. If the Input and Output columns are blank, then draw an arrow from the current activity to the successor activity. If there is input or output, then the developers determine if an input or output should be shown in the activity diagram. For example, on line 3 of Figure 14.8, the Get an Offer Letter activity produces Offer Letter as an output. However, the Output(to) entry does not show the activity ID number of the activity to receive the output; therefore, in the activity diagram, the Offer Letter is not depicted. Line 5 shows that the output is an Internship Letter, which is needed by activity 7. This is therefore shown as an object flow from activity 5 to activity 7. Moreover, the last entry of the line shows two conjunctive activities. This means a forking, as illustrated in the activity diagram. Note: activity 10 needs to be performed within 7–10 business days. This is shown in activity 10 with a pair of braces enclosing the timing constraint. Finally, the first line shows an input without a pair of parentheses that encloses an activity ID number. This means the input is not from any activity, but it is needed. It is shown as an object flow from nowhere in Figure 14.9.

14.5.3 Introducing Branching, Forking, and Joining

Next, conditional branching is introduced into the activity diagram produced in the last step. This is accomplished by examining each of the activities. A conditional branching is needed if one of the following holds:

- The verb-noun phrase that names the activity implies decision making that influences the outcome of the activity. Typically, the verb-noun phrase contains verbs such as "accept," "approve," "decide," "determine," and so forth. Alternatively, the verb-noun phrase may be "obtain approval (or acceptance) for . . . ," or "make decision on," and so on.

- The verb-noun phrase that names the activity implies checking, testing, or evaluation that influences the outcome of the activity. Typically, the verb-noun phrase contains verbs such as "check," "verify," "validate," "review," "evaluate," "assess," and so on.
- The activity may produce different outcomes that require different flows of control.

Consider, for example, the activity diagram in Figure 14.9. The Determine Eligibility activity is a decision-making process. The OIE may or may not approve a student's CPT application. Therefore, a conditional branching is used to model the decision-making activity. If the conditional branching was not used previously and needs to be added in this step, then additional activities may be introduced to handle the newly introduced cases, such as, an activity to notify the student that the CPT petition is not eligible.

The activities are examined to identify sequences of activities that can be performed in parallel. This is accomplished by using domain knowledge. Forking is introduced into the activity diagram to specify these parallel activities. Also identified are activities that need synchronization, that is, two or more activities must complete before another activity can begin. Joining is used to indicate synchronization in the activity diagram.

14.5.4 Refining Complex Activities

Real-world projects may involve "large" activities that include many other activities. These large activities need to be decomposed into a network of smaller activities to aid understanding and communication of design ideas. In this step, the development team examines the activity diagram and identifies activities that need refinements. This is accomplished in one of two ways:

1. Examining the relevant documentation that describes the activities. If the description of an activity implies that several application domain tasks need to be performed and/or the relationships between the tasks are not trivial, then that activity should be decomposed.
2. If no relevant documentation exists for an activity, then the development team writes a summary of how the activity is carried out. If the description includes several nontrivial steps and/or relationships between the steps are complex, then that activity should be decomposed.

14.5.5 Activity Modeling Review Checklist

The activity diagrams produced are checked using a review checklist. Below is an example of such a checklist:

1. Does the activity diagram describe the correct business process?
2. Is the activity diagram overly complex?
3. Is the activity diagram syntactically correct?

4. Is each conditional branching associated with a condition that can be evaluated?
5. Are the branching conditions mutually exclusive?
6. If the activity diagram is a refinement of an activity, then does the refinement satisfy the consistency rules presented in Section 14.3.3?

14.6 RELATIONSHIPS TO OTHER DIAGRAMS

Activity diagrams are related to other UML diagrams in a number of ways. An activity may be a use case, or suggest a use case. Such activities are interactive in nature, that is, each of these activities requires the actor to interact with the system to carry out the activity. In Figure 14.6, several such activities can be identified: Submit Hiring Request, Establish Project, and Create Project Account. In this regard, activity modeling is useful as an aid to identifying use cases. Sometimes, it may be difficult to identify use cases from high-level requirements. In these cases, the high-level requirements may be refined by lower-level requirements, from which the use cases are identified. An alternative approach is activity modeling, in which high level requirements are refined by decomposing activities to lower-level activities. Use cases are then identified from the activities that are interactive in nature. In addition to help in use case identification, the activity diagram is a useful tool for showing the workflow and control flow relationships among the use cases. These relationships include sequencing, conditional branching, concurrency, and synchronization.

An activity that is a use case suggests that actor-system interaction modeling and object interaction modeling should be applied to model the information processing task of the activity. On the other hand, a complex request in the sequence diagram may require an activity diagram to model the processing of the request. For example, a request to set up a faculty-led study-abroad program is a complex process. It needs the approval of various administrative entities, including the development of a memorandum of understanding with the host university, schedule the course, and brief the students, to list a few. An activity diagram showing the activities and the workflows can help the team understand the complex process and identify which tasks should be computerized. An activity may exhibit state-dependent behavior. There are many such examples. In these cases, the refinement of the activity should use state modeling rather than decomposition of the activity into another activity diagram. On the other hand, a state may represent a complex process. In this case, an activity diagram may be used as a refinement of the state activity.

For each object sent from one activity to another via an object flow, its class should appear in the design class diagram (DCD), or the domain model. If it is not the case, then the object class should be added to the DCD or the domain model. Additional object classes may be identified from the swim lanes. In particular, each swim lane that represents a human role identifies an object class. The object class should be included in the domain model, and in the DCD as well if the class must be implemented. The activities in the swim lane may identify operations for the class. A complex activity may decompose into lower-level activities or actions. Some of these may be operations of the class.

14.7 APPLYING AGILE PRINCIPLES

GUIDELINE 14.1 Value working software over comprehensive documentation.

Activity modeling must not be performed for the sake of documentation. It is performed only if the team needs to understand the activities and workflows to produce the working software. For example, activity modeling may be needed to implement an ERP system.

GUIDELINE 14.2 Active user involvement is imperative.

If the team needs to perform activity modeling, then active involvement of users is required. This is because the information processing activities and workflows of an organization is application specific, complex, and involves a lot of hidden information. Therefore, activity modeling requires active user involvement.

GUIDELINE 14.3 A collaborative and cooperative approach between all stakeholders is essential.

Active user involvement means that representatives of user communities must work with the team on a daily basis or at least several days a week. This requires the customer and users to commit their precious time and resources. In today's competitive business environment, the commitment is difficult to get and keep. Therefore, a collaborative and cooperative approach is essential.

GUIDELINE 14.4 Capture requirements at a high level; make them lightweight and visual. Do barely enough activity modeling.

If activity modeling is needed, then capture the activities and workflows at a high level and make them lightweight. This means that unnecessary details should be avoided. Construct the activity diagrams to be just clear enough to persuade the team to proceed with implementation. If necessary, the team can always return to activity modeling to refine the activity diagrams. That is, there is no need to produce a complete and detailed activity diagram.

14.8 TOOL SUPPORT FOR ACTIVITY MODELING

IBM Rational Modeler, Microsoft Visio, ArgoUML, and NetBeans UML Plugin provide activity diagram editing capabilities along with other features. The diagram editor lets the software engineer draw, edit, and manage activity diagrams.

14.9 SUMMARY

This chapter presents the importance of activity modeling. It reviews three prominent modeling tools–flowchart, Petri net, and data flow diagrams. These tools, among many others, contribute modeling concepts and constructs found in the UML activity diagram. It describes a UML activity diagram and the steps for activity modeling. The steps for activity modeling are influenced by the features of the three prominent activity modeling tools and the principle of separation of concerns. That is, in step 2, a preliminary activity diagram is constructed. This is basically a data flow diagram. It shows the activities and the control flows and object flows between the activities. Step 3 introduces conditional branching, forking, and joining to express complex relationships that exist among the control flows. In step 4, complex activities are decomposed, and decomposition consistency is checked.

At the end of this chapter, activity modeling is compared with the other modeling and design techniques presented in previous chapters. These include how to identify classes and their operations from an activity diagram and use these to update the design class diagram. Moreover, the usefulness of activity modeling as an aid to refinement of high-level requirements as well as use case identification is presented.

14.10 CHAPTER REVIEW QUESTIONS

1. What is activity modeling?
2. What is the usefulness of activity modeling?
3. What are the steps for activity modeling?
4. What are the rules to ensure that an activity is decomposed consistently?
5. How does activity modeling relate to the other analysis and design techniques such as object interaction modeling and state modeling?

14.11 EXERCISES

14.1 Refine the Obtain an Offer Letter activity discussed in Section 14.5.4 to produce an activity diagram, taking into consideration conditional branching, concurrency, and synchronization.

14.2 Develop a description for each of the following applications and apply the activity modeling steps to each of them:

- **a.** An online build-to-order application.
- **b.** A claim-handling system for an insurance company that issues home insurance as well as automobile insurance.

14.3 Produce an activity diagram that describes the steps for activity modeling

14.4 Produce an activity diagram that describes your academic department's undergraduate or graduate advising.

15 Chapter

Modeling and Design of Rule-Based Systems

Key Takeaway Points

- Business rules are decision-making rules. Decision tables are tabular specifications of business rules.
- The interpreter pattern lets business rules to change dynamically during system operation.

Previous chapters present modeling and design of several types of system including interactive, event-driven, and transformational systems. Another type of system is a rule-based system, which is used by businesses to make decisions. A software system may contain subsystems of different types. In particular, rule-based systems are often used as a component of a system to help decision-making. This chapter is devoted to the modeling and design of rule-based components. As an example of business rules, consider a point-of-sale shipping software. It has a *Ship Package* use case. The corresponding ship package controller has a function to compute the charge. The business rules for calculating a package's shipping charges are:

> The maximum limits for express packages within the U.S. are 150 lbs., and 119 inches in length and 165 inches in length and girth.[1] Packages that weigh 150 lbs. or less and exceed 108 inches in length or 130 inches in length and girth are considered oversized packages. Oversized packages are rated based on the greater of the package's actual rounded weight or dimensional weight.[2] In addition, a charge of $40 per oversized package applies.

Rules as such are called business rules, or decision logic. The informal specification of business rules has drawbacks. For example, an informal specification is more likely to be ambiguous. That is, different interpretations exist. Moreover, it does not explicitly display the relationships between the package parameters and the computed charges. Finally, it is difficult to check the completeness and consistency of the decision logic specification. Completeness means that the

[1]The girth of a package is (width + height) * 2.

[2]The dimensional weight of a package is (length * width * height)/194 for domestic shipping, and (length * width * height)/166 for international shipping.

specification has taken into account all possible cases or condition combinations. For example, if the business rules involve three binary conditions, then there are eight possible condition combinations. The specification should include all these cases. Consistency means that each condition combination should lead to only one unique course of action. This ensures that the same condition combination will not produce different results at different times. This chapter presents the decision table tool for specifying and analyzing decision logic. Throughout this chapter, you will learn the following:

- The definition of a decision table.
- The merits of a decision table.
- Methods for constructing a decision table.
- Completeness, consistency, and nonredundancy of a decision table.
- How to ensure that a decision table is complete, consistent, and nonredundant.
- The interpreter pattern.
- How to apply the *interpreter* pattern to design and implement rule-based systems.

15.1 WHAT IS A DECISION TABLE?

A decision table is a decision logic specification tool that displays the business rules as columns of a table. Figure 15.1 shows a decision table for the shipping business rules presented earlier. A decision table consists of six parts:

Rule numbers. The top row of the decision table shows the rule numbers. These columns are the rule columns. Each rule column represents a business rule. For example, the decision table in Figure 15.1 shows six rules.

Condition stubs. The first column of the upper portion of the decision table contains the condition stubs, which specify the conditions involved in the business rules. Figure 15.1 shows three conditions in the decision table.

Condition entries. The entries formed by the condition stub rows and the rule columns are condition entries. They specify the condition values for the rules. A dash in a condition entry is an "indifference." This means that whichever value is in the condition entry the outcome of the rule is the same. For example, rule 6 shows that if the package weight is greater than 150 pounds, the package is rejected. The two dashes in rule 6 mean that the length and girth values do not affect the outcome.

Action stubs. The first column of the lower portion of the table are the action stubs. They specify the possible actions. The decision table in Figure 15.1 shows four possible actions.

Action entries. The entries formed by the action stub rows and the rule columns are action entries. Most of the time, an action entry is either a blank, or an X. An action entry containing an X means the action is performed if the conjunction of the conditions are true. For example, the first rule states that "if the package weight is less than or equal to 150 pounds, the length is less than or equal to 108 inches, and the length plus girth is less than or equal to 130 inches, then rate the

condition stub | rule number | condition entry | indifference

	1	2	3	4	5	6
Weight ≤150 lbs	Y	Y	Y	Y	Y	N
Length (inches)	≤108	>108&≤119	≤108	>119	≤119	-
Length plus Girth (inches)	≤130	≤165	>130&≤165	–	>165	–
Rule Count	**1**	**2**	**1**	**3**	**2**	**9**
Rate by Weight	X					
Rate by greater of Weight and Dim. Weight		X	X			
Add $40 surcharge to each package		X	X			
Reject package				X	X	X

rule count | action stub | action entry

FIGURE 15.1 A decision table representing some shipping rules

package according to its actual weight." In some cases, a rule may execute more than one action, as for rule 2 and rule 3. If the order to execute the actions is important, then use serial numbers instead of an X to indicate the order. If the entries are not serial numbers, then the actions can be performed in any order.

Rule count. The rule count row records the number of condition combinations that the rule covers. These entries are useful for checking the completeness of the decision table.

15.2 USEFULNESS OF DECISION TABLE

Sequence diagrams are useful for showing the interaction between the objects through message passing. However, sequence diagrams are not suitable for showing the decision logic. Consider, for example, the *Ship Package* use case. After the user enters the package information and clicks the Calculate Charge button, the graphical user interface calls the compute charge method of the use case controller. The method implements the business rules for calculating the shipping charges. If the sequence diagram shows how the method computes the charges, then at least three UML combined fragments must be used to display the condition combinations and the corresponding actions. The sequence diagram will be complex and difficult to understand. A better approach suppresses the detail and shows only a UML note attached to the compute charge method. For example, the UML note may indicate "see Shipping Charge Decision Table in this document."

A decision table is also useful as a supplement to UML activity diagrams. Although an activity diagram can show branching, the decisions are made by an activity. For example, if an activity diagram were used to model the package shipping work-flow, then the decision to reject, or how to charge a package, is made in an activity. The outcome of the activity is displayed by using a diamond to show the branching to other activities. Activity diagrams do not show the decision logic. Decision tables complement activity diagrams by providing a means for visualizing the decision logic. Thus, the outcome of a decision table can be used to follow a specific branch to an activity. This completes the semantics of an activity diagram. In addition, decision tables also have the following advantages:

1. *Easy to understand.* Decision tables are easy to understand because they clearly display the cause and effect relationships between the condition combinations and the related actions.
2. *Easy to check.* It is easy to check the completeness, consistency, and nonredundancy of a decision table. Moreover, it is easy to review a decision table to determine whether it correctly specifies the business rules.
3. *Easy to implement.* It is easy to generate code from a decision table.
4. *It helps test-case generation and test-driven development.* The rules of a decision table are useful for generating functional test cases as well as boundary value test cases. Since the test cases can be produced and implemented before implementation, it helps test-driven development.
5. *Rules can be updated dynamically.* It is easy to apply the interpreter pattern to implement a decision table. This is presented in Section 15.8. The pattern allows a user to modify the business rules on the fly without needing to recompile the program. This capability is useful for businesses that need to update the business rules frequently, dynamically, and instantly.

15.3 SYSTEMATIC DECISION TABLE CONSTRUCTION

One way to construct a decision table is to systematically list the condition combinations and identify the actions for each of the condition combinations. Using this approach, the number of rules of the decision table is equal to the number of possible combinations of the conditions. Figure 15.2 displays a decision table that is

	1	2	3	4	5	6	7	8
Competitive Salary	Y	Y	Y	Y	N	N	N	N
Good Location	Y	Y	N	N	Y	Y	N	N
Nice Colleagues	Y	N	Y	N	Y	N	Y	N
Rule Count	1	1	1	1	1	1	1	1
Accept	X	X	X					
Hold				X	X			
Reject						X	X	X

FIGURE 15.2 Systematic decision table construction

constructed using this approach. The decision table describes the decision logic of a job seeker. Note the systematic arrangement of the condition values in the condition entries.

The systematic decision table construction method is easy to use because the condition entries are filled systematically. Each of the condition combinations is then examined and the appropriate actions are checked. One drawback of this approach is that the table must contain a rule for each of the condition combinations. If the number of combinations is large, then the size of the decision table is large. For example, there are 32 rules for a decision table with five binary conditions. However, some rules can be merged or consolidated to reduce the size of the decision table. The consolidated decision table is easier to understand and check because the redundancy is removed.

15.4 PROGRESSIVE DECISION TABLE CONSTRUCTION

The progressive decision table construction process produces the rules one at a time. It fills in the condition entries of each rule one by one. It is aimed to conclude each rule as soon as possible. That is, if the condition entries filled so far can determine the actions, then the appropriate action entries are checked, and the remaining condition entries are filled with the indifference symbol. The process then constructs the next rule by copying the nondash condition entries of the just-completed rule and changing one of the condition entries to a value that has not been considered previously. If the rule cannot lead to a decision, then enter values into the remaining condition entries until an action can be entered. The process is repeated until no new rules are created.

Example 15.1 Construct a decision table for the job seeker using the progressive approach.

Solution: We construct the decision table according to the decision making logic presented in Figure 15.2. We assume that the condition stubs are competitive salary, good location, and nice colleagues. First, enter Y into the first condition entry of the first rule, meaning that competitive salary is yes. According to Figure 15.2, this does not lead to an action. Therefore, we enter Y into the second condition entry of the firs rule. The rule so far says that the offer has competitive salary and good location. In this case, the job seeker accepts the offer. Therefore, we enter an indifference into the remaining condition entry and a cross into the accept entry of the first rule. The second rule is constructed by copying the first two condition entries of the first rule, and changing the good location from Y to N. The second rule so far says competitive salary but not a good location; of course, the job seeker would not accept the offer. Therefore, we enter Y into the remaining condition entry, that is, it has nice colleagues. In this case, the job seeker will accept the offer, so, the rule is completed. This process repeats and finally produces the decision table as shown in Figure 15.3.

	1	2	3	4	5	6
Competitive Salary	Y	Y	Y	N	N	N
Good Location	Y	N	N	Y	Y	N
Nice Colleagues	--	Y	N	Y	N	--
Rule Count	**2**	**1**	**1**	**1**	**1**	**2**
Accept	X	X				
Hold			X	X		
Reject					X	X

FIGURE 15.3 Progressive decision table construction illustrated

15.5 CHECKING FOR DESIRED PROPERTIES

Completeness, consistency, and nonredundancy are three important quality attributes of a decision table. These are defined as follows.

Definition 15.1 A decision table is complete if the rules cover all of the possible condition combinations.

The completeness of a decision table is important because it ensures that all possible cases of the business rules are taken into account. What would happen if a decision table is incomplete? If the development team implements the software according to a decision table that is not complete, then the software would not be able to process the missing cases. The completeness of a decision table is checked by comparing the sum of the rule counts with the total number of possible condition combinations. If the sum equals to the total number of possible combinations, then the table is complete, provided that the rule counts are correct. If the sum is less, then either the sum or the rule counts are incorrect, or some rules are missing. If the sum is greater, then either the sum or the rule counts are incorrect, or there are extra, redundant rules. For example, in Figure 15.1, there are three conditions. The first condition has two condition values, the second condition has three condition values, and the last condition has three condition values. Therefore, there are 18 possible condition combinations. The sum of the rule counts is also 18. Therefore, the decision table is complete.

Definition 15.2 A decision table is consistent if the condition combination of each of its rules is unique. A decision table is inconsistent if two or more rules have the same condition combination but different courses of actions.

The consistency of a decision table ensures that the same condition combination will lead to the execution of the same set of actions. If the team implements the software according to an inconsistent decision table, then the software would produce different results for the same input parameters, depending on which of the rules is applied.

Definition 15.3 A decision table is nonredundant if it does not contain two or more rules that can be replaced by a logically equivalent rule.

Consider, for example, the decision table in Figure 15.2. The decision table is constructed using the systematic decision table construction method, which often produces decision tables with redundancies. Consider rules 1 and 2, which differ on only one condition, that is, their actions are the same and their condition entries are the same except one. This means that regardless of whether the "Nice Colleagues" condition is Y or N, the job seeker will take the offer. Thus, the two rules can be merged into one with the condition entry for "Nice Colleagues" set to indifference. Similarly, rules 7 and 8 can be merged.

15.6 DECISION TABLE CONSOLIDATION

Decision table consolidation is the process to eliminate redundancies in a decision table. Figure 15.4 shows a decision table consolidation algorithm and an equivalent, decision table. The first while loop of the algorithm eliminates duplicate rules. The first if-then statement in the second while loop eliminates rules that are already covered by other rules. The second if-then-else statement in the second while loop checks for the existence of rules that differ on only one condition, that is, rules with identical

```
while (two or more rules are identical) {
   eliminate all but one of the rules
}

while (two or more unmarked rules differ on
        only one condition) {
   if (one of these rules has "-" for that condition)
      delete the other rules
   else
     if (the rules cover all the cases for that
        condition) {
        replace the rules with one that has "-" for
        that condition
     } else {
          marked the rules as visited;
     }
}
```

(a) Algorithm for decision table consolidation

	1	2	3	4	5
2 or more rules are identical	Y	N	N	N	N
2 or more unmarked rules differ on only one condition?	-	Y	Y	Y	N
1 of the rules has "-" for that condition?	-	Y	N	N	-
rules cover all cases of that condition?	-	-	Y	N	-
Rule Count	**8**	**2**	**1**	**1**	**4**
Delete all but one of the rules	1				
Delete other rules		1			
Replace the rules with one with "-" for that condition			1		
Mark rules as visited				1	
Goto this table	2	2	2	2	
Halt					X

(b) Decision table for decision table consolidation

FIGURE 15.4 Decision table consolidation algorithm

actions and identical condition entries except one that is different. If such rules exist and they cover all the cases for that condition, then these rules can be replaced by one of the rules with an indifference for that condition. This is because the replacement rule is equivalent to the rules replaced.

15.7 GENERATING CODE FROM A DECISION TABLE

It is relatively easy to generate code from a decision table. First, partition the rules according to the values of the first condition. Then rearrange the rules so that rules of the same partition are listed together. Second, partition the rules of each partition according to the values of the second condition and rearrange them similarly. Repeat this process for each of the remaining conditions. The result will look like the decision table in Figure 15.4(b). Now the rules are nicely arranged. Code can be generated easily.

15.8 USING A DECISION TABLE IN TEST-DRIVEN DEVELOPMENT

Test-driven development (TDD) means writing tests before implementing code so that the implementation can be tested sooner and often. Decision tables facilitate TDD because tests can be generated from the rules of a decision table before implementation. First, functional tests can be generated from a decision table to verify that the component under test (CUT) correctly implements the intended functionality. To generate functional tests, the condition entries of each rule are used to initialize the environment and input parameters of the CUT. The action entries are used to specify the expected result of the CUT. Besides functional tests, boundary value tests are useful for testing whether the CUT properly handles boundary values of an input variable or environment variable. A boundary value is a value that is located at the boundary of the value domain. Consider, for example, the shipping company decision table presented at the beginning of this chapter. The first condition defines a constraint on the weight of the package to be shipped, that is, the package weight must not exceed 150 pounds. From this, one can derive the following boundary values: −1 pounds, 0 pounds, 1 pounds, 149 pounds, 150 pounds, and 151 pounds. For each of these cases, the expected outcome of the CUT is specified. For example, it is expected that the CUT should display an error message when the weight is −1, 0, and 151 pounds. In addition to boundary values, extreme values are used to test the ability of the CUT in handling extreme cases. Consider again the shipping decision table discussed above. An extremely large weight, or dimension, can be used to test the CUT. The expected outcome of this test should be an error message.

15.9 DECISION TREES

Like decision tables, decision trees are commonly used to specify and analyze decision logic. For each decision table, one can construct a semantically equivalent decision tree, and vice versa. Figure 15.5 shows a job seeker's decision table and its

	1	2	3	4	5	6
Comp. Salary	Y	Y	Y	N	N	N
Good Location	Y	N	N	Y	Y	N
Nice Colleagues	--	Y	N	Y	N	--
Rule Count	2	1	1	1	1	2
Accept	X	X				
Hold			X	X		
Reject					X	X

(a) A job seeker's decision table

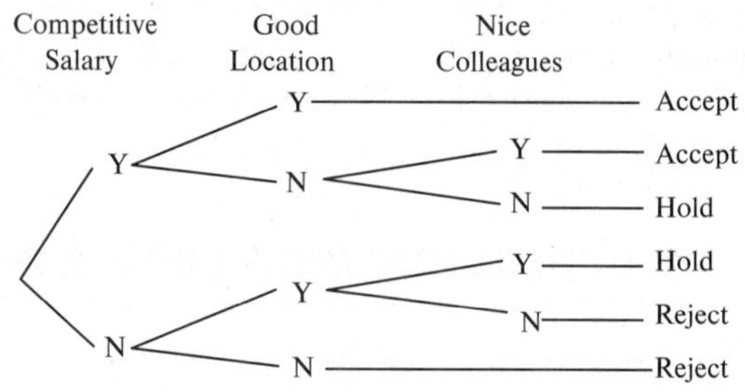

(b) An equivalent decision tree

FIGURE 15.5 A decision table and its equivalent decision tree

equivalent decision tree. As displayed in the decision tree, the nonterminal nodes, except the root, represent condition entries. The terminal nodes represent the actions. Each branch of the decision tree represents a rule. In comparison, the decision table representation is more compact than its decision tree counterpart. In addition, it is easier to check completeness, consistency, and nonredundancy for a decision table than a decision tree. For these reasons, decision tables are the focus of this chapter.

15.10 APPLYING THE INTERPRETER PATTERN

Many businesses need to modify the business rules. Sometimes, it is desirable to change the business rules on the fly. This eliminates the considerable time and effort to modify, compile, and test the code. A real-world story illustrates the importance. In the 1990s, several large telephone companies competed for customers with attractive discount policies. These were specified as business rules and implemented using conditional statements. Competition means that the companies need to modify the rules frequently and quickly. Unfortunately, modifying, rebuilding, and retesting large telephone software systems took weeks or months. One of the companies recognized the problem and implemented a novel solution. It allowed the company to modify the discount policies on the fly. This gave the company a very competitive advantage.

The technique used by the company is an application of the *interpreter* pattern (Figure 15.6). The pattern is useful for representing and processing business rules that must be modified dynamically. As its name suggests, the pattern interprets the business rules rather than compiling them into binary code and executing the code. Because no compilation is needed, the rules can be modified frequently and quickly.

Applying the interpreter pattern involves the following steps:

1. Define a grammar.
2. Construct a class diagram to represent the grammar.
3. Convert each conditional expression to be evaluated into a parse tree.

Name	Interpreter
Type	GoF/Behavior
Specification	
Problem	How to represent and process rules that need to modify frequently and quickly on the fly.
Solution	Represent the conditional expression of each rule as a parse tree with operators as nonterminal nodes and operands as terminal nodes. Represent the action part of each rule as a list of action commands. Apply a post-order traversal to evaluate the conditional expression and execute the list of commands if the evaluation result is true. When the rules are changed, the tree and the command list are updated.
Design	
Structural	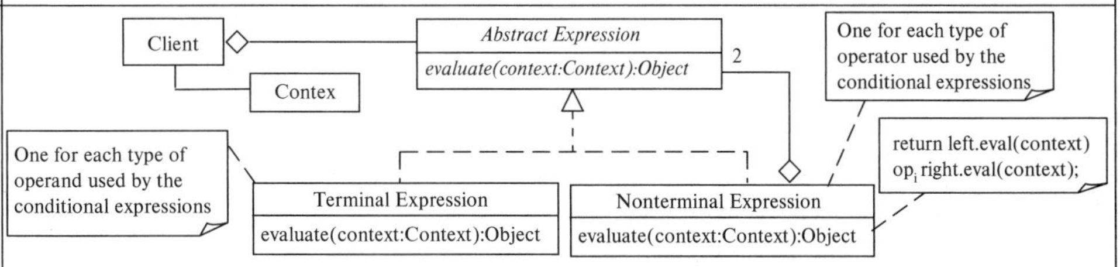
Behavioral	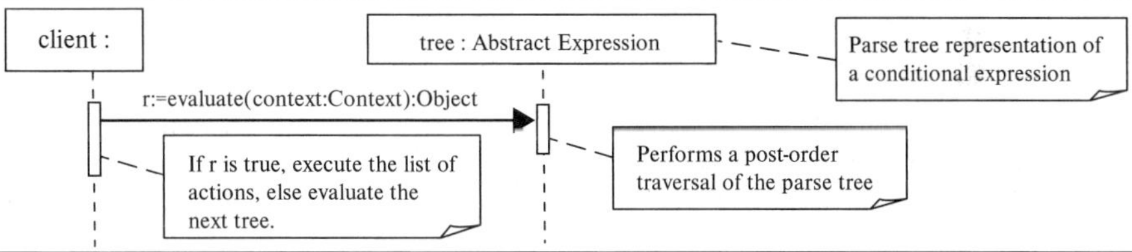
Roles and Responsibilities	• Abstract Expression: It defines a common interface for Terminal Expression and Nonterminal Expression. • Terminal Expression: It represents different types of operand such as int, boolean and string. • Nonterminal Expression: It represents different types of binary operator such as +, -, *, /, &&, ||, . (attribute accessor) etc. • Context: a collection, such as a hash table, that stores the objects and values used by the contitional expression. • Client: It may build the expression tree and invoke evaluate(context:Context) to perform a post-order traversal of the tree. If the evaluation of the conditional express returns true, then the client executes the list of actions associated with the rule.
Benefits	• It is easy to change the expression grammar. Simply change the structural design to add new types of operator or operand. • Rules can be changed on the fly. Simply modify or rebuild the expression tree and the command list accordingly. • It supports different and multiple semantics for the same expression grammar. For example, the result of 1+1 can be 2, 10 or 1 for decimal arithmetic, binary arithmetic and Boolean algebra, respectively.
Liabilities	• It is difficult to apply to languages that have a complex grammar such as C++ or Java. • More classes to design and implement. However, the implementation of the operator/nonterminal nodes is often "copy, paste and edit." • Performance may be an issue due to interpretation.
Guidelines	• Apply the interpreter pattern in cases where rules need to change on the fly, and performance is not a critical concern.
Related Patterns	• Composite: an expression tree may be stored in a composite with eval(c:Context):Object as one of its interface method. Another composite, with execute() as one of its interface method, may be used to store the actions, which are classified into primitive and composite actions called action plans. • Chain of responsibility may be used to chain the expression trees, ordered according to application-specific requirements. • Command: actions may be commands. • Observer: conditional part of a rule may be an observable and action part an observer. This decouples the condition and action parts and supports more flexible cause-effect relationships between conditions and actions. • Decorator: if the application requires different and/or multiple interpretations of the conditional expressions, then decorator may be used to implement the different interpretations as added functionalities.
Uses	• Business rule processing • Interpretation of languages with a simple grammar.

FIGURE 15.6 Specification of the interpreter pattern

4. Implement a context for looking up objects and constants used by the conditional expressions.
5. Create and evaluate the rules.

15.10.1 Defining a Grammar

The first step to applying the interpreter pattern is defining a grammar. For example, an expression is a logical expression, relational expression, or an arithmetic expression, and each relational expression consists of two arithmetic expressions and a relational operator.

15.10.2 Constructing a Class Diagram to Represent the Grammar

The second step is producing a class diagram to represent the grammar and evaluate conditional expressions. Figure 15.7 depicts such a class diagram. The figure shows that an expression (abbreviated as Expr) is a relational expression, an arithmetic expression, or a conjunction of two expressions. The figure also states that a relational expression is one of six comparison expressions (>=, >, ==, <=, < and !=), and each of them consists of two arithmetic expressions. For simplicity, Figure 15.7 assumes that all operands are integers. Thus, each eval method takes a Context object and returns an integer. Figure 15.7 also assumes that the eval methods of all conditional expressions including all relational expressions and conjunction return an integer value of 0 or 1, meaning false or true. The UML note attached to the Greater Than Expr class shows how its eval method is implemented. The implementation of the eval method for the Conjunction class uses the multiplication operator instead of the logical AND operator due to above

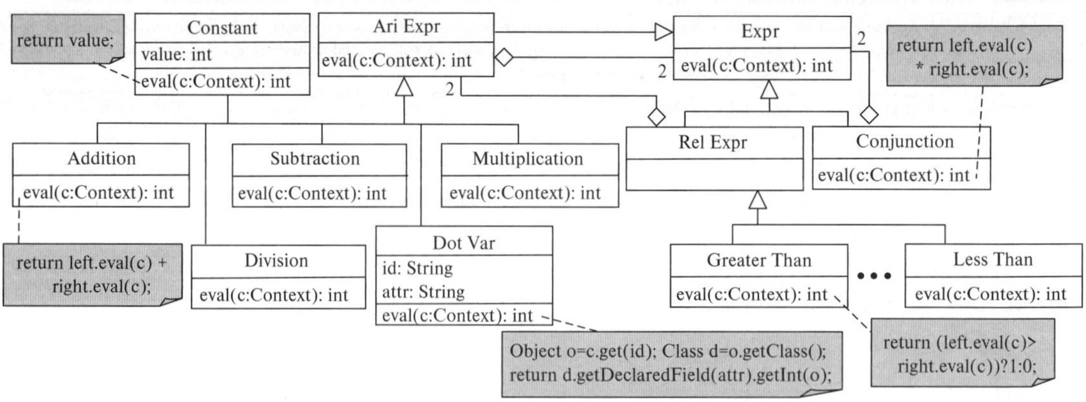

FIGURE 15.7 Class diagram for representing and evaluating conditional expressions

assumptions. Without the assumptions, we would have to use Object as the return type to unify Boolean values and integer values; in this case, the implementation of the eval methods would be more complex. Finally, the implementation of the eval method for the Dot Var class has to use Java reflection. This is because which object and which attribute of the object to be accessed are not known at compile time.

15.10.3 Converting a Conditional Expression into a Parse Tree

The third step is converting the conditional expression to be evaluated into a parse tree. It can be done by a simple parser or using a standard algorithm. As stated previously, the nonterminal nodes of the tree are operators and the leaf nodes are operands.

EXAMPLE 15.2

Convert the expression "order.qty * product.price>$200 && customer.years>5" into a parse tree.

Solution: Figure 15.8 shows the parse tree. The numbered circles and the numbered up arrows are not part of the parse tree. They show the post order traversal of the tree and the return values from the calls to the eval functions.

Note: post order traversal is already implemented by the recursive eval functions in Figure 15.7.

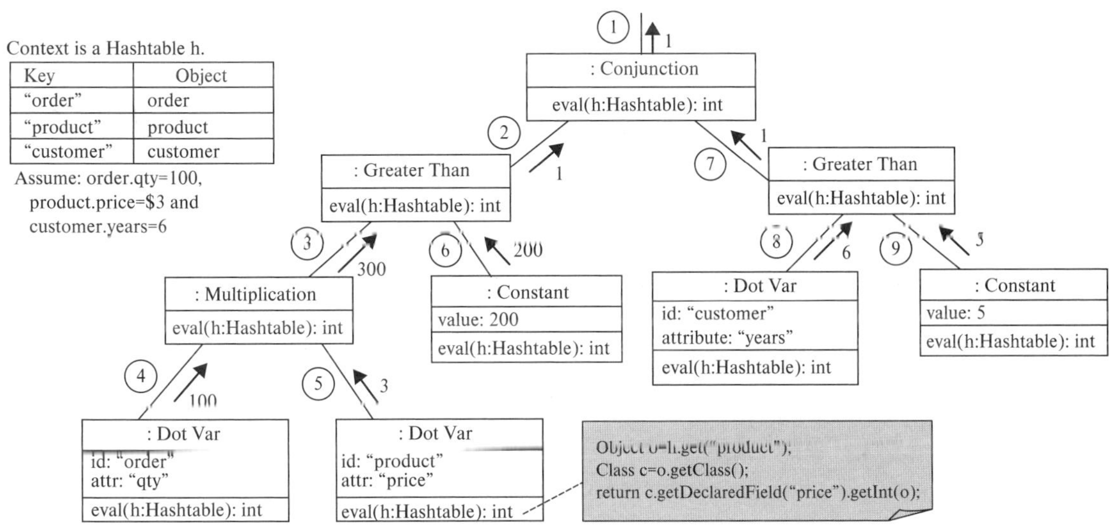

FIGURE 15.8 Parse tree for "order.qty*product.price>$200 && customer.years>5"

15.10.4 Implementing the Context

The next step is implementing and preparing the context for looking up the objects used by the conditional expressions. For most applications, one can use a hash table for this purpose. For instance, the hash table for above conditional expression would contain three objects: order, product and customer, with "order," "product" and "customer" as their respective keys.

15.10.5 Creating and Evaluating Business Rules

Finally, classes for representing the business rules as well as data structures to store the business rules are designed and implemented. A rule can be defined as consisting of a condition part and an action part. The condition part is a conjunction of conditional expressions, and the action part is a list of actions, which can be a linked list of actions. The simplest data structure to store the rules is a linked list, which allows the rules to be evaluated sequentially, beginning with the head of the linked list. The rules can be designed to satisfy different requirements, for example, only the first rule or all of the rules that are evaluated to true are executed. More sophisticated data structures to store the rules can use the composite pattern or the chain of responsibility pattern (Chapter 16).

EXAMPLE 15.3 Figure 15.9 shows the implementation of the interpreter pattern and evaluation of the expression order.qty * product.price>$200 & customer.years>5 as the condition part and the action part simply prints the message "the condition part is true."

15.10.6 Updating Rules Dynamically

Using the interpreter pattern, the business rules can be updated while the system is running. This is accomplished by implementing an *edit decision table dialog*. The user updates the decision table shown in the dialog and clicks the Submit button. The existing parse trees are replaced by the new parse trees created from the updated decision table. This approach does not require modification, compilation, testing, and debugging of the software system. It lets the business change the business rules quickly and dynamically.

15.10.7 Merits of the Interpreter Pattern

The interpreter pattern has the following benefits:

1. It is easy to extend and change the grammar. Whenever the grammar changes, the class diagram in Figure 15.6 is changed. Usually, such changes involves adding a few classes or changing the eval methods of a few classes.

```
public abstract class Expr {
  Expr left, right;
  public Expr(Expr l, Expr r) { left=l; right=r; }
  public abstract int eval(Hashtable h); }
public abstract class RelExpr extends Expr {
  public RelExpr(Expr l, Expr r) { super(l, r); } }
public class Conjunction extends Expr {
  public Conjunction(Expr l, Expr r) { super(l, r); }
  public int eval(Hashtable h)
  { return left.eval(h) * right.eval(h); } }
public class GreaterThan extends RelExpr {
  public GreaterThan(Expr l, Expr r) { super(l, r); }
  public int eval(Hashtable h)
  { return (left.eval(h)>right.eval(h))?1:0; } }
public abstract class AriExpr extends Expr {
  public AriExpr(Expr l, Expr r) { super(l, r); } }
public class Constant extends AriExpr {
  private int value;
  public Constant(int v)
  { super(null, null); value=v; }
  public int eval(Hashtable h)
  { return value; }
  public void setValue(int v)
  { value=v; } }
public class DotVar extends AriExpr {
  private String id, method;
  public DotVar(String id, String m)
  { super(null, null); this.id=id; method=m; }
  public int eval(Hashtable h) {
    try { Object o=h.get(id);
      Class c=o.getClass();
      Method[] m=c.getDeclaredMethods();
      Method p=null;
      for(int i=0; i<m.length; i++) { p=m[i];
         if (p.getName().compareTo(method)==0)
          break; }
      Integer x=(Integer)p.invoke(o, new Object[]{});
      return x.intValue();
    } catch(Exception e) { e.printStackTrace(); }
    return -1; }} // exception occurs
public class Multiplication extends AriExpr {
  public Multiplication(Expr l, Expr r) { super(l, r); }
  public int eval(Hashtable h)
  { return left.eval(h) * right.eval(h); } }
public class Action {
  public void execute()
  { System.out.println("Condition part is true."); }}
```

```
public class Rule {
  Expr condition; Action action; Rule next;
  public Rule(Expr c, Action a, Rule nx)
  { condition=c; action=a; next=nx; }
  public void eval(Hashtable h) {
    if (condition.eval(h)==1) action.execute();
    else if (next!=null) next.eval(h); } }
public class Interpreter {
  public static void main(String[] args) {
    Interpreter i=new Interpreter();
    Hashtable h=i.createContext(); Expr and=i.createTree();
    Rule r=i.createRule(and, new Action(), null);
     r.eval(h); }
  public Hashtable createContext()
  {  Order order=new Order(100);
    Product product=new Product(3);
    Customer customer=new Customer(6);
    Hashtable h=new Hashtable();
    h.put("order", order); h.put("product", product);
    h.put("customer", customer); return h; }
  public Expr createTree()
  {  // order.qty * product.price>$200 &&
     // customer.years>5
    DotVar order_qty=new DotVar("order", "getQty");
    DotVar product_price=new DotVar("product",
      "getPrice");
    Multiplication times=new Multiplication(order_qty,
      product_price);
    Constant c200=new Constant(200);
    GreaterThan gt=new GreaterThan(times, c200);
    DotVar customer_yrs=new DotVar("customer",
      "getYrs");
    Constant c5=new Constant(5);
    GreaterThan gt1=new GreaterThan(customer_yrs, c5);
    Conjunction and=new Conjunction(gt, gt1);
     return and; }
  public Rule createRule(Expr c, Action a, Rule next)
  {  return new Rule(c, a, next); }
public class Order {
  private int qty; public Order(int q){ qty=q; }
  public int getQty() { return qty; } }
public class Product {
  private int price; public Product(int p){ price=p; }
  public int getPrice() { return price; } }
public class Customer {
  private int yrs; public Customer(int y){ yrs=y; }
  public int getYrs() { return yrs; } } }
```

FIGURE 15.9 Sample code implementing the interpreter pattern in Figure 15.7

2. It is easy to implement, as shown by the UML notes attached to the functions in Figure 15.6.
3. It is easy to add interpretations. Consider, for example, a grammar that is originally defined for decimal algebra. If an interpretation for binary algebra is needed, then an operation that evaluates expressions in binary algebra can be added to the interface and implemented by the subclasses.
4. It allows the user to change the business rules on the fly without requiring the user to recompile the program—changes to the rules require only parsing the updated rules and reconstructing the parse trees.
5. It can avoid parsing if the rules are entered and updated through a dialog box, which implements the grammar rules by careful use of the input widgets such as text fields and selection lists.

One limitation is applying the pattern to a large, complex grammar is difficult. In this case, a compiler is a better choice. Another limitation is that interpretation runs slower than compiled code.

15.11 MACHINE LEARNING AND AI APPLICATION DEVELOPMENT

Rule-based systems work well when the rules can be formally and precisely formulated. However, for many real-world applications, this is extremely difficult, if not impossible. For example, it is impossible to implement a parser using grammar rules to analyze natural-language texts. Rules written in first-order logic cannot do the job either. This is because natural languages are very flexible and conventional parsers and logic are very rigid. Another example is X-ray image diagnosis. It requires medical knowledge as well as clinical experiences, which are impossible to formalize. In recent years, machine learning (ML) is increasingly applied to solve real-world problems that are not feasible with conventional rules-based systems. This section introduces the basic idea behind ML and how to design and implement AI applications.

15.11.1 Brief Introduction to Machine Learning

To overcome the limitations of the conventional rule-based systems, AI researchers rely on mining the plethora of existing data to discover valuable information, knowledge, or rules. For example, ML algorithms have been trained with millions of X-ray images and their diagnoses to discover a mapping from X-ray images to diseases. This mapping can be represented as a hypothesis function $h : X \rightarrow Y$, where X is a set of feature vectors that characterizes instances of the training dataset and Y the range of the h function. One technique used by ML to discover the hypothesis functions is called regression. This technique takes existing data as input and produces a hypothesis function that fits the existing data as close as possible. For example, if the existing data are two points $P1 = (0, 1)$ and

$P2 = (1, 3)$. Then the hypothesis function will be a linear function $h(x) = ax + b$, where a and b are constants. Using the existing data $P1$ and $P2$, regression will produce the function $h(x) = 2x + 1$. The reader can check that h exactly fits $P1$ and $P2$. For this simple example, we can find the exact function. But for many real-world applications, the hypothesis functions are very sophisticated and the exact functions may not exist.

There are two broad categories of regression algorithms: numerical regression and logistic regression. The former produces hypothesis functions with a numerical output, which may have an infinite number of possible values. For example, a hypothesis function for predicting the sale price of a house belongs to this category. Logistic regression is used to produce hypothesis functions with a limited number of possible values, such as "buy," "hold" or "sell" a stock. As such, this type of problem is called a classification problem. The trained ML algorithm is called a classifier. ML research has produced numerous regression algorithms and many tools that implement them are available.

15.11.2 A Workflow for Developing AI Applications

Figure 15.10 shows the workflow for developing AI applications including the creation of a ML model. It consists of five activities, described in the following paragraphs.

1. *Data Collection.* Data collection is extremely important because the quality of the dataset used to train the ML algorithms determines the quality of the ML models created. Data collection needs to consider the types of data to be collected, the features for which data will be collected, and data sources from which to collect the data. Depending on these, mechanisms to collect the data need to be implemented and executed to obtain the data.
2. *Dataset Generation.* Often, the raw data collected in the previous step must be processed to generate the dataset to train ML algorithms. This process may be manual, automatic, or semiautomatic. As an example, consider a simplistic stock recommendation application based on fundamental analysis. The theory of fundamental analysis believes that the price of a stock depends on a number of attributes including the price/earnings ratio (PE), the earnings growth rate (GROWTH), the PE/GROWTH ratio (PEG), the return on equity (ROE) and profit margin (MARGIN), among others. The values of these are real numbers, not suitable for ML to generate a decision tree classifier. They should be

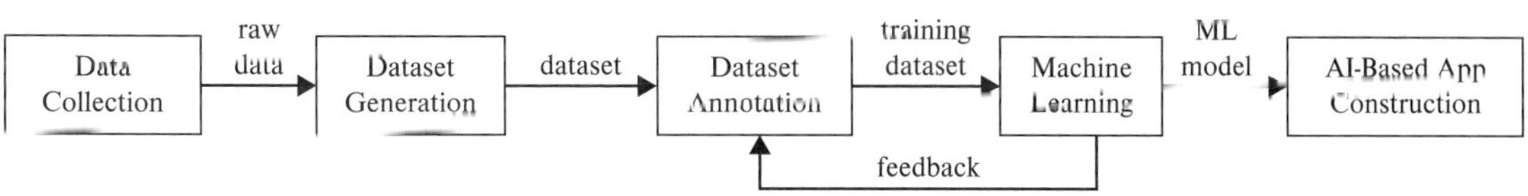

FIGURE 15.10 AI application development workflow

```
@relation    BuyStock
@attribute   TICKER        string          %   "%" begins a comment line
@attribute   PE            {high, low}     %   >20: high    <=20: low
@attribute   GROW          {high, low}     %   >20: high    <=20: low
@attribute   PEG           {high, low}     %   >2: high     <=2: low
@attribute   ROI           {high, low}     %   >15: high    <=15: low
@attribute   MARGIN        {high, low}     %   >15: high    <=15: low
@attribute   OUTPERFORM    {true, false}   %   Outperform S&P 500: true, else: false

@data
'ACMR'    high   high   low   high   high   true
'ALGN'    high   high   low   high   high   true
'BEAT'    high   high   low   low    low    false
'BSTC'"   low    high   low   high   high   false
'ENPH'    high   high   low   high   high   true
'EXEL'    high   high   low   high   high   true
'FND'     high   high   low   high   low    true
'GOOS'    high   high   low   high   high   false
...
```

FIGURE 15.11 Sample training dataset in Weka format

converted to nominal values such as high and low. Figure 15.11 shows instances of a dataset generated in the form required by Weka, an open source machine learning software. The upper portion shows the specification of the columns of the training dataset. Weka calls these attributes. There are seven attributes for the stock buying example: the first and the last are the stock ticker and the label, and the other are the five stock attributes described above. The label attribute of each training data item is usually entered manually. It tells the ML algorithm how to classify the data item so that the algorithm can learn. The lower portion shows part of the training dataset.

3. *Dataset Annotation.* The dataset generated may need to be annotated before it can be used to train a ML algorithm. Different types of data are annotated differently. The process can be manual, automatic, or semiautomatic. For example, the last feature (OUTPERFORM) in Figure 15.11 has been filled automatically by comparing the performances of the stocks with the performance of the S&P 500 Index during a period. If the stock outperforms the S&P 500 Index, then the annotation is true; otherwise, it is false.
4. *Machine Learning.* This step is carried out with a ML tool such as Weka, Apache Spark or Python, among others. The Weka software can be used with the Weka GUI or invoked from a program. Using the GUI mode to generate a model involves the following steps: (1) click the Explore button on the Weka GUI Chooser and then the Open file button on the Weka Explorer window to read in the training dataset, (2) in the Attributes section, check the attributes to be excluded then the Remove button to exclude them (e.g., the TICKER attribute in Figure 15.11 should be excluded because it is irrelevant to a stock's performance), (3) click the Classify tab then Choose followed by trees, and J48 to select the J48 classifier, (4) choose a test option such as cross-validation, (5) click the Start button to train and validate the classifier, the tool will show the result in the Classifier output

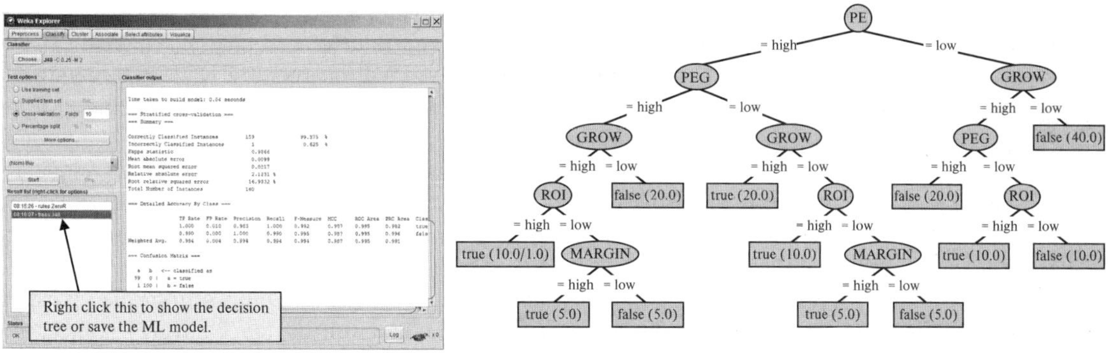

(a) J48-classifier outout

(b) Buy-stock decision tree

FIGURE 15.12 Using Weka GUI and a decision tree generated

panel (Figure 15.12(a)), (6) if the result is satisfactory, e.g., correctly identifies a high percentage of test instances, then right click the run item in the Result list at the lower-left corner of the Weka Explorer and select Visualize tree to show the decision tree, or select Save model to save the ML model. Figure 15.12(b) shows a decision tree created.

Calling Weka from a program is easy, as shown in Figure 15.13. The train method trains the J48 decision tree classifier. Note that the train method does not save the ML model. The classify method illustrates how to load and call a saved model to classify an unlabeled dataset.

```
package myweka;
import weka.core.converters.ConverterUtils.DataSource;
import weka.core.*;
import weka.classifiers.*;
import weka.classifiers.trees.J48;
import java.util.Random;
public class BuyStock{
  public Instances loadDataSet(String dataFile) {
    try {
      Data.Source source=new DataSource(dataFile);
      Instances dataset=source.getDataSet();
      if(dataset.classIndex()==-1) { // setting class attribute if needed
        dataset.setClassIndex(dataset.numAttributes()-1); }
      return dataset;
    } catch(Exception e) { return null; }
  }
  public void train(String dataFile) {
    try {
      Instances dataset=loadDataSet(dataFile);
      J48 tree=new J48(); // creates a J48 decision tree classifier
      tree.setOptions(new String[]{"-U"}); // unpruned tree
      Evaluation eval=new Evaluation(dataset);
      eval.crossValidateModel(tree, dataset,10, new Random(1));
      System.out.println(eval.toSummaryString
        ("\n=== Summary===\n", false));
    } catch (Exception e) { e.printStackTrace();}
  }
  public void classify(String dataFile) {
    try {
      ObjectInputStream ois=new ObjectInputStream(
        new FileInputStream(dataFile));
      Classifier classifier=(Classifier)ois.readObject();
      ois.close();
      Instances unlabeled=loadDataSet("stocks.arff");
      double clsLabel=classifier.classifyInstance
        (unlabeled.instance(0));
      unlabeled.instance(0).setClassValue(clsLabel);
      System.out.println("Classify to: "+unlabeled.instance(0));
    } catch(Exception e) { e.printStackTrace(); }
  }
  public static void main(String[] args) {
    BuyStock buyStock=new BuyStock();
    buyStock.train("training.arff");
    buyStock.classify("stocks.arff");
  }
}
```

FIGURE 15.13 Sample code to use Weka

5. *AI Application Construction.* The ML model produced and saved in the last step can be used by an AI application to process unlabeled dataset. Figure 15.14 depicts a high-level design that uses a saved ML model. The Dataset Generator is responsible for data collection, dataset generation and dataset annotation. Programs that have been implemented in steps 1–3 for these tasks can be reused. The Dataset Classifier is a simple program to load and call a saved ML model to classify an unlabeled dataset. For the stock buying example, the unlabeled dataset is similar to the one shown in Figure 15.11 but for a set of stocks to be analyzed. The classify method in Figure 15.13 illustrates how these can be done. The Result Processor is application dependent. It processes the output from the classifier according to requirements of the application. For the stock buying example, the Result Processor will recommend buying or not-buying a stock according to the outcome of the classify method.

15.11.3 Applying Patterns

Patterns are useful for designing and implementing an AI application because patterns can satisfy various requirements and design objectives. For example, there are fundamental analysis and technical analysis approaches for selecting stocks. While fundamental analysis considers a stock's PE, growth, profit margin, etc., technical analysis only considers the price movements of a stock. As a consequence, the training data for these two types of analysis are different. The abstract factory pattern (Chapter 16) or the factory method pattern (Chapter 17) can be applied to design and implement the Dataset Generator in Figure 15.14 so that it can generate different datasets for different analysis approaches and hide such differences from the client. The template method pattern can be applied to design and implement the Classifier to invoke different ML models for different stock analysis approaches.

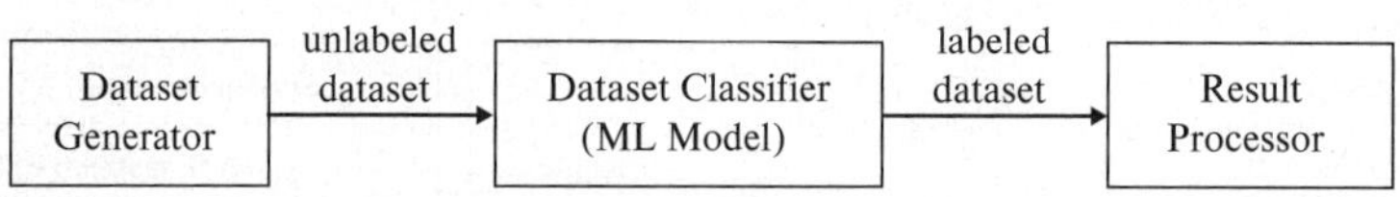

FIGURE 15.14 Overview of an AI application

15.12 SUMMARY

This chapter presents decision tables for specifying and analyzing business rules. It describes two methods for decision table construction, that is, the systematic method and the progressive method. The chapter also defines completeness, consistency, and nonredundancy of a decision table. It presents an algorithm for decision table consolidation. It also describes how to generate code from a decision table and relates a decision table to test-driven development.

Some businesses update their business rules frequently. Traditional approaches require modification to the conditional statements that implement the business rules. This in turn requires compilation, testing, and debugging. These activities usually take considerable time to carry out. The interpreter pattern allows change to the business rules without needing to recompile the software system. The approach presented in this chapter is easy to implement and use.

Finally, the advantages to specifying business rules using a decision table are summarized.

Rule-based systems only work for applications where the rules can be formally specified. Many real-world applications do not meet this requirement. This chapter presents ML to overcome this limitation. First, the basic idea behind ML is presented, followed by a workflow of activities for developing AI applications. Finally, hints for applying patterns to design and implement AI applications are described.

15.13 CHAPTER REVIEW QUESTIONS

1. What is a decision table?
2. What is the systematic decision table construction process?
3. What is progressive decision table construction?
4. What are the desired properties of a decision table?
5. How does one check that a decision table possesses the desired properties?
6. What is the interpreter pattern, and how is it used to implement a decision table?
7. What are the benefits of the interpreter pattern?
8. What is the basic idea behind ML?
9. What is the workflow of activities to develop an AI application?

15.14 EXERCISES

15.1 Perform the following for the business rules of the point-of-sale shipping software presented at the beginning of this chapter:

- **a.** Construct a decision table using the systematic decision table construction method.
- **b.** Consolidate the decision table and check the completeness, consistency, and nonredundancy of the result. Correct any errors, if any.
- **c.** Generate code from the consolidated, error-free decision table.

15.2 Do the following for the progressive decision table construction algorithm presented in this chapter:

- **a.** Construct a decision table for the progressive decision table construction algorithm using the progressive decision table construction method.
- **b.** Check the completeness, consistency, and nonredundancy of the decision table. Correct any errors, if any.
- **c.** Consolidate the error-free decision table and check the completeness, consistency, and nonredundancy of the resulting decision table.

15.3 Write an algorithm for checking the completeness of a decision table. The algorithm must also calculate the rule counts from the indifferences.

15.4 Convert your decision table completeness-checking algorithm into a decision table. Check the completeness, consistency, and nonredundancy of the decision table. Correct any errors.

15.5 Construct a decision table from the admission criteria described below. In addition, check the completeness, consistency, and nonredundancy of the decision table.

The computer science (CS) department of a university uses a set of admission criteria to process applications to its graduate program. Applications that clearly satisfy all the admission criteria are classified as accept. Applications that do not satisfy, or barely satisfy, the criteria are classified as reject. The remaining applications are marked as "pending investigation." Applicants must have paid the application fee. The admission criteria are the following:

- **a.** A four-year undergraduate degree in a technical area.
- **b.** A 3.2 grade point average (GPA) or higher on a 4.0 scale on the last two years of undergraduate course work.
- **c.** Relevance of the student's degree (background) to the curriculum. The ranking is high, average, and low.
- **d.** Ranking of the undergraduate degree-granting institution. The ranking is high, average, and low.
- **e.** A sum of verbal and quantitative scores of 1,150 or higher on the GRE and
  - i. GRE quantitative score $\geq$ 700
  - ii. GRE verbal score $\geq$ 400
- **f.** International applicants must have a test of English as a Foreign Language (TOEFL) score of $\geq$ 90 on the iBT, or a score $\geq$ 7.0 on the International English Language Testing System (IELTS).

15.6 Produce a grammar for the business rules you produce in exercise 15.5.

15.7 Construct a class diagram to represent the business rule grammar you produced in exercise 15.6. Show with UML notes how each of the classes implements its functions to interpret the semantics of the class.

15.8 Design a rule-based framework that allows the rules to change on the fly. That is, the rules can be stored in a text file and loaded into the memory when the system starts. The user can modify the rules by changing the text file. After modification, the user can reload the rules without having to restart the system. Produce a design class diagram to show the rule-based framework. Indicate the design patterns applied. Implement and demonstrate the rule-based framework.

15.9 Download and install the Weka open-source machine learning software. Learn to use the GUI mode to generate a decision tree using the J48 classifier from the weather.nominal.arff dataset, which is in the data folder under the Weka home directory.

part V

Applying Situation-Specific Patterns

16

Chapter

Applying Patterns to Design a State Diagram Editor

Key Takeaway Points

- Applying situation-specific patterns during the design process. Begin with the design problems encountered, select the right patterns, and apply them correctly.
- The pattern specifications are useful for verifying and validating designs that apply patterns, that is, ensuring that the right patterns are applied and applied correctly.

Chapter 10 presents the controller, expert, and creator patterns. These are three of the GRASP patterns. They can be applied to almost all software systems. Unlike GRASP patterns, the other patterns presented in this book are situation-specific patterns. That is, each solves a specific class of design problems. This is the key to understanding and applying these patterns. The patterns are also called the Gang of Four (GoF) patterns because the book [Gamma 1995] that was the first to publish them has four authors. The authors classified the situation-specific patterns into the following three categories:

Creational Patterns. Patterns in this category include abstract factory, builder, factory method, prototype, and singleton. They are concerned with the creation of objects to satisfy specific and various design objectives.

Structural Patterns. Patterns in this category include adapter, bridge, composite, decorator, facade, flyweight, and proxy. They are concerned with the representation and manipulation of class structures for different situations and design considerations.

Behavioral Patterns. Patterns in this category include chain of responsibility, command, interpreter, iterator, mediator, memento, observer, state, strategy, template method, and visitor. They are concerned with request processing, object behavior, communication and interaction, state behavior, dynamic update of business logic, algorithmic as well as other behavioral aspects of a design.

Applying situation-specific patterns to produce a good design is a challenging process. This is because patterns are abstractions of solutions to commonly encountered design problems. "Abstraction" means that patterns are described abstractly so they can be applied to solve different design problems. This is an advantage of patterns. However, the abstract descriptions of patterns make them difficult to understand and apply. Therefore, this chapter presents a problem-directed approach for applying patterns. That is, patterns are applied to solve design problems encountered during the design process, not for the sake of applying patterns. The design of a state diagram editor is used as the case study to introduce the patterns. The case study also helps to illustrate how the problem-directed approach applies the patterns. More specifically, the patterns solve the following state diagram editor design problems:

1. *Working with complex structures.* These design problems concern the representation, analysis, and manipulation of complex class structures.
2. *Creating and constructing complex objects.* These design problems concern how to construct objects that require a nontrivial construction process as well as use different families of products.
3. *Solving user interface design problems.* These design problems focus on commonly encountered user interface design problems, that is, problems related to working with a window system, keeping track of user interface states, decorating user interface widgets, and providing context-dependent help.

These are used to organize the presentation and illustrate how patterns are applied together to solve related design problems. However, the patterns are not limited to solving problems of only one of the above categories. As a matter of fact, each pattern can be applied to solve different categories of design problems. For example, some of the patterns presented in this chapter solve problems encountered during software maintenance, that is, how to modify an existing software system to enhance its functionality for ease of maintenance. Through the study of this chapter, you will learn the following:

- Techniques used by patterns.
- A problem-directed process for applying situation-specific patterns.
- A subset of situation-specific patterns.
- How to apply the process and patterns to the design of a state diagram editor.
- How to generate skeleton code to implement the patterns.

16.1 TECHNIQUES USED BY PATTERNS

The GoF patterns use a number of techniques to accomplish their design objectives. A good understanding of these techniques is essential for learning patterns. The techniques are:

- Program to an interface, not to an implementation
- Use polymorphism to provide behavioral variations
- Favor composition over inheritance
- Use delegation to support object composition

16.1.1 Program to an Interface

An interface specifies a collection of abstract operations and defines the service for all implementing classes. Program to an interface means variables should be declared to be an interface type, not an implementing class type. A variable of an interface type can refer to an object of any of the implementing classes. This accomplishes object polymorphism and dynamic binding. On the other hand, a variable of an implementing class type can only refer to objects of that class. This results in static binding.

16.1.2 Use Polymorphism to Provide Behavioral Variations

Polymorphism means one thing can assume different forms. There are function polymorphism and object polymorphism. Function polymorphism means functions with the same name but different signatures implement different functionalities. Object polymorphism means that a variable declared to be a parent class type or interface type can refer to an object of any of the subclasses. Because the subclasses implement different behaviors, changing the reference changes the behavior. Most of the GoF patterns (about 20 out of 23) use object polymorphism to provide behavioral variations.

EXAMPLE 16.1 How to use different sorting algorithms in different situations?

Solution: Assume that an application can selectively apply bubble sort, quick sort, and bin sort to sort a collection of numbers. The size of the collection and the characteristics of the elements determine which algorithm to apply. Figure 16.1 shows a design that uses polymorphism to provide behavioral variations. In this design, the sorting behavior is provided by three sorting algorithms. It also uses programming to an interface, that is, the sorter variable is declared to be of the Sorter interface type, not of any of the Bubble, Quick or Bin subclasses. This allows the sorter variable to refer to objects of any of the three subclasses, effectively achieving behavioral variations.

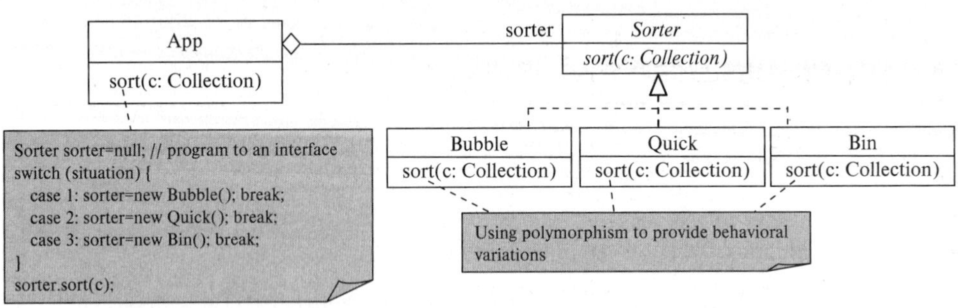

FIGURE 16.1 Use polymorphism to provide behavioral variations

16.1.3 Favor Composition over Inheritance

Inheritance increases reuse, that is, a child class can reuse the methods implemented by the parent class. Beside inheritance, one can also use composition to reuse the methods implemented by a class. These two approaches have pros and cons. Design patterns favor composition over inheritance because composition offers a number of benefits. The following example illustrates the differences.

EXAMPLE 16.2

A vending machine has a vending item dispenser, which also keeps track of the quantities of the vending items. Produce two designs that use inheritance and composition, respectively.

Solution: Figure 16.2(*a*) shows a design that uses inheritance, that is, the item dispenser is a subclass of a hash table. Therefore, the item dispenser inherits or reuses all the methods of a hash table. This design implies static binding, meaning that the dispenser is known to be a hash table at compile time. This binding cannot be changed during run time. Figure 16.2(*b*) shows a design that uses composition, that is, the item dispenser uses a collection to hold the vending items. Note that Collection is written in italic font in Figure 16.2(*b*). This means that it is an interface, which is a Java API. This design implies dynamic binding, meaning that the item dispenser can use any of the classes that implement the collection interface. Moreover, it can change to use a different implementing class at run time.

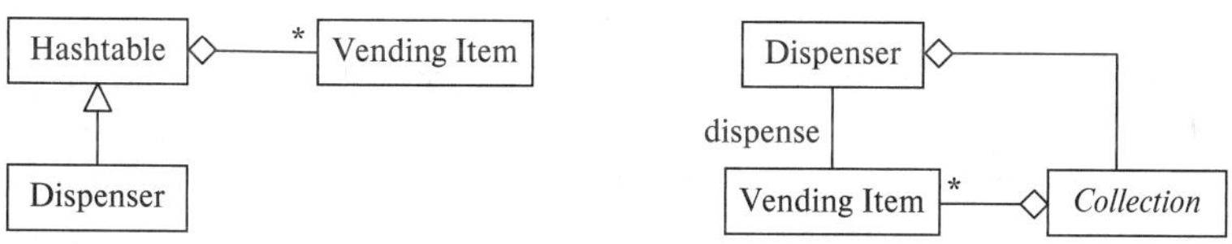

(a) Using inheritance - static binding
Dispenser cannot be other type of collection

(b) Using composition - dynamic binding
Dispenser can use any of the classes that implement the collection interface

FIGURE 16.2 Favor composition over inheritance

Composition offers a number of advantages over inheritance. First, composition can use any of the classes that implement the common interface whereas inheritance is restricted to reuse only the parent class. Second, composition is regarded as black-box reuse because it cannot override the implementation of the class that is reused. On the other hand, inheritance is considered white-box reuse because a subclass can override the implementation of the parent class. This implies the third difference, that is, inheritance breaks encapsulation while composition keeps encapsulation. Fourth, in an inheritance hierarchy, methods of a class are inherited by all of its descendants. This causes the so-called change impact propagation, meaning that changes to a method of the class affect all of its descendants. Such change impact is limited when using composition. Fifth, using composition, the aggregate class is not dependent on the data structure used by the component class thanks to black-box reuse. It is not the case for inheritance–a subclass may have to use the data structure implemented by the parent class. Finally, using inheritance, a subclass can override a method of the parent class. This can be accomplished in composition as well. That is, one can define a subclass of the component class and override methods of the component class in the subclass, then reuse the subclass instead of the component class.

16.1.4 Use Delegation to Support Composition

In Figure 16.1, the App class has a sort method, which a client object can invoke to sort a collection of elements. The UML note attached to that sort method shows how the method is implemented. The last statement of the UML note is sorter.sort(c), which means that the App class calls one of the concrete classes that implement the three sorting algorithms to sort. This is the so-called delegation mechanism. In other words, delegation is passing a request or part of it to one or more other classes. The advantage of doing so is information hiding–the client does not know that it is not the App object performs the sorting, it does not know which of the sorting subclasses sorts the elements. Because of information hiding, the client will not be affected when changes to the sorting subclasses take place. For example, the design allows more sorting algorithms to be added, or an existing algorithm to be removed. Delegation is often confused with function call. Delegation surely needs to call a function, but a function call is not necessarily a delegation.

16.2 PROCESS FOR APPLYING PATTERNS

Patterns to a software engineer are like tools to a carpenter. Both are designed to solve specific problems. To drill a hole, a carpenter uses a drill. Although a drill can also be used to hammer a nail, it is not designed for that purpose. Patterns are similar; each pattern solves a specific class of software design problems. The application of patterns should begin with the design problem encountered during the design process. The problem is used to identify a pattern that can solve the problem. Thus, pattern application is *problem-directed*. The opposite is the *pattern-directed* approach. That is, one wants to apply a pattern and looks for a problem to apply. This is similar to a carpenter's apprentice who acquires a new drill and wants to do something with it. The apprentice finds a loose nail and uses the drill to hammer the nail. Although the problem is fixed, the tool has been misused. Similarly, one can misuse patterns. That a pattern is applied in a design does not necessarily mean that the right pattern is applied and applied correctly. This remains true even if the implementation produces the correct result. Thus, the judgment should be whether the problem is solved by applying the right pattern correctly. These are *verification* and *validation* of pattern application. That is, "is the right pattern being applied," and "is the pattern applied correctly?"

This section presents a problem-directed process for applying situation-specific patterns. The process is explained as follows. The steps of the process are demonstrated throughout the rest of the chapter along with the presentation and application of the patterns.

Step 1. If a design problem is encountered

This step performs the design activities such as architectural design, object interaction modeling, state modeling, activity modeling, or deriving design class diagram as usual. If a design problem appears or some design idea is needed, then patterns are identified and applied to solve the design problem. How do you know that you encounter a design problem? You encounter a design problem if (1) you are not happy with your existing design because it is complex or has some potential problems such as difficulty to implement, change or test; (2) you feel that your design can be improved but you just don't know how; or (3) you scratch your head trying to find a solution for doing something. Anything similar to these indicates that you have a design problem. For example, during architectural design or object interaction modeling, the team recognizes that letting the controller access the database has potential problems such as tight coupling between the controller and the database, and overloading the controller with database access functions. Thus, a design problem emerges: how to avoid tight coupling between the controller and the physical database. Once the design problem is identified, the process continues with the following step.

Step 2. Search for patterns to solve the design problem

This step identifies patterns to solve the design problem. It involves the following three steps:

- First, reformulate the design problem to suppress detail and specifics. This helps look up the patterns. It should result in an abstract, or general formulation of the design problem. Sometimes, it is useful to summarize the design problem with a couple of keywords that precisely characterize the design problem.
- Second, use the reformulated design problem to look up patterns shown in Figure 16.3, which is a summary of the design problems solved by the patterns. In particular, search the second column of Figure 16.3 for patterns that can solve the design problem.
- The third step verifies that the selected pattern is the right one to apply, that is, the specification of the pattern is examined to ensure that it solves the design problem.

Step 3. Apply the selected patterns

In this step, the selected patterns are applied to the existing design. This is similar to the substitution operation in mathematics, where you replace variables of a formula with values to obtain a result. In pattern application, you view each pattern as a design template or "formula," and the classes in the pattern as "variables." You view the relationships between the pattern classes as the operators that connect the operands. To apply a pattern, you replace the pattern classes with classes in the existing design. In particular, you do the following. First, map the client class in the pattern to a class in the existing design. Second, map the other pattern classes beginning with the class that is accessed by the client class. If a pattern class does not have a counterpart in the existing design, then introduce a new class. Third, replace the generically named pattern classes and operations with their counterparts in the existing design. If a pattern class does not have a counterpart, then introduce it to the existing design and rename the class and its operations with application meaningful names, also taking into account its role in the pattern. Finally, change the behavioral design according to the pattern specification.

Abstract factory	You want to create objects of different families and hide from the client which family of objects is created.
Adapter	You want to convert one interface to another.
Bridge	You want to maintain a stable client interface while the implementation changes.
Builder	You want the flexibility to use different processes and different ways to perform the steps of a process.
Chain of responsibility	You want to process requests with request handlers but the exact handler to process a request is unknown in advance.
Command	You want to execute various operations in flexible ways including queuing, scheduling, undoing, and redoing operations.
Composite	You want a representation and a uniform interface to process objects of classes that exhibit recursive, part-whole relationships.
Decorator	You want to add functionalities to objects as well as removing them dynamically.
Facade	You want to simplify the client interface to interact with a web of components.
Factory method	You want to dynamically change the products created.
Flyweight	You want an economical way to create numerous occurrences of an object.
Interpreter	You want to process rules that need to modify frequently and quickly on the fly.
Iterator	You want a traversal mechanism that hides the underlying data structure.
Mediator	You want to decouple objects that interact with each other in a complex manner.
Memento	You want to store and restore state of an object and allow only the object to access the stored state.
Observer	You want to decouple event handlers from an event source so that you can add or remove handlers dynamically.
Prototype	You want to reduce number of classes, reusing copies of an object to avoid object creation cost, or using a dynamically loaded class.
Proxy	You want remote access, delayed access, controlled access, or keeping track of accesses to an object.
Singleton	You want to create at most one, or a limited number of, globally accessible instances of a class.
State	You want a low-complexity design to implement a state diagram.
Strategy	You want to selectively apply algorithms that implement the same functionality but differ in nonfunctional aspects (e.g., memory usage or performance).
Template method	You want to use different implementations of steps of a process or algorithm.
Visitor	You want to decouple type-dependent operations from their respective classes (to achieve high cohesion and designing "stupid objects").

FIGURE 16.3 Problems solved by situation-specific patterns

Step 4. Review the resulting design

In this step, the design is checked to ensure that the pattern is applied correctly and the design problem is solved. Moreover, the design indeed exhibits the benefits of the pattern and the liabilities are addressed.

16.3 CASE STUDY: STATE DIAGRAM EDITOR

This section presents a case study to use throughout the chapter—the design of a state diagram editor. For simplicity, the initial version of the editor can draw only flat state diagrams. A flat state diagram is one in which all states are atomic. That is, the states

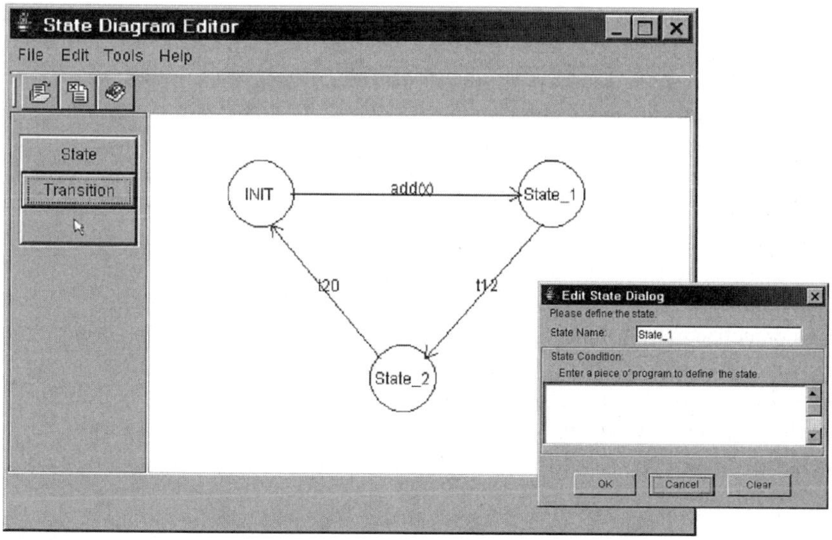

Microsoft

FIGURE 16.4 A state diagram editor

do not contain other states. The overall requirement of the state diagram editor is as follows:

> The state diagram editor shall allow a user to edit a new diagram or an existing diagram. The editor shall allow the user to add, delete, and edit states and transitions as well as undo and redo editing operations. The editor shall allow the user to perform other operations such as saving a diagram.

From the overall requirement, one can derive the *Edit State Diagram* use case, which allows the user to edit a new diagram as well as an existing diagram. Figure 16.4 shows a screen shot of the editor. The editor works as follows. To add a state, the user clicks the State button, the pointer changes to a cross hair. The user clicks anywhere in the drawing area, the editor draws a circle with a dummy state name, for example, State 1. To draw a transition from one state to another, the user clicks the Transition button, presses on the source state, drags to the destination state and releases. The editor draws an arrow line with a dummy transition name from the source state to the destination state. The user double-clicks a state or transition to launch an Edit Dialog to change the properties of the state or transition. According to the controller pattern presented in Chapter 10, the sequence diagram for the Edit State Diagram use case should contain an Edit State Diagram controller. The controller handles user requests such as adding, deleting, or moving, a state or transition, and updating the properties of a state or transition.

16.4 WORKING WITH COMPLEX STRUCTURES

The design of the state diagram editor needs to consider the data structures for representing and manipulating a state diagram in the computer. For example, when the user draws states and transitions, the editor needs to store them in some data structure. Conceptually, a state diagram consists of states and transitions. Therefore, a straight-forward design would define a state diagram as an aggregation of State objects and Transition objects. Moreover, each Transition object has a source state and a destination state. Another design uses an adjacency list. That is, a State Diagram object is an array of State objects, each of which has a reference to an array of outgoing transitions. Each Transition object stores the transition label, a reference to the destination state, and a reference to the next Transition object. These two designs do not consider composite states, that is, states that are state diagrams. Although this version of the editor is limited to flat state diagrams, the *design for change* principle suggests that the design should be easy to extend in the future to support composite states. With this design objective in mind, the design problem is *how to represent state diagrams where a state may contain other states?* In addition to representation, manipulation of complex class structures is also commonly seen in real-world applications. For example, the state diagram editor may need to run analysis algorithms to compute various properties such as the shortest path from one state to another state, the number of incoming and outgoing transitions for each of the states, and so on. The related design issues are *how to traverse a complex class structure, and how to apply analysis algorithms to objects of the class structure?* This section presents patterns that are useful for solving these design problems.

16.4.1 Representing Recursive Whole-Part Structures

As discussed above, the design of the state diagram editor needs to consider composite states. This means that the design has to consider *how to represent complex structures, in which a state object may include other state objects.* Such a design problem is common in software design. For example, a tree consists of nodes and edges, and a node can represent a subtree. A network consists of nodes and subnets. A system consists of subsystems and components, and a subsystem may contain other subsystems or components. The keywords are "recursive, part-whole" relationships. Looking up the patterns in Figure 16.3 finds the *composite* pattern. It is useful for processing complex class structures containing recursive part-whole relationships. The specification of the pattern in Figure 16.5 confirms that it is the right pattern. For example, the structural design shows that the Composite Component is an aggregation of Component. The inheritance relationship indicates that a Component is either a Primitive Component or a Composite Component. Thus, if Composite Component and Primitive Component 1 and 2 are substituted with State Diagram, State, and Transition, respectively, then a state diagram may contain states, transitions, as well as other state diagrams.

Applying Composite Pattern

Now, step 2 has identified the composite pattern to represent a state diagram. Step 3 of the pattern-application process is to apply the composite pattern to the existing design. To do this, we view the classes in the pattern as "variables," which we will replace with classes in the existing design. First, we determine which class in the existing design should substitute for the client class in the pattern, then the class accessed by the client class, and so on. Next, we replace the generically named operations of the pattern classes with operations of the corresponding classes in the existing design. If a pattern class does not have a counterpart in the existing design, then introduce it as a new class. Finally, add the relationships in the pattern into the existing design.

Name	Composite
Type	GoF/Structural
Specification	
Problem	How to represent recursive, part-whole relationships and allow the client to deal with primitive and composite components uniformly.
Solution	Define a common interface to unify the primitive and composite components so that the client can access them uniformly.
Design	
Structural	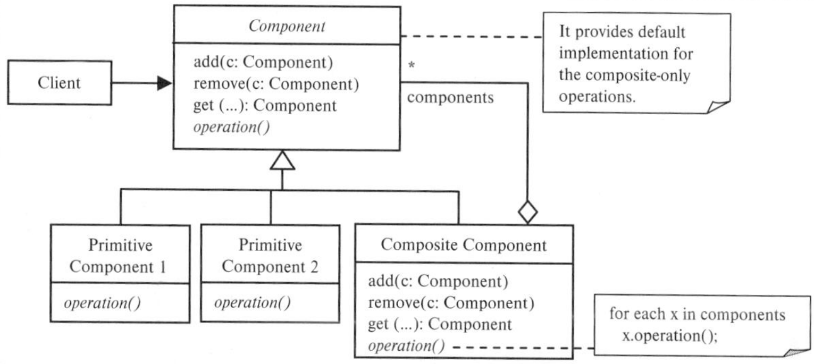
Behavioral	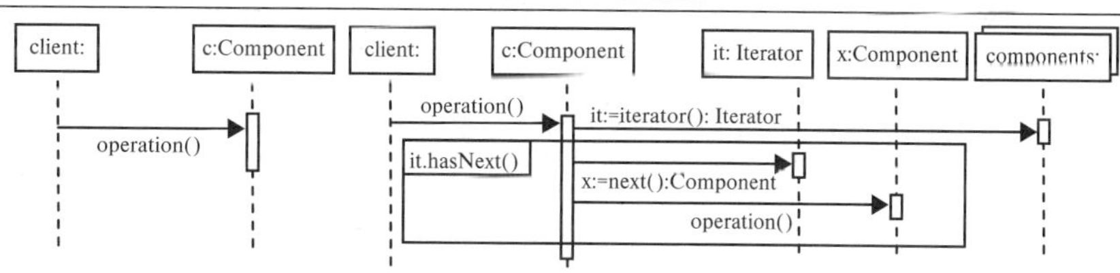 (a) c is a primitive component (b) c is a composite component
Roles and Responsibilities	• Component: It defines an interface for the client to access the composite as well as primitive components uniformly. It provides a default, do-nothing implementation for the composite-only operations such as add, remove and get. • Composite Component: It contains primitive and composite components and implements the composite-only operations. • Primitive Components: These components do not contain other components. They implement operation() to provide component-specific behavior. • Client: It creates, or obtains an instance of a subclass of Component and calls its functions.
Benefits	• It is useful for representing and manipulating complex class structures that exhibit recursive, whole-part relationships. • It provides a uniform interface for accessing and manipulating primitive as well as composite components. • It is easy to add a primitive or composite class. Simply add a subclass to Component.
Liabilities	The composite pattern requires the client to ensure that integrity constraints are not violated. For example, if the client removes a primitive component, it must also remove all of its relationships to other components.
Guidelines	• Use a collection of type Component to store primitive as well as composite components. • For each composite subclass, use only one collection to store all of its components; not one collection for each type of component!
Related Patterns	• Abstract Factory can create components of different types. • Strategy and Visitor are useful patterns for processing composite and primitive components. • Iterator can hide the underlying data structure used to store the components of a composite.
Uses	Applications that need to represent and process complex structures can benefit from Composite.

FIGURE 16.5 Specification of the composite pattern

EXAMPLE 16.3

Apply the composite pattern to the state diagram editor design.

Solution: First, we identify the client class in the editor design. As Figure 16.3 suggests, the client class invokes functions of the composite pattern, which represents a state diagram and its components. When editing a state diagram, the editor GUI receives user requests such as adding or deleting a state or transition. The GUI forwards such requests to the edit diagram controller, which updates the state diagram. Therefore, the edit diagram controller in the existing design should be the client class. Next, we map the other pattern classes to classes in the existing design. Figure 16.6 shows the mapping, where abstract classes and abstract operations are shown in italic font. Finally, the pattern classes and operations are renamed according to the mapping and the relationships in the composite pattern are added. The result is shown in Figure 16.7.

Class or Interface in Composite Pattern	Class or Interface in Existing Design
Client	Edit Diagram Controller
Component *operation()*	*DiagramElem* (new interface) *draw(g: Graphics)*
Primitive Component 1 operation()	State draw(g: Graphics)
Primitive Component 2 operation()	Transition draw(g: Graphics)
Composite Component operation()	State Diagram draw(g: Graphics) add(e:DiagramElem) remove (e: DiagramElem)

FIGURE 16.6 Mapping pattern classes to classes in existing state diagram editor design

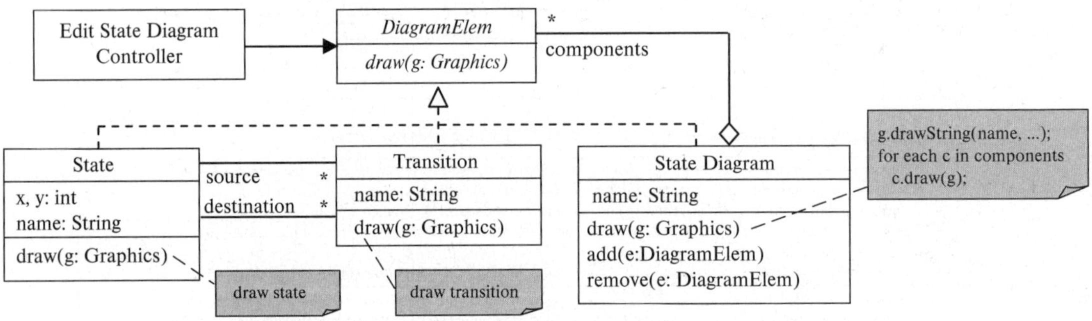

FIGURE 16.7 Part of state diagram editor design after applying composite pattern

Benefits and Liabilities of the Composite Pattern

Applying the composite pattern brings the following advantages to the design of the editor:

- It lets the editor store and process state diagrams, states, and transitions using one interface. The representation supports *recursive, whole-part* relationships.
- It provides a single, uniform interface for the controller to access the diagram elements. It hides the type of the diagram element from the controller; the controller does not need to know whether it is working with a primitive or composite component.
- It is easy to extend the editor to support other types of UML diagrams. Simply add the diagrams as composite diagram elements and their modeling concepts as primitive diagram elements.

The application of the composite pattern requires the controller to ensure the integrity of a state diagram. For example, when a state is moved or removed, then all the related transitions must be moved or removed accordingly.

16.4.2 Accessing Different Data Structures with Iterator

In Figure 16.7, the draw method of the State Diagram class calls each component of the state diagram to draw itself. This is an application of the expert pattern (Chapter 10). Different data structures can be used to store the components of a state diagram. The design for change principle suggests that the state diagram editor should allow the data structure to change. To satisfy this design objective, we can use the Java collection interface, which comes with a number of Java API classes that implement different data structures. However, if the data structure changes, then the code that accesses the data structure may need to change as well. For example, if the data structure changes from an array list to a hash table, then the code needs to change. So, we have a design problem: how to access elements of a collection while hiding the underlying data structure? Looking up Figure 16.3 finds the iterator pattern, which states "a traversal mechanism that hides the underlying data structure." The specification of the iterator pattern is given in Figure 16.8. The iterator pattern has been implemented as a Java API.

Name	Iterator
Type	GoF/Behavioral
Specification	
Problem	How to access elements of an aggregate without exposing the underlying data structure?
Solution	Define an iterator interface that a client can use to access the elements of an aggregate, and let concrete iterators implement the traversal algorithms for the concrete aggregates.
Design	
Structural	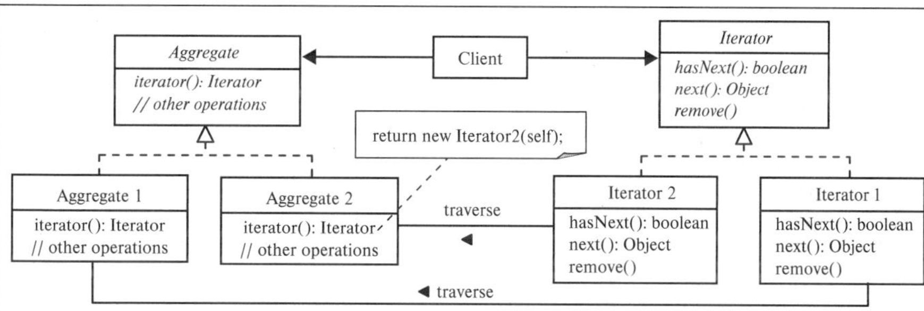
Behavioral	The concrete iterators implement the following behavior: • hasNext() returns true if there are more elements in the aggregate. • next() returns the next element in the aggregate. • remove() removes the last element returned by the iterator.
Roles and Responsibilities	• Aggregate, Aggregate 1 and Aggregate 2: These are the aggregate interface and concrete aggregates. • Iterator: It defines a common interface that provides operations for the client to access the elements of an aggregate. • Iterator 1 and Iterator 2: These represent the concrete iterators, each of which implements the algorithm to traverse a concrete aggregate. • Client: It invokes the iterator() method of a concrete aggregate to obtain the corresponding concrete iterator. It invokes the operations of the concrete iterator to access the elements of the concrete aggregate.
Benefits	• It hides the underlying data structure of the aggregate. • It supports different traversals of an aggregate (inorder, preorder, postorder). • It is easy to change the traversal at run time. • It is easy to add new traversals. • It simplifies the aggregate by moving the traversal operations to the iterator. • It allows more than one traversal on an aggregate at the same time provided that elements are not removed.
Liabilities	• It may violate encapsulation if the iterator needs to access the private data of the aggregate. • It may access an element twice or miss it completely during insertion into or deletion from the aggregate.
Guidelines	
Related Patterns	• Iterator can be used with Strategy, Visitor and Composite to access varying data structures.
Uses	Enumeration and Iterator of Java implement the iterator pattern.

FIGURE 16.8 Specification of the iterator pattern

Applying Iterator Pattern

EXAMPLE 16.4 Applying the iterator pattern to the design in Figure 16.7 produces the design in Figure 16.9. The Collection interface allows the State Diagram class to use different data structures to store its components. The iterator pattern hides the underlying data structure. This means that changing the concrete collection, e.g., from an array list to a hash table, at run time does not require change to the State Diagram class.

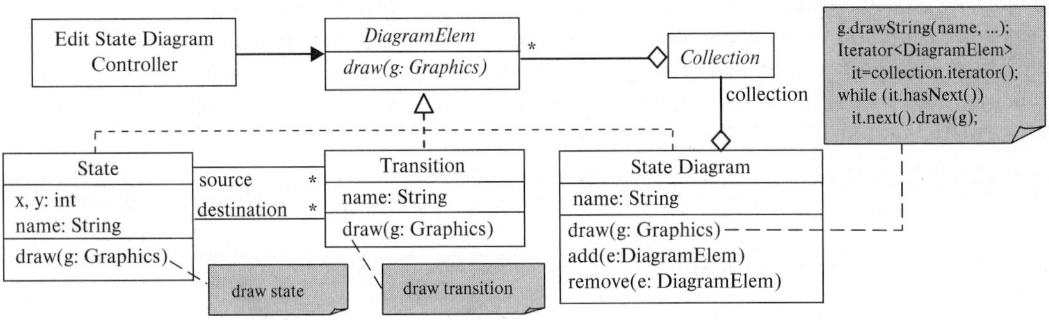

FIGURE 16.9 Applying composite and iterator patterns

Sample Code

EXAMPLE 16.5 Figure 16.10 shows a portion of the Java code that implements the design in Figure 16.9. Note that the State Diagram class uses only one collection to store State and Transition objects, not one collection for each type of object. Using multiple collections to store different types of object is a misuse of the composite pattern; it adds hundreds of lines of code and also uses conditional statements to process the different types of objects. These make the software even more difficult to understand, test and maintain.

Benefits of the Iterator Pattern

The iterator pattern brings the following benefits to a design:

- Supporting design for change. The iterator pattern hides the underlying data structure. It lets the underlying data structure to change without affect the client. This effectively supports the design for change software design principle.
- Supporting specific data structures. Certain applications require specific, ad hoc and/or evolving data structures. Iterator can hide such data structures from the client so that changes to the data structures will not affect the client.

```
public interface DiagramElem { void draw(Graphics g); }

public class State implements DiagramElem {
  private int x, y; private String name;
  public State(String name, int x, int y)
  { this.name=name; this.x=x; this.y=y; }
  public void draw(Graphics g)
  { g.setColor(Color.BLACK);
   g.drawOval(x, y, 40, 40);
   g.drawString(name, x+10, y+25);}
}

public class Transition implements DiagramElem {
  private String name; private  State source, destination;
  public Transition(String name, State s, State d)
  {  this.name=name;  source=s; destination=d; }
  public void draw(Graphics g) { /* draw a transition */ }
}

public class StateDiagram implements DiagramElem {
  Collection<DiagramElem> components=new
    ArrayList<DiagramElem>();
  public void add (DiagramElem e) { components.add(e); }
  public void remove (DiagramElem e)
  { components.remove(e); }
  public void draw(Graphics g) {
   Iterator<DiagramElem> it=components.iterator();
   while (it.hasNext()) { it.next().draw(g); }
  }
}

public class EditDiagramController {
  private static final int NONE=0, STATE=1, TRANS=2;
  private int choice=NONE;
  private StateDiagram diagram=new StateDiagram();
  public void stateBtnClicked() { choice=STATE; }
  public void transBtnClicked() { choice=TRANS; }
  public void canvasClicked(int x, int y) {
    switch (choice) {
      case STATE: State s=new State("state", x, y);
        diagram.add(s); choice=NONE; return;
      case TRANS: choice=NONE;
        // process transition
        return; }
  }
  public DiagramElem getDiagram() { return diagram; }
}
```

```
public class EditDiagramGUI extends JFrame {
  private EditDiagramController controller=
    new EditDiagramController();
  private JButton stateBtn=new JButton("State");
  private JButton transBtn=new JButton("Transition");
  private Canvas canvas=new Canvas();
  public EditDiagramGUI() {
    stateBtn.addActionListener(new ActionListener()
    { public void actionPerformed(ActionEvent e) {
        controller.stateBtnClicked(); }});
    canvas.addMouseListener(new MouseAdapter() {
      public void mousePressed(MouseEvent e) {
        int x=(int)e.getPoint().getX();
        int y=(int)e.getPoint().getY();
        controller.canvasClicked(x, y);
        canvas.setDiagram(controller.getDiagram());
        canvas.repaint();
      }
    });
    JPanel contentPane = (JPanel) getContentPane();
    contentPane.setLayout(new BorderLayout());
    canvas.setVisible(true);
    JPanel jPanel1=new JPanel();
    jPanel1.setPreferredSize(new Dimension(100, 200));
    jPanel1.add(stateBtn);
    jPanel1.add(transBtn);
    contentPane.add(canvas, BorderLayout.CENTER);
    contentPane.add(jPanel1, BorderLayout.WEST);
    setDefaultCloseOperation(EXIT_ON_CLOSE);
  }
  public static void main(String[] args) {
    EditDiagramGUI gui=new EditDiagramGUI();
    gui.setPreferredSize(new Dimension(800, 600));
    gui.setLocation(300, 300);
    gui.pack();
    gui.setVisible(true); }

class Canvas extends JPanel {
  private DiagramElem diagram;
  public Canvas() { super();
    setBackground(Color.WHITE); }
  public void setDiagram(DiagramElem d)
  { diagram=d; }
  public void paintComponent(Graphics g) {
    super.paintComponent(g);
    if (diagram!=null) diagram.draw(g); }
}}
```

FIGURE 16.10 Part of Java code that implements the design in Figure 16.9

16.4.3 Choosing Algorithms with Strategy

The state diagram editor should beautify a state diagram to please the eye. This requires the use of a layout algorithm. Many layout algorithms exist for computing a layout for a graph. These are applicable to state diagrams. The algorithms differ in layout quality, speed, and other aspects. The editor should allow the user to choose the layout algorithm. Design problems similar to this includes circuit layout, network routing, choosing discount policies, where algorithms to perform each of these tasks differ in nonfunctional aspects. Another example is printing a report. The print dialog usually provides various options for the user to choose including normal printing, best-quality printing. The keywords to look up the pattern to apply are "selectable algorithms," which find the *strategy* pattern. The specification of the strategy pattern is shown in Figure 16.11, which confirms that the pattern indeed solves the design problem.

<table>
<tr><td>Name</td><td>Strategy</td></tr>
<tr><td>Type</td><td>GoF/Behavioral</td></tr>
<tr><td>Specification</td><td></td></tr>
<tr><td>Problem</td><td>How to selectively apply interchangeable algorithms that implement the same functionality but differ in nonfunctional aspects.</td></tr>
<tr><td>Solution</td><td>Define an abstract class as the common interface to make the algorithms interchangeable. The client can choose the algorithm and delegate the work to the selected algorithm.</td></tr>
<tr><td>Design</td><td></td></tr>
<tr><td>Structural</td><td>
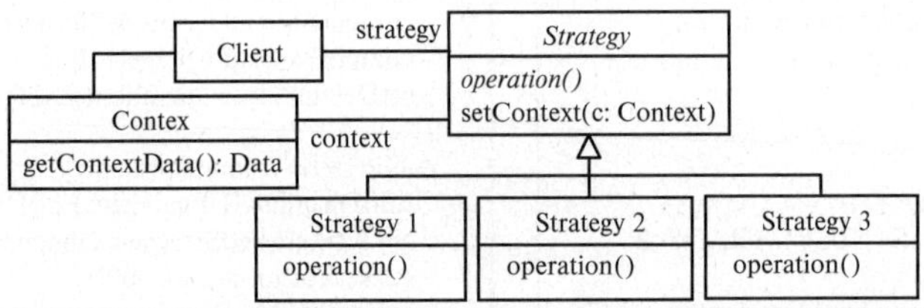

</td></tr>
<tr><td>Behavioral</td><td>
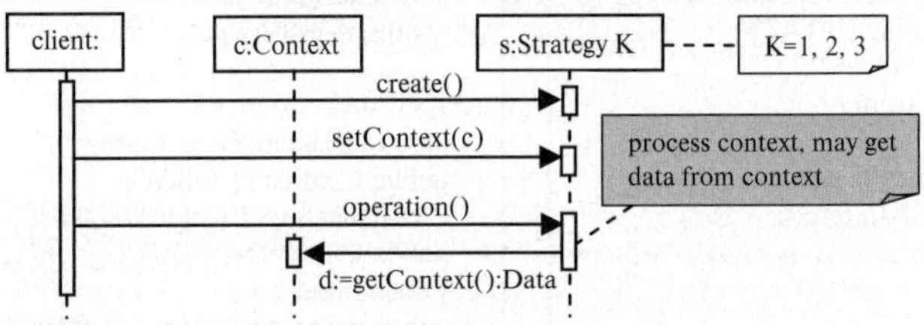

</td></tr>
<tr><td>Roles and Responsibilities</td><td>• Context: It represents what a concrete strategy processes.
• Strategy: It is an abstract class and defines a common interface to make the concrete strategies interchangeable.
• Strategies 1-3: These are the concrete strategies.
• Client: It selects the concrete strategy and invokes its operation to perform the task.</td></tr>
<tr><td>Benefits</td><td>• It facilitates the selection of algorithms.
• Compared to using conditional statements to select the algorithms, strategy makes the software easy to understand, implement, test and maintain.
• It is easy to add or remove strategies - simply add or remove Strategy subclasses.</td></tr>
<tr><td>Liabilities</td><td>• The client must know the available concrete strategies and how to select them.
• It may break encapsulation because a concrete strategy may need to access the data structure of the context.</td></tr>
<tr><td>Guidelines</td><td></td></tr>
<tr><td>Related Patterns</td><td>All of strategy, proxy, visitor, and decorator add functionality to existing objects but they fulfill different design objectives.</td></tr>
<tr><td>Uses</td><td>It is useful for applications that need to selectively apply algorithms in different circumstances.</td></tr>
</table>

FIGURE 16.11 Specification of the strategy pattern

Applying the Strategy Pattern

EXAMPLE 16.6

To apply the strategy pattern to the existing design, we first determine the mapping of the pattern classes to classes in the existing design. We examine the structural design and behavioral design of the strategy pattern shown in Figure 16.11. We find that the client invokes the strategies to operate on the context. To beautify a state diagram, the user must issue a request by clicking a beautify menu item and selecting from the submenu a layout algorithm. The request will be submitted to the editor GUI, which will invoke the beautify function of the edit diagram controller with the selected algorithm as the parameter. The controller then will invoke the selected layout algorithm to beautify the state diagram. Thus, the client class should be the edit diagram controller. The concrete strategies should be mapped to the layout algorithms, and the context should be mapped to the State Diagram class. Figure 16.12 shows the application of the strategy pattern to the design of the state diagram editor. In particular, Figure 16.12(*a*) shows the participants and their relationships and Figure 16.12(*b*) how the participants collaborate. The figure also shows the mapping between the editor classes and classes of the strategy pattern.

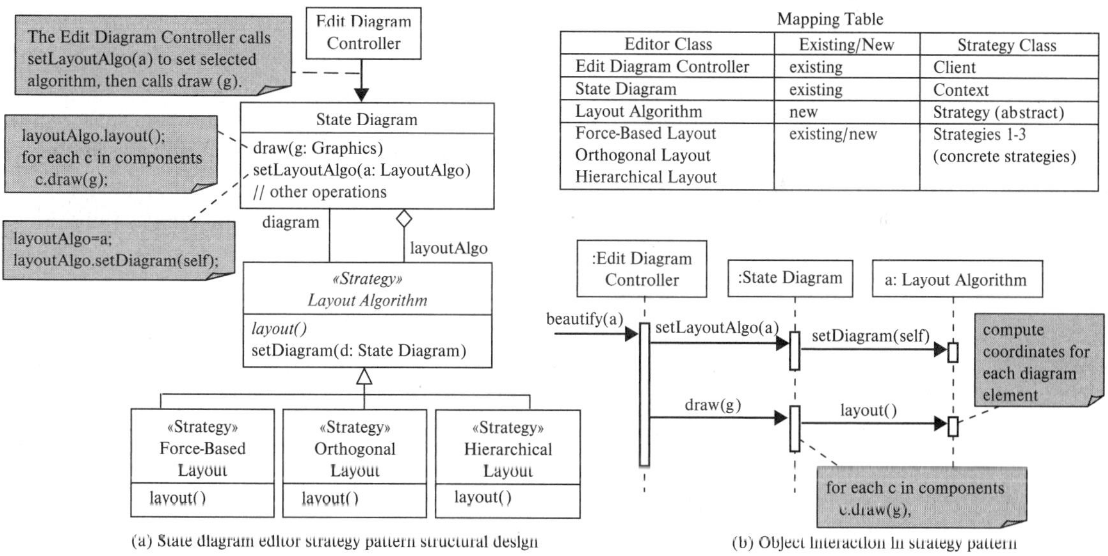

Editor Class	Existing/New	Strategy Class
Edit Diagram Controller	existing	Client
State Diagram	existing	Context
Layout Algorithm	new	Strategy (abstract)
Force-Based Layout Orthogonal Layout Hierarchical Layout	existing/new	Strategies 1-3 (concrete strategies)

FIGURE 16.12 Applying strategy to beautify a state diagram

Benefits of the Strategy Pattern

The strategy pattern brings the following benefits to the design of the state diagram editor:

- Designing "stupid objects." Each of the classes in Figure 16.12 knows how to do only one thing. Moreover, it need not use conditional statements to determine which of the layout algorithms to apply.

- Facilitating software reuse. The design in Figure 16.12 can reuse existing implementations of the layout algorithms. The adapter pattern can be applied to convert the desired interface to the interfaces of the existing implementations. On the other hand, the implementation of the strategy pattern in Figure 16.12 can be reused by other applications to layout other types of diagram.
- It is easy to add new layout algorithms–simply add strategy subclasses that implement the new layout algorithms.

16.4.4 Applying Type-Dependent Operations with Visitor

The state diagram editor may provide analysis capabilities such as reachability analysis and dead-state detection. Reachability analysis checks if every state is reachable from an initial state. A dead state is one that once the state machine enters the state, it remains in that state forever. Clearly, these analysis techniques need to analyze states and transitions. Moreover, the analysis performed on states is different from transitions simply because states and transitions are objects of different types. One commonly seen approach to accommodate this is using conditional statements to check the type of the object to be analyzed and perform the type-dependent analysis operation accordingly. Obviously, this increases the complexity of the design and implementation. It makes the code difficult to understand, test and change. Another design problem is which class should be assigned the analysis operations? If they are assigned to the State and Transition classes, then the cohesion of these classes may decrease because the analysis operations do not belong there. Hence, we have two design problems: how to deal with operations that are type dependent, and how to assign such operations to classes? The keyword here is type-dependent operations–how to deal with them and assign them to classes. Looking up Figure 16.3 finds the visitor pattern, which is intended "to decouple type-dependent operations from their respective classes." Figure 16.13 shows the specification of the visitor pattern.

Applying Visitor Pattern

The visitor pattern is useful for applying type-dependent operations on classes, usually in a class structure. There are numerous real applications. For example, visitor is often used with interpreter (Chapter 15) to provide different interpretations of the different types of expression. Another real-world application is using visitor to analyze bytecode for various purposes such as detecting malicious apps. There are 256 different bytecode instructions, which must be analyzed differently. If the instructions are treated as classes, then visitor can be apply to process the instructions differently.

In general, if a design needs to apply m type-dependent operations f1, f2, ..., fm to n classes C1, C2, ..., Cn, then one needs to perform the following:

1. Define a visitor interface containing n functions: visit (c: C1), visit (c: C2), ..., visit (c: Cn), that is, one for each type of object to be analyzed.
2. Define and implement m concrete visitors, that is, one for each type-dependent operation. Each concrete visitor implements visit (c: Ci) functions according to how the corresponding operation processes objects of Ci, i=1, 2, ..., n.

Name	Visitor
Type	GoF/Behavior
Specification	
Problem	How to decouple type-dependent operations from a class structure to achieve high cohesion and designing "stupid objects?"
Solution	Implement a hierarchy of visitor classes to provide type-dependent polymorphic operations. Let the objects of the class structure invoke the polymorphic operations of a concrete visitor.
Design	
Structural	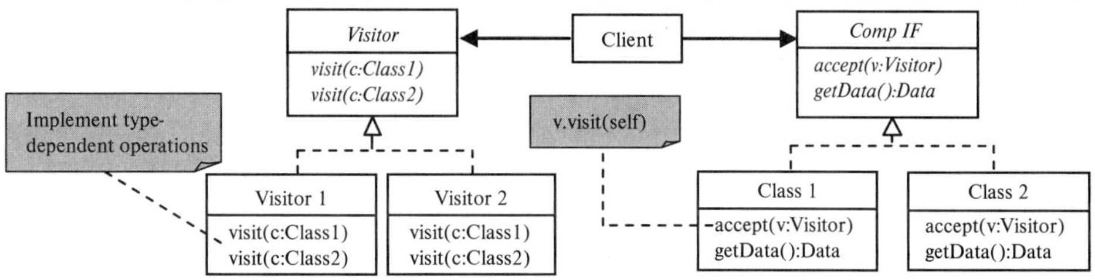
Behavioral	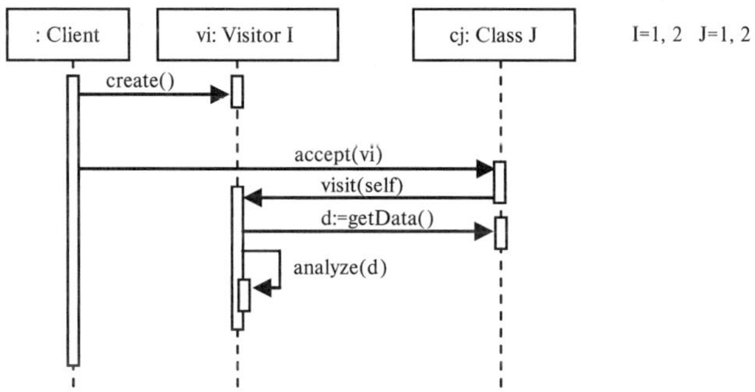
Roles and Responsibilities	• Visitor: This interface defines a polymorphic function visit(c: CJ) for each concrete class CJ in the class structure. • Visitors 1-2: These represent concrete visitors, each of which implements an algorithm or operation that processes different types of object differently because it uses polymorphic functions. • Comp IF: It defines an interface for all classes of the structure to be processed. • Classes 1-2: These concrete classes implement the accept(v: Visitor) methods as v.visit(self). Thus, exactly one of the visit methods of a concrete visitor v is executed. • Client: The client creates a visitor vi and uses it to call the accept(vi) method of each object in the structure.
Benefits	• High cohesion is achieved because each concrete visitor performs only one function. • The concrete visitor classes can be reuse to process other class structures. • It is easy to add concrete visitors. • Visitors can store intermediate results or states while they visit the class structure.
Liabilities	When adding a class CK to the class structure, every visitor needs to add and implement a visit(c: CK) function.
Guidelines	Define and implement separate visitor hierarchies for different class structures that do not have many classes in common.
Related Patterns	• Visitor and Iterator are often used together. The concrete iterator lets the concrete visitor visit each object in the structure. • Visitors can be singletons.
Uses	

FIGURE 16.13 Specification of the visitor pattern

3. Define an interface with an accept (v: Visitor) function and make the n classes implement this interface. The implementation is the same for all of the classes, that is, accept (v: Visitor) { v.visit (self); }, where "self" is a UML reserved word to mean the object itself, it is the same as "this" in C++ or Java.
4. To apply a type-dependent operation, create an object of the corresponding concrete visitor and use it to call the accept (v: Visitor) function of each object to be analyzed.

EXAMPLE 16.7 Perform reachability analysis on a state diagram as well as counting the number of states and transitions, respectively.

Solution: For simplicity, we assume that a state S is reachable if there is a directed path from an initial state to S. We do not consider guard conditions, which may prevent a transition from happening if it is evaluated to false. To apply the visitor pattern, we first define a visitor interface with two polymorphic functions, visit (s: State) and visit (t: Transition), because there are two types of object to analyze. Second, because there are two analysis functions, we define two concrete visitors, one for reachability analysis, and the other for counting the number of states and transitions. These concrete visitors are named RA and STC. Third, for each of the concrete visitors, we implement the two polymorphic functions according to how the analysis function processes states and transitions. For example, the STC visitor can store the state count and transition count in two integer attributes and increment the respective attribute when a state or transition is visited. Finally, we add accept (v: Visitor) to the DiagramElem interface and implement this in the State, Transition, and State Diagram classes. Alternatively, we could define a new interface with accept (v: Visitor) as the only function and have the State, Transition, and State Diagram classes implement this interface. In either case, the implementation for the State Diagram class is simply doing nothing, and the implementations for the State and Transition classes are the same and simply call the visit method of the visitor v passing the State or Transition object as the parameter. Figure 16.14 shows the resulting design. How the RA visitor works is detailed in the next example.

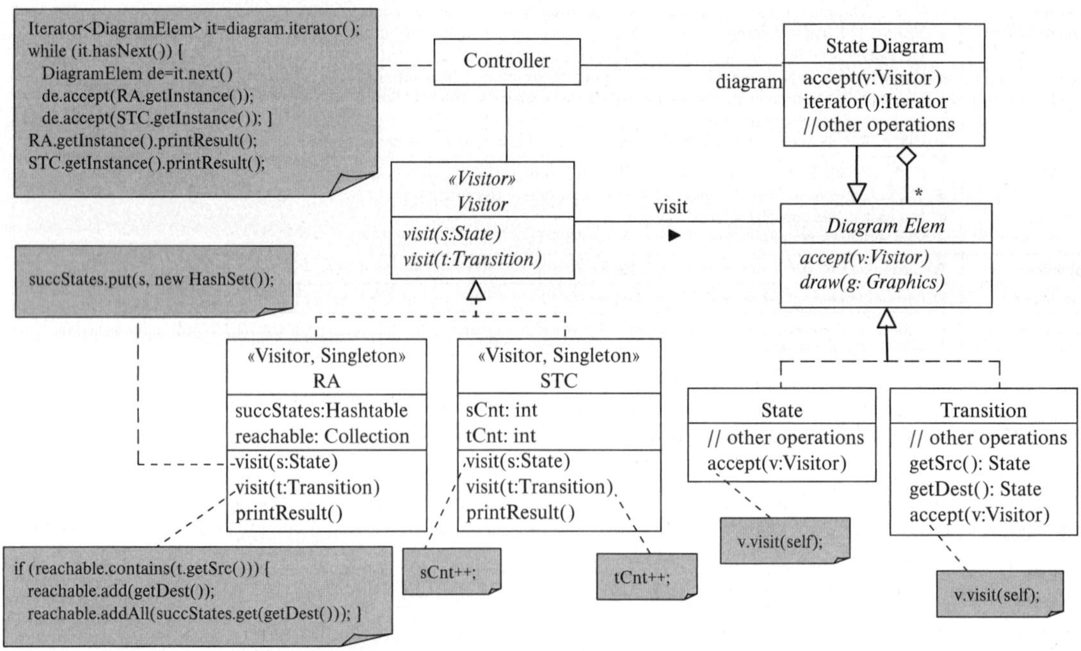

FIGURE 16.14 Applying visitor to analyze a state diagram

Sample Code

EXAMPLE 16.8

Figure 16.15 shows the code that implements the design in Figure 16.14. To save space, the package statements and import statements are omitted. The behaviors of the visit methods for the STC have been described in Example 16.7. It is not repeated here. The reachability analyzer maintains a hash table, succStates, to store the direct successor states of each state. Moreover, it uses a collection, called reachable, to store all of the reachable states; initially, it contains the initial state(s). The visit (s: State) method simply adds an entry to succStates with s as the key and a new hash set as the value. The visit (t: Transition) method checks if the source state of t is a reachable state, if so, the destination state of t and its direct successor states are added to the set of reachable states, else the destination state of t is added to the direct successor states of the source state of t.

The concrete visitors are implemented as singletons. To perform the analysis operations, the controller uses an iterator to retrieve every element of the state diagram and calls the accept (v: Visitor) method of that element two times, one with the RA singleton and the other with the STC singleton as the parameter. The accept (v:Visitor) method immediately calls the visit(s: State) or visit(t: Transition) method of the RA and STC singletons, respectively. After each element of a state diagram is visited, the concrete visitors print the results.

Benefits and Liabilities of the Visitor Pattern

The visitor pattern brings the following benefits to a design:

- Separation of concerns. The visitor pattern separates the analysis operations such as reachability analysis and counting states and transitions from the elements of a state diagram, and assigns such operations to the concrete visitors such as the RA and STC.
- High cohesion. The State and Transition classes achieve high cohesion because aggregate operations such as reachability analysis and counting states and transitions are not assigned to these classes. Aggregate operations process elements of a collection to compute a result; examples are compute average and maximum. In addition, the concrete visitors also achieve high cohesion because each of them is assigned only one responsibility.
- Designing "stupid objects." State, Transition, and the concrete visitor classes are assigned only one core functionality–State and Transition draw the respective shapes, and concrete visitors perform respective analysis operations. Moreover, no type checking is used to determine how to analyze a State or Transition object.
- It is easy to add new analysis operations–simply add concrete visitors that implement the new analysis operations.

```
public interface Visitor {
  void visit(State s); void visit(Transition t);
}

public class RA implements Visitor {
  private static RA instance=new RA();
  private Hashtable<State, HashSet> succStates;
  private Collection<State> reachable=new HashSet<State>();
  private RA() {
    succStates=new Hashtable<State, HashSet>(); }
  public static RA getInstance() { return instance; }
  public void visit(State s) {
    if (succStates.get(s)==null)
      succStates.put(s, new HashSet<State> ()); }
  public void visit(Transition t) {
    State src=t.getSrc(); State dest=t.getDest();
    if (reachable.contains(src)) { reachable.add(dest);
      reachable.addAll(succStates.get(dest));
    } else {
      if (succStates.get(src)==null)
        succStates.put(src, new HashSet<State>());
      succStates.get(src).add(dest); }}
  public void setInit(State s) { reachable.add(s); }
  public void printResult() {
    Iterator<State> it=succStates.keySet().iterator();
    while (it.hasNext()) {
      State s=it.next();
      System.out.println(s.getName()+" reachable is "+
        reachable.contains(s)); }
  }
}

public class STC implements Visitor {
  private static STC instance=new STC ();
  private int sCnt, tCnt; private STC () { }
  public static STC getInstance() {return instance; }
  public void visit(State s) { sCnt++; }
  public void visit(Transition t) { tCnt++; }
  public void printResult() {
    System.out.println(sCnt+" states, "+tCnt+" transitions."); }
}
```

```
public interface DiagramElem {
  void draw(Graphics g); void accept(Visitor v); }

public class State implements DiagramElem {
  private int x, y; private String name;
  public State(String name, int x, int y)
  { this.name=name; this.x=x; this.y=y; }
  public void draw(Graphics g)
  { g.setColor(Color.BLACK); g.drawOval(x, y, 40, 40);
    g.drawString(name, x+10, y+25);}
  public void accept(Visitor v) { v.visit(this); }
  public String getName() { return name; }
}

public class Transition implements DiagramElem {
  private String name; private State src, dest;
  public Transition(String name, State s, State d)
  { this.name=name; src=s; dest=d; }
  public void draw(Graphics g) { /* draw a transition */ }
  public State getSrc() { return src; }
  public State getDest() { return dest; }
  public String getName() { return name; }
  public void accept(Visitor v) { v.visit(this); }
}

public class Main {
  static DiagramElem createDiagram() {
    StateDiagram sd=new StateDiagram();
    State s0=new State("s0", 15, 15);
    State s1=new State("s1", 30, 15);
    Transition t0=new Transition("t0", s0, s1);
    sd.add(s0); sd.add(s1); sd.add(t0);
    // add other states and transitions
    RA.getInstance().setInit(s0);
    return sd; }
  public static void main(String[] args) {
    DiagramElem sd=createDiagram();
    Iterator<DiagramElem> it=((StateDiagram)sd).iterator();
    while (it.hasNext()) it.next().accept(RA.getInstance());
    RA.getInstance().printResult(); }
}
```

FIGURE 16.15 Sample code for Figure 16.14

The liabilities of the visitor pattern are:

- Adding new classes to the class structure may require considerable effort to change the concrete visitors unless the number of new classes and the number of concrete visitors are small.
- Breaking encapsulation if concrete visitors require access to the internal data structure of the classes to be analyzed.

16.4.5 Storing and Restoring Object State with Memento

One value-added feature of the state diagram editor is beautifying a state diagram. If the user does not like the result, the editor should allow the user to undo the operation. Besides using the command pattern to support undo and redo, storing and restoring the state of the diagram is a feasible approach. That is, before beautifying a state diagram, the edit controller saves the state of the diagram so that it can be restored per the user's request. Cloning the state diagram is one possible approach to accomplishing this, provided that deep-copying is implemented. However, security of some applications requires that only the object itself can access to the saved state. In this case, cloning is not an option because other objects can access to the saved state. Figure 16.3 shows that the memento pattern is the solution to this design problem. Figure 16.16 gives the specification of the memento pattern.

Name	Memento
Type	GoF/Behavior
Specification	
Problem	How to store and restore state of an object and allow only the object itself to access to the stored state.
Solution	Let the object save its state in a "lockbox" and set the pass code required to access the saved state.
Design	
Structural	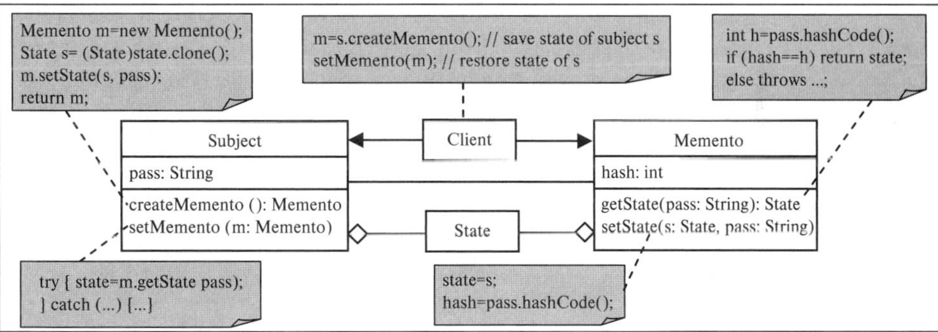
Behavioral	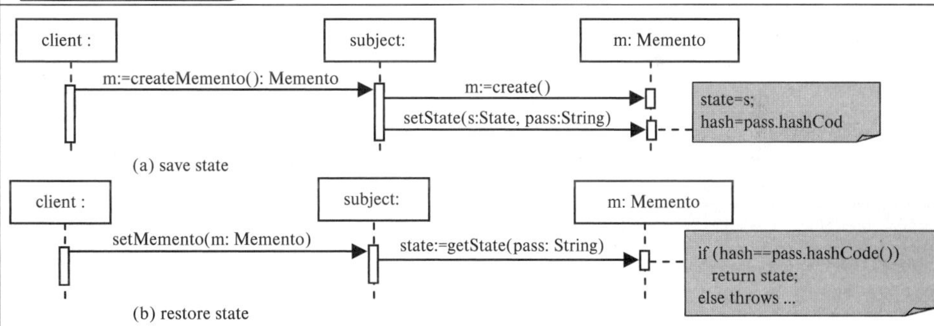
Roles and Responsibilities	• Subject: the object whose state need to save and restore. It saves its state in the "lockbox" and sets the pass code required to get the state back. • Memento: the "lockbox" to store the state of the subject. It saves the hash code of the pass code provided by the subject and uses the hash code to verify and ensure that the stored state is accessed only by the subject itself. • Client: It calls the subject to store and restore its state.
Benefits	• It is useful for saving and restoring states of sensitive object and allows only the object itself to access the saved state. Saving the hash code instead of a security key is more secure because a hash function is a one-way mapping. • Separation of concerns is achieved by moving storing and restoring state functions to the memento. • High cohesion is achieved because the subject can focus on its core functionality. • The memento is a "stupid object" because it does only one thing – storing and restoring the state of an object.
Liabilities	It may incur considerable overhead if a large state is copied between the subject and the memento.
Guidelines	
Related Patterns	Command can use Memento to store the state of an object for undoable operations.
Uses	

FIGURE 16.16 Specification of the memento pattern

Applying the Memento Pattern

EXAMPLE 16.9 Apply the memento pattern to save and restore a state diagram.

Solution: The memento pattern saves and restores the state of an object without exposing it to a third party. In the design in Figure 16.17, the Edit Controller maintains an instance of Memento. The memento stores the state of a state diagram. The intent of the memento pattern is ensuring that the Edit Controller, as the third party, cannot access the diagram state. The pattern achieves this by saving the hash code of a secret pass provided by the state diagram. To restore the original state, the diagram presents the secret pass to the memento. The memento ensures that the secret pass matches the saved pass before returning the saved state. In this way, the design ensures that only the state diagram can access the saved state. The design in Figure 16.17 uses the hashCode () function of the Java String API to generate the hash code from the pass and saves the hash code rather than the pass string. This provides security because a third party must know the original pass string to retrieve the diagram state.

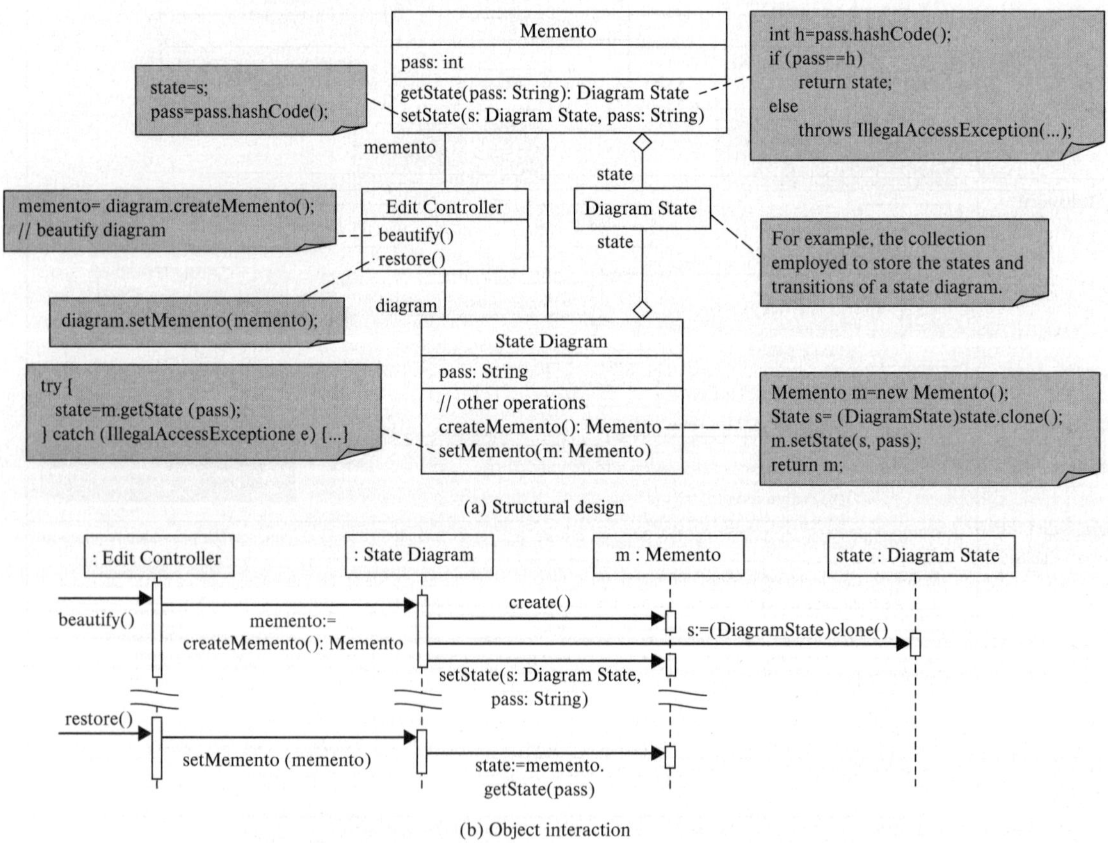

FIGURE 16.17 Storing and restoring state of an object with memento

16.5 OBJECT CREATION FOR DIFFERENT DESIGN OBJECTIVES

Section 16.3 presents patterns for representing and manipulating complex class structures. Sometimes, the application software needs to create such structures. For example, if the user wants to edit an existing state diagram, then the software needs to retrieve the diagram from a database, construct the composite, and call the composite to draw the state diagram. Applying patterns to creating and constructing complex objects is the focus of the next several sections.

16.5.1 Creating Families of Products

There are two versions of UML: UML 1.0 and UML 2.0. Both versions are used in practice. Therefore, it is desirable for the editor to be able to work with diagrams created for either version of UML. One way to provide this is using if-then-else statements. That is, the draw (...) methods in Figure 16.7 checks the UML version that is selected by the user and draws the elements using the notations of the selected version. But this approach is not good because the complexity is high, and maintenance is a nightmare if there are several versions of UML.

Another approach changes the interface of DiagramElem to include drawUML1(...) and drawUML2(...) operations. This approach reduces the complexity but maintenance is still a problem. To add or delete a UML version, each class of the composite must be changed. In the third approach, two versions of the DiagramElem class and its subclasses are defined, that is, UML 1.0 DiagramElem, UML 2.0 DiagramElem, UML 1.0 State Diagram, UML 2.0 State Diagram, and so forth. It is the responsibility of the client to create the State and Transition objects of the required version. Maintenance remains a problem because change to the client is required each time a new version is added or an existing version is removed.

A better design is based on the observation that once the user selects a version, all the diagram elements will be created for that version. That is, the selected version becomes the default until the user selects a different version. Therefore, it is not necessary to test the user's choice each time a diagram element is created. The question is how to create diagram elements using the notations for the default version without having to check the user's selection again and again. The *abstract factory* pattern described in Figure 16.18 provides a solution.

Applying the Abstract Factory Pattern

EXAMPLE 16.10

Apply abstract factory to support different versions of UML.

Solution: Figure 16.19 shows the abstract factory pattern applied to support different versions of UML. The Abstract Factory interface defines a common interface for creating State and Transition objects in either UML 1.0 or UML 2.0. Notice that the common interface has two functions; each begins with the word "create" followed by the name of the product to be produced. Verbs other than "create" could be used, such as "make." Naming the functions this way is a distinct characteristic of the abstract factory pattern. The input parameters of the functions are the values needed to create the products. For example, to create a state, the x, y coordinates of the origin of the state shape are needed. The return type of a function of the abstract factory can be the type of the abstract product, or the type of the concrete product produced. In Figure 16.19, the type of the concrete product is used. The UML 1.0 and 2.0 Factories are the concrete factories. They implement the Abstract Factory interface to produce the concrete products for UML 1.0 and UML 2.0, respectively. The client for the design in Figure 16.19 is Edit Diagram Controller. It has a setFactory (f: Abstract Factory) function, which stores the concrete factory f in its factory field. The client calls functions of this concrete factory to create concrete products of UML 1.0 or UML 2.0. Note that since the concrete factory is set by another object, the client does not know which concrete factory it uses. This in turn means that the client does not know the family of the products it uses.

Name	Abstract Factory
Type	GoF/Creational
Specification	
Problem	How to create objects of a selected family of classes but you don't want the client to be affected by the selection.
Solution	Define an object creation interface and let each subclass create the objects of the selected family of classes.
Design	
Structural	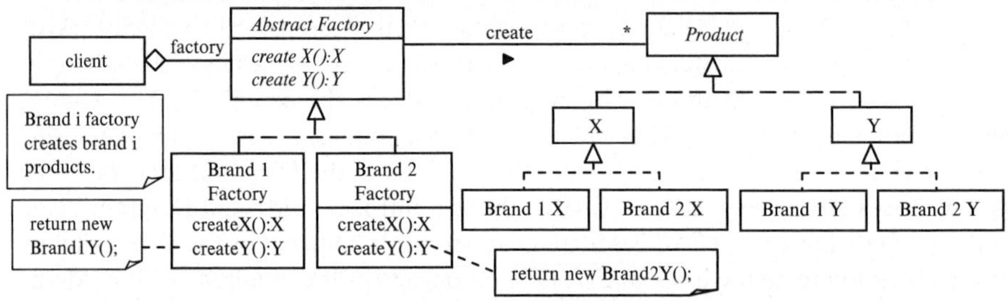
Behavioral	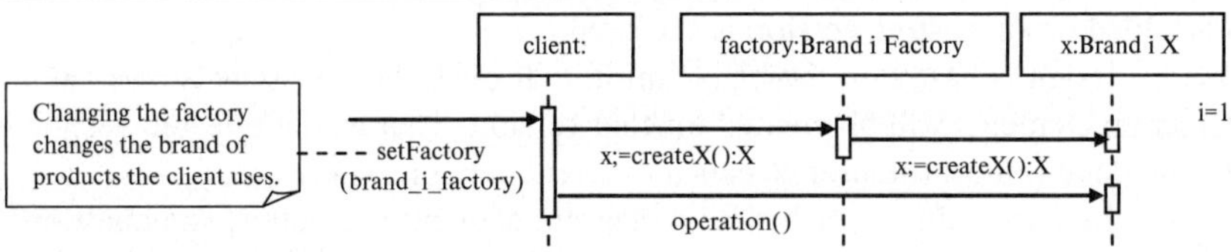
Roles and Responsibilities	• Product: Common interface for all products to be created. • X, Y: Common interfaces for different types of product. • Brand i X, Brand i Y: Concrete products of type X and type Y of different brands. For example, engine and brake of Compay-A, and engine and brake of Company-B. • Abstract Factory: It defines a common interface for the concrete factories. This interface includes a create method for each type of product to be created, e.g., createEngine(): Engine, createBrake(): Brake. • Brand 1 Factory, Brand 2 Factory: These are concrete factories, each creates all types of product for a given family or brand. By changing the concrete factory the client uses, products of different brands are created and used by the client. • Client: It uses a concrete factory to produce all types of product for a given brand. It may not know the concrete factory it uses if the factory is set by another object.
Benefits	• It provides a uniform interface for creating different brands of products. • A concrete factory can ensure the integrity of the products it creates. • It is easy to add new factories that do not require change to the abstract factory interface. • The client does not know which concrete factory and which family of products it uses.
Liabilities	• It is difficult and undesired to add factories that require change to the Abstract Factory interface.
Guidelines	
Related Patterns	• Abstract Factory often uses Factory Method. The Abstract Factory is an abstract class with factory methods; the concrete factories implement the factory methods to vary the brand of products created. • Prototype can be used to eliminate the product hierarchy if the products of different brands share the same behavior and relationships to other classes. For example, car components of different brands share the same behavior. • Builder can be used to produce complex products for Abstract Factory. Abstract Factory can produce products for Builder.
Uses	

FIGURE 16.18 Specification of the abstract factory pattern

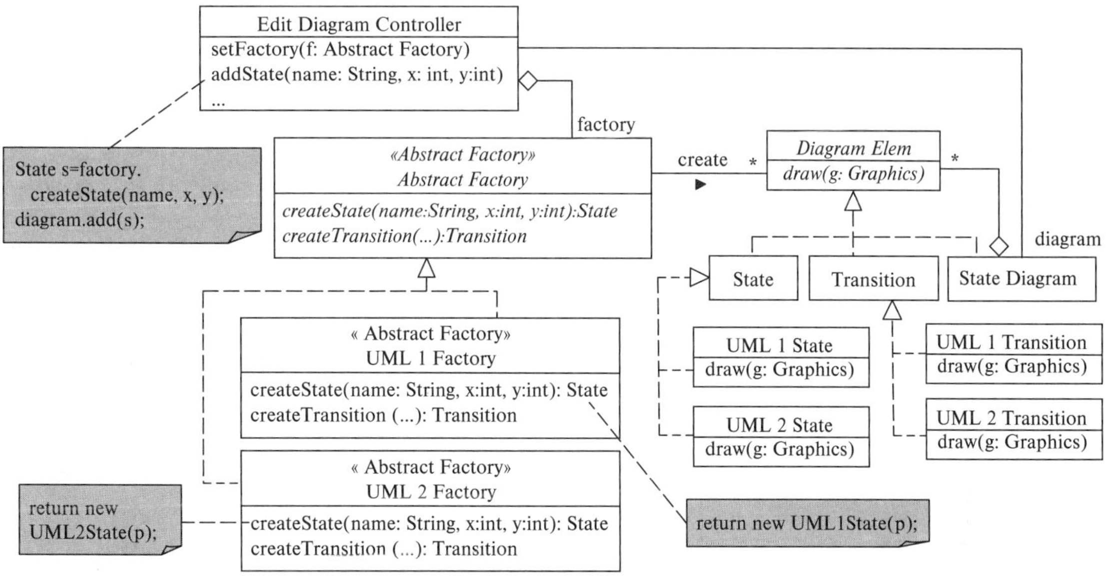

FIGURE 16.19 Supporting multiple versions of UML with abstract factory

Benefits and Liabilities of the Abstract Factory Pattern

The abstract factory pattern has the following benefits and liabilities:

- It is useful for applications that need to dynamically change the family of products produced.
- It is easy to add new factories provided that the new factories do not require a different interface. However, it is not easy to add factories that require a different interface.
- The concrete factories can enforce integrity constraints such as each transition must have a source and a destination state. Nevertheless, the pattern per se does not enforce such constraints; the concrete factories must implement constraint enforcement mechanisms.

16.5.2 Varying Process and Process Steps

The state diagram editor may provide semiautomated support to code generation, test generation, and test execution for state diagrams. These capabilities can be implemented by three functions, called genCode(), genTest(), and runTest(). These functions may be invoked in different orders to support conventional "write code first then test" as well as test-driven development (TDD), which advocates "write test first then code." This means dynamically changing the process from "generating code, generating tests, executing tests" to "generating test, generating code, executing tests." A state diagram may be implemented by using switch statements or the state pattern (Chapter 13). Similarly, test generation should support white-box testing and black-box testing. These mean that the steps of the process may change dynamically as well. Thus, we have a design problem that requires dynamically changing the process as well as the steps of the process.

Looking up Figure 16.3 finds the builder pattern, which supports "using different processes and different ways to perform the steps of a process." The specification of the builder pattern is given in Figure 16.20.

<table>
<tr><td>Name</td><td>Builder</td></tr>
<tr><td>Type</td><td>Gof/Creational</td></tr>
<tr><td>Specification</td><td></td></tr>
<tr><td>Problem</td><td>How to vary the construction process and the construction steps so that they can be combined in flexible ways to construct different products.</td></tr>
<tr><td>Solution</td><td>Decouple the construction process and the process steps into two separate hierarchies so that they can be combined in flexible ways.</td></tr>
<tr><td>Design</td><td></td></tr>
<tr><td>Structural</td><td>
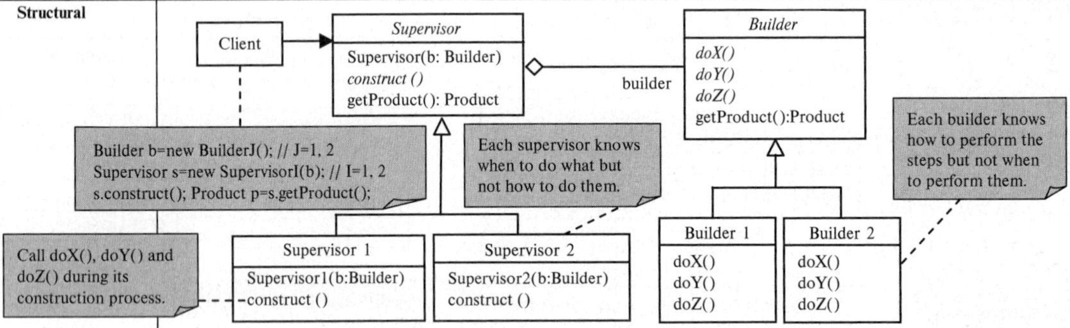

</td></tr>
<tr><td>Behavioral</td><td>
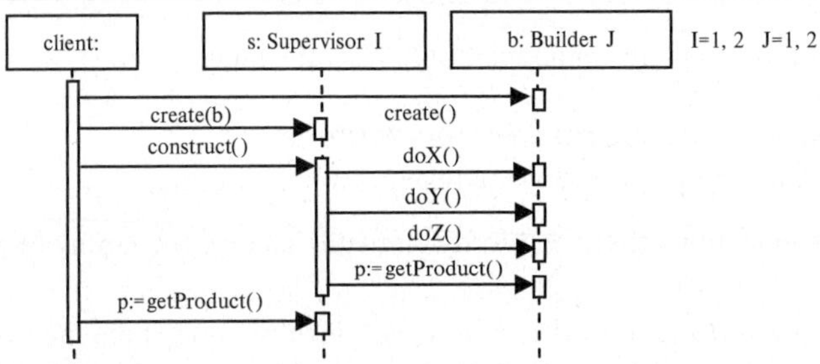

</td></tr>
<tr><td>Roles and Responsibilities</td><td>
• Supervisor, Builder: These define the common interfaces for the concrete supervisors and concrete builders.
• Supervisors 1-2: These represent the concrete supervisors. Each implements its own concrete construct process, which invokes the methods of a concrete builder to construct a product. It then retrieves the product from the builder. The supervisors know when to do what but not how to do them.
• Builders 1-2: These represent the concrete builders. Each implements the functions defined in the Builder interface to perform the concrete build steps.
• Client: It creates the desired supervisor and builder, invokes the construct() method of the supervisor, and retrieve the product from the supervisor.
</td></tr>
<tr><td>Benefits</td><td>
• Changing the construction process and construction steps can be done easily and dynamically.
• It supports separation of concerns - supervisors are concerned with construction process while builders are responsible for construction steps.
• It is easy to add concrete supervisors and concrete builders, provided that they do not require to change the existing supervisor interface and builder interface.
• The builder hides the representation and internal structure of the product from the supervisor.
• The supervisor can control the construction process at any level of detail.
</td></tr>
<tr><td>Liabilities</td><td></td></tr>
<tr><td>Guidelines</td><td>• Use Builder if both the process and process steps need to vary.</td></tr>
<tr><td>Related Patterns</td><td>
• Template Method and Factory Method vary only process steps whereas Builder supports variation of both process and process steps.
• Builder can be used to build complex objects for Abstract Factory. Abstract Factory can create products for Builder.
• Builder can be used to build complex Composite objects.
</td></tr>
<tr><td>Uses</td><td>Process automation can benefit from Builder. For example, a software engineering environment may support different software processes such as waterfall and agile. The development activities such as requirements, design, implementation, and testing are the process steps that implement different development methodologies such as structured analysis and structured design (SA/SD) and OO methodologies.</td></tr>
</table>

FIGURE 16.20 Specification of the builder pattern

The builder pattern is useful for applications that require the flexibility to change the construction process as well as the construction steps dynamically. For example, it has applications in computer-aided design and computer-aided manufacturing (CAD/CAM). The design process and the manufacturing process can change from product to product. In addition, the design steps and manufacturing steps also differ from product to product. The builder pattern is also useful for the design and implementation of enterprise resource planning (ERP) frameworks. In such applications, a supervisor is an abstraction of all possible workflow processes. The construction method of each concrete supervisor implements a concrete workflow. On the other hand, the Builder is an abstraction of all possible workflow activities. The concrete builders implement the activities differently to fulfill requirements of different organizations. Similarly, the pattern can be applied to software process automation to support different development processes such as waterfall and agile in combination with different methodologies that implement the development activities such as requirements, design, implementation, and testing. This lets a development organization select the process and methodology they want to use. One final note is that the builder pattern is not limited to product creation. In fact, it is applicable in all situations in which the process and the process steps need to vary independently and dynamically.

Applying the Builder Pattern

EXAMPLE 16.11

Apply the builder pattern to support conventional code-then-test and test-driven development, as well as different ways to generate skeleton code and test scripts.

Solution: Figure 16.21 shows a design that applies the builder pattern.

In Figure 16.21, the two concrete supervisors, CFD Spvr and TDD Spvr implement two different processes, one for conventional and the other for agile development. This is reflected in that they call the functions of a concrete builder differently. The

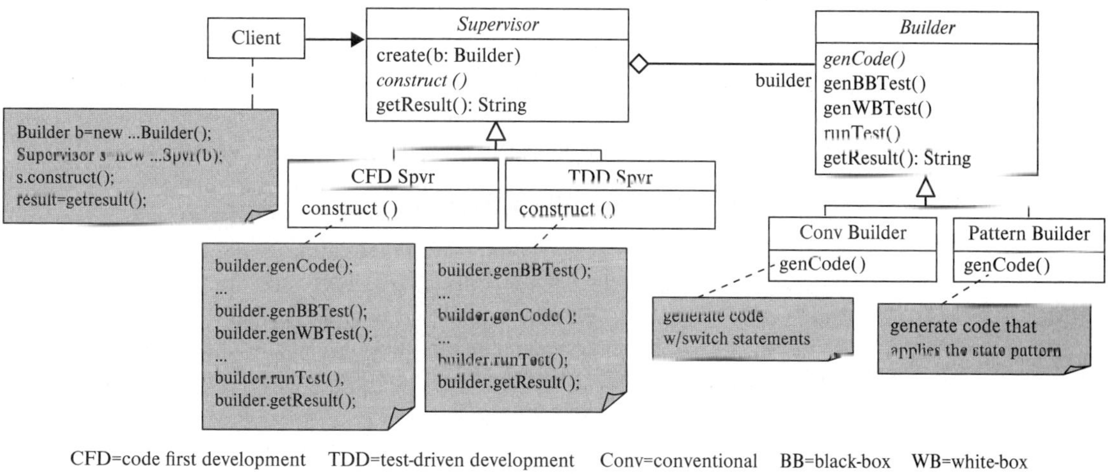

FIGURE 16.21 Applying builder pattern to support varying process and process steps

two concrete builders, Conv Builder and Pattern Builder, implement the code generation step differently—one generates conventional and the other generates state-pattern code. The design can support four different supervisor-builder combinations. The client can create a builder and a supervisor it wants, and call the construction method of the supervisor to carry out the construction process. The construction method in turn calls the builder to carry out the steps of the construction process. The genBBTest() and genWBTest() functions generate black-box and white-box tests, respectively. These and the runTest() function can be abstract in the Builder class and implemented by the concrete builders if test generation and execution also need to vary.

Sample Code

EXAMPLE 16.12 Implement the design in Figure 16.21.

Solution: Figure 16.22 shows the sample code for the design in Figure 16.21. The sample code is explained as follows. First, the builder abstract class implements visitor, defined in Figure 16.15, Example 16.8. This is because the concrete builders need to process State and Transition objects to generate code. This means that both the builder and the visitor patterns are applied. Second, the construction processes of the concrete supervisors show the generated skeleton code and test scripts to the user and require the user to modify the code and test scripts; these are indicated as in-line comments in Figure 16.22. Finally, only the implementation for the code generation methods is shown in Figure 16.22.

Benefits of the Builder Pattern

The builder pattern brings the following benefits to a design:

- It supports applications that require dynamically changing the process as well as process steps.
- It supports separation of concerns—the supervisor is responsible for telling the builder "when to do what" while the builder is responsible for "how to do them."
- It is easy to add concrete supervisors and concrete builders, provided that they do not require to change the existing supervisor and builder interfaces.

16.5.3 Reusing Objects with Flyweight

An eye-pleasing user interface could use icons to improve the look and feel of a state diagram. For example, each state could be displayed with an icon. The ordinary procedure to display an image icon is loading the image into the memory, and painting the image at a given location. Loading an image is often a time-consuming operation. Moreover, the image may occupy a large amount of memory. Therefore, it is not desirable to load the same image into the memory each time when a state is created because the states can share the same image. This means that one needs to load the image only once, and share it at places it is needed. This is the idea of the flyweight pattern, specified in Figure 16.23.

```
public class Supervisor {
  ArrayList<String> code=new ArrayList<String>();
  ArrayList<String> test=new ArrayList<String>();
  String result; protected Visitor builder;
  private StateDiagram diagram;
  public Supervisor(Visitor b) { builder=b; }
  public void setDiagram(StateDiagram d) { diagram=d; }
  public void construct() {
    Iterator<DiagramElem> it=diagram.iterator();
    while (it.hasNext()){ it.next().accept(builder);}}
  public String getResult() { return result; }
}

public class CFDSpvr extends Supervisor {
  public CFDSpvr(Visitor b) { super(b); }
  public void construct() { super.construct();
    ArrayList code=((Builder)builder).genCode();
    // here, show dialog for user to edit code
    test=((Builder)builder).genBBTest();
    test.addAll(((Builder)builder).genWBTest(code));
    // here, show dialog for user to edit test
    result=((Builder)builder).runTest(test); }
}

public class TDDSpvr extends Supervisor {
  public TDDSpvr(Visitor b) { super(b); }
  public void construct() { super.construct();
    test=((Builder)builder).genBBTest();
    // here, show dialog for user to edit test
    code=((Builder)builder).genCode();
    // here, show dialog for user to edit code
    result=((Builder)builder).runTest(test); }
}

public abstract class Builder implements Visitor {
  protected ArrayList<String> code=new ArrayList<String>();
  protected ArrayList<String> test=new ArrayList<String>();
  protected String result=""; public abstract ArrayList genCode();
  public ArrayList<String> genBBTest(){ return test; }
  public ArrayList<String> genWBTest(ArrayList code)
  { return test; }
  public String runTest(ArrayList test) { return result; }
}

public class PatternBuilder extends Builder {
  private Hashtable<State, HashSet> states=
    new Hashtable<State, HashSet>();
  private ArrayList<String> trans=new ArrayList<String>();
  public void visit(State s) {
    states.put(s, new HashSet<Transition>()); }
  public void visit(Transition t) { states.get(t.getSource()).add(t);
    if (!trans.contains(t.getName())) trans.add(t.getName()); }
  public ArrayList<String> genCode() {
    ArrayList<String> code=new ArrayList<String>();
    code.add("public class Subject {");
    code.add("   private State state; // init state");
    for(int i=0; i<trans.size(); i++) {   String f=trans.get(i);
      code.add("   public void "+f+" { state=state."+f+"; }"); }
    code.add("   public class State {");
for(int i=0; i<trans.size(); i++) {  String f=trans.get(i);
      code.add("     public State "+f+" { return this; }");
    } code.add("  }");
Enumeration<State> en=states.keys();
    while (en.hasMoreElements()) { State s=en.nextElement();
      code.add("  public class "+s.getName()+" extends State {");
      Iterator<Transition> it=states.get(s).iterator();
      while (it.hasNext()) { Transition t=it.next();
        code.add("     public State "+t.getName()+" {");
        code.add("       /* process "+t.getName()+" */");
      code.add("       return new "+t.getDest().getName()+"();}");
      } code.add("  }"); } code.add("}");
    Printer.getInstance().print(code, "Subject.java");
    return code; }
}

public class ConvBuilder extends Builder { private int n=0;
  Hashtable<State, Integer> sHash=new Hashtable<...>();
  Hashtable<String, HashSet> tHash=new Hashtable<...>();
  public void visit(State s) {  sHash.put(s, new Integer(n++)); }
  public void visit(Transition t) {
    if (tHash.get(t.getName())==null)
      tHash.put(t.getName(), new HashSet<Transition>());
    tHash.get(t.getName()).add(t); }
  public ArrayList<String> genCode() {
    Enumeration<String> functions=tHash.keys();
    ArrayList<String> code=new ArrayList<String>();
    code.add("public class SDCode {");
    Enumeration<State> en=sHash.keys();
    while (en.hasMoreElements()) { State s=en.nextElement();
      code.add("  private static final int "+
        s.getName().toUpperCase()+"="+
        ((Integer)sHash.get(s)).intValue()+";"); }
    code.add("  private int state=0;");
    while (functions.hasMoreElements()) {
      String f=functions.nextElement();
      code.add("  public void "+f+" {");
      code.add("    switch(state) {");
      Iterator<Transition> it=tHash.get(f).iterator();
      while (it.hasNext()) { Transition t=it.next();
        code.add("      case "+
          ((Integer)sHash.get(t.getSource())).intValue()+
          ": /* process transition "+t.getName()+" */;");
        code.add("        state="+
          ((Integer)sHash.get(t.getDest())).intValue()+
          "; break;"); }
      code.add("    }"+"\n"+"  }"); } code.add("}");
    Printer.getInstance().print(code, "SDCode.java");
    return code; }
}

public class Main {
    public static void main(String[] args) {
    StateDiagram sd=...// create state diagram
    Visitor b=new PatternBuilder();
    Supervisor tdd=new TDDSpvr(b); tdd.setDiagram(sd);
    tdd.construct(); String r=tdd.getResult();}
    // do the same for ConvBuilder and CFDSpvr here
}
```

FIGURE 16.22 Sample code for applying the builder pattern

<table>
<tr><td>Name</td><td>Flyweight</td></tr>
<tr><td>Type</td><td>GoF/Structural</td></tr>
<tr><td>Specification</td><td></td></tr>
<tr><td>Problem</td><td>How to create numerous occurrences of an object economically.</td></tr>
<tr><td>Solution</td><td>Let the occurrences of the object share part of the object that is sharable.</td></tr>
<tr><td>Design</td><td></td></tr>
<tr><td>Structural</td><td>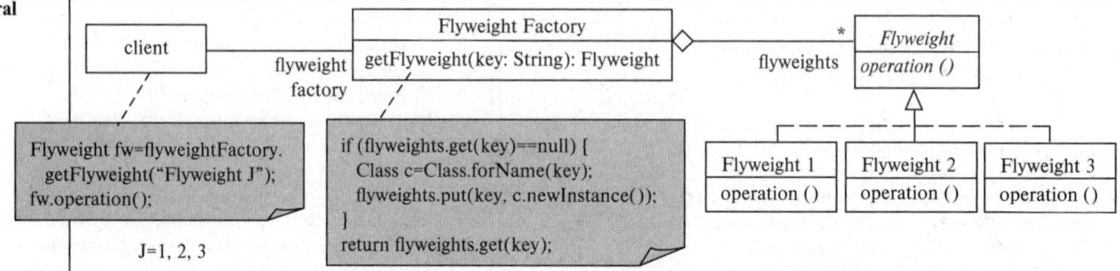
</td></tr>
<tr><td>Behavioral</td><td>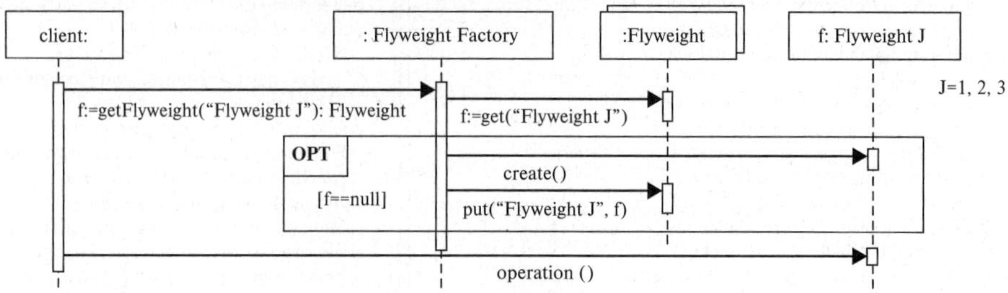
</td></tr>
<tr><td>Roles and Responsibilities</td><td>
• Flyweight: It defines a common interface for all of the concrete flyweight classes.
• Flyweights 1-3: These are the concrete flyweight classes, which implement the Flyweight interface.
• Flyweight Factory: It maintains a pool of concrete flyweight objects and lets the client obtain such objects. If a concrete flyweight object is not in the pool, it creates the object and saves it in the pool.
• Client: It obtains the concrete flyweight objects from the Flyweight Factory and uses them.</td></tr>
<tr><td>Benefits</td><td>
• It reduces memory consumption by sharing.
• It extends battery life for mobile devices.
• It improves object creation efficiency.</td></tr>
<tr><td>Liabilities</td><td>• It can only be applied if the flyweight is sharable.</td></tr>
<tr><td>Guidelines</td><td>• Apply Flyweight only if you can clearly identify sharable and non-sharable parts of an object.</td></tr>
<tr><td>Related Patterns</td><td>
• Singleton limits the number of instances of a class whereas Flyweight lets numerous occurrences of an object reuse a sharable part of the object.
• Prototype maintains a pool of prototype objects while Flyweight maintains a pool of sharable objects called flyweights.</td></tr>
<tr><td>Uses</td><td>
• Game or media applications where an image need to be painted at many different locations.
• Text editors to share the character images.
• Multiple-choice exam generators where different copies of the same exam can share the exam questions as flyweight.</td></tr>
</table>

FIGURE 16.23 Specification of the flyweight pattern

Applying the Flyweight Pattern

EXAMPLE 16.13 Apply the flyweight pattern so that all states can share an image icon. Solution: The simplest solution is to modify the State class as follows: (1) include a static image-icon field so that it can be shared by all State objects, (2) change the draw method to also paint the image icon at the location of the state. The modified code is shown below.

```
public class State extends DiagramElement {
   static ImageIcon icon=new ImageIcon("img/state.jpg");
   public State(String name, int x, int y) { super(name, x, y); }
```

```
public void draw(Graphics g)
{ g.setColor(Color.BLACK); g.drawOval(x, y, 40, 40);
  icon.paintIcon(null, g, x, y);
  g.drawString(name, x+10, y+25); }}
```

Nevertheless, this solution has limitations. First, although the image can be reused in other contexts, the code may not look nice and easy to comprehend. Moreover, it is not easy to use a different image icon. The flyweight pattern nicely solves these problems. Figure 16.24 shows the design that applies the flyweight pattern. The FW Factory class and its collection of flyweights let other objects reuse the State Icon. In addition, to change the icon used by the State objects, one only needs to retrieve a different flyweight from the flyweight factory.

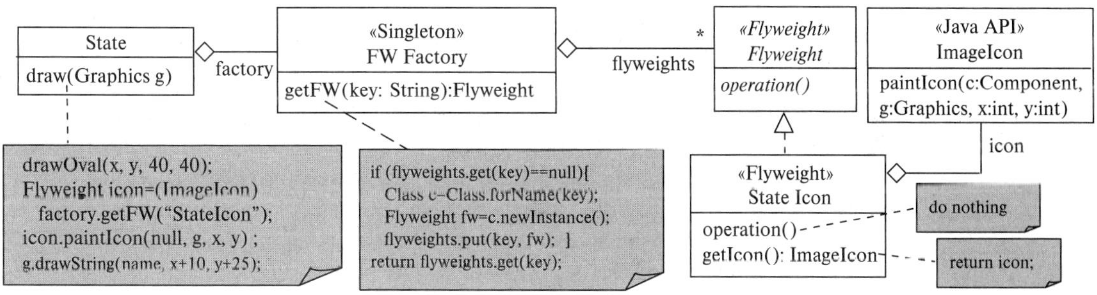

FIGURE 16.24 Applying flyweight pattern to editor design

Sample Code

EXAMPLE 16.14

The implementation of relevant classes of the flyweight pattern used to share an image icon is shown in Figure 16.25.

```
public interface Flyweight { void operation(); }

public class StateIcon implements Flyweight {
  ImageIcon icon=new ImageIcon("img/circle.jpg");
  public void operation() { }
  public ImageIcon getIcon() { return icon; }
}

public class FWFactory {
  private static FWFactory instance=new FWFactory();
  private Hashtable flyweights=new Hashtable<String, Flyweight>();
  public static FWFactory getInstance() { return instance; }
  public Flyweight getFW(String key) {
    if (fly weights.get(key)==null) {
      try { Class c=Class.forName(key);
            flyweights.put(key, c.newInstance());
      } catch (Exception e) { e.printStackTrace(); }
    } return (Flyweight)flyweights.get(key); }
}

public class State extends DiagramElement {
  public State(String name, int x, int y) { super(name, x, y); }
  public void draw(Graphics g) {
    g.setColor(Color.BLACK);
    g.drawOval(x, y, 40, 40);
    Flyweight fw=FWFactory.getInstance().
      getFW("flyweight.StateIcon");
    ImageIcon icon=((StateIcon)fw).getIcon();
    icon.paintIcon(null, g, x, y);
    g.drawString(name, x+10, y+25); }
}
```

FIGURE 16.25 Sample code for application of the flyweight pattern

Benefits of the Flyweight Pattern

- It is useful for sharing an object at numerous places of a software system.
- It reduces object creation time and memory consumption. As a consequence, it extends battery life and improves efficiency and performance.

16.6 DESIGNING GRAPHICAL USER INTERFACE AND DISPLAY

The design and implementation of the state diagram editor needs to handle many system-generated events such as button clicked, mouse clicked, mouse pressed, mouse dragged, and mouse released events. Responses to these events are state dependent. How to capture and handle such events is the focus of this section.

16.6.1 Keeping Track of Editing States

Editing operations exhibit state-dependent behavior. For example, if a user clicks the State button then anywhere in the canvas, the editor should draw a state shape. On the other hand, if the user clicks a state or transition shape without clicking the State button, the editor should select the state or transition. As discussed in Chapter 13, state-dependent behavior is usually modeled by a state diagram. Figure 16.26 shows a portion of the state-dependent behavior of the edit-diagram controller. For simplicity, it shows only the behavior for drawing a state or a transition.

As discussed in Chapter 13, a conventional approach to implement a state diagram uses nested-switch statements. One of the switches keeps track of the editor state and the other switch represents the transitions that can take place in a given state. The complexity of this approach is the number of states times the number of transitions. For example, in Figure 16.26, there are four states and seven transitions; hence, the complexity is 28, which is high. Moreover, it is not easy to add states or transitions because many cases of the switch statements need to change. Another approach lets the functions of a class implement the state behavior. The code generation method of the conventional builder class in Figure 16.22 uses this approach. Its complexity is lower but it is still not easy to add states or transitions. In summary, we need a low-complexity and easy-to-change approach to implement a state diagram. The state pattern (Chapter 13) solves this design problem.

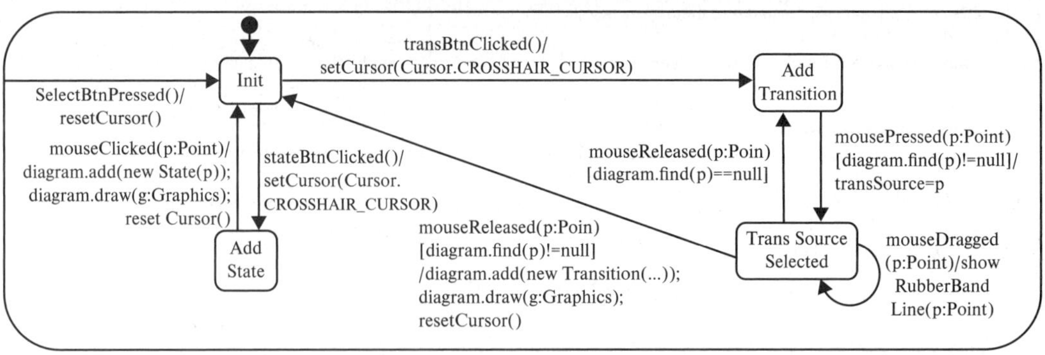

FIGURE 16.26 State-dependent behavior of the state diagram editor

Applying the State Pattern

EXAMPLE 16.15

Apply the state pattern to produce a design for the state diagram editor.

Solution: Figure 16.27 shows the design, which is explained as follows. First, the state diagram in Figure 16.26 has four states. Therefore, the design has a state class called CState and four state subclasses. The state diagram has seven transitions. So, the CState class has seven functions. The selectBtnClicked() function simply returns an instance of Init class, and the remaining six functions return "self," a UML keyword to denote the object itself; it means the same as "this" in C++ and Java. Each of the state subclasses overrides parent functions that correspond to a transition that goes out of the state. For example, in Figure 16.26, there are two transitions going out of the Init state. Therefore, the Init subclass overrides the stateBtnClicked() and transBtnClicked() functions. The UML note attached to the stateBtnClicked() method shows the functionality of the method. Finally, because Figure 16.26 describes the state behavior of the Edit Diagram Controller, therefore, the Subject class of the state pattern is mapped to the Edit Diagram Controller. At any given time, the controller has a state, which is indicated by the aggregation relationship in Figure 16.27. The controller also has seven functions, corresponding to the seven transitions. The implementation of each of these functions is simply calling the corresponding function of the state object. For example, the implementation of the mouseReleased(p: Point) function is "state := state. mouseReleased(p)."

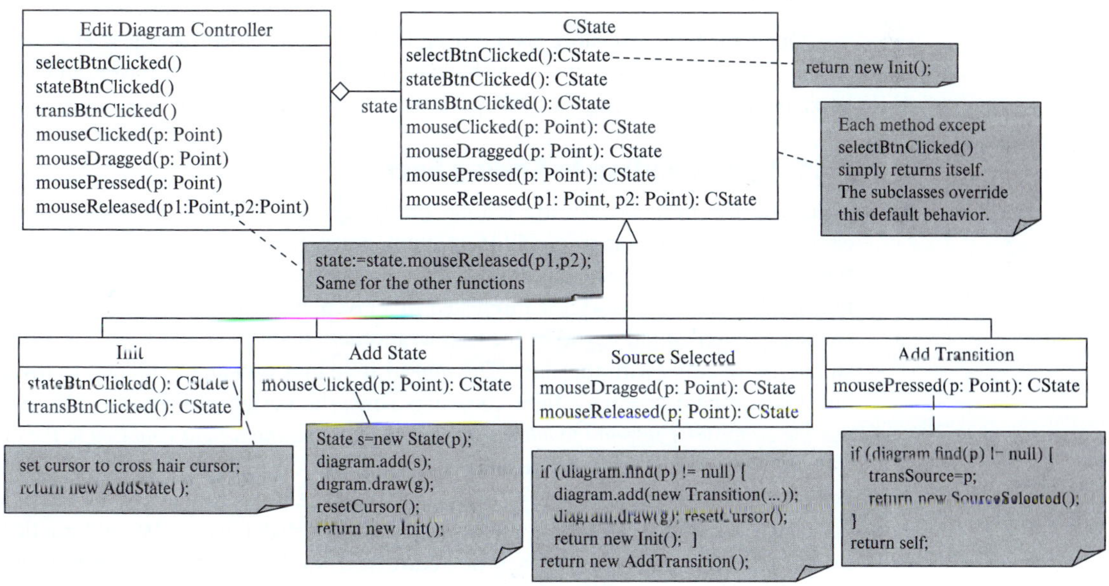

FIGURE 16.27 State diagram editor applying the state pattern

Sample Code

EXAMPLE 16.16 Figure 16.28 shows sample code that implements the design in Figure 16.27. It is explained as follows. First, it is based on the sample code given in Figure 16.15. New classes are added and some existing classes are modified. To save space, modified classes only show the portions that are either changed or added. Classes that are the same are not shown in Figure 16.28. Second, the state class and its subclasses are implemented as nested classes of the Edit Diagram Controller class. So is the Canvas class as a nested class of the Edit Diagram GUI. Third, in Figure 16.27, the stateBtnClicked() method of the Init class changes the cursor to crosshair. This implies that the method needs to call the setCursor(...) method of the Canvas class, which belongs to the presentation or GUI layer. This is not desirable because it creates a dependency on the Canvas. As a remedy, the sample code lets the Canvas sets the cursor to crosshair, as shown in the method body of the actionPerformed(...) method of the state button listener class. Similarly, reset cursor and drawing a rubber-band line are implemented in the GUI layer.

Benefits and Liabilities of the State Pattern

The state pattern has the following benefits:

- It reduces the complexity of the design and implementation of state dependent behavior as compared to conventional approaches.
- It is easy to add and remove states and transitions.
- It makes the state behavior easy to understand, implement, test, and maintain.

One liability is that more classes need to design, implement, and test. However, as shown in the sample code, the state class and its subclasses are small classes and easy to implement, understand, and test. This is a small price to pay but it is worth the benefits.

16.6.2 Responding to Editing Events

When the user performs editing actions, the system generates action events and delivers them to the state diagram editor. In many cases, the system delivers the events to the editor GUI object. The editor GUI object processes the events accordingly. Sometimes, more than one object is interested in a given event. For example, when a state shape is pressed and dragged by the user to another location, all the related transitions should move along with the state. The moved state may update the related transitions but this approach creates a tight coupling. Thus, the design problem to solve is *how can the editor GUI respond to editing events without creating a tight coupling to the event sources?* This design problem exists in many applications. For example, a spreadsheet needs to visualize its data using different views such as histogram chart, pie chart, and bar chart. When changes are made to the data, the views must update automatically. Looking up the pattern summary in Figure 16.3 finds the *observer* pattern, which decouples the event handlers from the event source so the handlers can be added and removed freely. The specification of the observer pattern in Figure 16.29 confirms that it is the right pattern to apply.

```
public interface DiagramElem { void draw(Graphics g); }

public class State implements DiagramElem {
  protected int x, y; private String name;
  public State(String n, int a, int b) {name=n; x=a; y=b; }
  public void draw(Graphics g) { g.drawOval(x, y, 40, 40);
   g.drawString(name, x+10, y+25);}
  public boolean contains(Point p) {
    int px=(int)p.getX(), py=(int)p.getY();
    return px>=x && px<=x+40 && py>=y && py<=y+40; }}

public class Transition implements DiagramElem {
  private String name; Point p0, p1;
  public Transition(String name, State s, State d)
  { this.name=name; int x0=s.x+20, y0=s.y+20, x1=d.x+20, y1=d.y+20;
    if (x0==x1) {
      if (y1>y0) { p0=new Point(x0, y0+20); p1=new Point(x0, d.y); }
      else { p0=new Point(x0, s.y); p1=new Point(x0, y1+20); } return; }
    double slope=(y1-y0)/Math.abs(x1-x0), a=Math.atan(slope);
    int dx=(int)(20*Math.cos(a)), dy=(int)(20*Math.sin(a));
    if (d.x>s.x) { p0=new Point(x0+dx, y0+dy); p1=new Point(x1-dx, y1-dy);
    } else { p0=new Point(x0-dx, y0+dy); p1=new Point(x1+dx, y1-dy); }}
  public void draw(Graphics g)
  { Graphics2D g2=(Graphics2D)g; g2.drawLine(p0.x, p0.y, p1.x, p1.y);
    double dx=(p1.x-p0.x), dy=(p1.y-p0.y), theta=0;
    if (dx==0) theta=Math.atan(dy/0.01); else
    { if (dx>0) theta = Math.atan(dy / dx);
      else theta =3.14+ Math.atan(dy/dx); }
    double alpha=60*3.14/180-theta;
    int x[]=new int[]{(int)(p0.x+dx-10*Math.sin(alpha)), p1.x,
      (int)(p0.x+dx-10*Math.cos(theta-30*3.14/180))},
    int y[]=new int[]{(int)(p0.y+dy-10*Math.cos(alpha)), p1.y,
      (int)(p0.y+dy-10*Math.sin(theta-30*3.14/180))};
    g2.drawPolyline(x, y, 3);
    g2.drawString(name, p0.x+(float)dx/2, p0.y+(float)dy/2); }}

public class StateDiagram implements DiagramElem {
  Collection<DiagramElem> c=new ArrayList<DiagramElem>();
  public void add (DiagramElem e) { c.add(e); }
  public void remove (DiagramElem e) { c.remove(e); }
  public State find(Point p) { Iterator<DiagramElem> it=c.iterator();
    while (it.hasNext()) { DiagramElem e=it.next();
      if (e.getClass().getName().indexOf("State")>=0)
        if (((State)e).contains(p)) return (State)e; } return null; }
  public void draw(Graphics g) {
   Iterator<DiagramElem> it=c.iterator();
   while (it.hasNext()) { it.next().draw(g); }}}

public class EditDiagramController {
  protected static final int INIT=0, ADDSTATE=1, ADDTRANS=2,
    SRCSELECTED=3;
  protected CState[] states=new CState[] { new Init(),
    new AddState(), new AddTransition(), new SrcSelected()};
  protected CState state=states[INIT]; public Point source;
  protected StateDiagram diagram=new StateDiagram();
  public void selectBtnClicked(){ state=state.selectBtnClicked(); }
  public void stateBtnClicked(){ state=state.stateBtnClicked(); }
  public void transBtnClicked(){ state=state.transBtnClicked(); }
  public void mouseClicked(Point p){ state=state.mouseClicked(p); }
  public void mouseDragged(Point p){ state=state.mouseDragged(p); }
  public void mousePressed(Point p){ state=state.mousePressed(p); }
  public void mouseReleased(Point p){ state=state.mouseReleased(p); }
  public StateDiagram getDiagram(){ return diagram; }

class Init extends CState {
  public Init(){ super(); }
  public CState stateBtnClicked(){ return states[ADDSTATE]; }
  public CState transBtnClicked(){ return states[ADDTRANS]; }}

class AddTransition extends CState {
  public AddTransition(){ super(); }
  public CState mousePressed(Point p){ State s=diagram.find(p);
    if (s!=null){ source=p; return states[SRCSELECTED]; } return this; }}}
```

```
class CState {
  public CState selectBtnClicked(){ return states[INIT]; }
  public CState stateBtnClicked(){ return this; }
  public CState transBtnClicked(){ return this; }
  public CState mouseClicked(Point p){ return this; }
  public CState mouseDragged(Point p){ return this; }
  public CState mousePressed(Point p){ return this; }
  public CState mouseReleased(Point p){ return this; }
}

class AddState extends CState { public AddState(){ super(); }
  public CState mouseClicked(Point p){ int x=(int)p.getX(), y=(int)p.getY();
    diagram.add(new State("State", x, y)); return states[INIT]; }}

class SrcSelected extends CState {
  public SrcSelected(){ super(); }
  public void setSource(Point p){ source=p; }
  public CState mouseDragged(Point p){ return this; }
  public CState mouseReleased(Point p){
    State s=diagram.find(source), d=diagram.find(p);
    if (d==null) return states[ADDTRANS];
    diagram.add(new Transition("trans", s, d)); return states[INIT]; }}

public class EditDiagramGUI extends JFrame {
  private EditDiagramController controller=new EditDiagramController();
  private JButton stateBtn=new JButton("State");
  private JButton transBtn=new JButton("Transition");
  private Canvas canvas=new Canvas();
  public EditDiagramGUI() {
    canvas.setDiagram(controller.getDiagram());
    stateBtn.addActionListener(new ActionListener(){
      public void actionPerformed(ActionEvent e) {
        setCursor(Cursor.CROSSHAIR_CURSOR);
        controller.stateBtnClicked(); }});
    transBtn.addActionListener(new ActionListener(){
      public void actionPerformed(ActionEvent e) {
        setCursor(Cursor.CROSSHAIR_CURSOR);
        controller.transBtnClicked(); }});
    canvas.addMouseListener(new MouseAdapter() {
      public void mouseClicked(MouseEvent e) {
        Point p=e.getPoint(); controller.mouseClicked(p); canvas.repaint();
        setCursor(Cursor.DEFAULT_CURSOR); }
      public void mousePressed(MouseEvent e) {
        Point p=e.getPoint(); canvas.source=p; controller.mousePressed(p); }
      public void mouseReleased(MouseEvent e) {
        controller.mouseReleased(e.getPoint());
        canvas.repaint(); canvas.mouseDragged=false;
        setCursor(Cursor.DEFAULT_CURSOR); }});
    canvas.addMouseMotionListener(new MouseMotionAdapter() {
      public void mouseDragged(MouseEvent e) {
        Point p=e.getPoint(); canvas.dest=p;
        canvas.mouseDragged=true; canvas.repaint(); }});
    JPanel contentPane = (JPanel) getContentPane();
    contentPane.setLayout(new BorderLayout());
    canvas.setVisible(true); JPanel jPanel1=new JPanel();
    jPanel1.setPreferredSize(new Dimension(100, 200));
    jPanel1.add(stateBtn); jPanel1.add(transBtn);
    contentPane.add(canvas, BorderLayout.CENTER);
    contentPane.add(jPanel1, BorderLayout.WEST);
    setDefaultCloseOperation(EXIT_ON_CLOSE); }
  public static void main(String[] args) {
    EditDiagramGUI gui=new EditDiagramGUI();
    gui.setPreferredSize(new Dimension(800, 600));
    gui.setLocation(300, 300); gui.pack(); gui.setVisible(true); }

class Canvas extends JPanel {
  Point source, dest; boolean mouseDragged;
  private DiagramElem diagram;
  public Canvas() { super(); setBackground(Color.WHITE); }
  public void setDiagram(DiagramElem d) { diagram=d; }
  public void paintComponent(Graphics g) {
    super.paintComponent(g); if (diagram!=null) diagram.draw(g);
    if (mouseDragged) {
      g.drawLine((int)source.getX(), (int)source.getY(),
        (int)dest.getX(), (int)dest.getY()); }}}}
```

FIGURE 16.28 Sample code for applying state pattern to editor design

Name	Observer
Type	GoF/Behavioral
Specification	
Problem	How to decouple change and related responses so that such dependencies can be added or removed freely and dynamically?
Solution	Provide a mechanism to add or remove many-to-one dependencies between objects so that when one object changes states, all its dependents are notified and updated automatically.
Design	
Structural	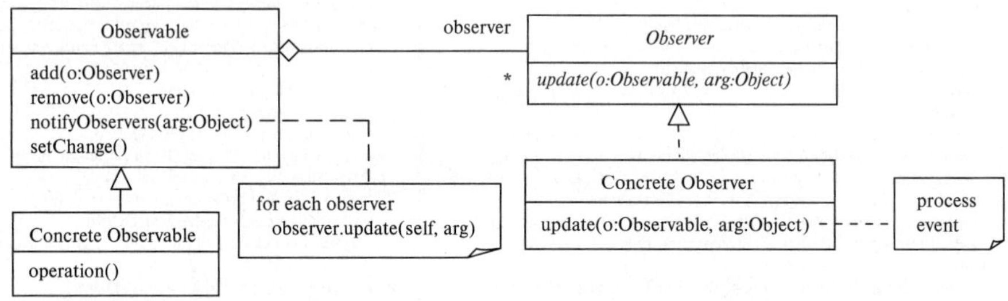
Behavioral	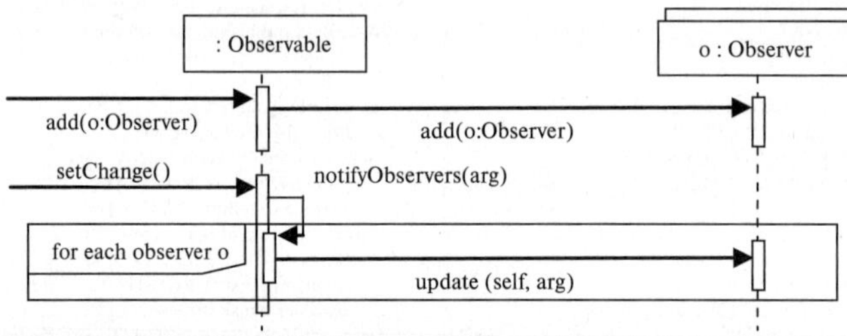
Roles and Responsibilities	• Observable: This class defines functions for adding, removing and notifying observers. • Concrete Observable: It extends the Observable class to add its own behavior such as operation(). It inherits the functions of the Observable class. • Observer: It defines an interface for all concrete observers. • Concrete Observer: It implements the update method to respond to the change.
Benefits	• Observers can be added to, or removed from the observer list of an observable without affecting the observable. • The Observable and the Observer classes can be reused independently. • It supports multicast and broadcast communication. The broadcast mechanism is inherited from the Observable class.
Liabilities	Unwanted concurrent update to a concrete observable may occur.
Guidelines	
Related P atterns	• Protection Proxy can be used to prevent unwanted concurrent update to a concrete observable.
Uses	• Observable and Observer are also Java APIs. The Java ActionLister API is a special case of the observer pattern.

FIGURE 16.29 Specification of the observer pattern

Figure 16.30 shows an application of the observer pattern to a real-world application where a table of data is visualized by different charts. The mapping between the real-world objects and the pattern classes are obvious. The Observer interface and the Observable class are also Java APIs, which implement the observer pattern. The Java Listener APIs are special cases of the observer pattern. In Figure 16.28, several listener APIs are used, including action listener, mouse listener and mouse motion listener. In Figure 13.20, we apply the observer pattern to notify the canvas to repaint the lawn each time the mower moves one step forward. The relationship between an observable and the observers resembles the relationship between a publisher (of a newsletter) and the subscribers (of the newsletter). Therefore, the observer pattern is also called the publisher-subscriber pattern.

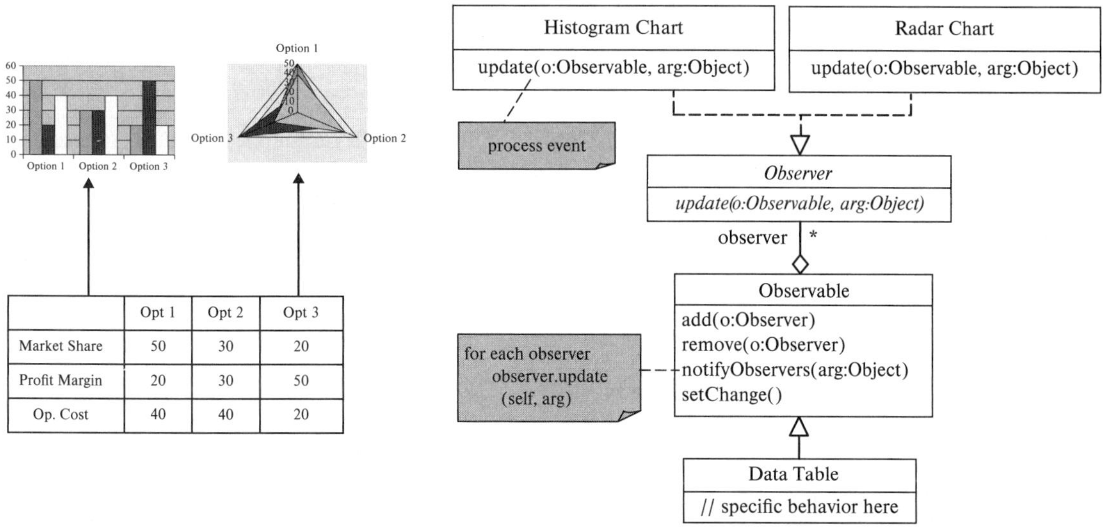

(a) An intuitive model of a real-world application

(b) Applying observer to the real-world application

FIGURE 16.30 Applying the observer pattern

16.6.3 Converting One Interface to Another

As discussed earlier, the use case controller keeps track of the editing states. This is achieved by using the state pattern. The controller defines and implements event-specific functions such as stateBtnClicked (), mouseClicked (p: Point), transBtnClicked (). One question remains to be answered. That is, *who should call these functions?* Ideally, the runtime environment should call these functions because it knows which event takes place. Unfortunately, the runtime environment does not know which of these functions to call because they are application specific. It can only deliver the event to a callback function. In Java, this is the actionPerformed (ActionEvent e) function of the registered Action Lister object. Thus, the design problem to be solved is *how to convert one interface to another.* Checking the pattern summary table finds the *adapter* pattern, which is detailed in Figure 16.31.

There are two types of adapters, shown in Figure 16.31(*a*) and Figure 16.31(*b*), respectively. Figure 16.32 compares these adapters. The class adapter uses inheritance while the object adapter uses object composition. The use of inheritance by the class adapter implies static binding and dependence of the adapter on the adaptee class. Static binding prevents the adapter to adapt to other classes. The dependence of the adapter class on the adaptee class means change impact may ripple from the adaptee class or its ancestor classes to the adapter class, which may require change to the adapter class. Moreover, if the adaptee class is a final class then the class adapter pattern cannot be used. Unlike class adapter, object adapter uses composition and dynamic binding. These allow the adapter to dynamically change the adaptee. This implies that the behavior of the adapter can be changed by changing the adaptee object. The object adapter can also override the behavior of the adaptee class. To do this, one defines a subclass of the adaptee class and overrides the behavior of the adaptee class in this subclass. The adapter then adapts to an object of the subclass. One disadvantage of object adapter is that it requires the creation of at least the adapter object and the adaptee object.

<table>
<tr><td>Name</td><td>Adapter</td></tr>
<tr><td>Type</td><td>GoF/Structural</td></tr>
<tr><td>Specification</td><td></td></tr>
<tr><td>Problem</td><td>How to convert one interface to another?</td></tr>
<tr><td>Solution</td><td>Define an interface as desired and let the implementing subclass adapt it to the existing interface.</td></tr>
<tr><td>Design</td><td></td></tr>
<tr><td>Structural</td><td>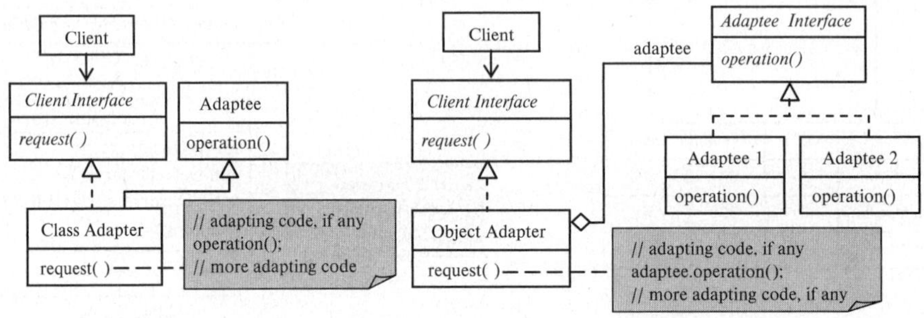

(a) Class adapter (b) Object adapter</td></tr>
<tr><td>Behavioral</td><td>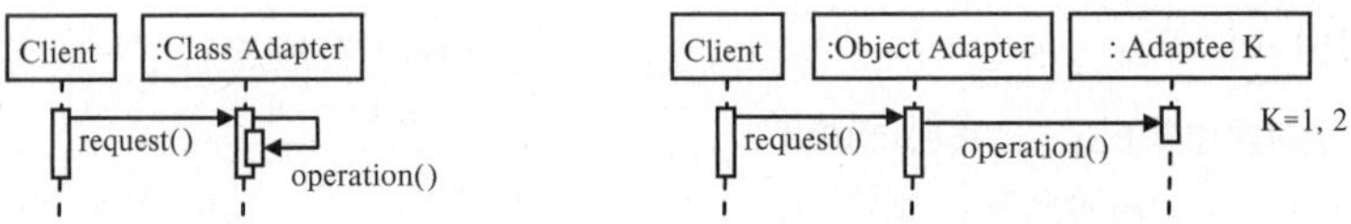

(a) Class adapter (b) Object adapter</td></tr>
<tr><td>Roles and Responsibilities</td><td>• Client Interface: It defines an interface to match the one that the client expects.
• Adapteee Interface: It defines a common interface for all implementing adaptee subclasses.
• Adaptee, Adaptee 1, Adaptee 2: These represent existing classes. The Adaptee Interface makes Adaptee 1 and Adaptee 2 interchangeable.
• Class Adapter, Object Adapter: These implement the Client Interface to adapt to an existing interface.</td></tr>
<tr><td>Benefits</td><td>• It converts one interface to another, facilitating reuse of existing software including commercial off-the-shelf software.
• Object adapter can dynamically change the adaptee.</td></tr>
<tr><td>Liabilities</td><td></td></tr>
<tr><td>Guidelines</td><td></td></tr>
<tr><td>Related Patterns</td><td>• Adapter is used after the software is implemented; Bridge is used during design to provide the flexibility.
• Adapter converts interfaces while Proxy adds functionality.
• Façade simplifies client interface and interaction to a web of objects.</td></tr>
<tr><td>Uses</td><td></td></tr>
</table>

FIGURE 16.31 Specification of the adapter pattern

Applying the Adapter Pattern

As a matter of fact, the various listeners in Figure 16.28 are object adapters because they convert the listener interfaces to the Edit Diagram Controller interface. To help understanding, Figure 16.33 shows an object diagram. It shows the relationships between relevant objects and how the action listeners convert the interfaces.

Benefits of the Adpater Pattern

The adapter pattern is often used as an after-fact remedy to fix the mismatch between two interfaces. It is useful when one wants to reuse an existing, or third-party, component, but its interface does not match the interface that the client expects. Use the class adapter when it needs to adapt only one adaptee class and this will not change

	Class Adapter	Object Adapter
Mechanism	Inheritance	Object composition
Pros	1. Reuses the implementation of the adaptee class. 2. The adapter can override the behavior of the adaptee class. 3. The runtime behavior of the adapter is easy to understand. 4. Each class adapter introduces only one adapter object.	1. Dynamic binding allows the adapter to change dynamically to adapt to objects of other adaptee classes. 2. The adapter can add functionality in addition to the functionality provided by the adaptee object. 3. It can define a subclass of the adaptee class and override the behavior of the adaptee class. The adapter can then adapt to an object of the subclass. 4. The behavior of the adapter can change dynamically by changing the adaptee object.
Cons	1. Static binding to an adaptee class prevents the adapter to adapt to other classes. 2. It breaks encapsulation because the adapter can override the behavior of the adaptee class. 3. If the adaptee class is a final class, then class adapter cannot be used. 4. The use of inheritance means dependency of the adapter class on the adaptee class and change to the adaptee class may affect the adapter class.	1. It is not as easy to override the behavior of the adaptee class. 2. The runtime behavior may be difficult to understand because the adapter can dynamically adapt to any of the classes in the adaptee inheritance hierarchy. 3. It requires the creation of at least an adapter object and an adaptee object.
Usage	Use class adapter if: 1. The adapter needs to adapt to only one adaptee class, and 2. No other adaptee class is anticipated.	Use object adapter if: 1. The adapter needs to adapt to different types of object. 2. Other adaptee classes or objects are anticipated. 3. The behavior of the adapter must change during execution time.

FIGURE 16.32 Comparing class adapter and object adapter

in the future. Use object adapter if there are more than one adaptee class, or the adapter needs to vary its behavior dynamically.

16.6.4 Request Handler Is Unknow in Advance

The state diagram editor may evaluate the quality of a state diagram and rank it accordingly. This can be done by using a set of assessment rules, which evaluate attributes

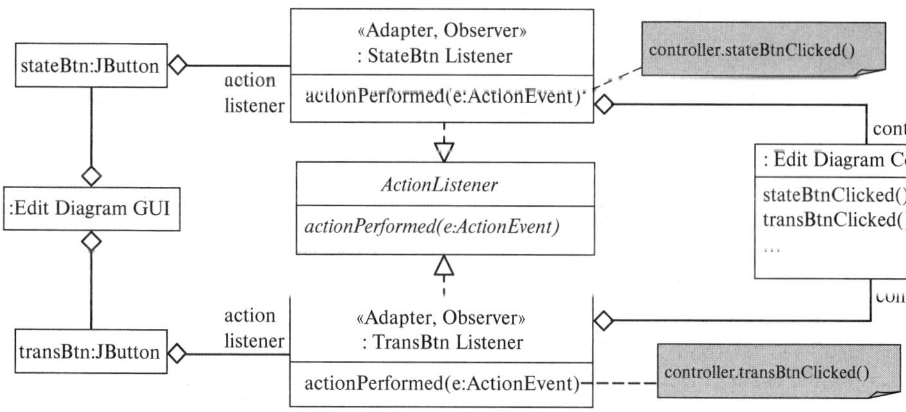

FIGURE 16.33 Converting interfaces from Action Listener to Edit Diagram Controller

of a state diagram. For example, a state diagram may be assessed by conformance to requirements, number of unreachable states and dead states, and number of nondeterministic transitions. Clearly, when evaluating a state diagram, which evaluation rule can be applied is unknown in advance. There are many such examples in the real world, including purchase order processing and stock recommendation. In purchase order processing, an employee can submit a purchase order to the team lead, who may be authorized to approve or disapprove it; otherwise, the purchase order is forwarded to the project manager. The manager may approve, disapprove, or forward the purchase order, and so on. In this case, who can handle the purchase order is unknown in advance. In stock recommendation, stocks are evaluated using rules that assess attributes of stocks and generate a ranking accordingly. In this case, which rule is evaluated to true for a stock is not known in advance. The design problem in these examples is different from the design problem solved by the observer pattern, where the observers or handlers for an observable are known in advance. Searching the patterns in Figure 16.3 finds the chain of responsibility pattern. Its specification is given in Figure 16.34.

The chain of responsibility pattern arranges request handlers one after another, forming a chain of handlers, each assigned a given responsibility. The handlers are ordered so that if a request cannot be handled by a handler, it may be handled by the successor. The purchase order processing example illustrates how the handlers are ordered. The rules to rank a state diagram should be ordered from hardest to satisfy to the easiest.

Applying the Chain of Responsibility Pattern

EXAMPLE 16.17 Extend the state diagram editor to include the ability to rank state diagrams as excellent, good, fair, and poor.

Solution: A state diagram can be evaluated by various criteria. For the sake of illustrating the design and implementation of the chain of responsibility pattern, we use only two criteria: correctness and completeness of state transitions. Let f be the set of state transitions stated in the requirements and t the set of state transitions in the state diagram. Then the correctness and completeness are defined as:

Correctness $Cr = | f \cap t | / | t |$
Completeness $Cp = | f \cap t | / | f |$

where $f \cap t$ is the set intersection of f and t, and represents transitions that are stated in the requirements and shown in the state diagram. In other words, these are considered correct transitions. The expression $| f \cap t |$ represents the number of correct transitions. Thus, correctness is defined as the percentage of transitions in the state diagram that are correct transitions. Likewise, completeness is the percentage of transitions stated in the requirements that appear in the state diagram. We assume that a state diagram will be ranked excellent, good, and fair if its correctness and completeness are at least 90%, 80%, and 70%, respectively. It is ranked poor if its correctness or completeness is less than 70%. Because we do not know in advance which rule can be applied, we design with the chain of responsibility pattern. Figure 16.35 shows the design of the relevant part of the state diagram editor. Figure 16.36 shows a sample implementation.

Name	Chain of Responsibility
Type	GoF/Behavioral
Specification	
Problem	How to process a request if the exact handler is not known in advance.
Solution	Chain the handlers from more specific to more general, and pass the request through the handlers until one that can handle it.
Design	
Structural	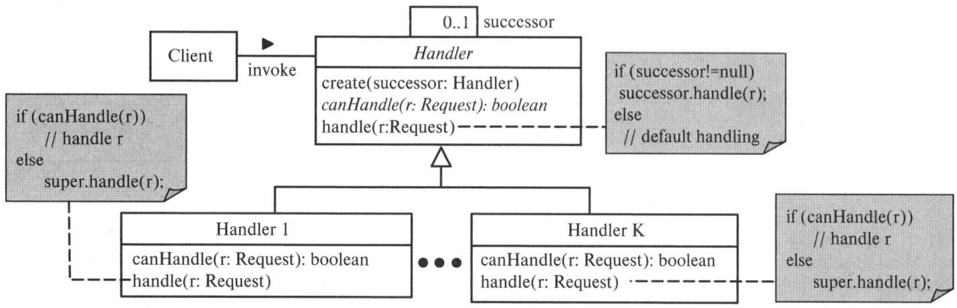
Behavioral	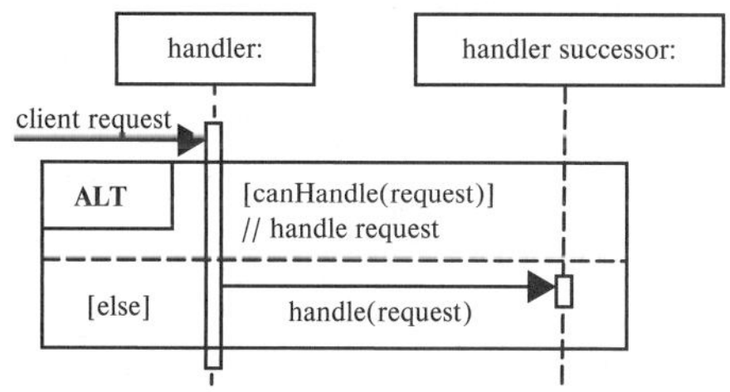
Roles and Responsibilities	• Handler: This abstract class defines a common interface and the successor relationship for the concrete handler subclasses. • Handler 1, ..., Handler K: These are concrete handlers, each of which handles only one specific request. If a handler cannot handler a request, it hands over the request to the next handler. • Client: It invokes the first handler of the chain of handlers to handle the request.
Benefits	• It avoids using conditional statements to check the request and handle it accordingly. • It supports separation of concerns because different concerns are assigned to different handlers. • It supports high cohesion and designing "stupid object" because each concrete handler knows how to process one specific request. Moreover, each concrete handler knows only its successor. • It is easy to add or remove concrete handlers. • The chain of handlers can be rearranged easily and dynamically. • Concrete handlers can form a tree or lattice, with the leaf nodes representing the most-specific handlers and the root representing the most-general handler.
Liabilities	• A request may not be handled if the chain does not have a handler to handle it. • It may affect performance if many handlers must try before a request is handled.
Guidelines	• Use Chain of Responsibility only if the exact handler for a request is not known in advance, else, use Observer instead. • Use Visitor if the concrete handlers perform type-dependent handlings.
Related Patterns	• Both Chain of Responsibility and Observer define a one-to-many relationship between a request/event and handlers. In Observer, a request is handled by zero or more handlers, which are known in advance. In Chain of Responsibility, a request is handled by zero or one handler, which is unknown in advance. • Visitor uses polymorphic functions to process different types of object differently whereas Chain of Responsibility uses handlers to process the same type of request differently.
Uses	• It can be used in a rule-based system to chain the business rules.

FIGURE 16.34 Specification of the chain of responsibility pattern

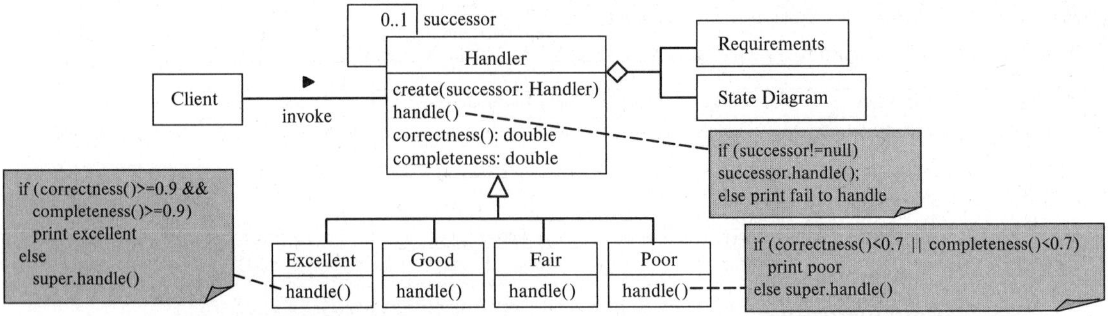

FIGURE 16.35 Applying chain of responsibility to rank state diagrams

```
public class Handler {
  public static Requirements r=
    new Requirements();
  public static StateDiagram d;
  protected Handler successor;
  public Handler(Handler s) { successor=s; }
  public void handle() {
    if (successor!=null) successor.handle();
    else System.out.println("Fail to handle.");
  }
  public double correctness() {
    HashSet a=(HashSet)d.t.clone();
    a.retainAll(r.f);
    return (double)a.size()/(double)d.t.size();
  }
  public double completeness() {
    HashSet a=(HashSet)d.t.clone();
    a.retainAll(r.f);
    return (double)a.size()/(double)r.f.size();
  }
}

public class Excellent extends Handler {
  public Excellent(Handler s) { super(s); }
  public void handle() {
    if (correctness()>=0.9 &&
      completeness() >=0.9)
      System.out.println("Excellent");
    else super.handle(); }
}

public class Fair extends Handler {
  public Fair(Handler s) { super(s); }
```

```
  public void handle() {
    if (correctness()>=0.7 &&
      completeness()>=0.7)
      System.out.println("Fair");
    else super.handle(); }
}

public class Good extends Handler {
  public Good(Handler s) { super(s); }
  public void handle() {
    if (correctness() >=0.8 &&
      completeness() >=0.8)
      System.out.println("Good");
    else super.handle(); }
}

public class Poor extends Handler {
  public Poor(Handler s) { super(s); }
  public void handle() {
    if (correctness()<0.7 || completeness()<0.7)
      System.out.println("Poor");
    else super.handle(); }
}

public class StateDiagram {
  HashSet<String> t=new HashSet<String>() {
    public Object clone() {
      HashSet s=new HashSet();
      Iterator<String> it=iterator();
      while (it.hasNext()) { s.add(it.next()); }
      return s;
    }
  };
  public void add(String ti) { t.add(ti); }
}
```

```
public class Requirements {
  Collection<String> f=new HashSet<String>();
  public Requirements(){
    for(int i=0; i<10; i++) f.add("f"+i); }
}

public class AssessController {
  Handler head;
  public AssessController() {
    Handler poor=new Poor(null);
    Handler fair=new Fair(poor);
    Handler good=new Good(fair);
    Handler head=new Excellent(good); }
  public void assess() { head.handle(); }
}

public class Main {
  static StateDiagram createSD(int k) {
    StateDiagram d=new StateDiagram ();
    Iterator<String> it=Handler.r.f.iterator();
    int i=0;
    while (it.hasNext() && i<k)
    { d.add(it.next()); i++; }
    return d;
  }
  public static void main(String[] args) {
    Handler.r=new Requirements();
    Handler.d=createSD(9);
    new AssessController().assess();
  }
}
```

FIGURE 16.36 Sample implementation of the design in Figure 16.35

It should be pointed out that in Figure 16.35 there are four concrete handlers for four recommendations. In practice, it may not be the case. For example, consider stock recommendation. A stock may be ranked strong buy, buy, hold, and sell. A strong buy recommendation can be issued for various reasons. For example, the stock is cheap, the stock exhibits favorable fundamental, or technical stock patterns. This implies that there are several concrete handlers, each of which ranks a stock as strong buy but using different evaluation criteria. Similarly, there are several handlers for each of the other ranks.

Benefits and Liabilities of the Chain of Responsibility Pattern

The chain of responsibility pattern brings the following benefits to a design:

- It greatly reduces complexity as compare to design and implementation that use nested conditional statements to determine how to handle a request.
- It is easy to introduce new concrete handlers to support requirements change, useful for agile development.
- The concrete handlers can be rearranged easily and dynamically. This is difficult with nested conditional statements.
- The concrete handlers can be organized to form a tree or lattice, resulting in a hierarchy of handlers. This is difficult to do with nested conditional statements.
- It supports separation of concerns by assigning separate handling responsibilities to different handlers.
- It results in high cohesion and "stupid objects" because each handler can do only one thing, and knows only one successor.

The liabilities of the pattern are:

- A request may not be handled because there is no handler that can handle it.
- It may incur performance penalty due to processing by a series of handlers.
- It may produce incorrect result if the concrete handlers are not chained properly. For example, the concrete handlers in Figure 16.36 are ordered Excellent, Good, Fair, and Poor. If they were ordered with Fair as the head handler, then an "excellent" state diagram would be ranked "fair."

16.6.5 Enhancing Display Capability with Decorator

Many software systems use scrollbars to facilitate viewing large documents and diagrams. Moreover, some users want to show borders that surround selected areas of the document or diagram. These functions could be provided by adding methods to the classes that represent documents or diagrams. However, doing so may result in assigning irrelevant responsibilities to these classes. Another approach is defining subclasses that extend the existing classes with such functionalities. This approach may result in a large number of subclasses. For example, if there are a half dozen functions and they can be combined with each other, such as diagrams with a border and scrollbars, then the number of combinations is $6! = 720$. The *decorator* pattern, described in Figure 16.37, allows the client to add or remove functionality freely and dynamically.

Applying the Decorator Pattern

Suppose that the state diagram editor allows the user to show or hide UML notes attached to diagram elements. Figure 16.38 illustrates how the decorator pattern accomplishes this. The figure illustrates how a state with a UML note is created and painted. First, the client creates a state and a UML note that decorates the state. The note is added to the state diagram composite. During repaint, the client calls the draw (g) method of the state diagram. The state diagram calls the draw (g) method of the UML note. The UML note calls the draw (g) method of the state and then calls its own drawNote (g) method. In this way, the state with a UML note is painted.

Name	Decorator
Type	GoF/Structural
Specification	
Problem	How to add or remove functionality to existing objects freely and dynamically?
Solution	Define an aggregate class of the existing class to provide the additional functionality. Define a common interface to hide the difference of the two classes.
Design	
Structural	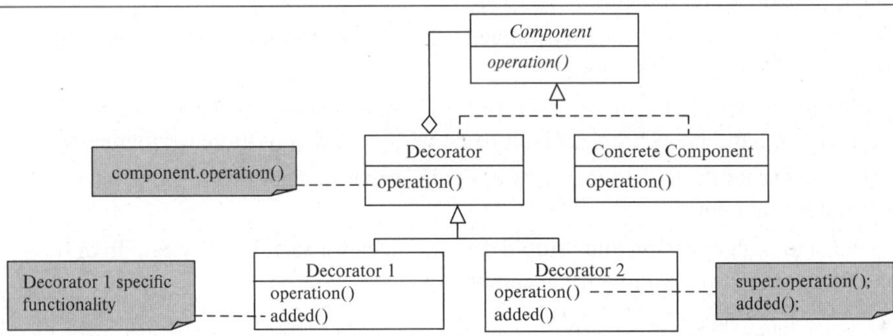
Behavioral	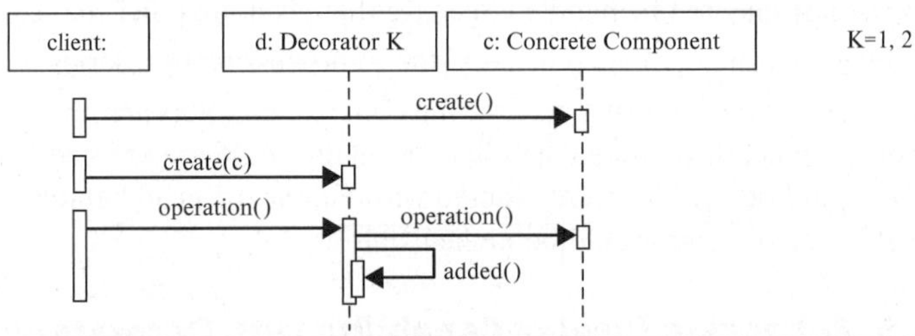
Roles and Responsibilities	• Component: It defines a common interface for Concrete Components and Decorators. • Concrete Component: It represents all concrete components to be decorated. • Decorator: The parent class for all concrete decorators. It invokes the operation of the concrete component decorated. • Decorators 1-2: These represent all concrete decorators. Through the parent Decorator, they invoke the operation of the concrete component decorated. They then invoke the added functionality.
Benefits	• Decorators can be added to, or removed from existing objects freely and dynamically. • New decorators can be added easily.
Liabilities	
Guidelines	
Related Patterns	• Template Method may simplify the implementation of concrete decorators. • Both Decorator and Visitor add functionality to existing classes. However, in Visitor the added functionality is type-dependent. • Decorator may be used with Interpreter: different decorators may interpret an expression differently.
Uses	• Encryption, decryption, compression, decompression are example applications of decorator. Some Java input/output APIs such as Filter Input Stream and its subclasses are decorators. • Decorator may be applied to add interpretation or semantics to the nodes of an abstract syntax tree.

FIGURE 16.37 Specification of the decorator pattern

Encryption, decryption, compression, and decompression of communication streams are other applications of the decorator pattern. That is, they add functionality to the communication streams. In Java, the pattern is applied to add functionality to an input stream or an output stream. Figure 16.39 shows the Filter Input Stream decorator. The Input Stream is the superclass of all classes that represent an

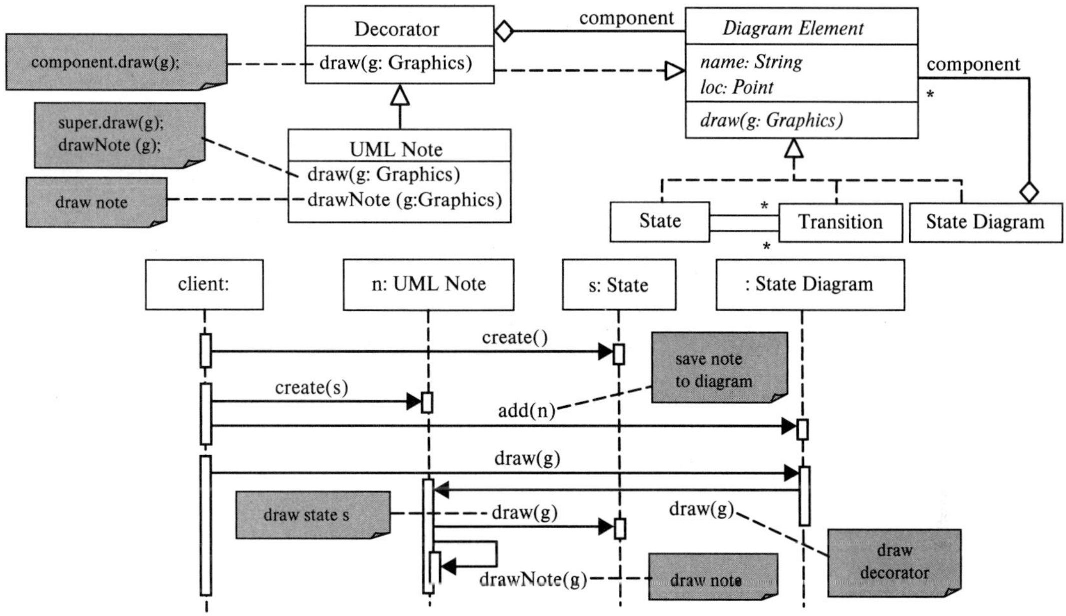

FIGURE 16.38 Decorating a state diagram

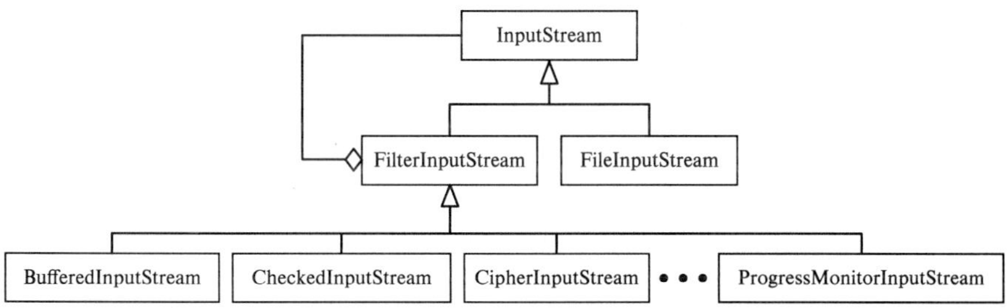

FIGURE 16.39 The FilterInputStream decorator

input stream of bytes. The Filter Input Stream class adds functionality to facilitate the processing of the input stream. Its subclasses are the concrete decorators. For example, the Buffered Input Stream provides the ability to buffer the input stream and set and reset marks in the input stream. The Checked Input Stream computes the checksum so that the client can use it to verify the integrity of the input data. The Cipher Input Stream adds cryptographic functions to the Input Stream. The Progress Monitor Input Stream decorator allows the user to monitor the progress when reading a large file. It displays a progress dialog if the input stream requires a while to read.

16.7 APPLYING AGILE PRINCIPLES

GUIDELINE 16.1 Responding to change.

Agile development advocates responding to change over following a plan. Patterns support design for change. Proper application of patterns results in software that is easy to change and extend. Thus, "responding to change" is supported. This means that the team anticipates future change and applies patterns to support design for change.

GUIDELINE 16.2 The team must be empowered to make decisions.

Patterns improve productivity and quality. Therefore, the team members should be trained, encouraged, and empowered to apply patterns. However, patterns must not be misused or abused (see the "good enough is enough" guideline below).

GUIDELINE 16.3 Values working software over comprehensive documentation.

Patterns must not be applied just for the sake of documentation. Patterns should be applied to improve quality of the working software and productivity of the team. This requires that the team knows how to apply the right pattern, at the right time, solve the right problem, in the right way. Moreover, the team must implement the patterns correctly.

GUIDELINE 16.4 Good enough is enough.

Patterns should be applied to solve design problems, not for the sake of decorating the design with patterns. Patterns must not be applied to solve trivial design problems, or problems that are not worth applying a pattern. For trivial problems, the application of patterns probably introduces more complexity than not applying them. Consider, for example, the drawing of a transition in the state diagram editor. It is true that sometimes a transition may consists of line segments plus an arrow line. These are easy to draw using Java Graphics. If the builder pattern is applied to draw the line segments, the arrow line, and the transition label, then the pattern is misused. Good enough is enough means that patterns should be applied when they are needed, not when they are wanted. It is not the case that the more patterns the better.

16.8 SUMMARY

This chapter presents situation-specific patterns, each of which solves a class of design problems. Pattern application is a challenge for beginners. Therefore, this chapter describes a problem-directed approach for applying patterns. It demonstrates the process with the design of a state diagram editor. That is, patterns are applied during the design process when design problems are encountered. Patterns are identified and applied to solve the design problems.

16.9 CHAPTER REVIEW QUESTIONS

1. What are design patterns?
2. What are the uses of design patterns?
3. How are design patterns described?
4. How does one apply design patterns?
5. When does one apply design patterns?
6. Can two or more patterns be applied to solve a design problem?
7. Can a pattern be applied twice to solve a design problem?
8. What is the relationship between design patterns and design principles?

16.10 EXERCISES

16.1 Produce sample code for the design in Figure 16.12.

16.2 What are the advantages of applying the visitor pattern to the state diagram editor as shown in Figures 16.14 and 16.15?

16.3 Discuss the similarities and differences of the two patterns in each of the following pairs of patterns. Moreover, give two situations that are not in the textbook or the lecture notes in which each pattern can be exclusively applied to exactly one situation. Describe how each pattern is applied and why the other pattern is not applicable.

- **a.** Decorator and visitor
- **b.** Memento and state
- **c.** Abstract factory and builder
- **d.** Strategy and visitor
- **e.** Flyweight and singleton
- **f.** Observer and chain of responsibility
- **g.** Abstract factory and creator

16.4 The preorder traversal processes the node visited first, and then the left child and the right child of the node. Write an algorithm to implement an iterator for the preorder traversal.

16.5 Design and implement a simple application that applies the controller, expert, iterator and composite patterns. When the application starts, it displays a window containing two buttons and a drawing area. The buttons are labeled "Circle" and "Box," respectively. When one of the buttons is clicked, and then the mouse is clicked in the drawing area, the corresponding shape is painted at the clicked location. The application should allow the user to draw multiple circles and/or boxes.

16.6 Design, implement, and test the subsystem for purchase order processing described in Section 16.6.4. Assume that there are three levels of approval authorities: project manager, engineering director, and cooperate finance. They can approve each purchase that is within \$10,000, \$100,000, and \$1 million, and not to exceed a total of \$100,000, \$1 million, and \$10 million per year, respectively.

16.7 Which other patterns can be applied to simplify the design and implementation of the purchase-order processing subsystem? How can this be accomplished? What assumptions must be made?

16.11 REFERENCES

[Gamma 1995] Erich Gamma, Richard Helm, Ralph Johnson and John Vlissides, "Design Patterns: Elements of Reusable Object-Oriented Software," Addison-Wesley, 1995.

17

Chapter

Applying Patterns to Design a Persistence Framework

Key Takeaway Points

- A *persistence framework* hides the database access functions from the business objects. It substantially reduces the impact to the business objects when the database is changed.
- The persistence framework applies the *bridge, command, factory method, prototype, proxy*, and *template method* patterns.

Chapter 16 presents a pattern application process and patterns for solving various design problems. The patterns are applied to the design of a state diagram editor. The state diagram editor needs to store the diagrams in a database. In procedural programming, the functions access the database directly, resulting in the so-called embedded code. It means that database queries are embedded in the procedural programs such as C code. Influenced by procedural programming, some programmers design and implement object-oriented systems the same way. That is, the object-oriented program lets business objects access the database directly. This approach has several problems. In this chapter, the problems are discussed and the design of a persistence framework is described. During this design process, several patterns are applied. As our case study, we will discuss how to design a persistence framework for a library information system (LIS). However, the result is applicable to all application systems that need to store and retrieve objects with a database. In this chapter, you will learn the following:

- What is a persistence framework, and why is it useful?
- What are the bridge, command, factory method, prototype, proxy, and template method patterns?
- How does one apply these situation-specific patterns to the design of the persistence framework?

17.1 PROBLEMS WITH DIRECT DATABASE ACCESS

Many applications need to store information to and retrieve information from a persistence storage such as the file system or a database. For example, an LIS uses a database to store information about documents and patrons. Chapter 6 presented a real-world case. The development team adopted a design that lets the business objects access an Ontologies OO-DBMS database directly as shown in Figure 17.1(*a*), where X denotes any object class. When the project approached its completion, the database vendor went into bankruptcy. This and the tight coupling to the database forced the team to change every business object because the database had to be replaced. The design in Figure 17.1(*a*) is not good because it is associated with a number of problems:

1. The controller has to know how to work with the database. This means that the controller has to know the database schemas, the data semantics, and how to query the database. For a relational database, this means that the controller has to know the tables, the meaning of each attribute, and how to query the database using SQL.
2. Since every use case controller works with the database, much database access code is duplicated. For example, the Checkout Document and Return Document use cases need to retrieve document information from the database. Such code is duplicated in both use case controllers.
3. If a different type of database is used, then all of the controllers have to change and such changes are costly.
4. If the database is located at a remote site, then the controller has to implement network communication protocols, *marshalling* and *unmarshalling.* (Marshalling converts an object to a format that is suitable for network transmission. Unmarshalling does the opposite.)
5. If the needed information is distributed over several databases, then the controller has to work with all of these databases.
6. If data access control is required due to security considerations, then the controller must also implement access control protocols.

17.2 HIDING PERSISTENCE STORAGE WITH BRIDGE

The problems identified in Section 17.1 imply that the controller in Figure 17.1(a) is assigned too many responsibilities. It is complex and difficult to understand, implement, test, and maintain. Moreover, the business objects are tightly coupled with the

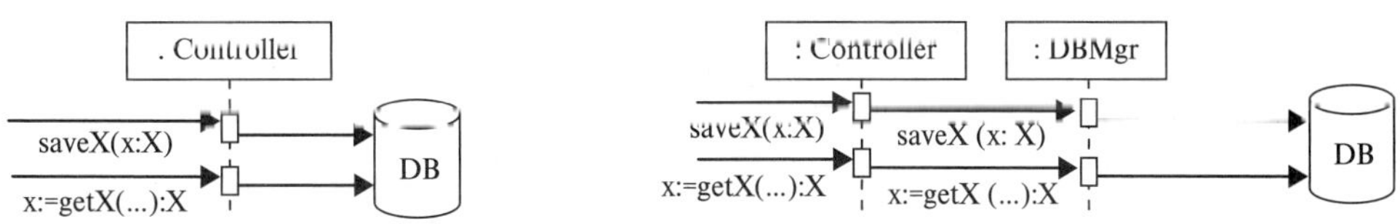

(a) Tight coupling between controller and database (b) Hiding database with a DB manager

FIGURE 17.1 Tight coupling and low coupling with a database

database. This implies that changes to the database will have significant impact on the business objects, that is, changes to the business objects are required. Frequently, such changes are difficult and costly. A better design should separate the database access responsibilities from the controller and assign them to a database manager (DBMgr), as shown in Figure 17.1(*b*). In this design, the controller is responsible for handling actor requests while the DBMgr handles database access. In this way, the DBMgr hides the database access from the business objects. Changes to the database will have little impact on the business objects. In most cases, the DBMgr delegates the requests from the controller to other objects, which access the database.

The bridge pattern can be used to accomplish the goals of the DB manager. The specification of the pattern is given in Figure 17.2. The main idea behind the bridge pattern is *decoupling the client interface from the implementation so that each of them can change independently*. It solves the problems discussed in Section 17.1 because the controller as the client is decoupled from the database access implementation. Therefore, change to the database implementation has little impact on the controller.

Name	Bridge
Type	GoF/Structural
Specification	
Problem	How does one maintain a stable client interface while the implementation changes?
Solution	Decouple the implementation from the client interface so that they can change independently.
Design	
Structural	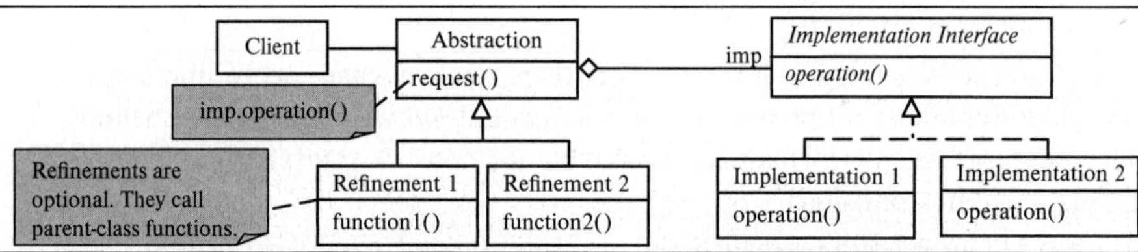
Behavioral	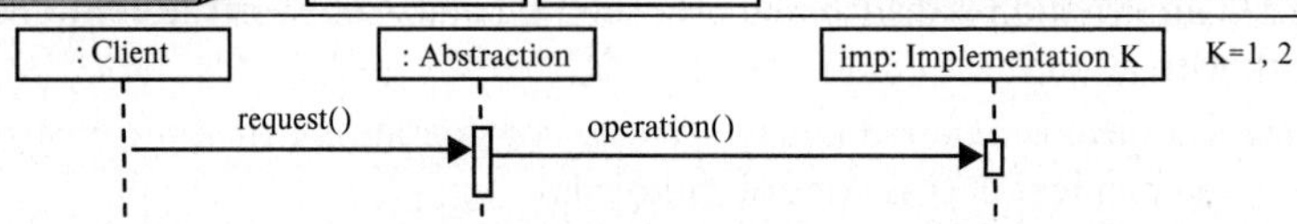
Roles and Responsibilities	• Abstraction: A class that maintains a stable client interface. It delegates client requests to the concrete Implementation 1 or Implementation 2 object. By changing the reference, the implementation changes. • Refinements 1-2: They are optional, and refine the interface of Abstraction, to provide different client interfaces. • Implementation Interface: It defines a common interface for all concrete Implementation subclasses. • Implementations 1-2: They represent all implementing subclasses that implement the functionality for different platforms.
Benefits	• It decouples the implementations from abstraction. • It maintains a stable client interface while allowing abstraction or implementation to change independently. • The client does not know which implementation is used. • It is easy to add concrete implementations. • The client is not affected by changes to implementation.
Liabilities	More classes to implement but the benefits are worth the extra effort.
Guidelines	• Apply the bridge pattern in cases where dynamically changing the implementation is required or anticipated. • The functions defined for the abstraction and implementation interface may have the same signature or different signatures.
Related Patterns	• Bridge is used "before the fact" while Adapter is used "after the fact." • Bridge is often confused with Strategy. Strategy lets the client select and use different algorithms. Bridge hides platform-specific implementations from the client.
Uses	Persistence framework, and desktop applications to support different window operating systems

FIGURE 17.2 Specification of the bridge pattern

Applying the Bridge Pattern

EXAMPLE 17.1

Apply the bridge pattern to provide a platform-independent persistent storage for objects of an LIS.

Solution: Figure 17.3 shows the design that applies the bridge pattern. The figure also shows the mapping between pattern classes and classes in the existing design. The DBMgr decouples the client from the database access implementation. The DBImpl Interface defines a common interface for the subclasses, which implement database access functions for various DBMS as needed. The DBMgr maintains a reference to a concrete database access implementation. When the client invokes a database access function such as getUser(...) of the DBMgr, the DBMgr delegates the request to the concrete database access implementation. In this way, the client is decoupled from the concrete implementation. The client is not affected by changes in the implementation as long as the DBMgr interface remains the same.

In Figure 17.3, the DBMgr and the DBImpl Interface contain the same set of operations. But it need not be the case. The two may contain different sets of operations. To save space, only four operations are shown in Figure 17.3. In general, if an application needs to store objects of N different classes, then the DBMgr will have at least N*2 operations, that is, for each class X, there are two operations, getX(. . .):X and saveX(x:X). In addition, the DBMgr may have other operations to search objects and generate statistical reports.

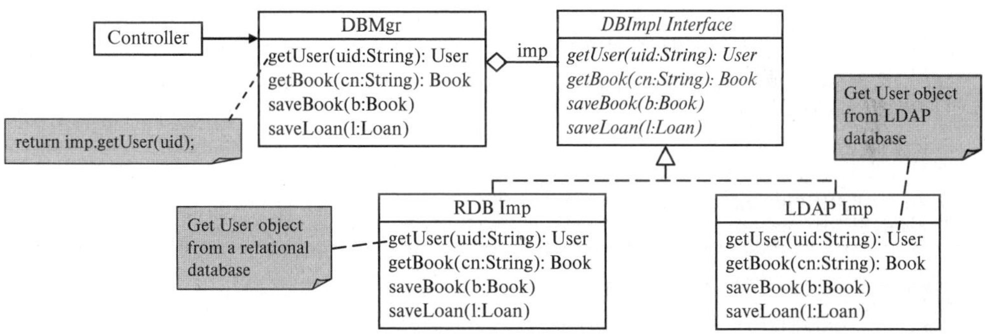

Editor Class	New/ Existing	Bridge Class	Editor Class	New/ Existing	Bridge Class
DB Impl Interface getUser(uid:String): User getBook(cn: String): Book saveBook(b: Book) saveLoan(l: Loan)	New	Implementation Interface operation()	LDAP Impl getUser(uid:String): User getBook(cn: String): Book saveBook(b: Book) saveLoan(l: Loan)	New	Implementation 2 operation()
RDB Impl getUser(uid:String): User getBook(cn: String): Book saveBook(b: Book) saveLoan(l: Loan)	New	Implementation 1 operation()	DBMgr getUser(uid:String): User getBook(cn: String): Book saveBook(b: Book) saveLoan(l: Loan)	Existing	Abstraction request()
			Controller	Existing	Client

FIGURE 17.3 Applying the bridge pattern

17.3 ENCAPSULATING DATABASE REQUESTS AS COMMANDS

Section 17.2 points out that if an application stores N classes of object, then a database access implementation will have at least 2*N operations. If N is large, then the database access implementation will contain thousands of lines of code. This makes the class difficult to understand and maintain. One solution to this problem is to distribute the responsibilities to other objects. This significantly reduces the size of the database access implementation. The *command* pattern described in Figure 17.4 can be used to implement the individual operations that access the database.

The ability to undo or redo a command is an attractive feature of the command pattern. To provide these capabilities, the Command Interface is extended with three additional operations, as shown in Figure 17.4(b):

1. undo(): This method simply reverses the execute() operation of the command.
2. redo(): This method simply reverses the last undo operation of the command.
3. reversible(): boolean: This method returns true if the command can be undone, else it returns false.

In addition to the three methods, an executed stack and an undone stack are used to store the executed commands and the undone commands, respectively. To undo the last operation, the reversible() function of the command at the top of the executed stack is called. If it returns true, then the command on the executed stack is popped and its undo() function is invoked. The command is pushed onto the undone stack. To redo the last undone operation, the command on the undone stack is popped and its redo() function is invoked. It is then pushed onto the executed stack.

Applying the Command Pattern

EXAMPLE 17.2 Figure 17.5 shows an application of the command pattern to the design of the persistence framework. The DBCmd interface defines a uniform interface for the concrete commands, which implement the database operations. There is a one-to-one correspondence between the database operations and the concrete commands. For example, the Get User class implements the getUser(. . .) operation of RDB Impl class. The data needed by the operation are passed as parameters to the constructor of the concrete commands. For example, the user id (uid) is passed to the constructor of the Get User class to be used by the execute() method to retrieve the User object. In Figure 17.5, the RDB Impl class is the Client. Its operations create the command objects and call their execute() methods to carry out the database operations. For example, the saveBook(b:Book) method creates a Save Book object and calls its execute() function to save the book.

Name	Command
Type	GoF/Behavioral
Specification	
Problem	How does one encapsulate operations so that their execution can be arranged flexibly and dynamically?
Solution	Define a uniform command interface and implement each operation as a command subclass so that the client can execute the command objects in flexible ways including undoing and redoing operations.
Design	
Structural	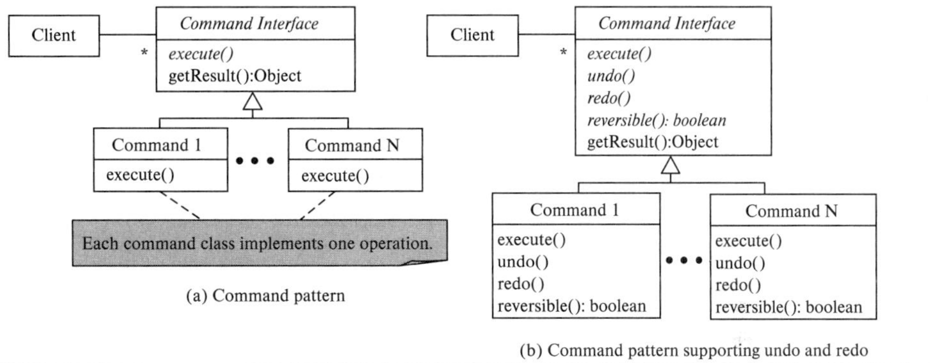 (a) Command pattern (b) Command pattern supporting undo and redo
Behavioral	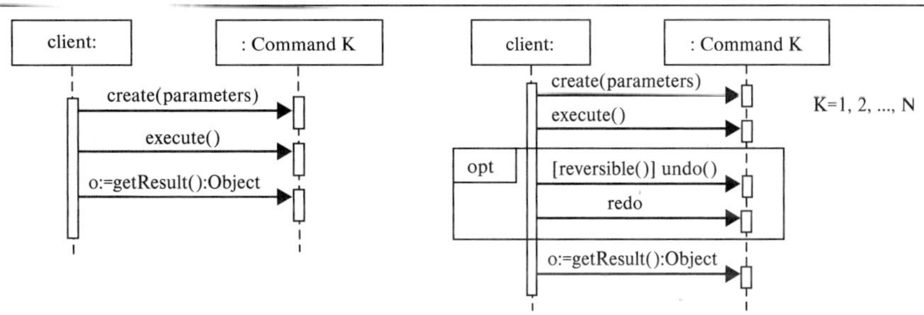
Roles and Responsibilities	• Client: It creates the desired command objects, invokes execute() methods in whichever order it wants, and gets the results. It may also queue the command objects and execute them at a later time. • Command Interface: It defines a uniform interface for the concrete command subclasses so that the client need not know which command it executes. The undo, redo and reversible operations let the client undo and redo commands. • Command 1-N: Each command subclass implements one operation and may undo or redo the operation.
Benefits	• It encapsulates operations as command objects, allowing the operations to be executed in flexible ways. • Commands can be composed to form composite commands using the composite pattern. • It is easy to add new commands. • It supports undo and redo operations. • It supports separation of concerns and high-cohesion design principles because different responsibilities are assigned to different command classes, and each command object does only one thing.
Liabilities	More classes to design and implement.
Guidelines	
Related Patterns	• Command is often confused with Bridge. The concrete command subclasses implement different functionalities but in Bridge the concrete implementations implement the same functionality but for different platforms. In Bridge, the client does not create or invoke the concrete implementation objects whereas in Command, the client creates and invokes the command objects. • Command differs from Strategy in that concrete strategies implement same functionality using different algorithms. • Command, Interpreter and Chain of Responsibility can be combined to design and implement rule based systems that support dynamic modification of rules.
Uses	Persistence framework to encapsulate database access operations; agent-oriented systems to encapsulate planned actions.

FIGURE 17.4 Specification of the command pattern

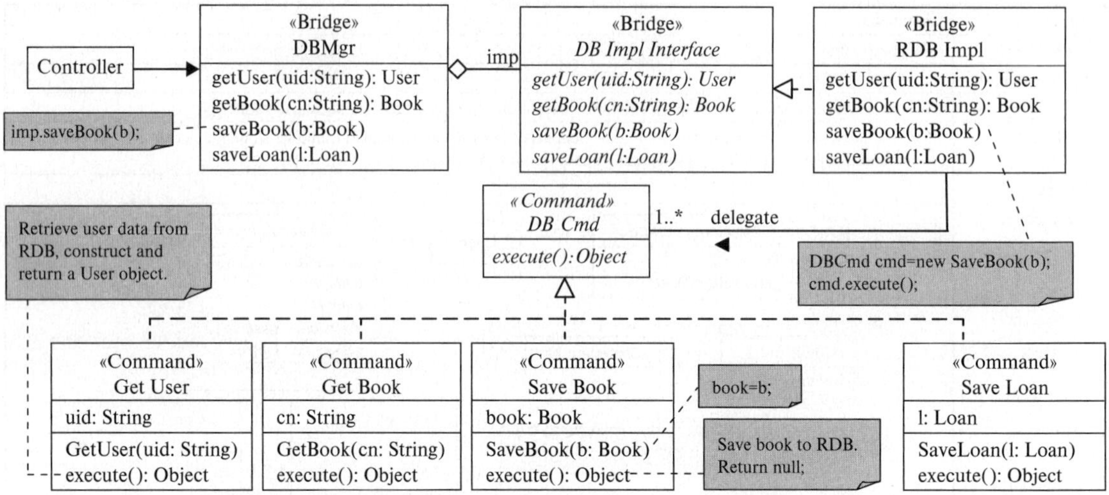

FIGURE 17.5 Applying the command pattern

Sample Code

EXAMPLE 17.3 Figure 17.6 shows the sample code that partially implements the design in Figure 17.5. Only the Get User command class and the RDB Impl class are implemented. It is assumed that User objects are stored in the User table with "uid" and "Name" as the column labels.

Benefits of the Command Pattern

The command pattern is applicable, but not limited, to the following situations:

- *Encapsulate requests as command objects.* By delegating a request to a command object, the code size of the delegating class is reduced. For example, a DBMgr usually has to process many different types of database requests. It may contain thousands of lines of code if it processes these requests itself. Delegating the requests to the command objects substantially reduces the code size of the DB manager.
- *The application needs to add new requests or functions.* It is easy to add concrete command classes that implement new operations. The command pattern has a simple interface. Moreover, the command objects are relatively independent. Therefore, it is easy to generate, compile, and load concrete command classes dynamically. This is useful for certain applications. For example, an intelligent system with learning ability may discover new actions. This means that the system needs to introduce new command classes during program execution.
- *The application needs to queue the requests and execute them at a different time.* For example, JUnit stores tests in a composite and executes them when the test runner is invoked. A rational agent generates plans of actions and executes them

```
public class DBMgr {
  private DBImplInterface imp;
  public DBMgr() { imp=Config.getInstance().getDB(); }
  User getUser(String uid) { return imp.getUser(uid); }
  Book getBook(String cn) { return imp.getBook(cn); }
  void saveBook(Book b) { imp.saveBook(b); }
  void saveLoan(Loan l) { imp.saveLoan(l); }
}

public interface DBImplInterface {
  User getUser(String uid); Book getBook(String cn);
  void saveBook(Book b); void saveLoan(Loan l);
}

public class Config {
  private static Config instance=new Config();
  private Config(){}
  public static Config getInstance() { return instance; }
  public DBImplInterface getDB() { return new RDBImpl(); }
}

public class Book {
  private String cn, title; private boolean isAvailable;
  public void setCN(String n) { cn=n; }
  public void setTitle(String t) { title=t; }
  public void setAvailable(boolean a) { isAvailable=a; }
}

public class User {
  private String uid, name;
  public void setUID(String uid) { this.uid=uid; }
  public void setName(String name) { this.name=name; }
}

public class Loan {
  private User patron; private Book book; Date dueDate;
  public Loan(User p, Book b) { patron=p; book=b; }
  public setDueDate(Date d) { dueDate=d; }
}

class GetBook implements DBCmd {
  String cn; GetBook(String cn) { this.cn=cn; }
  public Object execute() { ... }
}
```

```
public class RDBImpl implements DBImplInterface {
  public User getUser(String uid) {
    DBCmd cmd=new GetUser(uid); return (User)cmd.execute(); }
  public Book getBook(String cn) {
    DBCmd cmd=new GetBook(cn); return (Book)cmd.execute(); }
  public void saveBook(Book b) {
    DBCmd cmd=new SaveBook(b); cmd.execute(); }
  public void saveLoan(Loan l) {
    DBCmd cmd=new SaveLoan(l); cmd.execute(); }

interface DBCmd { public Object execute(); }

class GetUser implements DBCmd {
  String uid, username=..., password=...; Connection con=null;
  String driver="sun.jdbc.odbc.JdbcOdbcDriver";
  String url="jdbc:odbc:mydb";
  Statement stmt=null;
  public GetUser(String uid) { super(); this.uid=uid; }
  public Object execute() {
    User user=new User();
    try {
      Class.forName(driver); // load JDBC driver
      con=DriverManager.getConnection(url,
        username, password); // connect to database
       stmt=con.createStatement( );
      String query="select * from User where uid='"+uid+"'";
      ResultSet rs=stmt.executeQuery(query);
      user.setUID(rs.getString("uid"));
      user.setName(rs.getString("Name"));
       stmt.close(); con.close();
    } catch(Exception e) { e.printStackTrace(); } return user; }
}

class SaveBook implements DBCmd {
  Book book; SaveBook(Book b) { book=b; }
  public Object execute() { ... }
}

class SaveLoan implements DBCmd {
  Loan loan; SaveLoan(Loan l) { loan=l; }
  public Object execute() { ... }
}}
```

FIGURE 17.6 Sample code for applying the bridge and command patterns

at appropriate times. Updates to a database can be queued and committed at a later time. The command pattern lets the application store the command objects and execute them as scheduled.

- *The application needs to change the execution sequence of actions dynamically.* For example, a rational agent needs to generate and update plans at runtime to adapt itself to the changing world. The command pattern makes it easy to support such design objectives.
- *The application needs to support undoing and redoing operations.* Many applications need such capabilities. For example, all editor applications require these functions. Certain software fault-tolerant systems can recover from software faults.

When the system recovers, it may need to undo some of the operations performed previously. The command pattern is useful for such applications.

- *The application needs to log changes and redo them during system recovery.* Some approaches to software fault tolerance periodically save the system states. During recovery, the system returns to the previous state, and performs the logged operations. The command pattern is useful for the design and implementation of such systems.

17.4 HIDING NETWORK COMMUNICATION WITH REMOTE PROXY

Often, a database is located at another site or machine. In such cases, the database access implementation needs to communicate with a remote component, which accesses the remote database. In addition, network communication, and marshalling and unmarshalling are required. Network communication functions include connecting and disconnecting to the remote server, and communicating with the remote component using a communication protocol. These add functionality to the database access implementation. Previously, the implementation accesses a local database. Now the implementation needs to handle network communication, marshalling and unmarshalling. On the other hand, a remote component accesses the database instead of the local counterpart. These change the role of the local implementation. It becomes a placeholder or proxy for the remote component. This is the idea of the *proxy* pattern, described in Figure 17.7.

Figure 17.8 illustrates the four types of commonly used proxies. An application of a virtual proxy is delaying the loading of a large image until a request to display the image is received. At that time, the image is actually loaded. If no request to display the image is ever received, then the image is not loaded. In this sense, it improves performance and reduces memory consumption because images take time to load and memory space to store. An example of a protection proxy is access control, where the right to read, write or execute a resource is granted to the resource owner, a group of members, or the public. Another example is role-based access control (RBAC), where the right to read, write, or execute a resource is granted according to the role played by the user. Smart reference proxies implement mechanisms to make smart use of an object including:

1. Counting the number of references to the object so that memory space can be released when the count drops to zero. This reduces memory consumption.
2. Keeping track of which attributes of an object have been updated to improve database operation efficiency. For example, tax return forms have hundreds of fields. Sometimes, only a couple of fields are updated. In this case, rather than saving the entire form, only these attributes need to write back to the database.
3. Storing a large object to the database only when modification has been made. This improves the performance of the system.
4. Loading a persistent object into the memory when it is first referenced. For example, an Integrated Development Environment (IDE) may delay the loading of the

Name	Proxy
Type	GoF/Structural
Specification	
Problem	How does one provide a substitute for an object to control access to it?
Solution	Define a common interface and let the substitute encapsulate and control access to the object.
Design	
Structural	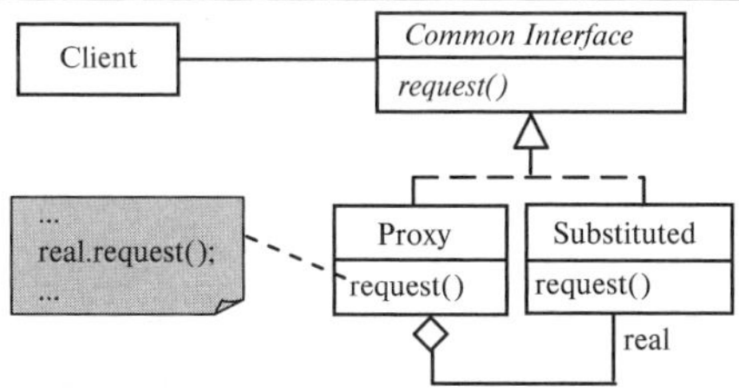
Behavioral	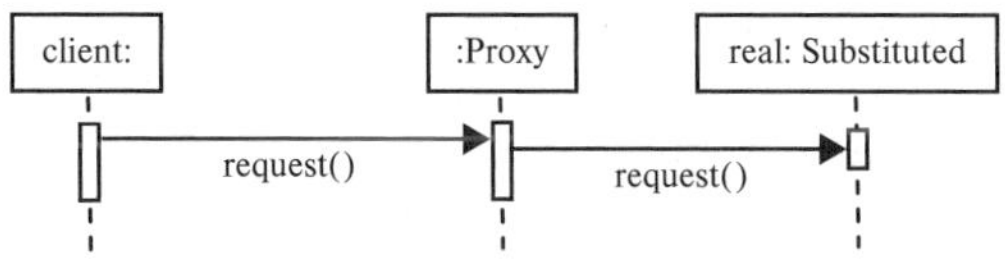
Roles and Responsibilities	• Substituted: It is the class of object to be controlled access. • Proxy: It creates, encapsulates, and controls access to the Substituted object. • Common Interface: It defines a common interface for the Substituted and Proxy.
Benefits	There are at least four types of proxy, providing various benefits: • Remote Proxy. It represents and acts on behalf of a remote object. • Virtual Proxy. It serves as a placeholder for an object that is expensive to create, or is memory intensive. The object need not be created until it is accessed. • Protection Proxy. It controls access to a real object according to access rights. • Smart Reference Proxy. It implements mechanisms to make smart use of the object.
Liabilities	
Guidelines	Apply the appropriate type of proxy according to the design problem to be solved.
Related Patterns	• Proxy adds functionality to an object permanently whereas functionality can be added or removed with Decorator. • Observers may cause inconsistent update to an observable. Proxy can be used to prevent concurrent update.
Uses	Persistence framework, role-based access control, concurrency control, memory management

FIGURE 17.7 Specification of the proxy pattern

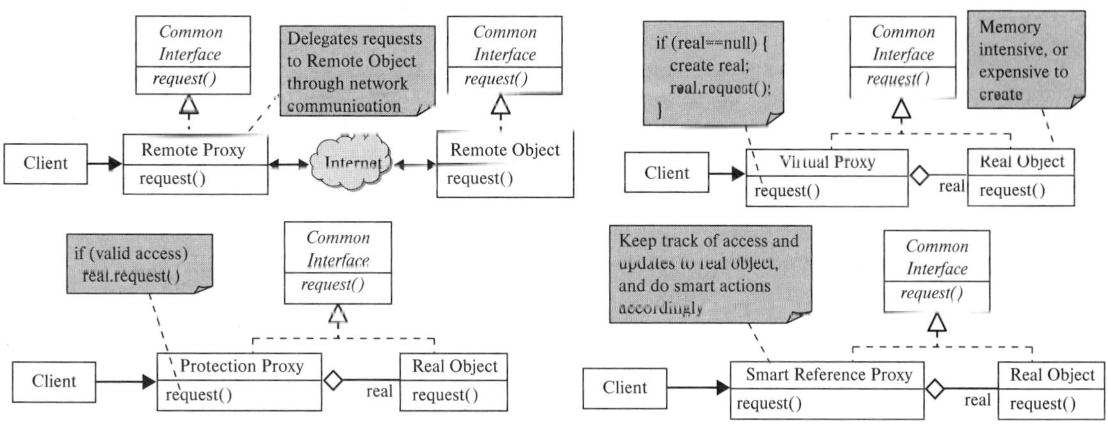

FIGURE 17.8 Four types of proxy illustrated

various analysis and design diagrams until they are accessed. This improves performance and resource utilization because not all of the diagrams will be viewed during a given session.

5. Locking and unlocking a shared object to avoid inconsistent update. For example, observers may update an observable object concurrently. In this case, a proxy can be used to lock and unlock the observable object to prevent concurrent update.

Applying the Proxy Pattern

EXAMPLE 17.4 Figure 17.9 shows the application of the remote proxy pattern to the design of the persistence framework. It assumes that the RDB database is a remote database. Thus, a remote proxy is used. The RDB Impl Proxy communicates with the RDB Remote Impl. The proxy acts on behalf of its remote counterpart. The design works as follows. The DBMgr creates an instance of RDB Impl Proxy. The DBMgr delegates requests from the controller to the proxy. The proxy handles network communication, marshalling and unmarshalling operations to communicate with its remote counterpart. The remote counterpart actually accesses the remote database. The design hides the remote database access component from the DBMgr. As a consequence, the DBMgr is not aware that the database locates at a remote site.

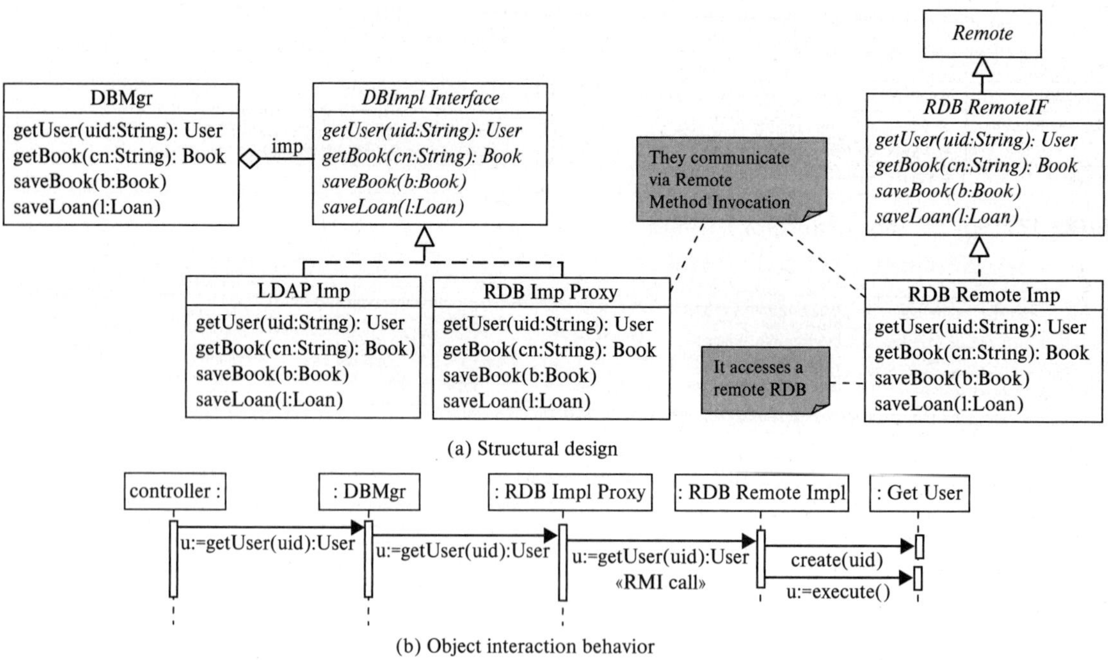

FIGURE 17.9 Applying the remote proxy pattern

Sample Code

EXAMPLE 17.5

Figure 17.10 shows a sample implementation of the design in Figure 17.9. It defines an RDB Remote IF interface, which extends the Java API Remote interface. The RDB Remote Impl class implements the RDB Remote IF to access the remote database. This is emulated by returning a User object. To transmit over the Internet, the User class needs to implement the Java API Serializable interface. On the local machine, the RDB Impl Proxy gets the User object from its remote counterpart and returns the object to the DBMgr. Figure 17.10 does not show the code for several classes: Config, DBImplInterface, and DBMgr because they are the same as in Figure 17.3. The Book and Loan classes are not shown because they can be treated similar to User.

```
import java.rmi.*;
public interface RDBRemoteIF extends Remote {
  User getUser(String uid) throws RemoteException;
  Book getBook(String cn) throws RemoteException;
  void saveBook(Book b) throws RemoteException;
  void saveLoan(Loan l) throws RemoteException;
}

import java.rmi.registry.*; import java.rmi.server.*; import java.rmi.*;
public class RDBRemoteImpl extends UnicastRemoteObject implements
   RDBRemoteIF {
  public RDBRemoteImpl() throws RemoteException { super(); }
  public User getUser(String uid) throws RemoteException {
    return new User(); }
  public Book getBook(String cn) throws RemoteException {
    return new Book(); }
  public void saveBook(Book b) throws RemoteException {
   System.out.println("Saving b to remote RDB."); }
  public void saveLoan(Loan l) throws RemoteException {
    System.out.println("Saving l to remote RDB."); }
}

import java.rmi.*;
import java.rmi.registry.*;
public class MyServer{
public static void main(String[] args) {
  try{
    RDBRemoteIF stub=new RDBRemoteImpl();
    Naming.rebind("rmi://localhost/mysql",stub);
  } catch(Exception e){ e.printStackTrace(); }
}}
```

```
import java.rmi.*;
public class RDBImplProxy implements DBImplInterface {
  public User getUser(String uid) {
    User u=null;
    try {
      RDBRemoteIF stub=(RDBRemoteIF)Naming.lookup
        ("rmi://localhost/mysql");
      u=stub.getUser("uid");
    } catch (Exception e) { e.printStackTrace(); }
    return u;
  }
  public Book getBook(String cn) { return null; }
  public void saveBook(Book d) { }
  public void saveLoan(Loan l) { }
}

public class Client {
  public static void main(String[] args) {
    DBMgr dbm=new DBMgr();
    User u=dbm.getUser("uid");
    if (u!=null && u.getClass().getName().indexOf("User")>=0)
      System.out.println("get user successful.");
    else System.out.println("get user failed."); }
}

public class User implements Serializable {
  private String uid; private String name;
  public void setUID(String uid) { this.uid=uid; }
  public void setName(String name) { this.name=name; }
}
```

FIGURE 17.10 Sample code for Figure 17.9

17.5 SHARING COMMON CODE WITH TEMPLATE METHOD

In Section 17.3, the command pattern is used to implement database access operations. In many cases, the execute() methods of the concrete command classes perform a similar sequence of operations:

```
(1) connect to the database   // same for all DB operations
(2) query the database        // different
(3) disconnect from database  // same for all DB operations
(4) process query result      // different
```

The concrete command classes for doing the database operations differ only in steps (2) and (4). The other steps are the same for all database access operations for a DBMS. These steps are duplicated in the command classes. The programmer needs to write duplicate code in the command classes. This extra effort invites more work when the shared steps are changed. This may cause inconsistent updates to the command classes. Many software engineers recognize these problems and use refactoring. That is, an abstract parent class is introduced. It implements the common steps and a template method to perform the four steps above. The database access command classes inherit the common steps and the template method from the parent class and implement only the steps that differ. This idea is captured in the *template method* pattern, described in Figure 17.11.

Name	Template Method
Type	GoF/Behavioral
Specification	
Problem	How does one vary steps of an algorithm dynamically without using conditional statements?
Solution	Define an abstract class with a template of the algorithm in which the steps to vary are treated as calls to abstract methods, called hook methods. The subclasses implement the hook methods to provide varying behavior.
Design	
Structural	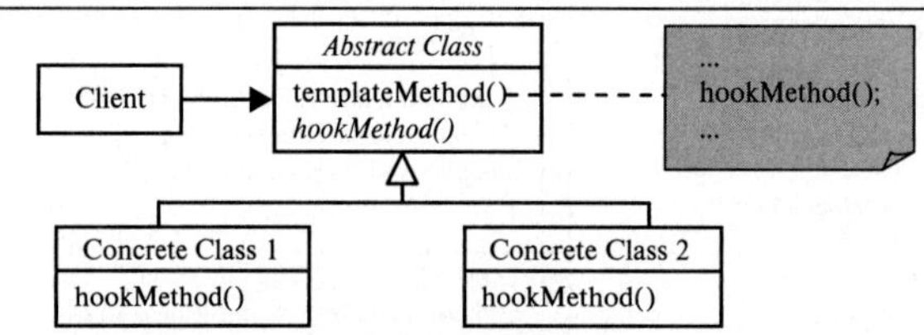
Behavioral	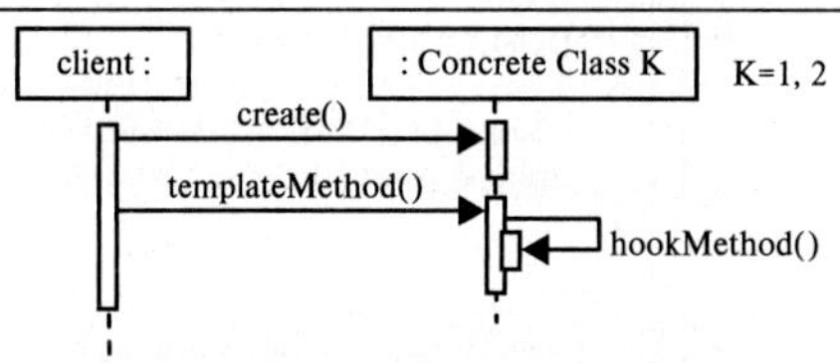
Roles and Responsibilities	• Client: It creates an object of the desired Concrete Class K, K=1, 2, and invokes its templateMethod(). • Abstract Class: It implements a template method in which the steps to vary are calls to abstract methods. • Concrete Classes 1–2: Each Concrete Class implements the abstract methods according to its own behavior.
Benefits	• It requires less effort to add concrete subclasses because duplicate code is eliminated. • It facilitates maintenance because change is needed at only one place. • It can vary the behavior of the template method by referring to an object of a different Concrete Class.
Liabilities	
Guidelines	
Related Patterns	• Factory Method is a special case of Template Method. That is, it is Template Method applied to object creation. • Template Method uses inheritance to vary part of an algorithm while Strategy uses delegation to vary the entire algorithm. • Strategy may benefit from Template Method if considerable common code is shared among the strategies. By using Template Method, the Concrete Strategy classes need implement only the steps that differ. • Builder supports varying of both the process and process steps whereas Template Method only allows the steps to vary. • Template Method is useful for implementing the construction process of a supervisor in the Builder pattern if the Concrete Supervisors share common code in their construction processes.
Uses	Template method is useful for code refactoring. It is widely used by programmers.

FIGURE 17.11 Specification of the template method pattern

Applying the Template Method Pattern

EXAMPLE 17.6

The template method pattern can be applied to improve the database access commands in the persistence framework. Figure 17.12 shows how to accomplish this. The DB Cmd class defines a template method–execute(). The hook methods are queryDB() and processResult() because they are different for different database access commands. The four command subclasses implement these hook methods. The client of the template method in Figure 17.12 is the RDB Impl class. The UML note of its saveBook(b:Book) method illustrates how the pattern is used. That is, it creates a Save Book object and calls the object's execute() method. Since Save Book inherits the execute() method from DB Cmd, the call in effect executes the template method. That is, it calls the connectDB() of DB Cmd, the queryDB() of Save Book, disconnectDB() of DB Cmd, and then processResult() of Save Book. The DB Cmd and the command subclasses apply two patterns–the command pattern and the template method pattern.

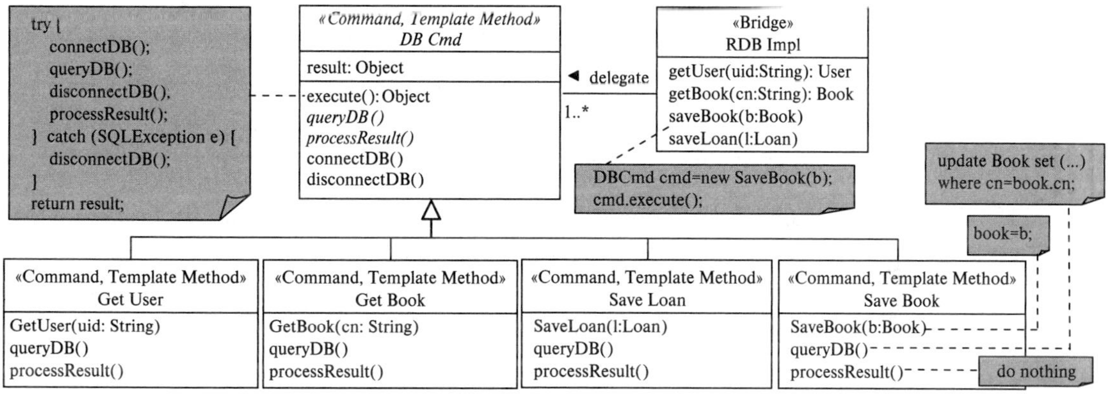

FIGURE 17.12 Applying template method to persistence framework

Sample Code

EXAMPLE 17.7

Figure 17.13 shows the implementation of the template method pattern as it is applied to the persistence framework. Only the DB Cmd class and its subclasses need to change. So, the other classes are not shown.

```
abstract class DBCmd {
  Connection con=null;
  String driver="..."; // set jdbc driver
  String url="..."; // set db url
  String username="username", password="password";
  ResultSet rs; Object result;
  public Object execute() {
    connectDB(); queryDB(); disconnectDB(); processResult();
    return result; }
  public abstract void queryDB();
  public abstract void processResult();
  public void connectDB() {
    try {
      Class.forName(driver); // load JDBC driver
      con=DriverManager.getConnection(url, username, password);
    } catch(Exception e) { e.printStackTrace(); }
  }
  public void disconnectDB() {
    try { con.close(); } catch(Exception e) { e.printStackTrace() ; }
  }
}

class GetBook extends DBCmd {
  public GetBook(String cn) {}
  public void queryDB() {} public void processResult() {}
}

class GetUser extends DBCmd {
  String uid;
  public GetUser(String uid) { super(); this.uid=uid; }
  public void queryDB() {
    try {
      Statement stmt=con.createStatement();
      String query="select * from User where uid='"+uid+"'";
      rs=stmt.executeQuery(query); stmt.close();
    } catch (SQLException e) { e.printStackTrace(); }}
  public void processResult() {
    User user=new User();
    try {
      user.setUID(rs.getString("uid"));
      user.setName(rs.getString("Name")); result=user;
    } catch(Exception e) { e.printStackTrace(); }}
}

class SaveBook extends DBCmd {
  public SaveBook(Book b) {}
  public void queryDB() {}
  public void processResult() {}
}
class SaveLoan extends DBCmd {
  public SaveLoan(Loan l) {}
  public void queryDB() {} public void processResult() {}
}
```

FIGURE 17.13 Sample code for template method in the persistence framework

Benefits of the Template Method Pattern

- It lets algorithms change behavior easily and dynamically.
- It is easy to add subclasses.
- It facilitates maintenance because the code is easier to understand and only one place needs to change.

17.6 RETRIEVING DIFFERENT OBJECTS WITH FACTORY METHOD

In the template method pattern, if one of the hook methods returns an object, which is used in the template method, then that method is called a factory method. The resulting pattern is the *factory method* pattern, described in Figure 17.14. The returned object is often referred to as the product. The factory method pattern lets the subclasses implement the factory hook methods. Thus, by varying the subclasses different products are created. This, in turn, changes the behavior of the template method because the product it uses is changed. The design and code in Figures 17.12 and 17.13 could be changed to apply the factory method. For example, the queryDB() method may return the Result Set, which is used by the processResult() method. The processResult() method may also return an object as the result. In the following, we will show an example of how to apply the factory method pattern to reverse engineer class diagrams and sequence diagrams, respectively.

Name	Factory Method
Type	GoF/Creational
Specification	
Problem	How does one vary the type of object used by an algorithm?
Solution	Define an abstract class with a template method of the algorithm, which uses objects returned by an abstract factory method implemented by subclasses to return objects of different types.
Design	
Structural	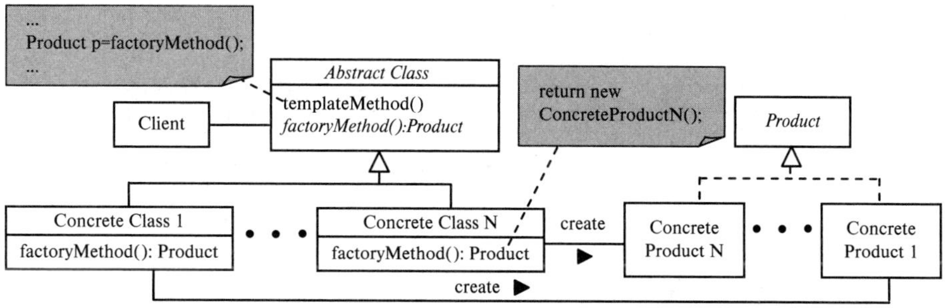
Behavioral	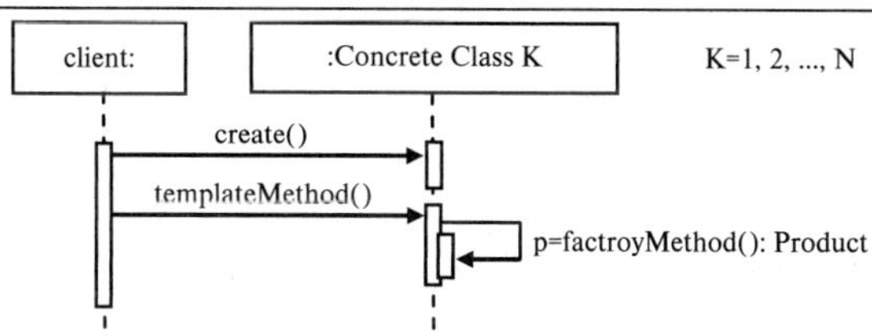
Roles and Responsibilities	• Client: It creates an object of the desired Concrete Class and invokes its templateMethod(). • Abstract Class: It implements a template method for an algorithm, which uses objects of varying classes returned by an abstract factory method. Its subclasses implement the factory method to return objects of different types. • Concrete Classes 1-N: Each concrete class implements the factory method to return an object of a certain type. • Product: It defines a common interface for the Concrete Product classes. • Concrete Products 1-N: These are concrete product types used by the template algorithm.
Benefits	Same as Template Method
Liabilities	
Guidelines	
Related Patterns	• Factory Method is a special case of Template Method. It is Template Method applied to object creation. • Factory Method is often used to implement the functions of a concrete factory in Abstract Factory.
Uses	It is widely used by programmers.

FIGURE 17.14 Specification of the factory method pattern

Applying the Factory Method Pattern

EXAMPLE 17.8

Figure 17.15 shows an application of the factory method in reverse engineering class diagrams and sequence diagrams. The reverse engineering process for both diagrams are the same, and involves three steps: (1) parse the source code to extract diagram elements, (2) compute layout for the diagram, and (3) display the diagram. The RE Factory has a template method called revEng() that implements the process. Because the steps are different for different diagrams, they are treated as factory methods, which are implemented by the two subclasses.

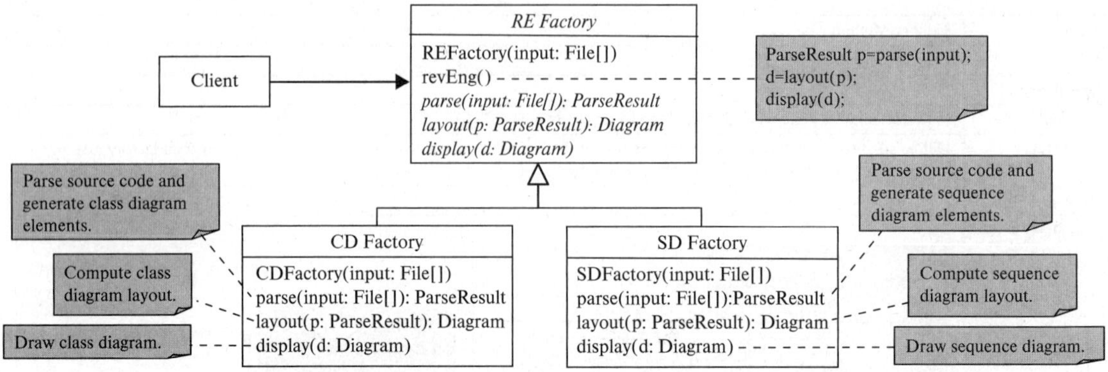

FIGURE 17.15 Reverse engineer class and sequence diagrams using factory method

The benefits of the factory method pattern are the same as the template method pattern.

17.7 REDUCING NUMBER OF CLASSES WITH PROTOTYPE

The persistence framework presented so far needs to implement at least N*2 command classes, where N is the number of classes whose objects need to be stored and retrieved with a database. A small application may need to store objects of 50 or so classes to a database. This means that one needs to design and implement 100+ command classes. A medium-sized application may have hundreds of such command classes. How to reduce the number of command classes is our design problem. Looking up Figure 16.3 finds the prototype pattern, specified in Figure 17.16.

To reduce the number of classes, the prototype pattern requires that the classes fulfill two criteria:

1. They must have the same behavior.
2. They must have the same relationships.

These imply that the classes differ only in their attributes. Thus, we need only one of these classes and use it to create an object and set its attribute values to produce a prototype for each of the classes. To create an object of an original class, one needs only to clone the prototype for that class.

Name	Prototype
Type	GoF/Creational
Specification	
Problem	How does one reduce the number of classes that share the same behavior and relationships (to other classes)?
Solution	Use one of the classes to create prototype objects of original classes by properly setting their attributes; objects of an original class can then be created by cloning its prototype.
Design	
Structural	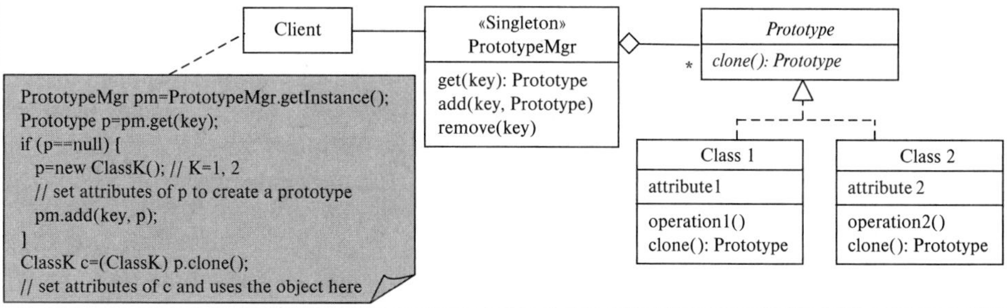
Behavioral	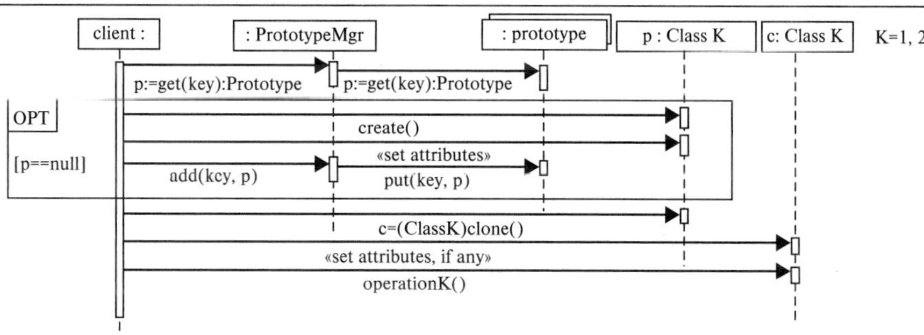
Roles and Responsibilities	• Client: It creates and saves the prototypes and uses them. • PrototypeMgr: It maintains a collection of prototypes, which are instances of Classes 1-2. • Prototype: It defines an interface containing a clone() method for all implementing prototype classes. • Classes 1-2: These are prototype classes, each of which has instances in the collection of prototypes.
Benefits	• It supports dynamically loaded classes (DLC), which cannot be referenced at compile time because the classes are available only at run time. The class loader creates and registers an instance of the DLC at run time when the DLC is loaded. • It is easy to add or remove prototypes at run time. • It improves the efficiency of object creation when cloning is more efficient than creating the object. • It reduces the number of classes.
Liabilities	• The implementation of the clone() method may requires deep copying if the copy and the original must be independent. • Implementing clone() may be difficult if the class is final or there are circular references.
Guidelines	Apply prototype to classes that share the same behavior and relationships, that is, their objects differ only in attribute values.
Related Patterns	• Abstract Factory may use Prototype to create the products. • Prototype may eliminate the product hierarchy of Abstract Factory, or reduce it to a single family of product classes. • Flyweight reduces the number of instances of a class whereas Prototype reduces the number of classes. Flyweight benefits from a sharable object while Prototype benefits from sharable behavior. They can be used together to accomplish both objectives in some applications.
Uses	See Benefits

FIGURE 17.16 Specification of the prototype pattern

Applying the Prototype Pattern

EXAMPLE 17.9 Try to apply the prototype pattern to reduce the number of command classes in the persistence framework.

Solution: To apply the prototype pattern, the command classes must share the same behavior and same relationships. In Figure 17.12, the command subclasses only share the same relationships to other classes. They do not share the same behavior. Therefore, the prototype pattern cannot be applied directly. We need to do something to make the subclasses share the same behavior. In other words, we should try to make their difference in behavior become difference in attribute values. To accomplish this, we find that retrieving objects from, and saving objects to a database are very different operations. We cannot make them to share the same behavior. Moreover, retrieving an association class is different from retrieving an ordinary class; this is also true for saving an association class. Therefore, the command subclasses are divided into four groups as follows:

1. Retrieving an ordinary class, examples are Get User and Get Book.
2. Saving an ordinary class, an example is Save Book.
3. Retrieving an association class, an example is Get Loan.
4. Saving an association class, an example is Save Loan.

In this example, we will only show how to apply the prototype pattern to reduce the number of classes for retrieving an object of an ordinary class. To identify the similarity and difference in behavior between Get User and Get Book, we construct a table as shown in Figure 17.17.

We find that for the queryDB() function, the two classes differ only in their query strings. This means that we can store the query string in an attribute instead of setting it in the queryDB() function. We find that for the processResult() function, the two classes differ in the type of object created, and the mapping between table column labels and class attributes. To eliminate the difference in the type of object created, we let the client create the object and store it in an attribute of type Object. The mapping between column labels and class attributes can be stored in a properties file, which is used to initialize an object of the Properties class, a Java API that extends Java Hashtable. We can store the file name in an attribute. To set the attribute values of the object created using the data retrieved from the database, we use Java reflection. Thus, the difference between behaviors becomes difference

	Get User Class	Get Book Class	Difference
queryDB()	query="select * from User where uid = "'uid'"; Statement stmt=con.createStatement(); resultSet=stmt.executeQuery(query);	query="select * from Book where cn = "'cn'"; Statement stmt=con.createStatement(); resultSet=stmt.executeQuery(query);	Query string
processResult()	User user=new User(); user.setUID(rs.getString("uid")); user.setName(rs.getString("Name")); result=user;	Book book=new Book(); book.setCN(rs.getString("cn")); book.setTitle(rs.getString("title")); result=book;	• Object recreated • Mapping between table column labels and attributes of the classes

FIGURE 17.17 Difference in behavior between Get User and Get Book classes

in attribute values, allowing us to apply the prototype pattern. This idea can be applied similarly to reduce the number of classes for the other groups of command subclasses of the DB Cmd class. Figure 17.18 shows an application of the prototype pattern to the design of the persistence framework. The attributes of the DB Cmd class are explained as follows:

- dbKey: String. This attribute stores the primary key value of the database record that stores data for the object to be retrieved or saved.
- query: String. This attribute stores the query string to retrieve or save an object. Its value is set by the client. Note that the query string is different for different types of objects and different types of database operations.
- map: String. This attribute stores the file name that defines the mapping between column labels and attribute names. The file contains a line of the format string1=string2 for each attribute of the class, where string1 is a column label and string 2 is an attribute name. The "=" sign can be any other character defined by the Java Properties API.
- rs: ResultSet. This attribute stores the query result of a database retrieval operation.
- object: Object. This attribute stores the object retrieved or to be saved.

Suppose that the client wants a "Get User" command. The client calls the PrototypeMgr to get a prototype using "GetUser" as the key. If the call returns null, the client creates an instance of the Get Object class and sets its attribute values as required to retrieve data and construct a User object. These include setting the query string, creating and setting a User object, and setting the column label to attribute name mapping file. The client then saves the Get Object instance in the collection of prototypes using "GetUser" as the hash key so that the instance will be available for cloning going forward. After saving the instance, the client calls the copy constructor of the Get Object class to create a copy of the Get Object instance, and uses the copy to retrieve a User object. A copy constructor takes in an object of the same class as the sole parameter, and creates an object that is a clone of the parameter. Instead of copy constructor, one can override the clone method of Java Object and invoke the clone method to create a copy. This requires that the Get Object class implements the Java Cloneable interface. Now, if the

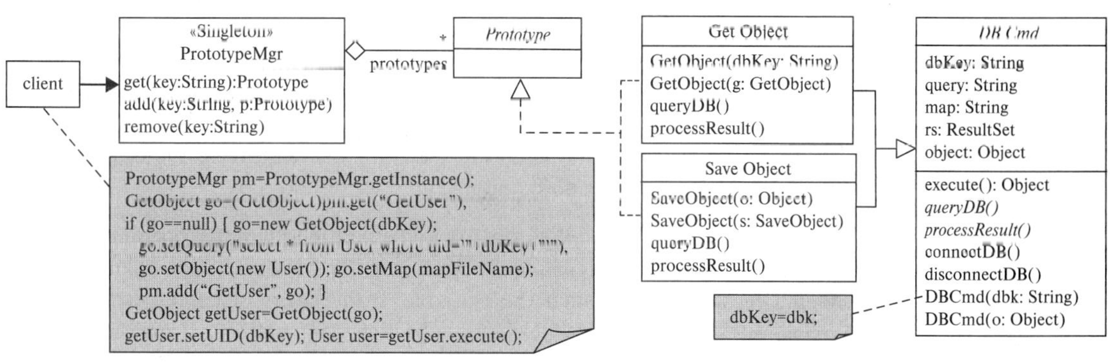

FIGURE 17.18 Applying prototype pattern to reduce number of classes

client wants a "Get Book" command, it repeats the same process but for retrieving a Book object. At the end of this process, the collection of prototypes will contain two Get Object instances, for retrieving User and Book objects, respectively. If the application needs to retrieve objects of 50 domain classes, then, instead of defining and implementing 50 command subclasses, one needs to define and implement only one class such as the Get Object class in this example.

Sample Code

EXAMPLE 17.10

Figure 17.19 shows the sample code that implements the design in Figure 17.18. It shows only four classes: PrototypeMgr, DB Cmd, Get Object, and Client. Instead of implementing the clone() method for the Get Object class, we implement a copy constructor. The queryDB() method uses the query strings to retrieve data for the object to be retrieved, and saves the query results in rs. The processResult() method processes the query result using Java Reflection and the mapping between column labels and attribute names to set the attribute values for the object to be retrieved.

Benefits and Liabilities of the Prototype Pattern

- The prototype pattern reduces the number of classes. If an application needs to retrieve and store objects of 50 domain classes with a database, then the pattern reduces the number of classes needs to design and implement from 100 to two.
- Prototypes can be added and removed easily and dynamically.
- One has the freedom to use or not use the prototype pattern. For example, it may not be easy to implement the idea presented in Examples 17.9 and 17.10 for retrieving a state diagram or a class diagram. In such cases, one does not need to apply the prototype pattern. Instead, one implements the command subclasses to retrieve the diagrams.
- The prototype pattern supports dynamically loaded classes (DLC). A DLC is a class that is available only at runtime, e.g., created during program execution using data collected dynamically.
- The prototype pattern can eliminate the product hierarchy associated with the abstract factory pattern and factory method pattern. Because the families of product have similar behaviors, for example, buttons and menu items of different window systems behave the same, we need only one button class and one menu item class for all of the window systems.

The prototype pattern requires one to implement the cloning operation. For some applications, deep copying is required because the copy and the original must be independent. This is difficult if the class has many layers of part-of relationships, or circular dependence relationships. Finally, the using reflection may slowdown the application, and compromise security. It is not suitable for performance or security sensitive applications.

```
public class PrototypeMgr {
  private static PrototypeMgr instance=new PrototypeMgr();
  private Hashtable<String, Object> prototypes=new Hashtable<...>();
  private PrototypeMgr() { /* load prototypes */ }
  public Object get(String key) { return prototypes.get(key); }
  public void add(String key, Object value) { prototypes.put(key, value); }
  public void remove(Object value) { prototypes.remove(value); }
  public static PrototypeMgr getInstance() { return instance; }
}

class GetObject extends DBCmd {
  Method[] methods=null;
  public GetObject(String dbKey) { super(dbKey); }
  public GetObject(GetObject go) {
    super(go.dbKey); this.con=go.con; this.driver=go.driver;
    this.url=go.url; this.username=go.username; this.rs=go.rs;
    this.password=go.password; this.query=go.query; this.map=go.map;
    try { this.object=go.object.getClass().newInstance(); }
    catch(Exception e) { e.printStackTrace(); }}
  public void queryDB() {
    try { Statement stmt=con.createStatement();
          rs=stmt.executeQuery(query); stmt.close();
    } catch (Exception e) { e.printStackTrace(); }}
  int findMethod(String attrName) { // method of object to set attribute
    String str="set"+attrName; str=str.toLowerCase();
    for(int i=0; i<methods.length; i++) {
      if (methods[i].getName().toLowerCase().indexOf(str)>=0) return i;
    } return -1; }
  public void processResult() {
    try { Properties prop=new Properties();
          prop.load(new FileReader(map));
          methods=object.getClass().getDeclaredMethods();
          Field[] attrs=object.getClass().getDeclaredFields();
          for(int i=0; i<attrs.length; i++) {
            String aName=attrs[i].getName();
            String cLabel=(String)prop.get(aName);
            Object value=rs.getObject(cLabel); int j=findMethod(cLabel);
            if (j>=0) { methods[j].invoke(object, value); }
            else { System.out.println("Cannot set "+attrs[i].getName()); }}
    } catch(Exception e) { e.printStackTrace(); }}
}
```

```
abstract class DBCmd {
  Connection con=null; String driver="..."; // set jdbc driver
  String url="..."; // set db url
  String userrname="username", password="password";
  String dbKey; String query; String map; ResultSet rs;
  Object object; // object retrieved or to be saved
  public DBCmd(String dbKey) { this.dbKey=dbKey; }
  public Object execute() {
    connectDB(); queryDB(); disconnectDB(); processResult();
    return object;
  }
  public abstract void queryDB(); public abstract void processResult();
  public void setQuery(String q) { query=q; }
  public void setObject(Object o) { object=o; }
  public void setMap(String fileName) { map=fileName; }
  public void connectDB() {
    try {
      Class.forName(driver); // load JDBC driver
      con=DriverManager.getConnection(url, username, password);
    } catch(Exception e) { e.printStackTrace(); }}
  public void disconnectDB() {
    try { con.close(); } catch(SQLException e) { e.printStackTrace(); }}
}

public class Client {
  public static void main(String[] args) {
    String dbKey="1234", String className="GetUser";
    PrototypeMgr pm=PrototypeMgr.getInstance();
    GetObject go=(GetObject)pm.get(className);
    if (go==null) {go=new GetObject(dbKey);
      String query="select * from User where uid='"+dbKey+"'";
      go.setQuery(query); go.setObject(new User());
      go.setMap("map.txt"); pm.add(className, go);
    }
    GetObject getUser=new GetObject(go);
    User user=(User)getUser.execute();
    System.out.println("uid="+user.getUID()+" Name="+user.getName());
  }
}
```

FIGURE 17.19 Sample code showing implementation of the prototype pattern

17.8 APPLYING AGILE PRINCIPLES

See Section 16.7 in Chapter 16.

17.9 SUMMARY

This chapter presents six situation-specific patterns. These are bridge, command, factory method, prototype, proxy, and template method. It also presents how to apply these patterns to the design of a data storage subsystem called a persistence framework. First, problems with direct database access are identified. Patterns are then applied to solve the problems and improve the design. This pattern application process is iterative during the design process.

17.10 CHAPTER REVIEW QUESTIONS

1. What are the general design problems solved by the bridge, proxy, command, template method, factory method, and prototype patterns?
2. How does the command pattern support undo and redo an operation?
3. What is a persistence framework, and how are patterns applied to design the framework? What are the benefits of applying the patterns?

17.11 EXERCISES

17.1 Discuss the similarities and differences of the two patterns in each of the following pairs of patterns. Moreover, give two situations that are not in the textbook or the lecture notes in which each pattern can be exclusively applied to exactly one situation. Describe how each pattern is applied and why the other pattern cannot be applied.

- **a.** Bridge and command
- **b.** Flyweight and prototype
- **c.** Singleton and prototype
- **d.** Abstract factory and factory method
- **e.** Adapter and proxy
- **f.** Bridge and strategy
- **g.** Adapter and bridge
- **h.** Decorator and proxy

17.2 Extend the design and implementation in Figures 17.18 and 17.19 to also support the other three groups of command subclasses: Save Object, Get Association Object and Save Association Object.

17.3 Design and implement a protection proxy that allows a client to access a protected object only if the client has the correct pass code. Moreover, only one client can access the object at any time.

17.4 Design and implement a persistence framework for accessing a local database using only the bridge and command patterns. The design does not need to consider that the database management system (DBMS) may change in the future. As tests, store and retrieve Book and Patron objects with the persistence framework. Choose your implementation language and DBMS, or as directed by your instructor.

17.5 Modify the design and implementation in exercise 17.4 to allow undo and redo database operations.

17.6 Design and implement a persistence framework to access a local database. The design should consider that the local DBMS may be replaced in the future. Choose your implementation language and DBMS, or as directed by the instructor.

17.7 Change the design and implementation of the persistence framework in exercise 17.6 to take into account that the persistence framework needs to support local as well as remote databases.

17.8 Describe two situations in which the prototype pattern can be applied to reduce the number of classes in one, but not the other situation.

17.9 Extend the design and implementation in Exercise 16.5 to support undo and redo operations. That is, if the undo button is pressed, the previous drawn shape is removed from the canvas. If the redo button is pressed, the previously undone operation is redone.

17.10 Describe a patient monitoring system, and produce a design of the system by applying 4–5 patterns presented in Chapters 10, 13, 15–17.

part VI

Implementation and Quality Assurance

18

Chapter

Implementation Considerations

Key Takeaway Points

- Everyone in the team should follow the same coding standards.
- Test-driven development, pair programming, and ping-pong programming improve the quality of the code.
- Classes should be implemented according to their dependencies to reduce the need for test stubs.

Previous chapters presented object-oriented analysis and design. The design activity produces the sequence diagrams, state diagrams, activity diagrams, and the design class diagram (DCD). Moreover, the classes are logically organized into packages. In this chapter, the design is converted into source code, which is compiled into executable programs. During this process, the team must consider several factors that affect the implementation. These include coding standards, how to organize the classes and web pages, how to translate the design into object-oriented programs, and how to assign the implementation work to team members. Throughout this chapter, you will learn the following:

- What are coding standards, and how do you implement them in your teamwork?
- How do you organize the source files and executable programs?
- How do you convert the design diagrams to code skeletons?
- How do you assign the implementation work to team members?
- How do you conduct test-driven development, pair programming, and ping-pong programming?

18.1 CODING STANDARDS

Defining and complying to coding standards are an important aspect of implementation. Experiences show that poorly written code requires rework, which increases development and maintenance costs. In the worst case, the code has to be abandoned.

On the other hand, a good practice of coding standards improves software productivity and quality while reducing cost and time to market. Therefore, most companies develop and require programmers to comply with company-specific coding standards. Good practices of coding standards require an understanding of the following, which are the focuses of this section:

1. What are coding standards?
2. Why use coding standards?
3. What are the guidelines for practicing coding standards?

18.1.1 What Are Coding Standards?

Generally speaking, coding standards are a set of rules that serve as requirements and guidelines for writing programs in an organization, or for a project. More specifically, coding standards should address the following:

1. Define the required and optional items of the coding standards.
2. Define the format and language used to specify the required and optional items.
3. Define the coding requirements and conventions.
4. Define the rules and responsibilities to create and implement the coding standards, as well as review and improve the practice.

The coding standards should define the required and optional items so that the programmers will know what to include. More importantly, if all projects use the same standards, then integration, collaboration, and software reuse are much easier to accomplish. Another advantage is that the list forms the basis for future improvement. Coding standards usually include the following major items:

1. *File header.* Many companies' coding standards require a file header at the beginning of each program file. It specifies the file location, version number, author, project, update history, and other useful information. Figure 18.1 provides a summary of file header items.
2. *Description of classes.* Many companies also require a functional description for each class. It includes:
   a. Purpose–a statement of the purpose of the class.
   b. Description of methods–a brief description of the purpose of each method, the parameters, return type, and other input and output such as files, database tables, and text fields accessed and updated by the method. The list should not include the ordinary get and set functions.
   c. Description of fields–a brief description of each field including the name of the field, data type, range of values, initialization requirement, and values of significance.
   d. In-code comments–comments that are inserted at places of the code to facilitate understanding and tool processing.

Figure 18.2 displays the file header from a real-world project and Figure 18.3 shows a part of the description of a class.

Item	Description
File name	full path name of the file that contains the program including the name of the hard drive
Version number	the version number and release number (useful for versioning, maintenance, and software reuse)
Author name	name of the programmer who creates the program file and writes the first version of the program
Project name	full name of the project for which the program is initially written
Organization	full name of the organization
Copyright	copyright information
Related Requirements	a list of requirements implemented by the program
List of classes*	a list of the names of the classes contained in the program file
Related documents	a list of related documents, and their URLs if available
Update history	a list of updates, each specifies the date of the update, who performs the update, what is updated, why the update, and possibly the impact, risks, and resolution measurements
Reviewers*	a list of reviewers and what each of them reviews
Test cases*	a list of test scripts along with their URLs if available
Functional Description	an overall description of the functionality and behavior of the program–that is, what the program does and how it interacts with its client.
Error messages	a list of error messages that the program may generate along with a brief description of each of them
Assumptions	a list of conditions that must be satisfied, or may affect the operation of the program
Constraints	a list of restrictions on the use of the program including restrictions on the input, environment, and various other variables

*optional item

FIGURE 18.1 Coding standards file header items

The coding standards should specify the language and format that should be used to describe the items. For example, the sentences used to specify the items should be in third person and simple present tense. Figure 18.2 illustrates an example format. The coding standards should specify the coding requirements and conventions. The difference is that requirements are compulsory and conventions leave the decision to the programmer. The organization and the project manager decide which rules are coding requirements and which are coding conventions. For convenience, no distinction is made between the two in the following presentation. Coding conventions include:

1. *Naming conventions.* These conventions specify rules for naming packages, modules, paths, files, classes, attributes, functions, constants, and the like. Naming conventions should help program understanding and maintenance. The names that are selected for the classes, attributes, functions, and variables should convey their functionality and semantics, and facilitate understanding of the program. Moreover, the names should be the same, or easily relate to the names in the design. Meaningless names such as "flag," "temp," "x," "y," "z," and the like, must not be used. In addition, names must not contain space, control characters, or special letters not allowed by a compiler.

```
/**
*  File Name : Rectangle.java
*
*  Object Oriented Testing Project
*
*  (c) Copyright 1998 (organization withheld)
*  ALL RIGHTS RESERVED
*
*  Input                      :   This class is constructed from input passed by the Layout
                                  class. This class is constructed by invoking the super class
                                  constructor. Refer to Shape.java for information on Input.
*  Output                     :   A Rectangle class to represent sequential statements is
                                  constructed and is used to draw a rectangle of the Flowgraph.
*  Supported Requirements     :   BBD_R19, BBD-R20, BBD-R23, BBD-R25, BBD-R26.
*  Classes in this file       :   Rectangle
*  Related Documents          :   BBD Analysis & Design Document
*                                 (GUI, Layout & Display)
*  Update History:
*
*  Date       Author              Changes
*  ---------------------------------------------------------------------------
*  6/20/98    Withheld                        Original
*
*
*  Functional Description     :   This file implements the Rectangle class of BBD Layout &
                                  Display Module. It is a subclass of Shape class. It generates
                                  the coordinates required for drawing a rectangle using AWT and
                                  stores them in Attributes[]. It also implements the draw
                                  method that draws the rectangle on the screen, inserts the
                                  associated text into it and places the node number by its side.
*  Error Messages             :
*  Constraints                :   The text associated with the Shape is printed in the Shape
                                  only when the zoomRatio is above 3.
*  Assumptions                :   It is assumed that the text will not be visible when the
                                  zoomRatio is less than 4 and hence it is not displayed.
*
**/
```

FIGURE 18.2 File header and functional description of a class

In Java, classes are stored in .java files with the same name as the class except inner classes. Class names have a capital initial. If the class name consists of several words, then each word has a capital initial and the words are lumped together like UndergraduateStudent. Attribute names, function names, and local variable names are like class names except that the first letter is not capitalized. Names for constants are all capital, like MAX.

2. *Formatting conventions.* Formatting conventions specify formatting rules used to arrange program statements. These include line break, indentation, alignment, and spacing. Most integrated development environments (IDE) define a default format, which can be changed according to the needs of the software development organization. In Figure 18.3, the formatting conventions are illustrated.
3. *In-code comment conventions.* If it is written properly, in-code comments facilitate program understanding and maintenance. Thus, the coding standards should

```
package bbd.display;
import java.io.*;
import java.awt.*;


/**
*
* Purpose                  :       This class is used for drawing a Rectangle Shape of the FlowGraph.
*
* Usage Instructions       :
*
* @author                  Withheld
* @Version                 Original
* @see                     java.awt.Graphics
* @see                     http://java.sun.com/products/jdk/1.1/docs/api/
*                          java.awt.Graphics.html#_top_
**/

public class Rectangle extends Shape
{

/**
*
* Method Name              :         Rectangle
* Purpose                  :         Constructor of the Rectangle class. It calls the super class
                                     constructor to initialize the class variables.
*
**/

  public Rectangle( String id, int Type, String shape, int number,
                    String code )
  {

    super( id, Type, shape, number, code );

  }

/**
*
* Method Name              :       setCoordinates
* Purpose                  :       It finalizes the coordinates of the Rectangle class at a zoomRatio
                                   = 5 and stores them in attributes.
* Miscellaneous            :       The attributes are initialized as follows. attributes[0] stores the
                                   x coordinate of the top left corner. attributes[1] stores the y
                                   coordinate of the top left corner. attribute[2] stores the width,
                                   whereas attribute[3] stores the height of the Rectangle.

*
**/

  public void setCoordinates( )
  {

    System.out.println( "setCoordinates for Rectangle called" );
    x = GRAPH_START_X + ( x * XGAP );
    y = GRAPH_START_Y + ( y * YGAP );

    attributes[0] = x - WIDTH/2;
    attributes[1] = y - HEIGHT/2;
    attributes[2] = WIDTH;
    attributes[3] = HEIGHT;

  }
...
```

FIGURE 18.3 Description of a class

define the requirements and guidelines including the locations where in-code comments must, or should be provided, and the formats to write the comments so that tools can process them.

Finally, rules and responsibilities for creating and implementing the coding standards as well as reviewing and improving the practice must be defined. For example, should the standards be applied to all the programs created, or just to some of the programs created? Should the coding standards be applied to test case scripts, or test case programs? Should the test case programs use the same coding standards? Who should be responsible for defining the coding standards, and who should be responsible for educating the programmers to follow, or comply with the standards? Answers to these questions require a definition of rules and responsibilities.

18.1.2 Why Coding Standards?

Coding standards are not just a set of documentation rules. Good practices of coding standards bring about a number of benefits. First, the standards define a common set of rules for writing programs in the organization or project. Without the standards, the teams and team members would not include the items or write whatever they think should be included. In this case, there is no consistency between the program files produced by different teams and team members. The coding standards ensure the consistency of the program files produced by the teams and team members. This greatly facilitates project management, software integration, software reuse, configuration management, software maintenance, and personnel transfer. Second, the coding standards make it easy to understand the programs because all program files describe the same items using the same format. Moreover, the standards ensure that important items are included and properly specified to reap the benefits. Third, the coding standards help code review and test case generation because the functional description and in-code comments help the reviewers and testers understand the program. Finally, the standards facilitate the use of tools such as JavaDoc and static analysis tools. JavaDoc generates html pages as online documentation for the classes. Static analysis tools check the code and in-code document to detect potential problems and violation of coding standards.

18.1.3 Guidelines for Practicing Coding Standards

Like everything else, coding standards could be overdone, resulting in standards that require everything to be documented in great detail. This is counterproductive because a lot of time and effort are wasted in describing things that are not important or obvious. Another problem is that the standards are defined but never implemented, checked, or enforced. The following guidelines are for practicing coding standards.

GUIDELINE 18.1 Define barely enough coding standards.

Coding standards should include only the most needed items. Barely enough coding standards are enough to reap the benefits while keeping the effort to a minimum. Barely enough coding standards should be determined by the stakeholders including the developers. This is because different domains, organizations, and projects should have different coding standards. For example, if the developers are familiar with the application domain, then the coding standards should require less. If the application is new, or difficult to understand for the developers, then the coding standards should require more descriptive information to be included in the program file.

GUIDELINE 18.2 The coding standards should be easy to understand and practice.

To reap the benefits of coding standards, developer support is essential. That is, the developers follow the coding standards when they write programs. This means that the standards should be easy to understand and practice; otherwise, the developers will give up sooner or later. Therefore, it is important to involve the developers. Moreover, the drafts of the coding standards should be reviewed and practiced by the developers, and modified according to feedback.

GUIDELINE 18.3 The coding standards should be documented and should include examples.

The first releasable version of the coding standards should be published as an official document. It should include examples to illustrate how to describe the required and optional items. This does not mean that the document should be a lengthy one. On the contrary, it should focus on what to do and how to do it.

GUIDELINE 18.4 Training on how to use the coding standards is helpful.

The training may require a couple of hours, but it is worthwhile because it helps the developers understand what is required. Moreover, the developers have the opportunity to ask questions to clear doubts.

GUIDELINE 18.5 The coding standards, once defined and published, should be practiced, enforced, and checked for compliance regularly.

If the coding standards are defined but not practiced, then they are useless. Therefore, it is important to put the standards into practice and check for their compliance regularly. Since the developers know that there will be a compliance check, they tend to comply. As time goes by, complying to the standards would become a part of the culture in the organization.

GUIDELINE 18.6 It is important to assign the responsibilities to individuals and make sure that all involved know the assignment.

Putting the coding standards to work requires clear assignment of responsibilities to individuals, that is, who is responsible for doing what. Moreover, the assignment should be announced at appropriate meetings to ensure that everybody knows his responsibilities. For example, the programmer is responsible for writing the file header, functional description, and the like. The reviewers are responsible for checking that the coding standards have been complied with. The configuration management personnel is responsible for making sure that all program files are properly reviewed and issues are addressed. These could be that the reviewers electronically sign their review reports indicating that issues are addressed as expected. Finally, it is important to establish checking mechanisms to ensure that everybody fulfills the responsibilities.

GUIDELINE 18.7 The practice of coding standards should involve stakeholders.

The success of standards practice depends on the support and cooperation of all stakeholders who are affected including the developers. Therefore, their opinions should be taken into consideration seriously by the management. It is worthwhile to spend time to communicate the rational, discuss issues, and resolve the issues.

18.2 ORGANIZING THE IMPLEMENTATION ARTIFACTS

One important decision concerning implementation is deciding on the directory structures to store the source code, binary code, bytecode, web pages, and test cases. It is important because the directory structure closely resembles the system architecture, which is defined in the early stage of the project (see Chapter 6: Architectural Design). The software architecture suggests the logical organization of the software artifacts, that is, grouping of the software artifacts into packages using UML package diagrams. Chapter 11 presented three approaches to organize the classes:

1. *Architectural-style organization.* This approach organizes the classes according to the building blocks of the software architecture.
2. *Functional subsystem organization.* This approach organizes the classes according to the functional subsystems of the software system.
3. *Hybrid organization.* This approach combines the architectural-style organization and the functional subsystem organization. Two approaches exist: the architectural-style functional subsystem organization and the functional subsystem architectural-style organization. Using the former, the classes in each of the architectural packages are organized according to the functional subsystems of the software system. This would organize the classes in the GUI package into several subpackages of the GUI package, including gui.circulation, gui.cataloguing, gui.purchasing, gui.usersvc, and gui.interlibraryloan. The functional subsystem architectural-style organization does the opposite.

The package structure is useful for deriving the directory structure used to store the source files and executable programs. For example, an interactive system typically has sequence diagrams like the one in Figure 18.4(*a*), where the Use Case GUI and Use Case Controller objects represent use case-specific GUI and controller. The GUI includes window-based, web-based, and other types of user interfaces. The Business Object represents business objects that participate in the business process of the use case. As discussed in Chapter 17, the DBMgr is a part of a persistence framework that includes a DB Proxy and DB commands to access a database, which may locate

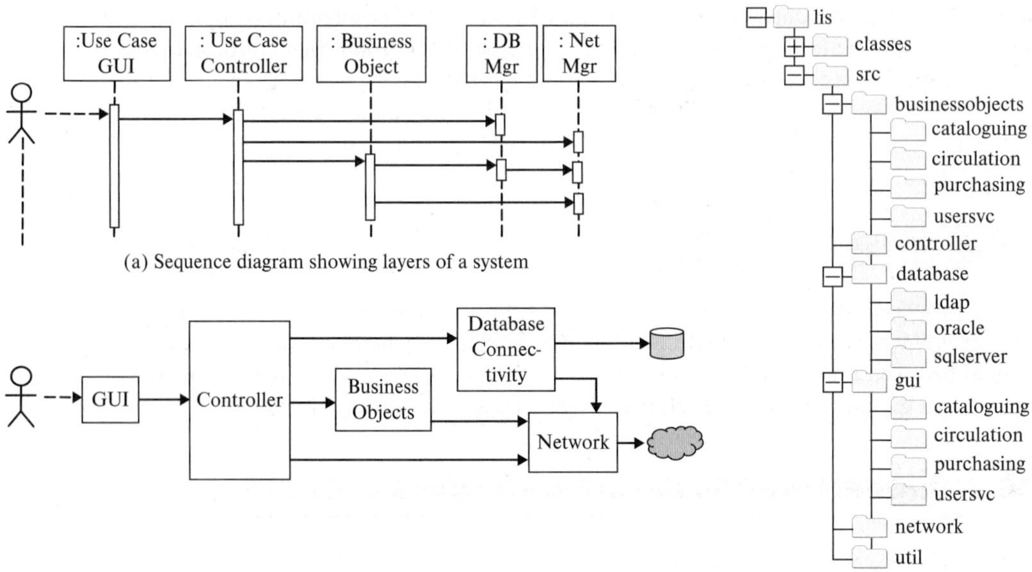

(a) Sequence diagram showing layers of a system

(b) Corresponding N-tier architecture

(c) Directory structure

FIGURE 18.4 N-tier architecture and directory structure

at a remote site. The Net Mgr is responsible for handling network communication and marshaling. It is a part of a network communication framework. The layers of an N-tier architecture are in one-to-one correspondence to the layers in the sequence diagram, as illustrated in Figure 18.4(*b*). The layers represent subsystems or components and are implemented as modules or packages. For example, the database layer includes the DBMgr class, the proxy classes, and the database access command classes. These classes belong to the database package and are stored in the database directory as shown in Figure 18.4(*c*).

The directory structure shown in Figure 18.4(*c*) is the result of applying the architectural-style functional subsystem organization. It assumes that the software system supports multiple database management systems (DBMS). Therefore, the proxy classes and the database-access command classes are grouped into DBMS-specific subsystems such as Oracle, SQL Server, and LDAP subsystems. These are subsystems of the database subsystem. Accordingly, the classes in these subsystems have DBMS specific package names such as “database.oracle,” “database.sqlserver,” and “database.ldap.” They are stored in the corresponding subdirectories under the database directory. The business objects form business-specific subsystems that often resemble their counterparts in the real world. For example, the business objects of a library information system can form circulation, cataloguing, purchasing, and user service subsystems. Therefore, classes belonging to these subsystems are stored in the circulation, cataloguing, purchasing, and usersvc subdirectories of the business objects directory. Similarly, the graphical user interface classes are stored in their respective subsystem's directories as shown in Figure 18.4(*c*). Organizing the classes into different subsystems, packages, and directories facilitates software reuse. For example, to reuse the database subsystem or one of its DBMS-specific components, one only needs to include the corresponding directory.

18.3 GENERATING CODE FROM DESIGN

As discussed in the introduction chapter, the object-oriented paradigm features seamless transition from analysis to design and from design to programming. Therefore, transition from design to implementation is relatively easy. Moreover, many IDEs can generate code skeletons from UML diagrams. However, depending on the implementation of the IDE, the code skeletons generated are different. If you don't use an IDE or don't want to use the code generated by an IDE, you can program yourself. This section presents rules for generating code skeletons from UML diagrams.

18.3.1 Implementing Classes and Interfaces

Mapping the classes and interfaces in the DCD to Java, C++, or C# is an easy and straightforward exercise because the modeling concepts correspond to the programming concepts nicely. Moreover, many IDEs can generate the classes and interfaces from UML class diagrams. It is therefore, not elaborated further in this book.

18.3.2 From Sequence Diagram to Method Code Skeleton

Sequence diagrams model the behavioral aspect of objects. As described in Chapter 11 (Deriving Design Class Diagram), the messages that are passed between the objects are used to identify operations of classes and relationships between the classes. This section illustrates the generation of the code skeletons for the functions of a class from a sequence diagram. Again, many IDEs provide this capability, but it is worthwhile to know the correspondence between design and implementation. Consider the sequence diagram in Figure 11.15. The long, narrow rectangle under the Checkout-Controller object indicates the execution of the checkout(cnList: String[ ]):String method of the CheckoutController. The arrow lines that go out from this rectangle represent calls to functions of other objects. The large box with "loop" at its upper-left corner represents a repetition statement. Thus, from the sequence diagram, one can generate the following code skeleton for the CheckoutController class:

```
public class CheckoutController {
   DBMgr dbm=new DBMgr();
   public String checkOut(String[ ] cnList) {
      String msg="";
      for (int i=0; i<cnList.length; i++) {
        Document d=dbm.getDocument(cnList[i]);
        Loan l=new Loan(p, d); dbm.save(l);
        d.setAvailable(false); dbm.save(d);
        // append d's info to msg;
      }
      return msg;
   } }
```

Clearly, the above code skeleton is incomplete. The programmer needs to fill in the missing parts such as how to initialize the Patron object p and what packages need to be imported. But the ability to generate code skeleton from the sequence diagram greatly simplifies the programming task.

18.3.3 Implementing Association Relationships

Given a class diagram, the mapping of its classes, attributes, operations, inheritance, and implementing relationships to code is straightforward. An aggregation relationship, such as class B is an aggregate of class A, is implemented by a reference from B to A to represent the fact that an instance of A is part of an instance of B. There are several approaches to implement association relationships. One approach uses reference or pointer, described as follows:

One-to-one association. A one-to-one association between class A and class B is implemented by A holding a reference to B if A calls a function of B, and/or by B holding a reference to A if B calls a function of A.

One-to-many association. A one-to-many association between class A and class B is implemented by A holding a collection of references to B if A calls the functions of B instances, or by B holding a reference to A if instances of B call a function of A.

Many-to-many association. A many-to-many association between class A and class B is similarly implemented by a collection of references from A to B, and vice versa.

In the above, using a reference from A to B as well as a reference from B to A improves performance if A calls B and B calls A. However, adding or removing an instance of the association requires change to both references. Another approach to implement association relationships introduces a new class to represent the relationship. For example, an association between class A and class B is implemented by defining a class, say AssocAB, that has references to both A and B and uses a private collection to hold its instances:

```
public class AssocAB {
    private static Collection instances;
    private A a; private B b;
    public AssocAB(A a, B b) {
        this.a=a; this.b=b;
    }
    public void add(AssocAB ab) { ... }
    public void add(A a, B b) { ... }
    public void remove(AssocAB ab) { ... }
    ...
}
```

The private collection should be carefully chosen according to the needs of accessing the elements. For example, if the access is sequential, then using an array list is sufficient. If random access is needed, then using a hash table is more convenient and more efficient.

18.4 ASSIGNING IMPLEMENTATION WORK TO TEAM MEMBERS

During the implementation phase, the classes in the DCD are assigned to team members to implement and test. Usually, the classes depend on each other. Therefore, they should be implemented and tested in some order. For example, if class B calls a method of class A, then A should be implemented and tested before B. If B is implemented before A, then testing B requires the construction of a dummy class to simulate A. The class is called a test stub. The use of test stubs has several drawbacks. It consumes time and effort. If the behavior of A is complex, the construction of the test stub could be difficult, if not impossible. The test stub is not the class it simulates. Therefore, testing with stubs has limitations. Retesting is always required when A is implemented. Therefore, the classes of a DCD should be implemented and tested according to their dependencies. In general, classes that other classes depend on should be assigned to team members who can complete the implementation fast. This allows the team to proceed with the implementation work without needing to wait for the completion of the other classes.

18.5 PAIR PROGRAMMING

Pair programming is an emerging programming technique that requires two people to program together at one machine, with one keyboard and one mouse. The two programmers play two different roles but both work on the same program simultaneously. While the one with the keyboard and the mouse focuses on the best way to implement the functionality, the other reviews the program as it is being typed. For convenience, these two roles are referred to as the writer and the reviewer. They are also referred to as the driver and observer, or other similar roles in the literature. The partners switch roles periodically or whenever they like, for example, switching roles between programming sessions. Each programming session lasts about one to three hours. The pairs are not fixed, they switch around all the time. If a team adopts pair programming, then all team members must learn to work with others. If two people cannot work together, they don't have to pair with each other.

The team divides the programming work into small tasks and assigns them to the pairs. Each task can be a class, a use case, or a package. Using the methodology described in this book, assigning classes to pairs works well. The technique presented in Section 18.4 can be used to assign the classes to the pairs. It is important to maintain constant communication between the pairs to exchange progress, issues, and changes that are needed. With test-driven development, to be presented in the next section, the partners work together to write test cases, implement the functionality, run the tests, modify the tests or program, and refactor the code. The partners discuss what to do next, why they do that, and how they do it. The writer then implements the ideas and the reviewer checks the code for correctness, completeness, consistency, and provides improvement suggestions. Pair programming brings a number of benefits, as follows:

1. It reduces pressure and brings fun to programming because there is always someone with whom to share the stress and joy of success.

2. It enhances team communication because the partners exchange ideas during pair programming. Moreover, pair-switching helps the team members gain insight into the components of the system. This improves productivity and quality.
3. It enhances mutual understanding and collaboration because pair programming lets the team members understand each other and learn from each other in various ways and aspects.
4. It tends to produce simpler and more efficient solutions faster because discussions stimulate creative thinking and help in problem solving.

Pair programming has a number of limitations:

1. It is not for everyone–there are programmers who prefer to work alone.
2. If it is not handled properly, the discussion between the partners can take a lot of time. Therefore, the discussions should focus on solving the problem and getting the work done.
3. It could be slow to start due to the need to adapt to the differences of the partners in education, experience, problem-solving approach, and coding style.
4. Other limitations are: (1) the partners have to be at the same location, (2) it may be difficult for the partners to find a meeting time due to conflicting schedules, and (3) it might not be as effective as systematic review methods in detecting defects.

A programming practice that is similar to pair programming is ping-pong programming. With ping-pong programming, one developer writes the tests and the other developer implements the functionality. Ping-pong programming goes along very well with test-driven development, presented in the next section. Ping-pong programming is an iterative process. First, the basic tests and functionality are implemented. The boundary or extreme cases are added incrementally until the functionality and tests are complete.

18.6 TEST-DRIVEN DEVELOPMENT

Conventional approach to implementation writes the program before writing the tests. In recent years, test-driven development (TDD) is increasing its popularity in the software industry. TDD requires the programmer to "write tests first, then implement the functionality." To write the tests, the programmer must understand the functionality. Tests are generally written for the functions of a class. Recent studies indicate that TDD can reduce prerelease defect densities by as much as 90%, compared to other similar projects that do not implement TDD. In addition, TDD improves programmer productivity. TDD works well for pair programming as well as solo programming.

18.6.1 Test-Driven Development Workflow

Figure 18.5 shows the TDD workflow. With TDD, the features of a class are implemented and tested incrementally. To save time and effort, it is not necessary to test the ordinary get and set functions. TDD performs the following steps:

1. *Prepare for test-driven development.* In this step, the skeleton code for the class is generated. The test coverage to be achieved is determined. A test coverage is a

quality criterion. For example, a 100% statement coverage means that the tests must execute each statement of the program at least once.

2. *Write tests.* In this step, the programmer selects the features to be implemented next, and designs and implements the tests for the features.
3. *Implement and test the features.* In this step, the programmer implements the features and runs the tests to ensure that the features are correctly implemented.
4. *Repeat until all features are correctly implemented.* Steps 2 and 3 are repeated until all the features are implemented and pass all the tests.
5. *Accomplish test coverage.* In this step, the programmer checks the test coverage, adds more tests, and modifies existing tests to ensure that the test-coverage objective is accomplished. The programmer may need to modify the program to pass the modified tests.

Step 1. Prepare for test-driven development.

Before TDD, the skeleton code for the class to be implemented is produced. It has all the functions including the get and set functions, also called getters and setters or accessors. Each function has an empty body, or returns a default value (null for returning an object). The class skeleton can be generated from the design class diagram (DCD). As a good software engineering practice, the skeleton code should include a file header that complies to adopted coding standards. In addition, the test coverage criteria are determined. Branch coverage is commonly used. It means that all branches of the

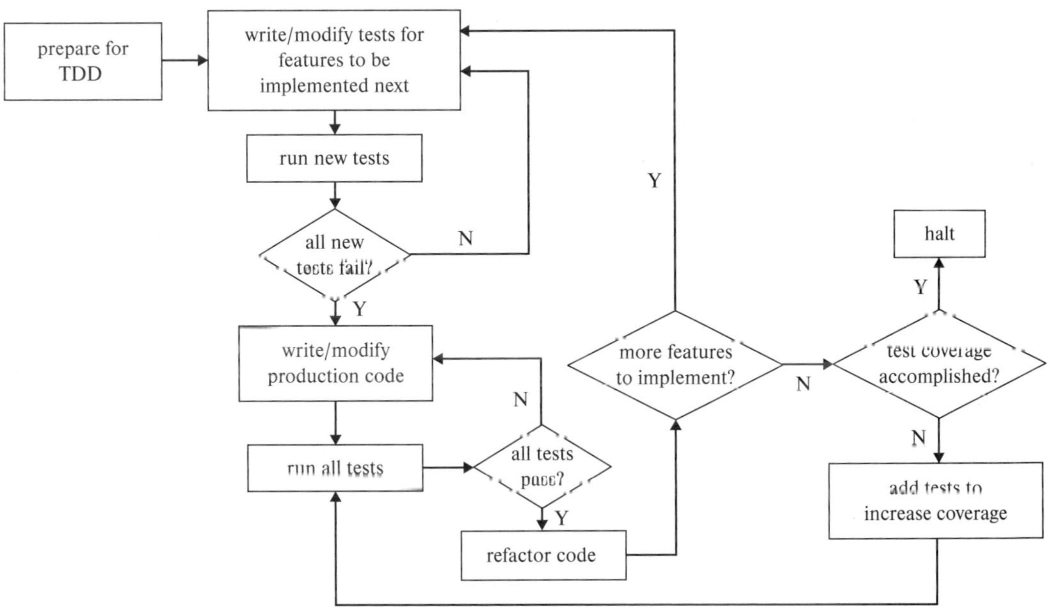

FIGURE 18.5 Test-driven development workflow

class must be tested at least once. For example, if a program contains only one if-then-else statement, then there are two branches because the condition has two outcomes. To achieve branch coverage, at least two tests are required. They must ensure that the program executes each branch correctly.

Step 2. Select features and write tests for the features.

In this step, the programmer selects the features to be implemented next. Often, features that realize high-priority requirements should be implemented first. A requirements traceability tool is useful in this regard. For example, during the requirements phase, requirements are ranked according to the customer's business priorities (Chapter 4). The requirement priorities determine the priorities of the use cases since use cases are derived from requirements (Chapter 7). The use case priorities, in turn, determine the priorities of the functions that are assigned to the objects during object interaction modeling (Chapter 9). Thus, the functions of a class in the DCD are prioritized. The priorities of the functions of a class may differ because they are derived from different use cases. A traceability tool should automatically track and capture such information during the development process. The selection of the features must also consider the dependencies among the features. For example, if function f2 calls function f1, or f2 uses data produced by f1, then f1 should be implemented no later than f2.

Once the features are selected, the programmer designs the tests according to the functionality of the features. Using a unit test tool such as JUnit, the programmer implements the tests. Appendix C contains a brief tutorial on how to use JUnit. The tests are run to test the features. Since the functionality is not implemented, the program should fail to pass each of the tests. If it is not the case, then the tests need to be strengthened and rerun until the program fails to pass the tests.

Step 3. Implement and test the features.

In this step, the programmer implements the features according to their functionality and runs the tests. The programmer may need to modify the program as well as the tests to remove errors. The programmer performs these activities until all the selected features are correctly implemented. The programmer then cleans up the production code as well as the test code. He or she also improves the structure, readability, and performance of the program. In-code documentation and comments are added as required by the codeing standards. These activities are called *refactoring.*

Step 4. Iterate until all features are implemented.

Steps 2 and 3 are repeated until all features of the class are implemented and the program passes all the tests.

Step 5. Ensure test coverage.

The programmer measures the test coverage using a coverage tool such as Emma or Cobertura. The programmer adds tests and reruns all the tests until the required test coverage is accomplished. During this step, refactoring is also performed.

18.6.2 Merits of Test-Driven Development

TDD is gaining popularity in the software industry because it brings a number of benefits to software development:

1. TDD requires the programmer to understand the functionality and implement testable features. Testability is an important attribute of software, especially software requirements. In this sense, TDD helps the team understand and improve the requirements.
2. TDD constantly validates the implementation with respect to the tests. It helps the team detect and remove defects. As a result, TDD produces high-quality code.
3. TDD focuses on the desired functionality first but also addresses the other quality aspects such as program structure and readability through refactoring.
4. TDD facilitates debugging because incremental implementation of the features makes it easy to locate and fix errors.

18.6.3 Potential Problems

There are a number of potential problems, which should be noted, although they are not specific to TDD:

1. The test cases may be too weak to ensure that the program indeed correctly implements the desired functionality. For example, the test cases only test that an object is stored in the database; it does not check that the attribute values are correctly stored.
2. The test cases may be too focused on the main functionality and overlook other cases that may cause the program to crash or behave incorrectly. For example, storing a null object into the database or an object with illegal attribute values should be tested but could be missing from the test cases.
3. The test cases or test scripts are themselves programs. If they are not written in accordance to coding standards and conventions, then the maintenance of these programs is a nightmare. Therefore, the refactoring activity should include refactoring of these programs. Moreover, the subject class and the test cases should comply to coding standards.

18.7 APPLYING AGILE PRINCIPLES

GUIDELINE 18.8 Develop small, incremental releases and iterate; focus on frequent delivery of software products.

Agility favors the development of small, incremental releases iteratively. This greatly reduces the risk of requirements misconception, a significant factor of project failure. Small, incremental releases make it easy to change the software to respond to users' feedback. The practice reduces the users' learning curve. As the increments are successfully deployed, the positive feeling of the team and the users increases. This, in turn, strengthens the collaboration and cooperation of the team and users.

GUIDELINE 18.9 Complete each feature before moving onto the next.

It is important to complete each feature before moving onto the next because agile development values working software. Implementing this principle means only completed features are counted, not partially completed features because the latter are not working software.

GUIDELINE 18.10 Test early and often.

Testing early and often allows the team to detect errors early and correct them much more easily. Test early and often applies to unit testing, as well as integration testing and acceptance testing. Modern tools such as IDEs and JUnit make it easy to implement this principle. For example, hundreds of tests can be run easily with such tools in just a few seconds. Frequent testings greatly improve the quality of the software.

GUIDELINE 18.11 Everybody owns the code–everybody is responsible for the quality of the code.

Collective code ownership improves teamwork because it encourages the team members to contribute to all program segments of the project. For example, extreme programming advocates anybody can change any line of code at any time. Collective code ownership requires that all code that is released into the source code repository must include unit tests that run at 100%. This implies that anyone who changes the code must ensure that the modified code also includes unit tests that run at 100%. Collective code ownership implements the agile principle that empowers the team to make decisions. Through this practice, the team members share their knowledge of the components of the system. It improves the team member's understanding of the components. It also reduces the risk of a team member leaving the project.

18.8 TOOL SUPPORT FOR IMPLEMENTATION

NetBeans and Eclipse are widely used tools in the implementation phase. They support many of the software development activities. They allow the programmer to create, edit, and manage program files and tests for multiple projects, compile and execute the programs and tests, track the test coverages, and debug the programs and tests as well as version control. Appendix C describes these tools in more detail.

18.9 SUMMARY

This chapter presents implementation considerations. These include coding standards, organization of implementation artifacts, converting design to programs, assigning implementation work to team members, and how to conduct test-driven development, pair programming, and ping-pong programming. The chapter also discusses applying agile principles during the implementation phase and tool support to implementation and test-driven development.

18.10 CHAPTER REVIEW QUESTIONS

1. What are coding standards, and why are they important?
2. How are design diagrams mapped to code?
3. What is test-driven development, its workflow, benefits, and potential problems?
4. What is pair programming, its benefits and limitations?
5. How does one assign the classes of a design class diagram to team members to implement?
6. How does one apply agile principles during implementation?

18.11 EXERCISES

Chapter 16 describes the design of a state diagram editor. It produces a number of design diagrams. The following three exercises are related to the design of the editor. Each program file must include the file header and description of classes using the format in Figures 18.2 and 18.3.

18.1 Produce a directory structure for the state diagram editor and assign the editor-related classes presented in Chapter 16 to the directories and subdirectories.

18.2 Implement the classes in Figure 16.7 using test-driven development. Use JUnit to write and run the test cases, and a code coverage tool to ensure that 100% branch coverage is accomplished.

18.3 Implement the classes in Figure 16.27 using test-driven development and pair programming. Form the pair yourselves or according to instructions given by the instructor. Use JUnit to write and run the test cases, and a code coverage tool to ensure that 100% branch coverage is accomplished.

18.4 Implement the persistence framework presented in Chapter 17. Assume that the application is a library information system and the database is a local database. Do this exercise using test-driven development, pair programming, and JDBC, or as instructed by the instructor. In addition, assume that the classes in Figure 11.6 have the following attributes:

Document(cn: String, title: String, author: String, publisher: String, ISBN: String, year: String, duration: String)

Loan(patron: Patron, document: Document, date: String, dueDate: String), the date has the format as "MM/DD/YYYY."

Patron(id: String, name: String, address: String, tel: String)

18.5 Implement the design of the business rules class diagram you produced in exercise 15.7.

18.6 Implement the design of the lawn mowing agent you produced in exercise 13.6.

18.7 Implement the graphical user interface for the state diagram editor presented in Chapter 16.

18.8 Design and implement a web page or two that allows the user to search for documents in a library information system. Do this exercise based on the persistence framework you produced in the above exercise. Use JSP or a technology as instructed by your instructor. An introduction to JSP is given in Appendix B. *Hint:* You need to design and implement a search use case controller that interacts with the DBMgr. You also need to extend the persistence framework to provide the search capability.

19 Chapter

Software Quality Assurance

Key Takeaway Points

- Software quality assurance encompasses a set of activities to ensure that the software under development or modification will meet functional and quality requirements.
- Software quality assurance activities are life-cycle activities.

The analysis, design, and implementation activities begin with a problem statement and lead to the production of an executable software system. The software process used to produce the software system, and how the process is carried out affect the quality of the software system. Therefore, it is important to pay attention to the process quality. Moreover, during this process, many software artifacts are produced. The quality of these software artifacts affects the quality of the software system. Therefore, it is important to ensure that these software artifacts are correct and satisfy other quality criteria, such as easy to understand. These mean that parallel to the development activities, there must be quality assurance activities to set the quality standards, perform the quality assurance activities, and check that the quality standards are met. These activities are collectively referred to as the *software quality assurance* (SQA) activities and the focus of this chapter. After you have read this chapter, you will understand the following:

- Benefits of software quality assurance.
- Software quality attributes, metrics, and indicators.
- Software validation and verification techniques.
- Software validation and verification in the life cycle.
- Software quality assurance functions.

19.1 BENEFITS OF SOFTWARE QUALITY ASSURANCE

The importance of software quality can never be overstated. Our society depends on software to perform almost everything. Software bugs cost billions of dollars owing to property damages, productivity losses, bodily injuries, and loss of lives. One of the software bugs is the Therac-25 bug, which caused the radiation therapy machine to deliver approximately 100 times the intended dose of radiation to patients from 1985 to 1987. Two of the patients died later from the accidents. Another software bug-related accident took place on June 4, 1996—an Ariane 5 rocket was destroyed 37 seconds after launching, due to an error in the 64-bit floating-point to 16-bit signed integer conversion code used by the flight computer, resulting in a loss of more than US$370 million. Although it is practically impossible to avoid all software-related accidents, effective SQA effort could prevent some of the accidents.

19.2 SOFTWARE QUALITY ATTRIBUTES

SQA begins with an understanding of software quality. Like a car or any other products, the quality of the product is determined by a number of factors. For example, the factors that affect the quality of a car include reliability, fuel efficiency, ease of handling, driving comfort, safety, and many other factors. Besides quality factors, people also pay attention to other factors of a car. These include the size of the car, number of doors, number of seats, and the shape and color of the car, among many others. These are descriptive factors because they describe some aspects of a car. Software is similar. It has quality factors and descriptive factors. Some authors think that "factors" are too informal because they could mean anything. Therefore, the literature uses *software attributes* to represent the factors that describe the software, including its quality:

Definition 19.1 A *software attribute* describes, or characterizes, one aspect of interest of the software.

Examples of software attributes include the size, complexity, performance, memory consumption, and many other factors of a software system or component. Some of the attributes are quality related, others are not. This leads to:

Definition 19.2 A *software quality attribute* is a software attribute that describes, or characterizes, a quality-related aspect of the software.

Consider, for example, it is commonly recognized that the effort required to understand, test, and maintain a software module increases significantly with the number of conditions used in the module. This is widely accepted as a complexity attribute of software. Some other commonly seen software quality attributes are as follows:

Reliability. The ability of the software to perform its required functions under stated conditions and produce correct and consistent results.

Robustness. The ability of the software to perform its required functions under rough or exceptional conditions.

Efficiency. The ability of the software to perform its functions and produce desired results with minimum expenditure of time and resources.

Interoperability. The ability of the software to interact and exchange information with other software.

Maintainability. The aptitude of the software to undergo repairs and evolution.

Testability. The aptitude of the software to permit all desired and applicable forms of assessment, including inspection, peer review, white-box testing, and black-box testing.

Portability. The aptitude of the software to permit itself to be transported to run on different operating environments or platforms.

Reusability. The aptitude of the software to permit itself to be used in a similar or different context with or without extension or customization.

Modularity. The aptitude of the software to facilitate integration or arrangement of its component modules.

Cohesion. The degree of relevance of the functions of a software module with respect to the module's core functionality.

Coupling. The degree of dependency and interaction between a module and other modules.

The International Standards Organization (ISO) and the Institute of Electrical and Electronics Engineers (IEEE) have developed respective quality models, each of which includes a hierarchy of quality attributes. Figure 19.1 shows these two models.

Software quality attributes are important aspects of a software system. For example, many businesses require that the software system must be reliable, highly available, easy to maintain, and interoperable. Such requirements are examples of nonfunctional requirements. This means that during the requirements elicitation phase, information relating to the quality aspects of a software system should be collected and used to derive such nonfunctional requirements. The quality attributes listed above could serve as a checklist for eliciting and deriving nonfunctional requirements. This means that a qualitative specification of nonfunctional requirements such as "the system must be reliable," or "the system must be easy to maintain" is not enough.

Functionality	Efficiency
o Suitability	o Time Behavior
o Accuracy	o Resource Behavior
o Interoperability	Maintainability
o Compliance	o Stability
o Security	o Analyzability
Reliability	o Changeability
o Maturity	o Testability
o Recoverability	Portability
o Fault Tolerance	o Installability
Usability	o Replaceability
o Learnability	o Adaptability
o Understandability	o Conformance
o Operability	

(a) ISO 9126 quality model

Efficiency	Portability
o Time economy	o Hardware independence
o Resource economy	o Software independence
Functionality	o Installability
o Completeness	o Reusability
o Correctness	Reliability
Reliability	o Non deficiency
o Security	o Error tolerance
o Compatibility	o Availability
o Interoperability	Usability
Maintainability	o Understandability
o Correctability	o Ease of learning
o Expandability	o Operability
o Testability	o Commucativeness

(b) IEEE Standard 1061 quality model

FIGURE 19.1 ISO and IEEE quality attributes

Qualitative formulation as such is ambiguous because different persons can interpret the same requirement differently. This leads to the study of quality measurements and metrics, presented in the next section.

19.3 QUALITY MEASUREMENTS AND METRICS

Software quality attributes state the important aspects of software. However, they are at most qualitative assessments of the software. The qualitative nature allows subjective evaluations. For example, person A may say that module M is complex, but person B may say it is not. A more objective approach is needed, leading to the following:

Definition 19.3 A *software measurement* is an objective and quantitative assessment of a software attribute.

For example, there are at least three objective and quantitative ways to measure the size of a module. One could measure the size of a module by the number of bytes of the module. Another measurement may count the number of lines of the source code. The third approach measures the size by the number of statements in the source code. Clearly, different measurement methods produce different results. Despite their differences, each of these approaches represents a way to measure the size of a module. With these measurements, it is possible to compare the sizes of two modules. For example, if the sizes of modules $M1$ and $M2$ are s1 and s2, then $M1$ is larger if s1 > s2, provided that they are measured by using the same approach. A potential problem is comparing s1 and s2 without knowing that the sizes of $M1$ and $M2$ are measured by different approaches. This could happen if s1 and s2 are just two integer numbers provided by two different parties. The same problem exists for other attributes. For example, there are at least two complexity measurements. One is the cyclomatic complexity proposed by McCabe, which computes the number of independent paths in a program. The other is the computational complexity or the big oh notation, which is a theoretical measure of the amount of time required to execute an algorithm. Therefore, it is necessary to standardize the measurements. This leads to:

Definition 19.4 A *software metric* is a standard software measurement.

The difference between metrics and measurements is that metrics are adopted as standard measurements. However, many software engineering publications do not distinguish metrics and measurements. This is because there is no officially declared "standard measurements." The metrics in use today become standard measurements because many authors refer to them as metrics. The literature has published numerous software metrics, which measure a wide variety of software attributes. For example, there are process metrics, project metrics, and product metrics. These are further decomposed into subcategories. That is, product metrics include quality metrics and other types of metric such as size metric. The quality metrics include the conventional quality metrics and object-oriented quality metrics. Some of the conventional metrics are applicable to object-oriented software. The object-oriented metrics are meaningful for object-oriented software only. It is the intention of this textbook to focus on a small number of the most discussed quality metrics. This is because even the quality metrics alone deserve a book of their own.

One advantage of software measurements and metrics is the ability to assess software in levels. For example, a module or class is considered big if it has more than a thousand lines of code. A big module or class is difficult to comprehend, test, and maintain. In this case, a thousand lines of code is an indicator of a big module. This leads to the following:

Definition 19.5 An *indicator* is a measurement or metric value, believed to have a significant implication.

As another example of indicator, a function is considered too complex if it contains ten or more atomic binary conditions. These examples show that indicators require measurements and metrics. That is, one computes a measurement or metric and then derives the indicator. Indicators are useful as warning signs as well as quality objectives to accomplish. For example, a tool that computes the size and complexity metrics could highlight big classes and highly complex classes with the red color. This allows the team to focus on quality improvement of these classes.

19.3.1 Usefulness of Quality Measurements and Metrics

Defining quality measurements and metrics consumes time and resources. Moreover, collecting data to compute the measurements and metrics requires considerable effort. Therefore, it is worthwhile to discuss the advantages of quality measurements and metrics. Quality measurements and metrics are quantitative assessment of software, including requirements specification, design, implementation, and documentation, among others. Quantitative assessments are preferred because they are associated with a number of advantages:

1. *Definition and use of indicators.* As discussed earlier, measurements and metrics allow definitions and use of indicators. While measurements and metrics compute specific values, indicators specify ranges of values of relative significance. Indicators let the team quickly spot problem areas as well as focus on the big picture. For example, if a class is big or highly complex, then design patterns may be applied to reduce these numbers.
2. *Directing valuable resources to critical areas.* Measurements, metrics, and indicators are useful for identifying areas that require more resources to design, implement, test, and maintain. These depend on the software artifacts being measured. For example, if a design has high complexity, then more resources might be needed to implement and test. If a class is big or highly complex, then more test resources and time should be allocated.
3. *Quantitative comparison of similar projects and systems.* For example, if the software sizes of two similar projects are substantially different, then further investigation is desirable to find out why. This applies to systems and other metrics.

4. *Quantitative assessment of improvement.* After training or using a methodology, the organization may want to find out the extent of improvement. Measurements and metrics play an important role in such assessments.
5. *Quantitative assessment of technology.* Are agile processes better than plan-driven approaches? How do agile methods compare with each other? Which of the UML-based tools should be used? Answers to these questions could be determined by experiments to quantitatively assess the technologies.
6. *Quantitative assessment of process improvement.* Many organizations adopt the capability maturity model integration (CMMI) or ISO 9001 to improve their software processes. Quantitative measurements are required by these models. Measurements and metrics allow the organization to define process improvement goals and measure the progress toward the goals.

The usefulness of the measurements, metrics, and indicators might not be obvious if one considers these without putting them in perspective. For any project of a certain size, the number of software artifacts produced is large. For example, many projects have hundreds of classes. It is impossible for the team members to examine the classes to find out which one is big, or complex. A tool, however, can quickly compute the metrics and highlight the warning spots. The team can examine these classes and take appropriate measures. This greatly saves time and effort.

19.3.2 Conventional Quality Metrics

Figure 19.2 shows some of the conventional quality metrics. These are classified into requirements metrics (R), design metrics (D), implementation metrics (C), and system metrics (S). They measure the quality aspects of a requirements specification, design, code, and system, respectively.

Requirements Metrics

The requirements unambiguity metric is based on the observation that a software requirements specification (SRS) is unambiguous if and only if each requirement stated in the SRS has only one interpretation. It is measured by the percentage of the requirements that are interpreted in a unique manner by all the reviewers. The requirements completeness metric is based on the assumption that the states of the system and the stimuli to the system as specified in the SRS are complete. That is, the SRS has included all possible states of, and all possible stimuli to, the system. To derive the metric, the system is viewed as a state transition machine, which maps each pair of a state and a stimulus to a state and produces a response.

$$f(state, stimulus) \longrightarrow (state, response)$$

The SRS is considered complete if the f function is complete. If the SRS specifies n_s states and n_i stimuli, then the total number of possible mappings is $n_s \times n_i$. Thus, by counting the number of unique functions (n_u) specified in the SRS, the completeness of the SRS can be measured. That is, if $n_u = n_s \times n_i$ then there is a function for each possible state and stimulus combination. In this case, the SRS is 100% complete. The requirements correctness metric is based on the observation that one would not know if a requirement is correct. One could only validate the correctness of a requirement

Quality Metrics	Type	Description	Calculation	Author
Requirements Unambiguity ($Q1$)	R	The ratio of the number of requirements that the reviewers are able to provide identical or semantically equivalent interpretations (n_{ui}) to the total number of requirements (n_r).	$Q1 = n_{ui}/n_r$	
Requirements Completeness ($Q2$)	R	The ratio of the number of unique functions specified in the requirements (n_u) to the number of all possible combinations of states and stimuli ($n_s \times n_i$), where n_s is the number of states and n_i the number of input or stimuli specified in the requirements.	$Q2 = n_u/(n_s \times n_i)$	Davis et al., 1993
Requirements Correctness ($Q3$)	R	The ratio of the number of validated correct requirements (n_c) to the total number of requirements ($n_r = n_c + n_{nv}$), where n_{nv} is the number of not-yet-validated correct requirements.	$Q3 = n_c/n_r = n_c/(n_c + n_{nv})$	
Requirements Consistency ($Q4$)	R	The ratio of the number of requirements that are not associated with conflicting interpretations ($n_r - n_{ci}$) to the total number of requirements (n_r), where n_{ci} is the number of requirements that are known to have conflicting interpretations by the reviewers.	$Q4 = (n_r - n_{ci})/n_r$	
Fan-In	D	The number of modules that calls a give module. A high fan-in module could mean: • it is a single point of failure. • it is assigned too many responsibilities. • its change affects many other modules.		
Fan-Out	D	The number of modules that are called by a given module. A high fan-out module could mean: • it is difficult to reuse because it requires many other modules. • it is affected by changes to any of the modules. • it may be difficult to understand due to interaction with the other modules.		
Cohesion	D	Measures the relevance of the functions in a module to the core functionality of the module. It is measured with six levels from 6 to 1: functional cohesion, communicational cohesion, procedural cohesion, temporal cohesion, logical cohesion, and incidental cohesion.	see Chapter 6, Architectural Design	
Coupling	D	Measures the dependencies among the modules. It has six levels from 6 to 1: data coupling, stamp coupling, control coupling, external coupling, common coupling, content coupling.		

FIGURE 19.2 Some conventional software quality metrics (*to be continued*)

Modularity	D	Measured by the cohesion and coupling metrics. High cohesion and low coupling imply high modularity.	Modularity = (a * Cohesion + b * Coupling)/(a + b), where a and b are weights on cohesion and coupling.	
Module Design Complexity (*mdc*)	D	The number of integration tests required to integrate a module with its subordinate modules. It is the number of decisions to call a subordinate module (d) plus one.	$mdc = d + 1$ d=number of conditional calls to subordinate modules in the structure chart.	
Design Complexity ($S0$)	D	The number of subtrees in the structure chart with module M as the root. Each conditional call to the subordinate modules of M creates one subtree.	$S0$(leaf) = 1 $S0(M) = S0(\text{child}_1)+...+S0(\text{child}_n)$ $+mdc$, where child is a distinct child, that is, it is counted only once.	McCabe and Butler, 1989
Integration Complexity ($S1$)	D	The minimal number of integration test cases required to integrate the modules of a hierarchical module structure or structure chart.	$S1 = S0 - n + 1$ where n is the number of modules in the module structure.	
Lines of Code	C	Number of lines of source code. A module with a large number of lines of code is difficult to understand, test, and maintain.	Lines of source code excluding comment-only lines.	
Cyclomatic Complexity (CC)	C	The number of independent control flow paths in a function. It is derived from the control flow graph of the function.	It can be computed by either one of three formulas: 1. Number of atomic binary conditions used by the function plus one. 2. #of edges - #of nodes + 2. 3. Number of closed regions in the flow graph plus 1.	McCabe, 1976
Reliability	S	The mean time between failure (MTBF), expressed as mean time to failure (MTTF) plus mean time to repair (MTTR).	Reliability = MTBF = MTTF + MTTR	
Availability	S	The degree to which a system or component is operational and accessible when required for use.	Availability = MTBF/(MTBF + MTTR)	

R=requirements, D=design, C=code, S=System

FIGURE 19.2 *(Continued)*

or could not validate it yet. Therefore, the formula uses the number of not-yet-validated requirements (n_{nv}) in the denominator. The requirements consistency metric counts the number of requirements that are conflicting with each other. For example, if the SRS has 100 requirements r1, r2, ... , r100 and ri and rj, $1 <= i, j <= 100$, are conflicting, that is, they cannot be satisfied at the same time, then the consistency is $(100 - 2)/100 = 98\%$. If none of the requirements are conflicting, then SRS is 100% consistent. An example of inconsistent requirements is that one requirement says "users shall be able to set the session logout time" while another requirement says "the webmaster shall set the session logout time for all users."

Design Metrics

The eight design metrics in Figure 19.2 are defined with a structure chart (or main program and subroutines architecture, Chapter 6) such as the one in Figure 19.3. In the structure chart, $M0 - M7$ are modules, the arrows represent module invocations,

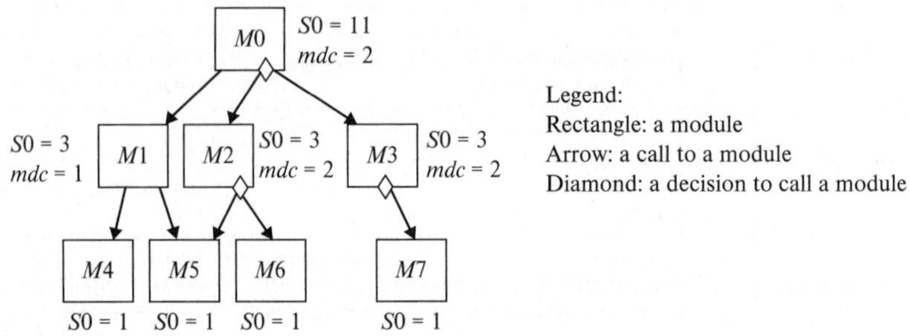

FIGURE 19.3 A structure chart with design complexity metrics

and the diamonds represent conditional calls. The module design complexity *mdc*(*M*) for a module M is calculated by:

$$mdc(M) = d + 1$$

where *d* is the number of diamonds that *M* has, and each diamond is a binary decision. The *mdc* is *d* plus one because a binary decision adds one integration test. This is explained as follows. Suppose *M* calls *A* and *B*. If there is no diamond, then one integration test is adequate to integrate *M* with *A* and *B*–that is, *M* calls *A* then calls *B*. Now suppose that a conditional call is added to *M*. Then there are three cases:

1. *M* calls *A*, then optionally calls *B*. This requires two tests. One tests *M* calls *A* then calls *B*, and the other tests *M* calls *A* and does not call *B*.
2. *M* calls either *A* or *B* conditionally. That is, if the condition is evaluated to true, then *M* calls *A* but not *B*. If the condition is evaluated to false, then *M* calls *B* but not *A*. Two tests are needed. One integrates *M* and *A*, and the other integrates *M* and *B*.
3. *M* calls *A* optionally and then calls *B*. This is similar to the first case.

Thus, each diamond or binary decision to call adds one. Therefore, $mdc = d + 1$. If the decision to call is not an atomic binary decision but an *N*-ary decision, then replace it with $N - 1$ binary decisions. In this case, the $mcd = N - 1 + 1 = N$. An atomic decision is one that does not contain AND or OR connectives.

The design complexity *S*0 is computed by:

$$S0(leaf) = 1, \text{ each leaf module is one subtree.}$$
$$S0(M) = \sum_{i=1}^{n} S0(M_i) + mdc(M)$$

where *M* calls the modules M_i, $i = 1, 2, \ldots, n$. The metric computes the effort required to understand the structured design. It is the effort to understand the subtrees in the hierarchy. Each distinct module itself is considered a subtree, that is, either itself if it is a leaf node or the subtree rooted at the module. If the module has a conditional call to its subordinate modules, then that binary condition creates an additional subtree, as discussed above.

EXAMPLE 19.1

Compute the design complexity for the structure chart in Figure 19.3.

Solution: The design complexity $S0$ of the modules are computed as follows:

$$S0(M4) = S0(M5) = S0(M6) = S0(M7) = 1$$

because they are leaf nodes.

$$S0(M1) = S0(M4) + S0(M5) + mdc(M1) = 1 + 1 + 1 = 3$$

because $M1$ does not have decisions so $mdc(M1) = 1$.

$$S0(M2) = S0(M6) + mdc(M2) = 1 + 2 = 3$$

because $M5$ has been used and not distinct, and $M2$ has one decision so $mdc(M2) = 2$.

$$S0(M3) = S0(M7) + mdc(M3) = 1 + 2 = 3$$

because $M3$ has one decision so $mdc(M3) = 2$.

$$S0(M0) = S0(M1) + S0(M2) + S0(M3) + mdc(M0) = 3 + 3 + 3 + 2 = 11$$

A simpler formula to use is:

$$S0(M) = N_{dm} + N_{abd}$$

where N_{dm} = number of distinct modules, that is, each is counted only once, and N_{abd} = number of atomic binary decisions to call a subordinate module. Using this formula, the design complexity of $M0$ in Figure 19.3 is:

$$S0(M0) = 8 + 3 = 11$$

because the chart has 8 modules and 3 binary decisions.

The integration complexity metric computes the minimal number of integration tests required to integrate the modules. The formula to use is:

$$S1(M) = S0(M) - n + 1$$

where n is the number of modules in the structure chart.

EXAMPLE 19.2

Compute the integration complexity for the design in Figure 19.3.

Solution: The integration complexity is:

$$S1(M0) = S0(M0) - N_{dm} + 1 = 11 - 8 + 1 = 4$$

That is, at least four tests are required. These test the following four subtrees created by the conditional calls:

11- $M0M1M4M5M2M5$

10- $M0M1M4M5M2M6$

0-0 $M0M1M4M5M3$

0-1 $M0M1M4M5M3M7$

where 11- means the decisions in $M0$ and $M2$ are true and the decision in $M3$ is immaterial. 10- means the decision in $M0$ is true, in $M2$ is false, and in $M3$ is immaterial.

The integration complexity formula can be simplified as well. Substitute the simpler formula for $S0$ in the formula for computing $S1$ results in:

$$S1(M) = S0(M) - N_{dm} + 1 = (N_{dm} + N_{abd}) - N_{dm} + 1 = N_{abd} + 1$$

That is, the integration complexity is the number of atomic binary decisions plus one. Using this formula to compute the integration complexity for the $M0$ module in Figure 19.3 results in

$$S1(M0) = N_{abd} + 1 = 3 + 1 = 4$$

Implementation and System Metrics

Two implementation metrics are shown in Figure 19.2: the number of lines of code metric and the cyclomatic complexity metric. The number of lines of code metric is straightforward and counts the number of lines of the source code. The cyclomatic complexity is presented in Chapter 20 and represents the number of independent paths through the program and the number of tests required. Figure 19.2 shows only two system-related metrics. However, there are many other system metrics. These include response time, throughput, performance, memory consumption, power consumption, resource utilization, and the like. The reliability metric uses the mean time between failure (MTBF) as the measurement. It is calculated as the sum of the mean time to failure (MTTF) and the mean time to repair (MTTR) of the system. That is, reliability is:

$$\text{MTBF} = \text{MTTF} + \text{MTTR}$$

EXAMPLE 19.3 First, suppose that MTTR = 0. That is, it requires no time to fix any failure; of course, this is practically impossible, but this assumption makes it easy to understand the formula. Suppose that during a 300-day period 10 failures occur to system A and 20 failures occur to system B. These result in

$$\text{MTBF(A)} = 300 \text{ days}/10 = 30 \text{ days}$$
$$\text{MTBF(B)} = 300 \text{ days}/20 = 15 \text{ days}$$

Since MTBF(A) > MTBF(B), A has a higher reliability than B. Now consider the case that it takes time to repair a failure. However, regardless of how long it takes to repair a failure, the time must be taken from the 30-day time for system A and the 15-day time for system B. That is, the MTTF is revised to MTTF(S) = MTBF(S) − MTTR(S). If it takes one day to repair each failure for system A, then the revised MTTF for A is MTTF(A) = MTBF(A) − 1 = 30 − 1 = 29. This does not affect the MTBF.

The system availability metric is computed by

$$\text{Availability} = \text{MTTF}/(\text{MTTF} + \text{MTTR})$$

Now the repair time is important because the longer the repair time, the shorter the MTTF. Moreover, the ratio of MTTF to MTTF + MTTR is smaller.

EXAMPLE 19.4

Compute the availability for system A for two cases, one assumes one day and the other three days to repair a failure, respectively.

Solution: The availability metric for one day to repair a failure is:

$$\text{MTTF(A)} = 30 - 1 = 29\text{, and}$$
$$\text{availability} = \text{MTTF}/(\text{MTTF} + \text{MTTR}) = 29/30 = 96.67\%$$

The availability metric for a three-day repair is:

$$\text{MTTF(A)} = 30 - 3 = 27$$
$$\text{availability} = \text{MTTF}/(\text{MTTF} + \text{MTTR}) = 27/30 = 90.00\%$$

That is, the longer it takes to fix the problems, the lower the availability of the system. This shows the importance to make the system easy to maintain.

19.3.3 Reusing Conventional Metrics for Object-Oriented Software

Many of the conventional metrics are reusable for object-oriented software. For example, all except the cyclomatic complexity metric are applicable to object-oriented software. It is obvious that the requirements metrics are applicable. The conventional design metrics can be applied to the architectural design. That is, they can be used to assess the design, in which the subsystems and components are treated as modules. They can also be applied to assess a component design, in which the classes are treated as modules. The applications of the fan-in, fan-out, coupling, and modularity metrics are straightforward. To apply the cohesion metric, simply treat the methods of a class as the functions of a module. The number of lines of code metric and the system metrics are applicable to object-oriented programs and systems as well because these metrics do not depend on object-oriented features.

19.3.4 Object-Oriented Quality Metrics

The object-oriented paradigm introduces a number of powerful features such as encapsulation, inheritance, polymorphism, and dynamic binding. Accordingly, there are a number of object-oriented measurements and metrics, proposed by Chidamber and Kemerer:

Weighted Methods per Class (WMC). The WMC for a class C is the sum of the complexity metrics of the methods of a class. It is computed as

$$WMC(C) = c_{m1} + c_{m2} + \cdots + c_{mn}$$

where c_{mi}, $i = 1, 2, \ldots n$, are the complexity metrics of the methods of C. The complexity metrics are purposely let open to allow any applicable complexity metrics to be used. This implies that the cyclomatic complexity metric discussed above can be used here.

EXAMPLE 19.5 Consider, for example, a Stack class implemented with a fixed-sized array and six methods: push(int x), pop(), top(), isEmpty(), isFull(), and Stack() as its methods. The push(int x) and pop() methods need to check if the stack is full and empty, respectively. Each of these has a cyclomatic complexity of 2. The other methods have a complexity 1. Thus, the WMC of the Stack class is 8.

The time and effort required to test and maintain a class increases with the WMC of the class. This is because there are more independent paths in its methods. It is likely that the conditional statements are introduced to test application-specific conditions. This means that it could be more difficult to use the class in other projects.

Depth of Inheritance Tree (DIT). The DIT for a class C is the longest inheritance path from a root to the class. Note that there could be more than one root. DIT is computed as:

DIT(C) = 0 if C does not have a parent class.

DIT(C) = 1 + max ({DIT(C'): C' is an immediate parent of C})

EXAMPLE 19.6 Figure 19.4 shows the class diagram of a software component. The DITs for some of the classes are:

DIT = 0 : EditCmd, GraphElem, TestModel

DIT = 1 : Edge, Node, Path

DIT = 2 : Clear, AddAll, DeleteOdd, DeleteEven, Empty, InitNode, Even, All, Odd

The ancestors of a class may reimplement some of the methods that the class uses; in such cases, the behavior of the class is affected. Therefore, the greater the DIT

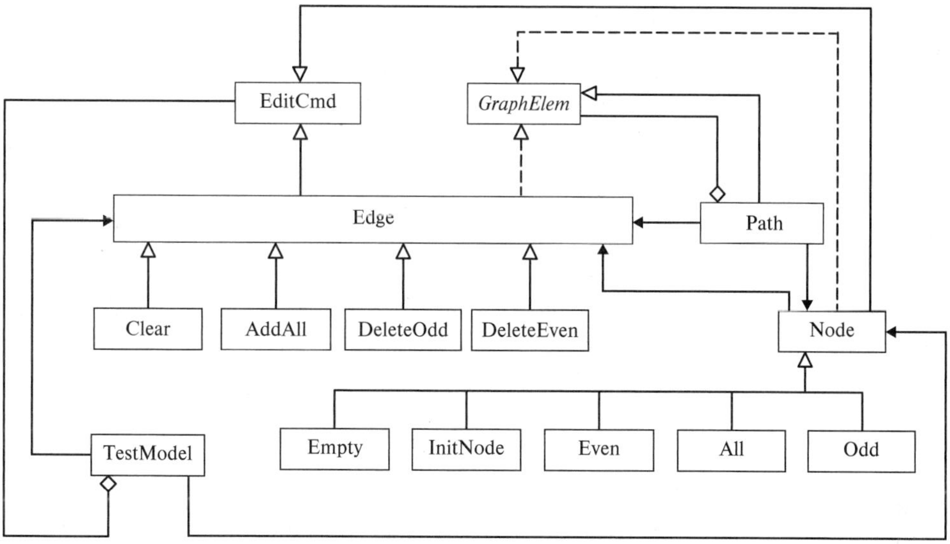

FIGURE 19.4 Class diagram for some classes of a state diagram editor

the more likely the class will inherit and use such methods. The behavior of the class could be more difficult to predict.

Number of Children (NOC). The NOC of a class C is the number of immediate children of C in an inheritance hierarchy:

$$NOC(C) = |\{C': C' \text{ is an immediate child of } C\}|$$

where $|S|$ denotes the number of elements in the set S.

EXAMPLE 19.7

The NOCs for some of the classes in Figure 19.4 are:

NOC = 0: Empty, InitNode, Even, TestModel, All, Odd, Path, Clear, Add All, Delete Odd, Delete Even because they do not have subclasses.

NOC = 2: EditCmd

NOC = 3: GraphElem

NOC = 4: Edge

NOC = 5: Node

Generally speaking, the greater the NOC the greater the likelihood of reusing features of C. If C is changed, then its children are affected. Since the children may use the inherited features, their behavior is affected by the behavior of the class and changes to the class.

Coupling Between Object Classes (CBO). The CBO of a class C is the number of classes it depends on:

$$\text{CBO(C)} = |\{\text{C': C depends on C'}\}|$$

where the depends-on relationships include inheritance and aggregation relationships such as a subclass depends on its parent class, and an aggregate class depends on its component classes. Moreover, a class may call or use other classes, creating dependencies on the other classes.

EXAMPLE 19.8 The CBO for some of the classes in Figure 19.4 are:

CBO = 0: EditCmd and GraphElem because they do not depend on other classes.

CBO = 2: Edge because it depends on EditCmd and GraphElem.

CBO = 3: TestModel, which depends on Node, Edge and EditCmd; Node, which depends on EditCmd, Edge and GraphElem; and Path, which depends on Edge, Node and GraphElem.

CBO = 1: The remaining classes in Figure 19.4.

The more classes that C depends on, the more difficult to test C. If the classes that C depends are not implemented or tested, then test stubs must be implemented to simulate their behavior. Since C depends on these classes, to understand C requires understanding of these classes. For example, to understand TestModel, one must understand EditCmd, Edge, and Node. To test TestModel, one needs to construct test stubs for EditCmd, Edge, and Node if they are not implemented and tested. Therefore, the greater the CBO the more difficult to understand, test, maintain, and reuse the class.

Response for a Class (RFC). The RFC is the number of methods of a class plus the number of methods called by a method of the class:

$$\text{RFC(C)} = |\{\text{m: m is a method of C or m is called by a method of C}\}|$$

The larger the RFC the more difficult to test and debug the class due to more complex interaction relationships and more effort required to understand the methods and prepare test cases and test stubs.

Lack of Cohesion in Methods (LCOM). The LCOM for a class C is the number of pairs of methods of C that do not share an attribute of C. Let A and M be the sets of attributes and methods of C, respectively. The LCOM of C is computed as follows.

$$\text{LCOM(C)} = |M| * (|M| - 1)/2 - |\{(x, y): (x, y \in M)(\exists z \in A)(x \text{ access } z \text{ and } y \text{ access } z)\}|$$

EXAMPLE 19.9

Calculate the LCOM for the Mower class in Figure 13.20 (excluding the nested classes).

Solution: The following table shows the attributes of the Mower class and methods that access each of the attributes. The last column shows the number of pairs of methods that access a common attribute. The last entry of the last column gives the total number of pairs of methods that share a common attribute. The Mower class has 13 methods, which has $13 * (13 - 1)/2 = 78$ pairs of method. Thus, the LCOM for the Mower class is $78 - 31 = 47$.

Attribute	Methods Accessing the Attribute						# of Pairs of Methods Accessing the Attribute
WIDTH	clear(East)						0
HEIGHT	clear(SE)	clear(SW)					0 (duplicate below)
timer	stop()	start()					1
x	getX()	clear(East)	clear(West)	fwd(West)	fwd(SE)	start()	$6 * (6 - 1)/2 = 15$
y	getY()	clear(SE)	clear(SW)	fwd(East)	fwd(SW)	start()	$6 * (6 - 1)/2 = 15$
state	actionPerformed(...)						0
this	actionPerformed(...)						0
Total # of pairs of methods accessing a common attribute							31

19.4 SOFTWARE VERIFICATION AND VALIDATION TECHNIQUES

Verification and validation are SQA activities to ensure that the software process and product confirm to established quality requirements. According to Barry Boehm, verification and validation are concerned with such questions as "are we building the product right?" and "are we building the right product?" That is, verification ensures that the process is carried out correctly, and validation ensures that the correct product is built. Validation is further divided into static validation and dynamic validation. Static approaches check the correctness of the product without executing the product while dynamic validation executes the product or a prototype. Software testing is a dynamic validation method that executes the system or its components. Software testing and static approaches are complementary. Each of them plays an important role in SQA. Inspection, walkthrough, and peer review are widely used static verification and validation techniques. These techniques are performed manually without executing the software. Therefore, they are referred to as *static verification* and *validation techniques.*

Software verification and validation are important because software is used in all sectors of our society. Today's software systems are extremely large and complex and process billions of transactions a day in the financial, retailing, manufacturing, transportation, telecommunications fields and many other sectors. Many software systems are embedded systems, real-time systems, or mission-critical systems. Failures of these software systems are financially very costly and politically unacceptable because the failures may incur recall of products, property damages, injury to human body, or even loss of human life. Therefore, the importance of software verification, validation, and testing can never be overstated.

19.4.1 Inspection

Inspection checks the product against a list of common errors, anomalies, and noncompliances to standards and conventions. It is similar to car inspection that is required in many countries. Car inspection checks the car against an inspection list of problems in a number of components. Each item is "mechanically" inspected to make sure that it works well. For example, turn on the headlight switch and check that the headlights are on. Similarly, code inspection aims at detecting commonly encountered programming errors such as:

- Use of uninitialized variables, objects, references, or pointers.
- Calling the wrong polymorphic function.
- Incorrect function invocation, for example, incorrect parameters are passed to the function, or the parameters are misplaced.
- Nonterminating loops or incorrect loop termination conditions.
- Mismatch in array dimensions, causing an array index out-of-bounds exception.
- Uncaught/unhandled runtime exceptions.
- Problems in the use of pointers, for example, memory is allocated but not released, leading to memory leak.
- Data flow anomalies, for example, objects are created but not used.
- Omitted reimplementation of a feature of the parent class, resulting in the invocation of the default implementation of the parent class.
- Incorrect, inconsistent, or incomplete business logic, for example:
  1. *incorrect business logic:* An if-condition is stated incorrectly.
  2. *inconsistent business logic:* The same condition should produce the same result but it does not, for example, an applicant with GPA = 3.0 is admitted at one place and rejected at another place.
  3. *incomplete business logic:* An if-condition without an else part when there should be one.
- Incorrect reference to data structures or data elements such as using the wrong data elements in computation.
- Errors in arithmetic, relational, or logical expressions such as mistyping "+" for "−", ">=" for ">", and "&&" for "| |".
- Incorrect I/O statements such as reading the wrong file, or processing the file format incorrectly.
- Incorrect invocation of library functions.
- Incorrect use of call by value and call by reference.

Applicability. All software artifacts, including requirements specification, domain model, use case specification, various design diagrams, program source code, static and dynamic pages, user interface design, test plan, and test cases.

Effectiveness. Effective in detecting common errors, anomalies, and noncompliance to standards and conventions.

Participants. One to three technical staff members.

Procedure. Similar to peer review (see Section 19.4.3).

Duration. Inspection meeting is usually not needed.

19.4.2 Walkthrough

Walkthrough manually executes the product using simple test data. Usually, the developer who produces the product leads the team to perform the walkthrough. The team checks the product step by step while reading aloud. It is designed to stimulate doubt and discussions. Walkthrough is similar to buying a car at the dealership. The sales rep shows and explains the features of a car to the buyer while the buyer asks questions to clear doubt and stimulate discussion.

Applicability. Expanded use case specification, various design diagrams, program source code, dynamic pages, user interface design, test cases.

Effectiveness. Useful to gain understanding or insight of complex functionality and behavior, especially products that involve complex algorithms, new algorithms, recursion, multithreading, real-time behavior, or concurrent update to shared resources.

Participants. Three to five technical staff members including the developer.

Procedure.

1. A product overview is presented to the participants if desired.
2. The developer loudly reads through the product and provides necessary explanations. The other team members ask questions and raise doubts. The developer answers the questions and provides justification. Action items are identified and recorded. A deadline for the developer to fix the problems is set.
3. The developer fixes the problems, produces a summary list, and obtains approval from the participants.

Duration. One to two hours per session.

19.4.3 Peer Review

In peer review, the product is reviewed by peers, who are guided by a list of review questions, designed to qualitatively assess aspects of the product. The following is a sample code review checklist:

1. Does the program correctly implement the functionality and conform to the design specification?
2. Do the implemented class interfaces conform to the interfaces specified in the design class diagram?

3. Does the implementation comply to the coding standards?
4. Compute a number of required quality metrics and identify those that are worse than the required indicators. A metrics calculation tool is very useful in this regard.
5. Are programming constructs used correctly and properly? For example, improper uses include using an array to store a large number of elements, loops without proper termination conditions, and uncontrolled update to shared variables.
6. Does the program correctly implement the algorithms and data structures?
7. Are there any errors or anomalies in the definition and use of variables such as memory is allocated but not released, variables are defined but not used, or variables are incorrectly initialized?
8. Are there any incorrect uses of logical, arithmetic, or relational operators, incorrect invocation of functions, incorrect interfacing to devices, or incorrect handling of device interrupts?
9. Are there any potential performance bottlenecks, or an inability to fulfill timing constraints?

The reviewers' assessments of the product may vary drastically because the assessments are heavily influenced by the reviewer's knowledge, experience, background, and criticality. Therefore, a review meeting is usually conducted to discuss the review results.

Applicability. Peer review is applicable to all software artifacts produced during the life cycle. These include requirements specification, domain model, use case specification, various design diagrams, program source code, static and dynamic pages, user interface design, test plan and test cases.

Effectiveness. Peer reviews are effective in detecting problems that require human judgment concerning the correctness, efficiency, user-friendliness, and other software quality attributes.

Participants. Three to five reviewers with the needed background or expertise.

Procedure.

1. A product overview is presented to the reviewers if desired. Each workable unit of product is assigned to a couple of reviewers to review. Each unit should require no more than one half of a day to evaluate. A review meeting is scheduled to take place one to two weeks later.
2. Guided by a review checklist, the reviewers evaluate the product and answer the review questions independently.
3. At the review meeting, the reviewers present their comments and suggestions and the developer answers questions and clarifies doubt. The participants also discuss ways to improve the product. Action items are identified and recorded. Most of the action items require the developer to fix the problems identified by the reviewers. However, in some cases, other developers may need to change their components to coordinate with the program under review. A deadline for completing the action items is set.

4. The developer fixes the problems and produces a list of responses that summarizes the solution of each problem. The reviewers may accept the changes or request additional improvements.
5. In some cases, a second review meeting is required. In these cases, the above steps are repeated.

Duration. One to two hours per review session.

The following are guidelines for peer review:

GUIDELINE 19.1 If the product requires a lot of effort to review, assign different parts of the product to different reviewers. Avoid having all reviewers review all parts of the product.

GUIDELINE 19.2 The aspect of the product reviewed by a reviewer should match the reviewer's experience and expertise. New graduates should not serve as reviewers, though they can be observers.

GUIDELINE 19.3 Avoid giving the reviewers too much to review in too little time.

GUIDELINE 19.4 No management personnel should be present in review meetings. The review comments should not be used as performance evaluations.

GUIDELINE 19.5 Ensure that the reviewers understand the product goals, constraints, and assumptions.

GUIDELINE 19.6 The reviewers are required to identify merits and strengths of the product and provide improvement suggestions, not just point out defects.

GUIDELINE 19.7 Avoid review sessions with many participants or longer than two hours.

GUIDELINE 19.8 The developer should inform the reviewers of any places of the product where feedback is sought because the developer is uncertain whether the solution is correct, appropriate, or adequate.

19.5 VERIFICATION AND VALIDATION IN THE LIFE CYCLE

Verification and validation are life-cycle activities. They should be performed in each of the phases to ensure that the process and products of each phase are correct. This section provides an overview of the inspection, walkthrough, and review activities in the life cycle. The checklists provided at the end of some of the chapters serve as sample checklists for these verification and validation activities. These checklists may be used with or without change.

Verification and Validation in the Requirements Phase

Verification and validation in the requirements phase aims at detecting errors and anomalies in the requirements specification and the analysis models including the domain model and use case diagrams. The techniques used include requirements review, inspection, walkthrough, and prototyping. There are three types of requirements review: technical review, customer review, and expert review (Chapter 4). These review activities are aimed at detecting different types of problems in the requirements specification. Technical review is an internal review, performed by technical staff such as the developers. It may combine inspection and peer review and check the requirements, constraints, use cases and domain model for completeness, consistency, unambiguity, traceability, and feasibility:

- *Completeness.* The completeness checks ensure that important application and domain-specific concepts are defined, the customer's business needs are addressed, important business cases, events and states are included, and the specification of the business rules is complete.
- *Consistency.* The consistency checks ensure that the application and domain concepts are defined and used consistently, and the specification of the business rules is consistent.
- *Unambiguity.* The unambiguity checks ensure that the application and domain concepts and business rules are described clearly and accurately.
- *Traceability.* The traceability checks ensure that the lower-level requirements correspond to the higher-level requirements, and the requirements–use case traceability matrix correctly describes the correspondence.
- *Feasibility.* The feasibility checks ensure that the team can deliver the system that satisfies the requirements and constraints under the budget and schedule constraints. Prototyping is often used in feasibility study to clear uncertainties.

Prototyping helps the development team understand the requirements. Prototypes are used to demonstrate the functionality and behavior to the users to solicit user feedback. This enables the team to avoid misunderstanding users' expectations, especially in user interface and interaction behavior. Prototypes are also used to assess the feasibility of the project. In this regard, prototypes help the development team to assess the feasibility of technical requirements and constraints such as timing, response time, and performance.

The simplest prototype could be a set of drawings that illustrate the user interfaces of the future system. The most sophisticated prototype could be a partially implemented system that the users can experiment with to gain hands-on experience. Which type of prototype to use is an application-dependent issue. For instance, applications that are mostly concerned with mission-critical operations would benefit from executable prototypes that demonstrate functionality, behavior, and performance. Applications that are end-user oriented would benefit from prototypes that demonstrate the user interfaces.

Chapter 5 presents the steps for constructing a domain model and a domain model inspection and review checklist. Besides inspection and review, walkthrough is useful for checking the correctness and completeness of a domain model. In domain model walkthrough, the model constructor, or one of the team members, explains the classes and relationships between the classes while the other team members examine the model, raise doubt, and make improvement suggestions. The inspection and review checklists at the end of Chapters 5 and 7 are useful for checking the domain model and use cases in the requirements phase.

Verification and Validation in the Design Phase

Verification and validation in the design phase are aimed at assessing the correctness of the design, how well the design satisfies the requirements and constraints, and other quality aspects of the design. Checking the correctness of the design is a validation activity to ensure that the design corresponds to the real needs of the customer. If the requirements and constraints correctly and adequately specify the real needs of the customer, then assessing the satisfiability of the design with respect to the requirements and constraints is a verification approach to ensure that the design corresponds to the customer's real needs.

Assessments of many quality aspects of the design are equally important. These include the architectural design, application of design principles and design patterns, security consideration, and consistency and completeness of the design. The review for architectural design is aimed at evaluating the architectural design with respect to the design principles, which are measured by quality metrics such as fan-in, fan-out, modularity, cohesion, and coupling. Chapter 6 and Chapters 8 through 11 included inspection and review checklists for assessing the design diagrams. Walkthrough is a useful technique for design verification and validation. It is applicable to the design specifications of the functional and behavioral aspects of the system, that is, the expanded use cases, sequence diagrams, state diagrams, activity diagrams, design class diagram, and decision tables.

Verification and Validation in the Implementation Phase

Inspection and peer review in the implementation phase are aimed to ensure the following:

- The source code correctly and adequately implements the functionality and behavior as expressed in the design specification, that is, the use case diagrams, expanded use cases, sequence diagrams, state diagrams, activity diagrams, decision tables, and design class diagram.
- The implemented interfaces and interaction behavior between the various components are consistent.
- The source code satisfies the organization's coding standards and quality metrics such as information hiding, high cohesion, low coupling, and acceptable cyclomatic complexity, for example, not to exceed 10.
- The programming constructs of the implementation language are used properly.

Walkthrough is an effective static validation technique for checking the correctness of a small segment of the source code. First, a small segment of the code to be analyzed is identified. Second, simple test data to exercise the code segment is prepared. The code is then manually executed with the test data as the input and the result of each execution step is checked for correctness. It is useful to record the intermediate results using a table, in which the columns represent the program variables and the rows represent the program statements executed. The entries of the table represent the values of the program variables as the program statements are executed step by step. Code walkthrough can be an individual exercise or a team exercise. It is very effective for checking the correctness of complex logic, recursive procedures, and simple concurrent programs.

19.6 SOFTWARE QUALITY ASSURANCE FUNCTIONS

The overall objective of SQA is to ensure that the software development process is carried out as required, and the software system meets the requirements and quality standards. Moreover, SQA should aim at continual improvement of the software process and quality standards. SQA, as an area of the software engineering discipline, is responsible for the research, development, and validation of cost-effective processes, methods, and tools to accomplish these goals. As a function in a software development organization, SQA has the additional responsibility to evaluate, select, and implement quality assurance processes, methods, and tools for the organization. Many software development organizations have an SQA component to take care of the SQA functions. Depending on the size of the organization, the SQA component can be a department, a division, a group, or a single person. SQA encompasses a wide variety of life-cycle activities or functions. These are generally classified into three broad categories of functions:

1. *Definition of processes and standards.* This function is aimed at developing and defining an SQA framework for the software development organization. It includes the development and definition of the development processes and methodologies, quality assurance processes, quality metrics, indicators, and standards as well as SQA procedures and policies.
2. *Quality management.* This function is performed for a specific software project and includes quality planning and quality control. That is, it produces a plan for adapting the SQA framework for the specific software project and ensures that the plan is correctly carried out. The quality plan specifies which items of the organizational SQA framework should be applied and how to apply to the software project.
3. *Process improvement.* This function performs activities to improve the development as well as quality assurance processes of the organization.

These activities are life-cycle activities because they are carried out in parallel with the software life-cycle process. For example, from the process point of view, SQA defines the development processes and methodologies to carry out the analysis, design, implementation, testing, and maintenance activities, and monitors the performance of such activities. From the product point of view, SQA defines quality attributes, metrics, indicators, standards and review checklists to ensure the quality of the software artifacts and the software system.

19.6.1 Definition of Processes and Standards

The definition of processes and standards function is responsible for developing and defining a framework for ensuring software quality for the whole organization. The framework generally should consist of the following items:

- Definition of software development, and quality management processes and methodologies.
- Definition of SQA standards, procedures, and guidelines for carrying out the SQA activities during the life cycle.
- Definition of quality metrics and indicators for quality measurement and assessment.

Definition of Process and Methodology

The importance of a software development process and a development methodology is discussed in Chapter 2, where several software process models are described. A software development methodology implements a software process. For example, the methodology presented in this book is an implementation of an agile unified process. The definition of processes and standards function may adapt one or more of the processes described in Chapter 2 and the supporting methodologies for the organization's software development projects. For some organizations, one development process and one methodology is adequate. For some other organizations, several different processes or methodologies are required to meet the needs of the software projects of the organization. In this case, the framework should specify the applicability, the advantages, and limitations of each process and methodology to help the project managers select them. The framework should also identify and define the software configuration management functions and tools to support such functions. That is, a mechanism to coordinate changes to the components of a system during the entire software life cycle.

The framework should define quality assurance processes to be used with the development processes. Quality assurance is not one size fits all, different development processes require different quality assurance activities. Figure 19.5 shows the SQA activities in the conventional and the agile processes, respectively. The figure provides a starting point for the SQA component to identify and specify the SQA activities to be performed during the phases of the development processes. In particular, during the requirements and design phases, conventional processes review the requirements and design specification, and verify and validate analysis and design models. Prototyping is performed to assess the feasibility of the project and validate design ideas. An acceptance test plan and an integration test plan are produced. Agile processes use a different set of techniques, shown in the third column of Figure 19.5. For example, agile methods use user stories, use cases, feature-driven development, and system metaphor (XP). Agile methods emphasize agile values, principles, and best practices.

During the implementation phase, conventional processes use coding standards, code review, inspection, and walkthrough as well as static analysis tools to ensure software quality. Agile processes use test-driven development, refactoring, pair programming, ping pong programming, stand-up meetings such as Scrum daily meetings, and coding standards to ensure quality of the code. During the integration and acceptance testing phase, conventional processes perform integration and acceptance testings. Agile processes use continuous integration or frequent builds, and user-performed

<table>
<tr><th>Software Development Activities</th><th>Conventional Process SQA Activities</th><th>Agile Process QA Techniques</th></tr>
<tr><td>Software requirements analysis</td><td>1. Requirements specification reviews
2. Evaluating requirements related metrics and indicators
3. Prototyping
4. Model validation
5. Planning for software acceptance testing</td><td rowspan="2">1. User stories, use case driven development, feature-driven development, system metaphor (XP)
2. Active user involvement, early customer feedback
3. Iterative and small increments
4. Feasibility study and prototyping (DSDM)
5. Release planning (XP)
6. Design for change
7. Brainstorming
8. Teamwork–value individuals and interaction, team decision making, frequent exchange</td></tr>
<tr><td>Software design</td><td>1. Software design review, inspection and walkthrough
2. Evaluating design related metrics and indicators
3. Use case based validation
4. Model checking
5. Planning for software integration testing</td></tr>
<tr><td>Software implementation</td><td>1. Code review, inspection and walkthrough
2. Static analysis checking
3. Evaluating code based metrics and indicators
4. Coding standards</td><td>1. Test-driven development
2. Refactoring
3. Pair programming (as on-the-fly code review)
4. Ping-pong programming
5. Stand-up meetings
6. Coding standards (XP)</td></tr>
<tr><td>Integration and system testing</td><td>1. Integration testing
2. Acceptance testing</td><td>1. Continuous integration (XP)
2. Functional tests by customers (XP)</td></tr>
<tr><td>Software operation and maintenance</td><td>1. Change analysis and control
2. Software re-engineering
3. Regression testing</td><td>1. User feedback
2. On-site customer
3. Responding to change</td></tr>
</table>

FIGURE 19.5 SQA in conventional and agile processes

acceptance testing. In the operation and maintenance phase, conventional processes apply change impact analysis, configuration change control, reengineering, and regression testing. Agile processes rely on user feedback during the iterative process, on-site customers, and respond to change to cope with changes during this phase.

Definition of SQA Standards and Procedures

Another responsibility of the SQA component is defining quality standards and procedures for all software projects to comply. These include process standards and product standards. The process standards define the requirements on the development processes and methodologies. This includes the selection of the processes and methodologies for the projects as well as standards that concern the application of the processes and methodologies during the life cycle of the project. For example, the process standards may require that every project must use a given process, or one of a number of processes such as the waterfall, unified, or agile processes. The standards may also require the use of a methodology, or one of a number of methodologies. The standards should also define lower-level requirements concerning the execution of the processes and methodologies. These include the software artifacts that each phase of the process should produce, and quality assurance standards and procedures to ensure the quality of the artifacts.

Sometimes, a specific project may require the use of a process or methodology that is not in the framework. This may be due to various reasons including technical reasons and political reasons. For example, the type of software to be developed requires a certain process or methodology. The customer demands the use of a certain process or methodology. Therefore, flexibility should be provided for the project to select a process or methodology. In this case, the standards should specify the requirements that the project-selected process or methodology should satisfy. For example, the standards may require that the development process selected must include configuration management or version control, formal reviews, and test-driven development.

The product standards define the requirements on the software artifacts produced during the life cycle. These include requirements on the structure, representation, format, checklists, and verification and validation activities. For example, the coding standards presented in Chapter 18 define the structure and format for all program files and the in-code documentation requirements. The review checklists and the verification and validation techniques presented earlier provide the basis for defining the requirements on the software artifacts.

The SQA standards are derived from the organization's software engineering goals including long-term and short-term goals and quality goals. Moreover, the organizational SQA standards should be defined based on one of the quality models such as the ISO 9001 or IEEE quality models. Software quality interplays with software productivity, cost, and time to market. Poor software quality incurs a lot of rework and bug fixing; and hence, it reduces productivity and increases cost and time to market. On the other hand, quality requires time and effort, but in the long run it increases productivity and reduces cost and time to market. Studies show that the delivered defects per thousand lines of code for CMMI (Chapter 23) level 1 to level 5 are 7.5, 6.24, 4.73, 2.28, and 1.05, respectively. That is, the improvement from CMMI level 1 to level 5 is 614%. Assume that the average cost to fix a field detect defect is $30,000. The savings are $193,500 per thousand lines of code. If the software system has 1 million lines of code, then the total savings are $193.50 million. Experience shows that it takes an average of two years to advance from one CMMI level to the next level. This means that a level-1 organization would take eight years to move from level 1 to level 5. If it invests $5 million per year in SQA to reach that goal, then the total costs are $40 million. Compared with the savings, the investment is worthwhile.

The SQA component also defines the procedures, policies, and guidelines for carrying out the SQA activities. For example, software verification and validation procedures and software configuration management procedures must be defined and clearly documented. The SQA component must also specify the policies and guidelines for applying the procedures. The policies answer questions such as "who is responsible for selecting the reviewers to review a program?" or "how many reviewers are required to review a program?" Finally, the SQA component should develop and document a process improvement process (PIP) for the organization.

Definition of Metrics and Indicators

Software quality assurance requires measurements so that quality can be assessed. Metrics and indicators are needed for measuring and assessing software quality. This function of the SQA component identifies and defines the metrics to be used to measure the process and product aspects of the projects in the organization, for example, how to measure the reliability of a software system, and how to measure the complexity of a class and a subsystem, respectively. Indicators are required to help the management and development teams focus on improvements and problem spots. For example, what is a reliable software system, what is a complex class, and so on. Indicators must be defined so that poor-reliability components/systems and complex classes can be detected easily. On the other hand, indicators for good software must be defined as well. These indicators help the management and development teams see the progress of process improvement. In general, it is useful to define three to five levels of indicators to show the progress of each aspect. To progress from one level to another, a typical team should spend a certain amount of effort, but the next level should be reachable within two years.

19.6.2 Quality Management

The definition of processes and standards function defines the SQA framework for the organization. The quality management function of the SQA adapts and implements the framework for each of the software projects of the organization. It consists of two activities:

1. *Quality planning.* This activity takes place at the beginning of each project. It produces a quality plan for the specific project.
2. *Quality control.* This activity takes place throughout the entire project. It monitors the execution of the quality plan as well as modifies the quality plan to respond to changes in the reality.

Quality Planning

Quality planning is performed at the beginning of each software project. Guided by the quality framework, this task produces a quality plan for, and according to the needs of, the software project. In most cases, the quality plan must comply with the standards defined in the organizationwide quality framework. The quality planning task defines the quality goals for the project and artifacts including the software system, identifies the applicable processes, methodologies, standards, procedures, and metrics to be used by the project, and produces a quality plan for the project. The plan should include at least the following sections:

1. *Purpose.* It specifies the purpose and scope of the plan as well as the product or system and its use.
2. *Management.* It specifies the project organization and team structure (see Chapter 23), including the team members, their roles and responsibilities. Most importantly, who will be responsible for the SQA functions and activities, and what are the roles and responsibilities of these team members.
3. *Standards and Conventions.* It specifies the SQA standards to be applied including documentation standards, structure (or format) standards, coding standards, and commentary standards.
4. *Reviews and Audits.* It specifies the types of review that will be performed including inspection and walkthrough, and the verification to ensure that the process is carried out correctly. It should specify the problem reporting and correction procedures.

5. *Configuration Management.* It specifies the configuration management activities of the project.
6. *Processes, Methodologies, Tools, and Techniques.* It specifies the processes, methodologies, tools, and techniques that will be used to develop the software system and conduct the SQA activities.
7. *Metrics and Indicators.* It specifies the metrics and indicators to be applied to measure and assess the software artifacts. Moreover, it should also specify the acceptable range of the metrics. For example, a cyclomatic complexity greater than 10 is not acceptable.

SQA Control

This SQA function ensures that the SQA plan is carried out correctly. SQA training could be one of the important activities of this function. The training is aimed to educate the developers of the importance of SQA, the organization's SQA standards and procedures, the available SQA tools as well as how to use the tools to perform SQA activities. Another responsibility of the SQA component is assisting the developers in performing the SQA activities. For example, in addition to training the walkthrough, inspection, and review techniques, the SQA component can help in the development of the inspection and review checklists.

This SQA function also collects SQA-related data and manages these data using an SQA database. Many different categories of SQA data need to be gathered, processed, and analyzed. At the minimum, information about field-detect defects must be collected and entered into the database for root cause analysis. It is intended to identify the software development activity that causes a software defect or problem. Root cause analysis helps the software development organization identify weaknesses in the software development life cycle. The result enables the organization to focus the improvement effort in those areas that improvement is most needed. The SQA component provides such process improvement recommendations to the management, and ensures that the accepted recommendations are properly implemented and incorporated into the process.

SQA encompasses many activities, components, and concepts. Figure 19.6 summarizes all these in an SQA domain model. For simplicity, the diagram does not show the attributes and methods. Explanation of the domain model is omitted because this section has described each of the classes and their relationships.

19.6.3 Process Improvement

A software development organization needs to continuously improve its process to stay in business. The term "process improvement" is not limited to improving only the process but all aspects of the development process. In other words, it means improving everything. Although agile development values individual and interaction over processes and tools, this does not mean that agile processes do not need process improvement. As a matter of fact, agile methods are improving from one version to another. Practices of agile methods in organizations are improving as well. That is, organizations are discovering better ways to adopt agile methods into their development environments.

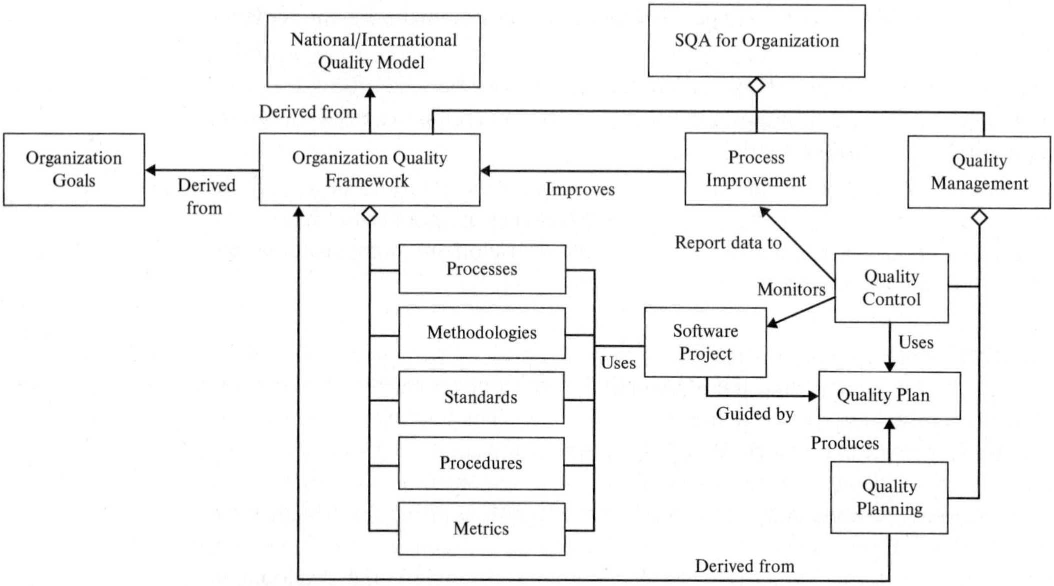

FIGURE 19.6 A domain model for SQA functions

The main focus of this function of the SQA component is the definition and execution of a PIP. The process should run continuously and iterate regularly, such as, every year or every two years. It should include at least the following activities:

1. *Defining metrics and data collection methods.* This phase defines the process aspects to be improved, the metrics to measure, the indicators to assess the improvement, and the data-collection mechanisms needed for computing the metrics. It should also specify: who, what, where, when, and how. That is, who should collect which pieces, where the data should be collected, when the data should be collected, and how to collect the data. For example, the reviewers should collect the lines of code and defects detected. The data should be entered into the SQA database.

   Different organizations have different priorities. Therefore, the aspects of the process to improve are different. Moreover, the mechanisms used to collect the data are organization and project dependent. All these need to be defined according to the organization's business objectives and environment. In addition, since the organization is changing, all these need to be modified regularly to reflect the changes.
2. *Collecting data for measuring the process.* During this phase, the data that are needed to compute the metrics are collected from various projects regularly. The process should define standards and procedures to ensure that the data are collected accordingly.
3. *Calculating the metrics and indicators.* The collected data are used to compute the metrics and indicators. Reports are generated for periodic review. The PIP should specify when this must take place. For example, it must take place quarterly, twice a year, annually, and so forth. The frequency is different for different organizations.

It is important to involve both the management and the developers in the decision-making process. This is advocated by the agile principle that "a collaborative and cooperative approach among the stakeholders is essential."

4. *Recommending improvement actions.* The reports generated in the last step are reviewed by a group of selected personnel. These may include management personnel, SQA personnel, and representatives from the various development teams. The composition of a group is organization dependent, but it is desirable to include representatives of all stakeholders. The review should generate a list of actions to improve the various aspects of the development process.

19.7 APPLYING AGILE PRINCIPLES

GUIDELINE 19.9 Good enough is enough.

SQA is good, but it is not the more the better. The organizational SQA framework should take into account the business goals and needs of the organization. For example, a CMMI level 1 organization would not be able to satisfy CMMI level 5 standards. If the organization's goal is to move to level 2, then the framework should specify level 2 standards and require all projects to comply.

Good enough is enough also means that the framework should not include everything. It should include only the items that are needed and contribute to the organization's business and quality goals. Moreover, SQA costs time and effort and affects productivity. Therefore, it is important to achieve the quality goals with the minimal effort. This means focusing on the quality aspects that have the biggest impact on quality and require the minimal amount of effort.

GUIDELINE 19.10 Keep it simple and easy to do.

Requiring software projects to comply to the quality standards is not an easy task. Collaboration of the project managers and developers is the key. This requires that the framework and the practices should be easy to understand and easy to comply. So keeping things simple and easy to do is important.

GUIDELINE 19.11 Management support is essential.

No SQA program can be a success without the support of the management. Therefore, a mutual understanding between the SQA component and management is important. On the one hand, the management of the organization should understand the importance of quality and SQA. On the other hand, the SQA component should understand the priorities and constraints of the management, and work with the management to help them solve their problems, including quality problems.

GUIDELINE 19.12 A collaborative and cooperative approach between all stakeholders is essential. The team must be empowered to make decisions.

The development of the quality framework, quality planning, and quality control are not the sole responsibilities of the SQA component. Quality is everybody's business. Therefore, it is important to involve all stakeholders that are affected in all of the SQA activities. That is, seeking input from the stakeholders, keeping the stakeholders informed, and soliciting feedback from the stakeholders. In particular, the SQA activities need support from the development teams. This means empowering the teams to make SQA decisions is the key to success.

GUIDELINE 19.13 Agile development values working software over comprehensive documentation.

Overemphasis on SQA could result in comprehensive documentation. For example, the SQA standards might require the development teams to produce various analysis and design diagrams and documents. Agile development values working software over comprehensive documentation. This means barely enough modeling and design–just enough for the team to understand the application, and communicate and validate the design ideas.

19.8 TOOL SUPPORT FOR SQA

Numerous tools exist to support SQA. Figure 19.7 shows some of the tools and their functions. Many of these are public domain or open source tools.

Name of Tool	Description
Checkstyle	A coding standard checking tool for Java. It can be configured to check almost any coding standards.
Chidamber & Kemerer Java Metrics (ckjm)	A Chidamber & Kemerer metrics calculation tool for Java.
Eclipse Metrics Plug-in	A metrics calculation and dependency analyzer plugin for the Eclipse IDE. It computes various metrics and detects cycles in package and type dependencies.
FindBugs	A static analysis tool that looks for bugs in Java code.
IBM Rational Logiscope	A software quality assurance tool that automates code reviews and detects error-prone modules for software testing.
Jindent	A source code formatter for Java. It also generates and completes Javadoc comments.
McCabe IQ Developers Edition	A quality measurement tool that performs static analysis and visualizes the architecture. It also highlights complex areas of the code to identify bugs and security vulnerabilities.
PMD	A Java source code analysis tool that looks for many potential problems.
Understand for Java	A reverse engineering, code exploration, and metrics calculation tool for Java source code.

FIGURE 19.7 Software tools supporting quality assurance

19.9 SUMMARY

This chapter presents software quality attributes, software quality metrics, and static verification and validation techniques such as peer review, inspection, and walkthrough. It also presents verification and validation in the life cycle. The SQA components of many software development organizations are responsible for the SQA functions, which include definition of processes and standards, quality management, and software process improvement. This chapter describes these functions and summarizes them in an SQA domain model. At the end of the chapter, how to apply agile principles to SQA is discussed.

19.10 CHAPTER REVIEW QUESTIONS

1. What are software quality attributes and quality metrics?
2. What are inspection, walkthrough, and review, and how do they differ from each other?
3. What are the three types of requirements review, and who performs each of these reviews?
4. What verification and validation activities are performed in each phase of the life cycle?
5. What are the three main functions of the SQA component in an organization?
6. What are the SQA activities in the conventional and agile processes, respectively?
7. What are the benefits of software quality assurance?

19.11 EXERCISES

19.1 What is the cyclomatic complexity of the flowchart in Figure 18.5? Apply the three approaches to compute the cyclomatic complexity, that is, counting the number of regions plus one, counting the number of atomic binary decision plus one, and counting the number of nodes and edges. Check that these results are identical. If not, explain why they are not identical.

19.2 Compute the conventional design metrics shown in Figure 19.2 for the design class diagram in Figure 11.6. *Hint:* Section 19.3.3 describes how this can be done. For conditional calls, check the design sequence diagram, where conditional calls may be indicated.

19.3 Compute the object-oriented quality metrics presented in Section 19.3.4 for the classes in Figure 16.15.

19.4 Practice peer review, inspection, and walkthrough on a number of sample requirements specifications, design specifications including diagrams, and source code. For the review and inspection, try to use the checklists presented in the previous chapters.

19.5 Exercise 4.2 produces the software requirements specification (SRS) for each of a telephone answering system, a vending machine, and a web-based only email system. Perform the three types of requirements review to these SRSs using the review checklists presented in Section 4.5.6. Write a review report for each of the SRSs.

20 Chapter

Software Testing

Key Takeaway Points

- Software testing is a dynamic validation technique.
- Software testing can detect errors in the software but cannot prove that the software is free of errors.
- Software testing increases the development team's confidence in the software product.

During the software development process, static checking such as inspection and code review are performed. These are useful for detecting certain types of error. However, static checking does not run the program; and hence, they cannot detect other types of error that require execution of the program. This is similar to test driving a car in addition to just visually checking it. A casual buyer would test drive the car with rather arbitrary driving scenarios. A cautious buyer would prepare test cases to assess different aspects of the car, for example, acceleration, high-speed driving, and brake effectiveness. These test cases are intended to establish a certain degree of confidence in the car–that is, that the car would perform to the expectation of the buyer. Software testing is similar and aims to check the correctness of the software and detect errors. It is complementary to static checks. Unlike casual testing as performed by some programmers, software testing aims to apply well-established testing methods and techniques to validate the software and detect errors. The following story may motivate the study of this topic.

Many years ago, I worked in a software company where I met a young, talented software engineer. Due to common interest, we quickly became good friends. We visited each other's office everyday, sometimes just to say hello. One day, he came to tell me that he would leave for a vacation because he finished testing his component. I was curious about how he tested his software. "Oh, that's easy," my friend said, "I tested to show that it works." I asked if he had used any test methods. He said that he did not. The answer did not surprise me because even today many computer science programs do not offer a course on software testing. Many software engineers perform unit tests like my friend. I told him to apply some of the test methods described in this chapter. Two weeks later, my friend showed up in my office. His face was pale and his hands were shaking. I asked what happened. "It was very scary," my friend said. "I found hundreds of bugs with the test methods you told me about the other day. If I had left for vacation, I would get into big trouble if the bugs were detected during integration testing." This story illustrates how important it is to perform testing using an effective test method. In this chapter, several effective test methods are described. In particular, you will learn the following in this chapter:

- Fundamentals of software testing.
- Software testing process.
- Conventional software testing techniques.
- Object-oriented software testing techniques.
- Software testing tools.
- Software testing in the life cycle.

20.1 WHAT IS SOFTWARE TESTING?

Software testing is both a discipline of software engineering and a process to ensure the correctness of a software system or component. As a discipline, it encompasses research, development, validation, and education of cost-effective software testing processes, methods, and techniques for use in practice. As a process, software testing is defined as follows.

> **Definition 20.1** *Software testing* is a dynamic validation activity to detect defects and undesirable behavior in the software being tested, and demonstrate that the software satisfies its requirements and constraints.

This definition indicates that testing serves two purposes. First, it aims to demonstrate that the software satisfies its requirements. These include functional as well as nonfunctional requirements. Second, testing is aimed at detecting errors and undesired behavior. The errors include semantic errors, logical errors, and computation errors, among many others. The undesired behavior refers to the behavior of the system that is not stated in the requirements and could be exploited to compromise the effectiveness, or security, of the system. Consider, for example, a web application that requires each user to login. Software testing of the login use case is to ensure that legitimate users with a valid password are able to login and the other cases are rejected. Moreover, if the requirements state that the account shall be made inactive after three fail attempts, then the test must also ensure that this is indeed the case. Clearly, the test generation process must take into account the various login scenarios, including valid, invalid, and scenarios that represent three or more failed attempts. The challenges are how to generate such tests, how to determine that the tests are effective in detecting errors, and when the test process should stop. Software testing as a discipline answers these questions and more.

20.2 WHY SOFTWARE TESTING?

Software testing is needed because static approaches to quality assurance have limitations. First, static approaches do not execute the program; and hence, they cannot detect errors that require execution. For example, polymorphism and dynamic binding imply that the type of an object is not known at compile time. This limits the effectiveness of static approaches. Second, inspection, walkthrough and peer review could not handle complexity very well due to human limitations. Studies show that it is common for an object-oriented program to contain a lengthy series of function calls that involve more than a dozen functions of different objects. It is difficult for a human being to trace the function calls to detect errors and anomalies. Software testing is invaluable for many embedded systems that use firmware or application-specific integrated circuits (ASIC). In such applications, the software is burned into the IC chips, which are very costly to change. The following story illustrates how much it costs if bugs are burned into the IC chips.

At the end of 1980s, a Hong Kong–based radio communications equipment provider made a fortune from selling its products in mainland China. To cope with competition, the company wanted to develop a new product and awarded the development contract to a small company in North America. Since it was a new product, changes to requirements were inevitable and testing time was reduced to meet the delivery schedule. An independent quality assurance consultant had warned the Hong Kong company that more testing was required, or it would have to expect an overwhelming number of product returns. Unfortunately, driven by its expected success, the Hong Kong company ignored the warning and authorized the production of the IC chips and the communication products. One month after the products were shipped to the customers, hundreds and thousands were returned and flooded the warehouse. The company lost every penny and went out of business quickly.

The importance of software testing is also justified by the use of software in process control systems, medical equipment and devices, and military applications, where failure can cause human injury or loss of life. These consequences are both politically unacceptable and economically undesirable. Besides these, software testing brings the following benefits:

1. Knowing that all software will be rigorously tested, the developers will be more conscious for developing error-free software.
2. Adopting cost-effective software testing methods and tools will significantly improve software quality. The story at the beginning of this chapter about the young software engineer applying these methods and detecting hundreds of bugs illustrates this.
3. Software testing adds another layer of quality assurance in addition to inspection, walkthrough, and peer review. This is similar to the benefits of test driving the car in addition to checking the car without driving it.
4. If a bug database is used to record the bugs detected during testing and field operation, then the information can be used to produce bug statistics and root cause analysis reports. These reports are very valuable for process improvement.

20.3 CONVENTIONAL BLACK-BOX TESTING

This section presents some of the well-known conventional black box testing techniques, which can be used to test the member functions of a class and provide a basis for learning object-oriented testing methods.

20.3.1 Functional Testing: An Example

Functional testing derives test cases from the requirements, or functional specification of the component under test (CUT). Functional testing is also referred to as black-box testing because it treats the CUT as a black box. In illustration, consider a purge function that eliminates duplicate elements from an integer list. The input to the purge function is a list of elements, denoted $L = A1, A2, \ldots, An$. The output of the function is a list of elements $L' = A1', A2', \ldots, Am'$, $m <= n$. The output list must not contain duplicate elements. This can be specified mathematically as:

$$(1)(\forall i')(\forall j')((i', j' <= m) \wedge (Ai' = Aj') \rightarrow (i' = j'))$$

This formula facilitates the derivation of test cases as follows:

Case 1: $n = 0$, $m = n$, the input is an empty list.

Case 2: $n = 1$, the input is a single-element list, which has two cases:

Case 2.1: $m < n$, an error is detected because the CUT deletes the only element that must not be deleted.

Case 2.2: $m = n$, expected.

Case 3: $n > 1$, the input list contains more than one element, two cases are possible:

Case 3.1: $m < n$, the input list contains duplicate elements, which are deleted.

Case 3.2: $m = n$, the input list does not contain duplicate elements.

From the above analysis, four test cases are generated: (1) an empty list, (2) a single-element list, (3) a list that contains duplicate elements, and (4) a list that does not contain duplicate elements. The outcome of all these test cases must satisfy the output condition, that is, the output list must not contain duplicate elements. Figure 20.1 illustrates the specification of the test cases and the tests derived from the test cases. In particular, Figure 20.1(a) specifies the test scenarios and the expected test outcome for each of the test scenarios. Figure 20.1(b) describes the concrete tests derived from the test scenarios. Each of the passing criteria entries specifies a condition that must be satisfied to pass the test. In the figure, they are EO – AO. This means that the expected output and the actual output must be the same. Sometimes, the passing criteria specify that the output values must fall between a certain range to pass the test. The figure shows four tests for the four test cases. This does not mean that the number of tests must be the same as the number of test cases. It can be more than or less than the number of test cases. That is, a test case may derive zero or more tests, depending on several factors. For example, the tester may skip a test case because it is trivial. More than one test for a test case are run to increase the chance of detecting an error. In Figure 20.1, the test cases and tests are specified using tables. Some authors use tuples to represent these. Since table rows and tuples are equivalent, these two representations are not different.

#	Description	Input	Expected Output
1	Test for an empty list	An empty list	Same as input
2	Test for a single-element list	A single-element list	Same as input
3	Test for duplicate elements	A list containing duplicate elements	The list with all duplicate elements removed
4	Test for no duplicate element	A list in which all elements are distinct	Same as input

(a) Purge program test case specification

#	Description	Input	Expected Output (EO)	Actual Output (AO)	Passing Criteria	Test Result
1	Test for an empty list	()	()	TBD	EO=AO	TBD
2	Test for a single-element list	(10)	(10)	TBD	EO=AO	TBD
3	Test for duplicate elements	(1,2,2,3,4,4,5)	(1,2,3,4,5)	TBD	EO=AO	TBD
4	Test for no duplicate element	(1,2,3,4,5)	(1,2,3,4,5)	TBD	EO=AO	TBD

TBD=to be determined

(b) Tests produced from the test case specification

FIGURE 20.1 Specification of test cases and tests

In the example, the output condition omits several cases that should be considered. For example, the elements in the resulting list must have the same order as in the input list. Moreover, every element in the resulting list must be an element in the original list, and vice versa. For simplicity, these conditions are not included. One important activity of software testing is implementing and running the tests to ensure that the CUT indeed passes the tests. These tasks can be accomplished by using a test tool. JUnit is widely used for implementing and running the tests for Java programs. How to use JUnit to accomplish these tasks is presented in Appendix C.

20.3.2 Equivalence Partitioning

In addition to testing by functionality as discussed in Section 20.3.1, there are three commonly used black-box testing techniques. These are equivalence partitioning, boundary value analysis, and cause-effect analysis. Equivalence partitioning divides the input and output domains into a number of disjoint subsets, and selects one test case from each of these disjoint subsets. For example, to test a telephony system, the telephone numbers are partitioned according to their area codes, and one phone number is randomly picked from each of these partitions to serve as the test case for the partition.

The key to equivalence partitioning is to identify an equivalence relation among the elements of an input domain. An equivalence relation is a reflexive, symmetric, and transitive relation. For example, "having the same area code" is an equivalence relation between telephone numbers. Another example is dividing mail by zip code and service type, such as first-class mail and express mail. Express mail is further divided into several subcategories. Equivalence partitioning is based on the assumption that elements belonging to the same partition possess the same characteristics or properties. Therefore, to test the software with respect to the characteristics, it is sufficient to use one of the elements from each of the partitions. The equivalence relation is

Case #	Input/Output		Partitions		Example	
	Type	Domain	Valid	Invalid	Valid	Invalid
1	Numeric	A range of values [*n*1, *n*2]	[*n*1, *n*2]	[-MIN, *n*1-1], [*n*2+1, MAX]	[1, 12]	[-MIN, 0], [13, MAX]
	Nonnumeric	A range of consecutive strings S1-S2	S1-S2	All strings except S1-S2	CS4300-CS4399	All strings except CS4300-CS4399
2	Numeric	Ranges of values [*n*1, *n*2], [*n*3, *n*4], $n_i<n_{i+1}$	[*n*1, *n*2], [*n*3, *n*4]	[-MIN, *n*1-1], [*n*2+1, *n*3-1], [*n*4+1, MAX]	[1, 5], [8, 12]	[-MIN, 0], [6, 7], [13, MAX]
	Nonnumeric	Ranges of consecutive strings S1-S2, S3-S4	S1-S2, S3-S4	All strings except S1-S2, S3-S4	CS430-CS439, CS450-CS459	All strings except CS430-CS439, CS450-CS459
	Nonnumeric	Regular sets	Regular sets	All strings except elements in the regular sets	CS4[35][0-9]	All strings except elements in CS4[35][0-9]
3	Numeric	A single value *n*	[*n*, *n*]	[-MIN, *n*-1], [*n*+1, MAX]	[3.0, 3.0]	[-MIN, 3.0), (3.0, MAX]
	Nonnumeric	A single string S	{S}	All strings except S	"USA"	All strings except "USA"
4	Numeric	An enumeration of discrete values {*n*1, ..., *n*k}	[*n*1, *n*1], ..., [*n*k, *n*k]	All integers except *n*1, ..., *n*k	{1, 5, 10, 25} or [1, 1], [5, 5], [10, 10], [25, 25]	All integers excluding 1, 5, 10, 25
	Nonnumeric	An enumeration of strings {S1, ..., S*n*}	{S1}, ..., {S*n*}	All strings except S1, ..., S*n*	{"jan", ..., "dec"} or {"jan"}, ..., {"dec"}	All strings except "jan", ..., "dec"
5	Boolean	{True, False}	{True}, {False}		{True}, {False}	

FIGURE 20.2 Rules for partitioning input spaces

application dependent. However, there are general partitioning rules as listed in Figure 20.2. In addition to partitioning the input into equivalence classes, test cases are also generated from the partitions of the output domain.

EXAMPLE 20.1

Apply equivalence partition test to the purge function discussed in Section 20.3.1.

Solution: The input to the purge program is an integer list. The purge program must process all such lists. Therefore, the input domain of the purge program is the set of all such lists. Applying an equivalence partition test is to partition this set into disjoint subsets and select one test case from each of the subsets. According to the functionality of the purge program, the input set is partitioned into two disjoint subsets, one of which consists of lists with duplicate elements while the other contains lists without duplicate elements.

EXAMPLE 20.2 One of the graduate admission criteria of a computer science department is *GPA* >= 3.0. However, if the student's undergraduate major is not computer science, then the student must take deficiency courses. Apply an equivalence partition test to this application.

Solution: The problem given above indicates that applicants with an undergraduate degree in computer science and *GPA* >= 3.0 are admitted unconditionally. Applicants with *GPA* < 3.0 are rejected. Applicants with *GPA* >= 3.0 but an undergraduate degree that is not computer science must take deficiency courses. Applying an equivalence partition test is to divide all the applicants into four disjoint subsets:

1. Partition 1 (*GPA* >= 3.0 and major == "CS"): This subset consists of applicants with *GPA* >= 3.0 and an undergraduate degree in computer science. This partition results in unconditional admissions.
2. Partition 2 (*GPA* >= 3.0 and major! ="CS"): This subset consists of applicants with *GPA* >= 3.0 but the undergraduate degree is not computer science. This results in admissions that require the student to take deficiency courses.
3. Partition 3 (*GPA* < 3.0 and major =="CS"): This subset consists of applicants with *GPA* < 3.0 and an undergraduate degree in computer science. This results in rejection.
4. Partition 4 (*GPA* < 3.0 and major! ="CS"): This subset consists of applicants with *GPA* < 3.0 and an undergraduate degree not in computer science. This also results in reject.

20.3.3 Boundary Value Analysis

Equivalence partitioning divides all possible input or output values into equivalence classes and selects test cases from each of the partitions. The boundary value analysis selects test cases at and near the boundaries of the equivalence classes. Therefore, the two test case generation methods complement each other. Figure 20.3 shows the rules for boundary value test case generation. The rules are also applicable to the output domain and generate test cases to cause the software to produce output values at the boundaries of the partitions of the output domain.

EXAMPLE 20.3 Apply boundary value test to the purge function in Section 20.3.1.

Solution: In Example 20.1, the input domain of the purge program is partitioned into two partitions. One consists of lists with duplicate elements and the other contains lists with no duplicate elements. Applying a boundary value test is to select test cases at the boundaries of these two subsets. The question is what are the boundaries of these two subsets? To determine these, the lists in each of the two subsets are ordered in some way. That is, the lists are sorted according to their lengths or number of elements in the list. The sorting, though performed only conceptually, shows that each subset contains an empty list, lists with only one element, lists with only two elements, . . . , and lists with a very large number of elements. Thus, the boundary value tests are: (1) an empty list, (2) a list with only one element, (3) a list with two elements, (4) a list of *N* elements with *N* equals to the specified upper limit of the length of any list, (5) a list with N-1 elements, and (6) a list of $N + 1$ element. Since the list is a container, a test for a null reference should be included.

Case #	Input/Output		Test Cases
	Type	Domain	
1	Numeric	A range of values [$n1$, $n2$]	$n1-1$, n, $n1+1$, $n2-1$, $n2$, $n2+1$
	Nonnumeric	A range of consecutive strings S1-S2	S1, S2, null string, empty string, very long string
2	Numeric	Ranges of values [$n1$, $n2$], [$n3$, $n4$], $n_i<n_{i+1}$	Same as 1 but for each range
	Nonnumeric	Ranges of consecutive strings S1-S2, S3-S4	S1, S2, S3, S4, null string, empty string, very long string
3	Numeric	A single value n	$n-1$, n, $n+1$
	Nonnumeric	A single string S	S, null string, empty string, very long string
4	Numeric	An enumeration of discrete values {$n1$, ..., nk}	$nj-1$, nj, $nj+1$, j=1, 2, ..., k
	Nonnumeric	An enumeration of strings {S1, ..., Sn}	S1, ..., Sn, null string, empty string, very long string
		A set of strings	Null string, empty string, one-char string, very long string
5	Boolean	{True, False}	{True}, {False}
6	Container	Instances of Container	(1) A null container reference, (2) an empty container, (3) a one element container, (4) one less than the maximum size of the container, (5) maximum number of elements, (6) if possible, one more element than the maximum size of container, (7) boundary test cases for container elements.

FIGURE 20.3 Rules for boundary value testing

EXAMPLE 20.4

Apply a boundary value test to the graduate admission example described in Example 20.2.

Solution: First, the ranges of values for each of the partitions obtained in Example 20.2 are determined. That is, for $GPA >= 3.0$, the range of values is 3.0–4.0 assuming that the maximal GPA is 4.0. For the degree major, the values are "CS" or "not CS." Next, the test cases are selected at the boundaries of the partitions as follows:

1. For Partition 1 ($GPA >= 3.0$ and major=="CS"), the test cases are the elements of the Cartesian product:
   {*GPA* == 2.99, *GPA* == 3.0, *GPA* == 3.01, *GPA* == 3.99,
   GPA == 4.00, *GPA* == 4.01} × {*major* == *null*,
   major == *empty string*, *major* == "*CS*", *major* == *a very long string*}

2. For Partition 2 ($GPA >= 3.0$ and major!="CS"), the major!="CS" condition implies a set of any strings not including "CS." Thus, the test cases are:
   $\{GPA == 2.99, GPA == 3.0, GPA == 3.01, GPA == 3.99, GPA == 4.00, GPA == 4.01\} \times \{major == null, major == empty\ string, major == a\ one\text{-}char\ string, major == a\ very\ long\ string\}$
3. For Partition 3 ($GPA < 3.0$ and major=="CS"), the test cases are:
   $\{GPA == -0.99, GPA == 0.00, GPA == 0.01, GPA == 2.99, GPA == 3.0, GPA == 3.01\} \times \{major == null, major == empty\ string, major == \text{"CS"}, major == a\ very\ long\ string\}$
4. For Partition 4 ($GPA < 3.0$ and major!="CS"), the test cases are:
   $\{GPA == -0.99, GPA == 0.00, GPA == 0.01, GPA == 2.99, GPA == 3.0, GPA == 3.01\} \times \{major == null, major == empty\ string, major == a\ one\text{-}char\ string, major == a\ very\ long\ string\}$

20.3.4 Cause-Effect Analysis

Cause-effect analysis is similar to the functional test example described in Section 20.3.1 except that a decision table (Chapter 15) is constructed to help the generation of the test cases. First, the dependencies between the input variables and the outcome of the CUT are identified. Second, values for the input variables are determined. Third, a decision table is constructed to show the correspondence between the input value combinations and the outcome of the CUT. Finally, test cases are derived from the rules of the decision table. As an example, consider the testing of a stack. For simplicity, only the push function is discussed. Figure 20.4 shows a decision table with stack reference and stack size as the input variables, and stack size, stack top, and exceptions as the output. The rule-count row is useful for completeness checking. That is, the sum of the integers on the row should equal the total number of all possible combinations of the values of the input variables. In this example, the stack reference input has two values and the stack size input has three values (i.e., stack size $= 0$, k and $k < n$, n). Therefore, the total number of combinations is 2 by 3 equals to 6. The sum is also 6. Therefore, the table has covered all possible cases.

From the decision table, four test cases are derived, which correspond to the four rules in the decision table. For example, the first test case is a null stack reference, corresponding to the first rule in the decision table. The second test case is an empty stack, corresponding to the second rule in the decision table, and so forth.

	1	2	3	4
Stack reference	null	not null	not null	not null
Stack size (max=n)	–	0	n	$k<n$
Rule count	3	1	1	1
Resulting stack size		1		k+1
Stack.top()		a		a
Exception	Null pointer exception		Stack full exception	

FIGURE 20.4 Cause-effect analysis of push(a) operation

20.4 CONVENTIONAL WHITE-BOX TESTING

Unlike black-box testing techniques, white-box testing derives test cases from the internal structure or logic of the CUT. Most white-box approaches generate test cases through the analysis of the source code.

20.4.1 Basis Path Testing

Basis path testing generates test cases to exercise the independent control flow paths, called basis paths, of the CUT. The basis paths are derived from the CUT's flow graph, which is constructed using a number of flow graph notations shown in Figure 20.5. Figure 20.6(b) shows a flow graph for the purge function in Figure 20.6(a); the nodes labeled B and E are the begin node and end node, respectively.

> **Definition 20.2** A *basis path* is a path from the B node to the E node and traverses a directed cycle at most once.

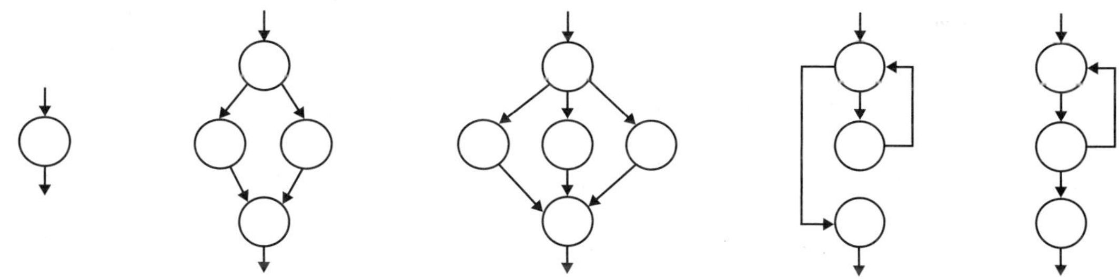

FIGURE 20.5 Flow graph notation and a flow graph

```
public LinkedList<Item> purge(LinkedList<Item> list) {
  if (list!=null) { // 1
    if (list.size()>=2) { // 2
      Item p=null, q=null;
      for(int i=0; i<list.size()-1; i++) { // 3
        p=list.get(i); // 4
        for(int j=i+1; j<list.size(); j++) { // 5
          q=list.get(j); // 6
          if (p.equals(q)) { // 7
            list.remove (q); // 8
          }
        }
      }
    }
  }
  return list; // 9
}
```

(a) Purge program

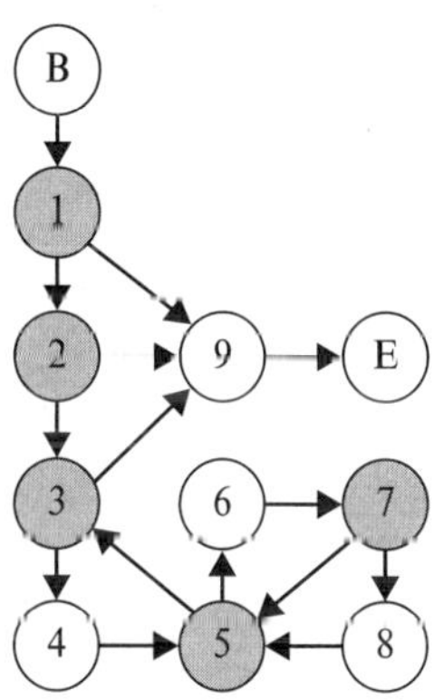

(b) Flow graph

FIGURE 20.6 Purge program and its flow graph

EXAMPLE 20.5 In Figure 20.6, the numbered nodes correspond to the numbers at the end of the statements in the program. The darkened nodes are the conditional nodes. When constructing a flow graph, it is recommended that compound conditions are decomposed into atomic conditions before drawing the flow graph. For example, A && B should be represented by two decision nodes representing A and B, respectively. This ensures that the correct number of test cases is generated.

The table below shows the basis paths and test cases along with expected test outcome.

	Basis Paths	Test Cases	Expected Outcome
1	B 1 9 E	list == nul	list == null
2	B 1 2 9 E	list.size() < 2	Same as input list.
3	B 1 2 3 9 E	list.size() >= 2 and without duplicates.	Same as input list.
4	B 1 2 3 4 5 3 9 E		
5	B 1 2 3 4 5 6 7 5 3 9 E		
6	B 1 2 3 4 5 6 7 8 5 3 9 E	A list with duplicates.	A list without duplicates and size is smaller.

Figure 20.7 shows the tests implemented in JUnit, a unit test tool for Java programs. A test class, such as PurgeTest in Figure 20.7, extends JUnit Test Case. The constructor of a test class takes a string parameter as the test case name, which can be any string. A test class contains tests, which are functions of the test class. JUnit requires that the function name of each of these functions begins with "test" such as testNullList in Figure 20.7. Moreover, these functions do not have parameters. Each of these functions test one aspect of the CUT. The setup and teardown functions are optional. They are called by JUnit to initialize the test class and clean up the context after testing. The test script in Figure 20.7 can be run from an integrated development environment (IDE) or invoked from the command line. See Appendix C2 and C3 for more information.

```
import java.util.*; import junit.framework.*;

public class PurgeTest extends TestCase {
  Purge purge; LinkedList list;
  ArrayList<Item> items=new ArrayList<Item>();
  public PurgeTest(String name) { super(name); }
  public void setUp() {
    purge=new Purge(); list=new LinkedList<Item>();
    for(int i=0; i<10; i++) { items.add(new Item(i)); }
  }
  public void testNullList() {
    boolean nullPointer=false; LinkedList output=null;
    try { output=purge.purge(output); }
    catch(Exception e) { nullPointer=true; }
    assertFalse(nullPointer); assertNull(output);
  }
  public void testEmptyList() {
    int size=list.size(); assertEquals(size, 0);
    LinkedList output=purge.purge(list);
    assertEquals(output.size(), size);
  }
  public void testOneElemList() {
    Item item=new Item(0); list.add(item);
    LinkedList output=purge.purge(list);
    assertTrue(output.size()==1 && output.contains(item));
  }
  public void testNoDuplicate() {
    for(int i=0; i<10; i++) { list.add(items.get(i)); }
    LinkedList output=purge.purge(list);
    assertEquals(output.size(), 10);
    for(int i=0; i<10; i++)
      assertTrue(output.contains(items.get(i)));
  }
  public void testDuplicate() {
    for(int i=0; i<10; i++)
    { list.add(items.get(i)); list.add(items.get(i)); }
    assertEquals(list.size(), 20);
    LinkedList output=purge.purge(list);
    assertEquals(output.size(), 10);
    for(int i=0; i<10; i++)
      assertTrue(output.contains(items.get(i)));
  }
  public static Test suite() { return new TestSuite(PurgeTest.class);}
  public void teardown() {}
}
```

FIGURE 20.7 JUnit test script for the purge program

20.4.2 Cyclomatic Complexity

The number of basis paths of the CUT is defined as the cyclomatic complexity of the CUT. It is determined in three equivalent ways. That is, either of these three approaches can be used to determine the cyclomatic complexity:

1. *Number of closed regions plus one.* This approach obtains the cyclomatic complexity by adding one to the number of closed regions in the flow graph. In Figure 20.6(b), there are five such regions; therefore, the cyclomatic complexity is 6.
2. *Number of nodes and edges.* In this approach, the cyclomatic complexity is the number of edges minus the number of nodes plus 2. In Figure 20.6(b), there are 15 edges and 11 nodes; therefore, the cyclomatic complexity is $15 - 11 + 2 = 6$.
3. *Number of atomic binary conditions plus one.* The cyclomatic complexity is the number of atomic binary conditions plus 1. In Figure 20.6(a), there are five atomic binary conditions. Therefore, the cyclomatic complexity is 6. When using this approach, treat each n-ary condition as $n - 1$ binary conditions. For example, a switch statement with three independent cases is counted as two atomic binary conditions.

It can be proved mathematically that the three approaches produce the same result. One way to prove this is by mathematical induction on the number of nodes in the flow graph. The cyclomatic complexity is useful for verifying the correctness of the flow graph. That is, the cyclomatic complexity computed by the three approaches must be the same. The metric is also useful for determining how many test cases are needed to test the basis paths.

20.4.3 Flow Graph Test Coverage Criteria

Flow graph-based test coverage criteria are defined as follows, ranging from the weakest to the strongest. The weakest criterion yields the lowest confidence on the CUT, while the strongest criterion provides the highest confidence on the CUT:

Node coverage. This criterion requires that each node of the flow graph must be visited at least once by the test cases. This is equivalent to the 100% statement coverage.

Edge coverage. This requires that each edge must be visited at least once by the test cases. It is equivalent to 100% branch coverage, meaning that every branch is tested at least once. A 100% node coverage does not necessarily imply 100% edge coverage. Consider, for example, an if (C) {S} statement. There are two edges; one for the true branch and the other for the false branch. A test case that satisfies C will achieve 100% node coverage. But the test case does not traverse the else edge. Therefore, it achieves only 50% edge coverage.

Basis path coverage. This requires that every basis path must be exercised at least once. Note that a 100% edge coverage does not necessarily imply 100% basis path coverage. Consider, for example, a program that consists of the following two statements: if (C1) {S1;} if (C2) {S2;}. Two test cases that satisfy both C1 and C2, and !C1 and !C2 will accomplish 100% edge coverage. But these test cases do not traverse the path in which C1 is not true and C2 is true.

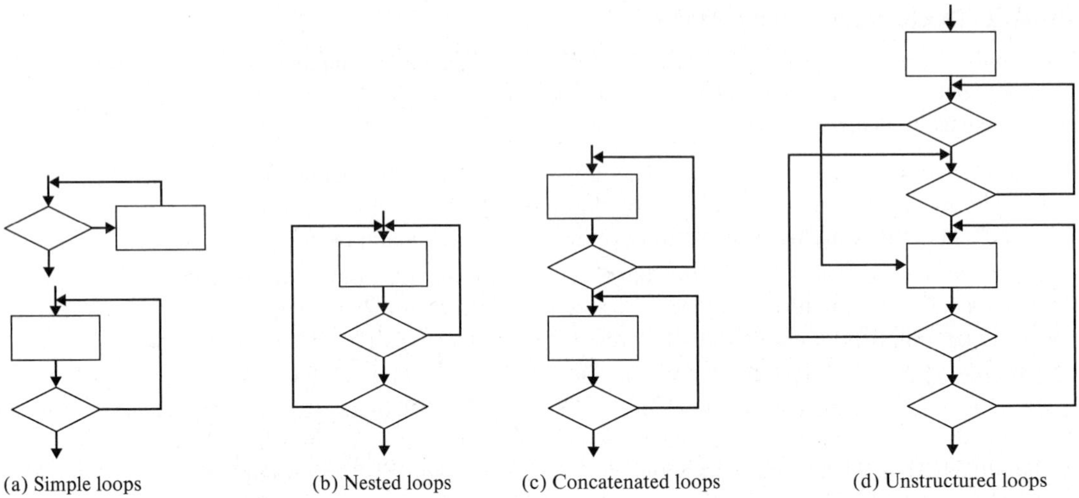

FIGURE 20.8 Four types of loops

All path coverage. This requires that every possible path is tested at least once. This is practically impossible because nested loops could create an excessive number of paths.

20.4.4 Testing Loops

All path coverage is practically impossible because many programs contain nested loops that iterate numerous numbers of times, resulting in countless number of paths. The question then is how to test the loops in a program. Beizer classifies all loops into simple loops, nested loops, concatenated loops, and unstructured loops, as illustrated in Figure 20.8. Beizer then suggests ways to test these loops.

Testing Simple Loops Boundary value analysis is applied to test a simple loop as follows:

1. Skip the loop.
2. One pass through the loop.
3. Two passes through the loop.
4. A typical number of iterations if not already done above.
5. One less than the maximum number of iterations.
6. The maximum number of iterations.
7. Attempt one more than the maximum number of iterations.

Testing Nested Loops

1. Begin with the innermost loop. Set all the outer loops to their minimum values.
2. Test the innermost loop for each of the following five cases: (1) minimum number of iterations, (2) minimum number of iterations plus one, (3) a typical number of

iterations, (4) maximum number of iterations minus one, (5) maximum number of iterations. If possible, attempt out-of-range values such as minimum number of iterations minus one and maximum number of iterations plus one.

3. Work outward, conducting tests for the next outer loop as follows:
   - Set all outer loops at their minimum values.
   - Exercise all nested loops with their typical values.
4. Repeat the above steps until all loops are tested.

Testing Concatenated Loops Two cases are considered when testing concatenated loops. If the loops are independent, then test them as simple loops. If the loop variable of one loop directly or indirectly depends on the loop variable of the other loop and the dependency occurs on the same path, then test them as nested loops.

Testing Unstructured Loops Unstructured loops are difficult to understand and test. The code should be rewritten to eliminate unstructured loops.

20.4.5 Data Flow Testing

Data flow testing focuses on the define-use relationships of selected program variables. A variable is defined if its value is updated at a program location. A variable can be used to evaluate a condition or compute a value. These are called *predicate use* or *p-use,* and *computation use* or *c-use,* respectively. In predicate use, there are at least two outcomes: the condition is evaluated to true, or it is evaluated to false. Each of these should be considered when testing the define-use relationship. A define-use path for a variable *v* is a path from the statement in which *v* is defined to the statement in which *v* is used, and *v* is not redefined between these two locations along the path. The define-use paths are different for c-use and p-use. Figure 20.9 illustrates these with a

```
      public int average(int offSet, int[ ] list) {
(1)     int n=min(offSet, list.length);
(2)     if (n <= 0)
(3)       return 0;
(4)     int sum=0;
(5)     for (int i=0; i<n; i++)
(6)       sum += list[i];
(7)     return (int)(sum/n);
      }
```

(a) Sample program

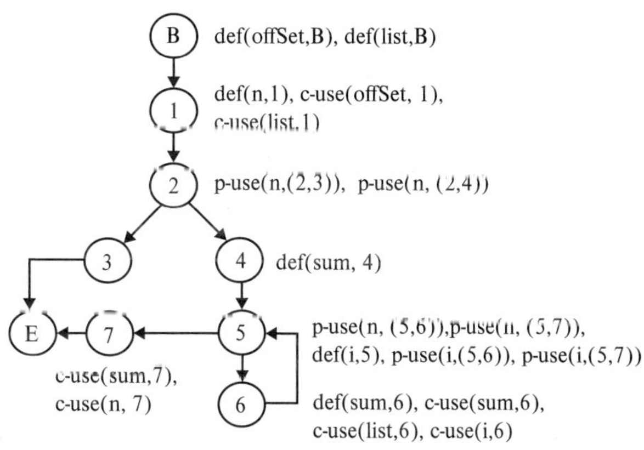

(b) Identifying data define-use

FIGURE 20.9 Identifying data define-use

Variable	c-use	p-use
offSet	(B, 1)	
list	(B, 1), (B, 6)	
n	(1, 7)	(1, (2,3)), (1, (2,4)), (1, (5,6)), (1, (5,7))
sum	(4, 6), (6, 6), (6, 7)	
i	(5, 6)	(5, (5,6)), (5, (5,7))

FIGURE 20.10 Intraprocedural data flow define-use chains

simple example, which computes the average of the first offSet elements of an integer list. The data define-use locations are identified and shown in Figure 20.9(*b*).

C-Use. For c-use, a define-use path is a path from the node containing the definition to the node containing the computation use. The c-use column of Figure 20.10 shows the c-use chains for the variables used in the program. In the figure, (1, 7) means the variable is defined at statement 1 and c-used at statement 7.

P-Use. For p-use, the define-use paths are the paths from the node containing the definition to each of the immediate successors of the node containing the predicate use. The p-use column of Figure 20.10 shows the p-use for the variables used in the program, where (1, (2,3)) means that the variable is defined at statement 1 and p-used at statement 2 and the result leads to executing statement 3.

Data flow testing is to ensure that the CUT is correct with respect to each of the c-use and p-use chains. For example, the c-use chain (1, 7) means generating test data that will cause the program to execute statement 1 and statement 7. The result produced by the CUT is checked for correctness. To achieve this, using offSet=1 will cause the CUT to execute these two statements. The result should be the value of the first element in the list. Of course, one can use offSet=2, and the result should be the average of the first two elements in the list. These tests ensure that the variable *n* is defined and c-used correctly. The other use chains are similar.

20.4.6 Coverage Criteria for Data Flow Testing

There are different levels of test coverages for data flow testing. In ascending order of degree of rigidness, the test coverages are:

All defines coverage. Each definition to some use is tested at least once. For example, with respect to the variable *n*, testing anyone of {(1,(2,3)), (1,(2,4)), (1,(5,6)), (1,(5,7)), (1,7)} is sufficient to satisfy this criterion.

All uses coverage. Each definition to each use is tested at least once. For example, with respect to the variable *n*, all of {(1,(2,3)), (1,(2,4)), (1,(5,6)), (1,(5,7)), (1,7)} must be tested at least once to satisfy this criterion.

All define-use paths coverage. All define-use paths from each definition to each use is tested at least once. For example, with respect to the variable *n*, all of {(1,(2,3)), (1,(2,4)), (1,(5,6)), (1,(5,7)), (1,2,4,5,7), (1,2,4,5,6,5,7)} must be tested at least once to satisfy this criterion. The last two elements in the set of paths indicate that there are two different paths from the definition to the c-use at node 7. The coverage criterion requires that each of these paths must be tested at least once.

20.4.7 Interprocedural Data Flow Testing

The last section presents test case generation based on data define-use paths within a function. This has been called intraprocedural data flow testing. There are many cases in which a variable is defined in one function and used in another function, resulting in interprocedural data flow testing. The derivation of interprocedural define-use paths are similar. Figure 20.11 shows the min(int x, int y) function that is called at statement 1 in Figure 20.9. By substituting offSet for x and list.length for y, respectively, the interprecedural define-use paths for offSet and list are identified. For offSet, the interprocedural define-use paths are: (B,(8,9)), and (B,9). For list, the interprocedural define-use paths are: (B, (8,10)), and (B,10). The test coverage criteria for interprocedural data flow testing are the same as the criteria for intraprocedural data flow testing.

20.5 TEST COVERAGE

The notion of *test coverage* is mentioned a few times during the presentation of the test methods in previous sections. It was not defined earlier because the term is somewhat abstract. It needs some contexts to help understanding. Now it is time to discuss and define the concept. One definition states:

> *Test coverage is defined as a percentage of certain software items that are tested (or exercised) over the total number of items of the same kind.*

Beizer defines test coverage as [Beizer 1990]:

> A measure or metric of test completeness with respect to a test selection criteria.

Mathur defines test coverage as [Mathur 2008]:

> Fraction of testable items such as basic block covered. Also a metric for test adequacy or "goodness of tests."

```
     public int average(int offSet, int[ ] list) {
(1)    int n=min(offSet, list.length);
(2)    if (n <= 0)
(3)      return 0;
(4)    int sum=0;
(5)    for (int i=0; i<n; i++)
(6)      sum += list[i];
(7)    return (int)(sum/n);
     }

     public int min(int x, int y) {
(8)    if (x<=y)
(9)      return x;
(10)   return y;
     }
```

(a) Program with an interprocedural call

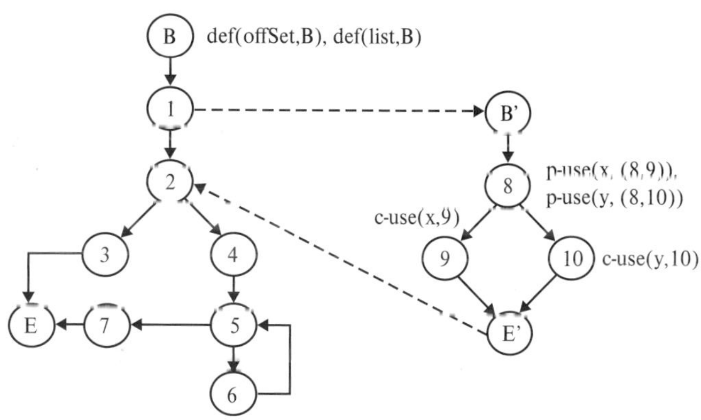

(b) Interprocedural data flow graph

FIGURE 20.11 Interprocedural data define-use

Other definitions exist in the literature. From a practical point of view, test coverage is both a quality goal and a measurement of the accomplishment of the quality goal. For instance, many software development organizations require a 100% branch coverage. This specifies a quality goal. It is a quality goal because 100% branch coverage may not be achievable for some programs. For example, no test set can exercise the false branch of the nested if-condition of the following hypothetic program. The tests can cover only three out of the four branches created by the two conditions, therefore, the coverage accomplished is 0.75 or 75%, which is a measurement or actual test coverage.

```
if (x > 1){
  if (2 * x > = 1)
    foo();
  else
    ba();
}.
```

A practical case is the goal to accomplish 100% statement coverage. Although this is not difficult to achieve for small programs, achieving 100% statement coverage is impossible for many large programs because some statements can never be reached. In summary, test coverage is used to specify the quality goal or test goal to be accomplished as well as a measurement of the extent of the accomplishment of the test goal. Sometimes, the test coverage is related to the test method, or test selection criterion. For example, the 100% basis path coverage is certainly related to the basis path testing technique. The test coverage criteria for data flow testing are only meaningful for data flow testing. However, the test coverage may be defined independent of the test method, or test selection criterion. Moreover, more than one test coverage criteria may be specified. For example, it is easy to specify the test coverage criterion for an equivalence partition test. For example, the test coverage is 100% partition coverage, or selecting at least one test case from each of the partitions. However, it is not easy to specify the coverage criterion for boundary value test. In this case, one may require 100% branch coverage–that is, generate and run boundary value test cases until the tests accomplish 100% branch coverage of the source code. Of course, this requires that the source code is available.

20.6 A GENERIC SOFTWARE TESTING PROCESS

So far several test methods are presented. Implicitly, each of them involves a test process, which defines the phases and activities to generate and carry out the tests. This section presents a generic test process as shown in Figure 20.12. All test methods presented in this chapter follow this process. This means that the process is useful for white-box testing and black-box testing. White-box testing derives test cases from the implementation such as the source code or executable code. Black-box testing generates test cases from the specification such as the requirements specification or design. Note in Figure 20.12, debugging is not a part of the test process.

The first step of the process is to create a test model from the specification or implementation and determines a test coverage. Test models can take many different

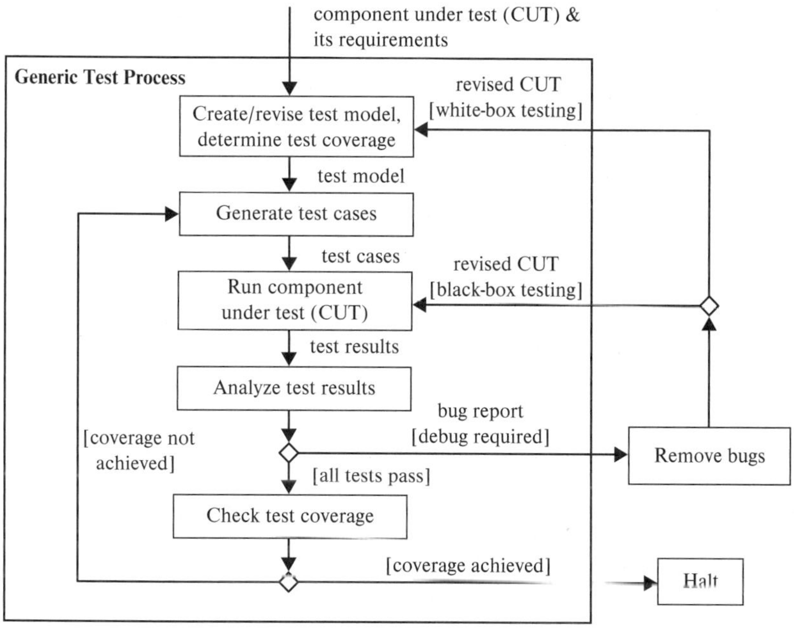

FIGURE 20.12 A generic software testing process

forms including flowchart, flow graph, state machines, expanded use cases, decision tables, and UML diagrams. For example, the test model for the basis path test method is a flow graph. The test model for the cause-effect test method is a decision table. The second step is generation of test cases. The test model facilitates the generation of the test cases and formulation of the test coverage criteria. For example, the basis path test method derives the test cases from the flow graph to cover each basis path (100% basis path coverage). The data flow test method derives the test cases from the define-use chains, which are identified from the test model. The test coverage criteria are specified based on the flow graph constructed for data flow testing. For example, the all define-use path coverage needs the flow graph to identify the paths. In addition to test cases, the second step also generates test data to instantiate the test cases. Consider, for example, the use of equivalence partition to test a telephony system. For each area-code partition, a concrete telephone number is required. The generation of this telephone number is test data generation. This results in concrete tests, that is, the set of concrete phone numbers, each of which is used to test an area-code partition. The third step is test execution or running the CUT with the tests. The next step is analyzing the test results. If there are failed tests, then debugging is performed, which is not a step of the test process. Debugging modifies the CUT to remove errors. If it is white-box testing, then the process is repeated. If it is black-box testing, then the modified CUT is rerun with the existing test cases. When all test cases pass, the last step is performed to check the test coverage. If it is accomplished, then the test process is completed successfully. If the coverage is still not achieved, then more test cases are needed and above process is repeated.

20.7 OBJECT-ORIENTED SOFTWARE TESTING

Section 20.4 presented conventional software testing techniques. These techniques are applicable to testing the methods of a class. This section presents object-oriented software testing techniques.

20.7.1 Use Case–Based Testing

Use case-based testing, as its name suggests, derives test cases from the use case specifications. More specifically, test cases are derived from the expanded use cases, which were studied in Chapter 8 (Actor-System Interaction Modeling). An expanded use case for a Register New User use case is shown in Figure 20.13, which helps to explain the test case generation steps. Each entry on the left column specifies the actor input and actor action. Each entry on the right column specifies the system response. These entries provide valuable information for test case generation, as the following steps illustrate:

Step 1. Identify actor input and actor actions.

In this step, the actor input variables and the actor actions that produce the input data are identified. Examples of an actor action include the user selecting an option on a selection list, or the user checking a checkbox. These actor actions are referred to as input producing actor actions. In Figure 20.13, three actor input elements are identified, that is, login ID, password, and retyped password.

Step 2. Determine input values.

In this step, the possible values for the input elements identified in the last step are determined. For each input element, three categories of values are specified, that is, valid values, invalid values, and values that could cause exceptions.

1. *Valid input.* This category refers to input that falls within the valid input domain and satisfies input requirements, if any. For example, a login ID is a string with a minimal and a maximal length.

UC1: Register a New User

Actor: New User	System: Web Application
	0) System displays homepage with a Register User link.
1) TUCBW user clicking the Register User link.	2) System displays a New User Registration Form.
3) User fills in the *login ID, password, retyped password* and clicks the Submit button. Actor input elements	3) System verifies the login ID and passwords, and 3.1) displays the Registration Successful page, or 3.2) displays an error message and asks the user to try again.
4) TUCEW the user seeing the Registration Successful page.	

FIGURE 20.13 Register New User expanded use case

Input Element	Type	Value Specification	Valid	Invalid	Exceptional Cases
Login ID	String	Length must be between 8 and 20 characters	Login ID satisfies value specification and is not used by another user	Login ID does not satisfy value specification or already exists in system	• Strings with length=0, 1, or a very large number; or • Strings with one or more spaces, control characters, or special characters
Password	Password	Length must be between 8 and 12 characters, and contain at least one alphabet, numeric, and special character	Password satisfies the password rule on the left	Password not satisfies the password rule	• Passwords with length=0, 1, or a very large number; • Passwords contain one or more spaces or control characters
Retyped password	Password	Same as password	Match with password	Retyped password does not match password, or is entered using copy-and-paste	

FIGURE 20.14 Identifying input values for use case–based testing

2. *Invalid input.* This category represents input values that are outside of the input domain or do not comply to input requirements. For example, a password is too short or does not match with the given login.
3. *Exceptional cases.* This category includes input values that may cause unusual behavior or unexpected results.

Figure 20.14 shows the result of this step.

Step 3. Generate test cases.

In this step, all of the possible combinations of the input values are listed. In principle, all these combinations are test cases. However, it is not necessary to run all of these because an equivalent subset is adequate. Therefore, the combinations are analyzed carefully to identify those that are needed. The following are the rules to apply:

1. If a combination has the potential to demonstrate the functional or behavioral correctness of the CUT, then keep it.
2. If a combination has the potential to detect an error in the CUT, then keep it.
3. If a combination is implied by some of the selected combinations, then delete it.
4. If it is not sure whether to keep or delete the combination, then keep it.

With these, six test cases are identified in Figure 20.15. Test cases 1 to 3 and 7 are useful for showing the correctness of the implementation. Test cases 5 and 13 may detect errors in the implementation. For each of the selected cases, specify the expected outcome and behavior of the CUT.

Step 4. Generate concrete tests.

This step generates the test data according to the test cases. The result is a list of concrete tests, as displayed in Figure 20.16.

Step 5. Implement and run the tests.

In this step, the tests are implemented and run in some test environment such as JUnit, which is presented in Appendix C. The test results are analyzed. If the

Test Case	Login ID	Password	Retyped Password	Expected Outcome
1	Valid	Valid	Valid	show Registration Successful page
2	Valid	Valid	Invalid	show Error Message
3	Valid	Invalid		show Error Message
~~4~~	~~Valid~~	~~Invalid~~	~~Invalid~~	
5	Valid	Exceptional	Valid	show Error Message
~~6~~	~~Valid~~	~~Exceptional~~	~~Invalid~~	
7	Invalid	Valid	Valid	show Error Message
~~8~~	~~Invalid~~	~~Valid~~	~~Invalid~~	
~~9~~	~~Invalid~~	~~Invalid~~	~~Valid~~	
~~10~~	~~Invalid~~	~~Invalid~~	~~Invalid~~	
~~11~~	~~Invalid~~	~~Exceptional~~	~~Valid~~	
~~12~~	~~Invalid~~	~~Exceptional~~	~~Invalid~~	
13	Exceptional	Valid	Valid	show Error Message
~~14~~	~~Exceptional~~	~~Valid~~	~~Invalid~~	
~~15~~	~~Exceptional~~	~~Invalid~~	~~Valid~~	
~~16~~	~~Exceptional~~	~~Invalid~~	~~Invalid~~	
~~17~~	~~Exceptional~~	~~Exceptional~~	~~Valid~~	
~~18~~	~~Exceptional~~	~~Exceptional~~	~~Invalid~~	

FIGURE 20.15 Test case generation for use case–based testing

Test Case	Login ID	Password	Retyped Password	Expected Result
1	"newuser@hmail.com"	"xft123%PLM"	"xft123%PLM"	show Registration Successful page
2	"newuser@hmail.com"	"xft123%PLM"	"yyyyyyyyy"	show Error Message
3	"newuser@hmail.com"	"zzzzzz"	"xft123%PLM"	show Error Message
5	"newuser@hmail.com"	"x"	"xft123%PLM"	show Error Message
7	"olduser@hmail.com"	"xft123%PLM"	"xft123%PLM"	show Error Message
13	"new user@hmail.com"	"xft123%PLM"	"xft123%PLM"	show Error Message

FIGURE 20.16 Use case–based tests for Register New User

CUT passes all the tests, then the test coverage is checked; otherwise correct the problem and repeat some of the previous steps. If the test coverage is achieved, then stop; otherwise repeat the previous steps with the aim of adding test cases to increase the test coverage.

20.7.2 Object State Testing with ClassBench

Many objects exhibit state-dependent behavior. For example, pushing an element onto a stack may increment the size of the stack or cause a stack full exception, depending on the state of the stack. Testing object state behavior is an important aspect of object-oriented software testing. This section presents the ClassBench approach proposed by

D. Hoffman and P. Strooper for object state testing [Hoffman and Strooper 1997]. As the running example, an integer set called IntSet is used. IntSet has a fixed size and five operations: add(int x), remove(int x), removeAll(), isMember(int x):boolean, and size(): int. The add operation throws duplicate exception and full exception and the remove operation throws not found exception.

Following the generic test process presented in Figure 20.12, the steps of the ClassBench approach is explained in the following.

Step 1. Create a test model and determine test coverage criteria. The ClassBench test model is a finite state machine, where the states represent the states of the CUT and the transitions represent executions of functions of the CUT. The test model is constructed to test the functionality and behavior of the CUT. Figure 20.17 shows a test model for the IntSet class, where the states are annotated with the sets they represent. The add-all transition adds 0, 1, 2, . . . , MAXSIZE to the set. The resulting state is labeled All. The delete-even and delete-odd transitions remove even numbers and odd numbers from the set represented by the All state. These result in the Even and Odd states, respectively.

Three test coverage criteria can be defined, in ascending order of rigidness:

1. *Node Coverage.* Visit each node of the test model at least once.
2. *Edge Coverage.* Visit each edge of the test model at least once.
3. *Path Coverage.* Traverse each path of the test model at least once, including repeated paths. This is considered too hard and practically impossible.

The ClassBench approach advises using edge coverage. Under this assumption, test cases are generated to exercise every edge of the test model. This is described next.

Step 2. Generate test cases. Each test case is a path of the test model, beginning from an initial state and ending at some state. Test case generation produces such test case paths until all edges are covered. For the test model shown in Figure 20.17(*a*), two test cases are derived as shown in Figure 20.17(b):

TC1: Empty, add-all, All, delete-odd, Even, clear, Empty.

TC2: Empty, add-all, All, delete-even, Odd, clear, Empty.

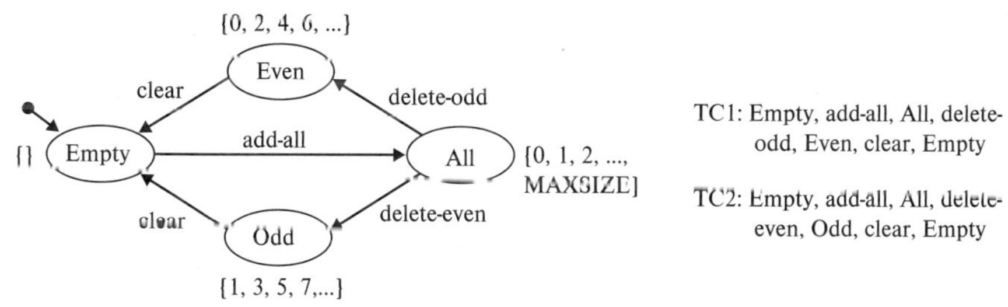

(a) A test model for the IntSet class

(b) A test case is a path from an initial state

FIGURE 20.17 A finite state model of an integer set

Step 3. Implement and run the test cases. The next step is to implement and run the test cases. Each test case could be implemented by following the states and edges in the test case path. When a state is visited, one checks that the CUT satisfies the state condition. When a transition is visited, the methods of the CUT are executed according to the semantics of the transition. Consider, for example, TC1: Empty, add-all, All, delete-odd, Even, clear, Empty. When the Empty state is visited, the size of the IntSet instance is checked to ensure that it is equal to zero. When the add-all transition is visited, the integers 0, 1, 2, . . . , MAX-1, MAX are added to the IntSet instance. When the All state is visited, the size of the IntSet instance is checked to ensure that it is MAX. Moreover, the CUT should contain the integers added.

Step 4. Analyze test results. Several approach can be used to analyze the test result. These include manual analysis as well as using assertions as in JUnit. Another approach is using test oracles. A test oracle is a piece of software that simulates the functionality and behavior of a CUT to facilitate checking of the test result produced by the CUT. Test oracles for object classes are object classes that simulate the CUT. The oracle has the same interface as the CUT, but its implementation is much simpler and less efficient.

As a test oracle for the IntSet class, one could implement an integer set using a bit set. It uses a boolean array bit[MAXSIZE] to simulate the functionality of IntSet. That is, bit[i] is true if the CUT contains integer i, for i = 0, 1, 2, ..., MAXSIZE-1. In addition, one overrides the equals method inherited from Object so that the oracle can compare its size and elements with the size and elements of the CUT. Figure 20.18 shows an implementation of TC1 in JUnit using a test oracle. It shows that whenever a state is visited, the state of the CUT is checked using the oracle. Whenever a transition is visited, the same operations are performed to the CUT and the oracle.

```
public class IntSetTest extends TestCase {
  IntSet cut; IntSetOracle oracle;
  public void setUp( ) {
    cut=new IntSet( ); oracle=new IntSetOracle( );
  }
  public void testCase1( ) {
    assertTrue(oracle.equals(cut));
    for(int i=0; i<MAXSIZE; i++)
      try {
        cut.add(i); oracle.add(i);
      } catch (Exception e)
      { e.printStackTrace( ); }
    assertTrue(oracle.equals(cut));
    for(int i=0; i<MAXSIZE; i=i+2)
    { try {
          cut.remove(i); oracle.remove(i);
      } catch (Exception e)
      { e.printStackTrace( ); }
    }
    assertTrue(oracle.equals(cut));
    for(int i=1; i<MAXSIZE; i=i+2) {
      try {
        cut.remove(i);
        oracle.remove(i);
      } catch (Exception e)
      { e.printStackTrace( ); }
    }
    assertTrue(oracle.equals(cut));
  }
}
```

FIGURE 20.18 Test oracle simplifies checking of test outcome

Step 5. Check test coverage. If code is available and code coverage criterion is determined in step 1, then the code coverage is checked in this step. For example, if the code coverage criterion is 100% branch coverage and the tests achieve the coverage, then the test process halts. If the coverage is not accomplished, then more test cases are needed to increase the coverage.

20.7.3 Testing Class Hierarchy

Inheritance is a unique feature of object-oriented programs. Testing an inheritance hierarchy should begin with the root class and work downwards. Conventional black-box and white-box test methods can be used to test the functions of a class, and the ClassBench approach can be applied to testing object state behavior. When testing a subclass, one may reuse some of the test cases from the parent class. One may need to generate new tests for testing a subclass. This section presents guidelines for determining which test cases to reuse and which new test cases need to be generated.

Let B be a subclass of class A. When testing class B, the following guidelines are applied:

1. New test cases including specification-based and/or program-based test cases are required for testing new features introduced by class B.
2. Inherited features should be retested in the subclass context. That is, the relevant test cases must be rerun when testing B.
3. Program-based test cases must be generated to test each redefined feature because the implementation has changed. Specification-based test cases from the parent class should be rerun in the subclass context to reveal an undesired side effect.

20.7.4 Testing Exception-Handling Capabilities

Exception handling is an important feature of object-oriented programming. Therefore, the exception-handling capability of the CUT should be tested. More specifically, two cases should be considered:

Case 1. The CUT throws exceptions.

In this case, testing is to ensure that the CUT correctly throws the exceptions. Figure 20.19(*a*) illustrates how to test the CUT in this case. That is, one tests that the CUT throws a set full exception when an element is added to a set that is already full.

Case 2. The CUT does not throw a potential exception.

In this case, testing is to ensure that the CUT either prevents, or catches and correctly handles the exception and enters into a desired state. For example, a CUT may store elements using an array, which may raise ArrayIndexOutOfBoundsException. But the CUT may check before adding to prevent it from happening, or catch and handle the exception. The CUT may do nothing and let the exception propagate to the upper level; in this case, an error is detected. Figure 20.19(*b*) shows how to test these cases.

```
public void testExceptionThrown( ) {
  boolean fullExc=false;
  try {
    for(int i=0; i<MAXSIZE+1; i++)
      cut.add(i);
  } catch (SetFullExc e) {
    fullExc=true;
  }
  assertTrue("SetFullExc not thrown.",
    fullExc);
}
```

(a) Testing for CUT that throws an exception

```
public void testExceptionPrevented( ) {
  boolean fullExc=false;
  try {
    for(int i=0; i<MAXSIZE+1; i++)
      cut.add(i);
  } catch (SetFullExc e) {
    fullExc=true;
  }
  assertFalse("SetFullExc thrown.",
    fullExc);
  // check that CUT is in a desired state
}
```

(b) Testing for CUT that can throw an exception but not explicitly specified

FIGURE 20.19 Testing exception-handling capabilities

20.8 TESTING WEB APPLICATIONS

Many web applications use objects to implement the software running in the server side. Therefore, teams that develop object-oriented applications must know how to test web applications. This section briefly describes a white-box approach for testing web applications.

20.8.1 Object-Oriented Model for Web Application Testing

A web application involves multiple types of documents that relate to each other in a complex manner. To help understand the documents and their relationships, a test model is constructed. The model is useful for deriving test cases. Figure 20.20 shows

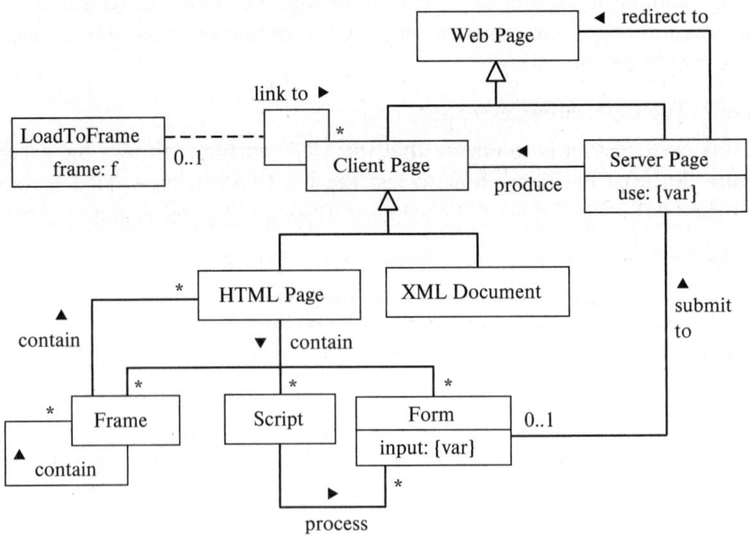

FIGURE 20.20 A generic web model for testing web applications

a class diagram that serves as a generic model for all web applications. The generic model is in fact a domain model that describes web documents such as static pages, server pages, forms, frames, and how they relate to each other. For example, an html page contains zero or more forms and each form is submitted to a server page. For a specific web application, an instance of this generic model can be produced automatically. It serves as the test model for the specific web application. For example, the object diagram in Figure 20.21 depicts a portion of a Study Abroad Management System (SAMS) website, where the log off arrow line means that it links each page inside the large rectangle to the logon.html page. The object diagram can be generated by using a web spider, or HttpUnit–a web test tool built on JUnit. The test model is useful for static analysis, defining test criteria, and generating test cases, described in the following sections.

20.8.2 Static Analysis Using the Object-Oriented Model

The test model shown in Figure 20.21 can be used to detect a number of anomalies. For example, pages that exist on the web server but do not appear in the test model are unreachable pages. A graph traversal can be performed to visit every link of a page to detect link errors, for example, the linked page does not exist. The model is also useful for assessing the design of a website. For example, customers want to find products they want easily and quickly. Customers give up and turn to a competitor's website after a few clicks if they cannot find the wanted product. This means that web designs

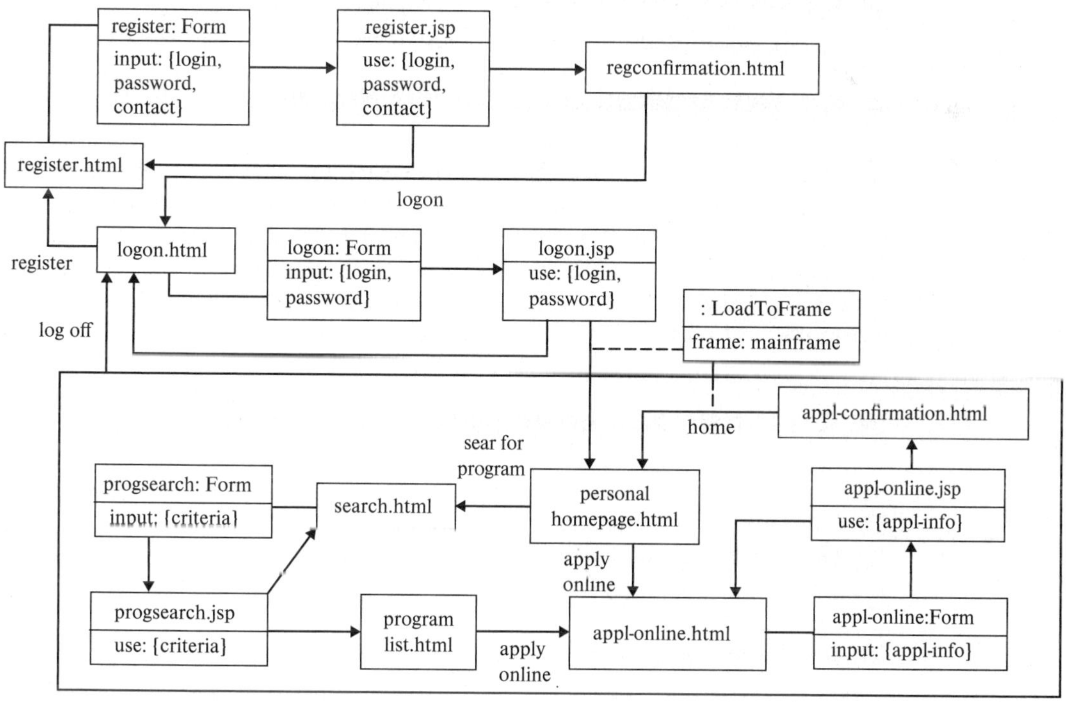

FIGURE 20.21 Part of a test model for SAMS

should show pages that the customer is looking for as quickly as possible. That is, the shortest paths to such pages must be short.

In many cases, the Form objects and JSP (or servlet) objects are in one-to-one correspondence. For example, the register form submits to the register.jsp, or the appl-online form submits to the appl-online.jsp. Moreover, the attributes and methods of the Java bean class used by the JSP page and the input fields of the form must correspond and follow JSP Java bean programming rules (see Appendix B for details). Static analysis can check these correspondences. It greatly reduces the testing and debugging time and effort spent to correct the correspondence errors. Of course, if the Java bean classes are generated from the forms, then the correspondence is automatically satisfied.

20.8.3 Test Case Generation Using the Object-Oriented Model

The Form and JSP objects shown in Figure 20.21 are useful for test case generation. Several test methods presented previously can be used to test the Java bean classes and the JSP pages. Cause-effect testing identifies combinations of a form's input variables and constructs a decision table to specify the test cases. Tests are then generated from the decision table. Partition testing divides the domains of the form's input variables and selects test data from the partitions to form tests. Boundary testing selects test data at the boundaries of the partitions. The test model also shows the variable define-use relationships. Therefore, data flow testing can be applied. In web applications, the variables are usually defined when a user enters their values into a form. They are used at nodes reachable from the form node. Thus, each path from the form node to a node that uses the input variable is a define-use path. Tests are produced and executed to exercise the define-use paths to satisfy the desired data flow coverage criterion.

20.8.4 Web Application Testing with HttpUnit

The test cases generated in the last section can be implemented and executed using the HttpUnit open source software. HttpUnit is an extension of JUnit to web application testing. It emulates browser behavior and allows a test case to send requests to and receive responses from the web server. Elements of a web page, such as forms, tables, and links are treated as objects. This facilitates the implementation and execution of test cases and analysis of test results. How to use HttpUnit to accomplish these tasks is described in Appendix C.

20.9 TESTING FOR NONFUNCTIONAL REQUIREMENTS

Software systems must also be tested with respect to nonfunctional requirements. These include performance testing, stress testing, and security testing, among others. It is beyond the scope of this book to cover these topics in detail. A brief description is provided in the following sections.

20.9.1 Performance and Stress Testings

Performance testing is aimed to assess several aspects of the software or system, including *system workload, throughput, response time, efficiency,* and *resource utilization*. Workload and throughput measure the amount of work that the system processes and produces. The measurement is application dependent, for example, the number of transactions processed per day, or the number of mail pieces processed per hour. Workload is sometimes measured in terms of peak workload and average workload. The response time is the amount of time that the system takes to process each request. Longer response time is expected when the system is fully loaded or overloaded.

Efficiency measures the amount of resources, such as CPU time and memory, that are required by the system to process a given workload, for example, a benchmark workload. Higher efficiency means less resources are required. Resource utilization measures the percentage of resources that are actually used by the system. If only 1–2% of the system's resources are actually used at any given time, then most of the investment in the resources is wasted. Stress testing is aimed at assessing the system's ability to withstand and process an extremely heavy workload, usually a magnitude that is multiple times of the workload that the system is designed to handle.

Performance testing and stress testing can be performed in many ways. The performance aspects of the system may be measured for a period of time while it is used by the users in the target environment. This approach is used for assessing the system's performance in the normal usage situation. For some applications such as telecommunication systems, special equipment, called test equipment, is used to conduct performance testing. Another approach to performance testing uses simulation. There are many simulation tools for performance testings.

Simulation-based performance testing involves a number of steps. The steps are different for different simulation approaches. An approach that uses profiling is described here. First, a user model is constructed. For example, a usage profile that describes the distribution of the different types of transaction can be produced from existing transaction logs. Next, a prototype transaction for each of the transaction types is constructed and used to produce the transaction instances. Finally, a random number generator is employed to generate the required workload to test the system according to the usage profile. Performance testing of web applications may use multiple client machines as well as simulated virtual machines to create the required volume of requests to test the performance of the web application.

20.9.2 Testing for Security

Conventional test methods and techniques are aimed at detecting errors in the software while demonstrating that the software accomplishes its intended functionality and behavior. They do not intend to detect the so-called unintended functionality and behavior, which can be exploited by adversaries to harm the system and its users. Testing for security, or security testing for short, fills this gap. More specifically, security testing is aimed at detecting security vulnerabilities that an adversary can exploit to compromise the security of the system.

White-box testing approaches are applied to detect security vulnerabilities and generate test cases. More specifically, static analysis tools analyze the code to detect patterns that are vulnerable. Test cases are then generated and executed to validate the tool-detected vulnerabilities. This approach helps to reduce the number of false positives produced by static analysis tools. Black-box testing approaches feed the system being tested with malicious input to break it. Test cases derived from requirements and known attack patterns are used to test the system. Random testing is another approach. One variation of random testing is input fuzzing. These approaches perform subtle modifications to the normal inputs and use the results to test the system. Security testing based on genetic algorithms is an improvement over fuzzing. While fuzzing randomly mutates the inputs, genetic algorithm-based approaches perform systematic fuzzing and also apply the ideas used by genetic algorithms. That is, they repeat the process, resulting in generations. During each iteration, the most effective test sets are selected to inject mutants. This could greatly improve the test effectiveness and efficiency.

20.9.3 Testing User Interface

Testing user interface is a special topic and deserves a book of its own. Therefore, it can be treated only briefly in this section. Unlike functional, performance, and security testings, user interface testing aims to uncover defects in the following areas:

1. *Defects in the look and feel of the user interface.* These include inconsistent, missing, incorrect, complex, poorly organized windows, dialogs, and web pages. The widgets and containers displayed in the windows, dialogs, and web pages may exhibit similar problems. If user interface requirements are specified, then checking the look and feel for conformance to the requirements is needed.
2. *Defects in data entry and output display.* Different applications require application-dependent input data entry and output display formats. For example, universities, hospitals, and banks use ID number, birthday, and phone numbers to retrieve information, respectively. The formats to enter these input data are different from application to application. User interface testing ensures that the system uses the correct input and output data, data types, and formats.
3. *Defects in the actor-system interaction behavior.* During the design phase, the expanded use cases specify the actor–system interaction behavior. User interface testing ensures that the system implements the interaction behavior.
4. *Defects in error handling.* Errors may be caused by the system or by the user. The system should handle such situations. Defects in error handling include not handling the errors, incorrect, inadequate, or inappropriate handling of errors.
5. *Defects in documentation and help facility.* Inconsistent, missing, incomplete, incorrect, complex, poorly organized, and poorly written online documentation and help facility are sources of these types of user interface defect.

Some of the user interface–testing activities can be done by using user interface test tools. For example, static analysis helps in the detection of missing actions in call-back functions and pages that are referenced but do not exist. The analysis may generate tests that simulate user input and user actions. However, user interface testing cannot be completely automated. Some of the test activities require human judgment, for example, to determine if the layout of a window, dialog, or web page is correct and appropriate.

20.10 SOFTWARE TESTING IN THE LIFE CYCLE

Software testing is a life-cycle activity, meaning that it should be taken into consideration in each of the life-cycle phases. The traditional life-cycle activities and their relationships to testing are illustrated using a V-shape diagram as shown in Figure 20.22. Agile processes selectively perform these activities during each iteration. The left leg of the V shape is mainly concerned with the construction activities of the system. During this period, only static testings are possible and are performed using inspection, walkthrough, and peer reviews, as described in Chapter 19 (Software Quality Assurance). Moreover, test plans are prepared to guide the dynamic validation, such as testing activities along the right leg using integration testing, acceptance testing, and system testing.

A test plan generally specifies the following items:

1. *Test objectives.* This specifies what the tests will accomplish. For example, the overall objective of system testing is to ensure that the system satisfies the system requirements and constraints. However, in practice, due to budget and schedule constraints, not all requirements and constraints could be tested. In such cases, the objectives should include a list of the requirements and constraints to be tested.
2. *Types of test.* This specifies which types of test will be performed on which parts of the system. These includc functional testing, structural testing, state testing, performance testing, stress testing, and testing for security, among others.

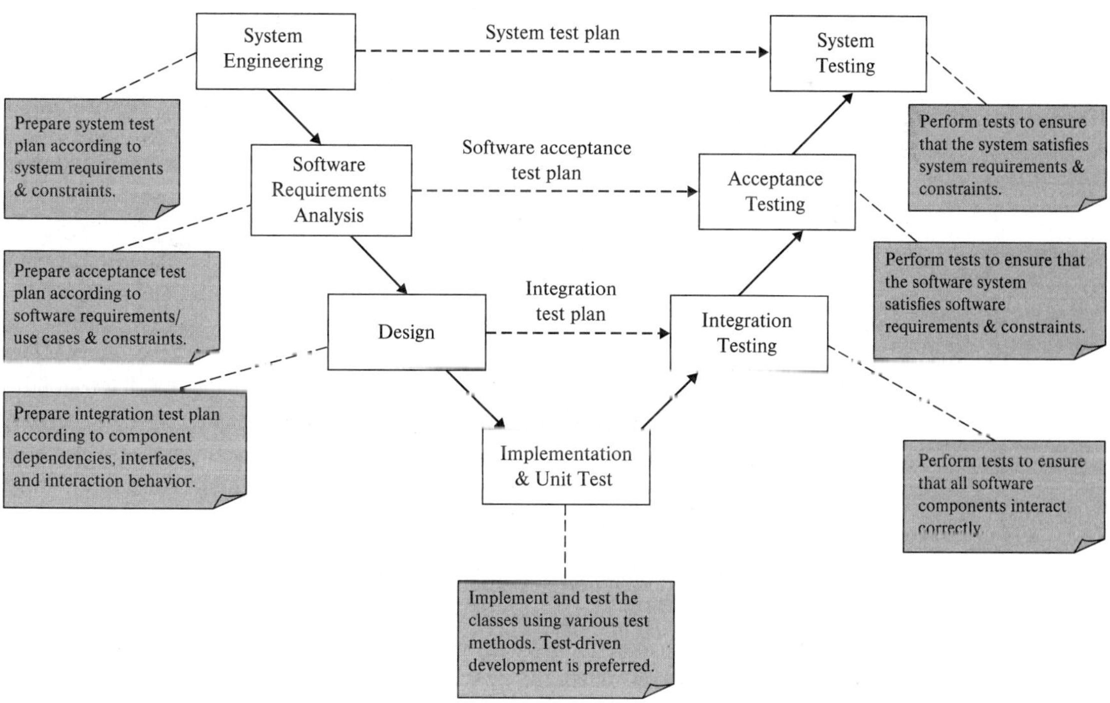

FIGURE 20.22 Software testing in the life cycle

3. *Test methods and techniques.* These specify the test methods and test techniques to be used to perform the tests. For example, "functional testing will use cause effect testing, equivalence partitioning, and boundary value analysis."
4. *Test cases.* These specify the test cases that must be performed during the testing phase. Typically, test cases for high-priority use cases and critical functionality of the system should be included. Refinements of the test cases may be needed during the testing phase to reflect the as-built functionality and behavior.
5. *Test coverage criteria.* These specify the test coverage criteria to be accomplished. For example, requirements coverage means that each requirement must be tested. Often, more than one type of coverage criteria is specified, for example, in addition to requirement coverage, many companies also require branch coverage.
6. *Documents needed.* The documents or artifacts that are needed for preparing the test cases, executing the tests, and analyzing the test results.
7. *Required resources.* These include human resources, hardware equipment, software components and software tools.
8. *Effort estimation and schedule.* The estimated effort required to perform the tests and a tentative test schedule.

Throughout the life cycle, testing is constantly performed, as shown in Figure 20.22 and discussed previously. In particular, during the system engineering phase, static testings such as inspection, walkthrough, and peer reviews are performed to ensure the correctness, completeness, and consistency of the system requirements and constraints. Prototyping may be employed to assess the feasibility of the project. A system test plan is prepared to mandate that high-priority system requirements and constraints must be tested and the types of test required.

During the system testing phase, the test cases specified in the system test plan are refined, and new test cases are generated to test the system. System testing ensures that the system satisfies the functional and nonfunctional requirements and constraints as stated in the system test plan. Black-box testing is the most common type of test, and performance testing, stress testing, and security testing are often required.

During the software requirements analysis phase, static testings and prototyping are performed to ensure the correctness, completeness, consistency, and feasibility of the software requirements and constraints. An acceptance test plan is generated to guide the acceptance testing. Use case–based test cases, described in Section 20.7.1, are ideal for acceptance testing. During acceptance testing, the acceptance test cases are run to demonstrate to the customer and users that the system satisfies the software requirements and constraints. The users may experiment with the system. User feedback is analyzed and used to improve the software accordingly. In some case, stress testing, performance testing, and security testing are performed.

During the software design phase, static testings are performed to verify that the design realizes the software requirements within the constraints. An integration test plan is produced. During the integration testing phase, the components are integrated and tested according to the integration testing strategy described in the integration test plan. It is aimed at detecting errors in component interfacing and interaction behavior.

Traditionally, integration and integration testing are performed using the following strategies:

- *Big bang.* All of the components of the software system are integrated and tested together. The drawback of this approach is that it is very difficult to debug.
- *Top-down integration.* The components of the software system are integrated and tested from the root of a component invocation tree and the process moves downwards. The assumption is that the components of the software system are structured according to the main-program-subroutines architectural style (see Chapter 6, Architectural Design). The drawback of this strategy is that test stubs are required to simulate the lower-level components. In addition, it cannot be applied to integration testing of classes that depend on each other in a complex manner.
- *Bottom-up integration.* The components of the software system are integrated and tested from the leaf components of a component invocation tree and the process moves up the hierarchy. The assumption is the same as the top-down integration strategy. The drawback of this strategy is that test drivers are required to invoke the lower-level components. The implementation and test order presented in Chapter 11 (Deriving Design Class Diagram) can be used as a bottom-up integration testing strategy.
- *Critical/high priority components first.* The critical or high-priority components are integrated and tested first. This strategy allows the critical or high-priority components to be exercised more often than the other components. However, both test stubs and test drivers are required to implement this strategy.
- *Available components first.* The components of the software system are integrated and tested whenever they are available. This strategy is used by many organizations and some of the agile methods such as extreme programming.

If the functions and interfaces of the individual components are implemented according to the design specification, then integration testing should proceed relatively smoothly. Unfortunately, many projects experience the so-called integration nightmare, meaning that the components do not work with each other, and debugging is difficult due to complex interdependencies and runtime effect. The most likely cause is inconsistencies in component interfacing and interaction. Inspection, code review, and integration testing are meant to detect such errors.

During the implementation and unit testing phase, the software components are implemented and tested by individual developers. Test-driven development is increasingly popular during recent years. Test-driven development means "write tests before writing the production code." It requires the programmer to understand the functionality prior to implementing the functionality. The combination of test-driven development and a code coverage tool ensures that the required functionality and code coverage criteria are satisfied. Chapter 18 (Implementation Considerations) describes the details.

After system testing, the product is installed and tested in the target environment. The tests are carried out by executing a subset of the test cases used during system testing. The test cases are selected according to changes to the environment parameters such as system setup, run conditions, and network configuration. It is to ensure that the system operates correctly in the customer environment.

20.11 REGRESSION TESTING

Changing a software system or its components is inevitable. This takes place during the development as well as the maintenance phases. Change alters the functionality, behavior, and performance. Therefore, retesting is required to ensure that the system or its components still satisfy the functional, performance, and security requirements. This type of testing is called regression testing. Often, regression testing executes all the existing test cases or a selected subset to ensure that the software system or its components pass the tests. Selecting a subset of the existing test cases can save time and effort. Test cases are selected according to the components that are changed or affected by the changes. Tools for selecting regression test cases have been developed. Some of the tools instrument and execute the software before making changes. This allows the tool to collect information about which test cases exercise which classes and methods. This information along with the changed and affected classes are used to select the test cases that need to be rerun. If XUnit (X refers to various programming languages such as J for Java and Cpp for C++) has been used during development testing, then regression testing simply reruns the XUnit test cases. However, XUnit test cases usually do not include system testing and user interface testing. In these cases, other regression testing tools such as Selenium IDE should be used. These tools record the user actions and play back the recorded test scripts during regression testing.

20.12 WHEN TO STOP TESTING?

Software testing is costly and time consuming. Therefore, it needs to know how much testing is adequate, or when to stop testing. In some cases, test coverage can be used as a minimum requirement, that is, testing stops when the test coverage is achieved. For example, if 100% requirement coverage or 100% branch coverage is accomplished, the test stops. In general, the stronger the coverage, the better the software quality. The "zero failure" method is another approach to determine when to stop testing. It is a decision technique that specifies the number of zero-failure test hours required before a software system can be released. The assumption is that the test cases are effective in detecting failures, and test execution time must not include debugging time.

As an example, consider the testing of a 33K line program. Suppose that 15 repairable failures have been detected and fixed in a total test execution time of 500 hours. No failure has been detected in the last 50 test hours. How many more zero-failure test hours are needed before deployment so that field detect failures will be limited to no more than one? To calculate the zero-failure hours, three input parameters are needed:

1. The projected average number of field detect failures *Nf*, or number of field detect failures per thousand lines of code. For the above example, $Nf = 1$, or $1/33\text{K} = 0.03$ field detect failures per thousand lines of code.
2. The total number of failures detected so far during testing, denoted *Nd*. For the above example, $Nd = 15$.
3. The total test-execution hours up to the detection of the last failure *Ht*. For the above example, $Ht = 450$.

The zero-failure test hours *Hz*, measured from the detection of the last failure, is computed by:

$$Hz = Ht * \left(ln\frac{Nf}{0.5 + Nf}\right) \Big/ \left(ln\frac{0.5 + Nf}{Nd + Nf}\right) = 450 * \left(ln\frac{1}{1.5}\right) \Big/ \left(ln\frac{1.5}{16}\right) = 77$$

Because 50 zero-failure hours has passed since the detection of the last failure, it needs 27 additional zero-failure hours of test execution time. During this period, testing continues as usual and no failure can occur; otherwise, the zero-failure hours must be calculated again and the testing continues.

20.13 APPLYING AGILE PRINCIPLES

GUIDELINE 20.1 Integrate testing throughout the life cycle; test early and often.

Agile practices develop small, incremental releases iteratively. During the iterative process, unit testing, integration testing, and acceptance testing are repeatedly performed. For example, in extreme programming, unit testing is performed continually. All tests must run flawlessly for the development to continue. In addition, extreme programming suggests continuous integration. That is, integrate and build the system many times a day, every time a task is completed. Continuous and frequent testings greatly improve the quality of the code.

GUIDELINE 20.2 Practice test-driven development.

Studies conducted at Microsoft in two different environments show that defect rate or defects per thousand lines of code decreases 4.2 times and 2.5 times between similar projects, one with test-driven development and one without. Development time also increased but not as significantly as the increase in quality. Other studies indicate that test-driven development can reduce prerelease defect densities by as much as 90%, compared to similar projects that do not implement test-driven development. Test-driven development also improves programmer productivity.

20.14 TOOL SUPPORT FOR TESTING

A wide variety of tools support software testing. These include unit test tools, integration test tools, acceptance test tools, and performance test tools. The XUnit family of tools is widely used for unit testing and regression testing. JCoverage, Cobertura, and Emma are some of the code coverage tools. NetBeans also includes a Code Coverage Plugin and a Load Generator for performance testing. Appendix C provides materials on how to use JUnit, and Cobertura. Other useful test tools are Selenium and MuJava. Selenium automates browser behavior so it can be used to test web applications. MuJava is a mutation test tool. It makes subtle changes called mutations to the CUT. The mutated CUT is then used to assess the effectiveness of a test set.

20.15 SUMMARY

This chapter presents software testing and its importance. It describes a generic test process and different test methods and techniques, including white-box, black-box, use case-based, state-dependent, and web application testing techniques. The chapter also describes how to test an inheritance hierarchy, exception-handling, and nonfunctional requirements. Static testing and dynamic testing in the life cycle are described.

20.16 CHAPTER REVIEW QUESTIONS

1. What is software testing and regression testing?
2. What are the benefits of software testing?
3. What is the generic testing process, and what are the activities of each of its phases?
4. What are the differences between casual programmer testing and systematic testing that uses a test method such as the ones described in this chapter?
5. What are white-box and black-box testings, and what are the similarities and differences between the two?
6. What are black-box test techniques and how do they differ from each other?
7. What are white-box test techniques and how do they differ from each other?
8. Can white-box testing be applied to test-driven development, and why?
9. What are the similarities and differences between the test-driven development process described in Chapter 18 and the generic test process described in this chapter? Are they contradictory to each other? Can they be used together, or combined?
10. What are the software testing-related activities in the life cycle?

20.17 EXERCISES

20.1 For the average function presented in Figure 20.9 do the following:

   a. Write a brief functional description for the function.
   b. Generate functional test cases based on the functional description.
   c. Identify and specify the partitions and generate partition test cases.
   d. Generate boundary value test cases.
   e. Implement the average function in a class; also implement the test cases using JUnit or any other test tool as designated by the instructor.
   f. Compile and run the test cases. Record any failures and errors that are reported. Analyze and briefly explain why each of the failures and errors occurs and how to fix them. Correct the failures and errors until the CUT passes all the test cases.

20.2 Perform basis path testing to the average function shown in Figure 20.9. Implement the CUT in Java and the test cases in JUnit, or according to instructions given by the instructor. Run the test cases and analyze the test results. Correct any problems and write a brief test report about the problems; include why they occur and how they are fixed.

20.3 Perform test-driven development to implement a singly-linked list that provides at least the following functions. *Note:* You are not allowed to use any Java API such as ArrayList and LinkedList as a replacement for the singly-linked list–i.e., you must implement the singly-linked list. Moreover, you are not allowed to implement a doubly-linked list.

- public void insert(Object o1, Object o2): insert object o1 in front of object o2 in the linked list.

- public Object find(String attrName, String attrValue): Returns the object with the given attribute name attrName with the given attribute value attrValue. If more than one such object is found, the first such object is returned. If not found, it returns null. You need to use Java reflection to do this. This function is, in fact, a polymorphic function, that is, the attrValue could be int, double, etc. But for this homework, you can assume that the attribute value is String type.
- public Object remove(Object obj): Removes the object referred to by the object reference obj from the linked list.
- public int size(): Returns the size of the linked list.

20.4 Apply cause-effect testing to test the singly-linked list. Implement the test cases in JUnit and measure the code coverage using Cobertura or other coverage tool as determined by the instructor. Your test cases must achieve 100% branch coverage. Cobertura is described in Appendix C.

20.5 Design equivalence partitioning and boundary value analysis test cases to test the singly-linked list and implement them in JUnit. Your test cases must achieve 100% branch coverage as measured by Cobertura or other coverage tool as determined by the instructor.

20.6 Repeat the last exercise, but instead of using equivalence partitioning and boundary value analysis, use basis path testing.

20.7 Repeat the last exercise, but instead of using basis path testing, apply the ClassBench state testing as described in Section 20.7.2.

20.8 Draw and fill the entries of a table that summarizes the test methods presented in this chapter. The table has one row for each of the test methods: equivalence partition, boundary value analysis, cause-effect, basis path, data flow (intraprocedural only), use case-based, ClassBench, web testing. The columns are:

a. Method, which shows the test methods presented in this chapter.

b. Test Model, which briefly describes what the test model is for the test method.

c. Test Case Generation, which briefly describes how the test cases are derived.

d. Test Coverage(s), which briefly specifies the applicable test coverage criteria.

20.9 Prove that the three approaches to compute the cyclomatic complexity are equivalent. *Hint:* Use mathematical induction. In addition, proof by contradiction can be used.

REFERENCES

Beizer, B. *Software Testing Techniques*. 2nd ed. Van Nostrand Reinhold, 1990.

Hoffman, D. and P. Strooper. "ClassBench: A Framework for Automated Class Testing," *Software Practice and Experience* 27, no. 5 (1997), pp. 573–597.

Mathur, A. *Foundations of Software Testing*. Addison-Wesley Professional, 2008.

part VII

Maintenance and Configuration Management

21 Chapter

Software Maintenance

Key Takeaway Points

- Software maintenance is modifying a software system or component after delivery to correct faults, improve performance, add new capabilities, or adapt to a changed environment. (IEEE Standard 610.12-1991)
- Software maintenance consumes 60%–80% of the total life-cycle costs; 75% or more of the costs are due to enhancements.

Previous chapters present the software development activities that lead to the release and installation of a software system in its operational environment. Often, the software system undergoes a beta testing phase, during which the users test run the system and report bugs and deficiencies. The development team removes the bugs and deficiencies. This period may take a few weeks or several months, depending on the nature of the application, complexity, and size of the software system. After beta test, the software system enters into its maintenance phase. The system is stabilizing in the first several months during which the users exercise more and more functions and become familiar with the system's behavior. Removal of bugs and deficiencies continues, but the rate should reduce significantly. This period is sometimes called the system aging period. As the world evolves, the system's functionality, performance, quality of service, or security can no longer satisfy the business needs. Enhancement to the system is required. In this case, a new project is established to identify new capabilities, and design and implement the new capabilities to enhance the software system. The new project will go through the steps as described in the previous chapters. In this way, the system evolves during the prolonged maintenance period. Software maintenance consumes 60%–80% of the total life-cycle costs; 75% or more of the costs are due to enhancements. Therefore, software maintenance is an important area of software engineering and deserves an entire book. This chapter serves as an introduction to the topic. After studying this chapter, you will learn the following:

- Fundamentals of software maintenance.
- Factors that require software maintenance.
- Lehman's law of system evolution.

- Types of software maintenance.
- Software maintenance process models and activities.
- Software reverse-engineering.
- Software reengineering.
- Software evolution
- Patterns for software maintenance

21.1 WHAT IS SOFTWARE MAINTENANCE?

Many software systems that were constructed decades ago are still in use today. These systems are called legacy systems. Many of the legacy systems will continue to operate in the next several decades. One of the reasons that these systems cannot retire is the high replacement cost. Another reason is that there is no guarantee that the new system will be as good as the replaced system. This is because legacy systems have embedded the collective knowledge, experience, intelligence and wisdom of thousands of software engineers, domain experts, and users during the last several decades. Even if replacing an old system is an option, it is too costly for an organization to replace an existing system frequently. The costs include system development cost, costs associated with lost productivity due to procurement, participation in requirements gathering, system design reviews, acceptance testing, user training, beta testing, and adapting to the new system. Therefore, after their releases, systems undergo a prolonged period of continual modifications to correct errors, enhance capabilities, adapting to new operating platforms or environments, and improving the system structure to make it possible for further changes. This process is called software maintenance, defined by the IEEE as follows:

Definition 21.1 Software maintenance is modifying a software system or component after delivery to correct faults, improve performance, add new capabilities, or adapt to a changed environment. (IEEE Standard 610.12-1991)

21.2 FACTORS THAT MANDATE CHANGE

After a system is released, installed, and operated in the target environment, update to the system is still needed. A number of factors mandate software change:

1. *Bug fixes.* Although the software system has been tested to achieve a desired test coverage, some vital bugs may occur during the operational phase. These require bug removal and regression testing to ensure that the modified software passes selected tests performed previously.
2. *Change in operating environment.* Changes in the hardware, platform,and system configuration may require modification to the software.

3. *Change in government policies and regulations.* Changes in government and industry policies and regulations may require changes to the software system to comply with the new policies and regulations.
4. *Change in business procedures.* Many software systems automate business operations. If the procedures of some of the business operations are changed, then the software system must be modified accordingly. For example, as security becomes important, many web-based applications require users to set up authentication questions and answers to better authenticate the users. Such changes are due to changes in business procedures and require changes to the software.
5. *Changes to prevent future problems.* Sometimes, changes to the software system are needed to prevent problems that could occur in the future. For example, redesign and reimplement a complex component to improve its reliability.

21.3 LEHMAN'S LAWS OF SYSTEM EVOLUTION

The Lehman's laws of system evolution are specified for the so-called E-type of systems. These are systems that cannot be completely and definitely specified. That is, system development for such a system is a wicked problem. On the other hand, the S-type systems are systems that can be completely and definitely specified. Their development is not a tame problem. Examples of such systems are mathematical software, chess playing software and the like. (See wicked problems in Chapter 2 for more detail.) The eight Lehman's laws are:

1. *Law of continuing change (1974).* After the system is released, changes to the system are required, and these continue until the system is replaced. Changes are due to reasons described in Section 21.2.
2. *Law of increasing entropy or complexity (1974).* The structure of the software system deteriorates as changes are made. This is because changes introduce errors, which require more changes. Changes often introduce conditional statements to handle erroneous situations, or check for invocation of new features. These increase the complexity of the system and coupling between the components. The result is that the system becomes more and more difficult to understand and maintain. Restructuring or reengineering is required to improve the structure of the system to reduce the maintenance cost.
3. *Law of self-regulation (1974).* The system evolution process is a self-regulating process. Many system attributes such as maintainability, release interval, error rate, and the like may appear to be stochastic from release to release. However, their long-term trends exhibit observable regularities. In fact, this law is universal. That is, it is not limited to system evolution. It is applicable to everything because everything is a system. Consider, for example, the stock chart for a public company. The daily prices may fluctuate, sometimes drastically. However, the long-term movements exhibit an upward, downward, or flat trend. This law is due to the eighth law–that is, the law of feedback systems. Indeed, the regularity is the result of the feedback loops, or interaction of factors that cancel each other as well as

enhance each other during a long period of maintenance activities. This law is also a generalization of the next three laws—law of conservation of organizational stability, law of conservation of familiarity, and law of continuing growth. These three laws state the regularities of three specific aspects.

4. *Law of conservation of organizational stability (1978).* The maintenance process for an E-type system tends to exhibit a constant average work rate over the system's lifetime.
5. *Law of conservation of familiarity (1978).* The average incremental growth of the system remains a constant during the system's lifetime.
6. *Law of continuing growth (1991).* E-type systems must continue its functional growth to satisfy its users.
7. *Law of declining quality (1996).* The quality of E-type systems will appear to be declining unless they are rigorously adapted to the changes in the operating environment.
8. *Law of feedback systems (1996).* The evolution process consists of multilevel, multiloop, and multiagent feedback systems that play a role in all the laws. That is, the other laws are due to the feedback behavior.

The law of increasing entropy implies that the system would be replaced because the cost to maintain it would exceed the cost of building a new system. This was true for operating systems, which were studied by Lehman and Belady. However, many organizations find that replacing a legacy application system is not an option because numerous business processes and business rules have been implemented in the legacy system during the prolonged maintenance process. Moreover, millions of records are stored in the databases. Due to inadequate documentation and the complexity of the system, no one really knows what is implemented and how to port the data records. Therefore, many legacy systems are still in use and companies spend hundreds of millions of dollars maintaining them each year.

21.4 TYPES OF SOFTWARE MAINTENANCE

The IEEE categorizes software maintenance into four types:

1. *Corrective maintenance:* Reactive modification of a software product performed after delivery to correct discovered faults.
2. *Adaptive maintenance:* Modification of a software product performed after delivery to keep a computer program usable in a changed or changing environment.
3. *Perfective maintenance:* Modification of a software product performed after delivery to improve performance or maintainability.
4. *Emergency maintenance:* Unscheduled corrective maintenance performed to keep a system operational. On the other hand, corrective maintenance is a planned maintenance activity.

As mentioned earlier, most of the maintenance costs are due to enhancements made to a software system. Therefore, some authors explicitly refer to this type of maintenance as enhancement maintenance.

21.5 SOFTWARE MAINTENANCE PROCESS AND ACTIVITIES

Software maintenance is an ongoing activity that continues until the system retires. Like software development, maintenance requires a process. During the history of software engineering, many maintenance process models have been proposed. This section reviews some of these process models. Regardless of which process model is used, software maintenance performs a set of basic activities. These include:

1. *Program understanding.* Software systems are large and complex. The maintenance software engineer must know the software before changing it. Therefore, program understanding is required.
2. *Change identification and analysis.* This activity identifies the needed changes, analyzes their impact, estimates the change effort, and assesses the change risks.
3. *Configuration change control* (CCC). Changes made to a component of the system may impact other components. Software engineers who maintain the affected components must be involved in the decision-making process. This requires the maintenance team to prepare an engineering change proposal (ECP). It serves to inform relevant stakeholders of the changes and solicits their feedback.
4. *Change implementation, testing, and delivery.* The approved changes are made to the existing system. Integration testing, acceptance testing, and system testing or regression testings are performed to ensure that the system is correctly modified.

21.5.1 Maintenance Process Models

Figure 21.1 shows some of the maintenance process models proposed in the literature. With the quick fix model in Figure 21.1(*a*), the source code and the necessary documentations are changed. The source code is compiled and the system is tested. The quick fix model can be applied to all types of maintenance. The iterative enhancement model in Figure 21.1(*b*) is an adaptation of the evolutionary development model to software maintenance. That is, changes are based on an analysis of the current system. The requirements specification and design of the current system are modified and used as the basis for implementing the changes. This process is repeated for each batch of changes. The full reuse model in Figure 21.1(*c*) differs from the iterative enhancement model in its emphasis in reusing the existing system's requirements specification, design, implementation, test cases, and other reusable components from a repository. With this model, software reuse processes and techniques are applied to reap the benefits of reuse. The model requires that there must be a repository of reusable components, and support for selecting and tailoring the reusable components must be available. The IEEE-1219 model shown in Figure 21.1(*d*) and the the ISO-12207 model in Figure 21.1(*e*) are similar to the iterative enhancement model. Figure 21.2 shows the correspondence between the models.

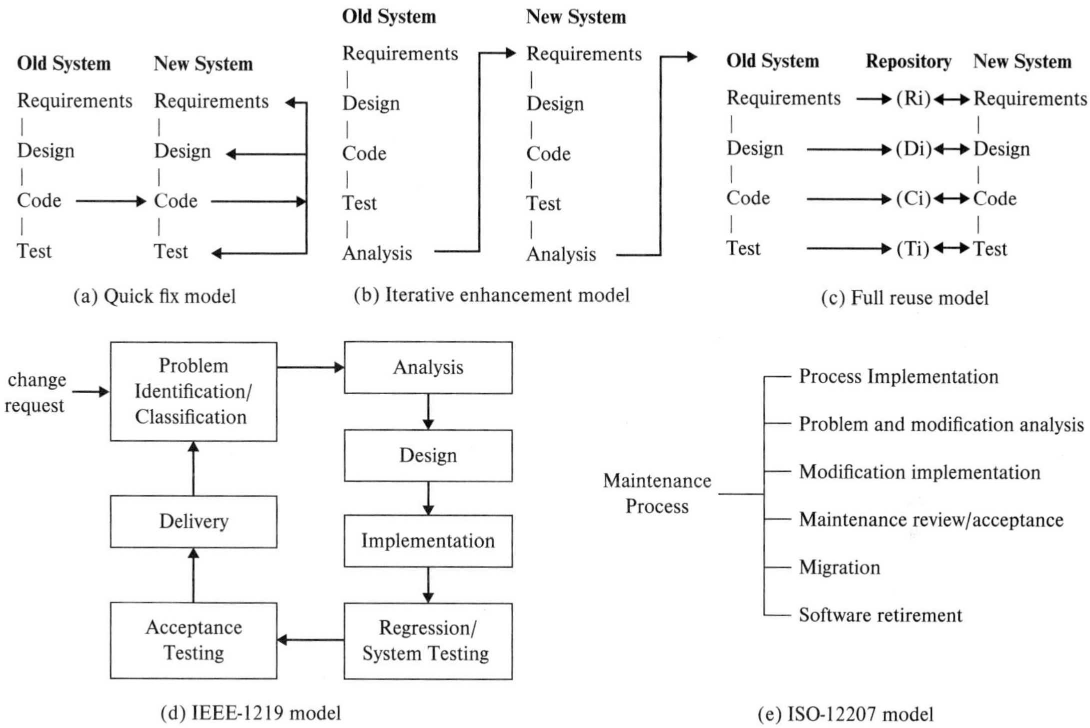

FIGURE 21.1 Different maintenance process models

Iterative Enhancement	IEEE	ISO
Analysis	Problem Identification/Classification	Problem and modification analysis
Requirement	Analysis	Modification implementation
Design	Design	
Code	Implementation	
Test	Regression/SystemTesting Acceptance Testing	Maintenance review/acceptance
	Delivery	Migration
		Software retirement

FIGURE 21.2 Mapping between the phases of three models

21.5.2 Program Understanding

To change a software system, the software engineer needs to understand the program. This is commonly referred to as program understanding or program comprehension. It involves a process that extracts the design and specification artifacts from the code and represents them in a mental model. This process is the opposite of the development process, which begins with a problem statement and ends with the production of the software running in the target environment. Different mental models are used to represent the design and specification artifacts that are recovered from the code. These include object-oriented models, control flow models,

Invocation Chain Length	1	2	3	4	5	6	7	8	9	10	11	12	13	14	15
Number of Chains	246	305	568	783	742	492	514	482	330	172	82	59	31	10	2

FIGURE 21.3 Invocation chains in the InterViews library

functional models, to mention a few. UML diagrams may serve as the object-oriented models. The flowchart and data flow diagram presented in Chapter 14 are examples of control flow models and functional models, respectively.

Many real-world systems consist of millions of lines of code and thousands of classes. In addition, object-oriented systems also exhibit complex interdependencies among the classes. For example, the InterViews library has 122 classes, more than 400 inheritance, aggregation and association relationships, and more than 1,000 member functions. The classes call each other, resulting in the so-called invocation chains. That is, function f1 calls function f2, which in turn calls function f3, and so on. Figure 21.3 shows the lengths of the invocation chains in the InterViews library. The data do not include calls that involve dynamic binding and function pointers (InterViews was implemented in C++).

The figure shows that two chains have a length of 14. This means 15 functions form a call sequence–that is, f1 calls f2, f2 calls f3, . . . , f14 calls f15. Thus, to understand the functionality, the maintainer needs to trace the 14 function calls and makes a note of what each function does, and then derives the functionality from the trace. The figure shows that most of the invocation chains call two to nine functions, and about 30% of the chains call more than a half a dozen functions. The complex relationships among the classes and the function invocation chains make object-oriented programs difficult to understand. Unfortunately, the InterViews library did not include any in-code comments. Each program file contains only a brief, generic file header stating the copyright information, and this is the only in-code comment. Thus, understanding a program is difficult without other supporting documents.

21.5.3 Change Identification and Analysis

Software maintenance needs to identify the needed changes based on the change events. Sometimes, more than one change is needed for a given event. All these changes should be identified. It is worthwhile to identify alternative changes to accommodate a change event. For example, if it is costly or time consuming to change a component and there are commercial off-the-shelf (COTS) alternatives, then changing the component as well as using COTS should be identified as alternatives. This information allows the change analysis step to evaluate the options and select a viable option to pursue. Sometimes, it is difficult to fix a component to remove the root cause, but it is relatively easy to change a different component to fix the problem, at least temporarily. In this case, these two alternatives should be identified. The changes identified are analyzed to:

1. Assess the change impact–that is, which other components will be affected by the changes made to a given component.
2. Estimate the costs and time required to implement the changes and test the result.
3. Identify risks and define resolution measures.

No. of classes changed	1	1	1	2	3	4	5	6	7	8	9	10
No. of classes affected, out of 122	51.07	61.75	74	63.31	84.63	95	2	86	83	89	83	85
Note	1	2	3	1	1	1	4	4	4	4	4	4

Total no. of classes changed: 57; total affected: 857.76; average affected: 15.05.
Note 1: Average over 20 cases; a number of classesare randomly selected and changed.
Note 2: One randomly selected class is deleted.
Note 3: Two randomly selected classes are deleted.
Note 4: A number of randomly selected classes are changed.

FIGURE 21.4 Change impact in maintaining object-oriented programs

Object-oriented software exhibits complex dependencies among the classes. Changes made to one class may affect many classes. This is also called the ripple effect. Figure 21.4 shows the change impact in the InterViews library discussed earlier. The data indicate that on average, 15 classes are affected when one class is changed. The first three cases indicate that changes made to one class could affect 51, 62, and 74 classes, respectively. However, in some case, change impact is limited. For example, in one case, five classes are changed but only two classes are affected. As discussed above, there are alternatives to fix a defect or solving a problem. Change impact analysis should consider the maintenance costs associated with the alternative ways to change the software. The number of alternatives should be limited to reduce the cost of change analysis. In addition to change impact, the risks associated with the changes are identified and measures are defined to resolve the risks if they do occur. The outcome of this step is used in the CCC step to determine if the proposed changes should be performed.

Change impact is identified by the dependencies among the classes. If a design class diagram is available and up to date, then the classes that are affected by changes to a class can be identified from the dependencies among the classes. However, for many real-world projects, the DCD does not exist or not match with code. In these cases, a reverse-engineering tool can be used to produce the implementation class diagram (ICD) from the code. The change impact can be derived from the design class diagram or the ICD as follows. If class B depends on class A, then changes to class A affect class B. Moreover, if class C depends on class B and class B depends on class A, then changes to class A also affect class C. This is because the dependency relation is a transitive relation. Class B depends on class A if one of the following holds. Figure 21.5 illustrates these cases with sample code.

1. Class B is a subclass of class A.
2. Class B is an aggregate of class A.
3. Class B uses class A, that is, one of the following is true:
   a. Class A is a parameter type of a function of class B.
   b. Class A is the return type of a function of class B.
   c. Class A is the type of a local variable of class B.
   d. Class B creates an object of class A.
   e. Class B calls a function of class A.
4. Class B is an association class for an association between class A and another class.

Change impact analysis using the DCD is associated with a number of problems. The DCD usually does not include implementation classes and their relationships.

Case	Description	Illustration	Explanation
1	Class B is a subclass of class A.	public class A { ... } public class B extends A {... }	Since B inherits features of A. Changes to A's features affect the behavior of B.

2	Class B is an aggregation of class A.	public class A { ... }
		public class B {
		  A a=new A(); ...
		}
			Class A is part of class B. Usually, B creates A means B closely uses A (see creator pattern in Applying Responsibility-Assignment Patterns). Thus, if A is changed, B is affected.

3	Class B uses class A.		

(a)	Class A is a parameter type of a function of class B.	public class B {
		  public void foo(A a) { ... }
		}
			Passing an object of class A to a function of B implies that the function uses the A object. Thus, changes to A affects B.

(b)	Class A is the return type of a function of class B.	public class B {
		  public A foo() {... }
		}
			B returns an object of A implies that B creates, uses or updates the A object or obtains it from somewhere. Thus, B depends on A.

(c)	Class A is the type of a local variable of class B.	public class B {
		  public void foo() {
		    A a=new A();
		    a.ba();
		  }
		}
			In this case, B creates the A object or gets it from somewhere and uses the A object. Thus, B depends on A.

(d)	Class B creates an object of class A.	see case 2 and case 3(c)	
(e)	Class B calls a function of class A.	see case 3(c)	

4	Class B is an association class for class A and another class.	public class B {
		  public B(A a, C c) {...}
		}
			Passing an object of class A to a function of B implies that the function uses the A object. Thus, changes to A affects B.

FIGURE 21.5 Illustration of dependencies between classes

Moreover, its classes and relationships may differ from their implementation counterparts. For example, an implemented class may have more functions than its design counterpart. These functions may call functions of other classes. Such dependencies may not exist in the DCD. Thus, change impact analysis based on the DCD may produce incorrect results. Finally, if the DCD is not available, then it is not possible to use this approach. Change impact analysis using a reverse-engineering approach offers a solution. This is described in Section 21.6.

21.5.4 Configuration Change Control

Section 21.5.3 shows that changes made to a class may ripple throughout the system, affecting many classes. In practice, the classes are developed by different teams and team members. If class A is changed and class B is affected, then the developer of class B needs to know that his class has been affected. This is necessary because changes to class B may be needed. Thus, changes to the components of a system must be made in a coordinated manner; otherwise, the project would become a chaos. The mechanism to coordinate changes to components of a system is called software configuration management. Configuration change control (CCC) is one of its components. It performs two main functions:

1. *Preparing an* ECP. Based on the change analysis result, the maintenance personnel prepares an ECP. The ECP consists of administrative forms, supporting technical and administrative materials that specify the proposed changes, the reasons for the changes, the affected components, and the effort, time, and cost required to implement the changes. The priorities of the changes are specified. A schedule to implement the changes is also described.
2. *Evaluating the* ECP. The ECP is reviewed by a configuration change control board (CCCB). The board consists of representatives from different parties including representatives of the development teams of the components that will be affected by the changes. If the review raises concerns, then the proposal is modified and resubmitted. In some cases, the proposal is rejected for various reasons. In this case, the proposal is archived for future reference.

21.5.5 Change Implementation, Testing, and Delivery

Once the ECP is accepted, the changes are implemented. For many real-world systems, the change incorporation activity needs to implement a set of changes, which may include all types of maintenance. The implementation is application dependent. It is not pursued further. The implementation is tested using the existing as well as new test cases. That is, regression testing and development testing are performed. The modified and tested system is then deployed to operate in the target environment. During the operation phase, bugs are recorded, various data such as system logs, transaction processing times, and data needed to compute desired metrics are collected. The data are used to compute metrics to assess the performance of the system. These results are useful for the next cycle of maintenance work.

21.6 REVERSE-ENGINEERING

The process that converts the code to recover the design, specification, and a problem statement is a reverse process of the development process. Therefore, this is called reverse-engineering.

21.6.1 Reverse-Engineering Workflow

Performing reverse-engineering manually is difficult. Therefore, tools are developed to automate the process. The main components of a reverse-engineering tool is shown in Figure 21.6. The tool takes the code as the input and displays the diagrams as the output. The first step of the reverse-engineering process extracts the software artifacts from the code. For example, to reverse-engineer an object-oriented program to generate a class diagram, the classes, their attributes and operations, and the relationships between the classes are extracted. The results are stored in a database. The artifacts are used to compute the diagram layout, that is, the coordinates that determine where to draw the classes, attributes, and relationships. Finally, a display component draws the diagram according to the layout.

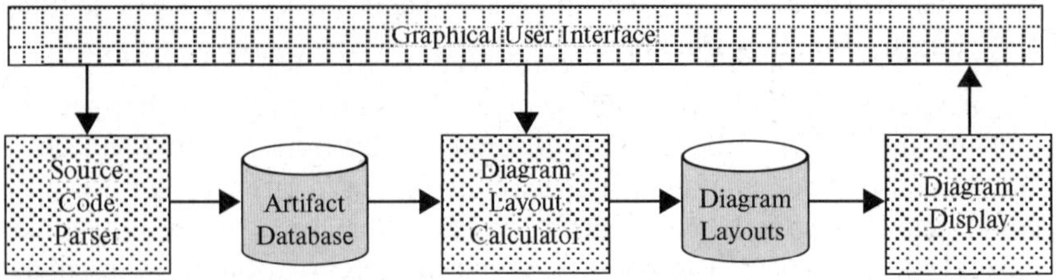

FIGURE 21.6 Components of a reverse-engineering tool

21.6.2 Usefulness of Reverse-Engineering

The diagrams produced by reverse-engineering have a number of uses:

Program understanding. The diagrams produced by a reverse-engineering tool facilitate understanding of the structure, functionality, and behavior of the software under maintenance. This is extremely useful when the system documentation is missing, outdated, or inadequate.

Formal analysis. Formal analysis techniques can be applied to the diagrams produced by a reverse-engineering tool to detect problems that may exist in the software. For example, software model checking applies the conventional model-checking technique to a software model produced by reverse-engineering.

Test case generation. The diagrams produced by reverse-engineering facilitate test case generation. For example, the basis paths of a flowchart diagram facilitate the generation of basis path test cases. The state diagram facilitates generation of state behavior test cases.

Software reengineering. The diagrams produced by reverse-engineering are useful for software reengineering–a process that restructures the software system to improve a certain aspect(s) of the software system. This is described in a later section.

21.6.3 Reverse-Engineering: A Case Study

In illustration, this section presents the OOTWorks testing and maintenance environment. It includes the following components, among others:

Object Relation Diagram (ORD). This component takes the source code and produces a UML class diagram showing the classes, their attributes and operations, and the relationships between the classes. The user can select the classes and relationships, and the attributes and methods of which classes to be displayed. The ORD utilities include:

- **Change Impact Analysis.** The user can select the classes to be changed and have the tool highlight the classes that are affected, based on the dependencies among the classes, as described in the last section.
- **Software Metrics.**This utility calculates software metrics including, for each class, the class size, number of lines of code, number of children, fan-in, fan-out, number of relationships, depth-in-inheritance-tree, and so on.

- **Version Comparison.** This utility takes as input two versions of the source code and displays the ORD for the old and new versions. Moreover, the new version highlights the classes added, changed, and affected. The old version highlights the classes deleted, changed, and affected.
- **Test Order.** This utility computes the order to test the classes so that the effort required to implement the test stubs is substantially reduced.

Block Branch Diagram (BBD). The BDD performs reverse-engineering of the functions of a class and displays the flowcharts for the functions. The BBD component also calculates and displays the basis paths of the function, highlights the basis path selected, and shows the variables that are used and modified.

Object Interaction Diagram. This component performs reverse-engineering of the source code to generate and display a sequence diagram that describes the interaction between the objects.

Object State Diagram. This component performs reverse-engineering of the source code to produce and display a state diagram that describes the state-dependent behavior of an object. The utilities include state reachability analysis and state-based fault analysis.

21.7 SOFTWARE REENGINEERING

Software reengineering is a process that restructures a software system or component to improve nonfunctional aspects of the software. As Lehman's laws indicate, software systems undergo continual changes. These cause the structure of the software system to deteriorate. As a consequence, the software becomes more difficult to comprehend and more costly to maintain. In this case, it is necessary to restructure the software system to reduce the maintenance cost.

21.7.1 Objectives of Reengineering

As discussed above, reengineering is required to improve the structure of the software system so that further maintenance activities can be performed cost effectively. Besides this, software reengineering is sometimes performed to improve the quality, security, and performance aspects of a software system. More specifically, software reengineering is often performed with one or more objectives in mind. The following is a list of such objectives:

1. *Improving the software architecture.* One important software reengineering objective is to improve the software architecture of an existing system. The need for improvement may be due to different reasons. Improving the software architecture is achieved by applying architectural design patterns, security patterns, and design patterns. For example, the controller pattern is often applied to decouple the graphical user interface from the business objects to improve the architecture.
2. *Reducing the complexity of the software.* The complexity of a system has significant impact on the quality and security of a software system. The complexity of a

software system or component can be measured in different ways. One complexity metric is the cyclomatic complexity, which was proposed by McCabe and discussed in Chapters 19 and 20. It measures the number of independent paths or control flows in a function. If the cyclomatic complexity is high, then the function is difficult to understand, implement, test, and maintain. Many patterns can be applied to reduce the complexity. These include observer, state, strategy, and other patterns.

3. *Improving the ability to adapt to changes.* This includes application of appropriate design patterns to improve the structure and behavior of the software system so that it is more adaptable to changes in requirements and operating environment. For example, the design of the persistence framework in Chapter 17 lets the system easily adapt to changes in the database management system. Applying this framework to an existing system improves its adaptiveness.
4. *Improving the performance, efficiency, and resource utilization.* During the system operation phase, data about various aspects of the system are collected and metrics are computed. These are valuable information for identifying places for improvement, for example, performance bottlenecks, poor workload distribution and poor resource utilization. Architectural styles, patterns, and efficient algorithms can be applied to improve the system. For example, virtual proxy, smart proxy, flyweight, and prototype can be applied to improve performance, object creation speed, and memory usage.
5. *Improving the maintainability of the software system.* Many patterns can be applied to make the software system easier to maintain. These include abstract factory, bridge, builder, chain of responsibility, command, composite, decorator, facade, factory method, flyweight, interpreter, iterator, mediator, observer, state, strategy, template method, and visitor.

21.7.2 Software Reengineering Process

A typical software reengineering process is shown in Figure 21.7. It involves the following activities:

1. **Identifying places that need improvement.** First, the software is analyzed to identify places where improvement is needed. Tools are useful for this task.
2. **Selecting an improvement strategy.** Next, improvement strategies are developed for the items that are identified to improve. Often, more than one strategy exist for each item that needs to be improved. The improvement strategies are analyzed to assess their change impact, and the time and cost required to implement the strategies. Based on the analysis result, an improvement strategy is selected.

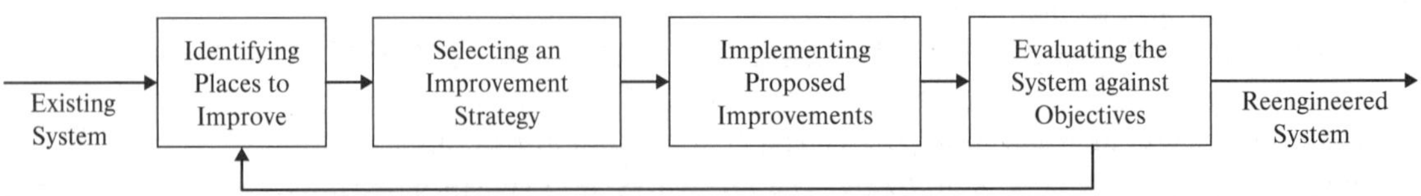

FIGURE 21.7 Software reengineering process

3. **Implementing the proposed improvements.** The proposed improvements are implemented. Testing and regression testing are performed to ensure that the reengineered software system satisfies the requirements.
4. **Evaluating system against objectives.** The modified system is evaluated against the objectives. If further improvement is needed, then the process is repeated.

21.7.3 Software Reengineering: A Case Study

This section illustrates how software reengineering improves software quality through a small case study. The system is the OOTWorks environment described in Section 21.6.3. The objective of the case study is to improve the OOTWorks environment using the tools of OOTWorks. The reengineering objectives discussed in Section 21.7.1 are taken into consideration. The case study performs the following steps, as described previously:

1. *Identifying places that need improvement.*
2. *Selecting an improvement strategy.*
3. *Implementing the proposed improvements.*
4. *Evaluating the system against improvement objectives.*

First, the metric calculation tool of OOTWorks is applied to identify places that need improvement. The tool indicates many places required improvements. One of these is the extremely high complexity of one of the methods of a metrics calculation class. The method calculates software metrics selected by the user. The software industry has an unofficial complexity threshold of 10, but the method has a complexity of 38. Examination of the code reveals that the method uses conditional statements to test if a metric is selected. If so, it was added to a vector of metrics. The complexity reflects the use of 38 conditional checks to determine which metrics need be computed. Moreover, the series of 38 conditional tests may slowdown the function. The following code shows the original implementation of the method:

```
public void itemStateChanged(ItemEvent e) {
    if (e.getItemSelectable()==noc) {
       if (noc.getState())
          metricsVector.add("noc");
       else metricsVector.remove("noc");
    }
    if (e.getItemSelectable()==nol) {
       if (nol.getState())
          metricsVector.add("nol");
       else metricsVector.remove("nol");
    }
    if (e.getItemSelectable()==fanin) {
       if (fanin.getState())
          metricsVector.add("fanin");
       else metricsVector.remove("fanin");
    }
    . . .
}
```

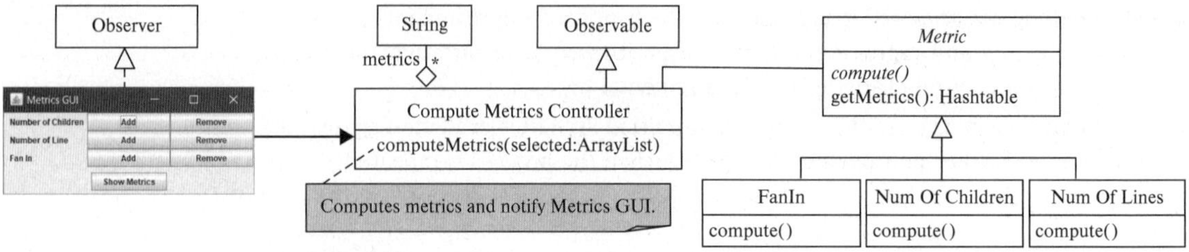

FIGURE 21.8 Reengineering metric calculation component of OOTWorks

The next step is to select an improvement strategy. The use of conditional statements implies behavior variations. That is, different metrics are calculated by using different algorithms. This suggests that polymorphism can be used to improve. Figure 21.8 shows the design.

An abstract class called Metric is defined. It has an abstract compute() method. The subclasses of Metric implement the compute() method to compute the metrics. Moreover, the Metrics GUI has a number of buttons for the user to select metrics. Each button has an action listener, which adds or removes a metric to or from a collection called selected. When the Show Metrics button is clicked, the computeMetrics() method of the controller is invoked. This method asks the each of the selected metrics to compute the metrics for the classes. It then notifies the Metrics GUI to display the result. Figure 21.9 shows a sample implementation.

```
public class NumOfChildren extends Metric {
  private static NumOfChildren instance=new NumOfChildren();
  public static NumOfChildren getInstance() { return instance; }
  private NumOfChildren() { super(); }
  public void compute() { metrics.put("A1", new Integer(1));
    metrics.put("A2", new Integer(2)); metrics.put("A3", new Integer(3)); }}
// Do as this class for the other metrics.
public class Canvas extends JPanel implements Observer {
  ArrayList<String> metrics=new ArrayList<String>();
  public Canvas() { super(); setSize(300, 200); }
  public void update(Observable o, Object arg) {
    metrics=(ArrayList<String>)arg; repaint(); }
  public void paintComponent(Graphics g) {
    super.paintComponent(g); if (metrics.isEmpty()) return;
    for(int i=0; i<metrics.size(); i++) {
      g.drawString(metrics.get(i), 20, 50+i*15); } metrics.clear(); }}
public class ComputeMetricsController extends Observable {
  private ArrayList<String> metrics=new ArrayList<String>();
  public void computeMetrics(ArrayList<Metric> selected) {
    for(int i=0; i<selected.size(); i++) { // compute metrics
      selected.get(i).compute();
      String row=selected.get(i).getClass().getName(); // metric name
      Hashtable<String, Integer> m=selected.get(i).getMetrics();
      Enumeration<String> keys=m.keys();
      while (keys.hasMoreElements()) { String cName=keys.nextElement();
        row+="   "+cName+"="+m.get(cName); } metrics.add(row); }
    setChanged(); notifyObservers(metrics); selected.clear(); }
```

```
public class MetricsGUI extends JFrame {
  ComputeMetricsController controller=new ComputeMetricsController();
  Canvas canvas=new Canvas();
  ArrayList<Metric> selected=new ArrayList<Metric>();
  public MetricsGUI() {
    init(); // this method creates and adds the buttons
    nocAdd.addActionListener(new ActionListener() {
      public void actionPerformed(ActionEvent ae) {
        selected.add(NumOfChildren.getInstance()); }
    });
    nocRemove.addActionListener(new ActionListener() {
      public void actionPerformed(ActionEvent ae) {
        selected.remove(NumOfChildren.getInstance());
        selected.trimToSize(); }
    }); // do the same for the other metrics' buttons
    show.addActionListener(new ActionListener() {
      public void actionPerformed(ActionEvent ae) {
        controller.computeMetrics(selected); }});
  }
  public static void main(String[] args) {
    MetricsGUI gui=new MetricsGUI(); gui.setSize(500, 400);
    gui.setLocation(300, 300); gui.validate(); gui.setVisible(true); }}

public abstract class Metric {
  Hashtable<String, Integer> metrics=new Hashtable<String, Integer>();
  public abstract void compute();
  public Hashtable<String, Integer> getMetrics() { return metrics; }}
```

FIGURE 21.9 Sample implementation of metrics calculation.

21.8 SOFTWARE EVOLUTION

Software evolution is the process that deals with changing requirements or operating environment after the initial release of a software system. It is a part of the adaptive maintenance activity. Most of the time, software evolution is to enhance the functionality of a software system. As stated at the beginning of this chapter, enhancements amount to 75% of the maintenance costs. This is because for some systems, software evolution may last several decades. During this prolong period of time, the system undergoes a series of modifications, made by different software engineers. As a consequence, the system's architecture may deteriorate, and the system's documentation may be missing, outdated, or inadequate. How to modify such systems is a challenge. This is the focus of this section.

Chapter 2 presents an overview of an agile unified methodology, in Figure 2.15, for developing software systems from scratch. The methodology has a planning phase and an iterative phase. The planning phase performs four activities: (1) requirements acquisition and domain modeling, (2) deriving use cases from requirements, (3) assigning use cases to iterations, and (4) designing system architecture. The iterative phase has six activities, performed during each iteration: (1) accommodate requirements change, (2) extending the domain model to include domain concepts introduced by the use cases assigned to the current iteration, (3) performing actor-system interaction modeling for the use cases assigned to the current iteration, (4) performing behavioral modeling (object interaction modeling, state modeling, and activity modeling), (5) deriving design class diagram, and (6) test-driven development (TDD), integration, and deployment. Chapters 4–15 detail the steps of the methodology. Software evolution or enhancing a software system can follow the same activities as depicted in Figure 2.15, but some of the activities should be performed differently. The following sections present how to carry out the activities to evolve a software system (with respect to functional enhancement).

21.8.1 Planning Phase

Requirements Acquisition and Domain Modeling

During this activity, the enhancement requirements are gathered using information collection techniques presented in Section 4.5.1. With consultation to the customer and users, the enhancement requirements can be classified into two categories: (1) requirements that introduce new use cases, and (2) requirements that require change to existing use cases. Sometimes, the customer or users may request that certain use cases be deleted for various reasons. It is a good practice to perform domain modeling to help understand the enhancement requirements as well as establishing a common understanding among the team members. If a domain model exists and it is up to date, then the domain model can be used as it is, or updated to include new domain concepts introduced by the enhancement requirements. If a domain model does not exist and the source code is available, then reverse engineering is performed to produce a class diagram from the source code, called an implementation class diagram (ICD). The ICD cannot be used as a domain model because it contains design and implementation classes such as graphical user interface classes, system configuration and system log classes as well as design pattern classes. All such classes must be removed from the ICD. If the existing code carefully names the domain classes and properly implements the relationships between the domain classes, the resulting ICD may be used as a domain model. If the resulting ICD does not help in understanding the application domain, then a domain model describing domain concepts relevant to the enhancement requirements may be constructed. The outcome of this activity is a prioritized list of enhancement requirements and optionally a domain model.

Deriving Use Cases from Enhancement Requirements

During this activity, three categories of use case are derived from the enhancement requirements:

1. New use cases. These are new use cases derived from the enhancement requirements. The steps presented in Chapter 7 (Deriving Use Cases from Requirements) can be applied.
2. Use cases to modify. These are existing use cases that need to be modified to address the enhancement requirements. For example, the Logon use case may need to be modified to support strong password. Usually, the customer or users tell the maintenance team which use cases need to be modified. The enhancement requirements specify the capabilities that need to be added to the existing use cases.
3. Use cases to delete. These are existing use cases that are no longer needed.

Like forward engineering, priorities are assigned to the use cases according to priorities of the enhancement requirements. Usually, low priorities are assigned to use cases to be deleted. Moreover, high-level use cases for the new and to-be-modified use cases are specified, and use case diagrams are produced to show the assignment of the use cases to new or existing subsystems. The new, to be modified and deleted use cases may be indicated in the use case diagrams.

Assigning Use Cases to Iterations

During this activity, the iteration duration is determined. Effort and time required to develop and deploy each of the use cases are derived using appropriate estimation methods, and the use cases are then assigned to the iterations (see Chapter 23).

Modifying System Architecture, If Needed

During this activity, the existing architectural design is modified, if needed, to address the enhancement requirements. For example, if the existing system uses a local database and the enhancements require the system to access a remote database, then the architectural design needs to change (see Chapter 17 for how to apply the proxy pattern to fulfill this requirement).

21.8.2 Iterative Phase

During the iterative phase, the use cases are developed and deployed iteratively. This lets the customer and users reap the benefits of enhancements as soon as they are available. For new use cases, the iterative activities are performed as in forward engineering. Therefore, they will not be covered in the following presentation.

Accommodating Requirements Change

During this activity, requirements change, if any, is addressed. As a consequence, the use cases as well as the iteration planning are modified accordingly.

Domain Modeling

During this activity, the existing domain model is expanded, if needed, to include domain concepts introduced by the use cases allocated to the current iteration. This includes addition, deletion, and modification of classes, attributes, and relationships.

Actor-System Interaction Modeling

Use cases to be modified require modification to existing expanded use cases, which may or may not exist. If they do not exist, then the team can try to run or ask the users to demonstrate the use cases, and reconstruct the expanded use cases. The team then updates the expanded use cases to satisfy the enhancement requirements.

For use cases to be deleted, the expanded use cases are deleted and archived. The expanded use cases can help in identifying classes, attributes, relationships, graphical user interface components, and web pages as candidates to modify or delete. For example, Figure 8.5 shows the expanded use case for the Add Program use case. If this use case were to be deleted, then the following items could be identified as candidates to delete:

1. The Add Program link on the Program Management submenu.
2. The Add Program form.
3. The program is added successfully message.
4. The program class if it is not used by other use cases directly or indirectly.

Behavioral Modeling

Behavioral modeling includes object interaction modeling, state modeling, and activity modeling. Behavioral models facilitate understanding and modification of the implemented behavior. During this activity, the behavioral models for the use cases that need to change are identified and modified. If a model does not exist, then the maintenance team can either create the model or uncover it from the implementation. Creating the models has been described in Chapter 9 (Object Interaction Modeling), Chapter 13 (Object State Modeling), Chapter 14 (Activity Modeling), and Chapter 15 (Modeling and Design of Rule-Based Systems). Tools may exist for reverse engineering some of the behavioral models from code.

To uncover the behavioral models, the team identifies the nontrivial steps from the expanded use cases. For each nontrivial step, do the following:

1. In the step that immediately precedes the nontrivial step in the expanded use case, identify the user interface widget such as a button, selection, or menu item that submits the actor request.
2. From the widget identified above, identify the call-back function of the listener, servlet or any object that processes the actor request.
3. Beginning with the call-back function, identify functions that are invoked by the call-back function, and functions that are called by such functions. In other words, trace the functions that call one after another in a depth-first fashion, skipping all sequential statements that do not contain a function call. The trace will not continue with database access functions because the persistence framework should take care of database access (see Chapter 17). Recover the sequence diagram or scenario while the functions are traced. A trace can discontinue at any level if the team deems that it has obtained enough insight of the implemented behavior. The trace may encounter code segments that implement state behavior, transformational behavior, or business rules if one of the following occurs:

    1) The current function contains nested if-then-else or nested switch statements. If the code evaluates combinations of values of two discrete variables, the evaluation result determines which block of code to execute, and each block of code contains a statement that sets the value of one of the two discrete variables, then the current function may implement state behavior. If so, uncover the state diagram from the code. The states of the state diagram are the values of the discrete variable, which is set in the blocks. The triggering events are the values of the other discrete variable.

    2) The current function contains a nested if-then-else or switch statement that checks the value of an attribute of the class and executes different blocks of code, moreover, each of the blocks of code contains a statement that sets the value of the attribute. In this case, the class may implement state behavior. The states are the values or ranges of values of the attribute that is checked. The transitions are the current function and other similar functions of the same class. If this is true, then uncover the state diagram from the code.

    3) The current function contains a series of if-then or if-then-else statements, or a nested if-then-else statement. In this case, analyze the code and determine if it is used to evaluate a set of business rules. If so, uncover the decision table from the code.

    4) The function calls that are traced seem to perform a transformation of input to substantially different output. In this case, analyze the code and determine if the code implements transformational behavior. If so, an activity model can be uncovered from the code.

The uncovered behavioral models are modified according to the use cases that need to change. This involves understanding the behavioral models, identifying places to change and making the changes.

For use cases to be deleted, the classes and functions that are candidates to delete are identified from their behavioral models. Any of these classes or functions can be deleted if it is not used by other use cases.

EXAMPLE 21.1

Uncover the behavioral models from the following code. It is assumed that the login function of the Login Controller is invoked by the Login JSP.

```
public class LoginController {
   private User user;
   public LoginResult login(String username,
      String password) throws
      DBException { UserDAO dao = new UserDAO();
      user = dao.getUser(username);
      if (user == null) return LoginResult.FAIL;
      boolean matches = PasswordUtil.match(password,
      user.getPassword()); LoginResult result =
      getResult(matches, user); return result;
   }
   private LoginResult getResult(boolean matches,
   User user) {
      if(!matches) return LoginResult.FAIL;
      if(user.isFirstLogin()) return
      LoginResult.FIRST_LOGIN; return
      LoginResult.SUCCESS;

   }
}
```

Solution: Figure 21.10 shows the implementation sequence diagram that is manually uncovered using the steps described above. Because the code does not exhibit state behavior, transformational behavior, or business rules, therefore, only the sequence diagram is uncovered.

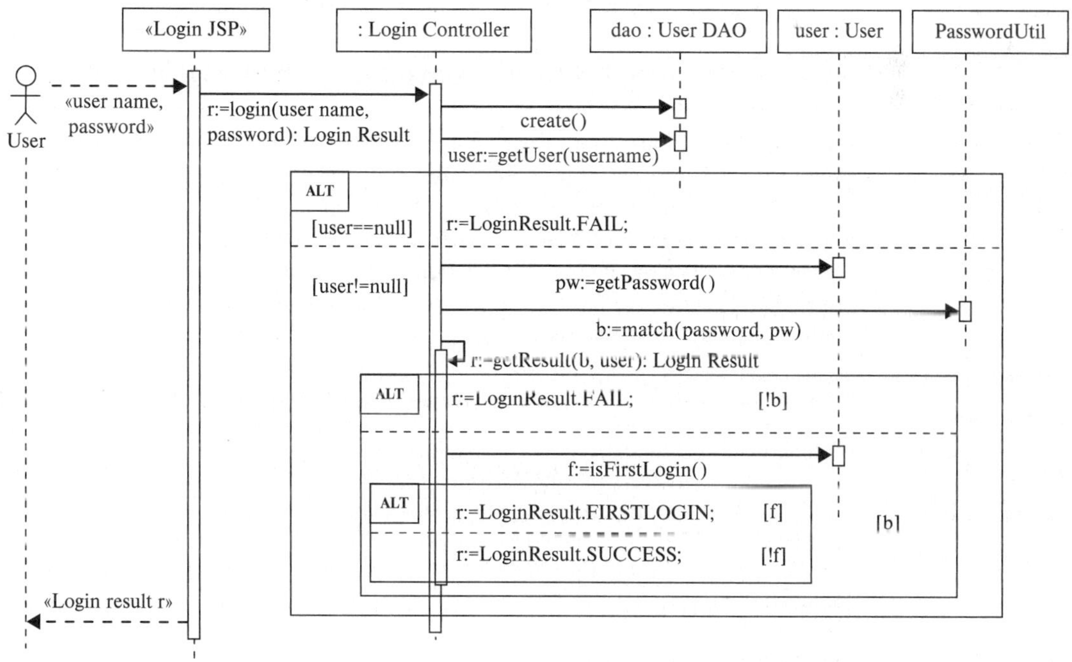

FIGURE 21.10 Implementation sequence diagram uncovered from the given code

The reader may find that the implementation sequence diagram in Figure 21.10 exhibits a design problem. That is, it uses PasswordUtil to verify the validity of the submitted login password. This violates the expert pattern, which suggests that this responsibility should be assigned to the User class rather than a third party. A better design should have part of the code as follows:

```
public LoginResult login(String username, String
password) throws DBException {
   UserDAO dao = new UserDAO();
   user = dao.getUser(username);
   if(user == null) return LoginResult.FAIL;
   return user.verify(password); // which returns
   // LoginResult.FAIL/SUCCESS/FIRSTLOGIN
}
```

Changing the implementation to above is a reengineering effort. Modifying the existing implementation to support two-factor login is a software evolution effort.

Test-Driven Development, Integration and Deployment

During this activity, the new and modified use cases are implemented using TDD. TDD is presented in Chapter 18 and not repeated here. For use cases that are deleted, one needs to delete GUI widgets, certain classes, functions, and attributes that are no longer needed. These items have been identified in previous activities. During this activity, these items are deleted if they are not used by other use cases. Integration testing, regression testing and acceptance testing are performed to ensure that the software system works and satisfies existing and enhancement requirements.

21.9 PATTERNS FOR SOFTWARE MAINTENANCE

As discussed previously, many patterns can be applied during the maintenance phase to improve the software system in various ways. This section presents two new patterns. The *facade* pattern is useful for simplifying the client interaction with a group of components. The *mediator* pattern simplifies the interaction between components of a system or subsystem. Patterns that can be applied during the maintenance phase are not limited to these two patterns. Therefore, other patterns that can be applied during maintenance are also reviewed.

21.9.1 Simplifying Client Interface with Facade

During software maintenance, it is commonly seen that a client component needs to invoke a group of components to accomplish a task. Consider, for example, the workflow shown in Figure 21.6. The client component needs to invoke a sequence of three components. In many cases, the client wants to recover the design from the code. It does not want to know the components and how to invoke them. A pattern to simplify the interface for the client is desirable. This is the facade pattern, described in Figure 21.11.

Name	Facade
Type	GoF/Structural
Specification	
Problem	How does one simplify the interface for a client that interacts with a web of components?
Solution	Decouple the client and the components with a class, called a façade, to interact with the components and provide a simple interface for the client.
Design	
Structural	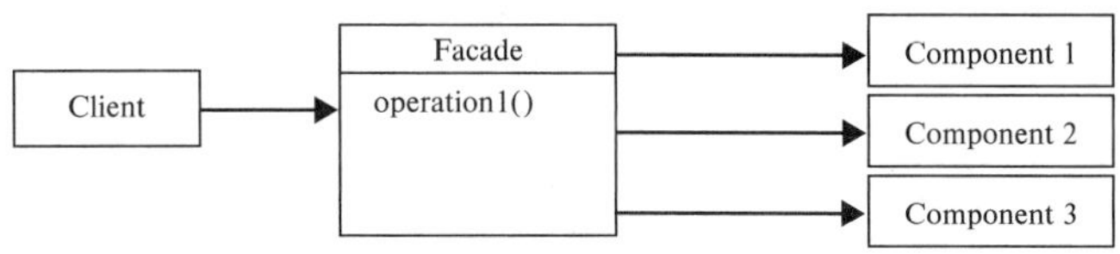 Diagram is illustrative only. The exact relationships between the facade and the components are application dependent.
Behavioral	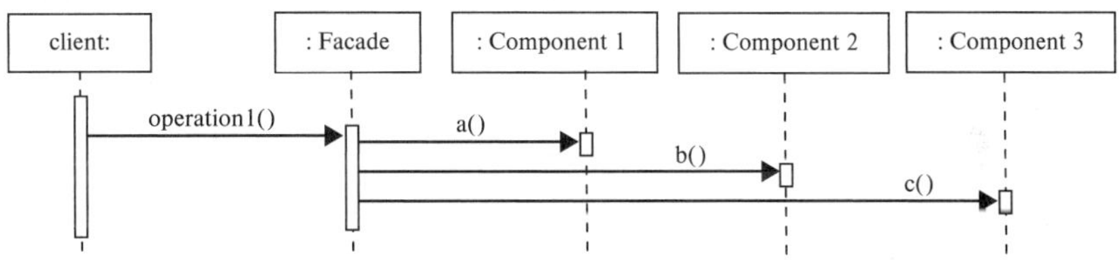 Diagram is illustrative only. The exact behavior is application dependent.
Roles and Responsibilities	• Facade: It defines a simple interface for the client and is responsible for interacting with the components for the client. • Components 1-3: These are the components that the client needs to interact. • Client: It interacts with the facade.
Benefits	• It simplifies the interface for the client. • It decouples the client from the components. Changes to the components will have little impact on the client. • The client still can access to the components if needed.
Liabilities	
Guidelines	
Related Patterns	• Facade simplifies the interface for the client while Mediator simplifies the interaction between a web of components. • Controller is a special case of Façade.
Uses	

FIGURE 21.11 Specification of the facade pattern

In the original design of the OOTWorks environment, the user needs to invoke the source code parser to extract the artifact. The user then invokes the layout component to compute the coordinates. Finally, the user invokes the display component to draw the diagram. This is not user-friendly. Therefore, the reengineering effort selects the facade pattern to improve the client interface. Figure 21.12 shows the application of the facade pattern to simplify the interface for the client. The benefits of applying the facade pattern to the existing design can easily be derived from the benefits listed in Figure 21.11.

21.9.2 Simplifying Component Interaction with Mediator

The facade pattern simplifies the client interface and lets the facade interact with the components. If the interaction between the components is complex, as hinted by the gray cloud shape in Figure 21.12, then the components may be tightly coupled with

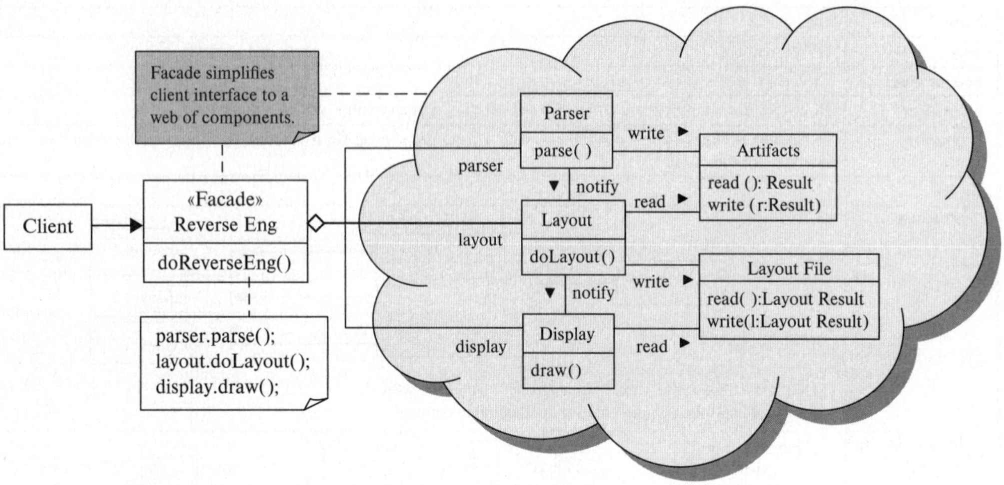

FIGURE 21.12 Facade simplifies client interface

each other. In the worst case, each component must know the presence of, and how to interact with, the other components. As a consequence, the components may be difficult to test, debug, maintain, and reuse. This kind of code is often seen during software maintenance. A solution to improve the design is to reduce the coupling between the interacting components.

The *mediator* pattern fulfills this objective. Figure 21.13 shows the specification of the pattern. The pattern assigns the responsibility of coordinating the interacting components to an object, called the mediator. The pattern replaces the component-to-component interaction in the existing design with the mediator-to-component interaction. The mediator defines the interface for the components to interact with it. It uses the existing interfaces of the components to interact with the components.

To illustrate, consider the design in Figure 21.12. The classes enclosed in the gray cloud shape interact with each other in a complex fashion. The interaction behavior is somewhat difficult to comprehend. In addition, a change to one class may affect the other classes. To improve, the mediator pattern is applied. Figure 21.14 shows the result. In the figure, the mediator interacts with the objects, which are decoupled from each other. The mediator coordinates the interaction.

21.9.3 Patterns for Software Maintenance

Many patterns presented in previous chapters are applicable during the maintenance phase. Figure 21.15 summarizes the patterns that can be applied during the maintenance phase. The first column is the pattern. The second column shows the types of maintenance for which the pattern can be applied. The third column briefly describes the use of the pattern and its benefits.

Name	Mediator
Type	GoF/Behavioral
Specification	
Problem	How does one simplify complex component-to-component interaction?
Solution	Introduce a mediator class to interact with each of the components and let this replace the complex m-to-m component interaction.
Design	
Structural	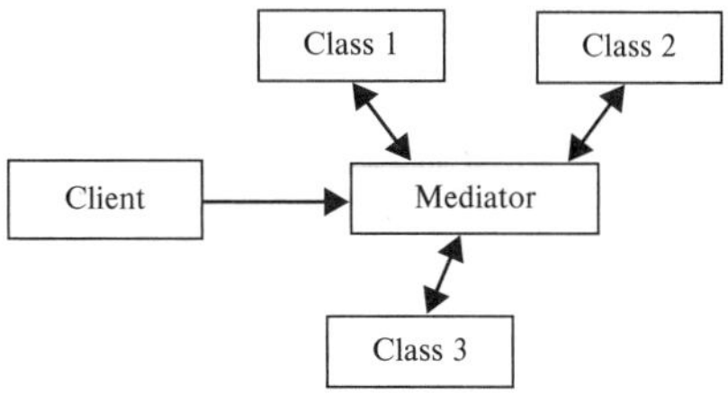
Behavioral	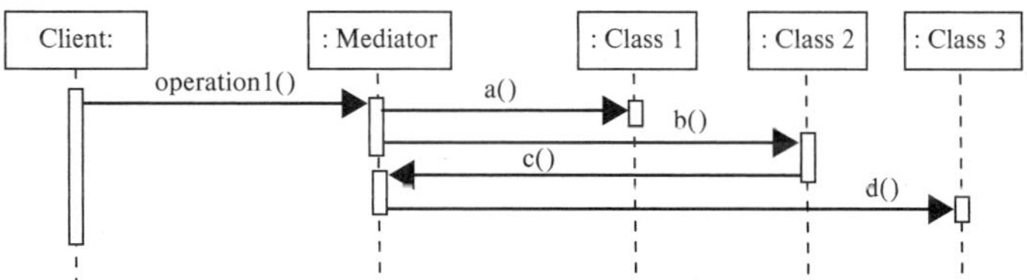 Diagram is illustrative only. The exact behavior is application dependent.
Roles and Responsibilities	• Classes 1-3: These are the classes that interact with each other forming an m-to-m interaction in an existing design. • Mediator: It is introduced to interact with each of the interacting classes. This 1-m interaction replaces the m-m interaction in the existing design. • Client: The client interacts with the mediator and through the mediator to interact with the components.
Benefits	• It simplifies the interaction of the components. • It facilitates understanding because the interaction behavior is simplified. • The components only need to interact with the mediator rather than all the components. • It facilitates reuse of the components because the components are decoupled from each other. • Change to one component has little impact on the other components because the mediator hides the components from each other. • It is easy to add or remove components. • It facilitates test-driven development because the component classes can be tested separately.
Liabilities	
Guidelines	
Related Patterns	State is often used to design and implement the state dependent behavior of a Mediator.
Uses	It is useful for designing and implementing the control element of an embedded system such as the cruise control. In this case, Classes 1-3 represent the driver classes that interact with the hardware devices.

FIGURE 21.13 Specification of the mediator pattern

21.10 APPLYING AGILE PRINCIPLES

Conventional approaches treat maintenance as a post development activity. For an agile project, maintenance begins with the delivery of the first increment or release–development is maintenance and maintenance is development. Figure 21.1 shows that

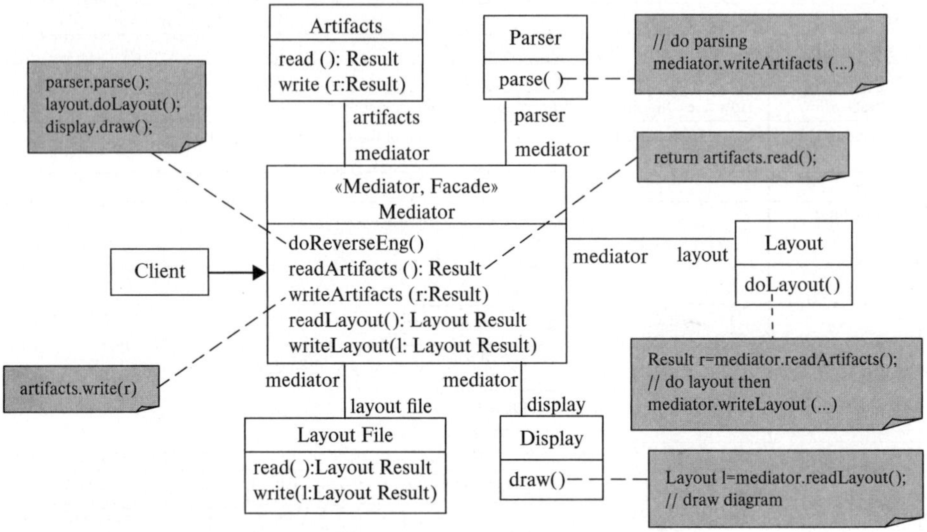

FIGURE 21.14 Mediator simplifies interaction between components

the maintenance process models also have the requirements, design, implementation, and testing phases as in the development process. This implies that the agile principles applicable to the development phases are also applicable to the phases of the maintenance process. Therefore, the following only presents principles that are specific to maintenance.

GUIDELINE 21.1 Good enough is enough.

Improving the structure of the software system is important because it reduces the maintenance costs. However, perfective maintenance is not aimed at obtaining the perfect architecture. In fact, the perfect or optimal architecture does not exist. A good enough architecture is good enough. This includes security architectures–a good enough security architecture is enough.

21.11 TOOL SUPPORT FOR SOFTWARE MAINTENANCE

Many software maintenance activities are tedious and time consuming. Moreover, software maintenance needs to coordinate the changes to ensure consistency. The resulting software system needs to be retested to ensure that it satisfies the requirements and constraints. The use of software tools can significantly reduce the time and effort. The following are some of the tools that are useful for software maintenance:

Reverse-engineering tools are useful for design and specification recovery. They aid program comprehension and identification of places that need improvement.

Pattern	Type	Example Applications/Benefits
Abstract factory	AEP	• Abstract factory can create objects that are environment or platform dependent. Thus, it can be applied to adaptive and perfective maintenance. • Abstract factory can be used to add new product families. Thus, it is applicable to enhancement maintenance.
Adapter	ACEP	• ACEP types of maintenance may reuse an existing component. Adapter can be used to adapt the existing interface. • It is useful for the full reuse process.
Bridge	AEP	• Bridge allows the interface and implementation to change independently. This makes the software easily adapt to changing environment. • New functionality can be added easily; and hence, it supports enhancement maintenance. • Applying bridge improves the ability of the software in many aspects including ease to maintain and adaptability to changes in requirements and environment.
Builder	AEP	• Builder can be used to enhance or improve the software to support new processes or new process steps. • Concrete supervisors and builders can adapt the software to changing environment. • Useful for maintaining enterprise resource planning (ERP) software.
Chain of responsibility, Controller, Observer	EP	• These patterns decouple event sources and handlers. Thus, it is easy to add handlers or sources to support enhancement and perfective maintenance. • Decoupling implies reduction of change impact; and hence, they facilitate software maintenance.
Command	EP	• Command is a special case of polymorphism. Therefore, it can be used to eliminate some of the conditional statements. Complexity is reduced. • It reduces the size of a class by delegating its functions to command objects. • It makes the software easy to add new type of command.
Composite	EP	• Composite simplifies the client's processing. • It improves the ability of the software to represent complex structures. • It makes the software easy to add new primitives or composites.
Decorator, Visitor	EP	• These patterns can add functionality to existing objects dynamically. New decorator or visitor can be added easily; and hence, they support enhancement maintenance. • They can remove functionality from an existing object and assign it to a decorator or visitor. This improves the cohesion of the object as well as reducing the use of conditional statements.
Facade, Mediator	P	• Facade simplifies the client interface and decouples it from the components. Mediator simplifies the interaction among the components. • They facilitate maintenance because (1) the software is easy to understand, and (2) decoupling reduces the change impact of the components. • They facilitate reuse. Facade makes the client easy to reuse the components. Mediator facilitates reuse of any of the components.
Factory method, Template method	AEP	• The concrete subclasses may implement environment or platform-dependent behavior; and hence, it can be used for adaptive maintenance. • Subclasses can be added easily; and hence, it facilitates enhancements. • These two patterns make the code easy to understand, modify, and reuse; and hence, it improves software maintainability.
Flyweight, Singleton, Virtual proxy, Smart reference proxy	P	• These patterns improve the efficiency or performance of the software. • Flyweight and singleton reduce the number of objects created. • Virtual proxy delays the creation of objects that are time consuming to create or memory intensive. • Smart reference proxy keeps track of object use; and hence, it improves performance and efficiency.

FIGURE 21.15 Patterns useful in the maintenance phase *(to be continued)*

Interpreter	EP	• Interpreter allows business rules to be updated dynamically. • It is easy to add or modify rules; and hence, it supports enhancement and perfective maintenance.
Iterator	P	• Iterator hides the implementation of the collection and makes maintenance easier.
Protection proxy	CE	• Protection proxy controls access to an object. • It can be used to add protection to correct security and concurrent access problems. Likewise, such protection can be added as enhancement to existing software.
Prototype	EP	• Prototype reduces the number of classes and hence maintenance is easier. • Prototype supports dynamically loaded classes. This can be explored to support dynamic addition of functionality.
State	EP	• State simplifies the design and implementation of state behavior. It makes the software easy to understand, test, and maintain. • New states and new events can be added easily; and hence, it supports enhancement maintenance.
Strategy	EP	• Strategy encapsulates algorithms as objects. Thus, it is easy to add new algorithms as enhancement maintenance. • It reduces the use of conditional statements to select the strategy; and hence, it makes the software easy to maintain.

Note: Type=maintenance type A=Adaptive, C=Corrective, E=Enhancement, P=Perfective

FIGURE 21.15 *(Continued)*

These tools are extremely valuable when the design documentation is missing, outdated, or inadequate.

Metrics calculation tools compute and display quantitative measurements of a software system. They help in identifying and highlighting places that need improvement. For example, classes that consist of thousands of lines of code are difficult to maintain and are more likely to be error prone. Classes that have an excessive number of functions may be assigned too many responsibilities. Methods with a high complexity are candidates for improvement.

Performance measurement tools such as software profilers can display execution times, invocation frequencies, and memory usage of various components of a software system. They are useful for identifying performance bottlenecks and memory-intensive components. Software reengineering may be needed to mitigate these problems.

Static analysis tools are useful for detecting violation of coding standards, incorrect use of types, existence of certain bugs and anomalies, and security vulnerabilities.

Change impact analysis tools are useful for assessing the scope of impact of proposed improvements. The change impact analysis results are the basis for the estimation of the effort required to perform the proposed improvements.

Effort estimation tools are useful for calculating the required time, effort, and costs to implement the proposed improvements.

Configuration management tools such as Concurrent Versions System and Subversion are useful for coordinating the changes to maintain the consistency of the software being reengineered.

Regression testing tools are useful for rerunning the test cases to ensure that the system satisfies the requirements and reengineering does not introduce new errors. Some of the tools can analyze the software and select a subset of test cases to rerun. This reduces the regression testing time and effort.

21.12 SUMMARY

This chapter presents the Lehman's laws of system evolution, types of software maintenance, and software maintenance process models. Reverse-engineering, reengineering, and patterns and tools that can be applied during the maintenance phase are described.

21.13 CHAPTER REVIEW QUESTIONS

1. What is software maintenance?
2. What are the factors that mandate change?
3. What are the Lehman's laws of system evolution?
4. What are the types of software maintenance?
5. What are the software maintenance process models?
6. What is change identification and analysis?
7. What are reverse-engineering and software reengineering?
8. What are the objectives of software reengineering?
9. What is the software reengineering process?
10. What patterns are useful for software maintenance?
11. How does one enhance a software system?

21.14 EXERCISES

21.1 Collect more than five articles from refereed journals, magazines, and conference proceedings. The articles must be about industry lessons learned or case studies regarding reengineering, restructuring, or reorganizing a software system. Write a survey article about these project experiences. The survey article should discuss the factors that cause the change, types of maintenance, the change process, reverse engineering, reengineering, patterns or architectural styles applied, and tools used by the projects. Limit the article to no more than 10 pages or as instructed by the instructor.

21.2 Collect more than five articles as in exercise 21.1. For this exercise, suggest and discuss your improvements to the reengineering projects described in the articles. For example, a project could have used a reverse-engineering or metrics tool, but it did not. A certain pattern could be applied to improve the system, but the project did not. Write a report to describe your improvement suggestions. Limit the report to no more than five pages or as designated by the instructor.

21.3 Describe how you would use a metrics tool to identify places that need improvement. Assume that you have the tool that can compute all the metrics and provide the capabilities you want.

21.4 Assume that right after you graduate, you are hired by the maintenance team of a financial company. Moreover, you are assigned to maintain an online security (e.g., stocks, mutual funds, exchange-traded funds, etc.) trading software. Describe and explain the responsibilities of this position. State the assumptions you wish to make.

21.5 This exercise is a continuation of the previous exercise (i.e., exercise 21.4). For this exercise, describe how you would fulfill your responsibilities to optimize your job performance. Describe also how you would obtain job satisfaction from doing the work. Limit the article to no more than five pages or as set by the instructor.

21.6 Suppose you are hired by an IT consulting company to work on a major reengineering project of a large, complex object-oriented software system. For this exercise, you have the freedom to make assumptions about the application domain and specific application of the software system. Assume that your team has 20 members. The members may work in groups. Write a brief article to do the following:

a. Describe how the project would proceed.

b. Describe which of the tasks you would like to be assigned to you, and why.

c. Assume that you are assigned the tasks you would like. Describe how you would carry out the tasks.

21.7 Discuss the similarities and differences between the patterns in each of the following pairs. Describe a unique situation in which one of the patterns should be applied and the other should not be applied.

1. Facade and mediator
2. Builder and facade
3. Observer and mediator
4. Facade and proxy.

Chapter 22

Software Configuration Management

Key Takeaway Points

- A baseline defines a significant state of progress of the system under development. It consists of a set of configuration items.
- Software configuration management (SCM) is baseline and configuration item management.
- SCM consists of configuration item identification, configuration change control, configuration auditing, and configuration status accounting.

During the software life cycle, numerous documents are produced. These include requirements specification, software design documents, source code, and test cases. These documents depend on each other. For example, a software design is usually derived from and dependent on the requirements specification. Classes depend on other classes. This means that changing the requirements specification requires changes to the design and changing one class requires changes to other classes. In general, changes made to a document may ripple throughout the project, affecting many other documents.

In software development, changes are inevitable because many events mandate changes to the software development documents. If changes to the documents are not coordinated, then inconsistencies may occur. For example, new requirements are added to the requirements specification, but the design document is not updated to reflect the new requirements. As a consequence, the software system that is eventually constructed will not satisfy the customer's needs and expectation. As another example, when changes are made to a class, other classes that directly or indirectly depend on the class must be updated. If this is not done properly, then the software system may behave abnormally. Therefore, one needs a way to control and track changes. In addition to change control, one also needs to track the progress of a software project. Using the traditional waterfall model, tracking the completion status of the phases is one way to track the progress of a software project. It is important to track the progress because the completion of one phase enables the development teams to start the work of the next phase. Project management requires the progress status information to make decisions, such as adjusting the project schedule, adding people to the project, and/or changing the functionality of the system.

This chapter presents concepts, activities, and techniques for controlling changes to the documents produced during the life cycle, and tracking the status of the soft-ware system and its components. These activities belong to SCM. Traditionally, configuration management only applies to the development of hardware elements of a hardware-software system. It is concerned with the consistent labeling, tracking, and change control of the hardware elements of a system. SCM adapts the traditional discipline to software development. In this chapter, you will learn the following:

- Basic concepts of SCM
- Functions of SCM
- SCM tools

22.1 THE BASELINES OF A SOFTWARE LIFE CYCLE

During the software development life cycle, numerous documents are produced. As each set of documents is produced and passes quality reviews, the project is moving closer toward its completion. In this sense, the successful productions of the needed software artifacts serve as measurements of the progress of the project. More specifically, the productions of such documents at significant check points, such as the end of the requirements phase, the end of the design phase, and so forth, act like the milestones of a long journey. These milestones let us know the progress status of the project and product. If the project reaches the milestones as scheduled, then the team knows that it will be able to complete the project on time; otherwise, the team needs to take action to resolve the discrepancy.

In SCM, the milestones are called *baselines*. A baseline denotes a significant state of the software life cycle. For example, sample base lines for the agile methodology in Figures 2.15 are shown in Figure 22.1. Each baseline is associated with a set of software artifacts or documents produced in the baseline. These artifacts or documents are called *software configuration items* (SCIs). In practice, each project defines its baselines and configuration items taking into con-sideration factors such as project nature, size, budget, and available resources. The concept of a baseline serves several purposes:

1. It defines the important states of progress of a project or product.
2. It signifies that the project or product has reached a given state of progress. That is, a baseline is established when the required SCIs are produced and pass the SQA reviews. At this point, the SCIs are checked in to the configuration management system. Once a configuration item is checked in to the configuration management system, changes to the item must go through a procedure to ensure that the changes will maintain the consistency of the configuration of the system.
3. It forms a common basis for subsequent development activities. Before the establishment of the requirements baseline, the teams could proceed with the design activities but changes to the requirements and use cases are to be expected. The establishment of the requirements baseline "freezes" the documents associated

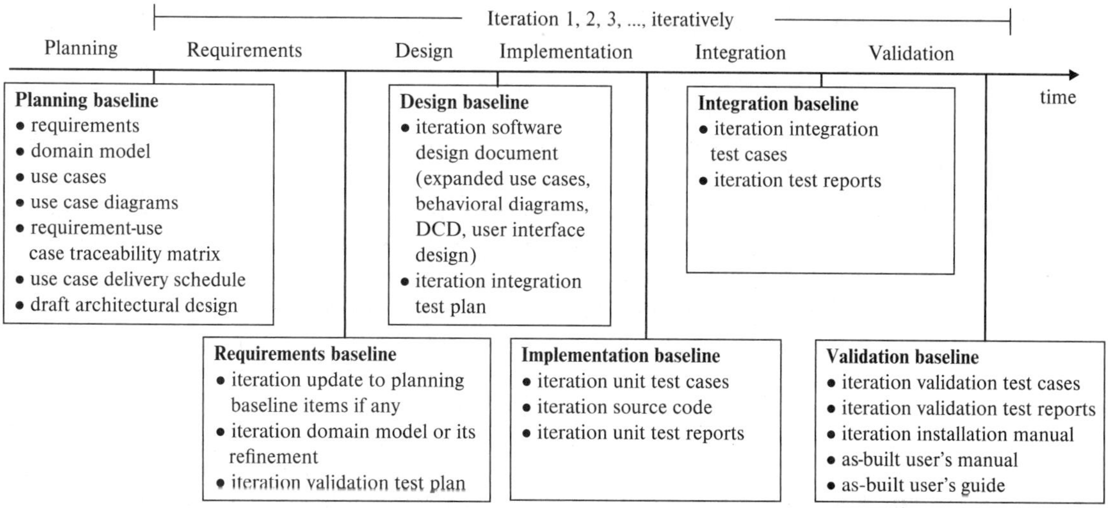

FIGURE 22.1 Sample baselines and configuration items

with the baseline, that is, changes can no longer be made freely. Needed changes must be documented and evaluated to assess their impact to configuration items produced in subsequent activities such as design diagrams and implementation.

4. It is a mechanism to control changes to configuration items as explained in the last bullet.

22.2 WHAT IS SOFTWARE CONFIGURATION MANAGEMENT?

Generally speaking, SCM is baseline management and configuration item management. Baseline management means defining a project's baselines and providing mechanisms to formally establish the baselines. That is, at the beginning of a project, the baselines of the project, the criteria to certify the baselines, and procedures to establish the baselines are defined. For example, a project may adopt the baselines in Figure 22.1. In this case, the criteria for establishing the planning baseline may be that the requirements, optionally a domain model, abstract and high-level use cases, a requirement-use case traceability matrix, a use case delivery schedule, and a draft architectural design are defined, reviewed, and the deficiencies are removed. The procedure for establishing the baseline may be that these documents are authorized to be checked in to the configuration management system. When all these documents are checked in, the baseline is established.

The configuration item management aspect of SCM is concerned with updates that are made to the baseline items. That is, before a document is checked in to the configuration management system, changes to the document can be made freely. However, once the document is checked in, then any update to the document must go through a change control procedure to coordinate the update.

22.3 WHY SOFTWARE CONFIGURATION MANAGEMENT?

For small projects that involve only a few developers working closely at one location, the need for SCM is not acute. The team members can talk to each other in person to synchronize the updates to the software artifacts they produce. However, many real-world software systems are developed by many teams and developers working on shared, interdependent software artifacts simultaneously, at different locations. In these cases, the work of one team cannot be started until other documents are produced. Therefore, mechanisms are needed to establish the baselines and publicize such information so that all of the teams are aware of the progress status of the project. Updates to the software artifacts must be carefully coordinated to allow the teams to assess the impact and avoid inconsistent update or overwriting the work produced by others.

Besides the need to synchronize the multiple distributed teams working together on a project, the need to maintain different versions of a software system requires SCM. Multiple versions of a system are needed to satisfy the needs of different customers, for example, different customers require different modules of the system. If a vendor has a few dozen customers, then the vendor may need to maintain dozens of versions of a software system to satisfy the needs of its customers. In addition, the vendor may need to maintain different releases of a software system. In some cases, there are subtle differences between the compilers from different compiler vendors. This means there are variations in the source code of the software system, resulting in different versions.

In summary, SCM is needed to coordinate the development activities of the multiple development teams and team members, as well as to support maintenance of multiple versions of a software system.

22.4 SOFTWARE CONFIGURATION MANAGEMENT FUNCTIONS

As depicted in Figure 22.2, SCM consists of four main functions. These are outlined below and detailed in the following sections.

- *Software configuration identification* defines the baselines, the configuration items, and a naming schema to uniquely identify each of the configuration items. This function is performed when a new project starts.
- *Configuration change control* exercises control on changes to the configuration items to ensure the consistency of the system configuration and successful cooperation between the teams and team members. This function is performed when change requests arrive, due to events that require changes.
- *Software configuration auditing* verifies and validates the baselines and configuration items, defines and executes mechanisms for formally establishing the baselines, and ensures that proposed changes are properly implemented.
- *Software configuration status accounting* is responsible for tracking and maintaining information about the system configuration. It provides database support to the other three functions.

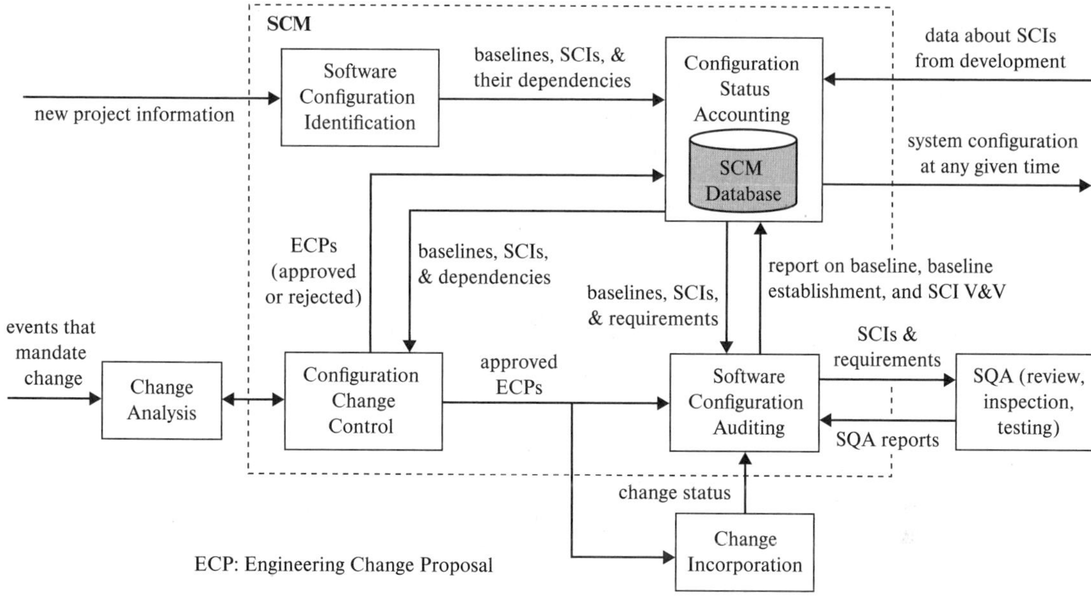

FIGURE 22.2 Software configuration management and process

22.4.1 Software Configuration Identification

During the software development process, numerous documents are produced, used, and updated. Not all documents must be placed under the control of SCM. Which documents need to be managed depend on various factors including project size, development process, and available resources. Software configuration identification defines the baselines and the SCIs for each of the baselines.

For projects that need to manage many configuration items, a model of baseline and configuration items is useful. Figure 22.3 shows a simple model in UML. Configuration items are classified into simple SCIs and composite SCIs. A Simple SCI does not include other configuration items. Examples are an expanded use case, a domain

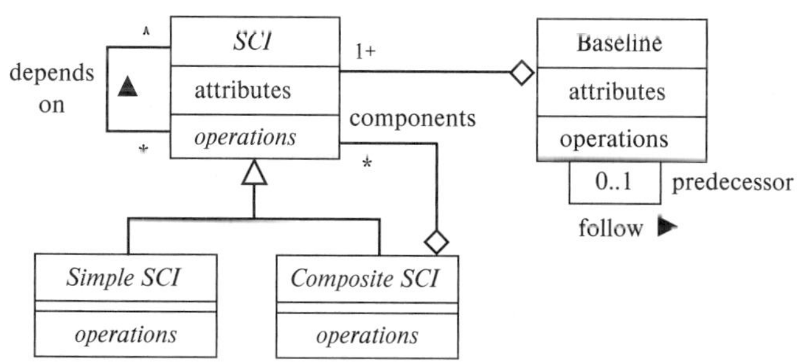

FIGURE 22.3 Modeling baselines and configuration items

model, a sequence diagram, and a design class diagram. A Composite SCI may contain other configuration items. For example, a design specification includes expanded use cases, sequence diagrams, and a design class diagram.

As shown in the model, changes to an SCI may affect other SCIs due to inheritance, aggregation, and association relationships. As an example of change impact due to an association relationship, consider a sequence diagram that is produced for an expanded use case. Obviously, if the expanded use case is modified, the sequence diagram may be affected and may need to be modified as well. As an example of change impact due to an aggregation relationship, consider a design specification that contains the expanded use case and sequence diagram. If the expanded use case is deleted, then the sequence diagram must be deleted. These imply that the design specification must be changed.

The abstract SCI class defines a set of attributes and operations that are common to all SCIs. Useful attributes include, but are not limited to, the following:

- *ID number*–A unique ID to identify the SCI. It should bear certain semantics to communicate the functionality of the SCI and the system or subsystem it belongs to. For example, a domain model constructed during iteration 1 for a library information system (LIS) may have an ID number like LIS-DM-It1.
- *name*–The name of the configuration item, for example, Checkout Document Expanded Use Case, Checkout Document Sequence Diagram, and so on.
- *document type*–The type of the document of the SCI, for example, requirements specification, domain model, design specification, test cases, and the like.
- *document file*–The full path name for the file that contains the SCI.
- *author*–The developer who creates the configuration item.
- *date created, target completion date, and date completed*–These are useful for tracking the status of the SCI.
- *version number*–This is used to keep track of the multiple versions of a configuration item.
- *update history*–A list of update summaries, each of which briefly specifies the update, who performs the update, and date of update.
- *description*–A brief description of the configuration item.
- *SQA personnel*–A technical staff who is responsible for the quality assurance of the configuration item.
- *SCM personnel*–A technical staff who is responsible for checking in the configuration item.

A simple SCI may have concrete operations to set and get attributes. It may also include operations for verifying and validating the SCI as well as computing metrics. A composite SCI has operations to add, remove, and get SCIs. Finally, a baseline has operations to add, remove, and get a predecessor as well as an SCI. To apply the model, each project extends the abstract leaf classes to provide concrete implementation of the abstract operations. In particular, a subclass is created for a set of SCIs that share the same behavior.

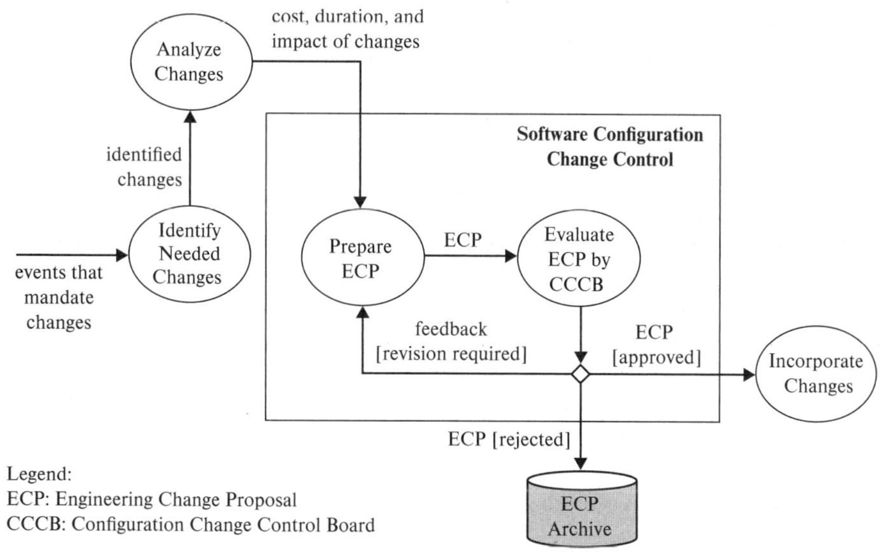

FIGURE 22.4 Software configuration change control

22.4.2 Software Configuration Change Control

As illustrated in Figure 22.4, SCCC involves the following activities but only two of them are SCCC functions:

1. *Identify changes required by various events.* Many events mandate changes to the SCIs. These events include:
    a. Software deficiencies, for example, the functionality is inadequate or incorrect, the performance is unacceptable.
    b. Hardware changes, for example, replacement of the computer or hardware devices.
    c. Changes to operational requirements, for example, a new security procedure requires that passwords must satisfy strong password rules and be changed periodically.
    d. Improvement and enhancement requests from customer and users, for example, improvement to user interface and actor-system interaction behavior are required.
    e. Changes to budget, project duration, and schedule are required, for example, the schedule needs to be adjusted to meet an emerging business situation, or the budget is cut and the system's capabilities must be reduced.
2. *Analyze changes.* When any of the events occur, the team needs to identify changes to the configuration items to respond to the change event. The changes are analyzed by respective experts who are the developers in most cases.

3. *Prepare an engineering change proposal.* The changes and analysis results are used to prepare an ECP. The ECP consists of administrative forms, and supporting technical and administrative materials that specify, among others, the following:
   a. Description of the proposed changes.
   b. Identification of originating organization or developer.
   c. Rationale for the changes.
   d. Identification of affected baselines and SCIs.
   e. Effort, time, and cost required to implement the proposed changes as well as the priority of each of the proposed changes.
   f. Impact to project schedule.
4. *Evaluate engineering change proposals.* The ECP is reviewed by a configuration change control board (CCCB), which consists of representatives from different parties, especially parties whose work and schedule will be affected by the changes. Three different outcomes are possible: (1) the proposal is rejected, in this case, it is archived; (2) changes to the proposal are required, in this case, it is returned to proposal preparation function; and (3) the proposal is approved, in this case, the changes are made.
5. *Incorporate changes.* The approved changes are made to the software system.

22.4.3 Software Configuration Auditing

The SCA function has the following responsibilities:

1. *Defining mechanisms for establishing and formally establishing a baseline.* A baseline can exist in one of two states: (1) a to-be-established (TBE) baseline, and (2) a sanctioned baseline. A TBE baseline is brought to existence when one of the associated documents is produced and entered into the SCM system. A sanctioned baseline is established when all of the associated configuration items are produced and pass SQA inspection, review and/or testing, and entered into the SCM system.
2. *Configuration item verification.* This ensures that what is intended for each configuration item as specified in one baseline or update is achieved in a succeeding baseline or update. For example, for each high-level use case allocated to an iteration in the requirements baseline, there must be an expanded use case in the design baseline that specifies how the system and the actor would interact to carry out the front-end processing of the use case.
3. *Configuration item validation.*This checks the correctness to ensure that the configuration item solves the right problem. Consider, for example, the Checkout Document use case of a LIS. Verification ensures that there is an expanded use case in the succeeding baseline. Validation ensures that the specification of the expanded use case indeed matches the user's expectation.
4. *Ensuring that changes specified in approved ECPs are properly and timely implemented.*

22.4.4 Software Configuration Status Accounting

Software configuration status accounting tracks and reports information about the configuration items. As depicted in Figure 22.2, it provides database support to the other three SCM functions. As such, the SCM database increases in complexity and amount of data that need to be maintained as the project progresses. Data that need to be stored include descriptive information about the SCIs and baselines, description of ECPs and their status, change status, deficiencies of a TBE baseline as a result of configuration auditing, relationships between the configuration items, and relationships between baselines and configuration items.

22.5 CONFIGURATION MANAGEMENT IN AN AGILE PROJECT

Agile projects welcome change and need to respond to changes rapidly. However, conventional configuration management involves a rigorous and often lengthy change control process. This greatly hinders and slows down the iterative development process. Therefore, only a few agile methods, such as Feature Driven Development (FDD) and Dynamic Systems Development Method (DSDM), explicitly require configuration change control. These methods consider SCM as a best practice. Although the rigor of a change control process is viewed as unfavorable for agile development, the other capabilities of SCM tools are useful for agile projects. In particular, version control, concurrency control, and rapid system build capabilities provided by version control systems and integrated development environments (IDEs) are highly valued and widely used by agile methods such as Crystal Clear, DSDM, FDD, and Extreme Programming (XP).

22.6 SOFTWARE CONFIGURATION MANAGEMENT TOOLS

SCM activities must maintain and process a lot of data and SCIs, which are related to each other in a complex manner such as trees with branches denoting releases, versions, and revisions. In addition, SCM tools need to notify relevant teams and team members of the state of the SCIs and changes to the SCIs. Concurrent updates to the SCIs may be needed to improve efficiency. Such updates require concurrency control to ensure consistency. Clearly, SCM tools are needed to support these activities. This section presents the capabilities of such tools.

The capabilities provided by SCM tools vary significantly. Some SCM tools provide full support to all SCM activities while others support only a subset of the SCM activities. Which SCM tools to use depend on the project. In general, large, mission-critical systems or distributed development require more SCM functions. Small, agile projects tend to use only version control tools. A typical SCM tool provides the following capabilities:

- *Version control.* The objective of version control is to manage the releases, versions, and revisions of a software system. It is used during the development process as well as the maintenance phase. The need for such a function has been discussed in the *"Why Software Configuration Management"* section.

- *Workspace management.* Software engineers work together to design and implement a software system. To coordinate the work of the software engineers, a central repository of software artifacts is needed. Workspace management provides local workspaces for the software engineers and the central repository for the software engineers to share their work. It allows the software engineers to check in local files to the repository, and check out repository files to their workspaces.
- *Concurrency control.* Software engineers may need to work on the same set of files simultaneously, which may result in inconsistent updates. Concurrency control provides mechanisms to enable or disable concurrent updates. If concurrent update is enabled, then the tool provides mechanisms to merge the concurrent updates and facilitate resolution of conflicts.
- *System build.* The system build capability allows the team to specify the system configuration, that is, which versions of which components should be included in a system. The SCM tool will automatically compile and link the components to produce the executable system.
- *Support to SCM process.* This capability is aimed at automating the SCM procedures described in previous sections.

Tools that provide version control, workspace management, and concurrency control include RCS, CVS and OpenCVS Subversion (SVN), IBM ClearCase, Git, and many others. RCS controls access to shared files through an access list of login names and the ability to lock and unlock a revision. CVS is a substantial extension of RCS and is a preinstalled plugin of NetBeans. Subversion is initially designed to replace CVS; and hence, it possesses all of the CVS capabilities. However, since its inception in 2000, Subversion has evolved beyond a CVS replacement and introduced a comprehensive set of advanced features. Figure 22.5 is a comparative summary of

	RCS	CVS/Subversion	ClearCase
Change management	Yes	Yes	Yes
Work on binary files	Yes	Yes	Yes
Architecture	Single machine	Client-Server	
Mode of operation	Individual files, exclusive mode of editing	Hierarchies of files and directories, concurrent editing	Hierarchies of files and directories, concurrent editing
Distributed	No	Yes	Yes
Platform supported	Linux/Unix, Windows	Usually Linux/Unix Server, client can run any major OS	Windows, Linux/Unix, z/OS, AIX
Support for offline use	Yes	Yes	Yes
Integration with IDEs	No	Integrated with NetBeans	Yes
Support for concurrent engineering	No	Yes	Yes
Revision tracking & audit	Yes	Yes	Yes
Free	Yes	Yes	No

FIGURE 22.5 A comparative summary of some versioning systems

some of the features of RCS, CVS, Subversion, and ClearCase. Appendix C.7 describes in detail how to use CVS and Subversion in NetBeans.

Tools that support system build include *make* and *ant*. Make is a UNIX/Linux utility and ant provides the functions of make to build systems using Java components. These tools let the software engineer specify a script or a sequence of commands. System build is accomplished by executing the script. Nowadays, system build is supported by almost all of the IDEs.

22.7 SUMMARY

This chapter presents the notion of a baseline and the baselines of a typical project. A baseline represents a significant achievement of the software project. The establishment of a baseline signifies that the project has reached a new status of progress. Besides this, the baselines also serve to control change to the software artifacts. Before a given baseline is established, all of the artifacts of the baseline can be modified freely. However, after the baseline is established, changes to the artifacts or SCIs must go through a change control process.

The functions of SCM are software configuration item identification, SCCC, SCA, and software configuration status accounting. These functions form the SCM process as shown in Figure 22.2. The SCM activities need to process a lot of data and software artifacts. Therefore, tools are needed to support SCM activities. This chapter presents the capabilities of SCM tools. How to use CVS and Subversion in the NetBeans IDE is given in Appendix C.7. Finally, the chapter summarizes the state-of-the-practice of SCM in agile methods. That is, although only a few agile methods require SCM, almost all agile methods use version control systems and system build tools such as an IDE.

22.8 CHAPTER REVIEW QUESTIONS

1. What are baselines? What are the baselines of the agile process described in this chapter?
2. What is SCM?
3. Why do we need SCM?
4. What are the functional components of SCM, and how do they relate to each other?
5. What is change control, what is the change control process, and why is change control needed in software development?
6. What are the functions of software configuration auditing?
7. What are the version control tools presented in this chapter, and what are their functions?

22.9 EXERCISES

22.1 Describe, with examples, how to use the model in Figure 22.3 to represent the baselines and the associated baseline configuration items in Figure 22.1. *Hint:* For this exercise, you do not need to construct the complete model; it is enough to show just how to represent a couple of baselines and a few associated configuration items.

22.2 Suppose that you work on a project to develop a library information system using the conventional waterfall process. Define the baselines for the project, identify and specify the configuration items for the baselines.

22.3 Suppose that during the implementation phase of the library information system project, a fatal design flaw is discovered in the architectural design. The architectural design must be modified. You are required to coordinate this activity. Therefore, you are required to addresses the following issues:

a. *Engineering change proposal (ECP).* What is an ECP, who should be responsible for writing the ECP, and what should be included in the ECP for this change?

b. *ECP evaluation board.* What is the name of the board or committee that will review and evaluate the ECP? What are the responsibilities of this organizational unit? Who are the possible members of this organizational unit? What are the possible outcomes of the review and evaluation process, and why?

c. *Post evaluation.* What are the possible actions to take place after the ECP is reviewed and evaluated, taking into account the possible outcomes of the ECP evaluation process?

22.4 Do the same as in exercise 22.2, except that the project uses one of the agile methods presented in Chapter 2.

22.5 Identify all possible SCIs for each of the agile methods described in Chapter 2.

part **VIII**

Project Management and Software Security

23 Chapter

Software Project Management

Key Takeaway Points

- Software project management is concerned with the management aspect of software engineering.
- Software project management is focused on effort estimation, planning and scheduling, software process, process improvement, and risk management.

Software systems are large, complex, intellectual products. Managing software development projects is different from managing projects in other engineering disciplines. This is due to the nature of software and software development. First of all, software is an intangible product–you cannot really see it, you cannot touch it, and you cannot accurately and directly measure it, but it exists. These properties make it difficult to estimate the effort required to develop a software product and measure the progress of the software project. Second, software development activities are intellectual activities. Today's software projects require a large number of software engineers working in teams. The teams and team members must communicate and collaborate to jointly carry out the development activities. These create challenges to software project management, especially in project organization, planning and scheduling of development activities, assigning work to project teams and team members, and monitoring the progress.

Effective communication is critical for software development and incurs extremely high communication overhead. This is because the content being communicated is intellectual, complex, abstract, and easy to misinterpret. Software project management has to consider software process and team organization to ensure effective communication and reduce communication overhead. Software project management must include risk management because many events could jeopardize the success of the project. Finally, the development and management processes must be integrated and continually improving.

Software project management is concerned with the management aspect of software engineering to increase software productivity and quality, and reduce software cost and time to market. This chapter presents software project management concepts and techniques to ensure that these management goals are accomplished, that is, that the budget is not overrun, and the product is delivered with the required functionality and quality, according to the schedule.

The importance of project management cannot be overstated. Two real-world stories, referred to as the National Health System (NHS) project and the Textile Process Control (TPC) project, illustrate this. The NHS project was reported in 2006 and involved a large IT consulting firm as the developer. The developer lost hundreds of millions of dollars due to cost overruns and the delayed delivery of the software system to the national health organization of an European country. The company paid a penalty of approximately $100M. The penalty would have been $500M if the contract had not been taken over by its competitor. The TPC project was about a small IT consulting company.[1] The company won a "death march" project to implement a system for a textile manufacturer in an eastern U.S. state. The project was a "death march" project because the analysis and design were carried out by another company. This means that the implementation team would not have the needed domain knowledge to implement the system. It would be an extremely lucky case if the analysis and design documents produced by the previous developer could truly communicate that knowledge. As expected, the implementation team could not deliver the system by the deadline. The company had to choose between two options–paying a huge lumpsum penalty to walk away or paying $1M per month until the system is delivered. These two stories partly reflect poor management decisions. They also illustrate the importance of good management to the success of a software project. In the following sections, you will learn the following:

- Project formats and team organization
- Estimation methods
- Software project planning and scheduling
- Risk management
- Process improvement

23.1 PROJECT ORGANIZATION

Managing a software project must address a number of issues relating to project organization. That is, how the teams are formed, how the teams and team members work together to carry out the life-cycle activities, what roles and responsibilities are needed in a software project, and factors that affect the project organization. This section deals with these issues.

23.1.1 Project Format

The project format is concerned with how the life-cycle activities are assigned to the project teams. Three project formats have been used in practice: *project-based format,*

[1]Private communication.

function-based format, and *hybrid format*. With the project-based format, each project is assigned to a project team, which performs all the life-cycle activities from the beginning of the project to the end. This format is applicable to all types of projects and is widely used. It lets the project team accumulate knowledge about the life-cycle activities, the application domain, and the system under development. These are essential for the success of the project and are valuable for future projects. It is desirable to include an expert in each functional area (i.e., analysis, design, implementation, testing, and deployment) in the team. However, this is not always feasible. For example, highly capable systems analysts and system architects are sometimes difficult to find and expensive to hire. Training, hiring an expert consultant, or learning on the job are possible solutions.

With the function-based format, each life-cycle activity is assigned to a team that is specialized in that functional area. That is, a requirements analysis team is responsible for the requirements analysis activity of a project, while a design team is responsible for the design activity of the project, and so on. The function teams work in a pipeline manner to perform the life-cycle activities of each project. The function-based format is more suitable for large corporations that are constantly involved in the development of many medium-scale and large-scale projects, to justify for the switching overhead between the function teams. The function-based format may not work for projects that require the development team to bring the knowledge about the system from one life-cycle activity to another. For example, the TPC project described at the beginning of this chapter failed because the implementation team did not participate in the analysis and design of the system. The knowledge of the process control application is critical to the implementation of the system. In other words, the function-based format is only suitable for well-defined and well-understood applications, which include system software, office automation systems, and so forth. The merits of the function-based format include:

1. Specialized teams tend to increase effectiveness and efficiency because the function teams can be formed by members who are experts in the functional areas.
2. It works well for a distributed development environment in which different functional activities are performed at different locations. For example, analysis and design are performed close to the customer site, implementation at a less-expensive location, and testing is carried out elsewhere.
3. It could result in lower development costs because of increased effectiveness and efficiency, a reduced number of high-paid analysts/architects, and reduced cost and increased utilization of special equipment such as analysis, design, and test tools.

The function-based format requires high-quality documentation, especially requirements specification and design specification. This is because the design team relies on the requirements specification to produce a quality design, and the implementation and test teams rely on the requirements and design documents to implement and test the system. These mean that in general the function-based format is not suitable for agile projects that emphasize light documentation.

The function-based format also requires that the team members possess sufficient domain knowledge. Therefore, it is not suitable for software development organizations with projects that come from a wide variety of application domains. It is most suitable for software product vendors that are specialized in a category of software products. These include system software vendors, word processor vendors, tax preparation software vendors, and many other specialized software vendors.

A combination of the project-based format and the function-based format is widely used in many software development organizations. For example, many systems are analyzed, designed, and implemented by one team and tested by another team. There are many cases in which the software requirements specification is produced by a system engineering team, designed and implemented by a software development team, and tested by a system testing team.

With the *hybrid format*, a project manager leads the project through the various function teams. Since the project manager participates in all the life-cycle activities, he or she carries with him or her the knowledge from one team to another. The manager also knows who to contact for more information. The hybrid format inherits the merits of the function-based format and overcomes its shortcomings.

23.1.2 Team Structure

The team structure is concerned with the organization of the project teams, that is, assigning roles and responsibilities to the team members. The commonly seen team structures include egoless team structure, chief programmer team structure, and hierarchical team structure. These are described below.

Egoless Team Structure

The egoless team structure is a project team model in which all team members participate in decision making and decisions are usually made by consensus. The team members work together and communicate with all the other team members. That is, the communication overhead is $N \times (N-1)/2$, where N is the number of team members. If N is large, then the overhead will be high. For example, a five-member team has an overhead of 10 while an eight-member team has an overhead of 28. Besides the communication overhead, the larger the team size, the more difficult to find a meeting time to accommodate all of the team members.

The egoless team structure is suitable for agile projects and projects that need to tackle challenging analysis and design problems. This is because egoless team structure values individuals and interaction, and creates an environment suitable for brainstorming–an effective technique for solving challenging problems. It is important to understand that it is impossible and not necessary to agree on everything at all times. This is because the team members come from different background and with different experiences. However, it is essential that the team members have a mutual understanding of why you want to do things that way. This mutual understanding allows the team members to work toward a common goal once a decision is made.

The egoless team structure may be less productive if the team is divided. In such cases, the issues should be resolved as quickly as possible so that the project can move on. Sometimes, the problem is due to different opinions; in such cases, the team may take a vote to resolve differences.

Chief Programmer Team Structure

The chief programmer team structure consists of a chief programmer, who leads the project, makes important design decisions, and supervises the other team members. The chief programmer may design and implement critical parts of the system and may consult with various specialists when making design decisions. The chief programmer structure reduces communication overhead because the team members communicate only with the chief programmer most of the time. In this case, the communication overhead is reduced to many-to-one from many-to-many. It may yield higher productivity because less time is spent in discussion and more time is spent in production. The FDD agile method uses this team structure. The ability of the chief programmer is critical for the success of the project. The chief programmer should possess a number of characteristic traits including strong technical abilities, good communication skills, management skills, and leadership. The chief programmer could be expensive and difficult to find. If the chief programmer resigns in the middle of a project and there is no suitable replacement, then the project could be in jeopardy.

Hierarchical Team Structure

The hierarchical team structure consists of a project manager, who supervises a number of senior software engineers, each in turn supervises a number of junior software engineers, and so forth. Major design decisions are made by the project manager and the senior software engineers, who also design and implement the system. The communication overhead includes the communication overhead between the project manager and the senior software engineers, and the communication overhead among the team members supervised by each of the senior software engineers. The hierarchical team structure can be viewed as combining the egoless team structure and the chief programmer team structure. Therefore, it has the benefits of the egoless and chief programmer structures. Today, many software development organizations use this structure.

23.2 EFFORT ESTIMATION METHODS

One important project management function is effort estimation. Effort estimation is required to plan and schedule a project. The effort is usually expressed as person-month or person-week. Thus a 96 person-months project would require eight software engineers working for one year. The average monthly salary of a software engineer multiplied by the number of person-months gives the total salary costs of the project. If the project has to be completed in six months, then 16 software engineers are required. However, such a compression in a project schedule may result in project failure or drastically increase project costs. When moving a pile of dirt, a team can double the workforce to reduce the time by half. However, it is not the case for creating software. This is because the increase in team size drastically increases the communication and coordination overhead. For example, the overhead is $8 * (8 - 1)/2 = 28$ and $16 * (16 - 1)/2 = 120$ for 8 and 16 persons, respectively. That is, the effort to communicate and coordinate increases substantially.

23.2.1 The Function Point Method

The function point (FP) of a system is a product of the gross function point (GFP) and the processing complexity adjustment (PCA). That is, $FP = GFP \times PCA$. The method involves six steps:

1. Determine the counts for each of five function categories and fill these in the FP worksheet shown in Figure 23.1.
2. Determine the complexity for each function category (simple, average, complex) and circle the corresponding entry in Figure 23.1.
3. Compute the GFPs. That is, multiply each function category count with the corresponding complexity value and sum up the products:

$$GFP = \sum_{i=1}^{5}(Count_i \times Complexity_i)$$

4. Assign a processing complexity PC_i, which is an integer value between 0 and 5, to each of the following 14 questions, with 0 indicates no influence, 1 incidental, 2 moderate, 3 average, 4 significant, and 5 essential:
   a. Does the system require reliable backup and recovery?
   b. Are data communications required?
   c. Are there distributed processing functions?
   d. Is performance critical?
   e. Will the system run in an existing, heavily utilized operational environment?
   f. Does the system require online data entry?
   g. Does the online data entry require the input transaction to be built over multiple screens or operations?
   h. Are the master files updated online?

	Function Category	Count	Complexity			Count × Complexity
			Simple	Average	Complex	
1	Number of user input		3	4	6	
2	Number of user output		4	5	7	
3	Number of user queries		3	4	6	
4	Number of data files and relational tables		7	10	15	
5	Number of external interfaces		5	7	10	
					GFP	

FIGURE 23.1 Gross function point worksheet

i. Are the inputs, outputs, files, or inquiries complex?
j. Is the internal processing complex?
k. Is the code designed to be reusable?
l. Are conversion and installation included in the design?
m. Is the system designed for multiple installations in different organizations?
n. Is the application designed to facilitate change and ease of use by the user?

5. Compute the processing complexity adjustment (PCA) for the whole system as follows:

$$PCA = 0.65 + 0.01 \sum_{i=1}^{14} PC_i$$

where 0.65 is an empirical constant ($0.65 \leq PCA \leq 1.35$).

6. Compute the function points

$$FP = GFP \times PCA$$

Clearly, the following invariant is true at all times:

$$GFP \times (1 - 0.35) \leq FP \leq GFP \times (1 + 0.35)$$

EXAMPLE 23.1 A shipping software is estimated to have the following function category counts: number of user inputs = 10, number of user outputs = 5, number of user queries = 8, number of data files = 30, number of external interfaces = 4. The complexity for each of these is simple.

The processing complexity values for the 14 questions are all average except that reliable backup and user-friendliness is essential (PC1 = 5 and PC14 = 5). Assume that the productivity of the development team is 60 function points per person-week. Estimate the effort required for this project.

Solution: First, enter the counts and circle the complexities in Figure 23.1 and compute the GFP:

$$GFP = 10 \times 3 + 5 \times 4 + 8 \times 3 + 30 \times 7 + 4 \times 5 = 304 \text{ FP}$$

The PCA is then computed:

$$PCA = 12 \times 3 + 2 \times 5 = 46$$

From these, compute the FP:

$$FP = GFP \times PCA = 304 \times 46 = 13984FP$$

Finally, the estimated effort is obtained:

$$E = FP/productivity = 13984/60 = 233 \text{ person-weeks}$$

The FP method has a number of merits. It is possible to estimate early in the life-cycle, for example, from the use cases. It can be used by a relatively nontechnical person. It is independent of the implementation language. Problems of the

FP method are that it is considered subjective by some authors, and for some projects the category counts may not be easy to obtain in an early development stage.

23.2.2 The COCOMO II Model

The COCOMO II is an update to the COCOMO model. COCOMO II takes into consideration modern software development practices. COCOMO II consists of three models: *Application Composition, Early Design*, and *Post-Architecture* models.

The Application Composition Model

The application composition model is used during the early stages of the life-cycle to estimate effort required to build a prototype. It is also used for projects that construct systems from commercial off-the-shelf (COTS) software components. Examples of such components-based systems include graphic user interface (GUI) builders, database or object managers, middleware for distributed as well as transaction processing, hypermedia handlers, smart data finders, and domain-specific components such as financial, medical, or industrial process control packages. Effort calculation using the application composition model involves seven steps:

1. Count the number of screens, reports, and 3GL components that will comprise the application.[2]
2. Determine the *complexity levels* of each of the screens and reports using Figure 23.2(*a*).
3. Look up the complexity weights for each of the screens, reports, and 3GL components from Figure 23.2(*b*).
4. Add the weighted counts of screens, reports and 3GL components to produce one number, called the *Object Point* (OP) count.
5. Estimate the percentage of reuse to be achieved, and compute the *New Object Points* (NOPs) to be developed in the project:

$$NOP = OP \times (100 - Reuse)/100$$

6. Determine the object point productivity from Figure 23.2(*c*), that is, the average of two capabilities shown in Figure 23.2(*c*).
7. Compute the person-month effort: Effort $PM = NOP/PROD$

EXAMPLE 23.2

The planning phase of a project needs to prototype a part of the system. The prototype requires four screens, three reports, and no 3GL component. Each screen has one view and accesses to one server data table. The first report has two sections

[2] 3GL stands for "third-generation programming languages," which include high-level programming languages such as C, C++, C#, and Java.

For Screens				For Reports			
# of Views Contained	# of data tables			# of Sections Contained	# of data tables		
	< 4	< 8	8+		<4	<8	8+
< 3	simple	simple	medium	0 or 1	simple	simple	medium
3–7	simple	medium	difficult	2 or 3	simple	medium	difficult
>8	medium	difficult	difficult	4+	medium	difficult	difficult

Note: The original table also takes into account the sources of the data tables, i.e., number of data tables from a server or a client. This table omits this distinction to simplify the process.

(a) Complexity levels

Object Type	Complexity Weight		
	Simple	Medium	Difficult
Screen	1	2	3
Report	2	5	8
3GL Component			10

(b) Complexity weight

Developers' experience & capability ICASE maturity & capability	Low	Very Low	Nominal	High	Very High
PROD (NOP/month)	4	7	13	25	50

(c) Object point productivity

FIGURE 23.2 FIGURE 23.2 Complexity levels for screens and reports

and does not use any data table. Each of the other two reports has more than three sections and accesses to four server tables. Fifty percent of the prototype will reuse existing components. The development environment is average (i.e., nominal) but the team has little experience in the application domain (i.e., low). Compute the effort for this project.

Solution: Each of the four screens is simple so each has 1 object point. The subtotal is 4. The first report is simple so it has 2 object points. Each of the other two reports has 8 object points; the subtotal is 16. The total is 22. Taking into consideration 50% reuse, so the new object point or NOP is 11. The average of low developer experience and capability and nominal ICASE maturity and capability is $(7+13)/2 = 10$. That is, PROD $= 10$. Thus, Effort $PM = NOP/PROD = 1.1$ person-month.

The Early Design Model

The early design model is used in the early stages of a software project when very little about the software size and the target environment is known. The basic formula for effort calculation is:

$$\text{Effort } PM = a \times size^b \times \prod_{i=1}^{n} EM_i$$

where $a = 2.94$ is a constant, b is computed using five project specific scale factors (SFs), *size* is the estimated software system size in thousand source lines of code or KSLOC, $n = 7$ denotes the number of effort modifiers, and EM_i are the effort modifiers. The following describes how to obtain these input parameters.

Estimate Software Size The software size in thousand source lines of code (KSLOC) can be estimated in two different ways: direct estimation or using function points (not the same as the FP method presented above). The approach that uses function points is described here. First, count each of the function types as follows:

- *External inputs.* Count each unique user data or control input type that updates an internal file.
- *External outputs.* Count each unique user data or control output type that leaves the software system.
- *Internal logical files.* Count each major group of user data or control information in the system including files that are generated, used, or maintained by the software system.
- *External interface files or interfaces.* Count files passed or shared between software systems.
- *External queries.* Count unique external queries that produce an immediate output.

For each of the counted items, determine the complexity level and then the weighted function points from Figure 23.3. Sum up the weighted function points for all of the counted items to produce an unadjusted function point (UFP) value.

For Internal Logical Files and External Interfaces				For External Outputs and Queries				For External Inputs			
#Records	#Data Elements			#File Types	#Data Elements			#File Types	#Data Elements		
	1-19	20-50	51+		1-5	6-19	20+		1-4	5-15	16+
1	Low	Low	Avg	0 or 1	Low	Low	Avg	0 or 1	Low	Low	Avg
2-5	Low	Avg	High	2-3	Low	Avg	High	2-3	Low	Avg	High
6+	Avg	High	High	4+	Avg	High	High	3+	Avg	High	High

(a) Determine function type complexity levels

Function Type	Complexity Weight		
	Low	Average	High
Internal Logical	7	10	15
External Interfaces	5	7	10
External Inputs	3	4	6
External Outputs	4	5	7
External Queries	3	4	6

(b) Determine function type complexity weights

FIGURE 23.3 Determine function points for each function type

Scale Factor	Description	Very Low	Low	Nominal	High	Very High	Extra High
PREC	Experience of the team with this type of project	6.20	4.96	3.72	2.48	1.24	0.00
FLEX	Flexibility that is given to the development team	5.07	4.05	3.04	2.03	1.01	0.00
RESL	Extent of design carried out, and risk elimination	7..07	5.65	4.24	2.83	1.41	0.00
TEAM	Teamwork	5.48	4.38	3.29	2.19	1.10	0.00
PMAT	Process maturity level (level 1 lower half and upper half are very low and low, respectively)	7.80	6.24	4.68	3.12	1.56	0.00

FIGURE 23.4 COCOMO II scale factors

Convert the unadjusted function points to thousand lines of source code or KSLOC as follows. First, look up a mapping table to determine the SLOC per UFP for the implementation language. The SLOC per UFP values are: Ada 71, APL 32, C 128, C++ 55, ANSI Cobol 85 91, Fortran 77 107, HTML 15, Java 53, Lisp 64, Modula 2 80, Pascal 91, PERL 27, Prolog 64, Spreadsheet 6, Unix Shell Scripts 107, Visual Basic 5.0 29, Visual C++ 34. Next, multiply the looked up value and the UFP value and divide the result by 1000 to produce the KSLOC.

Adjust Size for Requirements Volatility Requirements change could result in code that is developed but not delivered. If the discarded amount of code is not negligible, then it must be added to the estimated software size to adjust for requirements change.

Calculate Constant *b* The constant b takes into account five project and development team factors, called scale factors (SF), which can be looked up from Figure 23.4. The constant b is then computed using the following formula:

$$b = 0.91 + 0.01 \times (SF_1 + \cdots + SF5)$$

Cost Drivers for the Early Design Model There are seven cost drivers for the early design model. Their meanings and ranges of values are described below. The modifier values are listed in the order for Extra-Low, Very-Low, Low, Nominal, High, Very-High, Extra-High.

1. *Personnel Capability (PERS).* This reflects the analyst capability, programmer capability, and personnel continuity of the project team. The values are: 2.12, 1.62, 1.26, 1.00, 0.83, 0.63, 0.50.
2. *Product Reliability and Complexity (RCPX).* This is concerned with the requirements on software reliability and life-cycle-related documentation. Also considered is the complexity of the software and the size of the database. The values are: 0.49, 0.60, 0.83, 1.00, 1.33, 1.91, 2.72.
3. *Developed for Reusability (RUSE).* This is concerned with whether components of the software system must be developed with reuse in mind. The values are: n/a, n/a, 0.95, 1.00, 1.07, 1.15, 1.24.
4. *Platform Difficulty (PDIF).* This is concerned with execution time and main memory constraints as well as platform volatility. The values are: n/a, n/a, 0.87, 1.00, 1.29, 1.81, 2.61.

5. *Personnel Experience (PREX).* This is concerned with experiences with the application, programming languages, tools, and platform. The values are: 1.59, 1.33, 1.22, 1.00, 0.87, 0.74, 0.62.
6. *Facilities (FCIL).* This is concerned with the use of software tools and multisite development. The values are: 1.43, 1.30, 1.10, 1.0, 0.87, 0.73, 0.62.
7. *Required Development Schedule (SCED).* This is concerned with flexibility of development schedule expansion. The values are: n/a, 1.43, 1.14, 1.00, 1.00, 1.00, n/a.

Account for Effort to Reuse Components Effort is required to handle reusable components. This effort should be added to the computed effort estimate PM. The reuse effort could be computed by estimating the reused KSLOC less the amount of such code that is automatically generated, and divide the result by the productivity to adapt reused code.

The Post-Architecture Model

As the name suggested, the post-architecture model is used when the software architecture of the system has been developed. The post-architecture models share everything with the early design model except that there are 17 cost drivers as shown in Figure 23.5.

Driver	Description	VL	L	N	H	VH	XH
RELY	Required Software Reliability	0.82	0.92	1.00	1.10	1.26	–
DATA	Database Size	–	0.90	1.00	1.14	1.28	–
CPLX	Product Complexity	0.73	0.87	1.00	1.17	1.34	1.74
RUSE	Developed for Reusability	–	0.95	1.00	1.07	1.15	1.24
DOCU	Documentation Match to Life-Cycle Needs	0.81	0.91	1.00	1.11	1.23	–
TIME	Execution Time Constraint	–	–	1.00	1.11	1.29	1.63
STOR	Main Storage Constraint	–	–	1.00	1.05	1.17	1.46
PVOL	Platform Volatility	–	0.87	1.00	1.15	1.30	–
ACAP	Analyst Capability	1.42	1.19	1.00	0.85	0.71	–
PCAP	Programmer Capability	1.34	1.15	1.00	0.88	0.76	–
PCON	Personnel Continuity	1.29	1.12	1.00	0.90	0.81	–
APEX	Application Experience	1.22	1.10	1.00	0.88	0.81	–
PLEX	Platform Experience	1.19	1.09	1.00	0.91	0.85	–
LTEX	Language and Tool Experience	1.20	1.09	1.00	0.91	0.84	–
TOOL	Use of Software Tools	1.17	1.09	1.00	0.90	0.78	–
SITE	Multisites Development	1.22	1.09	1.00	0.93	0.86	0.80
SCED	Required Development Schedule	1.43	1.14	1.00	1.00	1.00	–

Legend: VL=very low, L=low, N=neutral, H=high, VH=very high, XH=extra high

FIGURE 23.5 Cost drivers for the post-architecture model

Compute Development Time with COCOMO II

The following is the formula to compute the required development time in COCOMO II, where $c = 3.67$, $d = 0.28$, and b is the constant computed earlier:

$$\text{Development Time } TDEV = c \times PM^{d+0.2\times(b-0.91)}$$

EXAMPLE 23.3 A real-time embedded process control software is estimated to have 52 KLOC. All of the scale factors and cost drivers are nominal except that the system requires very high reliability (1.26) and very high execution time constraint (1.29). Compute effort, duration, and number of developers required for this project using the post-architecture model.

Solution: First, compute the constant b as follows:

$$b = 0.91 + 0.01 \times (SF_1 + \cdots + SF5) = 0.91 + 0.01 \times (3.72 + 3.04 + 4.24 + 3.29 + 4.68)$$

$$= 0.91 + 0.01 \times 18.97 = 0.91 + 0.1897 = 1.0997$$

Next, compute the effort as follows:

$$PM = a \times size^b \times \prod_{i=1}^{n} EM_i = 2.94 \times 52^{1.0997} \times 1.26 \times 1.29$$

$$= 2.94 \times 52^{1.0997} \times 1.26 \times 1.29 = 2.94 \times 77.106 \times 1.26 \times 1.29$$

$$= 226.692 \times 1.26 \times 1.29 = 285.632 \times 1.29 = 368.465$$

The development time is:

$$TDEV = c \times PM^{d+0.2\times(b-0.91)}$$

$$= 3.67 \times 368.465^{0.28+0.2\times(1.0997-0.91)}$$

$$= 3.67 \times 368.465^{0.28+0.2\times0.1897}$$

$$= 3.67 \times 368.465^{0.28+0.2\times0.1897}$$

$$= 3.67 \times 368.465^{0.28+0.03794}$$

$$= 3.67 \times 368.465^{0.318}$$

$$= 3.67 \times 6.548 = 24 \text{ months}$$

Finally, the number of developers is:

$$N = PM/TDEV = 368.465/24 = 15.35$$

23.2.3 The Delphi Estimation Method

The Delphi estimation method relies on a group of experts to produce the estimation. It has the following steps:

1. Form a group of experts or experienced developers.
2. Present an overview of the system and its major components to the group.

3. Ask the experts to estimate independently the efforts required by the system and its components.
4. Ask the experts to present their estimates and the rationale behind the estimation.
5. Repeat the last two steps until a consensus estimation is reached.

The estimation may be improved by requiring the experts to produce pessimistic most likely, and optimistic estimates, denoted E_p, E_m, and E_o, respectively. The expected effort is then derived by the following formula:

$$\text{Expected Effort } E = (E_p + 4 \times E_m + E_o)/6$$

23.2.4 Agile Estimation

Agile processes welcome change. Therefore, agile estimation means that the effort estimates can and must change to match the reality. Agile processes believe that good enough is enough. Therefore, agile estimation relies on intuition and common sense, rather than mathematical formulas, to derive effort estimates. For example, to move a pile of dirt from one corner of the backyard to another, one would look at the pile of dirt and estimate that the job requires five person-hours, assuming that the tools available for the person are a shovel and a wheelbarrow. This approach bypasses any estimate of size and goes directly to an estimate of effort.

Using a conventional estimation method, the contractor would estimate the size of the pile, say 300 cubic feet, based on its dimensions. The contractor finds out that the capacity of the wheelbarrow is 6 cubic feet, perhaps from its label. Dividing the pile size by the capacity of the wheelbarrow implies that 50 trips are required. The contractor then estimates that it takes 3 minutes to load the wheelbarrow, 2 minutes to transport and unload the dirt at the other corner, and 1 minute to walk back. That is, each trip takes 6 minutes. So the estimated duration is 300 minutes or 5 hours.

In this example, the results are the same for the two different approaches. But this is because it is written like this. In reality, the two approaches will produce different results. Even if the results are the same, the processes and objectives are very different. The difference in the process is obvious and there is no need to elaborate. The difference in objective lies in the attempt to obtain an estimate as accurate as possible and the attitude toward a good-enough estimate. Conventional approaches to project management would commit to the estimate and schedule, but agile processes view that reestimation is the way of life. Consider, for example, if there is a big rock hidden under the surface of the pile of dirt, then the project will require many more hours to complete. Project management often encounters such a risk. Risks are due to uncertainties that could severely damage the project. Conventional and agile approaches manage risks very differently. Conventional approaches want a higher degree of certainty and prepare for risks with resolution measures. Agile approaches recognize that uncertainties always exist, and knowing which risks will occur is practically impossible. Therefore, agile processes would reestimate or reduce the scope of work to meet delivery schedule. That is, "as reality overtakes the plan, update the plan"—the extreme programming planning game.

Cohn suggests programmers estimate size with story points. A story point is a unit of measurement for expressing the overall size of a user story, feature, use case, or a piece of work. For example, a small, easy-to-implement use case is given 1 point, while a use case that is twice the size is given 2 points, and so forth. Used as a measurement, it is similar to a FP. However, it differs in the process to obtain the estimate. It relies on consensus of an overall estimate rather than a value that is computed from a number of parameters. In this regard, it works more like the Delphi estimation method. The planning poker game is one of the best techniques for agile estimation. It combines expert opinion (such as Delphi method), analogy, and divide-and-conquer into a fun process that results in quick and reliable estimates.

The participants of the planning poker game include all of the developers on the team–i.e., analysts, architects, programmers, testers, and database designers, and more. The participants are aware that, beyond a certain point, additional estimation effort yields very little value in terms of the accuracy of the estimate. The game requires prior preparation of a deck of cards for each participant. Each card in a deck has a valid story point written on it and it is big enough to be seen across the table in the meeting room. The cards may read 0, 1, 2, 3, 5, 8, 13, 20, 40, etc.–the Fibonacci numbers. The use of the Fibonacci numbers is based on the belief that the larger the size, the lower the accuracy of the estimate. The Fibonacci numbers provide room for possible errors. For example, if a use case is estimated to be twice the size of another use case that is estimated to be 2 points, then the size for the former is not 4 points but 5 points. The extra point is included to accommodate for possible errors in the estimation. Instead of Fibonacci numbers, the team can use a sequence of integers such that each is twice the previous one, for example, 1, 2, 4, 8, 16, . . . , or simply the natural numbers if so desired.

The planning poker game iterates the following steps:

1. At the start of the game, each participant is given a deck of cards. The participants are reminded that the goal is to obtain a good-enough estimate quickly but not to pursue an accurate estimate that will withstand all future scrutiny.
2. For each piece of work, such as a use case, to be estimated, the moderator reads the description and the product owner answers all questions concerning the product. The participants then perform the following three steps.
3. Each participant privately selects a card that represents his or her estimate. When all the participants finish the selection, they turn over their cards simultaneously so that all participants see all the estimates.
4. If the estimates differ significantly, then the participants that give the high and low estimates are asked to explain the rationale behind their estimates. If desired, the participants exchange their understanding of the story and discuss their estimates for a while.
5. The group repeats the last two steps until a consensus estimate is obtained. Sometimes, the discrepancies in the estimates are small and the moderator could ask the participants with the lower estimates if they are OK with the other estimates to resolve the discrepancies to quickly converge the estimates.

Two issues should be addressed when using the story point approach. The first issue is how to estimate a large size of work. The answer is divide-and-conquer, a well-known technique for solving large, complex problems. In this case, the piece of work or the use case is decomposed into a number of smaller pieces of work. Estimates are obtained for the smaller pieces of work. These estimates are then used to derive an estimate for the large piece of work.

The second issue is when to reestimate. The advantage of using a story point is that it is a relative concept, that is, the story points of a story are relative to the estimates of other similar or reference stories. This means that reestimation of a story is needed only when the size of a reference story is revised up or down due to any reason.

23.3 PROJECT PLANNING AND SCHEDULING

Project planning and scheduling are concerned with the scheduling of development activities and allocation of resources to the development activities. Project planning and scheduling are critical to the success of a project because poor planning may result in schedule slippage, cost overrun, poor software quality, and/or high maintenance costs.

23.3.1 PERT Chart

The program evaluation and review technique (PERT) chart is widely used for project scheduling. A PERT chart is an edge-weighted directed graph or digraph $G = (M, T, D)$, where M is the set of vertexes representing project milestones, D a set of labels denoting tasks durations, and $T \subseteq M \times M \times D$ the set of directed edges representing the project tasks and their durations. The digraph satisfies the following conditions:

- It does not have parallel edges.
- It does not have cycles, that is, the digraph is acyclic.
- It has exactly one source and one sink. The source represents the start of the project and the sink the completion of the project.

Figure 23.6(a) shows a PERT chart for a hypothetic project, where m0, m1, . . . , m5 are the milestones and T1 = 2, T2 = 1, . . .,T7 = 1 are the tasks and their durations in days, weeks, or months. m0 and m5 are the project start and project completion milestones. The PERT chart shows that m2 is established when task 1 is completed. The establishment of m2 allows task 3 and task 4 to start. Unlike m2, the establishment of m4 requires the completion of both task 4 and task 5.

PERT charts are widely used to produce project schedules and identify a project's critical path, which is the path with the longest total duration from the project start to the project completion. That is, it defines the total time required to complete the project. Any delay along the critical path will delay the completion of the project.

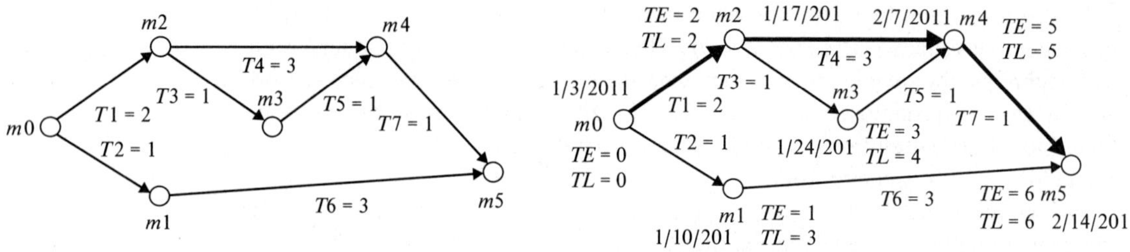

(a) A PERT chart (b) Project schedule and critical path

FIGURE 23.6 A PERT chart and its critical path

To produce a project schedule and identify the critical path, the following items are computed:

1. The *earliest start time* of each milestone m, denoted TE(m), is the earliest time that the milestone can be established. It is calculated as follows:

   $$\text{TE(m0)} = 0$$
   $$\text{TE(mi)} = \text{the longest total duration from m0 to mi}$$

   In Figure 23.6(*b*), the longest total duration from m0 to m3 is 3, from m0 to m5 is 6. Therefore, TE(m3) = 3, TE(m5) = 6.

2. The *latest completion time* of each milestone m, denoted TL(m), is the latest time that the milestone must be reached in order to meet the scheduled project completion date. It is computed as follows, where mn denotes the project completion milestone:

   $$\text{TL(mn)} = \text{TE(mn)}$$
   $$\text{TL(mi)} = \text{TE(mn)} - \text{the longest total duration from mi to mn}$$

   In Figure 23.6(*b*), TL(m5) = TE(m5)=6, because m5 is the sink. The longest total duration from m3 to m5 is 2 and the longest total duration from m2 to m5 is 4. Therefore, TL(m3) = TL(m5) – 2 = 6 – 2 = 4 and TL(m2) = TL(m5) – 4 = 6 – 4 = 2.

3. The critical path, which consists of the project start milestone along with every milestone that has identical earliest start time and latest completion time, that is, for all milestone m on the critical path, TE(m) = TL(m). In Figure 23.6(*b*), the critical path consists of the directed edges (m0, m2, T1), (m2, m4, T4), and (m4, m5, T7), as highlighted in the figure.

4. Specifying the earliest start date for each of the milestones, as shown in Figure 23.6(*b*).

The PERT chart in Figure 23.6(*b*) shows that two milestones–m_1 and m_3–are not on the critical path. Their earliest start time and latest completion time are different. More specifically, their latest completion time is greater than their earliest start time. The difference is called the *elapsed time,* which is the amount of time

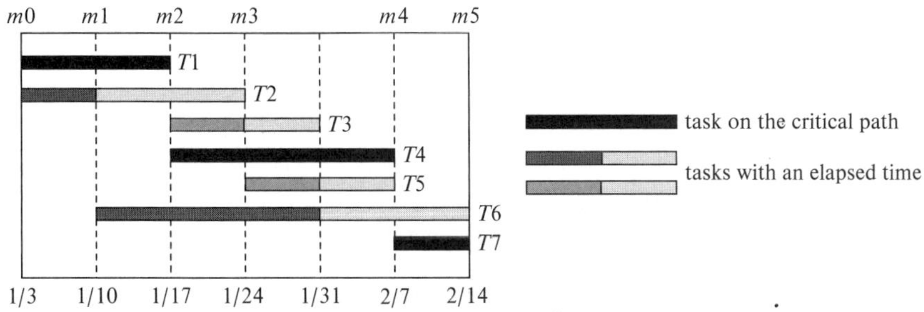

FIGURE 23.7 A Gantt chart showing the progression of tasks

that the milestone can be delayed without delaying the project completion time. It allows the project manager to adjust the schedule of the task according to project conditions.

23.3.2 Gantt Chart and Staff Allocation

The PERT chart is a useful tool for computing the earliest start time and latest completion time for each of the milestones as well as the earliest completion time of the project. But a PERT chart is not intuitive in showing the progression of the tasks and the amount of time available for each of the tasks. The Gantt chart is a better tool for highlighting such information.

Figure 23.7 shows a Gantt chart for the PERT chart in Figure 23.6(*b*). In a Gantt chart, the durations and elapsed times of the tasks are displayed as horizontal bars; each expands from the task's source milestone to the task's destination milestone. The milestones and their calendar dates are arranged chronologically along the horizontal axis. Gantt charts facilitate monitoring of project status and schedule.

In Figure 23.7, the dark bars represent the tasks on the critical path. Note that T4 starts immediately after T1 finishes and T7 starts as soon as T4 finishes. If any of these tasks delays its completion time, the project misses its deadline. Therefore, these are the critical tasks. On the other hand, T2 and T6 have elapsed times, giving the project manager some flexibility in scheduling. For example, T2 may start at m1 rather than at m0 if no programmer is available to perform T2 at the beginning of the project. In this case, T6 has to start a week later because T6 cannot start until T2 completes. The dependence of T6 on T2 is indicated by the same pattern used to fill the durations of these two tasks. It means that the delay in T2 causes the same delay in T6.

The construction of a Gantt chart from a PERT chart involves the following steps:

1. Draw a rectangle and mark the project milestones and their calendar dates chronologically along the horizontal axis. Add vertical guidelines to facilitate the reading of the milestones and calendar dates.
2. For each task, depict a horizontal bar from the source milestone of the task to the destination milestone of the task. Color the bars for the tasks on the critical path with a distinctive color. This step produces T1, T4, and T7 in Figure 23.7.

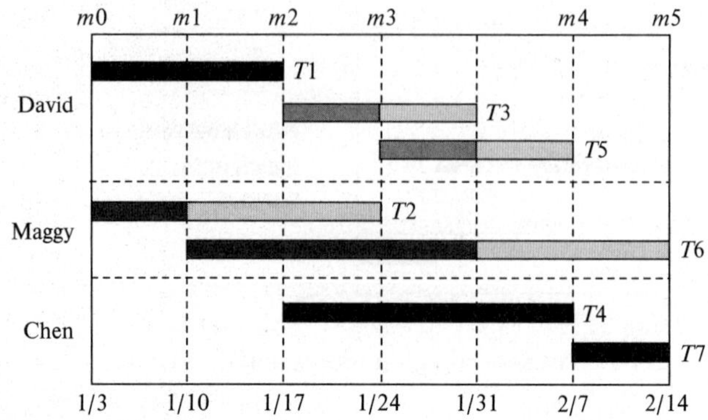

FIGURE 23.8 Allocating tasks to team members

3. Color the initial portions of the remaining bars to indicate the durations of the noncritical tasks. Use the same color or fill pattern to indicate the dependence of one task on another. For example, Figure 23.7 fills T2 and T6 with the same pattern to indicate that the start time of T6 depends on the completion time of T2.
4. If the destination milestone of a noncritical task has an elapsed time, then extend the bar proportionally to show the elapsed time. This step extends T2 with an elapsed time of two weeks in Figure 23.7.

The Gantt chart facilitates the allocation of the tasks to the developers. For the Gantt chart in Figure 23.7, assume that the task duration is equal to the task effort in person-weeks. Under this assumption, the total effort for the project is 12 person-weeks. Assume further that the team has three members: Chen, David, and Maggie. If the effort is to be equally divided among the team members, then each of them should be assigned four person-weeks of work. Figure 23.8 shows an allocation of the tasks to the members with a Gantt chart. Of course, in practice, the assignment of tasks to the team members must also consider the allocation of the tasks to match the expertise of the team members.

As shown in Figure 23.8, T1, T3, and T5 are assigned to David, T2 and T6 are assigned to Maggie, and T4 and T7 are assigned to Chen. Each of these members is assigned four person-weeks of work. David must complete T1 in two weeks; otherwise, the project completion time will be delayed. However, he has one week elapsed time for completing T3 and T5, as indicated by the one week elapsed time for these two tasks. Similarly, Maggie has two weeks elapsed time. Chen, however, has to complete T4 and T7 on schedule.

23.3.3 Agile Planning

Unlike conventional approaches that use PERT chart and Gantt chart, agile planning uses informal means such as a corkboard and a deck of story cards. Each story card describes the user story, its business priority, its story points, and the stories that it depends on. Post-it notes can be used instead. Story cards are preferred because they are easy to sort according to their business priorities and dependencies. An agile

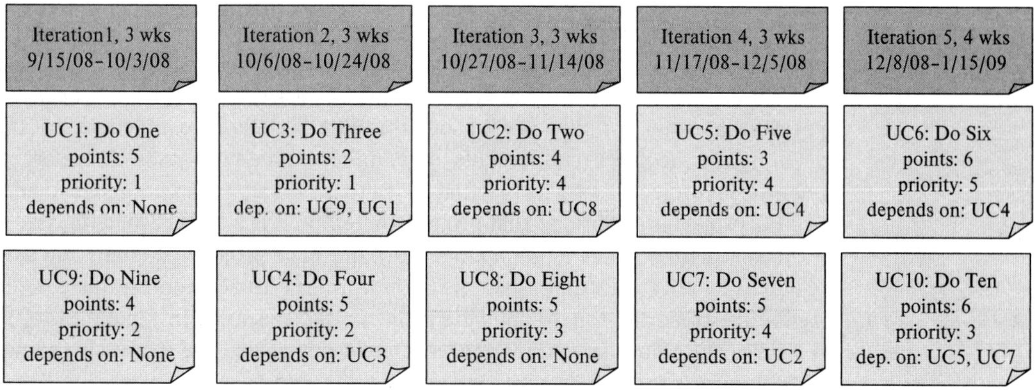

Assumptions: (1) The team can produce 3 points of work per week. (2) Priorities are ranked from 1 to 5 with 1 being the highest.

FIGURE 23.9 Planning increments with use cases and subsystems

plan can be produced quickly and easily by arranging the cards or Post-it notes in a conceptual grid. The columns represent the assignment of stories to the iterations. Figure 23.9 illustrates the use of Post-it notes to plan the deliveries of the use cases for a hypothetic agile project, where the iterations and durations are displayed at the top of the grid. The points measure the required effort to develop the use cases. It is assumed that the team can produce three points of work per week. This agile planning technique is associated with the following merits:

1. It is easy to ensure that high-priority use cases are developed and deployed early.
2. It is easy to ensure that the dependencies between the use cases are satisfied. For example, in Figure 23.9, UC1 and UC9 are assigned to iteration 1 and UC3 is assigned to iteration 2 because UC3 depends on UC1 and UC9, although UC9 has a lower priority than UC3.
3. It is easy to ensure that the sum of the points in each column is not greater than the team "velocity," which is the amount of work or points that the team can complete in one iteration.

23.4 RISK MANAGEMENT

Many contingencies could negatively impact a software project. Sometimes, the consequence of such an event is unbearable. The NHS project and the TPC project discussed at the beginning of this chapter could have been avoided if proper risk analysis had been performed. Such contingent events are commonly referred to as *risks*. The objective of risk management is to reduce the impact of such events if they occur. Proposed by Barry Boehm, risk management consists of six activities: (1) risk identification, (2) risk analysis, (3) risk prioritizing, (4) risk management planning, (5) risk resolution, and (6) risk monitoring. These are described in the following sections.

23.4.1 Risk Identification

Risks can be classified into universal project risks and project-specific risks. The universal project risks are risks that can occur to all projects while project-specific risks are risks that can occur only to a particular project. For example, schedule slip, budget overruns, and incorrect requirements are common to many projects. Therefore, these are universal project risks. The risk that is due to lack of domain knowledge to perform the TPC project is specific to that project; therefore, it is a project-specific risk.

It is a useful practice to maintain a list of universal project risk items and use it as a guide to identify risks that could occur in a project. To accomplish this goal, Barry Boehm identified the top 10 software project risks as shown in Figure 23.10, based on a survey of a number of experienced project managers. The figure also shows the corresponding risk management techniques.

During the risk identification step, universal software project risks and project-specific risks are identified. The list of top 10 software project risks shown in Figure 23.10 is useful for this purpose. Other useful means include consultation with experts and users, literature survey of similar projects, and comparison with experiences. Brainstorming is an effective approach to risk identification. The brainstorming session may involve various participants including the development team members, related experts, customer representatives, and users. To reduce effort, the project manager should limit the risk items to those that are likely to occur and would incur significant loss to the project.

	Risk Item	Suggested Risk Management Techniques
1	Personnel shortfalls	Staffing with top talent, job matching, team building, key personnel agreements, cross training.
2	Unrealistic schedules and budgets	Detailed multisource cost and schedule estimation, design to cost, incremental development, software reuse, requirements scrubbing.
3	Developing the wrong functions and properties	Organization analysis, mission analysis, operations-concept formulation, user surveys and user participation, prototyping, early users' manuals, off-nominal performance analysis, quality-factor analysis.
4	Developing the wrong user interface	Prototyping, scenarios, task analysis, user participation.
5	Gold-plating (i.e., adding nice features that are not required)	Requirements scrubbing, prototyping, cost-benefit analysis, designing to cost.
6	Continuing stream of requirements changes	High change threshold, information hiding, incremental development (deferring changes to later increments).
7	Shortfalls in externally furnished components	Benchmarking, inspections, reference checking, compatibility analysis.
8	Shortfalls in externally performed tasks	Reference checking, preaward audits, award-fee contracts, competitive design or prototyping, team-building.
9	Real-time performance shortfalls	Simulation, benchmarking, modeling, prototyping, instrumentation, tuning.
10	Straining computer-science capabilities	Technical analysis, cost-benefit analysis, prototyping, reference checking.

FIGURE 23.10 Top 10 software project risks and management techniques

23.4.2 Risk Analysis and Prioritizing

Risk analysis is concerned with the determination of the extent of damage of each risk, options to deal with the risk, and costs to implement the options. The analysis is aimed to determine which option to take, the cost to implement that option, and the extent of damage with that option. Risk analysis involves several basic concepts, that is, the loss probability, loss magnitude, and risk exposure. The loss probability is the estimated likelihood of occurrence of the risk. The loss magnitude is the estimated damage, in dollar amount, to the project if the risk occurs. The risk exposure is the expected damage, also in dollar amount, to the project; it is the product of the loss probability and the loss magnitude of the risk item.

Decision trees and decision tables are useful tools for evaluating the options and helping in the selection of a viable option. This is illustrated with a real-world project that uses an OO DBMS. An attractive design option is letting the business objects access the OO database directly. This option is easy to implement and would lead to better runtime performance. However, the risk is that the OO DBMS may not work as expected and have to be replaced. This is because the product is new and it is the first OO DBMS ever constructed. The loss probability or likelihood that could occur is 20%. The loss magnitude or costs to rewrite the software if this occurs are estimated to be \$2 1/2 million. The likelihood that the OO DBMS did not need to be replaced is 80%. Another option is *design for change,* that is, implementing the bridge pattern, presented in Chapter 17, to hide the OO database so that change to a different type of database can be accomplished easily. The cost estimate for implementing this option is \$150,000. There is an additional cost-to-implement classes needed by each new type of database; the estimate is \$10,000.

Figure 23.11 illustrates the analysis of these two options. The figure shows both a decision tree and a decision table. They are equivalent. More specifically, the rows of the table corresponds to the branches of the tree, and the columns of the table and the tree also correspond with each other. The merits of the decision table are that it is more compact and easier to construct. A decision table template in the form of a spreadsheet can be developed easily and used for future projects. The project manager only needs to enter the input parameters. The spreadsheet will compute the results automatically. The decision tree in Figure 23.11(*a*) is constructed by the following steps; the decision table can be constructed similarly:

1. Identify the options and all possible outcomes for each option. Identify also the loss probability and loss magnitude for each of the outcomes. The sum of the loss probabilities for each option should be one.
2. Do the following for each option that is identified:
   a. Expand the root with a new branch and label it with the name of the option. For the example described above, this expands the root with two branches, labeled "Design for Change" and "Direct DB Access," respectively.
   b. For each possible outcome of the option, do the following:
      i. Expand the tip of the option with a new branch and label it with the name of the outcome, the loss probability, and the loss magnitude.

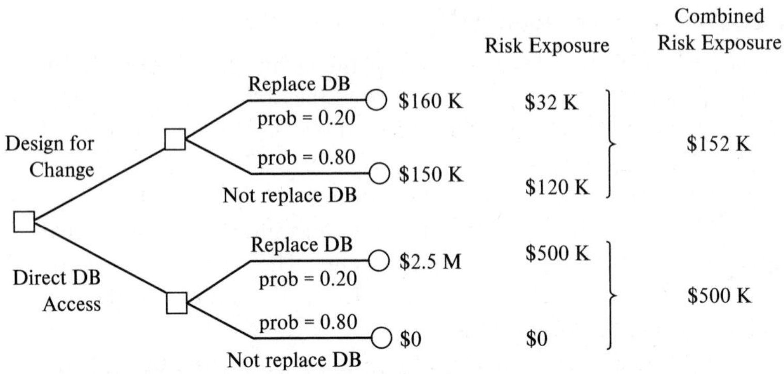

(a) Risk analysis using a decision tree

#	Option	Possible Outcome	Loss Probability	Loss Magnitude	Risk Exposure	Combined Risk Exposure
1	Design for Change	Replace DB	20%	$160,000	$32,000	$152,000
		Not replace DB	80%	$150,000	$120,000	
2	Direct DB Access	Replace DB	20%	$2,500,000	$500,000	$500,000
		Not replace DB	80%	$0	$0	

(b) Risk analysis using a decision table

FIGURE 23.11 Risk analysis of design options

ii. Compute the risk exposure of the outcome as the product of the loss probability and the loss magnitude of the outcome. Enter the result in the corresponding column.

c. Compute the combined risk exposure for the option as the sum of the risk exposures of all of the possible outcomes for the option. Enter the result in the corresponding column.

Figure 23.11 indicates that the design for change option has a lower combined risk exposure (i.e., $152K) than its counterpart (i.e., $500K). This means that design for change is a better choice.

The decision table and decision tree are useful for sensitivity analysis, that is, analysis of the impact of the input parameters on the combined risk exposures for the options. For instance, if the probability to replace the OO DBMS increases to 30% from 20%, then the combined risk exposure with design for change increases to $153,000, an increase of 0.6%. However, the combined risk exposure with no design for change increases to $750,000, a 50% increase. This analysis means if the loss probability of the risk is underestimated by 10%, then the costs to the project could be devastating. To cope with possible estimation errors, the so-called pessimistic, most likely, and optimistic estimates are used to derive an expected estimate, denoted E_p, E_m, E_o, and E_e, respectively:

$$E_e = (E_p + 4E_m + E_o)/6$$

The expected estimates are then used as the input parameters in the decision tree or decision table. The pessimistic, most likely, and optimistic estimates of loss probabilities and loss magnitudes may be obtained using the Delphi estimation method, described in Section 23.2.3, or the agile estimation method described in Section 23.2.4.

The risks are ranked according to their effects and combined risk exposures. Generally speaking, catastrophic risks and risks with a high combined risk exposure are high-priority risks. Expert opinion, project management experiences, and brainstorming are useful in assigning priorities to the risks.

23.4.3 Risk Management Planning

Risk analysis and prioritizing identify a list of risk items, compute their combined risk exposures, and rank them with priorities. The next step of risk management is producing a risk management plan to be carried out during the development process. The first step of risk management planning is developing strategies to address the risk items. The risk management techniques shown in the right-most column of Figure 23.10 are a useful guide. That is, project managers may examine the list to identify risk items or similar risk items that could occur for the project on hand. Other useful resources and techniques include expert opinion, project experiences, and brainstorming. The second step is to produce a risk management plan for tracking the risk items during the development life-cycle. For each risk item, the plan specifies the objective, the schedule of activities to be performed, who are responsible for performing the activities, how to perform the activities, and what are the needed resources.

23.4.4 Risk Resolution and Monitoring

Risk resolution is the implementation and execution of the risk reduction techniques specified and scheduled in the risk management plan. Risk monitoring ensures that the risk reduction strategies are implemented and executed according to schedule. It is aimed to ensure that the risk management process is a closed-loop process and progresses on track. Rather than monitoring all risk items, it is more effective to focus on the top-N risk items of the project, where N should be limited to 10, and depends on the project size, nature, and progress status. The top-N risk items should be reviewed regularly with upper management and frequently by the project manager. The status of the top-N risk items are updated to reflect changes of their rankings from the last review, number of months on the list, and risk-resolution status. Such a list is a useful tool to draw the project manager's attention to risk items that have moved up and persist on the list. These risk items may require upper management's attention to help resolve them quickly and effectively.

23.5 PROCESS IMPROVEMENT

A software process defines a series of activities for constructing a software system. The execution of a software process has to be monitored and data about various aspects of the process including productivity, quality, costs, and time to market should be collected. These data should be analyzed regularly to identify strengths and

Level	Name	Characteristics	Key Process Areas
1	Initial Level	• An ad hoc/chaotic process • No project management mechanism, no cost estimation, no project plans • Tools are not well integrated • Change control is lax • Senior management does not understand key issues	None
2	Repeatable Level	• An intuitive process that depends on individuals • Established basic project controls • Strength in similar work but facing significant risks with new challenges • Lacks an orderly framework for improvement	• Requirements management • Software project management • Subcontractor management • Software quality assurance • Software configuration management
3	Defined Level	• An organization-wide qualitative process is defined and implemented • A process group to improve process	• Organization process definition and focus • Training program • Integrated development and management • Software product engineering • Intergroup coordination • Peer reviews
4	Managed Level	A quantitative process with a process database, and a minimum set of quality and productivity measures	• Quantitative process management • Software quality management
5	Optimizing Level	An ever-improving process that is supported by • automatic data collection • using data to identify weaknesses • rigorous defect-cause analysis & defect prevention • numeric evidence to justify technology use • improvement feedback into process	• Defect prevention • Technology change management • Process change management

FIGURE 23.12 Levels of the Capability Maturity Model Integration

weaknesses of the process and the analysis result should be used to improve the process. The Capability Maturity Model Integration (CMMI) and the ISO 9000 Standards are widely used in process improvement. This section briefly describes the CMMI.

The CMMI was originally developed by the Software Engineering Institute (SEI) to assist the U.S. Department of Defense to assess the performance of the defense contractors. During the years, the CMMI has expanded its acceptance beyond the defense industry; currently, it is widely used by many software development organizations. The CMMI defines five levels of software capability maturity. As shown in Figure 23.12, each level has a number of key process areas that an organization should focus on to improve its software process. Each key process area is further decomposed into key practices and subpractices, which are omitted to conserve space.

The assessment of an organization's software process begins with an on-site visit by a team of software professionals, who examine several representative projects provided by the organization. On the first day, survey questionnaires are distributed and the responses to the survey are analyzed, resulting in an initial set of issues. On the second day, the team interviews the project leaders to clarify the initial set of issues and request explanatory materials. The team then refines the findings. On the third day, the team discusses the findings with representatives of each functional area. The team then finalizes the findings and prepares the briefing, which is given on the fourth day. The final report that gives the recommendations for improvement is sent to the organization about two months after the on-site assessment. Items that require immediate actions are given the highest priority. The CMMI model has a number of merits:

- It reflects the actual process improvement practices. For example, studies show that the delivered defect densities or delivered defects per 1,000 lines of code for CMMI level 1 to level 5 are 7.5, 6.24, 4.73, 2.28, and 1.05, respectively.
- For each level, it clearly defines the improvement goals and progress measures.
- The five maturity levels define a logical roadmap toward an optimizing process. The improvement from one level to the next higher level can usually be achieved in two years.
- The recommendation provides improvement priorities.

To improve the software process, an organization performs the following steps, which may serve as a self-study:

1. Evaluate the current process to gain an understanding of its status, that is, what is the maturity level of the current process.
2. Develop a vision for the desired process at the next higher maturity level, guided by the key process areas in Figure 23.12.
3. Define a plan of prioritized actions for improvement.
4. Implement the action plan.
5. Repeat the above steps to move to the next high level.

23.6 APPLYING AGILE PRINCIPLES

GUIDELINE 23.1 A collaborative and cooperative approach between all stakeholders is essential.

Project management deals with a lot of uncertainties. Effort estimation, planning, scheduling, and risk management are helpful but not silver bullets. Managing a software project is a wicked problem. Therefore, involving all stakeholders in the decision-making process is essential. The objective is not to reach an agreement, which is practically difficult if not impossible. Instead, it is aimed to reach a mutual understanding among the stakeholders. This mutual understanding is the basis for various parties to collaborate and cooperate.

GUIDELINE 23.2 Active user involvement is imperative. Customer collaboration is valued more than contract negotiation.

Agile development requires active involvement of the users because this is required to solve a wicked problem. However, in today's competitive work environment, the users won't have the time and effort to do so. One solution is that the customer assigns a dedicated, experienced user representative to the project. This means extra costs to the customer. If the customer does not collaborate, for example, does not assign such a person or ask the person to do this as a volunteer work, then even if the team wins the contract, the agile project may not be able to succeed.

GUIDELINE 23.3 Agile development values responding to change over following a plan.

Planning is important for a software project to succeed. However, the world changes. This means that the requirements must also change. It is important to respond to change. If the system is built with the existing requirements, then it won't be able to satisfy the customer's business needs. To the customer, the usefulness of the system is greatly compromised. That is why extreme programming defines this as the planning game–as reality overtakes the plan, update the plan.

GUIDELINE 23.4 Agile development values individuals and interactions over processes and tools.

Conventional approaches to project management emphasize processes and tools. These are good but not adequate. Agile development recognizes also the importance of individuals and interaction such as teamwork. Agility values these over processes and tools because processes and tools require individuals and teamwork to reap their benefits, as explained in Chapter 2.

GUIDELINE 23.5 Agile development values working software over comprehensive documentation.

For software, documentation is important, but it is not the silver bullet. After all, the team has to design, implement, and deliver the software that works in the target environment. Moreover, software development is a wicked problem. This implies that the real requirements and the desired design cannot be completely and definitely specified prior to implementing the code. The iterative nature of agile processes is part of the solution to tackling these problems. This leads to the next principle.

GUIDELINE 23.6 Good enough is enough.

Agile development suggests "barely enough modeling, but no more." This means performing modeling and design to the extent that is sufficient for the team to move on. That is, the extent that clarifies the doubt and establishes a common understanding among the team members of what needs to be implemented, and how.

23.7 TOOL SUPPORT FOR PROJECT MANAGEMENT

Many project management tools are available. These include commercial products and open-source software. Figure 23.13 provides a brief list.

Tool	Description	URL
Feng Office	An open-source project management tool.	http://sourceforge.net/projects/opengoo/?source=directory
IBM Engineering Workflow Management	A project management tool from IBM that supports life-cycle activity management for agile development.	https://www.ibm.com/products/ibm-engineering-workflow-management
MS Project	A comprehensive project management tool from Microsoft.	http://www.microsoft.com/project/
Oracle Project Management	A comprehensive project management tool from Oracle Corporation.	https://www.oracle.com/erp/project-portfolio-management-cloud/
Project-Open	A comprehensive open-source project management tool from]project-open[.	http://www.project-open.com/
web2Project	An open-source project management tool providing basic project management capabilities.	https://web2project.net/

FIGURE 23.13 A brief list of project management tools

23.8 SUMMARY

This chapter presents the basic functions of software project management. The project organizations include project-based, function-based, and hybrid organizations. The team structures include the egoless team structure, chief programmer team structure, and hierarchical team structure. Conventional effort-estimation methods include the FP estimation method, COCOMO II method, and Delphi method. The conventional project planning and scheduling methods are the PERT chart and Gantt chart. This chapter also presents agile estimation and agile planning. Project risk management involves risk identification, analysis, resolution, and monitoring. Finally, the chapter presents the CMMI model for process improvement. Knowledge of these project management functions enables the project manager to plan and schedule the development activities according to the project milestones to deliver the use cases and subsystems.

23.9 CHAPTER REVIEW QUESTIONS

1. What are the three project formats presented in this chapter? What are their pros and cons?
2. What are the team structures presented in this chapter? Which agile methods use which of the team structures?
3. What are the effort estimation methods, and how does each compute the effort, project duration, and number of persons required?
4. What is a PERT chart and a Gantt Chart? What are they used for?
5. What are agile estimation and agile planning? How do they differ from conventional approaches?
6. Why do we need risk management? What is the risk management process?
7. What is the capability maturity model integration (CMMI)? What are the maturity levels?

23.10 EXERCISES

23.1 Discuss in a brief article the pros and cons of the different team structures presented in this chapter. Discuss also their pros and cons with respect to agile projects.

23.2 Apply the COCOMO II Application Composite Model described in Section 23.2.2 to estimate the effort required to develop the Add Program use case for a Study Abroad web application for the Office of International Education (OIE) of a university. Assume that the object point productivity is nominal and no reuse of existing components is expected. The Add Program use case allows an OIE staff to add an overseas exchange program, such as French Language and Culture. This use case needs to display three web pages and a message as follows:

a. Initially, it displays a Welcome page, which consists of three frames. The main frame shows a description of the Study Abroad program. The top frame shows the OIE logo along with a row of buttons, such as OIE Home, About Study Abroad program, Contact Us, etc. The left frame shows a list of three menu items: Program Management, User Management, and System Settings. The Welcome page is displayed after an OIE staff member successfully logs into the system.

b. To add a program, the OIE staff clicks the Program Management item, which expands the item and shows a list of four menu items under the expanded item–Add Program, Update Program, Delete Program, and Import Programs.

c. The OIE staff clicks the Add Program item. The system displays an Add Program Form in the main frame of the page. The Add Program Form lets the OIE staff enter program information into the various fields. The OIE staff clicks the Submit button to save the program.

d. When the Submit button is clicked, the system saves the program into a database and displays a "program is successfully saved" message.

23.3 Make proper assumptions for the missing information in the Add Program use case description provided in the previous exercise and apply the function point method to estimate the required effort. Justify your assumptions and effort estimate.

23.4 Apply COCOMO II Early Design Model to estimate the effort required to develop the following use cases for the Study Abroad web application. Make necessary assumptions including the number of inputs, outputs, and the scale factors, cost drivers and the like. For example, you can assume average/nominal levels for all of the scale factors.

a. UC01. Search for Programs (Actor: Web User, System: SAMS)

This use case allows a user to search overseas exchange programs using a variety of search criteria such as subject, semester, year, country and region. The system searches the database and displays a list of programs, each of which includes a link to display the detail of the program.

b. UC02. Display Program Detail (Actor: Web User, System: SAMS)

This use case retrieves and displays the detailed description of a program, selected by clicking the link of the program displayed by the Search for Programs use case, or by giving the program ID or program name.

c. UC03. Submit Online Application (Actor: Student, System: SAMS)

This use case allows a student to apply to an overseas exchange program. The student fills in an application form and submits it. The system verifies the application, saves it in the database, and sets the status of the application to "submitted." The system also sends e-mail to the two faculty members requested by the student to write recommendation letters, and the academic adviser to approve the course equivalency form.

d. UC04. Login (Actor: Student, System: SAMS)

This use case allows a registered student to login to the system.

e. UC05. Logout (Actor: Student, System: SAMS)

This use case allows a student to logout from the system.

f. UC06. Edit Online Application (Actor: Student, System: SAMS)

This use case allows the student to edit an application that is not yet submitted.

g. UC07. Check Application Status (Actor: Student, System: SAMS)

This use case allows a student to check the status of an application, such as in-preparation, submitted, under-review, accepted, and rejected.

h. UC08. Submit Recommendation (Actor: Faculty, System: SAMS)

This use case lets a faculty member submit a recommendation on behalf of a student. The system saves the recommendation in the database.

i. UC09. Approve Course Equivalency Form (Actor: Advisor, System: SAMS)

This use case lets an academic adviser review and approve course equivalency forms submitted by students when they submit their online applications. Each form specifies the overseas courses that the student plans to use to substitute for the courses of the academic department.

23.5 Base on the estimates produced in the previous exercise, perform the following:

a. Identify the dependencies among the nine use cases for the Study Abroad application.

b. Assume that the team cannot work on a use case until the use cases that it depends on are completed. Assume that the completion of a use case marks a milestone. Produce a PERT chart schedule for developing the use cases.

c. Compute the earliest start time and latest completion time for each of the milestones.

d. Identify the critical path for the project.

e. Select a calendar date for the project start and fill in the calendar dates for the milestones.

23.6 Form a group of five students and practice agile estimation and planning for the 9 use cases of the Study Abroad application. Produce a brief report describing the process and the results obtained.

23.7 Identify top five possible risks for the SAMS project and develop risk resolution measures for them. Briefly justify your solution.

23.8 Suppose that a company is at level 1 of the CMMI. Propose a process improvement plan for the company to improve its process to level 5. Make necessary assumptions about the level-1 company.

24 Chapter

Software Security

Key Takeaway Points

- Software security is a proactive, rather than reactive, approach to constructing secure software.
- Consideration of software security should begin in the requirements phase and continue throughout the life cycle.

Computer system security has become a serious concern in recent years. The number of security vulnerabilities reported to the Computer Emergency Response Team Coordination Center (CERT/CC) has increased significantly during the last three decades. Several factors that contribute to this include an increase in system complexity, connectivity, and expansion of computer applications to all sectors of our society. Increasing complexity makes it more difficult to detect software design flaws and implementation bugs; these are often exploited by attackers to engineer attacks. Connectivity makes it possible for an attacker to access a computer system remotely. Finally, the expansion of computer applications attracts adversaries due to financial incentives. Although computer security problems already appeared in the 1980s, active R&D in computer security did not begin until 20 years ago.

Computer security covers a wide spectrum of areas and topics, including cryptography, security protocols, authentication and authorization, access control, intrusion detection, virus and malware, privacy, and software security, to mention a few. Some of these deserve a book or two of their own. The focus of this chapter is software security or "building secure software," that is, life-cycle activities that aim to produce more secure application software.

As pointed out by McGraw, current approaches to application security are reactive approaches–security is primarily based on finding and fixing known security problems. *Software security* is a proactive approach–start tackling the security problems from day one and continue throughout the entire software life cycle. Unfortunately, research in software security is still in its infant stage. Processes, methodologies, and techniques for the analysis and design of secure software have just begun to appear. Therefore, the materials presented in this chapter are expected to evolve. Upon completing this chapter, the student should understand the following:

- Basic concepts of software security.
- Importance of software security.
- Security attacks and defenses.
- Security requirements.
- Secure software design principles.
- Security patterns.
- Life-cycle activities for building secure software.

24.1 WHAT IS SOFTWARE SECURITY?

Software security and security software are different. The former means building secure software, that is, conducting all of the life-cycle activities with security in mind; security is built in the software rather than as an afterthought. Security software refers to software components that implement security functions such as encryption, decryption, authentication, and access control. A software system with some security functions does not necessarily imply that it is secure. However, software that connects to the network, or operates in a hostile environment, must include security functions to protect valuable resources. Software security is built-in during the following life-cycle activities:

1. *Modeling and analysis for security.* Modeling and analysis are performed in the early stage of the software project. The development team constructs models that show the resources that need protection and entities that access the resources. Such models help the development team identify, formulate, and validate security requirements.
2. *Design for security.* Design for security is performed during the architectural design and behavioral design phases. It applies security patterns and security design principles to ensure that security requirements are satisfied. It also takes into account anticipated change of security requirements.
3. *Secure coding.* Secure coding applies security principles and security patterns to produce secure code during the implementation phase.
4. *Test for security.* Test for security aims to detecting security vulnerabilities in the software. Conventional functional testing ensures that the software is correct with respect to the functional requirements. Security testing ensures that the software does not contain loopholes that attackers can explore to compromise the security of the system. It applies static as well as dynamic security-testing techniques to detect such vulnerabilities.

24.2 SECURITY REQUIREMENTS

Designing secure systems has to take into consideration security requirements, which define the capabilities of the software system to thwart attempted attacks and recover from successful attacks. Donald Firesmith defines 12 software-related security requirements, adapted below, with some of them modified, and the resilience and secrecy requirements added. Note that many of these are cross-cutting concerns. For example, identification requirements and authentication requirements are related. Authorization requirements follow authentication requirements.

Identification requirements specify the extent to which a system identifies the actors before interacting with them.

Authentication requirements specify the extent to which a system verifies the identity of its actors before interacting with them.

Authorization requirements specify the access and usage privileges of authenticated actors.

Immunity requirements specify the extent to which a system protects itself from infections by malicious programs such as computer viruses, worms, and Trojan horses.

Integrity requirements specify the extent to which a system ensures that its data and communications are not intentionally corrupted via unauthorized creation, modification, or deletion.

Intrusion detection requirements specify the extent to which a system detects and records attempted access or modification by unauthorized individuals or programs.

Nonrepudiation requirements specify the extent to which a system prevents any party that it has interacted with from denying all or part of the interaction.

Privacy requirements specify the extent to which a system protects the privacy rights of the stakeholders.

Secrecy requirements specify the extent to which a system conceals data and communication to prevent their contents from reading by unauthorized parts.

Security auditing requirements specify the extent to which a system enables security personnel to audit the status and use of its security functions.

Survivability requirements specify the extent to which a system survives the intentional loss or destruction of a component.

Resilience requirements specify the extent to which a system recovers from a successful attack.

System maintenance security requirements specify the extent to which a system prevents authorized modifications, such as defect fixes, enhancements, and updates, from accidentally defeating its security mechanisms.

24.3 SECURE SOFTWARE DESIGN PRINCIPLES

As discussed in previous chapters, best software design practices are guided by a set of software design principles. Secure software design is no exception. During the last three decades, the software engineering community and the software security community, especially the practitioners, had proposed a number of secure software design principles. The 10 best-known principles are found in the book by John Viega and Gary McGraw:

Principle 1. Secure the weakest link.

Identify and strengthen the weakest parts of the system until an acceptable level of risk is achieved.

Principle 2. Practice defense in depth.

Protect the system with layers of diverse defensive strategies so that there is a security measure to prevent a full breach in case other strategies turn out to be inadequate.

Principle 3. Fail securely.

Make sure that the system is in a secure state whenever failure occurs.

Principle 4. Least privilege.

Always limit the scope, extent, and amount of time of access to the absolute minimum.

Principle 5. Compartmentalize.

Design the system to consist of relatively independent, and mutually distrustful, components so that if a couple of components fail, the system will continue to operate, although its functionality may be reduced.

Principle 6. Keep it simple and stupid.

This software design principle can also be applied to building secure software. Highly complex software is more likely to fail and more difficult to detect security vulnerabilities through review, inspection, and testing.

Principle 7. Promote privacy.

Promote privacy for the users, systems, and code because information relevant to these entities is valuable for an adversary.

Principle 8. Remember that hiding secrets is hard.

Security is often about keeping secrets. It is much harder to do than most people think, and it is always a source of security risk.

Principle 9. Be reluctant to trust.

Skepticism is safer and better than grief when security is concerned. Don't trust anything without the desired confidence in security; don't trust even yourself because nobody is perfect. Review and test for security until the desired degree of confidence is truly established.

Principle 10. Use community resources.

Use community resources such as kernel functions and library functions that have been widely used and scrutinized. Repeated use without failure promotes trust although such resources may contain bugs that haven't been found. The *defer to kernel* security design pattern presented in the next section reiterates this principle.

24.4 SECURE SOFTWARE DESIGN PATTERNS

Previous chapters presented GRASP patterns and Gang of Four patterns. These software design patterns help software developers produce quality software while improving teamwork, communication, and productivity. Patterns are proven design solutions to commonly encountered design problems. This observation suggests to the software security community that recurring security problems could be solved by applying "*secure software design patterns,*" or security patterns in short. For example, today's software systems need to communicate with other systems over the Internet. How to protect the messages is a frequently encountered design problem. The *secure pipe* pattern (see Figure 24.1) provides a solution. As another example, systems need to check the access right of a subject to a certain resource. How to design the system to effectively accommodate this need is answered by the *check point* pattern.

Spyros Halkidis and Nikolaos Tsantalis investigated the effect of security patterns with respect to security attacks. Two e-commerce systems were involved in the study. One of the systems was designed and implemented with security patterns, and the other was not. The findings show that the system without security patterns has a high risk of being affected by the attacks, whereas the one that applies security patterns exhibits a significantly lower risk.

There are many security patterns and the pool is still expanding. Figure 24.1 shows a summary of some of these patterns, which represent only a small subset of the security patterns in the literature. The following example illustrates the application of some of these patterns.

It should be noted that some of the design patterns presented in previous chapters are also security patterns. For example, the protection proxy pattern described in Chapter 17 controls access to an object; and hence, it can be used to implement RBAC. The *N*-tier architecture resulting from the application of the controller, bridge, proxy, and command patterns forms a series of compartments. If the layers of the architecture are designed to require access privileges, then the resulting architectural design is an application of the privilege reduction pattern.

EXAMPLE 24.1 Apply security patterns to produce an architectural design for the SAMS system described in Appendix D.3 and previous chapters.

Solution: A design is shown in Figure 24.2, where several patterns are applied and explained below. The Single Access Point module is an application of both *single access point* and *privilege separation* patterns, that is, it is assigned the least privilege and serves as a single entry to the system. The *privilege reduction* pattern is also applied in the design of the architecture because the system is structured into a series of "compartments" that require different access privileges. For simplicity, some of the modules are labeled using the pattern names, such as Single Access Point, Check Point, and so forth.

Name	Intent/Problem Solved	Description, Participants, Responsibilities, & Interaction	Remarks
Privilege Reduction (A)	How does one compartmentalize a system? Decompose the system into mutually distrustful components.	A System consists of Mutually Distrustful Components that require different access privileges.	Also called Distrustful Decomposition.
Privilege Separation (A)	To be reluctant to trust, and practice least privilege.	Using/introducing a Least Privilege Module to decouple a Privilege-Elevated Module from an External Source.	A special instance of Privilege Reduction.
Defer to Kernel (A)	Prevent privilege elevation attacks through Privilege Separation and use of kernel functions.	A Client sends requests to a Server, which invokes functions of the Kernel to carry out operations that require elevated privileges.	It is a specialization of Privilege Reduction.
Single Access Point (A)	Provide only one entry to a system to facilitate user validation.	A Single Access Point serves as the only entry into the system. It collects and validates user information, and launches appropriate functions/applications.	May delegate validation to Check Point.
Check Point (A)	How does one organize checking of security policies and execution of countermeasures?	A Check Point uses Security Policy subclasses to check security policies and calls functions of Countermeasure in case of an attack.	Security Policy may be implemented as Strategy.
Secure Access Layer (A)	How does one interact with the security mechanism of an external system? Use or implement a secure access layer to interact.	An Application communicates through a Secure Access Layer, which communicates with an External System through a Lower Level Security Mechanism.	May use security mechanisms provided by the OS, network, or DBMS.
Secure Pipe (I)	How does one secure the connection between the client and the server, or between servers that require mutual authentication, confidentiality, or non-repudiation?	An Application creates a Secure Pipe at the system level to communicate with its client or partners. The Secure Pipe is an encrypted communication channel that provides the required security functionality such as mutual authentication, integrity, and privacy.	
Roles/RBAC (D)	How does one structure and manage role-based access control?	A Principal (such as actor/process) is associated with a Role, which has access privileges to Resource.	Multilevel RBAC supports hierarchical Role and Resource.
Session (I)	Multiple subjects want to share information but don't want to interact with each other.	Create a globally accessible container, called a Session object, to hold the shared variables. The subjects access the shared variables stored in the Session object.	
Input Validation (I)	An instance of a Check Point at the implementation level		
Secure Logger (I)	How does one protect system log data from unauthorized access?	An Application writes to a Secure Logger, which protects the log data. A Log Viewer reads the protected log and displays the log data.	

Legend: (A)=Architectural Level, (D)=Design Level, (I)=Implementation Level

FIGURE 24.1 Summary of some security patterns

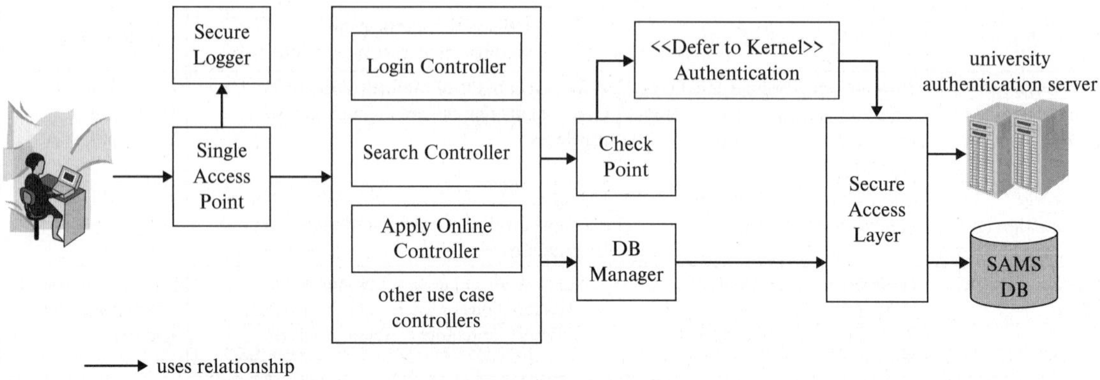

FIGURE 24.2 A secure architecture for the SAMS system

The controllers use the Check Point module to check security policies. In particular, the Login Controller uses Check Point to authenticate users. Instead of implementing its own authentication algorithm, Check Point utilizes an existing authentication service from a university authentication server. This illustrates an application of the *defer to kernel* pattern and the *use community resources* secure software design principle. The Apply Online Controller also uses Check Point to check authorization of the user to access the apply online functions and the online applications.

24.5 SEVEN BEST PRACTICES OF SOFTWARE SECURITY

Gary McGraw identifies seven best practices of software security in the software life cycle. Below is a summary, listed in descending order of effectiveness:

Code review, performed during the implementation phase, is aimed at finding implementation problems. These include oversights, omissions, misunderstanding, and "naive" assumptions, that is, trusting too much rather than being reluctant to trust. For example, a buffer overflow attack could be prevented if the code includes checks to ensure that the input size is less than the buffer size.

Architectural risk analysis, performed during the requirements, architectural design, and testing and integration phases, is aimed at identifying design flaws in the architecture and the design class diagram. Problems to be detected by architectural risk analysis include poor compartmentalization, inadequate protection of critical assets, failure to authenticate clients, or failure to control role-based access to resources.

Penetration testing, performed during the deployment and field operation phases, is aimed at finding architectural design flaws in the fielded environment. As such, the generation of penetration test cases should be guided by architectural risk analysis and focus on detecting security problems relating to the configuration and environmental factors.

Risk-based security testing, performed during the unit testing and system testing phases, is aimed at ensuring that the security functionality, such as authentication and authorization, is correct and adequate, and the security tests derived from attack patterns and risk analysis results achieve the desired coverage.

Misuse cases, identified during the requirements phase and used throughout the life cycle, specify attack scenarios. Modeling and analysis of misuse cases help the developer gain insight into potential security problems. This knowledge is valuable to architectural design, behavioral design, and security testing.

Security requirements, identified and formulated in the planning phase and evolve throughout the iterative development life cycle, specify the required protection to valuable assets. Security requirements promote the importance of security to the requirement level and form the basis for subsequent design, implementation, testing, and deployment activities.

Security operation, performed during the system operation phase, is aimed at setting up, monitoring, and understanding the behavior of the system that leads to successful attacks. This understanding provides valuable knowledge for enhancing the security of the software system.

24.6 RISK ANALYSIS WITH AN ATTACK TREE

The architectural risk analysis and misuse cases can benefit from the use of *attack trees,* which are derived from the fault tree analysis technique. An attack tree or a fault tree is an AND-OR tree, which is widely used in problem solving. The nodes represent problems to be solved, or goals to be accomplished. There are two types of node: AND-node and OR-node. An AND-node means that the problem is solved if all of its child problems are solved. An OR-node, which is the default, means the problem is solved if one of its child problems is solved. An example of an attack tree, which depicts some possible ways to compromise an account, is shown below. In this example, an asterisk indicates repetition, meaning that the subproblems are solved repeatedly. A node marked with "(AND)" is an AND-node; a node without "(AND)" is an OR-node, which is the default. In this example, the outline representation, rather than a graph representation is used. The outline representation is preferred because attack trees tend to be large for real-world applications.

```
Compromise an Account
   1. Use guessing (AND)* // i.e., 1 requires 1.1, 1.2 and 1.3
      1.1. Look up a login ID
      1.2. Guess the password
      1.3. Try to log in with the login ID and password
   2. Use a password cracker
   3. Apply man-in-the-middle attack (AND)
      3.1. Obtain the decryption key
      3.2. Intercept packets
      3.3. Decrypt intercepted packets
      3.4. Recover the password from the unencrypted packets
```

```
4. Apply social engineering attack
   4.1. Through the support center (AND)*
        4.1.1. Look up a user
        4.1.2. Collect information about the user
        4.1.3. Look up the user's login ID
        4.1.4. Call the support center to reset password
   4.2. Persuade the user through blackmail
```

Attack trees facilitate architectural design and behavioral design of secure software. The branches of an attack tree specify the possible ways and attempts of an attacker to attack the system. The attacks with a high-occurrence probability and significant damage to the business should be taken into consideration during the design process. For example, online banking systems and online brokerage systems could experience significant financial losses if their customers' accounts are compromised. The Compromise an Account attack tree depicts four options that an attacker could used to compromise an account. If the first three options are the most likely, then the design process must consider how to prevent, defend, and thwart such attacks, for example, by applying secure software design patterns or security software designed to defend against such attacks.

24.7 SOFTWARE SECURITY IN THE LIFE CYCLE

Figure 24.3 is a summary of the security-related activities in the development life cycle. This section presents an overview of these activities. The detail of each of these activities is described in subsequent sections.

During the planning phase, modeling and analysis of security threats are performed to identify potential security risks. From these, security requirements are derived and become part of the software development contract. Thus, the countability of the development team to deliver secure software is established. The security requirements are then associated with the use cases. The associations are represented in the requirement-use case traceability matrix, as described in Chapter 7 (Deriving Use Cases from Requirements). This ensures that each increment satisfies the related security requirements. In addition, misuse cases that describe how an attacker would attack the system are derived to guide the design and TDD activities. Secure software design principles and security patterns are applied to produce a preliminary software architecture.

During the iterative phase, changes to functional as well as security requirements are considered at the beginning of each increment, based on the feedback from the users. Changes to functional requirements may lead to changes to the security requirements and misuse cases, and possibly the software architecture. On the other hand, changes to security requirements may introduce additional functional requirements. Domain modeling should capture security-related domain concepts and relationships, for example, roles and resources accessed by the roles as well as related access privileges.

Design for security is an important consideration during actor-system interaction modeling, behavioral modeling, responsibility assignment, and deriving design class

Life Cycle Activity	Security Related Activities
Planning and Architectural Design	• Construct a domain model to help understand and identify security requirements • Identify security threats, and derive security requirements and misuse cases • Specify role-based access rights • Apply security principles and security patterns during architectural design, and review the architecture for security flaws • Produce a security test plan to guide the security test process
For each iteration, do the following:	
Accommodate Requirements Change	For changes in the requirements • Identify security threats, and derive or modify security requirements and misuse cases • Specify or modify role-based access rights • Modify architecture, and review the architecture for security flaws • Modify security test plan and high level test cases
Domain Modeling	Modify the domain to help understand security related domain concepts introduced by the use cases allocated to the current iteration
Actor-System Interaction Modeling Behavioral Modeling Responsibility Assignment Deriving Design Class Diagram	• Design for security, taking into account security requirements and misuse cases • Apply security design patterns and security design principles • Check for security related design flaws during design reviews
TDD, Integration, and Deployment	• Consider security requirements and misuse cases during TDD • Apply static security vulnerability analysis tools • Test for security, generate and run misuse case-based test cases • Perform penetration testing and misuse case testing

FIGURE 24.3 Security-related activities in the life cycle

diagrams. That is, these design activities should consider security risks and countermeasures to defend the system and its valuable resources. During TDD, integration and deployment, security requirements and misuse cases are used to generate test cases. Code review and inspection as well as static analysis tools are applied to detect security vulnerabilities.

24.7.1 Security in the Planning Phase

Deriving Security Requirements

Software security is aimed at building software systems that possess the ability to thwart security attacks and recover from successful attacks. The extent to which a software system shall accomplish these goals are specified as software security requirements. The derivation of security requirements should be carried out jointly with the customer and users as well as security personnel. The information-collection techniques described in Chapter 4 (Software Requirements Elicitation) can be applied during this process. The objective is to identify: (1) valuable assets that need protection, (2) which roles need what access privileges to which assets and for how long, (3) potential threats to the assets, (4) required countermeasures to possible attacks, and (5) recovery capabilities in cases of a successful attack. Domain modeling, described in Chapter 5, may be applied to capture security-related domain concepts and relationships if desired.

The use case diagrams produced during the planning phase are a good place to start. Use case diagrams depict the business processes, actors, and the subsystems that encompass the business processes. The business processes and subsystems are valuable business assets. In addition, the data or information resources that are accessed or processed by the business processes can be identified or inferred from the verb noun phrases that label the use cases. For example, from the *Reset Password* use case one can identify passwords as a valuable data asset or information resource that needs to be protected.

The actors and their associations to use cases shown in the use case diagrams specify which roles need access to which business processes. Moreover, from this and the data that are accessed or processed by the business processes, one can derive role to resource access privileges.

The actors shown in a use case diagram represent either outside sources or insiders. The CSI/FBI surveys indicate that insider misuses represent about 40%–60% of the security incidents reported during the last several years. Some other statistics show that 70%–80% of all computer-related frauds are committed by insiders. Insiders have direct physical access to the computer and network, and know the resource access controls. Insiders may misuse access privileges or view sensitive data that travel the network. *Separation of duties, least privilege,* and *individual accountability* are the countermeasures to these insider attacks.

The potential threats are identified by examining a list of attacks (or attack patterns) to determine which attacks could happen to which assets. Alternatively, the potential threats can also be identified with STRIDE, which stands for Spoofing, Tampering-with-Data, Repudiation, Information Disclosure, Denial-of-Service, and Elevation-of-Privilege attacks. That is, one analyzes the assets to identify which STRIDE attacks are possible.

It should be noted that the protection against each potential threat could involve a cost. Therefore, it is necessary to conduct a cost-benefit analysis to identify and prioritize the needed protections. To accomplish this, threats that could cause significant damages are identified. The costs of damages, the costs to repair the damages, the costs to recover from such damages, and the probabilities of occurrences of such threats are estimated. Techniques to accomplish these tasks include brainstorming, survey, and the Delphi method described in Chapter 23 (Software Project Management).

The benefit of the protection against a potential threat is the costs of damages minus the costs of protection. The expected benefit is the benefit times the probability of occurrence. Clearly, one wants to focus on the potential threats that have a high expected benefit. For these threats, one formulates security requirements so that the software under development will provide security mechanisms to defend the system and resources against such threats.

The following is a summary of the activities described above:

1. Identify valuable assets and potential threats, aided by the use case diagrams and known attacks such as STRIDE attacks, or the ones listed in Figure 24.4.
2. Conduct cost-benefit analysis to identify threats that are costly to ignore, costly to repair the damages, and costly to recover from such damages, and have a high probability of occurrence.

Attack	Description	Defense
Man-in-the Middle, Eavesdropping, Sniffing	Attacker secretly records, relays, and possibly modifies, the messages sent between two parties.	Use encryption, checksum, and challenge-response authentication
Race Condition	Attacker exploits security processes that occur in stages to cause the system to execute an operation for the attacker between the stages.	Ensure that security-critical processes are atomic or encapsulated
Buffer Overflow	Attacker causes a program to write beyond the bounds of a data object, leading to undesired behavior, e.g., changing the return address stack to cause the system to execute a program for the attacker.	Use safer versions of unsafe functions, or a type-safe programming language like Java and C#
Backdoor, Intrusion, Unauthorized Access	Attacker bypasses security mechanisms to gain access to a system, e.g., through debugging code, default login accounts, password cracking, or unprotected password files.	Remove all such access mechanisms and install intrusion detection and prevention software
Input Manipulation	Attacker manipulates one or more user input elements to cause the system to behave differently, e.g., inserting "../" or "..\" in a directory path strings provided by the user to cause the system to traverse an unintended directory.	Implement input validation using a white list, e.g., to ensure that the path name refers to an intended path
Denial of Service	Attacks exhausts the system's resources to significantly reduce the system availability to legitimate users.	
Website Defacement	Attack changes the appearance of a website to cause disruption or distraction of normal service.	Remove causes for unauthorized access to the web server and update to the web pages

FIGURE 24.4 Summary of some well-known attacks and possible defenses

3. For the threats identified in the last step, formulate security requirements to provide the protection to the assets, defend the system from possible attacks, and/or recover the application from successful attacks. The appropriate security requirements can be looked up from the list described in Section 24.2.
4. Update the requirement-use case traceability matrix to include the security requirements and relate them to the use cases.
5. If additional functional requirements and use cases are introduced, due to the addition of the security requirements, then repeat the above steps.

Identifying Misuse Cases

Building secure systems must ensure that the security requirements are complete and adequate, and the security mechanisms are properly implemented. If these conditions are not met, then attackers could exploit the flaws to launch attacks. In addition, some attacks bypass security measures, for example, through debugging code, default login accounts, or Trojan horses. Such uses of the system are called misuse cases.

EXAMPLE 24.2 Derive security requirements from the following use cases for the Study Abroad Management System (SAMS):

UC1: Search for Programs (actor: Web User, system: SAMS)
UC2: Display Program Detail (actor: Web User, system: SAMS)
UC3: Submit Online Application (actor: Student, system: SAMS)

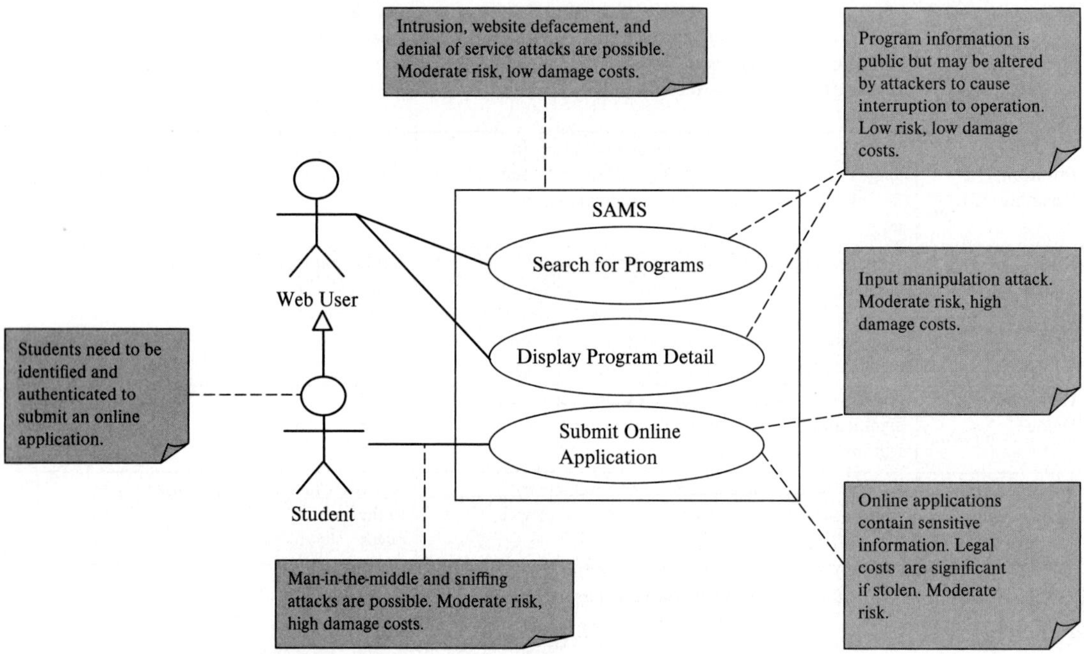

FIGURE 24.5 Identifying security threats

Solution: Figure 24.5 displays the use case diagram, which shows the business processes and the subsystem. These are the assets that may need protection. In addition, it identifies the information resources from the nouns of the verb-noun phrases that name the use cases, for example, "program," "program detail," and "online application." Based on the domain knowledge acquired or by consulting the customer and users, one can identify the assets that need protection, that is, assets that are crucial to the business and business operation. In this example, the exchange programs, program detail, and online applications are critical for the business of the Office of International Education.

Cost-benefit analysis identifies the potential threats, their damage costs, and occurrence probabilities or risks as shown in Figure 24.5 using UML notes. From the analysis result, one identifies input manipulation, man-in-the-middle, and sniffing attacks to be the threats that are associated with high damage costs and moderate occurrence probabilities. One also identifies online applications as the asset that must be protected. Thus, the following security requirements (SR) are formulated:

SR1. SAMS shall identify and authenticate all students who want to submit an online application.
SR2. SAMS shall allow students to access and only access their own accounts and online applications.
SR3. SAMS shall prevent all unauthorized accesses to student accounts and online applications including use of input manipulation.
SR4. SAMS shall detect, record, and notify the security administrator of suspicious attempts to gain access to student accounts and online applications.
SR5. SAMS shall encrypt all messages communicated between the system and students who are preparing or submitting an online application to prevent man-in-the-middle and sniffing attacks, and encrypt all student account information and online application data stored in the database.

Referring to the security requirements presented in Section 24.2, SR1 covers identification and authentication. SR2, SR3 and SR4 cover privacy. SR3 also deals with authorization, and SR4 also covers intrusion detection and non-repudiation. SR5 is about secrecy.

Note that the newly derived security requirements may lead to additional functional as well as security requirements. For example, SR1 above implies that SAMS must provide the capability for creating student login accounts. This, in turn, implies that students must be able to change and reset passwords, and more. Moreover, these functional requirements may lead to additional security requirements, for example, the reset password capability implies that the system must have a security mechanism to authenticate the student who wants to reset the password.

Misuse cases are use cases with hostile intent. Similar to use cases, a misuse case is a series of interactions that begins with an attacker, ends with the attacker, and accomplishes the intent of the attacker. In other words, a misuse case ends when the attacker's objective is achieved. The usefulness of misuse cases includes the following:

1. Misuse cases facilitate understanding, communication, and analysis of potential attacks to a system, although not all misuse cases lead to an attack or successful attack.
2. The description of a misuse case shows how an attacker would compromise the system. This information could be used during the design phase to guide the design of a secure architecture, and the design of secure system behavior, for example, actor-system interaction behavior, object interaction behavior, state behavior, and workflow activity behavior.
3. During the implementation phase, especially TDD and code review, misuse cases are useful for generating security test cases to test the implementation. Moreover,

the descriptions of the scenarios of the misuse cases enable the reviewers to focus on implementation problems that may lead to high-risk attacks.

4. Misuse cases that exploit configuration files and environment variables are useful for guiding the deployment process to protect the security of the system in the target environment.

Deriving misuse cases requires creative thinking. Brainstorming is highly recommended. To be effective, the brainstorming team should consist of approximately a half of a dozen participants including developers, information security experts, and users. The participants are guided by a list of known attacks and look for security problems belonging to the following categories:

- *Requirement-based misuse.* Look for missing, or inadequate security requirements that can lead to misuse attacks.
- *Design-based misuse.* Assume that the security requirements are adequate, and look for security problems that may result if the design fails to satisfy certain security requirements. For example, assume that access control to a database is a security requirement. A design-based security problem would occur if the design allows a client program to access the database directly. A potential attacker could exploit the design flaw to launch security attacks.

  Another category of design-based misuse is identified by attack patterns and security patterns. The former identifies design flaws that can be exploited by known attacks while the latter identifies design flaws that are addressed by secure software design patterns. For example, a pattern-based misuse case can be identified by assuming that the architectural design does not use a secure pipe to communicate sensitive information.
- *Implementation-based misuse.* Implementation-based misuse cases are identified from assumed security loopholes in the code, as well as from attack patterns that exploit implementation vulnerabilities. For example, inexperienced programmers may store passwords in clear texts. An implementation-based misuse could be identified by assuming that such a vulnerability exists. An input manipulation misuse case can be identified if input manipulation attack is a possibility for the system under development.
- *Bypass misuse.* Bypass misuse is identified by assuming that there are design, or implementation vulnerabilities that allow an attacker to bypass security mechanisms, for example, gaining access to the system through debugging code, or default login accounts. For example, using hard-coded user names and passwords to connect to a database is not uncommon. To ensure that such vulnerabilities do not exist, a misuse case could be derived. List of attack patterns and commonly seen security loopholes such as hard-coded passwords, default login accounts, and the like, can be used to improve the effectiveness of misuse case identification.
- *Tampering misuse.* Tampering misuse is identified from a list of known tampering attack patterns such as the use of a password cracker to discover a weak password.

Although misuse cases are useful, the potential misuse cases could be numerous. Therefore, the identification of misuse cases should be restricted to those that are most likely to occur and the consequences are politically or economically unacceptable.

EXAMPLE 24.3

Derive misuse cases for the SAMS application.

Solution: Identity theft or stealing personal information is among the bad things an attacker loves to do. An attacker has many options to accomplish this. He or she may try to gain access to the machine that hosts the database and then compromise the database security mechanism. The attacker may compromise a student account on SAMS and steal the student's information. He or she may also use this compromised account to try to obtain other students' information. This list of options may go on and on. For the purpose of our discussion, let us assume that the attacker wants to compromise a student's account and uses it to steal the student's information. In this case, three misuse cases, referred to as MC1, MC2, and MC3, are identified:

MC1: Compromise an Account. The attacker tries to compromise a weak-password account through repeatedly guessing or using a password cracker. This means there are two alternative misuse cases:(1) Compromise an Account by Guessing, and (2) Compromise an Account with a Password Cracker. For simplicity, only (2) is considered in this example.

MC2: Logon SAMS. This is the same as the Logon SAMS use case except that it is carried out by an attacker; and hence, it is treated as a misuse case because the functionality is illegally accessed.

MC2: Steal Information. After logging on the SAMS system, the attacker views and downloads the student's information.

Figure 24.6 shows the misuse case diagram and the high-level misuse cases, where the attacker and misuse cases are inverted, as proposed by Sindra and Opdalh.

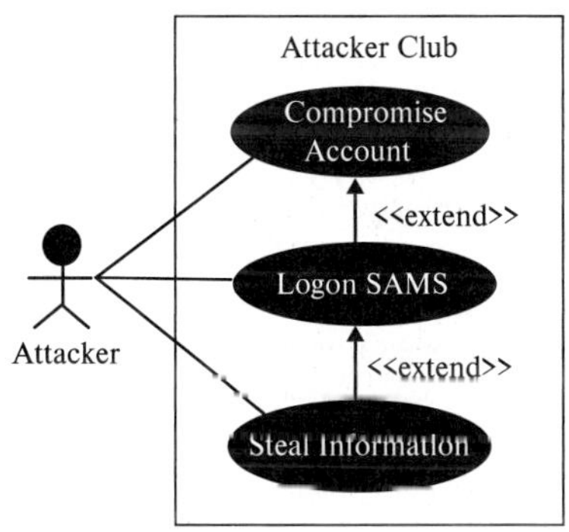

MC1: Compromise an Account
TMCBW the attacker launching a password cracker.
TMCEW the attacker seeing a matching pair of user name and password.

MC2: Logon SAMS
TMCBW the attacker clicking the Logon link on a SAMS web page.
TMCEW the attacker seeing the welcome message.

MC3. Steal Information
Precondition: The attacker already logged on.
TMCBW the attacker clicking the Edit/View Online Application link on a SAMS web page.
TMCEW the attacker seeing the detail of the online application.

Legend: Attacker — Steal Info: Misuse Case — ——— Association

TMCBW=This misuse case begins with, TMCEW=This misuse case ends with

FIGURE 24.6 Deriving misuse cases for SAMS

Producing a Secure Architecture

Sections 24.3 and 24.4 present secure software design principles and security patterns. They illustrate the application of some of the security patterns to the design of a software architecture for the SAMS web application. Designing a secure architecture for a software system involves risk analysis, and application of secure software design principles and patterns, as described by the following iterative steps:

1. Produce an architectural design that satisfies the security requirements and accounts for misuse cases.
2. Evaluate the architectural design to identify significant security risks.
3. Modify the architectural design to remove or mitigate the significant security risks.
4. Repeat the last two steps until an acceptable risk level is achieved.

Architectural design was presented in Chapter 6. One of the objectives of the design is to satisfy the requirements, including security requirements. The security requirements and high-risk misuse cases influence the design decisions. That is, the architectural design should include components and security patterns to provide the required security functions, and the ability to battle security attacks, mitigate attack damages, and recover from such attacks. The design should apply secure software design principles to enhance the security of the software architecture.

Applying secure software design patterns is similar to applying software design patterns. That is, identify the security problem first and then apply the appropriate security patterns. For example, if authentication is a requirement and the design problem is how to satisfy this requirement, then the *check point* pattern is applied. If authorization is a requirement and how to perform an authorization check is the design problem, then the check point and *role-based access control* (RBAC) patterns are applied.

The resulting architectural design should be analyzed with respect to the security requirements, secure software design principles, security patterns, and misuse cases. The objective is to detect potential security risks. For example, the architecture in Figure 24.2 indicates the use of a SAMS database, which stores student accounts and online applications. The security requirements indicate that *"SAMS shall prevent all unauthorized accesses to student accounts and online applications"* (SR3). From this requirement, a number of questions could be raised. For example, is the database protected from unauthorized access from within and outside of the OIE? Is encryption being used to protect sensitive information? As another example, *SR4 says that "SAMS shall detect, record, and notify the security administrator of suspicious attempts to gain access to the SAMS system and any of its components."* However, the architecture does not show which component will accomplish these functions. Thus, a security risk is identified.

Although it is not necessary for an architectural design to apply each of the secure software design principles and patterns, examining the architecture against these principles and patterns may lead to detection of security vulnerabilities. In this regard, one wants to identify places that a principle or pattern should be applied but it is not. This analysis may detect vulnerabilities or risks. For example, in Figure 24.2, the connection between a client computer and the SAMS web server is not secure. This means that submitted form data are subject to spoofing or eavesdropping attacks–a secure pipe should be used; and hence, a security vulnerability is detected.

The security risks identified by using security requirements, misuse cases, security principles, and patterns may overlap. This is because the identification mechanisms have overlapping objectives. For example, a requirement-based misuse case shares the same objective with the security requirement from which the requirement-based misuse case is derived. Similarly, security risks identified by bypass misuse cases may overlap with those identified by implementation-level security patterns. For example, input manipulation misuse cases and input validation patterns may identify the same security risks. Therefore, if two or more risk identification mechanisms share the same objective, then one needs to apply only one of them.

It is not desirable to resolve all of the security risks that are identified. This is because the benefit may not be worth the cost associated with the resolution of a certain risk. As discussed earlier, a cost-benefit assessment is desired. The objective is to identify the security risks that are more likely to be exploited and the attack consequences are unacceptable. This assessment is an application-dependent activity.

The architectural design is then modified to remove the security vulnerabilities that are vital to the security of the system. The appropriate security patterns are applied. For example, if the connection between the client browser and the SAMS web server is considered a vital security risk, then the architecture in Figure 24.2 is modified to include a secure pipe between the two.

24.7.2 Security in the Iterative Phase

Security in Requirements Change

Requirements change is a common practice in today's software development. Requirements can change as often as every day or every week, especially at the beginning of an agile project. Requirements change means new requirements are added, and existing requirements are modified or deleted. Deleting one or more requirements may lead to removal of related security requirements. This may lead to removal of related requirement-based misuse cases, and removal of related security mechanisms in the architectural design. On the other hand, adding functional requirements may lead to the addition of security requirements and misuse cases, and changes to the architectural design. Update to existing requirements can be processed similarly.

Review and inspection of the modified architectural design are carried out, guided by the security requirements, misuse cases, and secure software design principles and patterns, as described in the last section. Finally, the test plan and test cases are modified to reflect the changes to the requirements.

Security in Domain Modeling

During domain modeling, information relating to the security aspect of the application is also collected. The information should include at least the following:

- What are the valuable assets/resources including business processes, databases, and data files?

- What are the roles/job titles in the application?
- What are the responsibilities of each role, and what are the least access privileges for the role to fulfill its responsibilities?

The above information could be found in the security requirements and related documents such as security policy specifications and procedures. The information-collection techniques described in Chapter 4 (Software Requirements Elicitation) are applicable in this context. In many cases, interview is the most effective tool to collect the required security information. In addition to these, the use case diagrams are a valuable source. The roles, their responsibilities, and access privileges can be easily identified or derived from the use case diagrams.

The brainstorming, classification, and visualization steps of domain modeling are the same, and the resulting domain model should include security-related concepts, properties, and relationships. In particular, the model should include classes that represent the roles and resources accessed by the roles as well as association relationships that specify the least access privileges of the roles to the resources.

Security in Behavioral Design

The behavioral design activities include design of expanded use cases, sequence diagrams, state diagrams, activity diagrams, and derivation of a design class diagram. The security requirements and misuse cases are considered, and the secure software

EXAMPLE 24.4 Construct a part of a domain model for the SAMS application showing security-related concepts and relationships.

Solution: The solution is shown in Figure 24.7. For simplicity, attributes are not shown in the model. The model only depicts security related concepts and relationships to help understand and identify role-based access requirements.

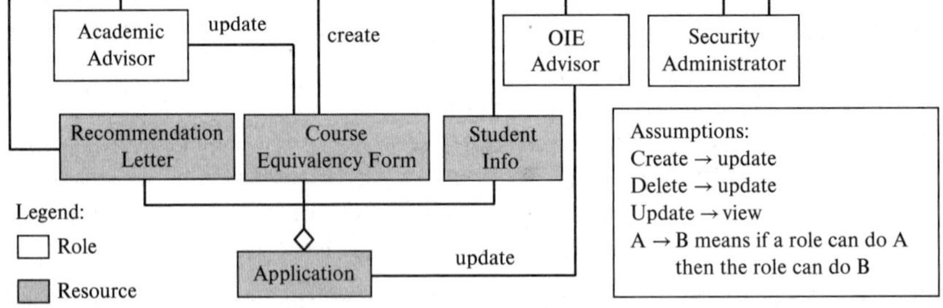

FIGURE 24.7 Part of a domain model showing security information

design principles and patterns are applied. The following paragraphs illustrate these ideas.

One commonly seen approach to verify a user-submitted password is comparing it with the password stored in the database. This approach violates the principle of "promoting privacy" because the user's password is unprotected. Another approach encrypts the password and stores the cipher text. The password is decrypted before verification. However, how to keep the encryption key secret is a challenge because Principle 8 tells us that "hiding secret is hard." Therefore, a better approach should hash the password and store the hash code. To verify a user-submitted password, the password is hashed and compared with the stored hash code. This approach makes it more difficult for others to steal the password.

Input manipulation attack or input validation pattern suggests that input from external sources should be validated before accepting them. Principle 9, "be reluctant to trust," suggests the same. If these are considered during behavior design, then the sequence diagrams will include input validators to validate the input from the web users.

Security in Implementation, Testing, and Deployment

Consideration of security during implementation, testing, and deployment involves the following activities:

1. *Guiding implementation with secure software design principles.*

   Many secure software design principles are applicable to implementation. These include *practice defense in depth, fail securely, keep it simple and stupid, promote privacy, remember that hiding secrets is hard, be reluctant to trust,* and *use community resources.* The *practice defense in depth* principle tells us to implement more than one security mechanism. For example, to defend against password cracking, one should implement strong password rules and disable the account after *N* failed login attempts. The *fail securely* principle suggests that valuable assets should be protected and no sensitive data should be left to the attacker when the system fails.

2. *Applying implementation-level security patterns.*

   Implementation-level security patterns are proven solutions to security problems at the implementation level. Applying implementation-level security patterns strengthens the security of the code. Implementation-level patterns include but are not limited to the input validation pattern, the secure logger pattern, and the defer to kernel pattern. Used at the implementation level, the defer to kernel pattern suggests using kernel functions or APIs that are proven to promote security rather than reinventing the wheels.

3. *Practice secure programming principles and practices.*

   During the years, a number of secure coding principles and practices have emerged and evolved. For example, Graff and Kenneth suggest the following: examine input data for malicious intent, perform bounds checking, check configuration files, check command line parameters, don't trust web URLs, be careful of web content, check web cookies, check environment variables, set valid initial data values, understand and correctly use file name references, be wary of indirect file references, be careful of how programs and data are searched, and pay special attention to the storage of sensitive information.

4. *Testing for security.*

Software security testing is a new, interdisciplinary area that involves both software engineering and information security. Approaches to software security testing are classified into two categories: static approaches and dynamic approaches. Static approaches include inspection, review and use of static analysis tools. These approaches can be applied to requirements, design, and code. With regard to security, the conventional code review and inspection checklist should be augmented with security-related review questions and inspection items to detect security vulnerabilities. The design of the review questions and inspection items should evaluate the code with respect to the security requirements, secure software design principles, patterns, misuse cases, and attack patterns.

Static analysis tools, also called code analyzers, are an aid to code review and inspection. These tools examine the software to detect security problems and vulnerabilities. Static analysis tools can check either the source code or the compiled code. Their functions include type checking, style checking, property checking, security analysis, bug finding, program verification, and program understanding. During the last several decades, many static analysis tools have been developed. The use of tools can drastically reduce time and effort. One problem of static analysis tools is that they tend to produce too many false positives or false alarms. Tremendous effort is required to examine the analysis result. Another problem is that a few tools report false negatives, that is, they do not detect some of the problems that actually exist.

All dynamic approaches to testing require execution of the program using a set of test cases. These approaches differ in the way in which the test cases are generated, and the test model that is used to generate the test cases. With regard to testing for security, the goal of a secure software test method is to generate test cases that can detect security problems as effectively and efficiently as possible. Many methods and tools for security testing have been proposed during the last two decades. Similar to conventional software testing methods and tools, security-testing methods and tools are also classified into black-box, white-box, and gray-box methods and tools, depending on the way in which the test cases are generated.

TDD is an emerging trend in recent years. It is a best practice to consider security during TDD. That is, security test cases should also be generated and run during TDD. This ensures not only the correctness of the functionality but also the desired degree of security of the implementation. Note that test for security should be performed for security functions as well as ordinary functions that have a security implication. For example, a component that implements strong password rules should be tested to ensure that the rules are implemented correctly. Moreover, the component should also be tested with boundary, extreme, and exceptional cases to ensure that it behaves properly under such circumstances.

If a component does not implement a security function but its execution has security implications, then the component should be tested for its security impact. For example, if a component accesses an object that contains sensitive information, then the component should be tested for proper access control, non-elevation of privilege, and failing in a secure state.

The misuse cases identified during the planning phase are useful for security test case generation. In particular, the attack scenario of each misuse case can be described by an "expanded misuse case," which is similar to a use case except that it has a hostile intent. The expanded misuse cases can be used to generate misuse case-based test cases (see Chapter 20 for use case-based test case generation).

5. *Perform penetration testing during deployment.* This is described in the "Seven Best Practices of Software Security" section.

24.8 APPLYING AGILE PRINCIPLES

GUIDELINE 24.1 Active user involvement is imperative

Security needs are different for different applications. The customer and users know what are the valuable resources of their business and the level of protection needed. Therefore, building secure systems requires active customer and user involvement. The team needs to work with the customer and users closely throughout the life cycle. In particular, active user involvement is critical during the requirements phase to identify and formulate the security requirements, and assign priority to the security requirements.

GUIDELINE 24.2 Good enough is enough. Keep it simple and straightforward.

There is no absolute security. Moreover, security is not free–it comes with development and operating costs. The level of protection to valuable resources differs from resource to resource; it is often situation dependent. Implementing security features that are not needed wastes time and money, not building a secure system. Sometimes, such requests could come from the director of the office of information security of the customer's organization. On the other hand, users of the organization do not think that such security requirements are needed. As such, there are conflicting opinions.

GUIDELINE 24.3 A collaborative and cooperative approach between all stakeholders is essential.

Security not only costs effort and money to build and operate, it costs convenience to comply to security procedures. With respect to security, different stakeholders have different opinions. The director of the office of information security tends to think the more security the better. This is because their sole responsibility is to stay away from trouble. On the other hand, the end users do not want the inconvenience associated with certain security procedures. Often, the users want the office of information security and the office of information technology to implement convenient measures to protect the valuable resources. In these cases, how to reach a viable solution requires a collaborative and cooperative approach between the stakeholders.

GUIDELINE 24.4 Agile development values customer collaboration over contract negotiation.

As discussed above, certain security features cause inconvenience to the users, and implementing convenient measures requires additional investment of the customer. For many real-world projects, security is not just a technical issue; it is largely a political decision in practice. Moreover, the need for security evolves during and after the system is built. Therefore, customer collaboration as well as mutual understanding among the stakeholders is very valuable and needed. In this regard, the team cannot remain purely technical.

24.9 SUMMARY

This chapter presents the notion of software security, that is, building secure software throughout the life-cycle activities. It discusses the importance of software security as well as secure software design principles and security patterns. Other techniques such as attack tree and misuse cases are described. Software security is an emerging, multidisciplinary area that involves software engineering, information security, operating systems, and computer networking, among others. The security area alone covers a broad spectrum of topics. These include cryptography, authentication, authorization, access control, intrusion prevention and detection, privacy, malware, and software security. This chapter serves as a brief introduction to the field of software security.

24.10 CHAPTER REVIEW QUESTIONS

1. What is software security, and why is it important?
2. What are the secure software design principles, and how do they differ from the software design principles presented in Chapter 6?
3. What are secure software design patterns, and how do they differ from the design patterns presented in the other chapters?
4. What are the software security activities in the life cycle?

24.11 EXERCISES

24.1 Identify and formulate security requirements for the online car rental project described in Appendix D.1.

24.2 Identify five of the most significant misuse cases for the online car rental project. Also specify the abstract, high-level, and expanded misuse cases for these five misuse cases. *Hint:* These are the same as abstract, high-level, and expanded use cases except that they have a hostile intent.

24.3 Produce a secure architectural design for the online car rental software. Indicate which secure software design principles and security patterns are applied.

24.4 Produce a domain model for the online car rental application. Include security-related domain concepts, their properties and relationships.

24.5 Produce sequence diagrams for the three most useful use cases for the online car rental application. Include and indicate in the sequence diagrams security mechanisms to satisfy the security requirements formulated previously.

24.6 Do the same exercises as above but use the National Trade Show Service (NTSS) system described in Appendix D.2.

A

Appendix

Personal Software Process: Estimation, Planning, and Quality Assurance

Appendix A is a continuation and supplement to the personal software process presented in Chapter 2.

A.1 EFFORT ESTIMATION IN PSP

During the training of the personal software process (PSP), the software engineer uses the To Date time and To Date % data recorded in the Project Plan Summary forms to improve the accuracy of estimation. The programming exercises are designed to make this a possibility. That is, the exercises are designed to satisfy the following assumptions. First, the work for the new job will be distributed in much the same way as prior jobs. Second, each project is small enough so that each phase involves only one task. Third, the work is similar enough so that the To Date % provides reasonably accurate task estimates. It is hoped that the software engineer who is trained in PSP will continue to fill the Time Recording Log and Defect Recording Log for all future projects. These data are then used for the planning and quality assurance of new projects. Various estimation methods and planning approaches can be used with PSP. These include the COCOMO model, the function point estimation method, the Delphi estimation method, PERT chart, and Gantt chart. These approaches were presented in Chapter 23. Clearly, the accuracy of the estimation and the accuracy of the plan can be improved by using the Time in Phase data recorded in the Project Plan Summary forms.

In addition to the widely known estimation methods, the *Proxy-Based Estimation* or PROBE method can also be used with PSP. A proxy is a substitute for the software to be estimated. The PROBE method is based on the assumption that the proxy is easier to estimate, and hence, it helps the estimation of the time required to develop the software. The proxy must satisfy the following criteria:

- The proxy size measure should closely relate to the effort required to develop the software. That is, it should have a close relationship to the resources required to develop the software.

- The proxy content of a system should be automatically countable. This suggests that the proxy should be a physical entity that can be precisely defined and automatically counted.
- The proxy should be easy to visualize at the beginning of a project. For example, classes, inputs, outputs, database fields, forms, and reports are easy to visualize and can be used as proxies.
- The proxy should be customizable to the needs of each project and developer. That is, the proxy should use data that are relevant to the new project at hand.
- The proxy should be sensitive to implementation variations that affect development cost or effort. That is, the proxy data should be available for different programming languages, design styles, and types of application.

The PROBE method uses proxy data of previous projects and linear regression to produce a linear function

$$T = f(S) = \beta_0 + \beta_1 \times S$$

where T is the development time, S the estimated proxy size, and β_0 and β_1 the coefficients derived by using linear regression. Since the size of the proxy is assumed to be easier to estimate and the proxy is closely related to the software, this linear function can then be used to estimate the actual development time for the software.

Divide-and-conquer is used to decompose a large project into a hierarchy of components, in which higher-level components are refined by lower-level components. This makes it easier to find proxies for the lower-level components. The time to synthesize the lower-level components is then added to the time required to develop a higher-level component.

Planning in PSP is similar to planning using other methods except that the recorded Time in Phase data and Interrupt Time data help the software engineer produce a more realistic schedule. The planning activity involves the following steps:

1. An estimate of the total development time required for the software is produced, as described in the previous paragraphs.
2. Allocate time to the development phases using the To Date % data recorded in the Project Plan Summary forms.
3. Estimate weekly task hours according to the personal data recorded for previous projects. For example, the Interrupt Time spent on other activities such as meetings, emailing, phone calls, and the like.
4. Calculate available hours that can be spent on the project each week, taking into consideration the commitments to other projects.
5. Sort the development tasks according to their dependencies and priorities.
6. Produce a schedule according to the order to perform the tasks, task durations, and time available each week.
7. Define the project milestones and list their planned completion dates.

A.2 SOFTWARE QUALITY ASSURANCE IN PSP

The PSP strategy to high-quality systems is to manage the defect content of all parts of a system. Thorough design and code reviews are effective ways to improve software quality and productivity. The following are PSP code review principles:

1. Personally review all of your own work before you move on to the next development phase.
2. Strive to fix all of the defects before you give the design or code to review by others.
3. Use a personal checklist and follow a structured review process. The personal checklist is produced from the Defect Recording Logs' that is, for frequent defect types, devise checks that are specific to detect the defects. The checklist is organized into sections, each of which focuses on detecting similar defects. The checklist is modified from time to time to reflect the improvement from using the PSP.
4. Follow sound review practices: review in small increments, do reviews on paper, and do them when you are rested and fresh.
5. Measure the review time, the sizes of the artifacts reviewed, and the number and types of defects you found and missed.
6. Use these data to improve your personal review process.
7. Design and implement your components so that they are easy to review.
8. Review your defect data to identify ways to prevent defects.
9. Review against coding standards.

A.3 DESIGN AND QUALITY

The PSP addresses the design issue from a defect prevention point of view and proposes four design templates. They are tabular substitutes of widely known design representations such as class diagram, scenario, structured English or pseudocode, and state diagram. Briefly, the design templates are:

1. *Functional Specification Template.* It is used to specify a class, its parent class, and the attributes and operations of the class. That is, it is a tabular specification of a class.
2. *Operational Specification Template.* It is a line-by-line specification of a scenario, that is, each line specifies the action performed by an object, along with a brief comment.
3. *Logic Specification Template.* It is similar to the specification of the program logic using Structured English or pseudocode.
4. *State Specification Template.* It specifies the states, state transitions, and guard conditions.

In addition to design templates, PSP uses several methods to verify a design. For example, it uses design standards to verify that a design performs its intended functionality. An execution table or a trace table is used to record the intermediate results or traces produced during the manual execution of a logic specification. A state specification is verified by manually tracing the states and transitions.

Appendix B

Java Technologies

This appendix provides a mini-tutorial to some of the commonly used Java technologies: Java Data Base Connectivity (JDBC), Swing, and Java Server Pages (JSP).

B.1 GETTING STARTED WITH DATABASE CONNECTIVITY

Almost all current real-world applications use a database. The most popular type of database is the relational database. A relational database uses tables to represent data and provides a query language for the user to access the database. The most popular query language is the Structured Query Language (SQL), which is commonly referred to as SQL. This section presents how to access a database from an object-oriented program. The objective is getting started with database connectivity quickly and easily.

B.1.1 What Is Database Connectivity?

The object-oriented world is quite different from the relational world. If a relational database is used to store objects, then there must be a mechanism to facilitate an object-oriented program to access the database to retrieve or store information. The so-called database connectivity accomplishes this. In particular, the Open Data Base Connectivity (ODBC) proposed by Microsoft is a C program interface to access a database. The Java Data Base Connectivity (JDBC) is a database access interface for Java.

As shown in Figure B.1, a Java application uses JDBC API, which in turn uses a JDBC/ODBC bridge and an ODBC driver, or a vendor-supplied JDBC driver to access the database. The JDBC API is described in the java.sql package.

B.1.2 Setting Up Data Sources

Before writing the program, you may need to set up the data source that links to the database you use. It depends on the database management system you use.

B.1.3 Accessing Databases from a Program

Using JDBC to access a database is relatively easy. As shown in Figure B.2, it involves four steps:

Step 1. Connecting to the database. The first step is connecting to the database, as shown in line (31). This includes loading the JDBC driver class in line (15) and establishing a connection to the database in line (21).

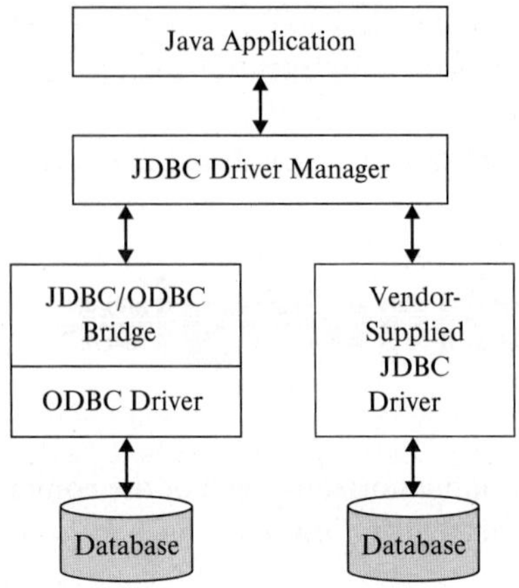

FIGURE B.1 Java Data Base Connectivity (JDBC)

Step 2. Querying the database. Lines (32)-(35) show the instructions to retrieve records from the database. The executeQuery(String sql) function of Statement retrieves the records from the database and returns the records in a ResultSet object. A ResultSet object is a data table that resembles a relation in a relational

```
(1) package database;
(2) import java.sql.*;
(3) import java.util.*;
(4) import java.io.*;
(5) // other import statements
(6) public class DBMgr {
(7)  Connection con = null;
(8)  String driver = “sun.jdbc.odbc.JdbcOdbcDriver”;
(9)  String url = “jdbc:odbc:mydb”;
(10)  String username;
(11)  String password;
(12)  Statement stmt = null;
(13)  public void connect() {
(14)   try { // load the JDBC driver
(15)     Class.forName(driver);
(16)   } catch(ClassNotFoundException e) {
(17)     System.err.println(“Failed to load driver.”);
(18)     return;
(19)   }
(20)   try { // connect to database
(21)     con=DriverManager.getConnection(url,
           username, password);
(22)   } catch (SQLException e) {
(23)     System.err.println(“Failed to connect.”);
(24)     return;
(25)   }
(26)  }
(27)  public ArrayList getClassX(String attrName,
        String attrValue) {
(28)   ResultSet rs=null;
(29)   ArrayList result=new ArrayList();
(30)   try {
(31)     connect();
(32)     stmt=con.createStatement();
(33)     rs=stmt.executeQuery(
(34)       “SELECT * FROM TABLEX ”+
(35)       “WHERE ”+attrName+“ = “+
               “‘“+attrValue+”’”);
(36)     while (rs.next()) {
(37)       ClassX x=new ClassX();
(38)       x.setAttr1(rs.getString(“attr1”));
(39)       x.setAttr2(rs.getString(“attr2”));
(40)       // other set attribute statements
(41)       result.add(x);
(42)     }
(43)     stmt.close(); con.close();
(44)   }
(45)   catch (SQLException e) {
(46)     return null;
(47)   }
(48)   return result;
(49)  }
(50) }
```

FIGURE B.2 Access a database from a Java program

database. The executeUpdate(String sql) of Statement should be used if the query is an insert, update, delete, or create table query. The method returns the row count for the number of rows affected.

Step 3. Processing query result. Lines (36)-(42) iterate over the table entries of the ResultSet object. In most cases, the entries of each row are used to set the attribute values of an object. The objects are appended to an ArrayList object, which is returned in line (48).

Step 4. Disconnecting from the database. This is shown in line (43).

The program in Figure B.2 is aimed to help the reader get started with JDBC. As such, the database user name and password are hard-coded. This implies a security problem because it is very easy to read the bytecode and discover the user name and password. A better solution should use encryption and save the user name and password in the memory and use them to connect to the database.

The driver string and database url can be defined in a properties file and loaded into a Properties object. These properties can then be retrieved by calling the getProperty(String propertyKey) method of the Properties object.

B.2 GETTING STARTED WITH SWING

Chapter 12 presents how to design the user interfaces for a given application. This section introduces graphical user interface (GUI) programming with Swing–a widget toolkit for Java. Swing is an extension of Java Abstract Window Toolkit (AWT). To distinguish, all components of Swing are preceded with a capital J, such as JFrame and JComponent, which extend AWT Frame and AWT Component. Swing is meant for implementing GUIs for stand-alone applications. The following presentation uses the state diagram editor GUI shown in Figure 16.4 to illustrate programming with Swing. Many IDEs greatly facilitate Swing programming. For example, the program segments displayed in this section can be easily produced by using the interactive GUI design capabilities of an IDE.

B.2.1 Creating Main Window with JFrame

First, one extends JFrame to create the main window. The following code creates a window with "State Diagram Editor" as its title and a menu bar:

```
package gui;
import javax.swing.*;
public class SDEFrame extends JFrame {
    JMenuBar jMenuBar1 = new JMenuBar();
    JMenu jMenuFile = new JMenu("File");
    JMenu jMenuEdit = new JMenu("Edit");
    JMenu jMenuTools = new JMenu("Tools");
    JMenu jMenuHelp = new JMenu("Help");

    public SDEFrame() {
        try { initComp();
```

```
        } catch (Exception ex) {
          ex.printStackTrace();
        }
      }
      private void initComp() throws Exception {
         setTitle("State Diagram Editor");
         jMenuBar1.add(jMenuFile); jMenuBar1.add(jMenuEdit);
         jMenuBar1.add(jMenuTools); jMenuBar1.add(jMenuHelp);
         setJMenuBar(jMenuBar1); setSize(800, 600);
      }
      /** exit application when the window is closed */
      protected void processWindowEvent(WindowEvent e) {
         super.processWindowEvent(e);
         if (e.WINDOW_CLOSING==e.getID()) System.exit(0);
      }
  }
```

To show the window, one needs a Main class, which creates an instance of SDE-Frame and makes it visible:

```
package gui;
import java.awt.Toolkit;
import javax.swing.SwingUtilities;
import javax.swing.UIManager;
import java.awt.Dimension;
public class Main {
  public Main() {
    SDEFrame frame = new SDEFrame();
    frame.validate();
    // Center the window
    Dimension screenSize = Toolkit.getDefaultToolkit().
       getScreenSize();
    Dimension frameSize = frame.getSize();
    frame.setLocation( (screenSize.width - frameSize.width) / 2,
                       (screenSize.height - frameSize.height) / 2);
    frame.setVisible(true);
  }
  public static void main(String[] args) {
         try { UIManager.setLookAndFeel(
              UIManager.getSystemLookAndFeelClassName());
         } catch (Exception exception) {
           exception.printStackTrace();
         }
         new Main();
  }
}
```

The reader can compile and run these programs to view the result.

B.2.2 Using Layout Managers to Arrange Components

This section describes how to use JPanel and Swing layout managers to arrange the components so that they will appear at appropriate places. A JPanel object is a container. One can add GUI components and other JPanel objects into a JPanel object. A layout manager or simply a layout arranges the components of a JPanel object in a predefined fashion. There are three basic layouts that are easy to use and solve most of the layout problems. These are BorderLayout, GridLayout, and FlowLayout. A border layout divides the rectangular area of a JPanel into five regions, the center region and four borders, referred to as north, south, east, and west regions. For example, to add a toolbar, the buttons, and a drawing area to the main window as shown in Figure 16.4, one can use border layout to place the toolbar in the north region of the content pane, which is the default container of a JFrame:

```
public class SDEFrame extends JFrame {
    // ...
    JButton openButton=new JButton();
    JButton closeButton=new JButton();
    JButton helpButton=new JButton();
    JToolBar jToolBar1=new JToolBar();
    // ...
    private void initComp() throws Exception {
        // ...
        ImageIcon openImg = new ImageIcon(getClass().
                getResource("openFile.png"));
        ImageIcon closeImg = new ImageIcon(getClass().
                getResource("closeFile.png"));
        ImageIcon helpImg = new ImageIcon(getClass().
                getResource("help.png"));
        openButton.setIcon(openImg); closeButton.setIcon(closeImg);
        helpButton.setIcon(helpImg); jToolBar1.add(openButton);
        jToolBar1.add(closeButton); jToolBar1.add(helpButton);
        getContentPane().setLayout(new BorderLayout());
        getContentPane().add(jToolBar1, BorderLayout.NORTH);
    }
}
```

A grid layout arranges components in a rectangular grid. Consider, for example, the layout of the three drawing buttons in Figure 16.4. One could add a JPanel, called westPanel, to the west region of the content pane and use a grid layout to arrange the buttons in the westPanel. With this implementation, the buttons will occupy the entire westPanel, leaving no space between the buttons. This won't look nice. The flow layout can be used to add space between the buttons and between the buttons and the borders of the westPanel. A flow layout arranges components in a left to right flow. More specifically, one adds to the westPanel three JPanel objects, which have flow layouts and each contains a button:

```
public class SDEFrame extends JFrame {
    // ...
    JButton stateButton=new JButton(" State ");
    JButton transitionButton=new JButton("Transition");
```

```
    JButton pointerButton=new JButton();
    private void initComp() throws Exception
        { // ...
        JPanel westPanel=new JPanel(new GridLayout(3, 1));
        JPanel stateBtnPanel=new JPanel();
        stateBtnPanel.setLayout(new FlowLayout());
        JPanel transitionBtnPanel=new JPanel();
        transitionBtnPanel.setLayout(new FlowLayout());
        ...
        getContentPane().add(westPanel, BorderLayout.WEST);
        westPanel.add(stateBtnPanel);
        westPanel.add(transitionBtnPanel);
        stateBtnPanel.add(stateButton);
        transitionBtnPanel.add(transitionButton);
        ...
    }
}
```

B.2.3 Processing Button Events with Action Listener

In Swing, when the user clicks a GUI button, an ActionEvent object is generated. The application should handle such events. In Swing, the ActionEvents are processed by ActionListener objects. For example, Figure 16.33 could be implemented in Swing as follows:

```
// package and import statements
public class EditDiagramGUI {
    EditDiagramController controller=new EditDiagramController();
    // Create the State and Transition buttons
    JButton stateButton=new JButton(" State ");
    JButton transButton=new JButton("Transition");
    // Create and add action listeners
    stateButton.addActionListener(new StateButtonListener());
    transButton.addActionListener(new TransButtonListener());

    // Define the action listeners as inner classes
    class StateButtonListener implements ActionListener {
        public void actionPerformed(ActionEvent e) {
            controller.stateBtnClicked();
        }
    }
    class TransButtonListener implements ActionListener {
        public void actionPerformed(ActionEvent e) {
            controller.transBtnClicked();
        }
    }
}
```

B.2.4 Implementing Drawing Capabilities

The drawing area or canvas is a JPanel. It may implement the MouseListener and MouseMotionListener interfaces to capture and handle mouse events. Alternatively, it may create and add MouseListener and MouseMotionListener objects to handle the mouse events. For example, in Figure 16.10, the Edit Diagram GUI class creates an anonymous Mouse Listener object and adds it to the canvas. When the canvas is pressed, this listener captures the event and calls the canvasClicked() method of the Edit Diagram Controller to handle the event. The Mouse Adapter class is a Java API, which implements the Mouse Listener interface to provide default implementations for the five Mouse Listener functions. Because of this, the code in Figure 16.10 only needs to override the mousePressed (MouseEvent e) method.

B.3 GETTING STARTED WITH JAVA SERVER PAGES

B.3.1 What Are Java Server Pages?

Web-based applications have become more and more popular. These applications rely on the so-called server pages to process requests submitted from a client browser. In the Java platform, the server pages are called Java Server Pages (JSP). Simply speaking, a JSP page contains html code with embedded Java program segments called scriptlets. To distinguish, a JSP file has jsp as its extension, for example, Login.jsp.

Before the advent of JSP, requests from and responses to a browser were processed by servlets, which are Java classes with such responsibilities. It is rather cumbersome to program servlets because println(. . .) statements are the only means to produce the responses, that is, the html pages sent to the client browser. JSP allows the programmer to layout the web page using html and process information using scriptlets. This makes server-side programming much easier.

B.3.2 JSP Workflow

Figure B.3 shows how JSP works. Requests containing a form submitted to a JSP page are processed by the JSP engine or container running on the web server. When a JSP page, such as, hello.jsp, is visited the first time, it is converted into a servlet, such as hello_jsp.class; or else the servlet is loaded into the JSP container and the bean(s) used by the servlet is identified. The JSP engine then extracts the form's data and uses them to set the attributes of the bean, which is a Java object. This is possible because the bean is written according to the Java coding convention and provides setter methods that correspond to the names of the input fields in the form. The JSP engine then executes the servlet, which in turn queries the bean and interacts with relevant business objects to process the request and produce the response. The response is then sent to the client. Note that JSP is case sensitive–if there is a case mismatch, your web application may not work or not work correctly.

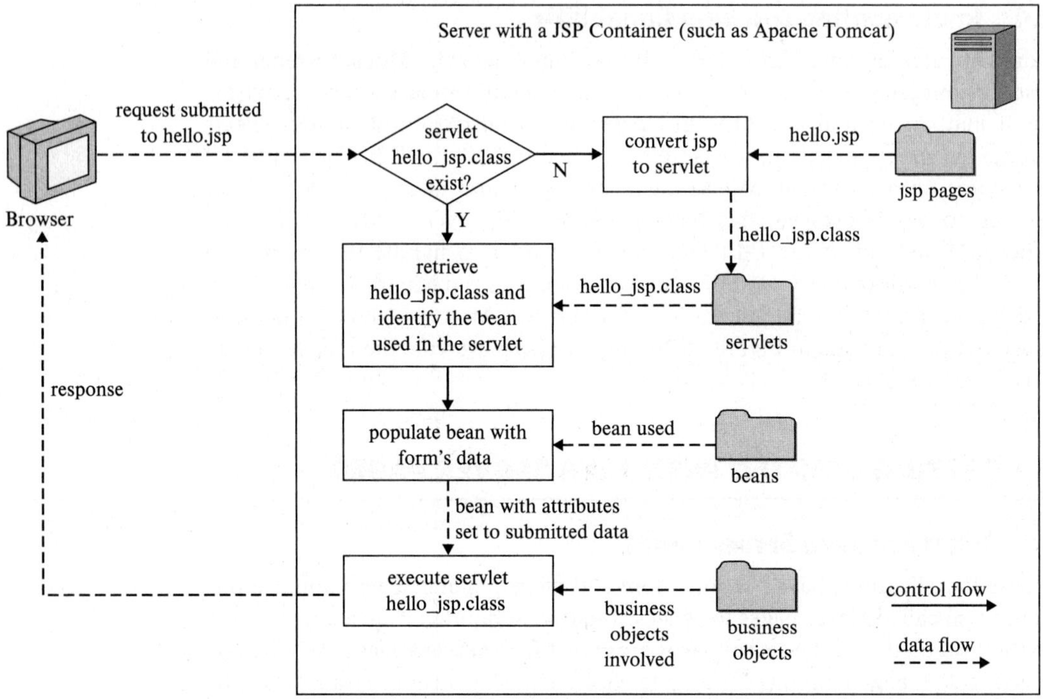

FIGURE B.3 Illustration of JSP workflow

B.3.3 Installing a Web Server with a JSP Container

The Apache Tomcat, or simply Tomcat, which is an open source from the Apache Software Foundation (ASF), is a widely used servlet container. It supports JSP and provides a "pure Java" HTTP web server environment for Java to run. Tomcat and related installation instructions can be obtained from http://tomcat.apache.org/.

B.3.4 Using Java Server Pages

This section presents how to use JSP pages with a simple example, tailored to illustrate the basic features of JSP. The example lets a student search for overseas exchange programs using a subject field and a term field. The web-based application returns a summary of programs satisfying the search criteria. In the following, the steps along with the development of the example are described.

Step 1. Produce an HTML page containing a form. In this step, an html page with a form for the user to enter the required input data is produced. The action attribute of the form tag is set to the JSP page that will process the request, for example, action="../pages/search.jsp." The method attribute is set to "post." Figure B.4(*a*) shows a sample html code for this page.

Step 2. Create a corresponding bean class. In this step, a Java class, called a Java bean, is created or generated (from the html file). The names of the

```
<html> <head> <title>Search for Oversea Programs</title> </head>
 <body> <form name="search" action="../pages/search.jsp" method="post">
  <table> <tr> <td>Search Criteria</td> </tr>
   <tr> <td colspan="2'>
    <table>
     <tr class="blackheading">
      <td align="right">Subject : </td>
      <td colspan="4" align="left" class="normaltext2">
       <input type="text" name="subject" id="subject" size="25" maxlength="20"/>
      </td>
     </tr>
     <tr class="blackheading">
      <td align="right">Term : </td>
      <td colspan="4" class="normaltext2" align="left">
       <input type="text" name="term" id="term" size="25" maxlength="45"/>
      </td> </tr>
     <tr height="20">
      <td colspan="2" align="center">
       <input type="submit" value="Submit"> 
       <input type="button" value="Cancel">
      </td>
      </tr>
    </table> </td>
   </tr>
  </table>
 </form>
 </body>
</html> a
```

(a) HTML page for entering search criteria

```
package beans;
public class SearchBean {
  String subject, term;
  public SearchBean() {...}
  public String getSubject() {
    return subject;
  }
  public void setSubject(String subject) {
    this.subject=subject;
  }
  public String getTerm() {
    return term;
  }
  public void setTerm(String term) {
    this.term=term;
  }
}
```

(b) Corresponding Java bean

FIGURE B.4 A form and the corresponding Java bean

attributes of the bean correspond to the names of the input fields of the form; these are case sensitive and follow the Java naming convention presented in the Coding Standards section (Chapter 18, Section 18.1.1). Moreover, the bean should have the ordinary getter and setter methods that are written ac cording to Java coding conventions. Figure B.4(*b*) shows the Java bean created.

Step 3. Create a JSP page to process the request. In this step, a JSP page to process the request is created. The JSP page may query the bean and process the input data, or passes the bean to a business object to process the request. The JSP page may include scriptlets and html code to process the request and display the output information. Figure B.5 shows a sample JSP page for the example, where the line numbers are added for explanation purpose.

The first three lines of the JSP page import the needed classes. Line (4) tells the JSP engine to create an instance of the SearchBean, called searchBean, and use it to store the input data. Line (5) causes the input data of all of the fields of the form to be stored in the bean, as indicated by the asterisk (*). Individual attributes can be set by multiple setProperty lines in each of which the asterisk is replaced by the attribute name.

Lines (6) and (7) are scriptlets that create an instance of SearchController and call its search (searchBean) method, which normally returns an array of Program

```
(1) <%@page import="controller.SearchController"%>
(2) <%@page import="beans.SearchBean"%>
(3) <%@page import="program.*"%>
(4) <jsp:useBean id="searchBean" scope="session" class="beans.SearchBean" />
(5) <jsp:setProperty name="searchBean" property="*"/>
(6) <% SearchController sc=new SearchController();
(7)     Program[ ] programs=sc.search(searchBean); %>
(8) <html> <head> <title>Search Result</title> </head>
(9) <body> <h2>Search Results</h2> <hr width="90%" />
(10) <% if(programs == null || programs.length == 0) { %>
(11) <p>No programs found, please <a href="../pages/search.html">try again</a>.</p>
(12) <% } else { %>
(13) <table width="90%" class="program" cellpadding="0" cellspacing="0">
(14) <tr> <td> Program Name </td> <td> Description </td> <td> Housing </td> <td> Fees </td> </tr>
(15) <% } for(int i=0; i<programs.length; i++) {
(16)      Program p=programs[i]; %>
(17)      <tr> <td> <%=p.getName()%> </td> <td> <%=p.getDescription()%> </td>
(18)      <td> <%=p.getHousing()%> </td> <td> <%=p.getFees()%> </td> </tr>
(19) <% } %>
(20) </table>
(21) <a class="back_link redlink" href="../pages/search.html">&lt;&lt; Back to Search</a>
(22) </body>
(23) </html>
```

FIGURE B.5 A JSP page to process a request and display output

objects. In this case, the searchBean object serves to pass the search criteria. Note the use of a pair of "<%" and "%>" strings to enclose Java source code in an html file.

Lines(8)-(23) are html code with scriptlets, which carry out necessary checking and computation to produce the response to the client. The assignment operator or the = sign that precedes a function call, such as =p.getName() on line (17), causes the return value to be displayed in the html page.

Step 4. Implement the other classes. In this step, the other relevant classes, such as SearchController and Program, are implemented.

Step 5. Build and deploy the web application. In this step, the bean classes and the business object classes are compiled into bytecode. To deploy the web application, the bytecode files, html files, JSP files, and image files are arranged in appropriate directories as shown in Figure B.6. The files including the directories are jarred to produce a web archive file, say jsptest.war. An IDE such as eclipse or NetBeans automatically produces the war file when it compiles the Java files.

The jsptest.war file is then placed in the appropriate directory according to the instructions given by the vendor of the web server and JSP engine. For Tomcat, the file should be placed in the webapps directory under the directory where Tomcat is installed, for example,

```
C:\...\Tomcat 6.0\webapps\jsptest.war.
```

Finally, start the web server according to the instructions given by the vendor.

FIGURE B.6 Directory structure for a .war file

Step 6. Run the example. Launch a web browser and enter in the address field

"http://localhost:8080/jsptest/pages/search.html"

and then press the Enter key. A search page is shown. Fill in the subject and term to search for and click Submit. If no error message occurs, then the browser should display a list of programs satisfying the search criteria.

Appendix C

Software Tools

This appendix presents some of the software tools used during implementation and testing. These include NetBeans, JUnit, and Cobertura.

C.1 NETBEANS

It is rather cumbersome to use a text editor to write Java programs, and the javac and Java commands to compile and run Java programs from the command prompt. These problems are overcome by integrated development environments (IDEs). An IDE is a software tool that provides support to a variety of software development activities, which include analysis, design, implementation, compilation, execution, testing, debugging, software quality assurance, software configuration management, and software project management. As an example, Figure C.1 shows a screen shot of Net-Beans. NetBeans is an open source IDE licensed under Common Development and Distribution License and General Public License. It is written entirely in Java, and hence, it can run on different platforms.

After installation, the user double-clicks the NetBeans icon in the desktop to launch it. The first thing to do is to create a project. This is accomplished by clicking File then selecting New Project to launch a dialog box. The dialog box lets the user select the category and type of project. To create a Java project, the user clicks Java in the Categories list and Java Application in the Projects list. The user then clicks the Next button to fill in project specific information. The window in Figure C.1 is a typical IDE window. It contains three panels, the project panel, the editor panel, and the navigator panel. The project panel, located at the upper-left corner of the main area, has three tabs. The Projects tab lets the user view the packages and libraries of each project. The Files tab lets the user view the files of each project. These include source files, .class files, and xml files that specify various project properties. The services tabs show the services that the user can use to access databases and web services.

The lower-left panel shows the functions and attributes of the class selected in the upper-left panel. The return types of the functions and the attribute types are also displayed. If the user double-clicks a function or attribute, the cursor in the editor panel will jump to that function or attribute so that the user can work on that feature. The editor has many code assistance features that make programming much easier and more pleasant. For example, the user can click the Run button and select Build Main Project, Run Main Project, or Test Project to compile, run, or test the project. It is beyond the scope of this book to provide a detailed presentation of an IDE. Fortunately, many IDE downloads come with an easy-to-learn tutorial, which the reader can follow to get familiar with the IDE.

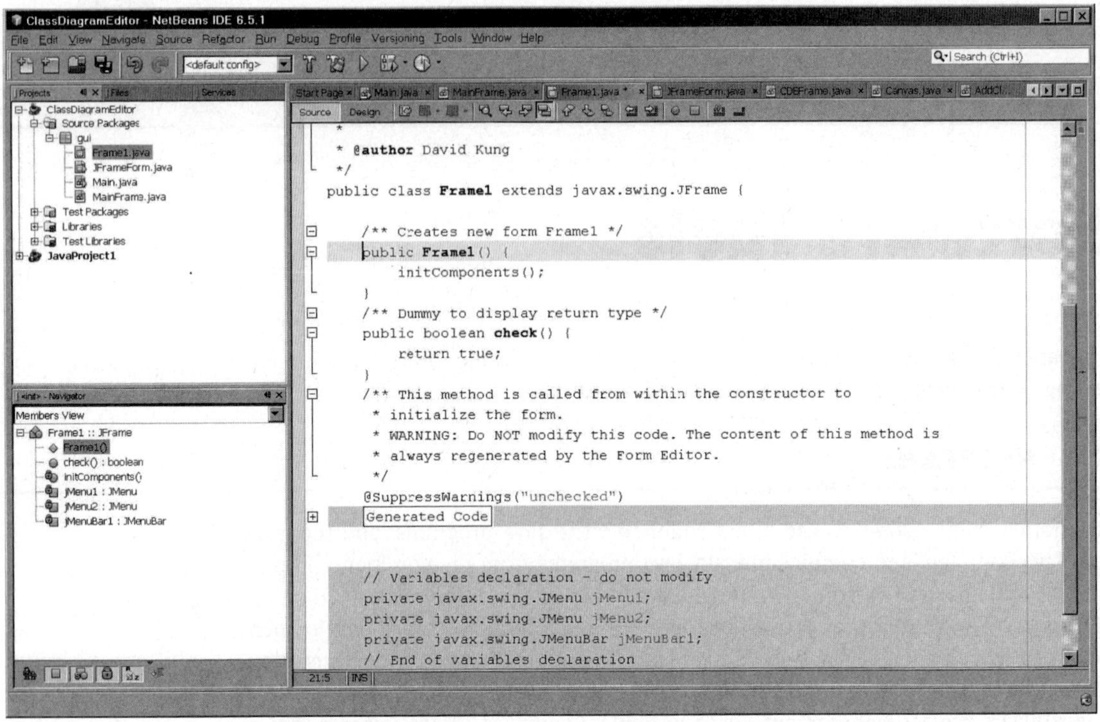

FIGURE C.1 Typical work areas of NetBeans

C.2 USING JUNIT

JUnit is a member of the XUnit family of test tools intended for unit testing and regression testing of Java programs. Other members of the XUnit family include, among others, CUnit for C, CppUnit for C++, xUnit.net for .Net, HtmlUnit for html, and HttpUnit for http. This section presents JUnit. The other tools are similar and are left to the reader. JUnit is an open-source Java unit testing framework, written by Erich Gamma and Kent Beck. The framework greatly facilitates the implementation and execution of test cases, and checking of test results. Once the test cases are implemented, they can be run again and again. This automates the regression test process. Implementing and running test cases in JUnit involves six simple steps. The purge example discussed earlier is used to illustrate these steps. More specifically, the four test cases derived in Section 20.3.1 are implemented. To use JUnit, one needs to encapsulate the purge() function in a class, called Purge.

Step 1. Create a subclass of TestCase.

In principle, all the test cases of a class are encapsulated in a class, which extends the TestCase class provided by the JUnit framework. This is illustrated in Figure C.2, where a class called PurgeTest is created as a subclass of TestCase.

```
package purge;
import java.util.*; import junit.framework.*;
public class PurgeTest extends TestCase {
  Purge purge; LinkedList list;
  ArrayList<Item> items=new ArrayList<Item>();
  public PurgeTest(String name) { super(name); }
  public void setUp() {
    purge=new Purge(); list=new LinkedList<Item>();
    for(int i=0; i<10; i++) { items.add(new Item(i)); }
  }
  public void testNullList() {
    boolean nullPointer=false;
    LinkedList output=null;
    try { output=purge.purge(output); }
    catch(Exception e) { nullPointer=true; }
    assertFalse(nullPointer); assertNull(output);
  }
  public void testEmptyList() {
    int size=list.size(); assertEquals(size, 0);
    LinkedList output=purge.purge(list);
    assertEquals(output.size(), size);
  }
  public void testOneElemList() {
    Item item=new Item(0); list.add(item);
    LinkedList output=purge.purge(list);
    assertTrue(output.size()==1 &&
      output.contains(item)); }
  public void testNoDuplicate() {
    for(int i=0; i<10; i++) { list.add(items.get(i)); }
    LinkedList output=purge.purge(list);
    assertEquals(output.size(), 10);
    for(int i=0; i<10; i++)
      assertTrue(output.contains(items.get(i))); }
  public void testDuplicate() {
    for(int i=0; i<10; i++)
    { list.add(items.get(i)); list.add(items.get(i)); }
    assertEquals(list.size(), 20);
    LinkedList output=purge.purge(list);
    assertEquals(output.size(), 10);
    for(int i=0; i<10; i++)
      assertTrue(output.contains(items.get(i)));
  }
  public static Test suite() {
    return new TestSuite(PurgeTest.class); } }
```

FIGURE C.2 TestCase class for testing Purge

The PurgeTest class declares an instance purge of Purge. It is called a fixture in terms of JUnit's terminology. This fixture is the class under test (CUT). It facilitates the test cases to access the CUT.

Step 2. Override setUp() and tearDown().

The setUp() and tearDown() functions are functions of the TestCase class. Subclasses should override these to implement test-specific setup and teardown. When JUnit executes the test cases, the setUp() function is called before calling each of the test methods that implements the test cases. The tearDown() function is called after executing each test method. In this example, the setUp() method simply reinitializes the fixture with a new instance of Purge. Thus, each test method tests its own copy of CUT. The PurgeTest class in Figure C.2 does not override the tearDown() function; it reuses the parent class' implementation.

Step 3. Implement the test cases.

In JUnit, test cases are implemented by functions named according to JUnit naming convention. That is, each function name begins with a "test" such as testEmptyList(), testOneElemList(), testNoDuplicate(), and testDuplicate() shown in Figure C.2. These implement the four test cases described in Section 20.3.1. In addition, a testNullList() function is implemented to test a null list. Each of these functions initializes the input list, calls the purge() function, and checks the resulting list. For example, the testOneElemList() method adds an item to the initially empty list, calls the purge() method, and then checks to ensure that the list is not changed. The checking is performed by the two assertTrue statements. The assertTrue(String message, boolean condition) function prints a message when the boolean condition is evaluated to false. The first of these statements checks the list size and ensures that the size is 1. The second assertTrue(. . .) statement ensures that the sole element in the list is named "item1." Besides assertTrue(. . .), many other polymorphic assert functions can be used, for example, assertEqual(. . .), assertFalse(. . .), assertNull(. . .), and so on. The JavaDoc API page for the Assert class describes these functions in detail.

Step 4. Write a public static Test suite() method.

This method specifies which of the test methods implemented in step 3 are to be executed by the test runner provided by JUnit. There are two ways to accomplish this: (1) the manual approach allows us to select which test cases to run, and (2) the automatic approach lets the test runner execute all of the test cases. The suite() method in Figure C.2 implements the automatic approach. If running all tests is time consuming or costly, then the manual approach is preferred. In this case, the suite() method is implemented as shown below. It creates an empty test suite and adds the desired test cases to it by calling the test suite's addTest method. The test suite is then returned to the caller.

```
public static Test suite() {
   TestSuite suite= new TestSuite();
   suite.addTest(new PurgeTest("testEmptyList") {
         protected void runTest()
         { testEmptyList(); }
   });
   // other suite.addTest(...) to add more test cases
   return suite;
}
```

Step 5. Compile the test cases and the CUT.

Before running the test runner, one must compile the test cases and the CUT. This is the same as compiling other Java programs except that the junit.jar file should be included in the class path and the test case java file(s) should be included in the source files to be compiled. The use of an IDE greatly simplifies this task–one would not need to type the class path and many source files.

Step 6. Run the test cases.

There are three test runners:

1. junit.awtui.TestRunner.
2. junit.swingui.TestRunner.
3. junit.textui.TestRunner.

Each of these is a Java class, and hence, they can be run as any other Java programs. These test runners differ in the user interfaces they provide, as the package

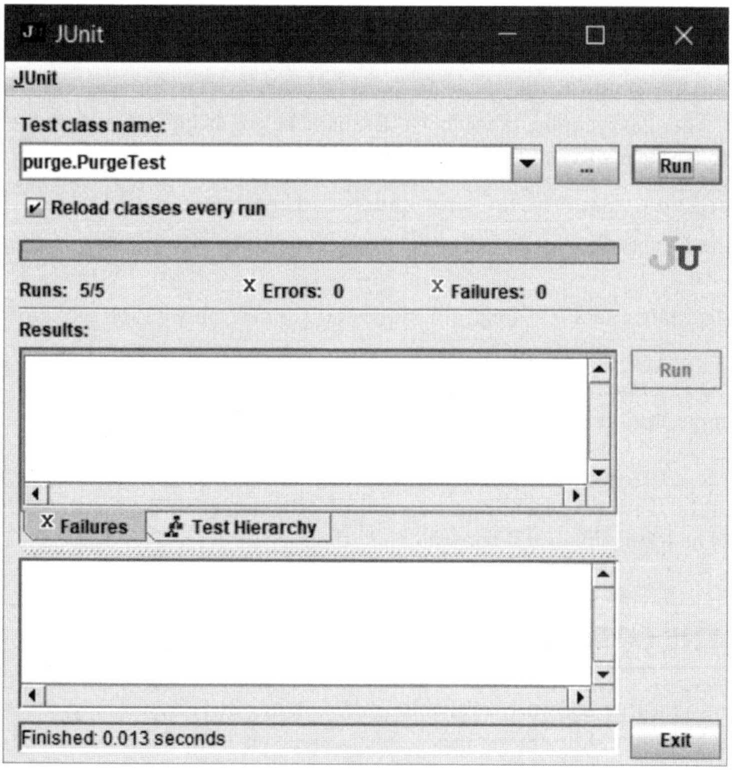

FIGURE C.3 User interfaces of JUnit test runners

names indicate. Figure C.3 displays the Swing test runner user interface after running the test cases shown in Figure C.2. The awt test runner user interface is similar and the text user interface prints the run result to the standard output. The text user interface facilitates the integration of JUnit into another tool. It is also useful when you want to implement your own graphical user interface to visualize the run result, for example, to display the result using a pie chart.

The JComboBox and the browse JButton located at the top of the Swing GUI lets the user select the test suite to run. After selection, the user clicks the Run button to run the tests. For example, the GUI shows that the purge.PurgeTest test suite is selected. The execution of the tests produces no error and no failure. The long, horizontal progress bar turns green to indicate that all tests passed. It would have been red if error or failure were detected. The detail of the error or failure wuold appear in the Results JScrollPane.

In JUnit, failures are anticipated failed conditions. It means that a test failed because an assertTrue(. . .) was evaluated to false. If the test case is designed and implemented correctly, then the failure indicates that an error (or bug) in the software is detected. Errors are unanticipated failed conditions that cause runtime exceptions, for example, divide by zero.

C.3 RUNNING JUNIT IN NETBEANS

Running JUnit within NetBeans is a convenient way to TDD. It is no different from running other Java applications in NetBeans. The following steps describe how to configure NetBeans to run the desired JUnit test runner:

1. Click Run– >Set Project Configuration– >Customize...
2. In the Project Properties purge dialog that is displayed, click Run in the Categories list.
3. In the Main Class text field, fill in the test runner you want to use, for example, "junit.swingui.TestRunner."
4. In the Arguments text field, enter the fully qualified TestCase subclass name, for example, "purge.PurgeTest."
5. Click OK.

To have JUnit execute the test cases in NetBeans, click the Run icon from the toolbar. The test runner GUI shows up and the execution result is displayed.

C.4 THE COBERTURA COVERAGE TOOL

Cobertura is a free software, available from GitHub. It is based on JCoverage and supports branch and line coverages. It also calculates cyclomatic complexity. It can be run from command line or NetBeans. Installation is easy–simply unzip it into a clean directory. Before running Cobertura in NetBeans, you must install the build script files:

1. Copy the build.xml and build.properties files under the Cobertura examples directory and rename the copies as cobertura-build.xml and cobertura-build.properties, respectively.
2. Copy/cut and paste the renamed files to your NetBeans project directory.
3. Edit the cobertura-build.properties file. In the cobertura.dir=../.. line, replace "../.." with the path that contains the cobertura.jar file. It should be the path to the cobertura directory. Save the updated file.

Another subtle step to take is to move your test case Java source files from the project test directory to the project src directory. This is because the Cobertura tasks only check the src directory for CUT and test case source files. You may change the cobertura-build.xml file to avoid moving the test files.

You need to compile the CUT and test cases, instrument the bytecode of the CUT, run the test, and collect test-coverage information. All these tasks are accomplished by a simple action. That is, you expand the cobertura-build.xml file in the Files view, right-click the **main** task and choose Run Target. You should see each task being executed and the status of the execution.

If all Cobertura tasks are built successfully, then you can view the coverage information in the reports directory under the project directory. For example, you can

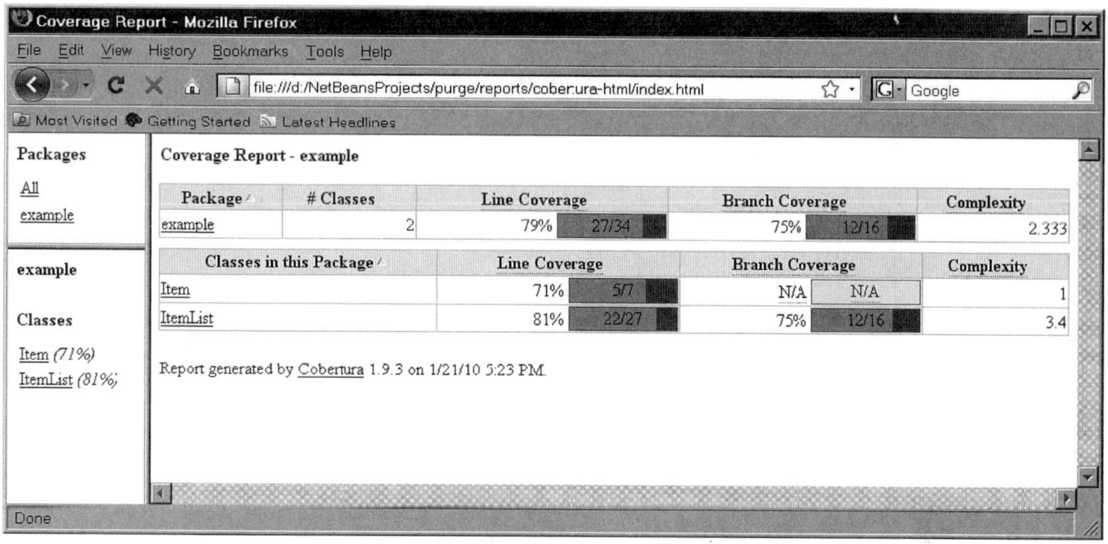

FIGURE C.4 Sample Cobertura Coverage Report

expand the cobertura-html directory to see a listing of html files. You can right-click the index.html file and select view from the pop-up menu to view the Coverage Report as shown in Figure C.4.

If you do the same for the index.html file under the junit-html directory, you will see the unit test results shown in Figure C.5.

C.5 USING CVS AND SUBVERSION IN NETBEANS

Many IDEs such as NetBeans and Eclipse support version control tools. The procedures to set up and use a version control tool in an IDE are similar. Therefore, this section only presents how to use CVS and Subversion in NetBeans IDE.

C.5.1 Creating a CVS Remote Repository

Figure C.5 lists some of the commonly used command line CVS commands. Before using CVS, you need to create a remote repository and grant access to a group of developers. In most cases, the repository is created on a UNIX or Linux machine. Therefore, you need to have a UNIX or Linux privilege account such as root. In the following, it is assumed that you have logged in as root or run a shell with the substitute user command as root (su - root). To create a CVS repository using csh, you perform the following steps:

1. Include “setenv CVSROOT /repository path” in your .cshrc in the root home directory, where “repository path” is the directory for the CVS root.

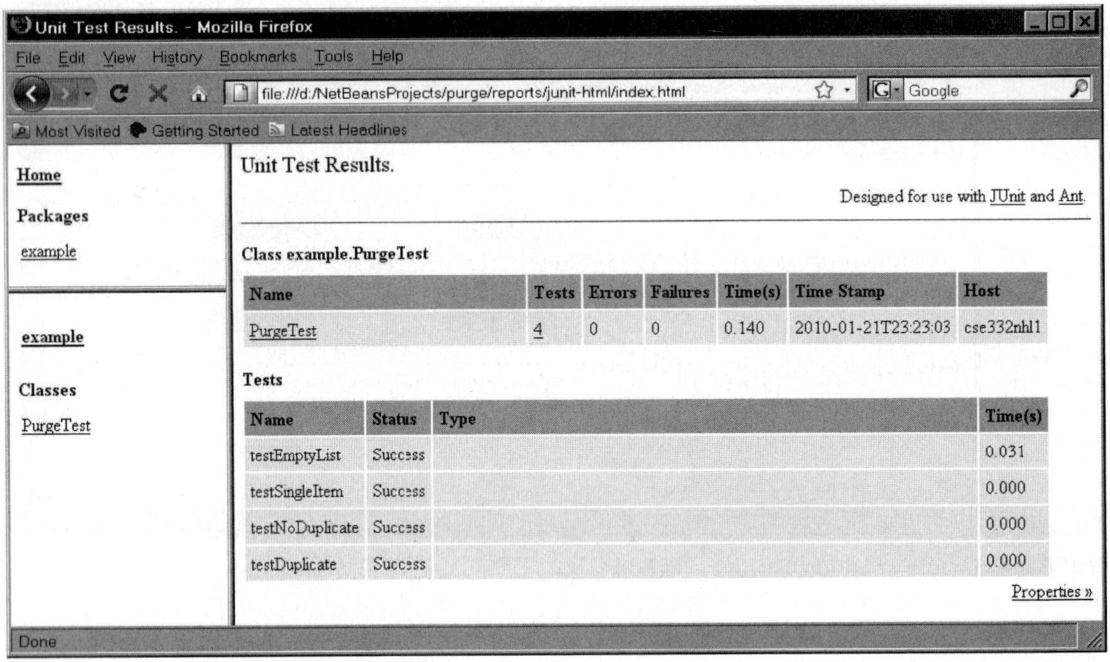

FIGURE C.5 Viewing unit test results in NetBeans

2. In the root home directory, execute the command

```
source .cshrc
```

This will set the environment variable CVSROOT to point to the repository path of your choice.

3. Execute the CVS init command as follows:

```
cvs init
```

This will initialize and set up the CVS repository. You need to do this only once.

4. Set up CVS as a user and a group by executing the following commands, where integers are unique group id number and user id number, which can be any integers that are not already used for the same purpose:

```
groupadd -g 50 cvsgrp
useradd -u 125 -g cvsgrp -d /u/cvs -s /bin/csh -c ''CVS Repository''
```

5. Set the ownership and access mode for the cvs user and cvsgrp for the CVSROOT directory and subdirectories:

```
chown -R cvs $CVSROOT
chgrp -R cvsgrp $CVSROOT
chmod -R g+s $CVSROOT
```

6. Check that the cvspserver entry is in the /etc/services file

```
grep cvs /etc/services
```

Command	Description
cvs init	Initialize a repository by adding the CVSROOT subdirectory and default control files.
cvs checkout modules ...	Create a private copy of the source for modules including at least one subdirectory.
cvs update	Bring your working directory up to date with changes from the repository. It must be executed from within the private source directory.
cvs commit file ...	Incorporate the changes you made to the files to the source repository.
cvs add file ...	Enroll new files in the cvs records for the modules that are checked out to your working directory. This takes effect when you execute the cvs commit command.
cvs remove file ...	Remove files from the repository. This takes effect when you execute the cvs commit command.
cvs export modules ...	Prepare copies of a set of source files for shipment off site.
cvs import	Incorporate a set of updates from off-site into the source repository, as a vendor branch.
cvs diff	Show differences between the files in the working directory and the source repository.
cvs status	Show file status.
cvs -H, or cvs -help	List available cvs commands, or display a command's usage information if a cvs command name is provided.
cvs -V, or cvs -version	Display cvs version information.

FIGURE C.6 Commonly used command line CVS commands

which should show the following lines:

```
cvspserver   2401/tcp \# CVS client/server operations
cvspserver   2401/udp \# CVS client/server operations
```

If grep does not print such lines, then add these lines to the /etc/services file.

7. Add an entry to /etc/inetd.conf to invoke CVS as a server

```
# CVS server
cvspserver stream tcp nowait root /usr/bin/cvs cvs
   --allow-root=/usr/local/src/cvsroot pserver
```

8. Tell the inetd daemon to reread the configuration file:

```
killall -HUP inetd
```

CVS is preinstalled in the NetBeans IDE; therefore, no setup is required to use it in the NetBeans IDE.

C.5.2 Setting Up Subversion in NetBeans

Subversion is open-source software resulting from an Apache Software Foundation project. It was initially designed to be a better CVS to replace CVS. Therefore, it has all the capabilities of CVS. Nevertheless, Subversion has evolved beyond a CVS replacement and offers a comprehensive set of advanced features. For example, directories, copying, updating, and deleting operations, and symbolic links are also versioned. A user can optionally lock a file before updating it to prevent concurrent modification; other users can read but not modify the locked file. For more Subversion features, see the Subversion online documentation.

The Subversion client software can be downloaded from either of the following websites, and installed according to the instructions that come with the download:

```
http://subversion.apache.org/
http://www.collab.net/downloads/netbeans
```

Alternatively, NetBeans users may install the bundled Subversion client as a NetBeans plugin. To accomplish this in NetBeans click Tools > Plugins and then the Available Plugins tab to show a list of available plugins. Select Subversion from the list and click the Install button. Follow the screen instructions to complete the installation process.

You need to specify the path to the Subversion client executable. For a Windows operating system, the executable is named "svn.exe." You can perform a systemwide search to locate the directory that contains the executable. Once the path to the directory containing the executable is identified, you click Tools > Options and then click the Miscellaneous icon at the top of the Options dialog window. Click the Versioning tab and select Subversion in the Versioning Systems list on the left. The IDE shows the dialog as in Figure C.7. Type in the path or click the Browse button to navigate to the directory that contains the svn client executable. Click the OK button and restart the NetBeans IDE.

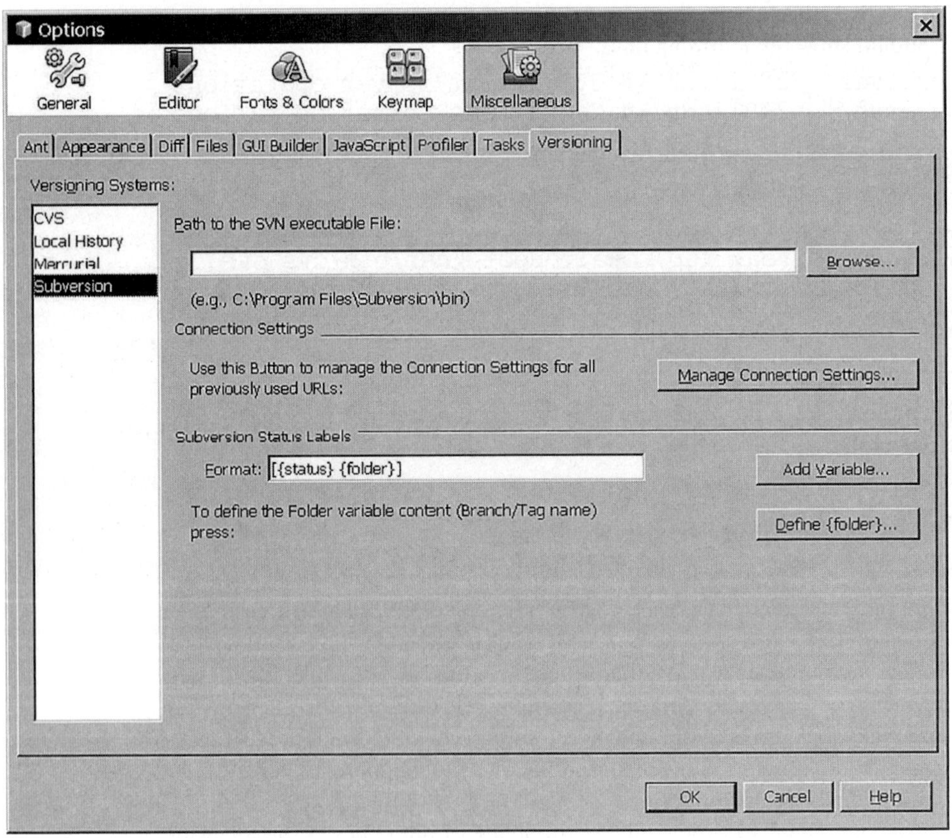

FIGURE C.7 Specifying path to Subversion client executable

You must have access to a Subversion repository. You can create a local repository using the svnadmin tool included in the Subversion client software. From a command prompt, type in the following:

```
svnadmin create /path/to/your/repository
```

C.5.3 Checking Out Files from a Repository

The previous two sections described how to set up CVS and Subversion in NetBeans. This and the next several sections present how to use either of these version control systems to perform version control tasks in NetBeans. Since the steps to perform the tasks are similar for CVS and Subversion, they are presented together. A slash is used to distinguish CVS and Subversion related terms, which are shown in italic font. For example, "choose Versioning > CVS/*Subversion* > Checkout" means "choose Versioning > CVS > Checkout," or "choose Versioning > Subversion > Checkout."

In most cases, the first thing to do is to check out shared files from a remote repository. This operation basically creates local copies of the files and directories you check out. You can then edit these files and commit your changes to the repository when you finish with your changes. The steps to check out files from a CVS or Subversion repository are the following:

1. From the menu bar of the NetBeans main window, choose Versioning > CVS/ *Subversion* > Checkout. A Checkout wizard appears, as shown in Figure C.8 for CVS.

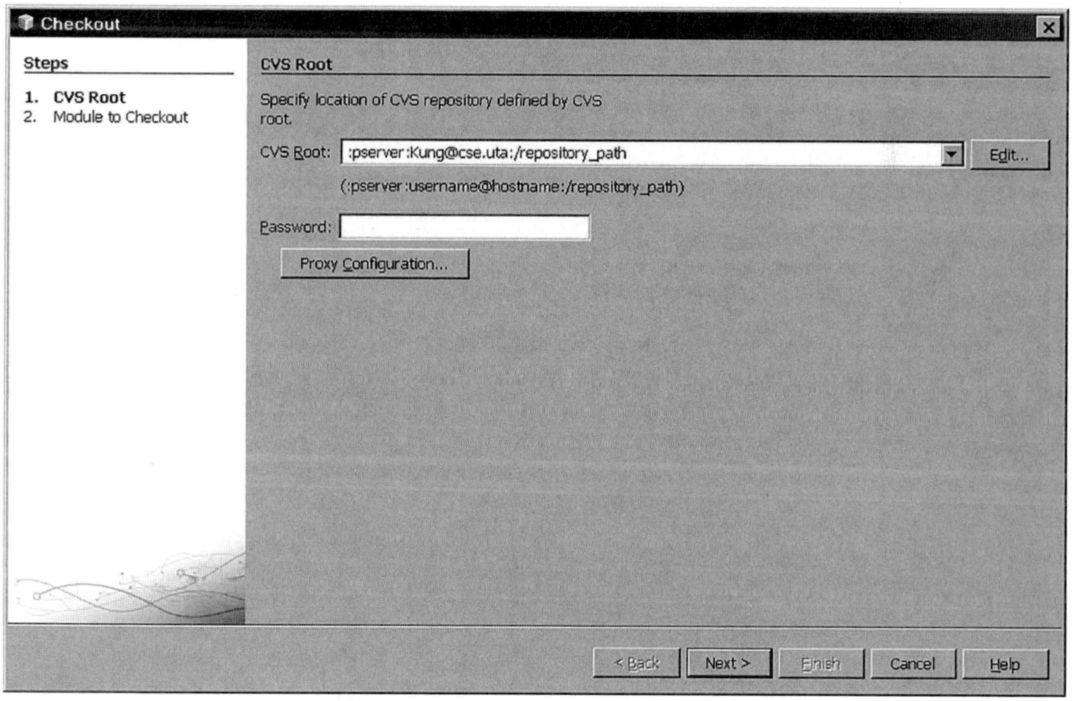

FIGURE C.8 Checking out files from a repository

2. In the CVS Root/*Repository URL* field, fill in the actual user name, host name, and repository path of the CVS root/*Subversion repository* directory on the remote host. In the Password field, fill in the required password. Alternatively, you can click the Edit button to display a dialog box, or click the down-arrow to select the protocol. These make the task easier because you don't have to cope with the syntax. NetBeans supports four different CVS root formats, where the last two formats require an external CVS executable:
   a. *Remote password server format*, which is the format used in Figure C.8, the syntax is
      ":pserver:username@hostname:/repository_path"
   b. *Access using Remote Shell (RSH) or Secure Shell (SSH) format*, the syntax is
      ":ext:username@hostname:/repository_path"
   c. *Access to a local repository format*, the syntax is
      ":local:/repository_path"
   d. *Access to a local repository using a remote protocol format*, the syntax is
      ":fork:/repository_path"

   For Subversion, NetBeans supports five types of connection protocols:
   a. *Direct repository access on local disk.* The URL format is file:
      ///repository_path.
   b. *Access via WebDAV protocol to a Subversion-aware server.* The URL format is http://hostname/repository_path.
   c. *Access via HTTP protocol with SSL encryption.* The URL format is https://hostname/repository_path.
   d. *Access via custom protocol to an svnserve server.*
      The URL format is svn://hostname/repository_path.
   e. *Access via SVN protocol through an external SSH tunnel.*
      The URL format is svn+ssh://hostname/repository_path.

   Depending on the CVS format or Subversion protocol used, you may need to provide additional information such as user name and password. After entering the needed information, click the Next button to proceed.
3. On the Modules/*Folders* to Checkout panel, specify the module/*folder* you want to check out in the Module/*Repository Folder(s)* field. Alternatively, you can click the Browse button to select the modules/*folders* in the repository. For CVS, the entire repository is checked out if you do not specify a module. In the Branch/*Repository Revision* field, specify a branch, revision number or tag for the checkout. The Browse/*Search* button allows you to choose from a list of all branches in the repository. Next, specify the local working directory, or click the Browse button to navigate to the desired local directory. For Subversion, leave the Scan for NetBeans Projects after Checkout option selected. Click the Finish button to start the checkout process.

   If the checked-out sources contain a project, the IDE will prompt you to open them in the IDE; otherwise, the IDE will prompt you to create a new project from the sources, and open the sources in the IDE.

C.5.4 Editing Sources and Viewing Changes

You can open a versioned project as described in the last section. You can also open a versioned project that you have created outside of NetBeans as if you were opening a NetBeans project. You can edit the files once the project is opened. The changes that you make will be highlighted with blue, green, and red, indicating lines that are changed, added, and removed since the earlier version. The versioning window presents a real-time view of the changes made in the local working copy for selected versioned directories. It opens by default in the bottom panel of the IDE, listing added, deleted, or modified files. It can be opened by clicking Window from the main menu then select Versioning > CVS/*Subversion*. It can also be opened by right-clicking a versioned file or directory and selecting CVS/*Subversion* > Show Changes. On the top of the versioning window are four action icons for the most common tasks. These are illustrated and explained in Figure C.9.

C.5.5 Viewing File Status

The IDE also displays the file names with different colors to indicate the file status as follows:

- *Blue.* This indicates that the file is locally modified.
- *Green.* This indicates that the file is locally added.
- *Red.* This indicates that the file contains conflicts between the local copy and the copy at the repository.
- *Gray.* This indicates that the file is ignored and will not be processed by update and commit commands. Files are ignored if they are not versioned.
- *Strike-through.*This indicates that the file is excluded from the commit command. Such files are still affected by other commands such as update.

C.5.6 Comparing File Revisions

Comparing local copies with the files in the repository is a common task of revision management. There are three ways to accomplish this: (1) right-click the versioned local file in the Files frame in the upper-left corner of the NetBeans IDE and select

Icon	Name	Description
	Refresh Status	Refresh the status of the selected files and folders to reflect any changes that may have been made externally.
	Diff All	Open the Diff Viewer to display a side-by-side comparison of local copies and the versions in the repository
	Update All	Update all selected files from the repository.
	Commit All	Commit local changes to the repository.

FIGURE C.9 Action icons in the versioning window

CVS/*Subversion* > Diff, (2) double-click a file in the Versioning window, or (3) click the Diff All icon in the toolbar at the top of the Versioning window. Performing either of these operations opens a graphical Diff Viewer in the main window of the IDE. The Viewer displays the local and the repository copies as well as the revisions in two side-by-side panels with the more current copy on the right. As described above, code segments that are changed, added, and deleted are highlighted with blue, green, and red, respectively.

C.5.7 Merging Changes from Repository

You can merge files from the repository with your local copies. For CVS, select the files or folders that you want to merge into your local copy in the Projects, Files, Favorites, or Versioning window and choose CVS > Merge Changes from Branch. In the dialog, select the branch of the repository you want to merge the changes from, or click the Browse button to select from a list of available branches. You can specify the tag in the Tag Name field, or click the Browse button to choose from a list of available tags. Click Merge to incorporate the changes found in the branch into your local copy of the file. The file status color changes to red if there are conflicts.

For Subversion, right-click the files or folders in the Projects, Files, or Favorites window and select Subversion > Merge Changes. In the dialog, in the Merge From field select One Repository Folder, Two Repository Folders, or One Repository Folder Since Its Origin. The last option port changes occurred between the folder's creation time and the revision number that you specify in the Ending Revision Field. In the Repository Folder field(s), enter or select the folder(s) from which you want to port changes. In the Starting Revision, and Ending Revision fields, enter the starting point and ending point of the ranges of changes you want to port, respectively. Click Merge to incorporate the changes. The file status changes to red if there are conflicts.

C.5.8 Resolving Conflicts

The versioning window shows the conflicts between the local copies and the repository copies in the Status column. All such conflicts must be resolved before you can commit the local changes to the repository. You can right-click a file with a conflict and choose CVS/*Subversion* > Resolve Conflicts to invoke the Merge Conflicts Resolver, which displays the two conflicting revisions side-by-side, highlighting the code segments that are different. You can click the Accept or Accept & Next button of one of the revisions to resolve the conflicts.

C.5.9 Updating Local Copies

It is recommended that all of the local files are updated before committing them to the repository. You can update your local copies with changes that other developers have committed to the repository by executing the update command. To do this, right-click a versioned file in the File pane and select CVS/*Subversion* > Update.

C.5.10 Committing Local Files to a Repository

You can commit local files or local directories by right-clicking the files or directories you wish to commit in the File pane and choosing CVS/*Subversion* > Commit. The

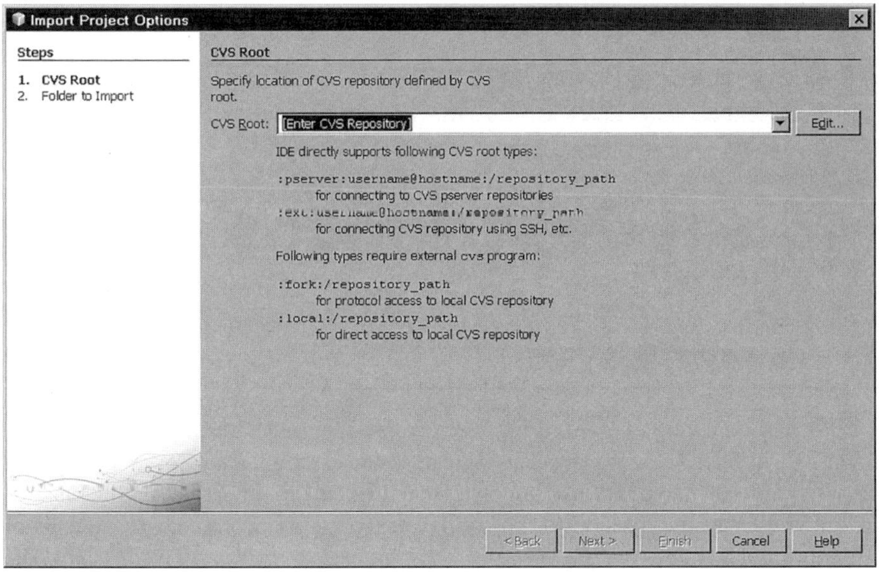

FIGURE C.10 Importing files into a remote CVS repository

IDS shows a Commit dialog with a Commit Message text area and a Files to Commit table. The table lists each file and directory, its status, the commit action, and the repository path. You can click a field in the Commit Action column to change the commit action, for example, you can exclude a file or directory from the commit.

C.5.11 Importing Files into a Repository

You can export files of an unversioned project into a remote repository. This is referred to as importing files into the repository. To do this, select an unversioned project, directory, or file and choose in the main menu Versioning > CVS/*Subversion* > Import into Repository. An Import wizard opens, as shown in Figure C.10. The wizard lets you specify the repository and folder, and the local files to import. When all these are specified, click the Finish button to start the importing process.

D Appendix

Project Descriptions

D.1 CAR RENTAL SYSTEM

A car rental company operates a number of rental locations throughout the metropolitan area. Since the company has a great business model and provides customer-friendly service, its business has boomed over the last several years. As the business has grown rapidly, the costs of running its business has also increased. In particular, as the job market becomes hot, the labor cost has doubled over the last several years. The company wants to find a solution to reduce its operating cost. The business operation of the company is described as follows. The description is not meant to be complete, and the company is flexible enough to consider any good improvement proposals.

Vehicles can be taken from one location and returned to the same location or to a different location with an additional charge. Although the company is, at present, concerned only with passenger cars, it may branch out into other forms of vehicle rentals in the future and would like to be able to use the same reservation system. The company has several different makes of cars in its rental fleet, from different manufacturers. Each make may have several models. For example, Toyota has Corolla, Camry, and more. The models are grouped into a small number of price classes. The customer must be able to select the make and the model he or she wants to rent. If the selected car is not available, the system should display a message telling the customer that the car is rented out and let the customer select another make and model, or have the system suggest similar models of a different make.

The company has a number of different rental plans available to customers. For example, there is a "daily unlimited miles plan" and a "weekend 10% discount plan." The company finds it important to have information available on the models of car, such as automatic or manual gear change, two or four doors, and sedan or hatchback. The rental prices may be different for different options and a customer will want to know such information when reserving a car. Currently, customers make reservations directly with the car rental company either in person or through the phone. The salespersons process the reservations manually using a reservation form and archive them in the file cabinet. No deposit is required at the time of reservation. The reservation is voided if the customer does not show up to sign the contract for more than a given period of time. Such reservation is honored only if there are still cars available to satisfy the request.

Sometimes a customer wishes to make a block reservation for several cars and to have the invoices for all rentals on the reservation handled together. As soon as a car is checked out to a customer, an invoice is opened. A single invoice may cover one or more rentals. Normally a customer will settle the invoice when the car is returned but, in some cases, the invoice must be sent to a company (such as the customer's employer). When the customer pays by a credit card, the rental charge will be processed through a credit card processing company.

A car may or may not be available for rental on a given day. Rental cars need frequent preventive maintenance and, in addition, any damage to a car has to be repaired as soon as possible. The company wants to keep track of the rental car purchase, repair, maintenance, and disposal information for business and tax purposes (e.g., depreciation of the rental cars).

D.2 NATIONAL TRADE SHOW SERVICE SYSTEM

The National Trade Show Services (NTSS) is a service provider that helps business customers create, promote, organize, and run national and international trade shows. Business customers contact NTSS for the services they need. Creating a trade show involves the design for the trade show, including professional services ranging from selection of a theme and a slogan to location and duration. Promoting a trade show includes advertisement activities. Organizing a trade show includes all activities before the trade show except creation and promotion. For example, inviting speakers, and registering participants and exhibitors. Running a trade show is the activity of on site registration, setting up the booths, conference rooms for seminars, reception, and distributing trade show materials. The NTSS creates an account for each customer to record service charges, payments received, and maintain the account balances.

A trade show can be regarded as an event. For example, the 2008 Consumer Electronics Show took place in the Las Vegas Convention Center during January 7–10, 2008 and the 2008 MacWorld Conference took place at the Moscone Center, 747 Howard Street, San Francisco, CA 94103 during January 14–18, 2008. An event has an organizer, which can be a person or an organization. For example, the CES was organized by the Consumer Electronics Association while the MacWorld was organized by Apple, Inc. An event has contact information and possibly a website that provides further information about the event. An event can belong to one or more predefined domains. For example, the CES and MacWorld belong to both Technology and Consumer Electronics. The list of predefined domains can change from time to time because new domains need be added and outdated domains need be removed.

A trade show is attended by different types of participants including the event organization staff, the invited and/or selected speakers, exhibitors, and observers. Except the event organization staff and the event organizer, all participants must register to attend a trade show events. The registration charges a fee, which is different for different trade show events. The event organization staff creates, prepares, and runs the event. The invited speakers are famous figures in the domain who were invited to give a keynote address at the event. The selected speakers are invited to speak at the event based on the evaluation of their proposals. The proposals are usually reviewed by a committee of reviewers, who are experts in the domain and willing to help. The status of a proposal includes pending review, accepted, and rejected. The exhibitors come to the trade show to exhibit their products or services. The exhibitors have to pay for the booths depending on the size of the booth (large, medium, or small). Booths are requested and rented for the whole duration of the event. Finally, the observers come to visit the trade show for various purposes.

D.3 STUDY ABROAD MANAGEMENT SYSTEM

This project will design, implement, test, and deploy incrementally a web-based application for the Office of International Education (OIE) of a university. The web-based application will allow students to search for overseas exchange programs using a variety of search criteria. The website will display the search result. The result is organized hierarchically to facilitate the navigation for the desired information. This document outlines the requirements, which are not meant to be precise or complete. Modifications and additions to this list of requirements are anticipated and welcome (students are encouraged to suggest new requirements). The students are expected to apply the agile unified process and methodology to perform the analysis, design, implementation, testing, and deployment of Study Abroad Management Systems. There will be three iterations; each is about one month. The project is not intended to be completed in one semester. It could be continued in a subsequent course or another course.

The following are the functional requirements (Rs):

R1 The web-based application must provide a search capability for overseas exchange programs using a variety of search criteria. The teams are responsible for eliciting, acquiring, and formulating the complete list of search criteria.

R2 The website must provide a hierarchical display of the search result to facilitate user navigation from a high-level summary to details about overseas exchange programs. The project teams are responsible for acquiring and defining the display layout by working with the OIE.

R3 The system must provide interactive as well as batch-processing means for OIE staff to enter the information about the exchange programs. This information is saved in a database.

[R3.1] For the interactive mode:

R3.1.1 The user interface must be web-based.

R3.1.2 The user interface must use as few windows as possible when the user-friendliness criterion is not compromised.

R3.1.3 The user interface must avoid unnecessary switches between keyboard action and mouse action when entering the data.

[R3.2] For the batch-processing mode:

R3.2.1 The system must be able to process at least one or two formats of structured files required and provided by the OIE.

R3.2.2 The system must provide a graphical user interface (GUI) for an OIE staff to enter the information about the data files to be processed. This GUI must be user-friendly and require minimal effort from the user.

R3.2.3 The system must be easily extendible to include other file formats and structures (how the data are organized in the file).

R4 Online application.

R4.1 The web-based application must provide the capability for students to submit online applications to overseas exchange programs. The process may begin by showing a checklist/to-do list. See R6 for details.

R4.2 The system must securely save the submitted applications in the database.

R4.3 The system must reply with a message showing the status of the application process. One possible message will be the to-do list that shows what still needs to be done to complete the application process.

R4.4 The system must generate and send an email to notify OIE staff according to preset notification preference.

R5 System administrator and staff users.

R5.1 The system must initially create an administrator account with a given password. The system administrator will have the privilege to create, update, and delete staff users. The system administrator is a staff user.

R5.2 The system must provide a password-protected, web-based user-interface for staff users to login and specify their individual email notification preference.

R5.3 The system must allow the administrator to specify systemwide email notification preferences, which will take precedence over the staff user's individually set preferences.

R6 The system must provide a checklist and to-do list to facilitate students to keep track of the application process.

R6.1 The list(s) must display what has been done and what needs to be done. The list may be different for different students and different overseas programs (the teams need to discuss with OIE to finalize it).

R6.2 Each list item must show only one to-do task.

R6.3 For each to-do task and if applicable, there must be a link to the appropriate page for completing the task.

R6.3 For each done task and if applicable, there must be a link to the appropriate page for updating the information that is already submitted.

R7 The website must allow an OIE staff to review and process online applications.

R7.1 On the staff home page (show after a staff has logged on), there must be a "Review Online Applications" link with a plus ('+') sign, when expanded, there will be several choices: (1) review newly assigned applications, (2) review processed applications, (3) review all applications. (The teams need to consult the OIE to finalize this requirement.)

R7.2 After a staff member selects the online applications to review, the system must display a table showing the summary information of the applicants, one online application on each row. Each row must include a link to an editable page so that the staff member can update the online application.

R7.3 After the staff member submits the update, the system must display a message showing the status of the update.

The project must take into consideration a number of quality requirements, including but not limited to the following:

- Reliability, the system must be thoroughly tested to ensure that the increments delivered to the OIE will be operational and highly available.
- Extensibility, the system must be easy to extend to provide new capabilities.
- Platform independence, the system must run on different platforms and support different database management systems.
- User-friendly interface, the system must provide a user-friendly interface that conforms to commonly used web-application user interface look-and-feel and man-machine interaction conventions.
- Security, the system must protect the contents of the website from malicious attacks and protect the privacy of its users.

D.4 UML CLASS DIAGRAM EDITOR

This team project will conduct analysis, design, implementation, and testing of a graphical editor (GED) for creating and editing UML class diagrams. This project is to be carried out by teams of five participants. The following is a list of soft-ware requirements. The project team can extend or refine the list with additional requirements:

1. GED shall allow the user to work with projects as follows:
   a. GED shall allow the user to create a new project. When this option is selected, GED shall ask the user for necessary project information and create the necessary directories and files for the new project.
   b. GED shall allow the user to open an existing project by selecting a project file from a given directory.
   c. GED shall allow the user to save a project.
   d. GED shall allow the user to delete a project. GED shall display a confirmation dialog.
   e. GED shall allow the user to close a project. GED shall prompt the user if there is unsaved work.
2. GED shall allow the user to work with UML class diagrams as follows:
   a. GED shall allow the user to create a new diagram in a given project. GED shall ask the user to provide a valid name and package or module for the diagram.
   b. GED shall allow the user to save a diagram.
   c. GED shall allow the user to save a diagram using a different diagram name and/or location.
   d. GED shall allow the user to open an existing diagram in a project.
   e. GED shall allow the user to edit an opened diagram using various editing operations including:
      i. Adding a new class: GED shall display a dialog to allow the user to enter class information like class name, attributes and types, operations and parameters, and types and return types.

ii. Updating a class: GED shall allow the user to change the class information.
iii. Deleting a class: GED shall allow the user to delete a class by prompting the user with a confirmation dialog.
iv. Adding a relationship: GED shall provide a user-friendly way to allow the user to add relationships between two or more classes.
v. Selecting one or more graphical elements: GED shall provide a user-friendly way to allow the user to select one or more graphical elements (classes, relationships, or their combination) of a UML diagram.
vi. Moving selected graphical elements: GED shall allow the user to move selected elements by dragging them to the desired place.
vii. Copying, cutting, and pasting: GEG shall provide the commonly used "copy & paste," and "cut & paste" capabilities.
viii. Deleting selected elements: GED shall allow the user to delete selected elements.
ix. Undo and redo: GED shall allow the user to undo or redo up to 10 editing operations (future extensions shall allow the user to define the number of undoable and/or redoable operations).

f. GED shall support object persistence through the use of a database or the file system. GED shall hide the persistent storage so that extension to support databases from different vendors and multiple databases can be easily made.

g. GED shall be designed using the software process and software methodology covered in the course and design patterns.

h. GED shall be tested at unit testing, integration testing, and acceptance testing levels using learned testing methods and available testing tools. Test cases shall be developed and test results documented.

3. GED shall generate Java or C++ skeleton source code according to user's selection.

E

Appendix

Object Constraint Language

The Object Constraint Language (OCL) can be used to formally specify invariants, operations, preconditions and postconditions of operations, initial values of attributes, derivation rules, and more. This appendix will use the example model shown in Figure E.1 to explain the OCL constructs.

E.1 RESERVED WORDS AND OPERATORS

Many OCL reserved words and operators share the same notations as in math and programming languages (PLs). Figure E.2 shows some of the commonly used, OCL-specific notations. These and other OCL constructs are detailed in the following sections.

E.2 CONTEXT AND INVARIANT

Every OCL expression is bound to a context implicitly when it is attached as a stereotype to a class in a UML diagram, or explicitly otherwise. The context specifies the class referred to in the OCL expression. An invariant states a condition that is true all the time. For example, as an invariant, every document must have zero or more copies. This is shown as "{ context Document inv: copies >= 0 }" in Figure E.1. The context specification may be dropped when an OCL expression is shown in a UML diagram and the context is clear.

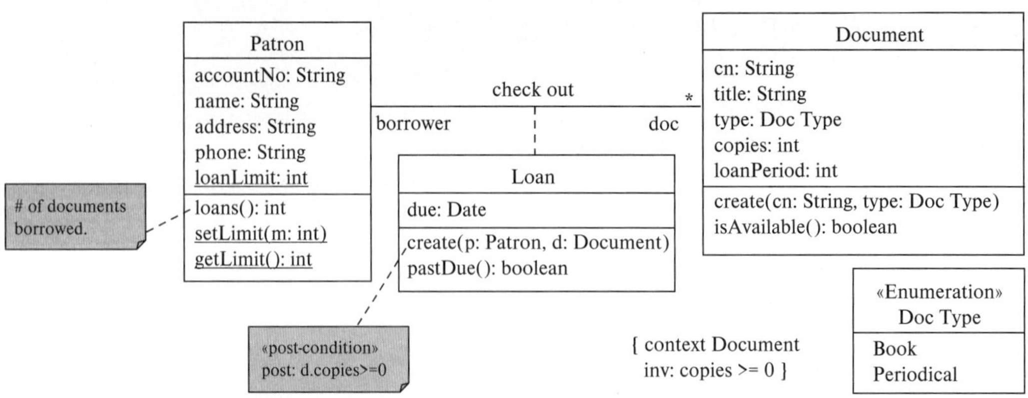

FIGURE E.1 Example model to explain OCL

Notation	Notion	Example
--	The rest of the line is a comment.	-- this is a comment
context	The class or type referred to by an OCL expression.	context Patron May be omitted in a stereotype connecting to a class in a UML diagram.
inv	Invariant, a condition that must be true all the time.	3 ways to express "every loan has a due date": context loan: Loan inv: loan.due <> null context Loan inv: self.due <> null context Loan inv: due <> null
self	One or any instance of the context. It is similar to "this" in OO programming.	
init	Attribute initialization.	context Document::copies: int init: 1 context Patron inv: self.loans()<=Patron::getLimit()
::	• Symbol to refer to a feature of a class. • Operator to invoke a static function of class. Non-static functions are invoked using the dot (".") operator.	
->	Navigation operator to apply a collection function.	contex Patron::loans(): int body: self.Loan->size() self.Loan is the set of loans to the patron, and the loans() function returns the size of the set.
body	Body of a query operation.	
derive	Derivation rule.	context Document::loanPeriod: int derive: if type=DocType::Periodical then 7 -- periodicals are 7 days else 30 -- books are 30 days endif
implies	Logical-implication operator.	context Document inv: loanPeriod=7 implies type=DocType::Periodical
@pre	Refer to the previous value of a feature in a post condition.	context Loan::create(p: Patron, d: Document) pre: d.copies > 0 and p.loans() < p::getLimit() post: d.copies=d.copies@pre - 1 and d.copies >= 0
pre, post	Pre- and post-conditions of an operation.	

FIGURE E.2 Some OCL reserved words and operators

E.3 ATTRIBUTE INITIALIZATION

Attributes of a class can be initialized by using the reserved word "init." Like an invariant, attribute initialization can be done in three different ways. Below is the way that uses the "self" reserved word:

```
context Patron::loanLimit: int init: 10
-- loanLimit of Patron is initialized to 10.
```

E.4 OPERATION SPECIFICATION

OCL can be used to specify operations of a class. This is accomplished by using the "body" reserved word. If the operation is a query operation, meaning that the operation returns a result, then the reserved word "result" is used to indicate the return result in a postcondition. As shown in Figure E.1, Loan is an association class for the checkout association between Patron and Document. The loans() query operation of the Patron class computes the number of loans for a patron. This operation can be specified as follows:

```
context Patron::loans(): Integer --returns number of loans to a patron
pre: self.Loan<>null             --if the patron has checked out some documents
body: result=self. Loan->size()  --return result is size of self.Loan
```

E.5 DERIVATION RULES

A derivation rule specifies how the value of an attribute is computed or derived. It is accomplished by using the "derive" reserved word:

```
context Document::loanPeriod: int
derive: if type=DocType::Periodical
        then 7    -- periodicals are 7 days
        else 30   -- books are 30 days
        endif
```

E.6 NAVIGATION OVER ASSOCIATION RELATIONSHIPS

Sometimes, one needs to express properties involving association relationships. This requires navigation over such relationships. Given a context, the objects that are associated with an instance of the context are obtained by using the role name at the other end of the association relationship. Because an association specifies a binary relationship between two classes, its instances are pairs of objects of the two classes. Therefore, the navigation result is always a set of objects of the class at the other end of the association. The size of the resulting set can be zero, one, or more than one. For example, the expression self.doc represents the set of documents checked out by a patron, where the context is Patron.

E.7 NAVIGATION TO AND FROM ASSOCIATION CLASSES

To navigate to association class, OCL uses the name of the association class. To navigate from an association class, OCL uses the role name at an end of the association:

```
context Patron::loans(): int post: result=self.Loan->size()
context Loan::docTitle(): String post: result=self.doc.title
```

E.8 COLLECTION TYPES

There are four collection types in OCL, which are subtypes of the abstract Collection type. The table below summarizes these collection types. The letter T enclosed in a pair of parentheses denotes the type of the elements of the collection. A collection can be specified using a literal, as shown in the last column.

	Duplicate Elements?	Elements Ordered?	Example
Set(T)	No	No	Set { 3, 2, 1, 5, 10 }
Bag(T)	Yes	No	Bag { 3, 4, 2, 3, 2 }
OrderedSet(T)	No	Yes	OrderedSet { 1, 2, 3, 5, 10 }
Sequence(T)	Yes	Yes	Sequence { 1, 2, 4, 4, 5, 6, 7, 7, 9, 10 } Sequence { 1..10 }

E.9 COLLECTION OPERATIONS

OCL provides many collection operations. The syntax for the select, reject, collect, forAll and exists operations is:

```
collection '->' ( 'select' | 'reject' | 'collect' |
'forAll' | 'exists' ) '(' [ v [ ':' Type ] '|' ]
boolean-expression ')'
```

1. select: this operation selects elements of a collection that satisfy a boolean expression. For example, the set of past-due loans for a patron can be expressed by using any of the following, where the context is Patron:

   ```
   self.Loan->select(pastDue()=true)
   self.Loan->select(loan: Loan | loan.pastDue()=true)
   self.Loan->select(loan | loan.pastDue()=true)
   ```

2. reject: this operation does the opposite of select, that is, not selecting elements of a collection that satisfy a boolean expression. For examples, the above past-due loans for a patron can be expressed as: self.Loan->reject (pastDue()=false).
3. collect: this operation produces a new collection of elements of a different type from the original collection. For example, let Patron be the context, then the set of titles of documents checked out by a patron can be expressed as: self. doc->collect(title). Although in this example, the collection of titles does not contain duplicate, the collect operation in general results in a bag rather than a set.
4. forAll and exists: these operations are like the universal and existential quantifiers in first-order logic. They are used to specify that all of, and respectively some of, the elements of a collection must satisfy a condition. For example, the following specifies an invariant that documents borrowed by a patron is either a book or a periodical:

   ```
   context Patron
   inv self.doc->forAll( d: Document | d.type =
   DocType::Book or d.type = DocType::Periodical )
   ```

Other collection operations include:

isEmpty,	true if collection is empty
notEmpty	true if collection is not empty
size	size of collection
count(elem)	number of occurrences of elem in collection
includes(elem)	true if collection contains elem
excludes(elem)	true if collection does not contain elem
includesAll(coll)	true if collection includes all elements of coll
including(elem)	append elem to collection

The iterate operation is similar to the iterator pattern and the iterator API in Java. It can be used to implement the above five operations. Its syntax is

```
collection -> iterate ( elem : Type1 ; acc :
Type2 = init-expr | do-expr )
```

This operation initializes the accumulator acc to the value of the init-expr, and executes do-expr for each elem of the collection. For example, if Patron is the context, then the set of past-due loans for a patron can be expressed as follows:

```
self.Loan->iterate( v : Loan; w : Set(Loan)=Set {} | if
v.pastDue()=true then w->including(v) )
```

E.10 LET OPERATION

The let operation can be used to define a variable in, and local to, any OCL expression so that it can be used multiple times in that expression. It syntax is:

```
Let var : Type = expr1 in expr2
```

For example, the following invariant states that a patron can borrow zero periodical if the patron has reached the loan limit, else the patron can borrow one or more periodicals:

```
context Patron inv: Let nPeri: Integer = self.doc->
select( type=DocType::Periodical)->size() in
   if loans()=loanLimit then nPeri = 0 else nPeri >= 1
```

Index

D

G

H

I

S

U